Eastern Hemisphere

HOLT

PEOPLE, PLACES, AND CHANGE

An Introduction to World Studies

Georgia Seventh Grade World Regions Standards: Africa and Asia

GEORGIA EDITION

Georgia GRADE 7 Standards

Standard	Sub-Standard	Why It Matters
HISTORICAL UNDERSTANDING **SS7H1** The student will identify important African empires	**a.** describe the development of African empires including Ghana, Mali, Songhai, and Ethiopia	The development of African empires was central to the history of the region and the progress of civilization. The culture of Africa today is influenced by the region's unique history.
	b. explain the importance of cities such as Timbuktu as a center of learning and Djenne as one of the oldest cities in Africa, and Zanzibar as a center of commerce.	African cities such as Timbuktu, Djenne were important centers of learning, scientific development, trade, and cultural exchange. Events there influenced the progress of civilization all over Africa.
	c. describe the significance of Sundiata, Mansa Musa, Sayyid Sa'id ibn Sultan and Zara Yakob	Great leaders such as Sundiata, Mansa Musa, Sayyid Sa'id ibn Sultan, and Zara Yakob shaped the history of African civilization, further enriching Africa's history.
SS7H2 The student will explain the reasons for the Africa independence movement	**a.** explain the origins of the slave trade in Africa and describe the trading routes to North Africa, Europe, and the Americas	The slave trade drastically transformed the history of Africa, Europe, and the Americas and affected the lives of millions of people.
	b. describe the development of European empires in Africa including the reasons for colonization, partitioning of Africa, and the approach to empire by Great Britain, France, and Belgium	The history of European colonization of Africa affected the continent's progress and modernization. The legacy of colonization can still be seen in Africa today.
	c. describe the nationalist movements in colonial Africa including Kenya and Nigeria, Ghana, and the Belgian Congo	Nationalist movements in Africa transformed the political organization of the region. Political structures in Africa today still reflect the ideals of these movements.
	d. analyze the impact of the colonial period on the development of Africa	The colonial period of Africa drained the region of its resources and hampered its growth. Africa is still attempting to overcome its history of colonialization.
SS7H3 The student will describe major developments in Africa since independence	**a.** explain the problems faced after independence by countries such as Kenya and Nigeria	Independence has not resolved all of Africa's problems. Nations such as Kenya and Nigeria still struggle with issues ranging from political disorder to disease to economic crisis.

Standard	Sub-Standard	Why It Matters
	b. explain the experience of South Africa (apartheid) including the origins of and ending of apartheid and the roles of Nelson Mandela and F. W. deKlerk.	Apartheid and the struggle to end it were the defining factors of South Africa's recent history.. Though apartheid no longer exists, its legacy can be seen in the country's social, political, and economic challenges.
	c. describe problems created by the health issues including AIDS and starvation,	Health issues have had a significant impact on the development of Africa and the lives of Africans, millions of whom suffer from AIDS or other diseases.
	d. explain the problems created by repeated civil war in Africa including Democratic Republic of the Congo (Zaire) and Rwanda	Civil war in regions of Africa has had a devastating impact on African peoples and hampered the economic development of countries such as the Democratic Republic of the Congo and Rwanda.
	e. explain the problems created by governmental corruption and one-party rule as seen in Zimbabwe	Corrupt governments have limited the spread of democracy in Africa and caused great hardship for the citizens of many countries.
	f. explain the origins of the pan-Africa movement and its importance to the development of the African Union	Seeking peace and economic development, many African countries have banded together to improve their societies. These countries' actions will have a tremendous effect on Africa's future.
SS7G1 The student will be able to describe and locate the important physical and human characteristics of Africa	**a.** describe and locate major physical features to include Sahara, Savannah, Sahel, Tropical Rain Forest, Congo River, Nile River, Zambezi River, Niger River, East African Mountains (Ethiopian Highlands), Drakensberg Mountains, Atlas Mountains, Kalahari Desert, Lake Tanganyika and Lake Victoria	Africa is the world's second largest continent and has a wide variety of physical features. These features have been a major force in shaping the lives of Africa's people throughout history.
	b. describe and locate the nations of South Africa, Zimbabwe, Tanzania, Rwanda, Mozambique, Democratic Republic of the Congo, Ghana, Mali, Mauritania, Sierra Leone, Sudan, Egypt, Ethiopia, Libya, Kenya, Chad	Though Africa's many countries share some common bonds, each has its own unique history, society, and culture.

Georgia GRADE 7 Standards

Standard	Sub-Standard	Why It Matters
SS7G2 The student will discuss the impact of government policies and individual behaviors on the African environment	**a.** explain how pollution has affected countries such as Kenya, Egypt, and South Africa and actions taken by government and individuals	Pollution of the air, water, and earth threaten the health and safety of people all over Africa, forcing governments and people to seek ways to remedy the problem.
	b. explain the impact of the extraction of natural resources on the environments of Kenya, Chad, and Nigeria	Many African countries, including Kenya, Chad, and Nigeria, depend on mining for their economic survival. However, mining has led to environmental problems that these countries must now try to correct.
	c. explain the importance of water as a natural resource in countries such as Egypt, Sudan, Mali, and Chad	Much of northern Africa is desert, and water is very scarce. As a result, the people of Egypt, Sudan, Mali, Chad, and other north African nations have learned to consider water one of their most valuable resources.
	d. explain ways in which countries such as Kenya, South Africa, and Mali have worked to improve the African environment	Realizing that their environments are important resources and potential sources of income, many African nations have taken steps to protect and improve the natural landscape.
	e. explain the impact of deforestation and desertification on the environment in such countries as Cote d'Ivoire, Kenya, and Botswana	Economic activities such as farming and mining have caused the destruction of forests and the expansion of the desert into once fertile lands, often with catastrophic effects on people's lives and livelihoods.
SS7G3 The student will explain the impact of location, climate, physical characteristics, natural resources and population size on African countries	**a.** describe the impact location has on countries such as Chad, Egypt, and South Africa, with regard to trade, migration, agriculture, and industry	Africa is a huge continent with varied features. Because of this variation, each country's location within Africa greatly affects how its people live and work.
	b. explain the impact of physical features such as deserts, mountains, rivers, and proximity to the ocean have on countries such as Ethiopia, Sudan, Morocco	Wherever they live, people must adapt to their natural environments and to the features that make up those environments.

Standard	Sub-Standard	Why It Matters
	c. explain the distribution of natural resources in Africa and how that has affected the development of countries such as Chad, Sudan, and South Africa	Africa is rich in natural resources, but these resources are not evenly distributed across the continent. Countries like South Africa that are rich in valuable resources have prospered, while other countries have been less fortunate.
	d. describe the effect the Sahara, Sahel, Savannah, and Tropical Rain Forest have on where people live, the type of work they do, and transportation	Africa's different regions have very different climates. Some of these climates are pleasant places to live, while others are harsh and make travel and transportation difficult.
SS7G4 The student will describe the cultural characteristics of different people who live in Africa	**a.** describe the religions, customs, and traditions of the Arab, Ashanti, Bedouin, Khoikhoi and San, Ibo, and Swahili ethnic groups	Africa is home to thousands of different cultural and ethnic groups. Each of these groups has its own traditions and customs, which together create a rich cultural tapestry in Africa.
	b. evaluate how the literacy rate of countries such as Sudan, South Africa, and Egypt has affected their development	Education and literacy vary widely across Africa. In many cases, a correlation can be made between a country's literacy rate and its level of economic development.
	c. trace the spread of the Bantu peoples and explain the impact this had on Africa	Speakers of Bantu languages were the ancestors of many of the people who live in Africa today. The cultures of these early peoples helped shape modern Africa.
	d. explain the major literary (including literature Nobel laureates Wole Soyinka, Nigeria; Naguib Mafuz, Egypt; Nadine Gordimer, South Africa), artistic, and music forms of people in the region.	The arts, including writing and music, have long been important in African cultures. Studying Africa's art, literature, and music can help people better understand other aspects of African culture.
SS7CG1 The student will demonstrate an understanding of the modern governments of Africa	**a.** describe the structure of the national governments in the modern African nations of Morocco, Kenya, Libya, and South Africa including type of government, form of leadership, type of legislature, and the role of the citizen	Africa's governments range from military dictatorships to elected democracies to hereditary monarchies. The type of government a country has helps shape its economic development and culture.

Standard	Sub-Standard	Why It Matters
	b. explain the problem and impact of civil war and conflict in Africa	For decades, many countries in Africa have been torn about by terrible civil wars. These wars have caused political instability, economic hardships, and other problems for the countries.
SS7E1 The student will describe different *economic systems (traditional, command, market, mixed)* and how they answer the basic economic questions: *What to produce? How to produce? For whom to produce?*	**a.** explain the basic types of economic systems found in South Africa, Egypt, Nigeria, and Morocco	The type of economic system present in a country affects what types of products it can create, how those products will be created, and who will benefit. These factors are key to the economic development of a country.
SS7E2 The student will give examples of how *voluntary trade* benefits buyers and sellers in Africa over time	**a.** analyze the development of voluntary trade including trans-Saharan trade, Middle East and Asian trade routes	Trans-Saharan trade and trade with the Middle East and Asia made many African empires very rich and helped to shape their cultures.
	b. explain how trade barriers including the Sahara and the Tropical Rain Forest have affected development of trade within Africa	Parts of Africa, including the vast Sahara and the humid tropical rain forests of Central Africa, are difficult to cross. People had to develop ways to bypass these physical barriers in order to develop trade routes.
	c. describe how international trade requires a system for *exchanging currency* between and among nations and identify examples of currencies from nations such as Egypt, South Africa, Nigeria, and Chad	Because each country in Africa has its own system of currency, they have had to develop systems of currency exchange to make trade easy and manageable.
	d. explain the function and purpose of the South African Development Community (SADC) and the Economic Community of West African States (ECOWAS)	Many countries in Africa want to improve their level of economic development but are not able to do so alone. To help their economies improve, these countries have banded together in international communities that have the potential to become major players in world economics.
SS7E3 The student will describe the factors that influence *economic growth* and examine their presence or absence in such African countries as Chad, South Africa, Nigeria, and Kenya	**a.** describe the importance of *investment in human capital,* including the health, education, and training of people	To have a prosperous economy, a country needs a trained work force, which economists call human capital. Many African countries lack such a work force, often due to health crises or insufficient educational resources.

Standard	Sub-Standard	Why It Matters
	b. describe how factors such as political stability, education, and health issues inhibit or enhance *investment in capital goods,* including factories, machinery, and new technology	A major challenge facing African countries seeking to improve their economies is their lack of capital goods like factories and machines. Political and social problems have kept many countries from developing or obtaining the goods they need for their economies to improve.
	c. describe how *natural resources,* including land, air, water, minerals, time, and other gifts of nature have affected economic development	Without natural resources, countries cannot improve their economies. Some African countries are still learning how to best use the resources they have.
	d. analyze the *role of entrepreneurs* who take the risks of organizing productive resources	Individual investors play a major role in developing a country's economy. In Africa, such entrepreneurs have created businesses in hundreds of different fields.
SS7H4 The student will describe development of the three major religions that originated in the Middle East	**a.** explain the origins of Judaism as seen in the Hebrew peoples	Judaism is one of the oldest religions that is still practiced today. Elements of Judaism also influenced later religions, especially Christianity.
	b. explain the origins and spread of Christianity to 312 CE	Christianity and its teachings have had an immeasurable influence on the history of the world.
	c. explain the origins and spread of Islam to 1258 CE including the religious, cultural and military factors	Islam influenced the history and culture of many regions of the world and affected the progress of civilization and learning for humankind.
	d. explain the origins of the division between Sunni and Shia Muslims	The division between the Sunni and Shia Muslims still exists today, affecting politics and religious issues in the Middle East today.
SS7H5 The student will describe importance of the Ottoman Empire to Asia	**a.** describe the origins of the Ottoman empire	The Ottoman Empire dominated southwestern Asia for centuries. The legacy of the Ottoman Empire can still be found in the architecture and culture of the region today.

Georgia GRADE 7 Standards

Standard	Sub-Standard	Why It Matters
	b. describe the geographic expansion of the Ottoman empire	The political and military power of the Ottoman Empire influenced the history and culture of Asia, Africa, and Europe.
	c. explain the impact of the Ottoman Empire with regard to trade and religion on the region	The Ottoman Empire had a tremendous influence on trade and religion in the vast regions to which it spread. The course of economic and religious history was changed in these regions.
	d. discuss the importance of the break up of the Ottoman Empire after World War I	The breakup of the Ottoman Empire after World War I altered the history of the Middle East and southeastern Europe, influencing the political and economic life in those regions even today.
SS7H6 The student will describe major developments in the Middle East during the 20th century	**a.** explain the historical reasons for the establishment of the modern state of Israel in 1948, including anti-Semitism in Europe, Zionism, and the Holocaust	The state of Israel was created in 1948, setting off a chain reaction of events that has shaped life in the Middle East ever since.
	b. describe the continuing conflicts between Israel and the Arab world	The continuing conflict between Israel and the Arab world is one of the worlds' most divisive and problematic political challenges, influencing the everyday lives of people in the region and beyond.
	c. explain the economic impact of oil on the region	The Middle East is the world's greatest supplier of oil, and as such has great influence in international economic affairs.
	d. explain U.S. involvement and interest in North Africa/Southwest Asia to include the Persian Gulf War, the invasion of Afghanistan, and Operation Iraqi Freedom	The United States has played a major role in many regions of Africa, Southwestern Asia, and beyond, affecting the politics, economy, and society in those regions as well as in the United States.

Standard	Sub-Standard	Why It Matters
SS7G5 The student will be able to describe and locate important physical and human characteristics in Southwestern Asia (Middle East)	**a.** describe and locate major physical features of the Middle East to include the Jordan River, Tigris River, Euphrates River, Golan Heights, West Bank, Gaza Strip, Suez Canal, Strait of Hormuz, Persian Gulf, Black Sea, Caspian Sea, Red Sea, Arabian Sea	The natural and man-made physical features of the Middle East have greatly influenced where and how people live in the region.
	b. describe and locate the following nations in the Middle East: Israel, Jordan, Saudi Arabia, Iran, Iraq, Syria, Lebanon, Kuwait, and Afghanistan	The countries of the Middle East are frequently mentioned in the media, often due to economic concerns or political issues.
SS7G6 The student will evaluate the impact of government policies and individual behaviors on Southwest Asia's environment	**a.** describe the environmental issues facing the countries of the Middle East including industrial pollution, water rights, extraction of natural resources	The Middle East's success in the oil industry has not come without cost, as some aspects of the industry can cause great harm to the region's natural environments.
	b. explain the problems associated with developing governmental policies in the Middle East concerning environmental issues such as water rights and extraction of natural resources such as oil	To protect their environments, the governments of the Middle East have to take action. However, their actions could hurt their countries' economies if oil production and other activities are limited.
SS7G7 The student will explain the impact of location, climate, physical characteristics, natural resources and population size on various Southwestern Asian countries	**a.** describe the impact of location on trade, agriculture, and industry of Middle Eastern countries such as Israel, Jordan, Iran, and Saudi Arabia	The Middle East, located at the crossroads of three continents, is situated in an excellent location for trade. Various countries in the region have had very different experiences with agriculture and resources, however, based on their locations.
	b. describe the impact climatic conditions have on the Middle East and how that has impacted the development of agriculture and increased the importance of water in the Middle East	Southwest Asia is one of the world's driest regions. The region's dryness continues to create issues with which the people of the region have to deal.
	c. explain the distribution of natural resources and how that has affected the development of countries such as Saudi Arabia, Israel, Jordan, Iraq, Iran, and Kuwait	The Middle East is rich in mineral resources, especially oil. However, these resources are not evenly distributed, and countries have developed very differently as a result.

Georgia GRADE 7 Standards

Standard	Sub-Standard	Why It Matters
	d. describe how the geography of the Middle East has affected the population in terms of where people live, the type of work they do, and transportation	The Middle East's desert climate and harsh terrain are still major factors in shaping people's lives there.
SS7G8 The student will describe the diverse cultural characteristics of the people who live in Southwestern Asia	**a.** describe the major Middle Eastern ethnic groups such as Arab, Jewish, Berber, Druze, Bedouin, Kurd, Turk, Persian, and Armenian, including where they live, their religion, customs, and traditions	The Middle East is home to millions of people from dozens of different ethnic groups. Interactions between these groups affect daily life for all people in the region.
	b. evaluate the effect of the literacy rate on the development of Middle Eastern countries such as Syria, Iran, Israel, and Saudi Arabia	Literacy is one of the many factors that affects the economic development of countries around the world.
	c. explain the major literary, artistic, and musical forms of Israel, Saudi Arabia	The literature, art, and music of the Middle East reflect the beliefs and values of the people who live there.
SS7CG2 The student will describe the different political structures of the Middle East	**a.** explain the basic structure of the national governments in Turkey, Jordan, Iran, Saudi Arabia and Israel to include type of government, form of leadership, type of legislature, and the role of the citizen	The governments of the Middle East make decisions every day that affect people not only in the region but all around the world.
	b. explain the role of religion in governance in the Middle East	More than in many parts of the world, religious ideas play a major role in shaping government policies in the Middle East.
SS7E5 The student will describe different *economic systems (traditional, command, market, mixed)* and how they answer the basic economic questions: *What to produce? How to produce? For whom to produce?*	**a.** explain the basic types of economic systems found in Israel, Saudi Arabia, and Turkey	The economic systems of Middle Eastern countries regulate the production of a substantial portion of the world's oil supply.

Standard	Sub-Standard	Why It Matters
SS7E6 The student will give examples of how *voluntary trade* benefits buyers and sellers across time	**a.** analyze the importance of trade to Middle Eastern nations with regard to the exporting of oil and other natural resources and the importing of industrial and agricultural commodities	Although Middle Eastern countries have grown rich from the export of oil, many have to buy food from other countries to ensure their people's survival.
	b. define types of *trade barriers* that exist in the Middle East including both physical barriers such as limited rivers and deserts and political issues that produce trade barriers	The Middle East depends on trade for its survival, but trade can be difficult due to harsh physical conditions and political conflicts with other countries.
	c. illustrate how international trade requires a system for *exchanging currency* between and among nations and identify examples of currencies from Israel, Saudi Arabia, and Jordan	Many Middle Eastern countries are major players in international trade, and their currencies are used to buy goods from countries around the world.
	d. explain the significance of the Organization of Petroleum Exporting Countries (OPEC)	A union of Middle Eastern and other countries, OPEC controls most of the world's production and sale of oil.
SS7E7 The student will describe the factors that influence *economic growth* and examine their presence or absence in Middle Eastern countries such as Israel, Lebanon, Turkey, Saudi Arabia and Iran	**a.** describe *investment in human capital,* including the health, education, and training of people	The success of Middle Eastern economies depends on having a productive workforce—people who are healthy, educated, and trained for their jobs.
	b. describe *investment in capital goods,* including factories, machinery, and new technology	Without proper equipment, a country cannot thrive economically.
	c. describe the *role of natural resources,* including land, air, water, minerals, time, and other gifts of nature	Every country in Southwest Asia depends at least in part on its natural resources for its economic survival.
	d. analyze the *role of entrepreneurs* who take the risks of organizing productive resources	The economic success of Middle Eastern nations has been due in large part to the actions of entrepreneurs, or individual business owners.
SS7H7 The student will explain the growth and development of Southern and Eastern Asia	**a.** trace the origins and spread of Hinduism and Buddhism	Hinduism and Buddhism, two of the world's largest religions, greatly affected the history and culture of Southern and Eastern Asia.

Georgia GRADE 7 Standards

Standard	Sub-Standard	Why It Matters
	b. explain the importance of the Silk Road in the movement of goods and ideas to other parts of the world	The Silk Road influenced the history of many regions around the world by facilitating the movement of goods and the spread of ideas.
	c. describe the technological contributions of China including the development of paper, tea, and gunpowder and of India including the use of cotton clothing, the Arabic numeral system, and the game of chess	China's and India's technological contributions influenced the course of world history.
SS7H8 The student will describe the policies of China that led to isolation and the reaction to western desire to trade with China	**a.** explain why in the 15th century China ceased to trade with other parts of the world	China's dramatic move to cease trade with the rest of the world transformed the nation, influencing its economic and cultural history and reshaping its relations with other countries.
	b. describe the reaction of China to efforts by European nations to force relations with China including limited areas of trade and the leasing of Hong Kong to Great Britain	The forced opening of China to trade transformed the culture and economy of China, particularly Hong Kong, where the legacy of its British ties are apparent today.
SS7H9 The student will describe the major developments eastern Asia during the 20th century.	**a.** describe the condition of Japan, China, and Korea after WWII	After years of fighting during World War II, Japan, China, and Korea were forced to begin rebuilding their economies. Korea and China, however, also faced challenges of the rise of communism, which still exists in the region today.
	b. explain the rise of Mao Zedong to power, including the long march, the establishment of communism, the Great Leap Forward, and the Cultural Revolution	The rise of communism has had a major impact on the history of China and other parts of the world in the 1900s and 2000s, influencing the region's economy, politics, culture, and daily life.
	c. describe the collapse of colonialism in Asia including India and Indo-China	The collapse of colonialism led to political and economic challenges in various regions of Asia. Countries such as Vietnam are still dealing with the legacy of colonialism.
	d. describe the Korean War including the reasons for the existence of a North and South Korea	The conflict of the Korean War led to the creation of North and South Korea and transformed the region of East Asia.

Standard	Sub-Standard	Why It Matters
	e. describe the Vietnam War including the causes, results, and the reunification of Vietnam	The Vietnam War had a significant impact on the politics, society, emigration, and economics of Vietnam, and dramatically affected the United States.
	f. explain the rebuilding of Japan after World War II	The rebuilding of Japan after World War II was a major success, leading to economic prosperity for Japan and the region as a whole.
SS7G9 The student will be able to describe and locate important physical and human characteristics in Southern and Eastern Asia	**a.** describe and locate major physical features in Southern and Eastern Asia to include Himalayan Mountains, Mekong River, Ganges River, Indus River, Brahmaputra River, Huang He (Yellow River), Yangtze (Chang Jiang) River, Gobi Desert, Indian Ocean, Bay of Bengal, Korean Peninsula, Bering Strait, Yellow Sea, Sea of Japan, South China Sea, and Honshu	The physical features of Southern and Eastern Asia have shaped the ways of life and economic activities of the people who live there.
	b. describe and locate the following nations in Southern and Eastern Asia: India, Bangladesh, Pakistan, Vietnam, Myanmar, Sri Lanka, Thailand, Indonesia, Malaysia, China, Philippines, Japan, North and South Korea, Russia, and Georgia	About half of the world's people live in the countries of Southern and Eastern Asia.
SS7G10 The student will evaluate the impact of government policies and individual behaviors on Southern and Eastern Asia's environment	**a.** describe environmental problems nations such as India, Indonesia, and Pakistan in Southern Asia are facing such as pollution of the Ganges River, air pollution, such as the Asia Brown Cloud, and overpopulation	Because Southern Asia's population is so high, environmental problems such as pollution and overpopulation threaten the health of millions of people each year.
	b. explain the problems nations in Southern Asia such as India, Pakistan and Indonesia have in developing policies concerning environmental issues such as pollution of rivers, industrial pollution, and the extraction of natural resources, including the destruction of the rain forest	The governments of Southwest Asia have experienced problems in creating and enforcing laws to control environmental problems, some of which cause problems for countries outside the region as well.

Georgia GRADE 7 Standards

Standard	Sub-Standard	Why It Matters
	c. describe the environmental problems, such as overpopulation, industrial pollution, and flooding, facing countries in Eastern Asia including China, Japan, and South Korea	The countries of East Asia have political and economic ties to other countries around the world, so their problems also affect other countries, including the United States.
	d. explain efforts by governments and industries in China, Japan, and South Korea to meet environmental problems such as overpopulation, industrial pollution, and flooding	The continued economic success of East Asia countries depends in part upon their success in dealing with environmental problems.
SS7G11 The student will explain the impact of location, climate, physical characteristics, natural resources and population size on Southern and Eastern Asian countries	**a.** describe the impact of location on trade, agriculture, and industry on India, Pakistan, Indonesia, China, and Japan	The location of the countries of South and East Asia on the Indian and Pacific Oceans ties their economies to other countries that border these oceans, including the United States.
	b. describe the impact climatic conditions have on the population distribution, agriculture and industrial development in Southern and Eastern Asia	Climate is a huge influence on where and how people live in the countries of Southern and Eastern Asia.
	c. explain the distribution of natural resources and how that has affected the development of countries such as Bangladesh, India, China, and Japan	Many Southern and Eastern countries depend on natural resources for their economic livelihood, so the distribution of those resources has a tremendous impact on the region's future.
	d. describe how the geography of Southern and Eastern Asia has affected the population in terms of where people live, the type of work they do, and transportation	Southern and Eastern Asia are home to nearly half of the world's people. Factors such as climate and vegetation are crucial in determining where and how these people live.
SS7G12 The student will describe the diverse cultural characteristics of the people who live in Southern and Eastern Asia	**a.** describe the predominant religious practices, customs, and traditions of the people of India, Indonesia, China, and Japan	Many religions, including Buddhism, Hinduism, Islam, Confucianism, and Shinto, shape the lives and cultures of the people of Southern and Eastern Asia.

Standard	Sub-Standard	Why It Matters
	b. evaluate the effect of the literacy rate on the development of countries such as India, Indonesia, China, and Japan	The countries of Southern and Eastern Asia have very different levels of economic development, and studying each country's literacy rate can provide a clue to understanding those differences in development.
	c. explain the major literary, artistic, and musical forms of India, China, and Japan	India, China, and Japan are known for their unique styles of literature, art, and music, styles that have influenced artists and writers from around the world.
SS7CG3 The student will demonstrate an understanding of modern governments of Southern and Eastern Asia	**a.** describe the structure of the national governments of India, Indonesia, China, and Japan including the type of government, form of leadership, the type of legislature, and the role of the citizen	As the most populous and developed countries in Southern and Eastern Asia, India, Indonesia, China, and Japan have great influence over other countries in the region and their governments.
SS7E8 The student will describe different *economic systems (traditional, command, market, mixed)* and how they answer the basic economic questions: *What to produce? How to produce? For whom to produce?*	**a.** explain the basic types of economic systems found in India, China, and Japan	India, China, and Japan are all major trading partners of the United States. The economic system practiced in each country affects the level and type of trade the United States carries on with it.
SS7E9 The student will give examples of how voluntary trade benefits buyers and sellers across time	**a.** analyze how India has benefited from increased trade with other countries since 1991	Since 1991, India has become a major economic force in Southern and Eastern Asia, and its economic activities influence economic matters worldwide.
	b. analyze the impact of trade on modern Japan	Japan has one of the strongest economies in the world today, an economy based largely on international trade.
	c. explain the importance of the Pacific Rim in trade and economic development	Because East Asia is located on the Pacific Ocean, its economies are tied to those of other countries that border the Pacific, including the United States.
	d. describe why Southern and Eastern Asia are becoming a significant factor in international trade	In recent years, many countries—including the United States—have turned to Southern and Eastern Asian countries as trade and industry partners.

Georgia GRADE 7 Standards

Standard	Sub-Standard	Why It Matters
	e. define types of *trade barriers* that exist in Southern and Eastern Asia, especially for countries such as India and Indonesia and how those barriers are being overcome	Countries such as India and Indonesia will become even greater economic powers after they have overcome the barriers that currently limit their trade.
	f. illustrate how international trade requires a system for *exchanging currency* between and among nations and identify examples of currencies from India, China, and Japan	Because India, China, and Japan are such powerful trading countries, their currencies can be accepted and exchanged in many other countries around the world.
SS7E10 The student will describe the factors that cause *economic growth* and examine their presence or absence in Southern and Eastern Asian countries such as Pakistan, India, China, and Indonesia	**a.** describe *investment in human capital,* including the health, education, training of people, and the impact of poverty on economic development	The continued success of the economies of Southern and Eastern Asian countries hinges on their abilities to find well-educated and well-trained employees.
	b. describe *investments in capital goods,* including factories, machinery, and new technology	Southern and Eastern Asia's capital goods are key to their economic success.
	c. describe the *role of natural resources,* including land, air, water, minerals, time, and other gifts of nature	The availability of natural resources varies widely among countries in this region, so economic leaders in each country must plan how to deal with what they have.
	d. analyze the *role of entrepreneurs* who take the risks of organizing productive resources	Although entrepreneurs have long been a factor in the economic systems of some countries, such as Japan, in other countries they are just beginning to play a significant role.

HOLT Eastern Hemisphere

PEOPLE, PLACES, AND CHANGE

An Introduction to World Studies

GEORGIA EDITION

HOLT, RINEHART AND WINSTON

A Harcourt Education Company

Orlando • Austin • New York • San Diego • Toronto • London

THE AUTHORS

Prof. David M. Helgren is Director of the Center for Geographic Education at San Jose State University in California, where he is also Chair of the Department of Geography. Prof. Helgren received his Ph.D. in geography from the University of Chicago. He is the coauthor of several geography textbooks and has written many articles on the geography of Africa. Awards from the National Geographic Society, the National Science Foundation, and the L. S. B. Leakey Foundation have supported his many field research projects. Prof. Helgren is a former president of the California Geographical Society and a founder of the Northern California Geographic Alliance.

Prof. Robert J. Sager is Chair of Earth Sciences at Pierce College in Lakewood, Washington. Prof. Sager received his B.S. in geology and geography and M.S. in geography from the University of Wisconsin and holds a J.D. in international law from Western State University College of Law. He is the coauthor of several geography and earth science textbooks and has written many articles and educational media programs on the geography of the Pacific. Prof. Sager has received several National Science Foundation study grants and has twice been a recipient of the University of Texas NISOD National Teaching Excellence Award. He is a founding member of the Southern California Geographic Alliance and former president of the Association of Washington Geographers.

Prof. Alison S. Brooks is Professor of Anthropology at George Washington University and a Research Associate in Anthropology at the Smithsonian Institution. She received her A.B., M.A., and Ph.D. in Anthropology from Harvard University. Since 1964, she has carried out ethnological and archaeological research in Africa, Europe, and Asia and is the author of more than 300 scholarly and popular publications. She has served as a consultant to Smithsonian exhibits and to National Geographic, Public Broadcasting, the Discovery Channel, and other public media. In addition, she is a founder and editor of *Anthro Notes: The National Museum of Natural History Bulletin for Teachers* and has received numerous grants and awards to develop and lead in-service training institutes for teachers in grades 5–12. She served as the American Anthropological Association's representative to the NCSS task force on developing Scope and Sequence guidelines for Social Studies Education in grade K–12.

While the details of the young people's stories in the chapter openers are real, their identities have been changed to protect their privacy.

Cover and Title Page Photo Credits: (child image) Steve Vidler/Nawrocki Stock Photo; (bkgd) Image Copyright © 2003 PhotoDisc, Inc./HRW

ISBN 0-03-043224-3

6 7 8 9 032 2007 Printing

HOLT
PEOPLE, PLACES, AND CHANGE
Eastern Hemisphere

CONTENTS

UNIT 2 Southwest and Central Asia 70

Notes from the Field

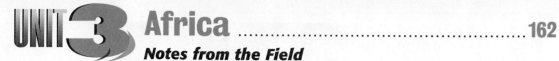

UNIT 3 Africa 162

Notes from the Field

UNIT 4 South Asia 292
Notes from the Field

UNIT 5 East and Southeast Asia 342
Notes from the Field

REFERENCE SECTION

FEATURES

FEATURES

Connecting to Science

Connecting to Technology

COULD YOU SURVIVE?

CASE STUDY

FOCUS ON

FEATURES

Geo SKILLS

HANDS on GEOGRAPHY

MAPS

FEATURES

FEATURES

ATLAS
CONTENTS

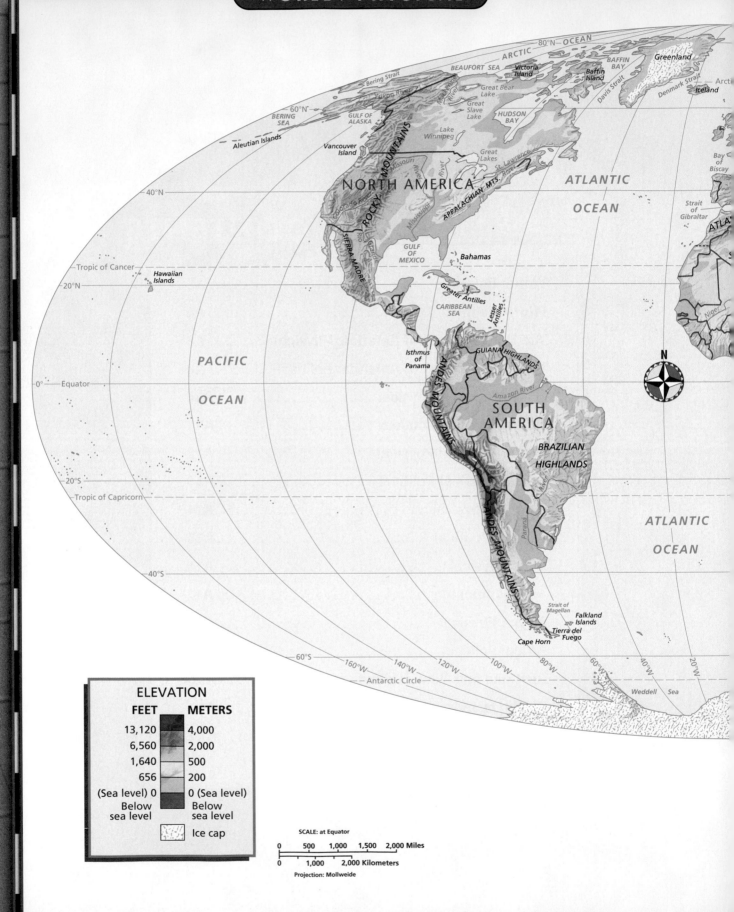

ELEVATION

FEET	METERS
13,120	4,000
6,560	2,000
1,640	500
656	200
(Sea level) 0	0 (Sea level)
Below sea level	Below sea level

Ice cap

SCALE: at Equator

0   500   1,000   1,500   2,000 Miles

0   1,000   2,000 Kilometers

Projection: Mollweide

ARCTIC 80°N OCEAN

North Cape
BARENTS SEA
KARA SEA
LAPTEV SEA
EAST SIBERIAN SEA

Yenisei River
Lena River
Kolyma River

EUROPE
BALTIC
ALPS
BLACK SEA
MEDITERRANEAN SEA

URAL MOUNTAINS
Ob River
Volga River
Lake Baikal

60°N
SEA OF OKHOTSK
KAMCHATKA PENINSULA

Sakhalin Island

ARAL SEA
CASPIAN SEA
Balqash Lake
ALTAY MOUNTAINS
GOBI
Amur River

Hokkaido

ASIA
40°N
SEA OF JAPAN
Honshu

HIMALAYAS
Huang He
Chang River
Shikoku
Kyushu

SAHARA
AFRICA

ARABIAN PENINSULA
RED SEA
Euphrates River
Persian Gulf
Nile River

THAR DESERT
Ganges River

EAST CHINA SEA

Taiwan
Tropic of Cancer
20°N

PACIFIC OCEAN

ARABIAN SEA
Bay of Bengal
Philippine Islands
SOUTH CHINA SEA

Sri Lanka
Strait of Malacca
MALAY PENINSULA
Borneo
Celebes
New Guinea
Solomon Islands
Equator 0°

Congo River
Lake Tanganyika
Lake Victoria

Sumatra
Java
CORAL SEA
New Hebrides
Fiji Islands

INDIAN OCEAN

Madagascar
Mozambique Channel

GREAT SANDY DESERT
New Caledonia
20°S

KALAHARI DESERT
GREAT VICTORIA DESERT
AUSTRALIA
GREAT DIVIDING RANGE
Darling River
Tropic of Capricorn

Cape of Good Hope

TASMAN SEA
North Island
NEW ZEALAND
South Island

Tasmania
60°S

20°E 40°E 60°E 80°E 100°E 120°E 140°E 160°E

ANTARCTICA

Denmark Strait
Iceland
North Cape
10°E 20°E 30°E 40°E
BARENTS SEA
KARA SEA
KJØLEN MTS.
URAL MTS.

N

NORTH SEA
BALTIC SEA
Volga River
60°N

0 250 500 750 Miles
0 250 500 750 Kilometers
Projection: Mollweide

British Isles
50°N

ATLANTIC OCEAN
Bay of Biscay
ALPS
Rhine River
Danube River
BLACK SEA

40°N
MEDITERRANEAN SEA
Strait of Gibraltar
Crete
Euphrates R.

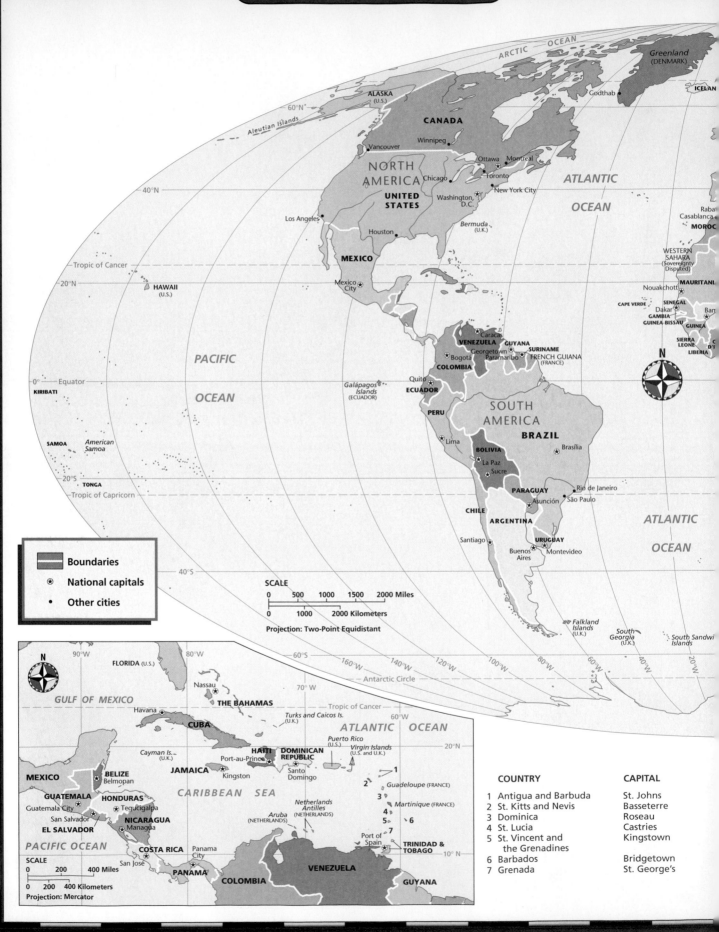

ARCTIC OCEAN

Greenland
(DENMARK)

ICELAN

Godthab

ALASKA
(U.S.)

60°N

CANADA

Aleutian Islands

Vancouver

Winnipeg

NORTH
AMERICA

Ottawa Montreal

40°N

Chicago

Toronto

ATLANTIC

UNITED
STATES

Washington,
D.C.

New York City

OCEAN

Rabat
Casablanca

Los Angeles

Bermuda
(U.K.)

MOROC

Houston

WESTERN
SAHARA
(Sovereignty
Disputed)

MEXICO

Tropic of Cancer

20°N

HAWAII
(U.S.)

Mexico
City

Nouakchott

MAURITANI

CAPE VERDE

SENEGAL
Dakar
GAMBIA
GUINEA-BISSAU

Ban

GUINEA

PACIFIC

Caracas

Georgetown

VENEZUELA GUYANA SURINAME
Paramaribo FRENCH GUIANA
(FRANCE)

SIERRA
LEONE

C

D'I

LIBERIA

N

Bogotá

COLOMBIA

OCEAN

Galápagos
Islands
(ECUADOR)

Quito

ECUADOR

0° Equator

KIRIBATI

SOUTH
AMERICA

PERU

BRAZIL

Brasília

SAMOA

American
Samoa

Lima

BOLIVIA

Rio de Janeiro

La Paz
Sucre

20°S

TONGA

PARAGUAY

São Paulo

Tropic of Capricorn

Asunción

CHILE

ARGENTINA

ATLANTIC

URUGUAY

OCEAN

40°S

Santiago

Buenos
Aires

Montevideo

SCALE

0 500 1000 1500 2000 Miles

0 1000 2000 Kilometers

Projection: Two-Point Equidistant

Falkland
Islands
(U.K.)

South
Georgia
(U.K.)

South Sandwi
Islands

60°S

180°W

160°W

140°W

120°W

100°W

80°W

60°W

40°W

20°W

Antarctic Circle

N

90°W

80°W

FLORIDA (U.S.)

70°W

Nassau

GULF OF MEXICO

THE BAHAMAS

Tropic of Cancer

60°W

Havana

Turks and Caicos Is.
(U.K.)

ATLANTIC OCEAN

CUBA

Puerto Rico
(U.S.)

20°N

Cayman Is.
(U.K.)

HAITI DOMINICAN
REPUBLIC

Virgin Islands
(U.S. and U.K.)

Port-au-Prince

1

MEXICO

BELIZE
Belmopan

JAMAICA

Kingston

Santo
Domingo

2

Guadeloupe (FRANCE)

GUATEMALA

HONDURAS

CARIBBEAN SEA

3

Martinique (FRANCE)

Guatemala City

Tegucigalpa

Netherlands
Antilles
(NETHERLANDS)

4

San Salvador

NICARAGUA

Aruba
(NETHERLANDS)

5

6

EL SALVADOR

Managua

Port of
Spain

7

PACIFIC OCEAN

COSTA RICA

Panama
City

TRINIDAD &
TOBAGO

10°N

SCALE

San José

0 200 400 Miles

PANAMA

COLOMBIA

VENEZUELA

GUYANA

0 200 400 Kilometers

Projection: Mercator

COUNTRY	CAPITAL
1 Antigua and Barbuda	St. Johns
2 St. Kitts and Nevis	Basseterre
3 Dominica	Roseau
4 St. Lucia	Castries
5 St. Vincent and the Grenadines	Kingstown
6 Barbados	Bridgetown
7 Grenada	St. George's

ARCTIC OCEAN

RUSSIA
⊛ Moscow

EUROPE

⊛ Astana

KAZAKHSTAN

Ulaanbaatar ⊛

MONGOLIA

Harbin •

GEORGIA
Istanbul
Ankara ⊛
ARMENIA
TURKEY
Baku ⊛
AZERBAIJAN
NICOSIA
CYPRUS
SYRIA
Beirut
LEBANON
Damascus ⊛
Tripoli
Jerusalem ⊛
ISRAEL
Amman
JORDAN
Cairo ⊛

UZBEKISTAN
Tashkent ⊛
TURKMENISTAN
Ashgabat ⊛
Tehran •

Almaty •

ASIA

Beijing ⊛
Tianjin •

NORTH
KOREA
P'yŏngyang ⊛
Seoul ⊛
SOUTH
KOREA
Pusan •

JAPAN
Tokyo ⊛
Yokohama •
Nagoya •
Osaka •

40°N

TAJIKISTAN

KYRGYZSTAN

CHINA

Baghdad ⊛
IRAQ
KUWAIT
BAHRAIN
QATAR OMAN

Kabul ⊛
AFGHANISTAN

Islamabad ⊛

Wuhan •
Chongqing •

Shanghai •

LIBYA

EGYPT

SAUDI
ARABIA
Riyadh ⊛

UNITED ARAB
EMIRATES

Karachi •

PAKISTAN

Delhi •
New
Delhi ⊛

NEPAL Kathmandu ⊛

BANGLADESH
Dhaka ⊛

BHUTAN

Calcutta •

Guangzhou •

Hong
Kong

Taipei •

TAIWAN

Tropic of Cancer

20°N

AFRICA

CHAD
N'Djamena ⊛

SUDAN
Khartoum ⊛

ERITREA
Asmara ⊛
YEMEN
Sanaa ⊛

OMAN

Muscat •

INDIA

Mumbai •
(Bombay)

MYANMAR
(BURMA)

Yangon •
(Rangoon)

LAOS
Hanoi ⊛

Manila •

Northern
Marianas
(U.S.)

PACIFIC
OCEAN

Guam (U.S.)

MARSHALL
ISLANDS

CENTRAL
AFRICAN
REPUBLIC

CAMEROON
EQUATORIAL
GUINEA

ETHIOPIA
Addis Ababa ⊛

SOMALIA

THAILAND
Chennai •
(Madras)
Bangkok ⊛

VIETNAM

CAMBODIA
Phnom Penh ⊛

PHILIPPINES

PALAU

DJIBOUTI

SRI
LANKA

Ho Chi
Minh City •

BRUNEI

FEDERATED STATES
OF MICRONESIA

GABON
REP.
OF THE
CONGO
Kinshasa ⊛
DEMOCRATIC REP.
OF THE CONGO

UGANDA
KENYA
Nairobi ⊛
RWANDA
BURUNDI

Colombo ⊛

MALDIVES

Kuala
Lumpur ⊛
MALAYSIA

Singapore •
SINGAPORE

INDONESIA

NAURU

Equator

KIRIBATI

0°

SEYCHELLES

TANZANIA
Dar es Salaam •

PAPUA
NEW
GUINEA

Port Moresby •

SOLOMON
ISLANDS

TUVALU

Luanda ⊛

MALAWI

INDIAN OCEAN

Jakarta •
Surabaya •

EAST TIMOR

ANGOLA

ZAMBIA
Lusaka ⊛

MOZAMBIQUE

COMOROS

MADAGASCAR
Antananarivo ⊛

VANUATU

New Caledonia
(FRANCE)

FIJI

20°S

ZIMBABWE
Harare ⊛

NAMIBIA

hoek

Gaborone ⊛
BOTSWANA

Réunion
(FRANCE)

MAURITIUS

AUSTRALIA

Tropic of Capricorn

Pretoria ⊛
Maputo ⊛
Johannesburg •
SWAZILAND

LESOTHO

SOUTH
AFRICA

Town

Sydney •
Canberra ⊛
Melbourne •

NEW
ZEALAND

Wellington ⊛

ANTARCTICA

Tasmania

20°E 40°E 60°E 80°E 100°E 120°E 140°E 160°E 60°S

	COUNTRY	CAPITAL
1	Czech Republic	Prague
2	Slovakia	Bratislava
3	Slovenia	Ljubljana
4	Croatia	Zagreb
5	Bosnia and Herzegovina	Sarajevo
6	Macedonia	Skopje
7	Serbia and Montenegro	Belgrade
8	Lithuania	Vilnius
9	Latvia	Riga
10	Estonia	Tallinn

SCALE

0   250   500   750 Miles

0   250 500   750 Kilometers

Projection: Mollweide

Arctic
Circle

ICELAND
⊛ Reykjavik

NORWAY

SWEDEN

FINLAND
Helsinki ⊛

60°N

St. Petersburg •

RUSSIA

Oslo ⊛
Stockholm ⊛
⊛ 10

NORTH SEA

UNITED
KINGDOM

DENMARK
Copenhagen ⊛

⊛ 9

⊛ 8

Minsk ⊛
Moscow ⊛

BELARUS

Dublin ⊛
IRELAND

NETHERLANDS
Amsterdam ⊛
The Hague •
London ⊛
Brussels ⊛
BELGIUM

Berlin ⊛
Warsaw ⊛

GERMANY
POLAND

Kiev ⊛

50°N

ATLANTIC

OCEAN

Paris ⊛
LUXEMBOURG
Bern ⊛
SWITZERLAND
LIECHTENSTEIN

⊛ 1
Vienna ⊛
AUSTRIA
⊛ 2
Budapest ⊛
HUNGARY
⊛ 3 ⊛ 4

UKRAINE

MOLDOVA
Chişinău ⊛

FRANCE

ITALY

MONACO
ANDORRA
Corsica
(FRANCE)

SAN MARINO
Rome ⊛
VATICAN CITY

ROMANIA
Bucharest •
⊛ 7
⊛ 5
BULGARIA
⊛ 6 ⊛ Sofia

BLACK SEA

PORTUGAL

Madrid ⊛
Lisbon •
SPAIN

Balearic
Is.
(SPAIN)

Sardinia
(ITALY)

Tirana ⊛
ALBANIA

40°N

GREECE

Athens ⊛

Gibraltar (U.K.)

MEDITERRANEAN

Sicily

SEA

Crete

MALTA

To understand the relative locations of Alaska and Hawaii, as well as the vast distances separating them from the rest of the United States, see the world map.

PACIFIC OCEAN

MEXICO

Kauai
Niihau
Oahu
Molokai
Maui
Lanai
Kahoolawe
PACIFIC OCEAN
Mauna Kea 13,796 ft. (4,206 m)
Hawaii
SCALE
0   75   150 Miles
0   75   150 Kilometers

Alaska inset:
ARCTIC OCEAN
Arctic Circle
RUSSIA
BROOKS RANGE
Bering Strait
St. Lawrence Island
St. Matthew Island
Nunivak Island
Yukon River
Kuskokwim River
Tanana River
ALASKA RANGE
Mount McKinley 20,320 ft. (6,194 m)
CANADA
GULF OF ALASKA
Kodiak Island
Alexander Archipelago
BERING SEA
Aleutian Islands
Attu Island
PACIFIC OCEAN
SCALE
0   250   500 Miles
0   250   500 Kilometers
Projection: Albers Equal Area

CANADA

MESABI RANGE

Isle Royale

Lake Superior

Lake Huron

Lake Michigan

Lake Ontario

Lake Erie

Wisconsin River

Mississippi River

Des Moines River

Illinois River

Wabash River

P L A I N S

Lake of the Ozarks

ARK PLATEAU

OUACHITA MTS.

White River

Red River

edo and ur reservoir

ine River

C O A S T A L —

Pearl River

Mississippi Delta

Chandeleur Islands

GULF OF MEXICO

N

Ohio River

Scioto River

Allegheny River

ALLEGHENY PLATEAU

CUMBERLAND PLATEAU

Lake Barkley

Cumberland River

Kentucky Lake

Tennessee River

GREAT SMOKY MTS.

BLUE RIDGE MOUNTAINS

A P P A L A C H I A N

Kanawha River

Monongahela R.

Potomac River

Susquehanna River

Finger Lakes

ADIRONDACK MTS.

CATSKILL MTS.

P L A T E A U

M O U N T A I N S

Hudson R.

Delaware R.

Delaware Bay

Chesapeake Bay

James River

Roanoke River

P I E D M O N T

A T L A N T I C   C O A S T A L   P L A I N

Coosa River

Alabama R.

Tombigbee River

Chattahoochee River

Oconee River

Savannah River

Altamaha River

Sea Islands

P L A I N

St. Lawrence River

St. Lawrence Seaway

Lake Champlain

GREEN MTS.

WHITE MTS.

LONGFELLOW MTS.

St. John River

Penobscot River

Connecticut River

Cape Cod

Long Island Sound

Long Island

ATLANTIC OCEAN

Pamlico Sound

Cape Hatteras

Okefenokee Swamp

FLORIDA PENINSULA

Cape Canaveral

Lake Okeechobee

The Everglades

Cape Sable

Florida Key

Straits of Florida

THE BAHAMAS

CUBA

ELEVATION

FEET	METERS
13,120	4,000
6,560	2,000
1,640	500
656	200
(Sea level) 0	0 (Sea level)
Below sea level	Below sea level

Ice cap

SCALE

0	250	500 Miles
0	250	500 Kilometers

Projection: Albers Equal Area

PACIFIC OCEAN

WASHINGTON
Strait of Juan de Fuca
Puget Sound
Seattle
Olympia ★
Tacoma
Spokane •
Portland •
Columbia River
★ Salem
• Eugene
OREGON

Franklin D. Roosevelt Lake
Pend Oreille
Flathead Lake
Helena ★
MONTANA
Fort Peck Lake
Missouri River
River
Yellowstone
• Billings

IDAHO
Boise ★
Snake River
Yellowstone Lake

WYOMING
Casper •
Cheyenne ★

Lake Sakakawea
NORTH DAKOTA
Bismarck ★
Fargo •
Red River
Lake Oahe
SOUTH DAKOTA
Pierre ★
Sioux Falls •

NEBRASKA
Platte River
Omah
Lincoln ★

Cape Mendocino
Shasta Lake
Goose Lake
Pyramid Lake
Reno •
Carson City ★
Lake Tahoe
NEVADA
Sacramento river
Berkeley
Oakland
San Francisco
San Francisco Bay
Sacramento •
• Stockton
• Modesto
San Joaquin R.
San Jose •
Monterey Bay
• Fresno
CALIFORNIA
• Bakersfield
Las Vegas •
Colorado River
Lake Mead
Los Angeles •
Long Beach •
Channel Islands
Anaheim •
Santa Ana
Salton Sea
• San Diego

Great Salt Lake
Utah Lake
★ Salt Lake City
• Provo
UTAH
Green River
Lake Powell

COLORADO
★ Denver
• Colorado Springs

KANSAS
Arkansas River
Topε
• Wich

ARIZONA
Phoenix ★
Gila River
• Tucson

Santa Fe ★
NEW MEXICO
• Albuquerque

Canadian River
OKLAHOMA
Oklahoma City ★
Keystone Lake
Eufa
• Amarillo
• Lubbock

Gulf of California

El Paso •
Pecos River

TEXAS
Abilene •
• Odessa
Fort Worth •
Da
Colorado River
Brazos River
★ Austin
San Antonio
Rio Grande
Amistad Reservoir
Corpus Christi •
• Laredo
Padre Island

MEXICO

To understand the relative locations of Alaska and Hawaii as well as the vast distances separating them from the rest of the United States, see the world map.

Kauai
Niihau
Oahu
Honolulu •
Molokai
HAWAII
Lanai
Kahoolawe
Maui
PACIFIC OCEAN
Hawaii
22°N
N
19°N

SCALE
0   75   150 Miles
0   75   150 Kilometers

ARCTIC OCEAN
Arctic Circle
RUSSIA
Bering Strait
Nome •
180°
St. Lawrence Island
St. Matthew Island
Nunivak Island
Yukon River
• Fairbanks
65°N
CANADA
ALASKA
• Anchorage
60°N
Kodiak Island
GULF OF ALASKA
Juneau •
Alexander Archipelago
55°N

BERING SEA
SCALE
0   250   500 Miles
0   250   500 Kilometers
Projection: Albers Equal Area

Attu Island
A l e u t i a n   I s l a n d s
PACIFIC OCEAN

CANADA

MINNESOTA
Duluth

Minneapolis
★St. Paul

WISCONSIN
Madison ★
Milwaukee

IOWA
Cedar Rapids
Davenport
Des Moines

Lake Superior

Lake Michigan

Lake Huron

MICHIGAN
Grand Rapids
Lansing
Flint
Detroit
Ann Arbor

Rockford
Chicago
Gary
South Bend
Fort Wayne
Peoria

INDIANA
Springfield
Indianapolis

ILLINOIS

St. Louis
Jefferson City
Evansville

Lake of the Ozarks

Kansas City

MISSOURI
Springfield

Fayetteville

ARKANSAS
Little Rock ★

MISSISSIPPI

Shreveport

LOUISIANA
Beaumont
Baton Rouge ★
New Orleans

GULF OF MEXICO

Toledo
Cleveland
Youngstown
Akron

OHIO
Dayton
Columbus
Cincinnati

Louisville
Frankfort
Lexington

KENTUCKY

Lake Barkley
Kentucky Lake

Nashville ★
Knoxville

TENNESSEE
Chattanooga
Memphis
Huntsville

Birmingham
Atlanta ★

ALABAMA
GEORGIA
Columbus
Macon
Montgomery ★

Jackson ★

Mobile

Chandeleur Islands

Tallahassee ★

FLORIDA

Orlando
Tampa
St. Petersburg
Lake Okeechobee

Fort Lauderdale
Miami

Cape Sable
Florida Keys
Straits of Florida

CUBA

St. Lawrence River

Lake Ontario

Lake Champlain

MAINE
Augusta ★

Montpelier ★

VT.
N.H.
Concord ★

Buffalo
Rochester
Syracuse
Albany

NEW YORK

Lake Erie

PENNSYLVANIA
Allentown
Harrisburg
Pittsburgh
Philadelphia

Susquehanna River

MASS.
Springfield
Worcester
Boston
Providence

CONN.
Hartford
New Haven
Bridgeport
R.I.

Cape Cod

Long Island Sound
Long Island

Newark
New York City
Jersey City
Trenton

N.J.

DELAWARE
Dover
Delaware Bay

Baltimore
MD.
Annapolis ★
⊛ Washington, D.C.
Arlington
Alexandria

WEST VIRGINIA
Charleston ★

VIRGINIA
Richmond ★
Roanoke
Newport News
Portsmouth
Norfolk

Chesapeake Bay

Cape Hatteras

Winston-Salem
Greensboro
Durham
Raleigh ★

NORTH CAROLINA
Charlotte

SOUTH CAROLINA
Columbia ★

Savannah

Savannah River
Sea Islands

Jacksonville

ATLANTIC OCEAN

THE BAHAMAS

Cape Canaveral

Legend:
Boundaries
⊛ National capitals
★ State capitals
• Other cities

N

SCALE
0   250   500 Miles
0   250   500 Kilometers
Projection: Albers Equal Area

NORTH AMERICA: PHYSICAL

ARCTIC OCEAN

EUROPE

ASIA

North Pole

POLAR ICE PACK

Queen Elizabeth Islands

Ellesmere Island

Greenland

Denmark Strait

St. Lawrence Island

Bering Strait

BERING SEA

Nunivak Island

BROOKS RANGE

BEAUFORT SEA

Banks Island

Baffin Bay

Cape Farewell

Davis Strait

Mt. McKinley 20,320 ft. (6,194 m)

ALASKA RANGE

Yukon River

Victoria Island

Baffin Island

Kodiak Island

GULF OF ALASKA

YUKON PLATEAU

Mackenzie River

Great Bear Lake

Southampton Island

Hudson Strait

LABRADOR SEA

Alexander Archipelago

Peace River

Great Slave Lake

Coats Island

Queen Charlotte Islands

Lake Athabasca

Mansel Island

Vancouver Island

Athabasca River

Hudson Bay

Anticosti Island

Newfoundland

Mount Rainier 14,410 ft. (4,392 m)

PACIFIC OCEAN

Saskatchewan River

Nelson River

CANADIAN SHIELD

St. Lawrence River

GULF OF ST. LAWRENCE

Prince Edward Island

Cape Breton Island

Columbia R.

COAST RANGE

CASCADE RANGE

Lake Winnipeg

Cape Mendocino

Snake River

Lake Superior

Lake Huron

Lake Ontario

Cape Cod

BLACK HILLS

Missouri River

Lake Michigan

Lake Erie

Long Island

APPALACHIAN MOUNTAINS

ATLANTIC OCEAN

SIERRA NEVADA

CENTRAL VALLEY

GREAT BASIN

DEATH VALLEY

Great Salt Lake

Platte River

INTERIOR PLAINS

Ohio R.

Cumberland R.

PIEDMONT

Bermuda

COAST RANGES

Mount Whitney 14,494 ft. (4,419 m)

COLORADO PLATEAU

Colorado River

Arkansas River

OZARK PLATEAU

Tennessee River

Mississippi River

Cape Hatteras

ATLANTIC COASTAL PLAIN

ROCKY MOUNTAINS

GREAT PLAINS

Red River

Tropic of Cancer

Guadalupe Island

GULF OF CALIFORNIA

BAJA CALIFORNIA

SIERRA MADRE OCCIDENTAL

Rio Grande

Brazos River

GULF COASTAL PLAIN

Cape Canaveral

FLORIDA PENINSULA

GULF OF MEXICO

Florida Keys

Straits of Florida

Bahamas

SIERRA MADRE ORIENTAL

Cuba

Greater Antilles

Hispaniola

Puerto Rico

Lesser Antilles

Jamaica

Popocatépetl 17,887 ft. (5,452 m)

YUCATÁN PENINSULA

CARIBBEAN SEA

Trinidad

SIERRA MADRE DEL SUR

Lake Nicaragua

CENTRAL AMERICA

ISTHMUS OF PANAMA

SOUTH AMERICA

Equator 0°

ELEVATION

FEET		METERS
13,120		4,000
6,560		2,000
1,640		500
656		200
(Sea level) 0		0 (Sea level)
Below sea level		Below sea level

Ice cap

N

SCALE

0   250   500   750   1,000 Miles

0   250   500   750   1,000 Kilometers

Projection: Azimuthal Equal Area

NORTH AMERICA: POLITICAL

ARCTIC OCEAN

ASIA

EUROPE

North Pole

ICELAND

Point Barrow

Queen Elizabeth Islands

Ellesmere Island

Greenland (DENMARK)

BEAUFORT SEA

Banks Island

Baffin Bay

ALASKA (U.S.)

Anchorage

Victoria Island

Baffin Island

Great Bear Lake

Southampton Island

Hudson Strait

Kodiak Island

Juneau

Alexander Archipelago

Great Slave Lake

Coats Island

Mansel Island

LABRADOR SEA

Cape Farewell

Queen Charlotte Islands

Hudson Bay

PACIFIC OCEAN

Edmonton

CANADA

Anticosti Island

Newfoundland

Vancouver Island

Vancouver

Calgary

Lake Winnipeg

St. Pierre and Miquelon (FRANCE)

Seattle

Portland

Winnipeg

Lake Superior

Quebec

Cape Breton Island

Prince Edward Island

Cape Mendocino

Minneapolis

Lake Michigan

Lake Huron

Lake Ontario

Lake Erie

Ottawa

Montreal

Toronto

Boston

Cape Cod

ATLANTIC OCEAN

Milwaukee

Detroit

Cleveland

New York City

San Francisco

San Jose

Salt Lake City

Chicago

Columbus

Philadelphia

Denver

Kansas City

Indianapolis

St. Louis

Baltimore

Washington, D.C.

Los Angeles

San Diego

UNITED STATES

Memphis

Norfolk

Bermuda (U.K.)

Tijuana

Phoenix

Atlanta

Cape Hatteras

Dallas

Birmingham

Austin

San Antonio

Houston

New Orleans

Jacksonville

Cape Canaveral

Tropic of Cancer

Monterrey

GULF OF MEXICO

Florida Keys

Miami

THE BAHAMAS

Turks and Caicos Islands (U.K.)

ST. KITTS & NEVIS

ANTIGUA & BARBUDA

MEXICO

Nassau

DOMINICAN REPUBLIC

Puerto Rico (U.S.)

San Juan

Guadeloupe (FRANCE)

Guadalajara

Mexico City

Havana

CUBA

DOMINICA

Puebla

Mérida

Cayman Is. (U.K.)

HAITI

Virgin Is. (U.S., U.K.)

Martinique (FRANCE)

BARBADOS

Kingston

Port-au-Prince

Santo Domingo

ST. LUCIA

Belmopan

JAMAICA

ST. VINCENT AND THE GRENADINES

GRENADA

BELIZE

CARIBBEAN SEA

Netherlands Antilles (NETHERLANDS)

GUATEMALA

HONDURAS

Guatemala City

Tegucigalpa

Aruba (NETHERLANDS)

TRINIDAD AND TOBAGO

San Salvador

NICARAGUA

EL SALVADOR

Managua

Panama Canal

COSTA RICA

San José

Panama City

PANAMA

SOUTH AMERICA

Equator

Legend

- Boundaries
- ⊛ National capitals
- • Other cities

N

SCALE

0 — 500 — 1,000 Miles

0 — 500 — 1,000 Kilometers

Projection: Azimuthal Equal Area

CENTRAL
AMERICA

CARIBBEAN SEA

N

ATLANTIC
OCEAN

Panama
Canal

GULF
OF
PANAMA

Margarita
Island

Tobago
Trinidad

Orinoco River
Delta

Lake
Maracaibo

Cauca
River

Magdalena
River

LLANOS

Meta
River

Orinoco River

Angel Falls

GUIANA

HIGHLANDS

Devil's Island
Cape Orange

Malpelo
Island

Mount Tolima
18,425 ft. (5,616 m)

Orinoco River

Amazon
River
Delta

Galápagos
Islands

0° Equator

Mount Chimborazo
20,561 ft. (6,267 m)

GULF OF
GUAYAQUIL

Marañón
River

Caquetá
River

Japurá
River

Amazon
River

Rio Negro

AMAZON

BASIN

Amazon River

Tapajós
River

Tocantins River

Equator 0°

Juruá
River

Ucayali River

Purus

Madeira
River

Xingu
River

BRAZILIAN

10°S

ANDES

Mount Huascarán
22,205 ft. (6,768 m)

PACIFIC

OCEAN

Beni River

Mamoré

Ancohuma Peak
20,958 ft. (6,388 m)

MATO GROSSO
PLATEAU

Araguaia

São Francisco River

HIGHLANDS

10°S

ATACAMA DESERT

ANDES

Pilcomayo River

CHACO

Paraguay
River

BRAZILIAN
PLATEAU

20°S

Tropic of Capricorn

San Ambrosio
Island

San Félix Island

Salado River

Paraná River

Uruguay River

Tropic of Capricorn

Juan Fernández
Islands

Mount Aconcagua
22,834 ft. (6,960 m)

Salado River

Rio de la Plata

30°S

ATLANTIC

OCEAN

PAMPAS

Colorado
River

Chiloé
Island

CHONOS
ARCHIPELAGO

PATAGONIA

ANDES

GULF OF SAN MATÍAS

GULF OF
SAN JORGE

Cape Tres Puntas

40°S

Bahia
Grande

Strait of
Magellan

Falkland
Islands

South
Georgia
Islands

TIERRA DEL
FUEGO

CAPE HORN

50°S

ELEVATION

FEET		METERS
13,120		4,000
6,560		2,000
1,640		500
656		200
(Sea level) 0		0 (Sea level)
Below sea level		Below sea level

SCALE

0   250   500   750   1,000 Miles

0   250   500   750   1,000 Kilometers

Projection: Azimuthal Equal Area

SOUTH AMERICA: POLITICAL

CENTRAL AMERICA

CARIBBEAN SEA

ATLANTIC OCEAN

N

Barranquilla
Cartagena
Caracas
Lake Maracaibo
VENEZUELA
Georgetown
Paramaribo
GUYANA
Cayenne
Medellín
Bogotá
SURINAME
FRENCH GUIANA (FRANCE)
COLOMBIA
Cali
Malpelo Island (COLOMBIA)
Orinoco River
Rio Negro
Quito
ECUADOR
Equator 0°
Equator
Guayaquil
Amazon River
Belém
Galápagos Islands (ECUADOR)
Amazon River
Marañón River
BRAZIL
Recife
PERU
Trujillo
Ucayali River
PACIFIC OCEAN
Callao
Lima
Lake Titicaca
Arequipa
BOLIVIA
La Paz
Lake Poopó
Brasília
São Francisco River
Salvador
Sucre
Belo Horizonte
PARAGUAY
Campinas
São Paulo
Rio de Janeiro
Tropic of Capricorn
Tropic of Capricorn
Paraguay River
Asunción
Curitiba
San Félix Island (CHILE)
San Ambrosio Island (CHILE)
CHILE
Paraná River
Pôrto Alegre
Uruguay River
Juan Fernández Islands (CHILE)
Córdoba
Valparaíso
Santiago
Rosario
URUGUAY
Buenos Aires
Montevideo
ATLANTIC OCEAN
Río de la Plata
ARGENTINA

Legend
- Boundaries
- ⊛ National capitals
- • Other cities

SCALE
0   250   500   750   1,000 Miles
0   250 500 750 1,000 Kilometers
Projection: Azimuthal Equal Area

Strait of Magellan
Falkland Islands (U.K.)
South Georgia Island (U.K.)
Tierra del Fuego

EUROPE: PHYSICAL

ASIA

URAL MOUNTAINS

BARENTS SEA

KOLA PENINSULA

White Sea

Pechora River

Dvina River

North Dvina River

Kama River

Ural River

Volga River

Don River

CASPIAN SEA

Mt. Elbrus (5,642 m)
18,510 ft

CAUCASUS MTS.

SEA OF AZOV

CRIMEAN PENINSULA

BLACK SEA

SOUTHWEST ASIA

NORTHERN EUROPEAN PLAIN

Lake Onega

Lake Ladoga

Rybinsk Reservoir

Dnipro River

Dnestr River

Nistru River

CARPATHIAN MTS.

TRANSYLVANIAN ALPS

BALKAN PENINSULA

SEA OF MARMARA

AEGEAN SEA

Rhodes

Crete

Daugava R.

NORTH PLAINS

GULF OF FINLAND

BALTIC SEA

Vistula River

Oder River

Elbe River

Danube River

DINARIC ALPS

ADRIATIC SEA

APENNINES

Tiber River

TYRRHENIAN SEA

Sicily

Malta

MEDITERRANEAN SEA

AFRICA

NORTH CAPE

ARCTIC OCEAN

KJØLEN MOUNTAINS

GULF OF BOTHNIA

Lake Vättern

Lake Vänern

Kattegat

Skagerrak

NORWEGIAN SEA

Arctic Circle

Iceland

Faeroe Islands

Shetland Islands

Orkney Islands

Hebrides

BRITISH ISLES

IRISH SEA

PENNINES

Thames River

English Channel

NORTH SEA

Rhine River

Seine River

Loire River

ALPS

Mont Blanc
15,781 ft (4,810 m)

Lake Geneva

Rhône River

PYRENEES

Garonne River

Ebro River

Bay of Biscay

Cape Finisterre

IBERIAN PENINSULA

Douro River

Tagus River

Guadiana River

Guadalquivir River

Strait of Gibraltar

Corsica

Sardinia

Balearic Islands

ATLANTIC OCEAN

ELEVATION
FEET   METERS
13,120   4,000
6,560   2,000
1,640   500
656   200
0   0 (Sea level)
(Sea level)
Below   Below
sea level sea level

Ice cap

SCALE
0   250   500 Miles
0   250   500 Kilometers
Projection: Azimuthal Equal Area

A14 • Atlas

EUROPE: POLITICAL

Boundaries
⊛ National capitals
• Other cities

SCALE

Projection: Azimuthal Equal Area

ASIA: PHYSICAL

ELEVATION

FEET	METERS
13,120	4,000
6,560	2,000
1,640	500
656	200
(Sea level) 0	0 (Sea level)
Below sea level	Below sea level

Ice cap

NORTH AMERICA

Wrangel Island

New Siberian Islands

Aleutian Islands

KAMCHATKA PENINSULA

BERING SEA

SEA OF OKHOTSK

CENTRAL RANGE

Sakhalin Island

Kuril Islands

Hokkaido

Honshu

Shikoku

Kyushu

SEA OF JAPAN

Korea Strait

Okinawa

Ryukyu Islands

Taiwan

Luzon Strait

Luzon

Philippines

Mindanao

EAST CHINA SEA

YELLOW SEA

NORTH CHINA PLAIN

BOHEA HILLS

SOUTH CHINA SEA

Hainan

GULF OF TONKIN

PACIFIC OCEAN

New Guinea

MAOKE MOUNTAINS

AUSTRALIA

ARAFURA SEA

BANDA SEA

Celebes

CELEBES SEA

Borneo

Moluccas

JAVA SEA

Bangka

Java

Sumatra

Mentawai Islands

Strait of Malacca

MALAY PENINSULA

GULF OF THAILAND

INDOCHINA PENINSULA

Chao Phraya River

Mekong River

Xi River

Chang

Hong River

Huang

He

QIN LING

GREAT WALL

GREATER KHINGAN RANGE

GOBI

MONGOLIAN PLATEAU

STANOVOY MOUNTAINS

KOLYMA MTS.

CHERSKIY RANGE

VERKHOYANSKY RANGE

YABLONOVY RANGE

Aldan River

Lena River

Amur River

Shilka River

SAYAN MOUNTAINS

ALTAY MOUNTAINS

CENTRAL SIBERIAN PLATEAU

S I B E R I A

TAYMYR PENINSULA

North Land

Franz Josef Land

Novaya Zemlya

KARA SEA

LAPTEV SEA

BARENTS SEA

Tunguska River

Lower Tunguska River

Angara River

Yenisey River

WEST SIBERIAN PLAIN

Ob River

Irtysh River

Ishim River

KAZAKH UPLANDS

Balqash Lake

TIAN SHAN

TARIM BASIN

TAKLIMAKAN DESERT

KUNLUN MOUNTAINS

PLATEAU OF TIBET

Mount Everest 29,035 ft. (8,850 m)

HIMALAYAS

Brahmaputra River

Nu River

Salween River

Irrawaddy River

ANDAMAN SEA

Andaman Islands

Nicobar Islands

Bay of Bengal

Sri Lanka

EASTERN GHATS

DECCAN PLATEAU

Godavari River

WESTERN GHATS

Ganges River

INDO-GANGETIC PLAIN

THAR DESERT

Indus River

Sutlej River

HINDU KUSH

PAMIRS

KYZYL KUM

KARA KUM

Amu Darya

Syr Darya

TURAN LOWLAND

ARAL SEA

URAL MOUNTAINS

Ural River

CASPIAN SEA

GREAT SALT DESERT

IRANIAN PLATEAU

ZAGROS MTS.

PERSIAN GULF

GULF OF OMAN

Strait of Hormuz

ARABIAN SEA

Socotra Island

GULF OF ADEN

RUB' AL-KHALI

AN-NAFUD

SYRIAN DESERT

Tigris River

Euphrates River

ANATOLIAN PLATEAU

Mount Ararat 16,945 ft. (5,165 m)

CAUCASUS MTS.

Bosporus

SEA OF AZOV

BLACK SEA

Cyprus

SINAI PENINSULA

RED SEA

MEDITERRANEAN SEA

EUROPE

AFRICA

Lakshadweep Islands

Maldives

INDIAN OCEAN

N

SCALE

0   500   1,000 Miles

0   500   1,000 Kilometers

Projection: Modified Oblique Conic

Tropic of Cancer

Arctic Circle

Equator

ASIA: POLITICAL

Boundaries
⊛ National capitals
• Other cities

PACIFIC OCEAN

INDIAN OCEAN

AUSTRALIA

EUROPE

AFRICA

RUSSIA

MONGOLIA

CHINA

KAZAKHSTAN

INDIA

JAPAN

NORTH KOREA

SOUTH KOREA

TAIWAN

PHILIPPINES

VIETNAM

LAOS

THAILAND

CAMBODIA

MYANMAR (BURMA)

MALAYSIA

SINGAPORE

INDONESIA

BRUNEI

EAST TIMOR

SRI LANKA

MALDIVES

NEPAL

BHUTAN

BANGLADESH

PAKISTAN

AFGHANISTAN

IRAN

IRAQ

SAUDI ARABIA

YEMEN

OMAN

UNITED ARAB EMIRATES

QATAR

BAHRAIN

KUWAIT

JORDAN

SYRIA

LEBANON

ISRAEL

CYPRUS

TURKEY

GEORGIA

ARMENIA

AZERBAIJAN

TURKMENISTAN

UZBEKISTAN

TAJIKISTAN

KYRGYZSTAN

SCALE

1000 Miles

1000 Kilometers

500

Projection: Two-Point Equidistant

AFRICA: PHYSICAL

EUROPE

CENTRAL ASIA

SOUTHWEST ASIA

MEDITERRANEAN SEA

Azores

Madeira Islands

Strait of Gibraltar

ATLAS MOUNTAINS

Canary Islands

GULF OF SIDRA

LIBYAN DESERT

QATTARA DEPRESSION

Suez Canal

PERSIAN GULF

S A H A R A

AHAGGAR MOUNTAINS

AIR MTS.

TIBESTI MOUNTAINS

Nile River

Lake Nasser

NUBIAN DESERT

RED SEA

Tropic of Cancer

Cape Blanc

EL DJOUF

Cape Verde Islands

Cape Verde

Niger River

Senegal R.

S A H E L

FOUTA DJALLON

S U D A N

CHAD BASIN

Lake Chad

White Volta

Black Volta

Lake Volta

Benue River

ADAMAWA MTS.

SUDAN BASIN

Blue Nile

White Nile

Lake Tana

ETHIOPIAN HIGHLANDS

HORN OF AFRICA

SOMALI PENINSULA

GULF OF ADEN

Cape Palmas

GULF OF GUINEA

Ubangi River

Congo River

Cape Lopez

CONGO BASIN

Lake Albert

Lake Edward

RIFT VALLEY

Lake Turkana

Mount Kenya 17,058 ft. (5,199 m)

ATLANTIC OCEAN

Kasai River

Lake Kivu

Lake Victoria

SERENGETI PLAIN

Mount Kilimanjaro 19,340 ft. (5,895 m)

INDIAN OCEAN

Equator

Ascension

MITUMBA MOUNTAINS

WESTERN RIFT VALLEY

Lake Tanganyika

EASTERN RIFT VALLEY

MASAI STEPPE

Zanzibar

Seychelles

Cuanza River

Lake Rukwa

Lake Mweru

Cape Delgado

Comoro Islands

Lake Malawi (Nyasa)

NAMIB DESERT

Lake Kariba

Zambezi River

Victoria Falls

Okavango Delta

KALAHARI BASIN

Madagascar

Mauritius

Réunion

KALAHARI DESERT

Limpopo River

Tropic of Capricorn

Mozambique Channel

Vaal River

Orange River

DRAKENSBERG MOUNTAINS

GREAT KARROO

Cape of Good Hope

ELEVATION

FEET	METERS
13,120	4,000
6,560	2,000
1,640	500
656	200
(Sea level) 0	0 (Sea level)
Below sea level	Below sea level

N

SCALE

0 — 500 — 1,000 Miles

0 — 500 — 1,000 Kilometers

Projection: Azimuthal Equal Area

AFRICA: POLITICAL

EUROPE

CENTRAL ASIA

SOUTHWEST ASIA

MEDITERRANEAN SEA

Azores (PORTUGAL)

Madeira (PORTUGAL)

Strait of Gibraltar
Casablanca • Rabat ⊛   Algiers ⊛ Tunis
MOROCCO   **TUNISIA**   Tripoli ⊛

Canary Islands (SPAIN)
El Aaiún •
WESTERN SAHARA (Claimed by Morocco)

ALGERIA   **LIBYA**   **EGYPT**
Alexandria •
Giza • Cairo ⊛
Suez Canal

Tropic of Cancer

MAURITANIA   Nouakchott ⊛   **MALI**   **NIGER**   **CHAD**   Khartoum ⊛   **ERITREA**   Asmara ⊛
Lake Nasser
RED SEA

CAPE VERDE   Praia ⊛
SENEGAL   Dakar ⊛   Bamako ⊛   *Niger River*   Niamey ⊛   **SUDAN**   *Blue Nile*   **DJIBOUTI**   Djibouti ⊛
Banjul ⊛ **GAMBIA**   **BURKINA FASO**   *Lake Chad*   N'Djamena •   GULF OF ADEN
Bissau ⊛   **GUINEA**   Ouagadougou ⊛   **NIGERIA**   *White Nile*   **ETHIOPIA**
GUINEA-BISSAU   Conakry ⊛   **CÔTE D'IVOIRE** **GHANA**   **BENIN**   **TOGO**   Abuja ⊛   Addis Ababa ⊛
Freetown ⊛   Yamoussoukro ⊛   Lomé ⊛   Lagos •   **CENTRAL AFRICAN REPUBLIC**   **SOMALIA**
SIERRA LEONE   Abidjan • Accra ⊛   Portò-Novo ⊛   Bangui ⊛
Monrovia ⊛   **CAMEROON**   **UGANDA**   **KENYA**   Mogadishu •
LIBERIA   Malabo •   Yaoundé ⊛   Kampala ⊛   Nairobi ⊛

N

EQUATORIAL GUINEA   *GULF OF GUINEA*
SÃO TOMÉ AND PRÍNCIPE   **REPUBLIC OF THE CONGO**   *Congo River*   Kisangani •   **RWANDA**   Kigali ⊛   *Lake Victoria*   **INDIAN OCEAN**
São Tomé •   Libreville ⊛   **GABON**   **DEMOCRATIC REPUBLIC OF THE CONGO**   Bujumbura ⊛   **BURUNDI**   Victoria ⊛
Equator   Brazzaville ⊛   **TANZANIA**   **SEYCHELLES**
CABINDA (ANGOLA)   Kinshasa ⊛   Dodoma ⊛   Mombasa •
Luanda ⊛   *Lake Tanganyika*   Zanzibar • Pemba •   Dar es Salaam •

ATLANTIC OCEAN

ANGOLA   Lubumbashi •   *Lake Malawi (Nyasa)*   **COMOROS**   Moroni ⊛
ZAMBIA   **MALAWI**   Lilongwe ⊛
St. Helena (U.K.)   Lusaka ⊛   *Zambezi River*
Harare ⊛   **MOZAMBIQUE**   Antananarivo ⊛   **MAURITIUS**
NAMIBIA   **ZIMBABWE**   Port Louis ⊛
Bulawayo •   **MADAGASCAR**   *Réunion (FRANCE)*
BOTSWANA   Tropic of Capricorn
Windhoek ⊛   Gaborone ⊛   Pretoria ⊛   Maputo •
Johannesburg •   Mbabane ⊛   **SWAZILAND**
Bloemfontein ⊛   Maseru ⊛   **LESOTHO**
Orange River   **SOUTH AFRICA**
Cape Town •

Legend

	Boundaries
⊛	National capitals
•	Other cities

SCALE

0 — 500 — 1,000 Miles
0 — 500 — 1,000 Kilometers

Projection: Azimuthal Equal Area

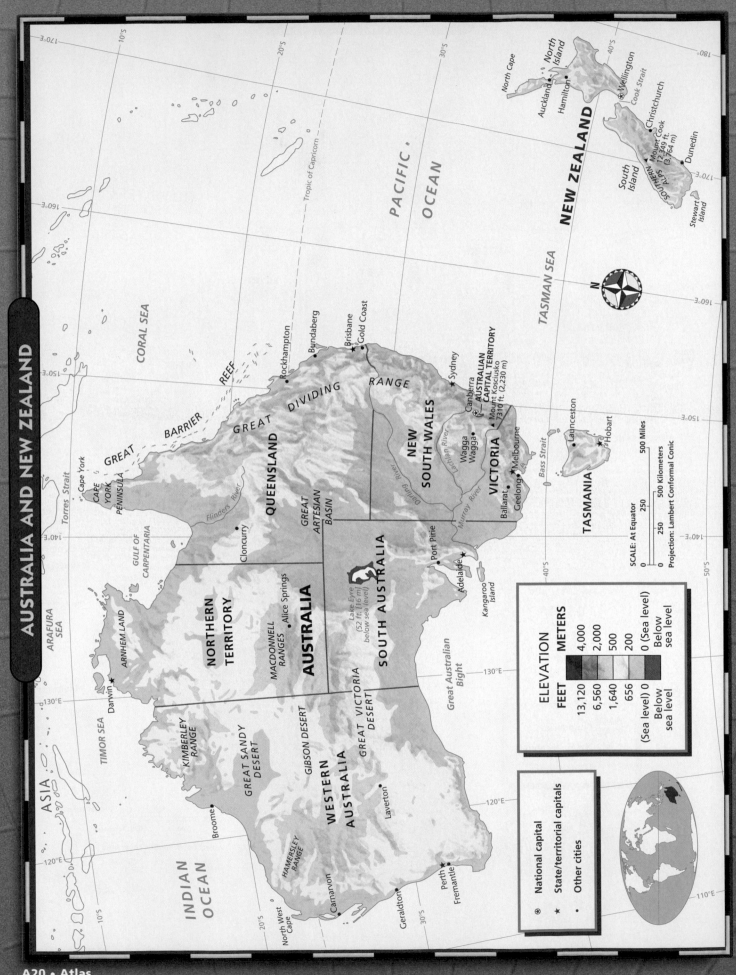

AUSTRALIA AND NEW ZEALAND

NEW ZEALAND

North Cape
North Island
Auckland • Hamilton
Wellington
⊗ Cook Strait
Christchurch
South Island
Mount Cook
12,349 ft.
(3,764 m)
SOUTHERN ALPS
Dunedin
Stewart Island

PACIFIC OCEAN

TASMAN SEA

N

CORAL SEA

GREAT BARRIER REEF
Tropic of Capricorn

Cape York
CAPE YORK PENINSULA
Torres Strait

GREAT DIVIDING RANGE

Rockhampton
Bundaberg
Brisbane
Gold Coast

QUEENSLAND

Flinders River

GREAT ARTESIAN BASIN

Cloncurry

NEW SOUTH WALES

Sydney
Canberra ⊗
AUSTRALIAN CAPITAL TERRITORY
Mount Kosciusko
7,310 ft. (2,230 m)

Lachlan River
Wagga Wagga
Darling River
Murray River

VICTORIA
Melbourne
Geelong ★
Ballarat •

Launceston
TASMANIA
Hobart ★
Bass Strait

GULF OF CARPENTARIA

NORTHERN TERRITORY

Alice Springs
MACDONNELL RANGES

AUSTRALIA

Lake Eyre
(52 ft. [16 m]
below sea level)

SOUTH AUSTRALIA

Port Pirie
Adelaide ★
Kangaroo Island

Great Australian Bight

130°E

ARNHEM LAND
Darwin ★
ASIA

TIMOR SEA

ARAFURA SEA

KIMBERLEY RANGE

GREAT SANDY DESERT

GIBSON DESERT

GREAT VICTORIA DESERT

WESTERN AUSTRALIA

Laverton •
120°E

HAMERSLEY RANGE

North West Cape
Canarvon
Geraldton

Perth ★
Fremantle

INDIAN OCEAN

Broome •

10°S
20°S
30°S

110°E
120°E
130°E

ELEVATION

FEET	METERS
13,120	4,000
6,560	2,000
1,640	500
656	200
(Sea level) 0	0 (Sea level)
Below sea level	Below sea level

SCALE: At Equator
0   250   500 Miles
0   250   500 Kilometers
Projection: Lambert Conformal Conic

⊗ National capital
★ State/territorial capitals
• Other cities

NORTH POLE

EUROPE

KARA SEA

BARENTS SEA

NORWEGIAN SEA

ASIA

LAPTEV SEA

GREENLAND SEA

Iceland

ATLANTIC OCEAN

ARCTIC OCEAN

150°E

+ NORTH POLE

30°W

Arctic Circle

80°N

Greenland (DENMARK)

70°N

70°N

PACK ICE

Queen Elizabeth Islands

NORTH MAGNETIC POLE

Baffin Bay

60°N

International Date Line

60°N

Baffin Island

180°

BERING SEA

BEAUFORT SEA

50°N

PACIFIC OCEAN

150°W

120°W

90°W

60°W

NORTH AMERICA

SCALE

| 0 | 250 | 500 | 750 Miles |
| 0 | 250 | 500 | 750 Kilometers |

Projection: Polar Azimuthal Equidistant

PACIFIC OCEAN

120°W

SOUTH AMERICA

180°

150°W

AMUNDSEN SEA

90°W

BELLINGSHAUSEN SEA

PACK ICE

60°W

ROSS SEA

MARIE BYRD LAND

ANTARCTIC PENINSULA

ELLSWORTH LAND

Vinson Massif 16,066 ft. (4,897 m)

RONNE ICE SHELF

PACK ICE

WEDDELL SEA

International Date Line

ROSS ICE SHELF

MAUD MOUNTAINS

QUEEN

Mount Markham over 14,275 ft. (over 4,351 m)

EDITH RONNE LAND

FILCHNER ICE SHELF

ATLANTIC

POLAR

SOUTH POLE

COATS LAND

150°E

PLATEAU

30°W

OCEAN

SOUTH MAGNETIC POLE

ADELIE LAND

ANTARCTICA

ICE CAP

0°

WILKES LAND

QUEEN MAUD LAND

60°S

60°S

120°E

SHACKLETON ICE SHELF

AMERICAN HIGHLAND

70°S

Antarctic Circle

50°S

INDIAN OCEAN

90°E

ENDERBY LAND

30°E

50°S

60°E

SCALE

| 0 | 250 | 500 | 750 Miles |
| 0 | 250 | 500 | 750 Kilometers |

Projection: Polar Azimuthal Equidistant

GEOGRAPHY & MAP SKILLS

HANDBOOK

Studying geography requires the ability to understand and use various tools. This Skills Handbook explains how to use maps, charts, and other graphics to help you learn about geography and the various regions of the world. Throughout this textbook, you will have the opportunity to improve these skills and build upon them.

CONTENTS

GEOGRAPHIC

Vocabulary

- globe
- grid
- latitude
- equator
- parallels
- degrees
- minutes

- longitude
- prime meridian
- meridians
- hemispheres
- continents
- islands
- ocean

- map
- map projections
- compass rose
- scale
- legend

MAPPING

THE EARTH

The Globe

A **globe** is a scale model of Earth. It is useful for looking at the entire Earth or at large areas of Earth's surface.

The pattern of lines that circle the globe in east-west and north-south directions is called a **grid**. The intersection of these imaginary lines helps us find places on Earth.

The east-west lines in the grid are lines of **latitude**. These imaginary lines measure distance north and south of the **equator**. The equator is an imaginary line that circles the globe halfway between the North and South Poles. Lines of latitude are called **parallels** because they are always parallel to the equator. Parallels measure distance from the equator in **degrees**. The symbol for degrees is °. Degrees are further divided into **minutes**. The symbol for minutes is ´. There are 60 minutes in a degree. Parallels north of the equator are labeled with an *N*. Those south of the equator are labeled with an *S*.

The north-south lines are lines of **longitude**. These imaginary lines pass through the Poles. They measure distance east and west of the **prime meridian**. The prime meridian is an imaginary line that runs through Greenwich, England. It represents 0° longitude. Lines of longitude are called **meridians**.

Lines of latitude range from 0°, for locations on the equator, to 90°N or 90°S, for locations at the Poles. See **Figure 1**. Lines of longitude range from 0° on the prime meridian to 180° on a meridian in the mid-Pacific Ocean. Meridians west of the prime meridian to 180° are labeled with a *W*. Those east of the prime meridian to 180° are labeled with an *E*. See **Figure 2**.

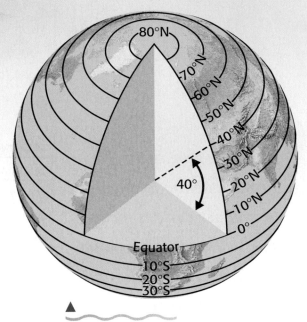

Figure 1: The east-west lines in the grid are lines of latitude.

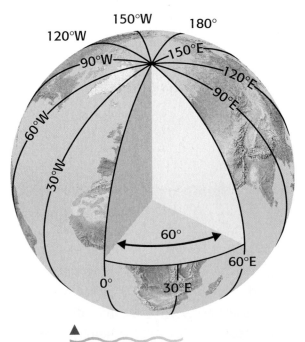

Figure 2: The north-south lines are lines of longitude.

NORTHERN HEMISPHERE

SOUTHERN HEMISPHERE

Figure 3: The hemispheres

The equator divides the globe into two halves, called **hemispheres**. See **Figure 3**. The half north of the equator is the Northern Hemisphere. The southern half is the Southern Hemisphere. The prime meridian and the 180° meridian divide the world into the Eastern Hemisphere and the Western Hemisphere. The prime meridian separates parts of Europe and Africa into two different hemispheres. To prevent this, some mapmakers divide the Eastern and Western hemispheres at 20° W. This places all of Europe and Africa in the Eastern Hemisphere.

Our planet's land surface is organized into seven large landmasses, called **continents**. They are identified in **Figure 3**. Landmasses smaller than continents and completely surrounded by water are called **islands**. Geographers also organize Earth's water surface into parts. The largest is the world **ocean**. Geographers divide the world ocean into the Pacific Ocean, the Atlantic Ocean, the Indian Ocean, and the Arctic Ocean. Lakes and seas are smaller bodies of water.

EASTERN HEMISPHERE

WESTERN HEMISPHERE

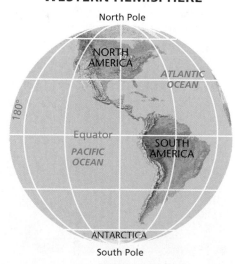

YOUR TURN

1. Look at the Student Atlas map on page A4. What islands are located near the intersection of latitude 20° N and longitude 160° W?
2. Name the four hemispheres. In which hemispheres is the United States located?
3. Name the continents of the world.
4. Name the oceans of the world.

MAPMAKING

A **map** is a flat diagram of all or part of Earth's surface. Mapmakers have different ways of showing our round Earth on flat maps. These different ways are called **map projections**. Because our planet is round, all flat maps lose some accuracy. Mapmakers must choose the type of map projection that is best for their purposes. Many map projections are one of three kinds: cylindrical, conic, or flat-plane.

Figure 4: If you remove the peel from the orange and flatten the peel, it will stretch and tear. The larger the piece of peel, the more its shape is distorted as it is flattened. Also distorted are the distances between points on the peel.

Figure 5A: Paper cylinder

Cylindrical projections are designed from a cylinder wrapped around the globe. See **Figure 5A**. The cylinder touches the globe only at the equator. The meridians are pulled apart and are parallel to each other instead of meeting at the Poles. This causes landmasses near the Poles to appear larger than they really are. **Figure 5B** is a Mercator projection, one type of cylindrical projection. The Mercator projection is useful for navigators because it shows true direction and shape. The Mercator projection for world maps, however, emphasizes the Northern Hemisphere. Africa and South America appear smaller than they really are.

Figure 5B: A Mercator projection, although accurate near the equator, distorts distances between regions of land. This projection also distorts the sizes of areas near the poles.

Conic projections are designed from a cone placed over the globe. See **Figure 6A**. A conic projection is most accurate along the lines of latitude where it touches the globe. It retains almost true shape and size. Conic projections are most useful for areas that have long east-west dimensions, such as the United States. See the map in **Figure 6B**.

Figure 6A: Paper cone

▲ Figure 6B: Conic projection

Flat-plane projections are designed from a plane touching the globe at one point, such as at the North Pole or South Pole. See **Figures 7A** and **7B**. A flat-plane projection is useful for showing true direction for airplane pilots and ship navigators. It also shows true area. However, it distorts true shape.

◄ Figure 7A: Flat plane

▲ Figure 7B: Flat-plane projection

The Robinson projection is a compromise between size and shape distortions. It often is used for world maps, such as the map on page 76. The minor distortions in size at high latitudes on Robinson projections are balanced by realistic shapes at the middle and low latitudes.

YOUR TURN

1. What are three major kinds of map projections?
2. Why is a Robinson projection often used for world maps?
3. What kind of projection is a Mercator map?
4. When would a mapmaker choose to use a conic projection?

MAP ESSENTIALS

In some ways, maps are like messages sent out in code. Mapmakers provide certain elements that help us translate these codes. These elements help us understand the message they are presenting about a particular part of the world. Of these elements, almost all maps have directional indicators, scales, and legends, or keys. **Figure 8**, a map of East Asia, has all three elements.

A directional indicator shows which directions are north, south, east, and west. Some mapmakers use a "north arrow," which points toward the North Pole. Remember, "north" is not always at the top of a map. The way a map is drawn and the location of directions on that map depend on the perspective of the mapmaker. Maps in this textbook indicate direction by using a **compass rose** ①. A compass rose has arrows that point to all four principal directions, as shown in **Figure 8**.

Figure 8: East and Southeast Asia—Physical

Mapmakers use scales to represent distances between points on a map. Scales may appear on maps in several different forms. The maps in this textbook provide a line **scale** ②. Scales give distances in miles and kilometers (km).

To find the distance between two points on the map in **Figure 8**, place a piece of paper so that the edge connects the two points. Mark the location of each point on the paper with a line or dot. Then, compare the distance between the two dots with the map's line scale. The number on the top of the scale gives the distance in miles. The number on the bottom gives the distance in kilometers. Because the distances are given in intervals, you will have to approximate the actual distance on the scale.

ELEVATION

FEET		METERS
13,120		4,000
6,560		2,000
1,640		500
656		200
(Sea level) 0		0 (Sea level)
Below sea level		Below sea level

The **legend** ③, or key, explains what the symbols on the map represent. Point symbols are used to specify the location of things, such as cities, that do not take up much space on a large-scale map. Some legends, such as the one in **Figure 8**, show which colors represent certain elevations. Other maps might have legends with symbols or colors that represent things such as roads. Legends can also show economic resources, land use, population density, and climate.

Size comparison of Canada to the contiguous United States

Physical maps at the beginning of each unit have size comparison maps ④. An outline of the mainland United States (not including Alaska and Hawaii) is compared to the area under study in that chapter. These size comparison maps help you understand the size of the areas you are studying in relation to the size of the United States.

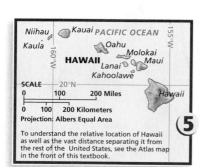

Niihau Kauai PACIFIC OCEAN
Kaula   Oahu
          HAWAII Molokai
               Lanai Maui
          Kahoolawe

SCALE   20°N
0   100   200 Miles
0   100   200 Kilometers
Projection: Albers Equal Area

Hawaii

To understand the relative location of Hawaii as well as the vast distance separating it from the rest of the United States, see the Atlas map in the front of this textbook.

Inset maps are sometimes used to show a small part of a larger map. Mapmakers also use inset maps to show areas that are far away from the areas shown on the main map. Maps of the United States, for example, often include inset maps of Alaska and Hawaii ⑤. Those two states are too far from the other 48 states to accurately represent the true distance on the main map. Subject areas in inset maps can be drawn to a scale different from the scale used on the main map.

YOUR TURN

Look at the Student Atlas map on pages A4 and A5.

1. Locate the compass rose. What country is directly west of Madagascar in Africa?

2. What island country is located southeast of India?

3. Locate the distance scale. Using the inset map, find the approximate distance in miles and kilometers from Oslo, Norway, to Stockholm, Sweden.

4. What is the capital of Brazil? What other cities are shown in Brazil?

WORKING
WITH MAPS

The Atlas at the front of this textbook includes two kinds of maps: physical and political. At the beginning of most units in this textbook, you will find five kinds of maps. These physical, political, climate, population, and land use and resources maps provide different kinds of information about the region you will study in that unit. These maps are accompanied by questions. Some questions ask you to show how the information on each of the maps might be related.

Figure 9: East and Southeast Asia—Climate

Mapmakers often combine physical and political features into one map. Physical maps, such as the one in **Figure 8** on page S6, show important physical features in a region, including major mountains and mountain ranges, rivers, oceans and other bodies of water, deserts, and plains. Physical-political maps also show important political features, such as national borders, state and provincial boundaries, and capitals and other important cities. You will find a physical-political map at the beginning of most chapters.

Mapmakers use climate maps to show the most important weather patterns in certain areas. Climate maps throughout this textbook use color to show the various climate regions of the world. See **Figure 9**. Colors that identify climate types are found in a legend with each map. Boundaries between climate regions do not indicate an immediate change in the main weather conditions between two climate regions. Instead, boundaries show the general areas of gradual change between climate regions.

Figure 10: East and Southeast Asia—Population

POPULATION DENSITY

Persons per sq. mile	Persons per sq. km
520	200
260	100
130	50
25	10
3	1
0	0

● Metropolitan areas with more than 2 million inhabitants

○ Metropolitan areas with 1 million to 2 million inhabitants

Population maps show where people live in a particular region. They also show how crowded, or densely populated, regions are. Population maps throughout this textbook use color to show population density. See **Figure 10**. Each color represents a certain number of people living within a square mile or square kilometer. Population maps also use symbols to show metropolitan areas with populations of a particular size. These symbols and colors are shown in a legend.

Land Use and Resources maps show the important resources of a region. See **Figure 11**. Symbols and colors are used to show information about economic development, such as where industry is located or where farming is most common. The meanings of each symbol and color are shown in a legend.

Figure 11: East and Southeast Asia—Land Use and Resources

RESOURCES
- Coal
- Natural gas
- Oil
- Nuclear power
- Hydroelectric power
- Gold
- Silver
- Other minerals
- Seafood

LAND USE
- Commercial farming
- Subsistence farming
- Forest
- Nomadic herding
- Limited economic activity
- Manufacturing
- ● Major manufacturing and trade centers

YOUR TURN

1. What is the purpose of a climate map?
2. Look at the population map. What is the population density of the area around Qingdao in northern China?
3. What energy resource is found near Ho Chi Minh City?

USING
GRAPHS, DIAGRAMS, CHARTS, AND TABLES

Bar graphs are a visual way to present information. The bar graph in **Figure 12** shows the imports and exports of the countries of southern Europe. The amount of imports and exports in billions of dollars is listed on the left side of the graph. Along the bottom of the graph are the names of the countries of southern Europe. Above each country or group of countries is a vertical bar. The top of the bar corresponds to a number along the left side of the graph. For example, Italy imports $200 billion worth of goods.

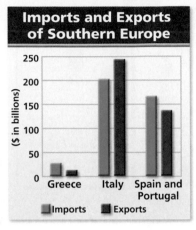

Figure 12: Reading a bar graph

Often, line graphs are used to show such things as trends, comparisons, and size. The line graph in **Figure 13** shows the population growth of the world over time. The information on the left shows the number of people in billions. The years being studied are listed along the bottom. Lines connect points that show the population in billions at each year under study. This line graph projects population growth into the future.

Figure 13: Reading a line graph

A pie graph shows how a whole is divided into parts. In this kind of graph, a circle represents the whole. The wedges represent the parts. Bigger wedges represent larger parts of the whole. The pie graph in **Figure 14** shows the percentages of the world's coffee beans produced by various groups of countries. Brazil is the largest grower. It grows 25 percent of the world's coffee beans.

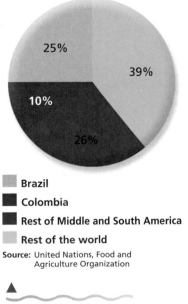

Source: United Nations, Food and Agriculture Organization

Figure 14: Reading a pie graph

Age structure diagrams show the number of males and females by age group. These diagrams are split into two sides, one for male and one for female. Along the bottom are numbers that show the number of males or females in the age groups. The age groups are listed on the side of the diagram. The wider the base of a country's diagram, the younger the population of that country. The wider the top of a country's diagram, the older the population.

Some countries have so many younger people that their age structure diagrams are shaped like pyramids. For this reason, these diagrams are sometimes called population pyramids. However, in some countries the population is more evenly distributed by age group. For example, see the age structure diagram for Germany in **Figure 15**. Germany's population is older. It is not growing as fast as countries with younger populations.

Germany's Population 2000

Male | Female

95+
90–94
85–89
80–84
75–79
70–74
65–69
60–64
55–59
50–54
45–49
40–44
35–39
30–34
25–29
20–24
15–19
10–14
5–9
0–4

4 3 2 1 0 1 2 3 4   age
Population (in millions)

Source: U.S. Census Bureau

Figure 15: Reading an age structure diagram

Figure 16: Reading an elevation profile

Each unit atlas includes an elevation profile. See **Figure 16**. It is a side view, or profile, of a region along a line drawn between two points.

Vertical and horizontal distances are figured differently on elevation profiles. The vertical distance (the height of a mountain, for example) is exaggerated when compared to the horizontal distance between the two points. This technique is called vertical exaggeration. If the vertical scale were not exaggerated, even tall mountains would appear as small bumps on an elevation profile.

In each unit and chapter on the various regions of the world, you will find tables that provide basic information about the countries under study.

The countries of Spain and Portugal are listed on the left in the table in **Figure 17**. You can match statistical information on the right with the name of each country listed on the left. The categories of information are listed across the top of the table.

Graphic organizers can help you understand certain ideas and concepts. For example, the diagram in **Figure 18** helps you think about the uses of water. In this diagram, one water use goes in each oval. Graphic organizers can help you focus on key facts in your study of geography.

Time lines provide highlights of important events over a period of time. The time line in **Figure 19** begins at the left with 5000 B.C., when rice was first cultivated in present-day China. The time line highlights important events that have shaped the human and political geography of China.

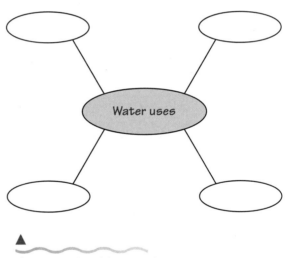

Spain and Portugal

COUNTRY	POPULATION/ GROWTH RATE	LIFE EXPECTANCY	LITERACY RATE	PER CAPITA GDP
Portugal	10,102,022 0.1%	72, male 80, female	93%	$18,000
Spain	40,217,413 0.1%	75, male 82, female	97%	$20,700
United States	290,342,554 0.9%	74, male 80, female	97%	$37,600

Source: Central Intelligence Agency, *The World Factbook 2003*

▲

Figure 17: Reading a table

Water uses

▲

Figure 18: Graphic organizer

Historic China: A Time Line

Qin becomes China's first dynasty
200s B.C.

Rise of Ming dynasty
1368

Cultural Revolution
1966–1976

| 5000 B.C. | A.D. 1 | 1000 | 1200 | 1400 | 1600 | 1800 | 2000 |

5000 B.C.
First rice farmers cultivate the area near the Chang River

206 B.C. – A.D. 220
Han dynasty dominates China

1200s
Mongols invade China

1912
Republic is established with the overthrow of the Manchu dynasty

1989
Government troops crush protesters in Tiananmen Square

▲

Figure 19: Reading a time line

Corn: From Field to Consumer

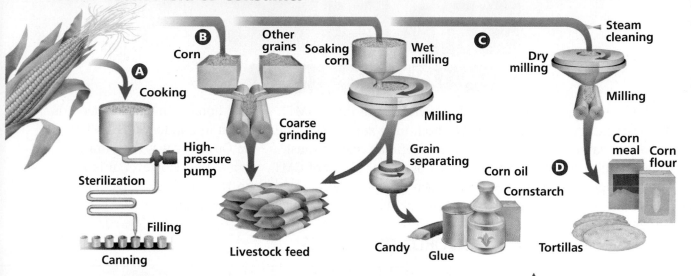

Figure 20: Reading a flowchart

A Corn can be processed in a variety of ways. Some corn is cooked and then canned.

B Corn is ground and used for livestock feed.

C Corn also might be wet-milled or dry-milled. Then grain parts are used to make different products.

D Corn by-products, such as cornstarch and corn syrup, are used to make breads, breakfast cereals, puddings, and snack foods. Corn oil is used for cooking.

Flowcharts are visual guides that explain different processes. They lead the reader from one step to the next, sometimes providing both illustrations and text. The flowchart in **Figure 20** shows the different steps involved in harvesting corn and preparing it for use by consumers. The flowchart takes you through the steps of harvesting and processing corn. Captions guide you through flowcharts.

YOUR TURN

1. Look at the statistical table for Spain and Portugal in Figure 17. Which countries have the highest literacy rate?

2. Look at the China time line in Figure 19. Name two important events in China's history between 1200 and 1400.

3. Look at Figure 20. What are three corn products?

READING
A TIME-ZONE MAP

The sun is not directly overhead everywhere on Earth at the same time. Clocks are set to reflect the difference in the sun's position. Our planet rotates on its axis once every 24 hours. In other words, in one hour, it makes one twenty-fourth of a complete rotation. Since there are 360 degrees in a circle, we know that the planet turns 15 degrees of longitude each hour. ($360° \div 24 = 15°$) We also know that the planet turns in a west-to-east direction. Therefore, if a place on Earth has the sun directly overhead at this moment (noon), then a place 15 degrees to the west will have the sun directly overhead one hour from now. During that hour the planet will have rotated 15 degrees. As a result, Earth is divided into 24 time zones. Thus, time is an hour earlier for each 15 degrees you move westward on Earth. Time is an hour later for each 15 degrees you move eastward on Earth.

By international agreement, longitude is measured from the prime meridian. This meridian passes through the Royal Observatory in Greenwich, England. Time also is measured from Greenwich and is called Greenwich mean time (GMT). For each time zone east of the prime meridian, clocks must be set one hour ahead of GMT. For each time zone west of Greenwich, clocks are set back one hour from GMT. When it is noon in London, it is 1:00 P.M. in Oslo, Norway, one time zone east. However, it is 7 A.M. in New York City, five time zones west.

WORLD TIME ZONES

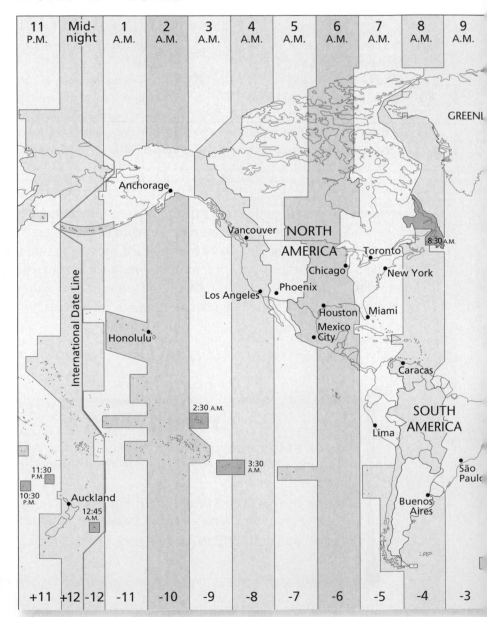

As you can see by looking at the map below, time zones do not follow meridians exactly. Political boundaries are often used to draw time-zone lines. In Europe and Africa, for example, time zones follow national boundaries. The mainland United States, meanwhile, is divided into four major time zones: Eastern, Central, Mountain, and Pacific. Alaska and Hawaii are in separate time zones to the west of the mainland.

Some countries have made changes in their time zones. For example, most of the United States has daylight savings time in the summer in order to have more evening hours of daylight.

The international date line is a north-south line that runs through the Pacific Ocean. It is located at 180°, although it sometimes varies from that meridian to avoid dividing countries.

At 180°, the time is 12 hours from Greenwich time. There is a time difference of 24 hours between the two sides of the 180° meridian. The 180° meridian is called the international date line because when you cross it, the date and day change. As you cross the date line from the west to the east, you gain a day. If you travel from east to west, you lose a day.

YOUR TURN

1. In which time zone do you live? Check your time now. What time is it in New York?

2. How many hours behind New York is Anchorage, Alaska?

3. How many time zones are there in Africa?

4. If it is 9 A.M. in the middle of Greenland, what time is it in São Paulo?

GEOGRAPHIC DICTIONARY

GULF
a large part of the ocean that extends into land

OCEAN
a large body of water

CORAL REEF
an ocean ridge made up of skeletal remains of tiny sea animals

PENINSULA
an area of land that sticks out into a lake or ocean

BAY
part of a large body of water that is smaller than a gulf

ISTHMUS
a narrow piece of land connecting two larger land areas

ISLAND
an area of land surrounded entirely by water

DELTA
an area where a river deposits soil into the ocean

STRAIT
a narrow body of water connecting two larger bodies of water

SINKHOLE
a circular depression formed when the roof of a cave collapses

WETLANDS
an area of land covered by shallow water

RIVER
a natural flow of water that runs through the land

LAKE
an inland body of water

FOREST
an area of densely wooded land

COAST
an area of land near the ocean

VALLEY
an area of low land between hills or mountains

MOUNTAIN
an area of rugged land that generally rises higher than 2,000 feet

VOLCANO
an opening in the Earth's crust where lava, ash, and gases erupt

CANYON
a deep, narrow valley with steep walls

GLACIER
a large area of slow-moving ice

HILL
a rounded, elevated area of land smaller than a mountain

PLAIN
a nearly flat area

DUNE
a hill of sand shaped by wind

OASIS
an area in the desert with a water source

DESERT
an extremely dry area with little water and few plants

PLATEAU
a large, flat, elevated area of land

UNIT 1

An Introduction to World Geography and Cultures

Iceberg in sea ice, Antarctica

Carnival parade in Valletta, Malta

A Physical Geographer in Mountain Environments

Professor Francisco Pérez studies tropical mountain environments. He is interested in the natural processes, plants, and environments of mountains. **WHAT DO YOU THINK?** *What faraway places would you like to study?*

I became attracted to mountains when I was a child. While crossing the Atlantic Ocean in a ship, I saw snow-capped Teide Peak in the Canary Islands rising from the water. It was an amazing sight.

As a physical geographer, I am interested in the unique environments of high mountain areas. This includes geological history, climate, and soils. The unusual conditions of high mountain environments have influenced plant evolution. Plants and animals that live on separate mountains sometimes end up looking similar. This happens because they react to their environments in similar ways. For example, several types of tall, weird-looking plants called giant rosettes grow in the Andes, Hawaii, East Africa, and the Canary Islands. Giant rosettes look like the top of a pineapple at the end of a tall stem.

I have found other strange plants, such as rolling mosses. Mosses normally grow on rocks. However, if a moss plant falls to the ground, ice crystals on the soil surface lift the moss. This allows it to "roll" downhill while it continues to grow in a ball shape!

I like doing research in mountains. They are some of the least explored regions of our planet. Like most geographers, I cannot resist the attraction of strange landscapes in remote places.

Rosette plants, Ecuador

La Digue Island, Seychelles

Understanding Primary Sources

1. What are three parts of the environment that Francisco Pérez studies?

2. Why do some plants that live on separate mountains look similar?

Sturgeonfish

CHAPTER 1

A Geographer's World

Hand-held compass

Chart of the Mediterranean and Europe, 1559

GPS (global positioning satellite) receiver

Read to Discover

1. What role does perspective play in the study of geography?
2. What are some issues or topics that geographers study?
3. At what three levels can geographers view the world?

Vocabulary

perspective
spatial perspective
geography
urban
rural

Reading Strategy

VISUALIZING INFORMATION Look at the photographs in this section. What do you see in the photographs that would tell you about some of the topics geographers study? Write your answers on a sheet of paper.

Perspectives

People look at the world in different ways. Their experiences shape the way they understand the world. This personal understanding is called **perspective**. Your perspective is your point of view. A geographer's point of view looks at where something is and why it is there. This point of view is known as **spatial perspective**. Geographers apply this perspective when they study the arrangement of towns in a state. They might also use this perspective to examine the movement of cars and trucks on busy roads.

Geographers also work to understand how things are connected. Some connections are easy to see, like highways that link cities. Other connections are harder to see. For example, a dry winter in Colorado could mean that farms as far away as northern Mexico will not have enough water.

Geography is a science. It describes the physical and cultural features of Earth. Studying geography is important. Geographically informed people can see meaning in the arrangement of things on Earth. They know how people and places are related. Above all, they can apply a spatial perspective to real life. In other words, people familiar with geography can understand the world around them.

This fish-eye view of a large city shows highway patterns.
▼

✔ **READING CHECK:** (*The World in Spatial Terms*) What role does perspective play in the study of geography?

The movement of people is one issue that geographers study. For example, political and economic troubles led many Albanians to leave their country in 1991. Many packed onto freighters like this one for the trip. Geographers want to know how this movement affects the environment and other people.

Interpreting the Visual Record

Movement How do you think Albania has been affected by so many people leaving the country?

Geographic Issues

Issues geographers study include Earth's processes and their impact on people. Geographers study the relationship between people and environment in different places. For example, geographers study tornadoes to find ways to reduce loss of life and property damage. They ask how people prepare for tornadoes. Do they prepare differently in different places? When a tornado strikes, how do people react?

Geographers also study how governments change and how those changes affect people. Czechoslovakia, for example, split into Slovakia and the Czech Republic in 1993. These types of political events affect geographic boundaries. People react differently to these changes. Some people are forced to move. Others welcome the change.

Other issues geographers study include religions, diet (or food), **urban** areas, and **rural** areas. Urban areas contain cities. Rural areas contain open land that is often used for farming.

✔ **READING CHECK:** *The Uses of Geography* What issues or topics do geographers study?

Local, Regional, and Global Geographic Studies

With any topic, geographers must decide how large an area to study. They can focus their study at a local, regional, or global level.

Local Studying your community at the local, or close-up, level will help you learn geography. You know where homes and stores are located. You know how to find parks, ball fields, and other fun places. Over time, you see your community change. New buildings are constructed. People move in and out of your neighborhood. New stores open their doors, and others go out of business.

Regional Regional geographers organize the world into convenient parts for study. For example, this book separates the world into big areas like Africa and Europe. Regional studies cover larger areas than local studies. Some regional studies might look at connections like highways and rivers. Others might examine the regional customs.

Global Geographers also work to understand global issues and the connections between events. For example, many countries depend on oil from Southwest Asia. If those oil supplies are threatened, some countries might rush to secure oil from other areas. Oil all over the world could then become much more expensive.

Region The southwest is a region within the United States. One well-known place that characterizes the landscape of the southwest is the Grand Canyon. The Grand Canyon is shown in the photo at left and in the satellite image at right.

✔ **READING CHECK:** *The World in Spatial Terms* What levels do geographers use to focus their study of an issue or topic?

Section Review 1

Define and explain: perspective, spatial perspective, geography, urban, rural

Reading for the Main Idea

1. How can a spatial perspective be used to study the world?

2. Why is it important to study geography?

Critical Thinking

3. **Drawing Inferences and Conclusions** How do threatening weather patterns affect people, and why do geographers study these patterns?

4. **Drawing Inferences and Conclusions** Why is it important to view geography on a global level?

Organizing What You Know

5. **Finding the Main Idea** Copy the following graphic organizer. Use it to examine the issues geographers study. Write a paragraph on one of these issues.

Issues geographers study

Read to Discover

1. What tools do geographers use to study the world?
2. What shapes Earth's features?
3. How do humans shape the world?
4. How does studying geography help us understand the world?

Vocabulary

absolute location
relative location
place
region
movement
diffusion
human-environment interaction

Reading Strategy

TAKING NOTES Taking notes while you read will help you understand and remember the information in this section. Write down the headings in the section. As you read, fill in notes under each heading. Underline the most important details you find.

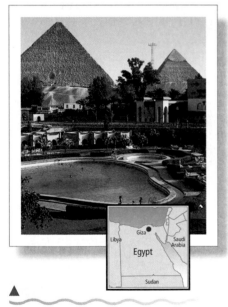

The location of a place can be described in many ways.

Interpreting the Visual Record

(*Location*) **Looking at the photo of this hotel in Giza, Egypt, and at the map, how would you describe Giza's location?**

Learning Geography

The study of geography has long been organized according to five important themes, or topics of study. One theme, location, deals with the exact or relative spot of something on Earth. Place includes the physical and human features of a location. Human-environment interaction covers the ways people and environments affect each other. Movement involves how people change locations and how goods are traded as well as the effects of these movements. For example, when people move they may bring animals, diseases, and their own culture to a new place. Region organizes Earth into geographic areas with one or more shared characteristics.

Another way to look at geography, however, is to study its essential elements, or most important parts. In 1994, several geographers and teachers created national geography standards called *Geography For Life*. The six essential elements they created to organize the study of geography are The World in Spatial Terms, Places and Regions, Physical Systems, Human Systems, Environment and Society, and The Uses of Geography. Because the six essential elements and the five themes share many of the same properties, both will be used throughout this textbook. Look for labels on questions, photographs, maps, graphs, and charts that show which geography theme or essential element is the main focus. In this section we discuss several topics related to the geography themes and essential elements. Here you will discover the relationship between these two ways of learning about our world.

✓ **READING CHECK:** (*The Uses of Geography*) What are the five themes of geography? What are the six essential elements?

The World in Spatial Terms

This element focuses on geography's spatial perspective. As you learned in Section 1, geographers apply spatial perspective when they look at the location of something and why it is there.

Location The term location can be used in two ways. **Absolute location** defines an exact spot on Earth. For example, the address of the Smithsonian American Art Museum is an absolute location. The address is at 8th and G Streets, N.W., in Washington, D.C. City streets often form a grid. This system tells anyone looking for an address where to go. The grid formed by latitude and longitude lines also pinpoints absolute location. Suppose you asked a pilot to take you to 52° north latitude by 175° west longitude. You would land at a location on Alaska's Aleutian Islands.

Relative location describes the position of a place in relation to another place. Measurements of direction, distance, or time can define relative location. For example, the following sentences give relative location. "The hospital is one mile north of our school." "Canada's border is about an hour's drive from Great Falls, Montana."

A geographer must be able to use maps and other geographic tools and technologies to determine spatial perspective. A geographer must also know how to organize and analyze information about people, places, and environments using geographic tools.

✓ **READING CHECK:** (*The World in Spatial Terms*) What two ways describe location?

Places and Regions

To help explain why many areas of the world are similar to or different from one another, geographers organize Earth's surface into different places and regions. The Places and Regions essential element deals with how people have created regions based on Earth's features and how culture and other factors affect how we see places and regions.

Place Our world has a vast number of unique places and regions. A **place** can be described both by its physical location and by its physical and human features. Physical features include coastlines and landforms. They can also include lakes, rivers, or soil types. For example, Colorado is flat in the east but mountainous in the west. This is an example of a place being described in terms of its landforms. A place can also be described by its climate. For example, Greenland has long, cold winters. Florida has mild winters and hot, humid summers.

▲

(*Place*) Places can be described by what they do not have. This photo shows the result of a long period without rain.

Movement People travel from place to place on miles of new roadway.

Region A **region** is an area of Earth's surface with one or more shared characteristics. Many of the characteristics that describe places can also be used to describe regions. Regions vary in size. Some are very large, like North America. Others are much smaller, like the Florida Keys. Regions are also different from the surrounding areas. For example, Silicon Valley is a region in California that is known for its many computer companies and engineers.

What defines a region? Some regions have boundaries that are easy to define. For example, natural vegetation regions have similar plants. Deserts, forests, and grasslands are examples of natural regions with fairly clear boundaries. A region can also be described as cultural, economic, or political.

✓ **READING CHECK:** *Places and Regions* What features can you use to describe a place?

Physical Systems

Physical systems shape Earth's features. Geographers study earthquakes, mountains, rivers, volcanoes, weather patterns, and similar topics and how these physical systems have affected Earth's characteristics. For example, geographers might study how volcanic eruptions in the Hawaiian Islands spread lava, causing landforms to change. They might note that southern California's shoreline changes yearly, as winter and summer waves move beach sand.

Geographers also study how plants and animals relate to these nonliving physical systems. For example, deserts are places with cactus and other plants, as well as rattlesnakes and other reptiles, that can live in very dry conditions. Geographers also study how different types of plants, animals, and physical systems are distributed on Earth.

✓ **READING CHECK:** *Physical Systems* What types of physical systems do geographers study?

Men in rural Egypt wear a long shirt called a *galabia*. This loose-fitting garment is ideal for people living in Egypt's hot desert climate. In addition, the galabia is made from cotton, an important agricultural product of Egypt.

Interpreting the Visual Record

Human-Environment Interaction **How does the *galabia* show how people have adapted to their environment?**

Human Systems

People are central to geography. Geographers study human systems, or the human activities, movements, and settlements that shape Earth's surface. Human systems also include peoples' customs, history, languages, and religions.

Movement Geographers study the **movement** of people and ideas. When people move, they may go to live in other countries or move within a country. Geographers want to know how and why people move from place to place.

People move for many reasons. Some move to start a new job. Some move to attend special schools. Others might move to be closer to family. People move either when they are pushed out of a place or when they are pulled toward another place. In the Dust Bowl, for example, crop failures pushed people out of Oklahoma in the 1930s. Many were pulled to California by their belief that they would find work there.

Geographers also want to know how ideas or behaviors move from one region to another. The movement of ideas occurs through communication. There are many ways to communicate. People visit with each other in person or on the phone. New technology allows people to communicate by e-mail. Ideas are also spread through films, magazines, newspapers, radio, and television. The movement of ideas or behaviors from one region to another is known as **diffusion**.

The things we produce and trade are also part of the study of human systems. Geographers study trading patterns and how countries depend on each other for certain goods. In addition, geographers look at the causes and results of conflicts between peoples. The study of governments we set up and the features of cities and other settlements we live in are also part of this study.

✓ **READING CHECK:** (*Human Systems*) What are some reasons why people move?

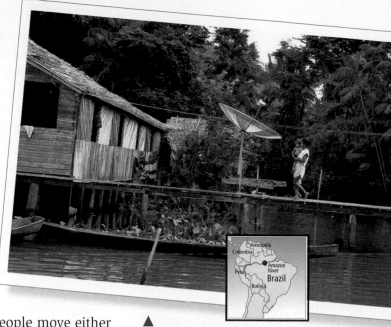

▲
A satellite dish brings different images and ideas to people in a remote area of Brazil.
Interpreting the Visual Record How might resources have affected the use of technology here?

▲
This woman at a railway station in Russian Siberia sells some goods that were once unavailable in her country.

Environment and Society

Human actions, such as using oil or water, affect the environment. At the same time, Earth's physical systems, such as climate or natural hazards, affect human activities. Our survival depends on what Earth provides. Many geographers consider the relationship between people and the environment a central focus of geography.

Human-Environment Interaction Geographers study how people and their surroundings affect each other. This relationship between people and the environment, or **human-environment interaction**, can be examined in three ways. First, geographers study how humans depend on their physical environment to survive. Human life requires certain living and nonliving resources, such as freshwater and fertile soil for farming.

Geographers also study how humans change their behavior to be better suited to an environment. These changes or adaptations include the kinds of clothing, food, and shelter that people create. These changes help people live in harsh climates.

Finally, humans change the environment. For example, farmers who irrigate their fields can grow fruit in Arizona's dry climate. People in Louisiana have built levees, or large walls, to protect themselves when the Mississippi River floods.

✓ **READING CHECK:** (*Environment and Society*) How might people change to live in certain environments?

The Uses of Geography

Geography helps us understand the relationships among people, places, and the environment over time. Understanding how a relationship has developed can help in making plans for the future. For example, geographers can study how human use of the soil in a farming region has affected that region over time. Such knowledge can help them determine what changes have been made to the soil and whether any corrective measures need to be taken.

✓ **READING CHECK:** (*The Uses of Geography*) How can studying geography help plan for the future?

▲
Open-air markets like this one in Mali provide opportunities for farmers to sell their goods.

Homework Practice Online
Keyword: SK5 HP1

Section Review 2

Define and explain: absolute location, relative location, place, region, movement, diffusion, human-environment interaction

Reading for the Main Idea

1. (*The World in Spatial Terms*) How do geographers study the world?

2. (*Physical Systems*) What shapes Earth's features? Give examples.

Critical Thinking

3. **Finding the Main Idea** How do humans shape the world in which they live?

4. **Analyzing Information** What benefits can studying geography provide?

Organizing What You Know

5. **Summarizing** Copy the following graphic organizer. Use it to identify and describe all aspects of each of the six essential elements.

Element	Description

Read to Discover

1. What is included in the study of human geography?
2. What is included in the study of physical geography?
3. What types of work do geographers do?

Vocabulary

human geography
physical geography
cartography
meteorology
climatology

Reading Strategy

READING ORGANIZER Before you read this section, create a three column chart. Title the columns Human Geography, Physical Geography, and Working as a Geographer. As you read, write information that you learn about each topic on your chart.

Human Geography

The study of people, past or present, is the focus of **human geography**. People's location and distribution over Earth, their activities, and their differences are studied. For example, people living in different countries create different kinds of governments. Political geographers study those differences. Economic geographers study the exchange of goods and services across Earth. Cultural geography, population geography, and urban geography are some other examples of human geography. A professional geographer might specialize in any of these branches.

✓ **READING CHECK:** (*Human Systems*) How is human geography defined?

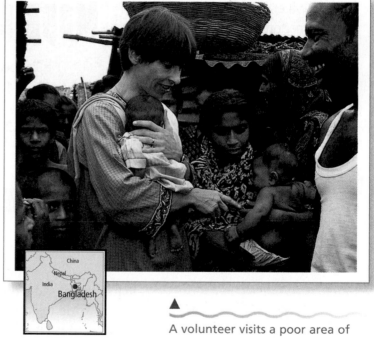

▲
A volunteer visits a poor area of Bangladesh. Geographers study economic conditions in regions to help them understand human geography.

Physical Geography

The study of Earth's natural landscapes and physical systems, including the atmosphere, is the focus of **physical geography**. The world is full of different landforms such as deserts, mountains, and plains. Climates affect these landscapes. Knowledge of physical systems helps geographers understand how a landscape developed and how it might change.

CONNECTING TO *Technology*

A mapmaker creates a digital map.

Computer Mapping

Maps are tools that can display a wide range of information. Traditionally, maps were drawn on paper and could not be changed to suit the user. However, computers have revolutionized the art of mapmaking.

Today, mapmakers use computers to create and modify maps for different uses. They do this by using a geographic information system, or GIS. A GIS is a computer system that combines maps and satellite photographs with other kinds of spatial data—information about places on the planet. This information might include soil types, population figures, or voting patterns.

Using a GIS, mapmakers can create maps that show geographic features and relationships. For example, a map showing rainfall patterns in a particular region might be combined with data on soil types or human settlement to show areas of possible soil erosion.

The flexibility of a GIS allows people to seek answers to specific questions. Where should a new road be built to ease traffic congestion? How are changes in natural habitat affecting wildlife? These and many other questions can be answered with the help of computer mapping.

Understanding What You Read
1. How could a GIS help people change their environment?
2. What social, environmental, or economic consequences might future advances in GIS technology have?

Knowledge of physical and human geography will help you understand the world's different regions and peoples. In your study of the major world regions, you will see how physical and human geography connect to each other.

✓ **READING CHECK:** (*Physical Systems*) What is included in the study of physical geography?

Working as a Geographer

Geography plays a role in almost every occupation. Wherever you live and work, you should know local geography. School board members know where children live. Taxi drivers are familiar with city streets. Grocery store managers know which foods sell well in certain areas.

They also know where they can obtain these products throughout the year. Local newspaper reporters are familiar with town meetings and local politicians. Reporters also know how faraway places can affect their communities. Doctors must know if their towns have poisonous snakes or plants. City managers know whether nearby rivers might flood. Emergency workers in mountain towns check snow depth so they can give avalanche warnings. Local weather forecasters watch for powerful storms and track their routes on special maps.

Some specially trained geographers practice in the field of **cartography**. Cartography is the art and science of mapmaking. Today, most mapmakers do their work on computers. Geographers also work as weather forecasters. The field of forecasting and reporting rainfall, temperature, and other atmospheric conditions is called **meteorology**. A related field is **climatology**. These geographers, known as climatologists, track Earth's larger atmospheric systems. Climatologists want to know how these systems change over long periods of time. They also study how people might be affected by changes in climate.

Governments and a variety of organizations hire geographers to study the environment. These geographers might explore such topics as pollution, endangered plants and animals, or rain forests. Some geographers who are interested in education become teachers and writers. They help people of all ages learn more about the world. Modern technology allows people all over the world to communicate instantly. Therefore, it is more important than ever to be familiar with the geographer's world.

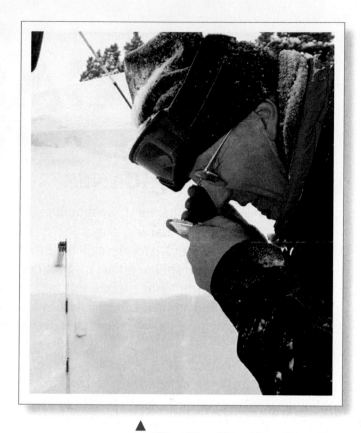

▲
Experts examine snow to help forecast avalanches. They study the type of snow, weather conditions, and landforms.

✔ **READING CHECK:** (*The Uses of Geography*) What types of work do geographers perform?

Homework Practice Online
Keyword: SK5 HP1

Section Review 3

Define and explain: human geography, physical geography, cartography, meteorology, climatology

Reading for the Main Idea

1. (*Human Systems*) What topics are included in the study of human geography?

2. (*The Uses of Geography*) How do people who study the weather use geography?

Critical Thinking

3. Finding the Main Idea Why is it important to study physical geography?

4. Making Generalizations and Predictions How might future discoveries in the field of geography affect societies, world economies, or the environment?

Organizing What You Know

5. Categorizing Copy the following graphic organizer. Use it to list geographers' professions and their job responsibilities.

Cartographer —makes maps —studies maps		

CASE STUDY

HOW GEOGRAPHERS TRACK HURRICANES

As you learned in Chapter 1, geographers called climatologists study Earth's atmosphere. Sometimes large circulating storms called hurricanes develop in the atmosphere above tropical oceans. Hurricanes often move over land and into populated areas. When a hurricane approaches land, it brings strong winds, heavy rains, and large ocean waves.

Climatologists try to predict where these storms will travel. They want to be able to warn people in the hurricane's path. Early warnings can help people be better prepared for the deadly winds and rain. It is a difficult job because hurricanes can change course suddenly. Hurricanes are one of the most dangerous natural hazards.

The map below shows the path of Hurricane Fran in 1996. Notice how Fran moved to the west and became stronger until it reached land. It began as a tropical depression and became a powerful hurricane as it passed over warm ocean waters.

One way of determining a hurricane's strength is by measuring the atmospheric pressure inside it. The lower the pressure, the stronger the storm. Hurricanes are rated on a scale of one to five. Study Table 1 to see how wind speed and air pressure are used to help determine the strength of a hurricane.

Hurricane Mitch formed in October 1998. The National Weather Service (NWS) recorded Mitch's position and strength. They learned that Mitch's pressure was one of the lowest ever recorded. The

Table 1: Saffir-Simpson Scale

HURRICANE TYPE	WIND SPEED MPH	AIR PRESSURE MB (INCHES)
Category 1	74–95	more than 980 (28.94)
Category 2	96–110	965–979 (28.50–28.91)
Category 3	111–130	945–964 (27.91–28.47)
Category 4	131–155	920–944 (27.17–27.88)
Category 5	more than 155	less than 920 (27.17)

Source: Florida State University, <http://www.met.fsu.edu/explores/tropical.html>

Path of Hurricane Fran, 1996

SCALE
0   300   600 Miles
0   300   600 Kilometers
Projection: Miller Cylindrical

30 mph Wind speed (in miles per hour)
1006 mb Atmospheric pressure (in millibars)
O Tropical depression
◉ Tropical storm
𝕹 Hurricane
▨▨▨ Fran's path

Sept. 6 989 mb 35 mph
Sept. 5 954 mb 100 mph
Sept. 2 976 mb 70 mph
Sept. 4 956 mb 100 mph
Aug. 31 984 mb 61 mph
Aug. 29 984 mb 65 mph
Aug. 27 1006 mb 30 mph
Aug. 25 1007 mb 30 mph
Aug. 24 1007 mb 30 mph
Sept. 3 977 mb 75 mph
Sept. 1 982 mb 65 mph
Aug. 30 990 mb 65 mph
Aug. 28 997 mb 52 mph
Aug. 26 1007 mb 30 mph

GULF OF MEXICO
ATLANTIC OCEAN
CARIBBEAN SEA
PACIFIC OCEAN

90°W 80°W 70°W 60°W 50°W 40°W 30°W 20°W 30°N 20°N 10°N

Table 2: Hurricane Mitch, 1998 Position and Strength

DATE	LATITUDE (DEGREES)	LONGITUDE (DEGREES)	WIND SPEED (MPH)	PRESSURE (MILLIBARS)	STORM TYPE
10/22	12 N	78 W	30	1002	Tropical depression
10/24	15 N	78 W	90	980	Category 2
10/26	16 N	81 W	130	923	Category 4
10/27	17 N	84 W	150	910	Category 5
10/31	15 N	88 W	40	1000	Tropical storm
11/01	15 N	90 W	30	1002	Tropical depression
11/03	20 N	91 W	40	997	Tropical storm
11/05	26 N	83 W	50	990	Tropical storm

Source: <http://www.met.fsu.edu/explores/tropical.html>

NWS estimated that Mitch's maximum sustained surface winds reached 180 miles per hour.

Hurricanes like Mitch cause very heavy rains in short periods of time. These heavy rains are particularly dangerous. The ground becomes saturated, and mud can flow almost like water. The flooding and mudslides caused by Mitch killed an estimated 10,000 people in four countries. Many people predicted that the region would not recover without help from other countries.

In the southeastern United States, many places have emergency preparedness units. The people assigned to these groups organize their communities. They provide food, shelter, and clothing for those who must evacuate their homes.

You Be the Geographer

1. Trace a map of the Caribbean. Be sure to include latitude and longitude lines.
2. Use the data about Hurricane Mitch in Table 2 to plot its path. Make a key with symbols to show Mitch's strength at each location.
3. What happened to Mitch when it reached land?

This satellite image shows the intensity of Hurricane Mitch. With advanced technology, hurricane tracking is helping to save lives.

Review and Practice

Define and Identify

Identify each of the following:

1. perspective
2. spatial perspective
3. geography
4. urban
5. rural
6. absolute location
7. relative location
8. place
9. region
10. movement
11. diffusion
12. human-environment interaction
13. human geography
14. physical geography
15. cartography
16. meteorology
17. climatology

Review the Main Ideas

18. What is geography?
19. What do urban areas contain? What do rural areas contain?
20. What are three ways to study geography? Give an example of when each type could be used.
21. What kind of directions would you give to indicate a place's absolute location? Its relative location?
22. How can a place be described?

23. What are some ways to define a region?
24. What are some reasons why people move?
25. How do some people adapt to better suit their environment?
26. Why is cartography important?
27. What types of jobs do geographers do?

Think Critically

28. **Analyzing Information** How can a geographer use spatial perspective to explain how things in our world are connected?
29. **Drawing Inferences and Conclusions** When and how do humans relate to the environment? Provide some examples of this relationship.
30. **Summarizing** How are patterns created by the movement of goods, ideas, and people?
31. **Finding the Main Idea** How are places and regions defined?
32. **Finding the Main Idea** How does studying geography help us understand the world?

Map Activity

33. On a separate sheet of paper, match the letters on the map with their correct labels.

    Africa
    Antarctica
    Asia
    Australia
    Europe
    North America
    South America

Writing Activity

Write a letter persuading another student to enroll in a geography class. Include examples of professions that use geography and relate that information to the everyday life of a student. Be sure to use standard grammar, spelling, sentence structure, and punctuation.

Ⓘ internet connect

Internet Activity: go.hrw.com
KEYWORD: SK5 GT1

Choose a topic to explore online:
- Learn to use online maps.
- Be a virtual geographer for a day.
- Compare regions around the world.

Social Studies Skills Practice

Interpreting Maps

Study the following map of the state of California. Use what you know about location to answer the questions.

1. How would you describe the relative location of Los Angeles?

2. If you were in San Francisco, how would you describe the relative location of Yosemite National Park?

3. What would you use on this map to find the absolute location of places?

4. What is the absolute location of Los Angeles?

Analyzing Primary Sources

Read the following quote from geographer Dr. Reginald G. Golledge. Then answer the questions.

"As I was growing up in Australia, my family moved frequently, largely from one small town to another . . . The small-town environment and the surrounding countryside favored the development of a state of mind that constantly asked, 'What's over the next hill? How far is it to the river? Where are the wild berries and fruits located?'"

Source: *Geographical Voices: Fourteen Autobiographical Essays*

1. Did Dr. Golledge grow up in a rural area or an urban area?

2. How do you think Dr. Golledge's childhood experiences led him to become a geographer?

3. As a child, was Golledge interested more in human geography or physical geography?

4. Which two of the five geography themes best describes the questions Dr. Golledge asks?

CHAPTER 2

Planet Earth

Diver, coral, and fish, Fiji Islands

Quartz crystals

Erupting volcano

Tornado in Saskatoon, Canada

Read to Discover

1. What processes build up the land?
2. What processes shape Earth's surfaces?
3. How has topography affected human history and culture?

Vocabulary

landforms   erosion
topography   plain
plate tectonics   alluvial fan
subduction   floodplain
earthquakes   delta
lava   glaciers
fault   terraces
weathering

Reading Strategy

TAKING NOTES Taking notes while you read will help you understand and remember the information in this section. Write down the headings in the section. As you read, fill in notes under each heading. Underline the most important details you find.

Building Up the Land

Landforms are shapes on Earth's surface. The shape, height, and arrangement of landforms in a certain place is called **topography**. The theory of **plate tectonics** helps explain how Earth's topography formed and how it changes. According to this theory, Earth's surface is divided into several large plates, or pieces. There are also a number of smaller plates. These plates move very slowly—just inches per year.

Plate Tectonics

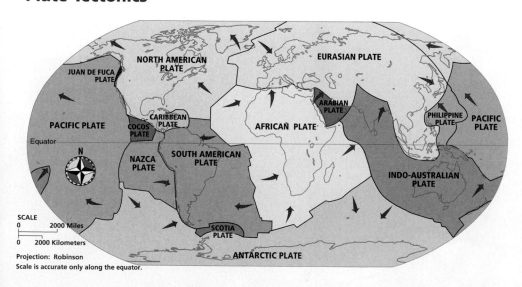

The plates that make up Earth's crust are moving, usually a few inches per year. This map shows the plates and the direction of their movement.

☐ internet connect

GO TO: go.hrw.com
KEYWORD: SS Tsunami
FOR: Web sites about the
tsunami of December 26,
2004, and its aftermath

On December 26, 2004, a massive earthquake in the Indian Ocean off the coast of Indonesia triggered a giant wave, called a tsunami. The tsunami struck coastlines in Indonesia, India, Sri Lanka, Thailand, and several other countries in the region. The waves are known to have killed some 150,000 people, and tens of thousands remain missing. Here, a man in Thailand searches the rubble for his belongings.

▼

Colliding Plates Some plates collide as they move. **Subduction** occurs when one plate moves underneath another. In subduction zones, volcanoes and **earthquakes** are common. An earthquake is a sudden, violent movement along a break within the outer layers of Earth's crust.

Look at the Plate Tectonics map on the previous page and find the Pacific plate. Where the Pacific plate moves against neighboring plates, volcanoes and earthquakes are common. In fact, the edge of the Pacific plate is called the Ring of Fire because it is rimmed by active volcanoes. The region's earthquakes and volcanoes have killed thousands of people and caused terrible destruction. Several major earthquakes have hit California in recent years. Local authorities along the West Coast are constantly preparing for future earthquakes. Scientists predict that one of the strongest earthquakes in U.S. history may occur in the San Francisco Bay area within the next 30 years.

In some places, colliding plates have other results. Instead of sinking, one of the plates may crumple up and form a mountain range. The Andes in South America and the Himalayas in Asia formed in this way.

Other Plate Movements In other parts of the world, plates move away from each other. From the gap, hot **lava**, or melted rock from deep in the Earth, may emerge. The lava may build up, forming a mountain range. This process is happening in the Atlantic Ocean where the Eurasian plate and the North American plate are moving away from each other.

Tectonic plates can also slide past each other and cause earthquakes. In California the Pacific plate is sliding northwestward along the edge of the North American plate. This movement has created the San Andreas Fault zone. A **fault** is a fractured surface in Earth's crust where a mass of rock is in motion.

✓ **READING CHECK:** (*Physical Systems*) What are three ways that tectonic plates move?

Shaping Earth's Surface

The forces of plate tectonics build up the land. At the same time, water, wind, and ice constantly break down rock and move rocky material. This process of breaking down landforms and creating new ones is called **weathering**.

Heat, Water, and Chemical Action Weathering breaks rocks into smaller pieces in several ways. Heat can cause rocks to crack. Water may then get into the cracks. If the water freezes, the ice expands with a force great enough to break the rock. Water can also work its way underground and slowly dissolve minerals such as limestone. This process sometimes carves out caves. In some areas small plants called lichens attach to bare rock. Chemicals in the lichens gradually break down the stone. All these processes eventually break rock down into sediment, in the form of gravel, sand, silt, or clay. Then water, ice, or wind can move the sediment and create new topography with it. This process of moving rocky material or sediment to another place is called **erosion**.

Moving water is the most common force that erodes the land. Flowing water carries sediment. This sediment eventually forms different kinds of landforms depending on where it is deposited. For example, a river flowing from a mountain range onto a flat area, or **plain**, may deposit sediment there. The sediment sometimes builds up into a fan-shaped form called an **alluvial fan**. A **floodplain** is created when rivers flood their banks and deposit sediment. A **delta** forms where a river carries sediment all the way to the ocean. The sediment settles to the bottom where the river meets the ocean. The Nile and Mississippi Rivers have two of the world's largest deltas.

Waves in the ocean or lakes also shape the land they touch. Waves can shape beaches into great dunes, such as on the shore of Long Island. Oregon's jagged coastline also shows how waves can erode land.

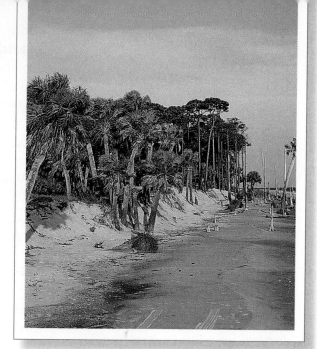

Erosion wears away Earth's surface at an island beach off the Florida coast. **Interpreting the Visual Record** (Place) **What physical process is causing erosion on this beach?**

Ocean water turns muddy as the Mississippi River pushes sediment out of its delta.

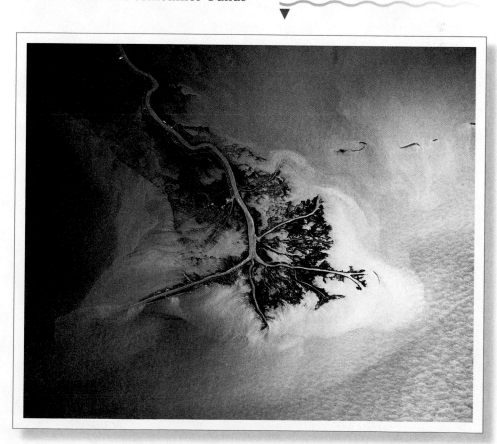

Ice and Wind Action In high mountain settings and in the coldest places on Earth one finds **glaciers**. These large, slow-moving rivers of ice can move tons of rock.

Glaciers covered most of Canada and the United States during the last ice age—or period of extreme cold. As they advanced, the glaciers carved out gashes in Earth's surface. Glaciers dug the Great Lakes. As the ice melted and retreated, tons of rock and sediment were left behind.

Wind also shapes the land. Strong winds can lift soil into the air and carry it far away. On beaches and in deserts, wind drops sand, which piles up into dunes. In addition, blowing sand can wear away rock. The sand acts like sandpaper to polish jagged edges and rough surfaces.

Erosion and Soil These processes of breaking down Earth's surface create deposits of soil. People need soil to grow food. Erosion, however, can also remove soil from farmers' fields. Heavy rainfall can wash away soil. Strong winds can blow it away.

Over the centuries, however, people have developed ways to conserve our precious soil. Some farmers plant rows of trees to block the wind. Others who farm on steep hillsides build **terraces** into the slope. Terraces are horizontal ridges like stair steps. By slowing the downhill rush of water the terraces keep the soil in place. They also provide more space for growing crops.

✔ **READING CHECK:** (*Physical Systems*) What forces cause erosion?

Rice paddies like these in Indonesia are common throughout island Southeast Asia.

Interpreting the Visual Record

(*Human-Environment Interaction*)

How have farmers limited erosion in the rice paddies pictured below?

▼

People and Topography

Topography has quite a bit to do with human history and culture. Those effects are so big, however, that we may not see them easily.

Landforms and Life Why do you live where you live? Perhaps your parents moved to your city to take jobs in the tourist industry. Do tourists visit your area partly because of its landforms, such as mountains? Or maybe your town grew up on a river delta. People could farm the delta's fertile soil. They could also use either the river or the sea for trade and travel. What are some more ways that your area's topography may have influenced its growth?

Reading a Topographic Map

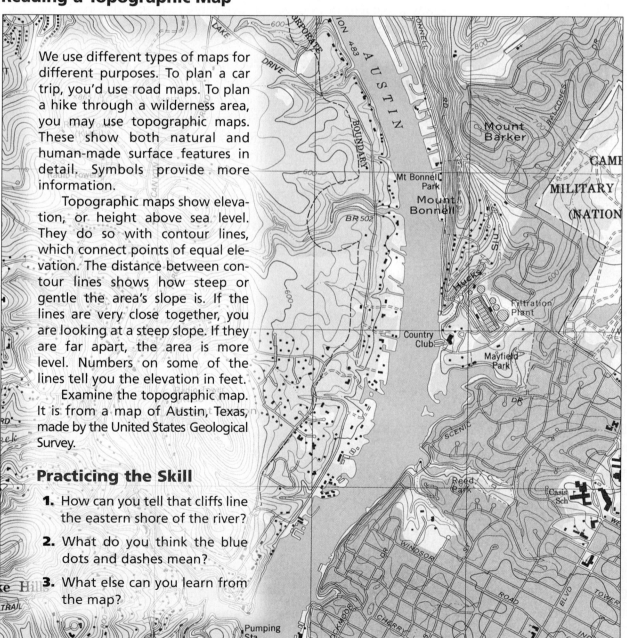

We use different types of maps for different purposes. To plan a car trip, you'd use road maps. To plan a hike through a wilderness area, you may use topographic maps. These show both natural and human-made surface features in detail. Symbols provide more information.

Topographic maps show elevation, or height above sea level. They do so with contour lines, which connect points of equal elevation. The distance between contour lines shows how steep or gentle the area's slope is. If the lines are very close together, you are looking at a steep slope. If they are far apart, the area is more level. Numbers on some of the lines tell you the elevation in feet.

Examine the topographic map. It is from a map of Austin, Texas, made by the United States Geological Survey.

Practicing the Skill

1. How can you tell that cliffs line the eastern shore of the river?

2. What do you think the blue dots and dashes mean?

3. What else can you learn from the map?

In 1914 an enormous canal was completed across the Isthmus of Panama, linking the Pacific and Atlantic Oceans. Workers used millions of pounds of explosives and steam-powered shovels to cut through much of the landscape.

Interpreting the Visual Record

(Human-Environment Interaction)

Through what landforms did the Panama Canal workers have to dig?

Landforms affect the history of entire countries. For one example, start by looking at a map of India. You will see that the Ganges River crosses a broad plain before emptying into the Bay of Bengal. This river has brought sediment down from the Himalayas for countless centuries. It dropped the sediment on the plain, forming a vast area of excellent farmland. Many invaders have attacked India, trying to win this rich plain for themselves.

Here is an example of how landforms affected language. Find the island of New Guinea on a map of Southeast Asia. Notice how mountainous it is. These mountains have isolated New Guinea's peoples so much that many languages developed. In fact, more than 700 different languages are spoken on the island today.

Changing Landforms For thousands of years, people have changed Earth's surface to suit their needs. They have dug canals for irrigation ditches and carved terraces for farms. They have created artificial hills on which to build temples. People have even held back the sea to claim more dry land. Today, engineers build dams to control river flooding. They drill tunnels through mountains instead of laying roads over the mountains. Thus, while earthquakes, volcanoes, weathering, and erosion change Earth's surface, people do so also.

✓ **READING CHECK:** (**Environment and Society**) What are some landforms that could affect human history and culture?

Homework Practice Online
Keyword: SK5 HP2

Section Review 1

Define and explain: landforms, topography, plate tectonics, subduction, earthquakes, lava, fault, weathering, erosion, plain, alluvial fan, floodplain, delta, glaciers, terraces

Reading for the Main Idea

1. (*Physical Systems*) What events are common where tectonic plates collide?

2. (*Physical Systems*) How do rivers create new landforms?

Critical Thinking

3. **Comparing and Contrasting** How are weathering and erosion different?

4. **Making Predictions**
   How may the lives of people who live in the mountains or on plains be different?

Organizing What You Know

5. **Categorizing** Copy the following graphic organizer. Use it to describe the results of each force of erosion or weathering.

   heat ⇨
   cold ⇨
   water moving through limestone ⇨
   chemicals in lichens ⇨
   waves ⇨
   glaciers ⇨
   wind ⇨

Section 2 Water and Air

Read to Discover

1. Where is water found on Earth?
2. What is the water cycle?
3. How do people and water affect each other?
4. What are short-term and long-term results of air pollution?

Vocabulary

tributary
groundwater
aquifers
water cycle
evaporation
water vapor

condensation
precipitation
acid rain
ozone layer
global warming
greenhouse effect

Reading Strategy

READING ORGANIZER Before you read this section, create a spider map. Label the circle Water and Air. Create a leg for each of these topics: Geographic Distribution of Water, The Water Cycle, Water and People, and The Air We Breathe. As you read the section, fill in the map with details about each topic.

Geographic Distribution of Water

Water is essential for life. The presence or absence of water in a place affects whether people can live there. Water, therefore, is part of both physical and human geography. Throughout this book, you will see how water or its lack determines what life is like around the world.

The oceans contain about 97 percent of Earth's water. Another 2 percent is locked in the ice of Earth's polar regions and glaciers. Only about 1 percent is freshwater in lakes, streams, rivers, and below Earth's surface.

Earth's freshwater resources are not evenly distributed. Some places are extremely dry. Dry states such as Nevada have few natural lakes. Others have many lakes and rivers. For example, in the United States, Minnesota has more than 11,000 lakes. Some areas have too much water. Floods can make survival difficult in places where rainfall is very heavy or where rivers burst their banks.

Mountain glaciers like this one can move slowly downhill. This photo shows the face of a glacier. Here chunks may break off, or calve, and form icebergs.

Interpreting the Visual Record What dangers may these kayakers face?

▼

Groundwater

Precipitation

Runoff

Well

Groundwater

In some areas where rainfall is scarce, there is enough groundwater to support agriculture.
Interpreting the Visual Record How do people gain access to groundwater?

Pivoting sprinklers irrigate these circular cornfields in Kansas.
Interpreting the Visual Record
(*Human-Environment Interaction*)
Why may irrigation be necessary in these fields?

Surface Water Water may collect at high elevations, where rivers begin. The first and smallest streams that form are called headwaters. When these headwaters meet and join, they form larger streams. In turn, these streams join with others to form rivers. Any smaller stream or river that flows into a larger river is a **tributary**. For example, the Missouri River is a major tributary of the Mississippi River.

A lake may form where a river flows into a low-lying area. Most lakes are freshwater, but some are salty. For example, the Dead Sea in Southwest Asia is actually a lake that is much saltier than the ocean. When the lake water evaporates, it leaves behind salts and minerals, making the lake salty.

Most of Earth's water is in the oceans. The Pacific, Atlantic, Indian, and Arctic Oceans are connected. This vast body of water covers about 70 percent of Earth's surface. These oceans also include smaller areas called seas and gulfs. The Gulf of Mexico and the Mediterranean Sea are two examples of smaller ocean areas.

Groundwater Not all surface water immediately returns to the atmosphere through evaporation. Some water from rain, snow, rivers, and lakes seeps into the ground. This **groundwater** trickles down until all the tiny spaces in the soil and rock are filled. In some places, the groundwater collects in water-bearing layers of rock, sand, or gravel called **aquifers**. Some aquifers are quite large. For example, the

The Water Cycle

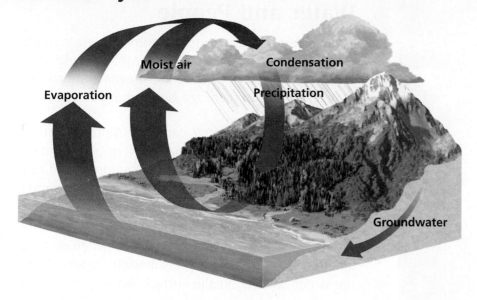

Evaporation · **Moist air** · **Condensation** · **Precipitation** · **Groundwater**

The circulation of water from one part of the hydrosphere to another depends on energy from the Sun. Water evaporates, condenses, and falls to Earth as precipitation.
Interpreting the Visual Record (*Place*)
How would a seasonal increase in the amount of the Sun's energy received by an area change the water cycle in that area?

Ogallala Aquifer stretches across the Great Plains from Texas to South Dakota. Many Americans get their water from wells—deep holes dug down to reach an aquifer's groundwater. Elsewhere, groundwater may bubble up from an aquifer as springs.

✓ **READING CHECK:** (*Physical Systems*) Where is most of Earth's surface water found?

Flooded streets are a way of life during the wet monsoon season in Tamil Nadu, India.

The Water Cycle

The circulation of water from Earth's surface to the atmosphere and back is called the **water cycle**. The total amount of water on the planet doesn't change. Water, however, does change its form and its location.

The Sun's energy drives the water cycle. **Evaporation** occurs when the Sun heats water on Earth's surface. The heated water evaporates, becoming a gas called **water vapor**. As the water vapor cools, **condensation** happens. This is the process by which water changes from a gas into tiny liquid droplets. These droplets join together to form clouds. If the droplets become heavy enough, **precipitation** occurs— that is, the water falls back to Earth. This water can be in the form of rain, hail, sleet, or snow. The entire cycle of evaporation, condensation, and precipitation repeats over and over.

✓ **READING CHECK:** (*Physical Systems*) What are the three main steps in the water cycle?

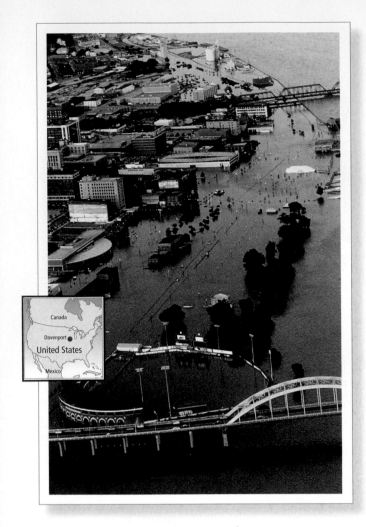

Davenport, Iowa, located on the Mississippi River, suffered severe flooding when heavy rains caused the river to rise above its banks.

Water and People

Water plays a vital role in our survival. As a result, you will often see events and problems related to water in the news. Some of those events are natural disasters. Some of them are issues that people create.

Water Hazards Water can be extremely destructive. Thunderstorms, especially when accompanied by hail or tornadoes, can damage buildings and ruin crops. Heavy rains can cause floods, the world's deadliest natural hazard. Of every ten people who die from natural disasters, four die in floods. Some floods occur in usually dry places when a large amount of rain falls in a short amount of time. Then the water collects on the surface instead of soaking into the hard, dry ground. Normally dry creekbeds can suddenly gush with rushing water. People and livestock are sometimes caught in these flash floods.

Floods also happen in low-lying places next to rivers and on coastlines. Too much rain or snowmelt entering a river can push the water over the river's banks. Powerful storms, especially hurricanes, can cause ocean waters to surge into coastal areas. Is your region ever threatened by floods? What causes floods where you live?

Water Conservation In those places where there isn't enough water, however, many people try to use as little as possible. Scientists have developed new water management methods for saving the precious liquid. Many modern factories now recycle water. Farmers can irrigate their crops more efficiently. Cities build water treatment plants to purify water that might otherwise be wasted. Some people in dry regions use desert plants instead of grass for landscaping. As a result, they use less water in their yards.

An Omani man collects water from a local *falaj*, or aqueduct. These channels are dug to carry water from desert springs to farms and villages. **Interpreting the Visual Record** (*Human-Environment Interaction*) **How does this method of irrigation differ from modern methods?**

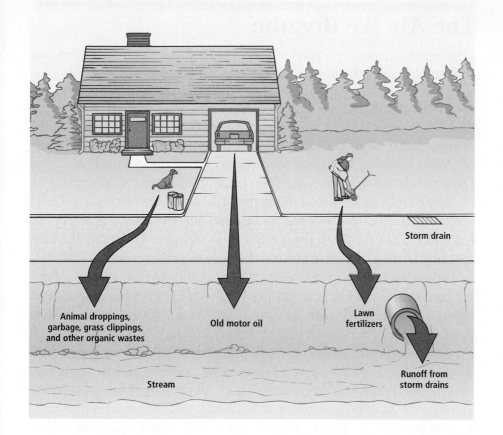

Animal droppings, garbage, grass clippings, and other organic wastes

Old motor oil

Lawn fertilizers

Storm drain

Stream

Runoff from storm drains

◄

Most of the water that goes down drains, or wastewater, flows through pipes to a wastewater treatment plant. There the polluted water is treated before being returned to a river or a lake. Most of the wastewater from homes is easy to purify. However, industrial wastewater and storm runoff from streets and fields contain toxic substances that are difficult to purify.

Interpreting the Diagram What are some sources of pollution created by this single home?

Water management is often a local environmental issue. Growing cities may want to pump more groundwater from an aquifer, while farmers say they need that water for their crops. In dry areas, businesses that use large amounts of water, such as golf courses or fish farms, may draw criticism. What are the water management issues in your community?

Water Pollution Even where water is plentiful, it may not be clean enough to use. Polluted water can carry disease-causing bacteria or substances that harm people and animals.

Water pollution has many causes. Agriculture and industry are two main ones. When farmers use too many chemical fertilizers and pesticides, these chemicals ooze into local streams. Industrial waste may drain poisons or metals into the water supply. Heavy rain can wash motor oil from parking lots into groundwater. In addition, some poor communities don't have quality sewer systems for household wastes. Although most countries try to keep their water clean, sometimes the cost of doing so is higher than they can afford.

Pollution may spread far from its source. Rivers carry chemicals from distant factories to the oceans. There, pollution can sicken or kill fish and shellfish. People who eat these foods from polluted waters can get sick.

✓ **READING CHECK:** (*Environment and Society*) What are some causes of water pollution?

The Air We Breathe

Like water, air is necessary for survival. Just as human activities can pollute our water, they can also pollute our air.

Air Pollution Air pollution comes from several sources. Burning fuels for heating and running factories releases chemicals into the air. A major cause of air pollution is exhaust from the hundreds of millions of motor vehicles on the planet. Particularly in big cities, all these chemicals build up in the air. They create a mixture called smog.

Some cities have special problems with smog. Denver, Los Angeles, and Mexico City, for example, lie in bowl-shaped valleys that trap air pollution. On some days, the air in these cities gets so thick with smog that officials urge residents to stay indoors to protect their health.

When air pollution combines with moisture in the air, it can form an acid similar in strength to vinegar. When it falls to the ground, this liquid is called **acid rain**. It can damage or kill trees. Acid rain can even kill fish.

Many countries have laws to limit pollution. However, pollution is an international problem. Winds can blow polluted air away, but just to another place. Pollution can easily blow from one country to another. It can even pass across continents. As a result, countries that keep their own air clean can still suffer from other countries' pollution.

Pollution and Climate Change Smog and acid rain are short-term effects of air pollution. Air pollution may also have long-term effects by changing Earth's atmosphere. Certain kinds of pollution damage the **ozone layer** in the upper atmosphere. This ozone layer protects living things by absorbing harmful ultraviolet light from the Sun. Damage to Earth's ozone layer may cause human health problems such as skin cancer.

Another issue of growing concern is **global warming**—a slow increase in Earth's average temperature. The Sun constantly warms Earth's surface. The gases and water vapor in the atmosphere trap some of the heat. This process helps keep Earth warm. Without the atmosphere, heat would escape into space, and we would freeze. The process is called the **greenhouse effect**. In a greenhouse the Sun's heat passes through the glass roof but is then trapped inside. Evidence suggests that pollution causes the atmosphere to trap more heat. As a result, Earth would get warmer.

Heavy smog clouds the Los Angeles skyline. **Interpreting the Visual Record** (*Human-Environment Interaction*) **What problems do you think smog would create in everyday life?**

The Greenhouse Effect

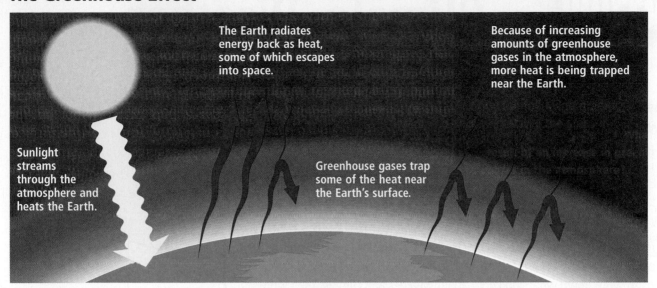

The Earth radiates energy back as heat, some of which escapes into space.

Because of increasing amounts of greenhouse gases in the atmosphere, more heat is being trapped near the Earth.

Sunlight streams through the atmosphere and heats the Earth.

Greenhouse gases trap some of the heat near the Earth's surface.

Scientists agree that Earth's climate has warmed during the last century. Not all agree, however, on the explanation. Most scientists say that air pollution caused by people has made temperatures rise. Burning fuels such as oil and coal is listed as the main culprit. Other scientists think warmer temperatures have resulted from natural causes. There is also disagreement about what has caused the thinning of the ozone layer.

✔ **READING CHECK:** (*Environment and Society*) How may air pollution affect Earth's climate?

The Earth's atmosphere acts like the glass in a greenhouse. Sunlight passes through the atmosphere and heats the Earth. As heat radiates up from the Earth, some heat escapes into space. The rest of the heat is trapped by gases in the atmosphere.

Interpreting the Diagram **What is one result of an increase in greenhouse gases in the atmosphere?**

Section Review 2

Homework Practice Online

Keyword: SK5 HP2

Define and explain: tributary, groundwater, aquifers, water cycle, evaporation, water vapor, condensation, precipitation, acid rain, ozone layer, global warming, greenhouse effect

Reading for the Main Idea

1. (*Environment and Society*) What are some hazards that water can create?

2. (*Environment and Society*) What are the main causes of air pollution?

Critical Thinking

3. **Analyzing Information** Why would protecting groundwater from pollution be important?

4. **Making Generalizations and Predictions** What may happen if air pollution continues to increase?

Organizing What You Know

5. **Sequencing** Copy the following graphic organizer. Use it to describe the steps in the water cycle.

Climate, Weather, and Vegetation

Read to Discover

1. What factors create climate and weather?
2. How are climate, plants, and animal life related?

Vocabulary

weather
climate
prevailing winds
currents
rain shadow

Reading Strategy

FOLDNOTES: TRI-FOLD Create a **Tri-Fold** FoldNote as described in the Appendix. Label the columns "Know," "Want," and "Learn." Use the main ideas to write down what you know about weather and climate. Then write down what you want to know. After you study the section, write down what you learned.

▲
Wildlife eat the summer vegetation in the Alaskan tundra.
Interpreting the Visual Record Why is there snow on the mountain peaks during summer?

Factors Affecting Climate and Weather

Weather is the condition of the atmosphere at a certain time and place. **Climate** refers to the weather conditions in an area over a long period of time. Weather and climate then help determine what kind of plants grow in a certain place.

Several factors determine a region's climate. Some of the forces that affect whether it will be sunny or rainy today are related to what is happening on the other side of the planet. Other forces are local.

The Sun Solar heat, or heat from the Sun, makes life possible on Earth. It also affects our weather and climate. The Sun doesn't heat Earth evenly, however. Because Earth is a sphere, areas closest to the North Pole and the South Pole don't receive direct rays from the Sun. Also, because Earth is tilted on its axis, areas away from the Sun receive less heat. Regions closer to the equator receive more heat. Therefore, the higher a place's latitude, the less solar heat it gets and the colder its climate.

Each year is divided into periods of time called seasons. Each season is known for a certain type of weather, based on temperature and amount of precipitation. Winter, spring, summer, and fall are examples of seasons that are described by their average temperature. "Wet" and "dry" seasons are described by their precipitation. The seasons change as Earth orbits the Sun. As this happens, the amount of solar energy received in any given location changes.

Winds Solar heat doesn't stay in one place. It moves around the planet. Otherwise, some places would be much hotter and others much colder than they are now. Winds, created by changes in air pressure, move the heat.

You may think of air as weightless, but it isn't. Cold air weighs more than warm air. When air warms, it gets lighter and rises. Colder air then moves in to replace the rising air. Wind is the result of this process.

Winds blow in great streams of air around the planet. Winds that blow in the same direction over large areas of Earth are called **prevailing winds**. These winds then make a region warmer or colder, drier or wetter, depending on from where they blow.

Some regions on Earth, particularly in the tropics, have seasons tied to precipitation rather than temperature. Shifting wind patterns are one cause of seasonal change. For example, in January winds from the north bring dry air to India. By June the winds have shifted, coming from the southwest and bringing moisture from the Indian Ocean.

As Earth revolves around the Sun, the tilt of the poles toward and away from the Sun causes the seasons to change. The day when the Sun's vertical rays are farthest from the equator is called a solstice. Solstices occur twice a year—about June 21 and about December 22. The days when the Sun's rays strike the equator directly are called equinoxes. These days mark the beginning of spring and fall.

Interpreting the Diagram At what point is the North Pole tilted toward the Sun?

The Seasons

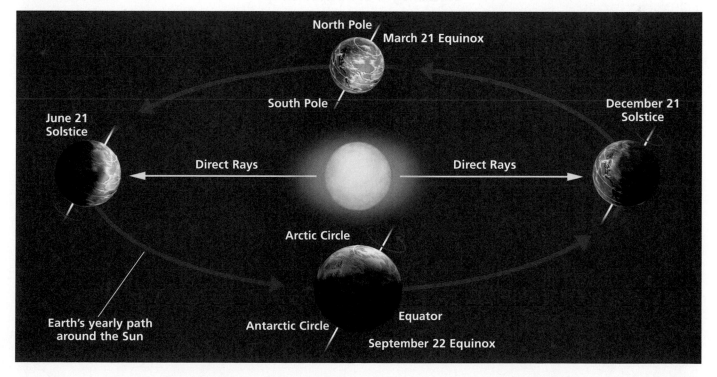

North Pole
March 21 Equinox
South Pole
December 21 Solstice
June 21 Solstice
Direct Rays
Direct Rays
Arctic Circle
Earth's yearly path around the Sun
Antarctic Circle
Equator
September 22 Equinox

This infrared satellite image shows the Gulf Stream moving warm water from lower latitudes to higher latitudes. The dark red shape alongside Florida's east coast is the Gulf Stream.

Oceans and Currents Winds move ocean water in the same general directions as the air above it moves. Warm ocean water from near the equator moves in giant streams, or **currents**, to colder areas. Cold water flows from the polar regions to the tropics. So, just as wind moves heat between places, so do ocean currents.

The Gulf Stream is an important ocean current. It moves warm water north from the Gulf of Mexico to the east coast of the United States. It then moves across the Atlantic Ocean toward Europe. The warm air that moves with it keeps winters mild. As a result, much of western Europe has warmer winters than areas in Canada that are just as far north.

Distance from the ocean also affects a region's climate. Water heats and cools more slowly than land. Therefore, coastal areas don't have the wide differences in temperature that areas in the middle of continents have. For example, Kansas City has colder winters and hotter summers than San Francisco. The cities are at about the same latitude, but Kansas City is in the continent's interior. In contrast, San Francisco lies on the Pacific Ocean.

Reading a Weather Map

Weather maps show atmospheric conditions as they currently exist or as they are forecast for a particular time period. Most weather maps have legends that explain what the symbols on the map mean. This map shows a cold front sweeping through the central United States. A low-pressure system is at the center of a storm bringing rain and snow to the Midwest. Notice that temperatures behind the cold front are considerably cooler than those ahead of the front.

You Be the Geographer According to this map, what region is experiencing the highest temperatures?

Landforms and Precipitation

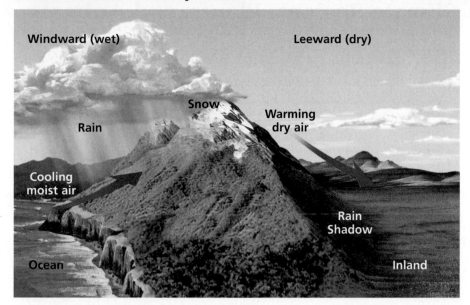

Windward (wet)   Leeward (dry)

Snow

Warming
dry air

Rain

Cooling
moist air

Rain
Shadow

Ocean   Inland

Moist air from the ocean cools as it moves up the windward side of a mountain. The water vapor in the air condenses and falls in the form of rain or snow. The drier air then moves down the leeward side of a mountain. This drier air brings very little precipitation to areas in the rain shadow.

Pictured in the bottom photo are mountains in the western part of the Sierra Nevada in Sequoia National Park. The top photo shows part of the eastern slope of the same range near Bishop, California.
(Place) **How does the vegetation of these places differ? What causes the difference?**

Elevation and Mountain Effects

Have you seen photos of Kilimanjaro, a mountain in East Africa? The mountain has snow on it all year although it is only about 250 miles from the equator. How can this be?

An increase in elevation—height on Earth's surface above sea level—causes a drop in temperature. This happens because the air is less dense at higher elevations. Thus the base of a mountain may be hot while the top is covered with ice.

Elevation has another effect on weather and climate. Warm, moist air blowing against a mountainside will rise. As it rises, it cools and forms clouds. Precipitation falls from the clouds. The side of the mountain facing the wind often gets heavy rain. By the time the air reaches the other side of the mountain it has lost most of its moisture. This can create a dry area called a **rain shadow**. Compare some of the physical maps and climate maps in the unit atlases to find examples of this effect.

✔ READING CHECK: *Physical Systems*
What are the main factors affecting climate and weather?

Climate Regions, Plants, and Animals

The chart below describes the 12 main climate types in terms of weather. Climate affects what kind of plants, or vegetation, can grow in a certain area. For example, if your region has a tundra climate, you won't be able to grow palm trees in your yard. Palm trees need a much warmer climate.

In turn, vegetation helps determine what animals are present. If you live in a desert, you won't see tree-dwelling monkeys, except in a zoo! What plants and animals live in your area?

World Climate, Plant, and Animal Regions

Climate	Major Weather Patterns	Vegetation	Animals You May See in the Climate Region (Animals Vary by Region.)
HUMID TROPICAL	warm and rainy all year	rain forest	bats, tree frogs, monkeys, jaguars, tigers, snakes, parrots
TROPICAL SAVANNA	warm all year, with rainy and dry seasons	grassland with scattered trees	anacondas, lions, elephants, gazelles, ostriches, hyenas rhinoceroses, zebras
DESERT	dry and sunny	a few hardy plants such as cacti	lizards, scorpions, snakes, bats, bobcats, coyotes
STEPPE	semiarid, hot summers with cooler winters	grassland and a few trees	antelope, wild horses, kangaroos, coyotes, camels
MEDITERRANEAN	dry, sunny, warm summers and mild, wetter winters	scrub woodland and grassland	deer, elk, mountain lions, wolves
HUMID SUBTROPICAL	hot, humid summers and mild, humid winters; rain all year	mixed forest	alligators, deer, bears, squirrels, foxes, snakes, many species of birds
MARINE WEST COAST	cloudy, mild summers and cool, rainy winters	evergreen forest	wild boars, deer, bears, seals
HUMID CONTINENTAL	four distinct seasons; long, cold winters and short, warm summers	mixed forest	wolverines, wild boars, deer, badgers, beavers, ducks
SUBARCTIC	long, cold winters and short, warm summers; low	evergreen forest	rabbits, moose, elk, wolves, lynxes, bears
TUNDRA	cold all year, little precipitation	moss, lichens, low shrubs, marshes during the summer	rabbits, reindeer, wolves, foxes
ICE CAP	freezing cold all year	no vegetation	animals that depend on the sea, such as polar bears, seals, and penguins
HIGHLAND	wide range of temperatures and precipitation amounts, depending on elevation	forest to tundra vegetation, depending on location and elevation	wide range of animals, depending on location, elevation, and vegetation

World Climate Regions

Major World Ocean Currents
← Cool currents
← Warm currents

Low Latitudes	HUMID TROPICAL		**Middle Latitudes**	MEDITERRANEAN		**High Latitudes**	SUBARCTIC
	TROPICAL SAVANNA			HUMID SUBTROPICAL			TUNDRA
Dry	DESERT			MARINE WEST COAST			ICE CAP
	STEPPE			HUMID CONTINENTAL			HIGHLAND

go.hrw.com
Homework Practice Online
Keyword: SK5 HP2

Section Review 3

Define and explain: weather, climate, prevailing winds, currents, rain shadow

Reading for the Main Idea

1. (*Physical Systems*) How does the Sun's heat affect temperature and winds?

2. (*Physical Systems*) What effect does the Gulf Stream have on Europe's climates?

Critical Thinking

3. Drawing Inferences From looking at the map, why do you think central Asia is very cold in winter and often hot in the summer?

4. Finding the Main Idea Why may a mountaintop and a nearby valley have wide differences in temperature?

Organizing What You Know

5. Summarizing Copy the following graphic organizer. Use it to summarize the 12 climate types.

Climate	Weather	Vegetation	Animals

Planet Earth • 37

Read to Discover

1. What are the most important renewable resources?
2. How do the main energy resources differ?
3. How do we use mineral resources?
4. How do resources affect people?

Vocabulary

renewable resources
nonrenewable resources
deforestation
reforestation
fossil fuels

petroleum
hydroelectric power
geothermal energy
solar power

Reading Strategy

TAKING NOTES As you read this section, list the natural resources mentioned in the text. Beside each resource, write R if the resource is renewable and N if the resource is nonrenewable.

▲
A row of poplar trees divides farmland near Aix-en-Provence, France.

(*Human-Environment Interaction*) **What effect will these trees have on erosion?**

Using Renewable Resources

The landforms, water, climate, and weather of a place all affect the people who live there. Another factor that affects daily life is the resources available to them. A resource is any material that is part of Earth and that people need and value.

Some of Earth's resources are renewable, while others are nonrenewable. **Renewable resources**, such as soil and forests, are those that natural processes continuously replace. **Nonrenewable resources** are those that can't be replaced naturally after they have been used. Once they've been used, they're gone forever!

You read in Section 1 about the need to preserve soil, since it is essential to survival. Soil qualifies as a renewable resource because natural processes create more of it. For example, when a tree dies and falls to the forest floor, the tree decays and adds valuable nutrients to the soil. Bacteria and other organisms break down the wood and turn it into humus. However, these processes are very slow. Soil that required hundreds of years to build up can be washed away in a few seconds.

Forests Forests are renewable resources because we can plant new trees. People use trees for many products. Wood products include lumber for buildings and furniture. Plastics and some fabrics use wood in the manufacturing process. Cooking oils, medicines, nuts, and rubber are among the many products that trees supply. In addition, trees and other plants release oxygen into the atmosphere. We enjoy forests for hiking and camping. Wildlife depends on forests for food and shelter.

Like soil, forests can be destroyed much faster than they can grow. In some places, forests are not being replaced as quickly as they are cut down. This loss of forest areas is called **deforestation**. People can reverse the trend by planting new trees. This practice, called **reforestation**, is important for both people and wildlife.

Resources and Land Management

The preservation of renewable resources is often part of larger land management issues. For example, suburbs spring up on what was valuable farmland. Fertile soil there can no longer grow food. Or, a developer may want to build a shopping mall in a forested area. Residents may prefer to preserve the trees within a park. These and similar local environmental issues are debated across the United States as towns and cities grow.

✓ **READING CHECK:** *Environment and Society* How can people help preserve forest resources?

▲

Human-Environment Interaction
Villagers work on a reforestation project in Cameroon.

Human-Environment Interaction
Development at the edge of Danville, California, is replacing farmland and rangeland.

▼

Human-Environment Interaction Deep underground, a miner digs coal in a narrow tunnel.

Wind turbines are just one source of electricity. **Interpreting the Visual Record** Human-Environment Interaction **How does this photo show human adaptation to the environment?**

Energy Resources

Most of the energy we use comes from the three **fossil fuels**: coal, petroleum, and natural gas. Fossil fuels were formed from the remains of ancient plants and animals. These remains gradually decayed and were covered with sediment. Over long periods of time, pressure and heat changed these materials. They became completely different solids, liquids, or gases. All fossil fuels are nonrenewable resources.

For thousands of years, people have burned coal for heat. Burning coal pollutes the air, however. Modern ways of burning coal produce less pollution, but cost more money. **Petroleum** may be the fossil fuel with which you are most familiar. When it is first pumped out of the ground, petroleum is a dark oily liquid called crude oil. It is then processed into gasoline, diesel and jet fuels, and heating oil. Burning these fuels also creates air pollution. The cleanest-burning fossil fuel is natural gas, which is usually found near petroleum deposits.

Renewable Energy Resources Energy sources besides fossil fuels exist. Their big advantage is they are cleaner, in general. Renewable energy sources aren't available everywhere, however. They may also cost more money. Some of these energy sources have other drawbacks too.

France has 59 nuclear reactors like this one and depends on nuclear power for about 77 percent of its energy.

Clean Energy Sources The most commonly used renewable energy source is **hydroelectric power** — the production of electricity by waterpower. Dams harness the energy of falling water from rivers to run generators that produce electricity. Although hydroelectric power doesn't pollute the air, it does affect the environment. The lakes that form when dams block rivers may drown farmland and forests. Fish and wildlife habitats are also affected.

Wind has powered sailing ships and windmills for centuries. Now wind has a new use. It can create electricity by turning a system of fan blades called a turbine. "Wind farms" with hundreds of wind turbines have been built in windy places. The heat of Earth's interior — **geothermal energy** — is another clean source of power. People can use the energy directly to heat water, or they can generate electricity with it. **Solar power** — heat and light from the Sun — can heat water or homes. Special solar panels also absorb solar energy to make electricity.

Nuclear Power The last major renewable energy resource is nuclear power. Although operating a nuclear power plant doesn't release pollution into the air, it does produce waste materials that will be deadly for many centuries. Management of these wastes is a serious problem. In addition, some nuclear power plants have had serious accidents. A nuclear accident in Chernobyl in Ukraine killed people, caused cancer in survivors, and poisoned farmland.

✓ **READING CHECK:** (*Environment and Society*) What are the main advantages of using renewable energy sources?

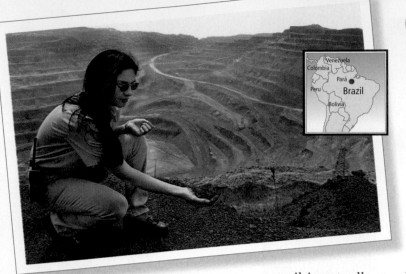

Mineral Resources

Energy resources are not the only nonrenewable resources that come out of the ground. We also use solid substances called minerals. Examples include metals, rocks, and salt.

Minerals fulfill many needs. Look around you to see just a few of the ways we use minerals. Your school is probably built on steel girders made from iron. The outside walls may be granite, limestone, or other types of rock. Window glass is made from quartz, a mineral found in sand. The "lead" in your pencil is actually graphite, another mineral. Metals are everywhere—from the staples through your homework papers to the coins in your wallet and the watch on your wrist.

Because they are nonrenewable, we need to conserve mineral resources. Recycling common items, such as aluminum cans, will make the supply of these resources last longer. It also reduces the amount of energy that factories use to convert metal into useful objects.

✔ **READING CHECK:** *Environment and Society* How can people conserve mineral resources?

Resources and People

Why does it matter what resources an area has, or how much it has of a resource? Actually, resources affect culture, history, and current events.

Resources and Wealth As you read this book, you will find that some places are rich in resources of many kinds. For example, the United States has fertile soil, forests, oil, metals, and many other resources. These riches have allowed our country to develop its economy. Our resources provide raw materials for various industries, from building houses to making cars. We also grow huge amounts of food. Partly because the United States has such a powerful economy, we also have great power in world affairs.

In contrast, some other countries are poor in resources. There, few industries grow, and people don't have many choices about how to earn a living. Some countries have large amounts of some resources but not of others. For example, Saudi Arabia is rich in oil but lacks water for growing food. Saudi Arabia pays other countries for food with the profit it earns on oil.

Resources and Daily Life The resources available to people affect how they live. In this country we have many resources. We can choose among many different ways to dress, build our homes, eat, travel, and entertain ourselves. People of other cultures may have fewer choices because they have fewer resources. Or, their environments may offer resources that we don't use.

Consider people who live in a rain forest, far from any city or factory. These people depend on the resources in their environment for all their needs. They may craft containers by weaving plant fibers together or canoes by hollowing out tree trunks. Their musical instruments are not electric guitars, but perhaps flutes made from bamboo. What kinds of songs would they sing? These forest people would be more likely to sing about finding food than about new cars.

✓ **READING CHECK:**
(*Environment and Society*) How does the lack of resources affect people?

This Brazilian rain forest is being cleared by burning.
(*Human-Environment Interaction*)
How do you think the loss of land affects people who live in the rain forest?

Homework Practice Online
Keyword: SK5 HP2

Define and explain: renewable resources, nonrenewable resources, deforestation, reforestation, fossil fuels, petroleum, hydroelectric power, geothermal energy, solar power

Reading for the Main Idea

1. (*Environment and Society*) What are fossil fuels, and how are they used?

2. (*Environment and Society*) What are the main renewable energy sources?

Critical Thinking

3. Analyzing Information How are preserving soil and forest resources related to resource and land management?

4. Making Generalizations and Predictions How may a country that has only one or two valuable resources develop its economy?

Organizing What You Know

5. Categorizing Copy the following graphic organizer. Use it to describe the mineral resources that may be used in a typical home.

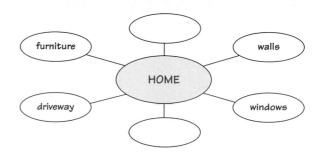

furniture — HOME — walls
driveway — windows

Planet Earth • 43

Define and Identify

Idenfity each of the following:

1. topography
2. plate tectonics
3. erosion
4. tributary
5. water cycle
6. global warming
7. climate
8. rain shadow
9. nonrenewable resources
10. geothermal energy

Review the Main Idea

11. What is the theory of plate tectonics and how does it work?
12. What may occur when tectonic plates move away from each other?
13. How is water involved in erosion?
14. What methods are used to protect soil from erosion?
15. What percentage of Earth's water is freshwater? What covers 70% of Earth's surface?
16. What are the three phases of the water cycle? What drives the water cycle?
17. What are the two main causes of water pollution?
18. Why may one country suffer from another country's air pollution?
19. What parts of the Earth receive the most solar heat? Why?

20. What makes wind?
21. Explain why Kansas City has more extreme seasons than San Francisco.
22. Why may the base of a mountain be hot while the top is covered in ice?
23. Why is it important to preserve renewable resources such as soil and forests?
24. What problems are associated with fossil fuels?
25. What are some examples of renewable energy resources?
26. What are minerals used for?

Think Critically

27. **Drawing Inferences and Conclusions** Why are we developing alternative energy sources?
28. **Finding the Main Idea** How are the Earth's land, water, and atmosphere related?
29. **Understanding Cause and Effect** How may a dam affect a river and its surrounding areas?
30. **Drawing Inferences and Conclusions** How do the laws that govern and restrict pollution both help and hurt people?
31. **Making Generalizations and Predictions** Why is pollution a global concern?

Map Activity

32. Match the letters on the map with their correct labels.
    Humid subtropical
    Steppe climate
    Marine west coast climate
    Mediterranean climate
    Desert
    Humid tropical
    Tropical savanna

Writing Activity

Imagine you are writing a report about your region of the United States for students around the world. Use your textbook, the library, and the Internet to research the landforms, climate, resources, and history of your region. Then write a few paragraphs highlighting what you discover.

☑ **internet** connect

Internet Activity: go.hrw.com
KEYWORD: SK5 GT2

Choose a topic to explore online:
- Learn more about using weather maps.
- Discover facts about Earth's water.
- Investigate earthquakes.

Social Studies Skills Practice

Interpreting Graphs

The United States uses different resources to meet its energy needs. Study the following graph and answer the questions.

Energy Consumption in the United States, 2002

Source: Energy Information Administration

1. What percentage of the nation's energy consumption is renewable?

2. Which fossil fuel is used the most?

3. Based on what you have learned in this chapter, which renewable resources provide the cleanest energy?

4. Why do you think solar, wind, and geothermal energy are not a commonly used resource?

Analyzing Primary Sources

In 1906, San Francisco experienced the most powerful earthquake recorded in the United States. Read the following account of the disaster from Peter Bacigalupi, one of San Francisco's shop owners. Then answer the questions.

"I was awakened from a sound slumber by a terrific trembling, which acted in the same manner as would a bucking broncho . . . My bed was going up and down in all four directions at once, while all about me I heard screams, wails, and crashing of breaking china-ware and nick-nacks. A great portion of plaster right over the head of my bed fell all around me, and caused a cloud of dust, which was very hard to breathe through . . . I started to walk downtown, and arriving within eight blocks of the business section, noted that there were hardly any panes of glass left in any of the show windows . . . Buildings were tumbled over on their sides, others looked as though they had been cut off short with a cleaver."

1. Was there any warning that the earthquake was about to occur?

2. What effect did the earthquake have on Mr. Bacigalupi's house?

3. What did he witness when he walked around the city?

4. How do you think communities can prepare for earthquakes such as this one?

CHAPTER 3

The World's People

The Colosseum, Rome, Italy

1998 Olympic opening ceremony, Nagano, Japan

Easter Island, Chile

Read to Discover

1. What is culture?
2. Why are cultural symbols important?
3. What influences how cultures develop?
4. How did agriculture affect the development of culture?

Vocabulary

culture
culture region
culture traits
ethnic groups
multicultural
race
acculturation

symbol
ethnocentrism
domestication
subsistence agriculture
commercial agriculture
civilization

Reading Strategy

READING ORGANIZER Before you read, create a chart with columns titled Term, Definition, Example. Write each of the terms above in the left column. As you read write the definition and give an example in the other two columns.

Aspects of Culture

The people of the world's approximately 200 countries speak hundreds of different languages. They may dress in different ways and eat different foods. However, all societies share certain basic institutions, including a government, an educational system, an economic system, and religious institutions. These vary from society to society and are often based on that society's **culture**. Culture is a learned system of shared beliefs and ways of doing things that guides a person's daily behavior. Most people around the world have a national culture shared with people of their own country. They may also have religious practices, beliefs, and language in common with people from other countries. Sometimes a culture dominates a particular region. This is known as a **culture region**. In a culture region, people may share certain **culture traits**, or elements of culture, such as dress, food, or religious beliefs. West Africa is an example of a culture region. Culture can also be based on a person's job or age. People can belong to more than one culture and can choose which to emphasize.

Race and Ethnic Groups Cultural groups share beliefs and practices learned from parents, grandparents, and ancestors. These groups are sometimes called **ethnic groups**. An ethnic group's shared culture may include its religion, history, language, holiday traditions, and special foods.

When people from different cultures live in the same country, the country is described as **multicultural** or multiethnic. Many countries

Dance is an example of a culture trait. Dancers from central Texas perform a traditional Czech dance.

▼

World Religions

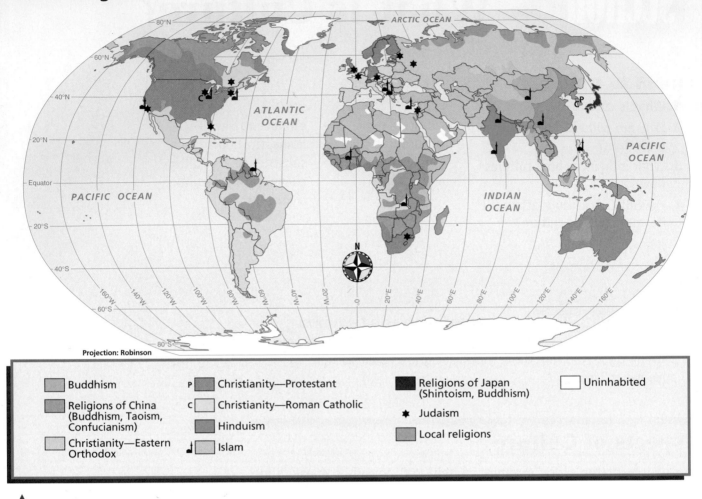

Projection: Robinson

	Buddhism	P	Christianity—Protestant		Religions of Japan (Shintoism, Buddhism)		Uninhabited
	Religions of China (Buddhism, Taoism, Confucianism)	c	Christianity—Roman Catholic	★	Judaism		
	Christianity—Eastern Orthodox		Hinduism		Local religions		
			Islam				

▲
~~~~~
Religion is one aspect of culture.

A disc jockey plays Cuban music for the large Cuban ethnic group of Miami, Florida.

▼

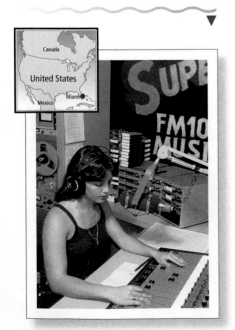

are multicultural. In some countries, such as Belgium, different ethnic groups have cooperated to form a united country. In other cases, such as in French-speaking Quebec, Canada, ethnic groups have frequently been in conflict. Sometimes, people from one ethnic group are spread over two or more countries. For example, Germans live in different European countries: Germany, Austria, and the Czech Republic. The Kurds, who are a people with no country of their own, live mostly in Syria, Iran, Iraq, and Turkey.

Race is based on inherited physical or biological traits. It is sometimes confused with ethnic group. For example, the Hispanic ethnic group in the United States includes people who look quite different from each other. However, they share a common Spanish or Latin American heritage. As you know, people vary in physical appearance. Some of these differences have developed in response to climate factors like cold and sunlight. Because people have moved from region to region throughout history, these differences are not clear-cut. Each culture defines race in its own way, emphasizing particular biological and ethnic characteristics. An example can be seen in Rwanda, a country in East Africa. In this country, the Hutu and the Tutsi have carried on a bitter civil war. Although both are East African, each one considers itself different from the other. Their definition of race involves height and facial features. Around the world, people tend to identify races based on obvious physical traits. However, these definitions of race are based primarily on attitudes, not actual biological differences.

Cultural Change Cultures change over time. Humans invent new ways of doing things and spread these new ways to others. The spread of one culture's ways or beliefs to another culture is called diffusion. Diffusion may occur when people move from one place to another. The English language was once confined to England and parts of Scotland. It is now one of the world's most widely spoken languages. English originally spread because people from England founded colonies in other regions. More recently, as communication among cultures has increased, English has spread through English-language films and television programs. English has also become an international language of science and technology.

People sometimes may borrow aspects of another culture as the result of long-term contact with another society. This process is called **acculturation**. For example, people in one culture may adopt the religion of another. As a result, they might change other cultural practices to conform to the new religion. For example, farmers who become Muslim may quit raising pigs because Islam forbids eating pork.

✓ **READING CHECK:** (*Human Systems*) What is the definition of culture?

Cultural Differences

A **symbol** is a sign that stands for something else. A symbol can be many things such as a word, a shape, a color, or a flag. People learn symbols from their culture. The sets of sounds of a language are symbols. These symbols have meaning for the people who speak that language. The same sound may mean something different to people who speak another language. The word *bad* means "evil" in English, "cool" to teenagers, and "bath" in German.

If you traveled to another country, you might notice immediately that people behave differently. Some people, however, may see the differences in other cultures as inferior to their own. This view is called **ethnocentrism**. Many people may even have an ethnocentric view toward the foods some cultures eat. For example, they may think it is disgusting that the Inuit of Canada eat whale blubber. To the Inuit, however, eating blubber is perfectly normal.

✓ **READING CHECK:** (*Human Systems*) How do symbols reflect differences among societies and cultures?

 Movement Some immigrants from China settle in New York City's Chinatown.

GO TO: go.hrw.com
KEYWORD: SK5 CH3
FOR: Web sites about the world's people

Fans cheer for the U.S. Olympic soccer team.

Interpreting the Visual Record Why do you think symbols such as flags create strong emotions?

A couple prepares for a wedding ceremony in Kazakhstan.

The layout of Marrakech, Morocco, is typical of many North African cities.

Interpreting the Visual Record *Place*
How are the streets and houses of Marrakech different from those in your community?

Spain
Morocco
Marrakech ●
Algeria

Development of a Culture

All people have the same basic needs for food, water, clothing, and shelter. People everywhere live in families and mark important family changes together. They usually have rituals or traditions that go with the birth of a baby, the wedding of a couple, or the death of a grandparent. All human societies need to deal with natural disasters. They must also deal with people who break the rules of behavior. However, people in different places meet these needs in unique ways. They eat different foods, build different kinds of houses, and form families in different ways. They have different rules of behavior. Two important factors that influence the way people meet basic needs are their history and environment.

History Culture is shaped by history. A region's people may have been conquered by the same outsiders. They may have adopted the same religion. They may have come from the same area and may share a common language. However, historical events may have affected some parts of a region but not others. For example, in North America French colonists brought their culture to Louisiana and Canada. However, they did not have a major influence on the Middle Atlantic region of the United States.

Cultures also shape history by influencing the way people respond to the same historical forces. Nigeria, India, and Australia were all colonized by the British. Today each nation still uses elements of the British legal system, but with important differences.

Environment The environment of a region can influence the development of culture. For example, in Egypt the Nile River is central to people's lives. The ancient Egyptians saw the fertile soils brought by the flooding of the Nile as the work of the gods. Beliefs in mountain spirits were important in many mountainous regions of the world. These areas include Tibet, Japan, and the Andes of South America.

Culture also determines how people use and shape their landscape. For example, city plans are cultural. Cities in Spain and its former colonies are organized around a central plaza, or square, with a church and a courthouse. On the other hand, Chinese cities are oriented to the four compass points. American cities often follow a rectangular grid plan. Many French city streets radiate out from a central core.

✓ **READING CHECK:** (*Human Systems*) What are some ways in which culture traits spread?

Development of Agriculture

For most of human history people ate only wild plants and animals. When the food ran out in one place, they migrated, or moved to another place. Very few people still live this way today. Thousands of years ago, humans began to help their favorite wild plant foods to grow. They probably cleared the land around their campsites and dumped seeds or fruits in piles of refuse. Plants took root and grew. People may also have dug water holes to encourage wild cattle to come and drink. People began cultivating the largest plants and breeding the tamest animals. Gradually, the wild plants and animals changed. They became dependent on people. This process is called **domestication**. A domesticated species has changed its form and behavior so much that it depends on people to survive.

Domestic sheep can no longer leap from rock to rock like their wild ancestors. However, the wool of domestic sheep is more useful to humans. It can be combed and twisted into yarn.

Domestication happened in many parts of the world. In Peru llamas and potatoes were domesticated. People in ancient Mexico and Central America domesticated corn, beans, squash, tomatoes, and hot peppers. None of these foods was grown in Europe, Asia, or Africa before the time of Christopher Columbus's voyages to the Americas. Meanwhile, Africans had domesticated sorghum and a kind of rice. Cattle, sheep, and goats were probably first raised in Southwest Asia. Wheat and rye were first domesticated in Central Asia. The horse was also domesticated there. These domesticated plants and animals were unknown in the Americas before the time of Columbus.

This ancient Egyptian wall painting shows domesticated cattle.

Interpreting the Visual Record Can you name other kinds of domesticated animals?

Agriculture and Environment Agriculture changed the landscape. To make room for growing food, people cut down forests. They also built fences, dug irrigation canals, and terraced hillsides. Governments were created to direct the labor needed for these large projects. Governments also defended against outsiders and helped people resolve problems. People could now grow enough food for a whole year. Therefore, they stopped migrating and built permanent settlements.

Types of Agriculture Some farmers grow just enough food to provide for themselves and their own families. This type of farming is called **subsistence agriculture**. In the wealthier countries of the world, a small number of farmers can produce food for everyone. Each farm is large and may grow only one product. This type of farming is called **commercial agriculture**. In this system companies rather than individuals or families may own the farms.

Agriculture and Civilization Agriculture enabled farmers to produce a surplus of food—more than they could eat themselves. A few people could make things like pottery jars instead of farming. They traded or sold their products for food. With more food a family could feed more children. As a result, populations began to grow. More people became involved in trading and manufacturing. Traders and craftspeople began to live in central market towns. Some towns grew into cities, where many people lived and carried out even more specialized tasks. For example, cities often supported priests and religious officials. They were responsible for organizing and carrying out religious ceremonies. When a culture becomes highly complex, we sometimes call it a **civilization**.

✓ **READING CHECK:** *Environment and Society* In what ways did agriculture affect culture?

Homework Practice Online
Keyword: SK5 HP3

Section Review 1

Define and explain: culture, culture region, culture trait, ethnic groups, multicultural, race, acculturation, symbol, ethnocentrism, domestication, subsistence agriculture, commercial agriculture, civilization

Reading for the Main Idea

1. *Human Systems* How can an individual belong to more than one cultural group?

2. *Human Systems* What institutions are basic to all societies?

Critical Thinking

3. **Drawing Inferences and Conclusions** In what ways do history and environment influence or shape a culture? What examples can you find in the text that explain this relationship?

4. **Analyzing Information** What is the relationship between the development of agriculture and culture?

Organizing What You Know

5. **Summarizing** Copy the following graphic organizer. Use it to describe culture by listing shared beliefs and practices.

Culture

Economics and Population

Read to Discover

1. What is economics?
2. How are industrialized countries different from developing countries?
3. What are the different types of economic systems?
4. Where do most people on Earth live?

Vocabulary

gross national product
gross domestic product
industrialized countries
literacy rate
developing countries
third-world countries
free enterprise
market economy
command economy
tradition-based economy
mixed economy
one-crop economy
exports
imports
interdependence
birthrate
death rate
population density
overpopulation
migration
emigrant
immigrant

Reading Strategy

FOLDNOTES: FOUR-CORNER FOLD Create a **Four-Corner Fold** described in the Appendix. Title the flaps The Economy, Developed and Undeveloped Countries, Types of Economies, and Population. As you read, write what you learn about each topic beneath its flap.

The Economy

All of the activities that people do to earn a living are part of a system called the economy. This includes people going to work, making things, selling things, buying things, and trading services. Economics is the study of the production, distribution, and use of goods and services.

Economic Indicators A common means of measuring a country's economy is the **gross national product** (GNP). The GNP is the value of all goods and services that a country produces in one year. It includes goods and services made by factories owned by that country's citizens but located in foreign countries. Most economists use **gross domestic product** (GDP) instead of GNP. GDP includes only those goods and services produced within a country. GDP divided by the country's population is called per capita GDP. This figure shows individual purchasing power and is useful for comparing levels of economic development.

Economic Activities Economists divide economic activities into four industries—primary, secondary, tertiary, and quaternary (see chart on the next page). A country's economy is usually based on one or more of these activities.

Shoppers crowd a street in Tokyo, Japan.

Economic Activities

ECONOMIC INDUSTRIES	DESCRIPTION	TYPES OF ACTIVITIES	EXAMPLE	
Primary industry	Involves natural resources or raw materials	Farming, fishing, mining, forestry	Dairy farmer feeds his cows.	
Secondary industry	Makes finished products using natural resources or raw materials	Manufacturing and construction	Factories make cheese.	
Tertiary industry	Handles goods that are ready for sale	Trucking, restaurants, grocery stores	Grocery stores sell cheese.	
Quaternary industry	Collects information	Research and management	A technician inspects dairy products in a lab.	

Interpreting the Chart Which economic industry involves selling goods?

A monorail in Sydney, Australia takes passengers throughout the city's central business district.
Interpreting the Visual Record *Place* What in this photo suggests that this is a city in an industrialized country?

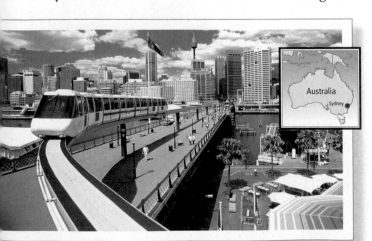

Australia
Sydney

The World's Rich and Poor

Economists divide the countries of the world into two groups. They use various measures including GNP, GDP, per capita GDP, life expectancy, and literacy to determine a country's stage of development. Developed countries like the United States, Canada, Japan, and most European countries are the world's wealthiest. They are called **industrialized countries**.

Industrialization occurs when a country relies more on manufacturing and less on agriculture. In industrialized countries, many people work in manufacturing, service, and information industries. These countries have strong secondary, tertiary, and quaternary industries. They have good health care systems. Industrialized countries also have good systems of education. The **literacy rate**, or the percentage of people, who can read and write is high.

Most people in industrialized countries live in cities and have access to telecommunications systems— systems that allow long-distance communication. The level of technology in most countries is usually measured by how many telephones, televisions, or computers are in use.

Developing countries make up the second group. They are in different stages of moving toward development. About two thirds of the world's people live in developing countries. These countries are poor. People often work in farming or other primary industries earning low wages. Cities in developing countries are often very crowded. Many people move to cities to find work. Most people are not educated. They usually have little access to health care or telecommunications.

Some developing countries have made economic progress in recent decades. South Korea and Mexico are good examples. These countries are experiencing strong growth in manufacturing and trade. However, some of the world's poorest countries are developing slowly or not at all.

One Planet, Four Worlds Some people also refer to developing countries as **third-world countries**. These countries lack the economic opportunities of most industrialized countries. Some industrialized countries are called first-world and second-world countires. First-world countries include the United States, Canada, Western Europe, Japan and Australia. Second-world countries include Russia, the former Soviet republics, China, and Eastern Europe.

Third-world countries in Latin America, however, experience some economic growth. Countries like Haiti, however, show no economic growth. They are known as fourth-world countries.

✓ **READING CHECK:** What are some of the differences between industrialized and developing countries?

This photo shows daily life in a village in eastern Afghanistan.
Interpreting the Visual Record (Place)
What in this photo suggests that this village is in a developing country?

Interpreting the Chart Which countries have the highest literacy rates?

Comparing Developed and Developing Countries

COUNTRY	POPULATION	POPULATION GROWTH RATE	PER CAPITA GDP	LIFE EXPECTANCY	LITERACY RATE	TELEPHONE LINES
United States	290.3 million	0.9%	$ 37,600	77	97%	194 million
France	60.1 million	0.4%	$ 26,000	79	99%	35 million
South Korea	48.2 million	0.7%	$ 19,600	75	98%	24 million
Mexico	104.9 million	1.4%	$ 8,900	72	92%	9.6 million
Poland	38.6 million	0.0%	$ 9,700	73	99%	8 million
Brazil	182.1 million	1.1%	$ 7,600	71	86%	17 million
Egypt	74.7 million	1.8%	$ 4,000	70	57%	3.9 million
Myanmar	42 million	0.5%	$ 1,700	55	83%	250,000
Mali	11.6 million	2.8%	$ 900	45	46%	23,000

Source: Central Intelligence Agency, *The World Factbook 2003*

Making a Living

Countries organize their economies in different ways. Most developed countries have an economic system called **free enterprise**. This system is organized around the production and distribution of goods and services. The United States operates under a free enterprise system. There are many benefits of this system. Companies are free to make whatever goods they wish. Employees can seek the highest wages for their work. People, rather than the government, control the factors of production. Factors of production are the things that determine what goods are produced in an economy. They include the natural resources that are available for making goods for sale. They also include the capital, or money, needed to pay for production and the labor needed to manufacture goods. The work of entrepreneurs is another factor of production. Entrepreneurs are people who start businesses in a free enterprise system.

Business owners in a free enterprise system sell their goods in a **market economy**. In such an economy, business owners and customers make decisions about what to make, sell, and buy. In contrast, the governments of some countries control the factors of production. The government decides what, and how much, will be produced. It also sets the prices of goods to be sold. This is called a **command economy**.

Some countries with a command economy are communist. Communism is a political system where the government owns almost all the factors of production. Only five countries in the world are communist today—China, Cuba, Laos, North Korea, and Vietnam.

The third type of economy is called a **tradition-based economy**. This type of economy is based on customs and tradition. Economic activities are based on laws, rituals, religious beliefs, or habits developed by the society long ago. The Mbuti people of the Democratic Republic of the Congo practice a tradition-based economy.

Large shopping malls, such as this one in New York City's Trump Tower, are common in countries that have market economies and a free enterprise system. Shoppers here can find a wide range of stores and goods concentrated in one area.

ECONOMICS

Money Management

A country's economy can be affected by how well its citizens manage their money. If you have a job, the money you make is called your income. You can either spend your money, save it, or invest it. *Investing* means using your money in ways that will make more money. For example, you can by stock, or shares, in a company that performs well. When you sell the stock you purchased, the original value of your money, hopefully, has gone up. Investing and saving money benefits both you and your country's economy. The U.S. economy benefits because your invested dollars are at work growing U.S. businesses.

Buying shares of stock, represented by certificates like these, is a way to invest money.

What if you need to buy something you cannot afford? You can buy it on credit, promising a bank or credit card company that you will pay back the money owed, with interest. If you buy too much on credit, you may not be able to pay all of your debts, which can hurt you financially. This means you will not have money for saving and investing. Likewise, when a country borrows too much money without paying it back, its economy may falter.

What choices does a person have when managing his or her income?

Another economic system is called a **mixed economy**. Most countries have this type of economy. Their economy is based on at least two of the economic systems you've learned about. For example, the United States has a market economy but certain things are regulated by the government.

Finally, some countries in tropical and subtropical regions have a **one-crop economy**. Their economy is based on a single crop, such as bananas, sugarcane, or cacao.

Buying and Selling International trade plays a large role in a country's economy. A country's **exports** include products sold to other countries. On the other hand, a country's **imports** include products a country buys from other countries. Imported products are usually things that aren't produced or available in the country that is buying the item. For example, Japan must import many agricultural products from other countries. Because Japan is a relatively small island, it does not have enough land suitable for crop growing.

Getting the Goods In international trade a condition known as **interdependence** occurs between countries when they depend on each other for resources or goods and services. An industrialized country may depend on the raw materials of a developing country. However, the developing country depends on the finished goods and technology of the industrialized country. For example, Mexico exports crude oil to the United States. In return, the United States exports computer equipment to Mexico.

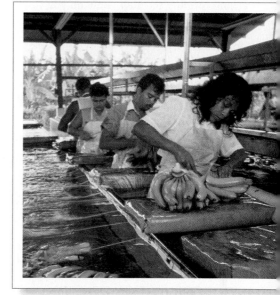

▲
At a plantation in Costa Rica, workers wash bananas before shipping them around the world.

Interpreting the Visual Record

(Movement) **Why may having a one-crop economy cause problems for a country?**

 READING CHECK: (*Human Systems*) What are the four types of economies?

Six Billion and Counting

In 1960, the world's population hit three billion. Since then the world's population has grown to over six billion. More than 90 percent of this population growth was in the developing countries of Africa, Latin America, and Asia. More than a quarter of the world's six billion people are between the ages of 10 and 24. About 86 percent of these young people live in developing countries.

World of People Some countries are very crowded. Others are only thinly populated. People who study these differences in the world's population are called demographers. They collect information, or demographics, which include population size, and the ages and gender of the population. They also determine **population density**, or how many people live closely together. Population density is calculated by dividing a country's population by its area—stated in either square miles or square kilometers. When a country has an extremely high population density, it may be suffering from **overpopulation**. An overpopulated country usually cannot support its people without outside help.

People are spread unevenly across Earth. Some places are crowded with people, while others are empty. Where do most of the world's people live? Asia is the world's most populated region. China and India both have more than a billion people! In addition, Indonesia, Pakistan, Japan, and Bangladesh each have over 100 million people.

The regions on this map that are shaded dark purple have a high population density.

Interpreting the Map How do you think the patterns on this map will change over the next 100 years? Why?

▼

World Population Density

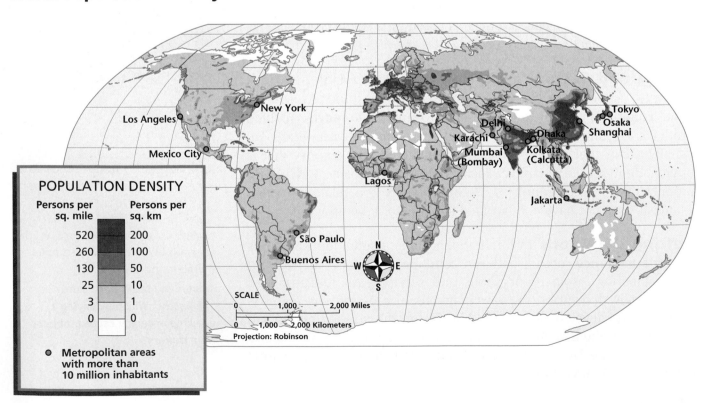

POPULATION DENSITY

Persons per sq. mile	Persons per sq. km
520	200
260	100
130	50
25	10
3	1
0	0

● Metropolitan areas with more than 10 million inhabitants

SCALE
Projection: Robinson

Growing Pains Births add to a country's population. Deaths subtract from it. The number of births per 1,000 people in a year is called the **birthrate**. Similarly, the **death rate** is the annual number of deaths per 1,000 people. The birthrate minus the death rate equals the rate of natural population increase. This number is expressed as a percentage. The birthrate in developing countries is more than double that of industrialized countries. For example, the birthrates of Niger and Bulgaria are very different. Niger has the world's highest birthrate. Most women in Niger have about seven children. On the other hand, Bulgaria has the world's lowest birthrate. Most Bulgarian women only have one child.

On the Move Throughout history, people have moved from place to place looking for better opportunities. People are constantly moving within their own country or across international borders. This movement of people is called **migration**. One person or a group migrate either for a short period of time or permanently. There are several different types of migration. Someone who leaves one place for another is called an **emigrant**.

On the other hand, an **immigrant** is someone arriving from another country. A migrant worker is someone looking for work by regularly moving from place to place. Some people move to other countries for opportunities they don't have in their homeland. Most people emigrate for economic reasons.

✓ **READING CHECK:** (*Human Systems*) What region of the world has the most people?

Define and explain: gross national product, gross domestic product, industrialized countries, literacy rate, developing countries, third-world countries, free enterprise, market economy, command economy, tradition-based economy, mixed economy, one-crop economy, exports, imports, interdependence, birthrate, death rate, population density, overpopulation, migration, emigrant, immigrant

Reading for the Main Idea

1. (*Environment and Society*) What geographic features influence population density?

2. (*Human Systems*) What characteristics do developed nations share?

Homework Practice Online

Keyword: SK5 HP3

Critical Thinking

3. **Finding the Main Idea** What are the different economic systems? Describe each.

4. **Drawing Inferences and Conclusions** What causes overpopulation and how can it be prevented?

Organizing What You Know

5. **Summarizing** Copy the following graphic organizer. Use it to study your local community and classify the businesses in your area.

Primary Industries	Secondary Industries	Tertiary Industries	Quaternary Industries
• •	• •	• •	• •

Read to Discover

1. What is globalization? How are people around the world connected?

2. Why are refugees a global problem? What causes famine? How do people in need get help?

Vocabulary

globalization
popular culture
refugees
famine
humanitarian aid
drought

Reading Strategy

READING ORGANIZER Before you read, create a spider map. Label the center oval Global Connections. Draw seven legs and label them Technology, Cities, Travel, Trade, Sports, Refugees, and Assistance. As you read, write what you learn about these topics beneath each of the legs.

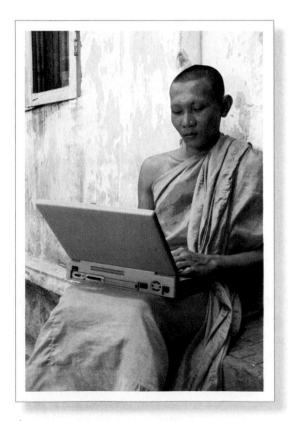

▲
A Buddhist monk in Cambodia may use this laptop computer to log on to the Internet.

Living in a Small World

In just seconds an e-mail message sent by a teenager in India beams all the way to a friend in the United States. A businesswoman in Singapore takes a call from her cell phone from an investor in New York. With just a few taps on a computer's keyboard, anyone in the world can also immediately access the Internet. These are all examples of how small our world has become with the use of cell phones, e-mail, the Internet, and satellite television.

Global Tech Thanks to these technologies, people around the world communicate and do business with each other faster than anyone ever thought possible. **Globalization** is the term most often used to describe how time and distance in the world seem to be shrinking. Globalization is also used to describe how countries are increasingly linked through **popular culture** and a global economy. Popular culture includes things people across the world share such as movies, literature, music, clothing, and food. For example, you can find the American restaurant, McDonald's, in almost every major world city today. Kids throughout the world exchange Pokemon trading cards from Japan. Millions read Harry Potter.

Speaking Globally Almost 6,000 languages are spoken today. English, however, is the language of globalization. As a result, a quarter of the world's population speaks English for global business, communications, higher education, diplomacy, aviation, the Internet, science, popular music, entertainment and international travel. American news channels and movies are seen everywhere. For example, CNN uses satellites to broadcast in English to millions of TV sets around the world.

Cultural Centers Even with fast communication, globalization wouldn't be possible without major cities. As transportation and cultural centers, cities provide the perfect place for different people to exchange goods and ideas. For example, Miami is sometimes called the "Gateway to Latin America." As an international port and multi-cultural city, many companies that operate in Latin America are headquartered in Miami. Many other global cities also depend on their geographical location for international business. Seattle and San Francisco have economic ties to major Asian cities located across the Pacific Ocean, such as Tokyo and Hong Kong.

This restaurant in Ecuador provides visitors with Internet access.

Ships dock in Miami, Florida.
Interpreting the Visual Record
(*Movement*) **What in this photo suggests that Miami is a major international city?**

Travel Ills There's a downside, however, to life in a well-connected world. You can board a plane at any major airport today and travel to just about anywhere in the world. Some people, however, carry more than just their luggage on to these flights. They can also carry diseases. For example, in 2003, one woman who didn't realize she was infected with the contagious disease called SARS, traveled from China to Toronto, Canada. As she made contact with several people in Toronto, they too came down with the disease. However, steps are now taken to prevent people with contagious diseases from boarding international flights.

Quick Trades Globalization not only links the world's people, it also connects businesses and countries. For centuries, people have traded. But, never as fast as today. Through the use of the Internet it is quick and simple to order goods from anywhere in the world. For example, a shoe retailer in Chicago can find a Web site that links them to someone in China who makes the sneakers they need. The order is then flown to Chicago the following day. That afternoon the sneakers are sold to customers.

Made in the USA? Check the label on your shoes, other clothing, or book bag to see where it's made. It probably doesn't say the United States. Why? Most clothing and a lot of electronic equipment are imported to the United States from other countries. Many international companies build their factories in places where workers will work for less money than American workers. By hiring cheap labor, these companies lower their manufacturing costs. As a result, these products usually have a lower price tag than products made in the United States.

World Sports You've already learned that money, ideas, and goods are traded in the global economy. But, did you also know that people could be exchanged as well? For example, more and more baseball players from Latin America and Asia are now playing professionally in the United States. In addition, many American and European soccer teams frequently trade players across the Atlantic.

✔ **READING CHECK:**
(*Human Systems*) What are some examples of globalization?

Fans of Hideki Matsui—a professional baseball player from Japan—show their support as they watch him play for the New York Yankees.

Interpreting the Visual Record
(Movement) **How is this sign an example of globalization?**

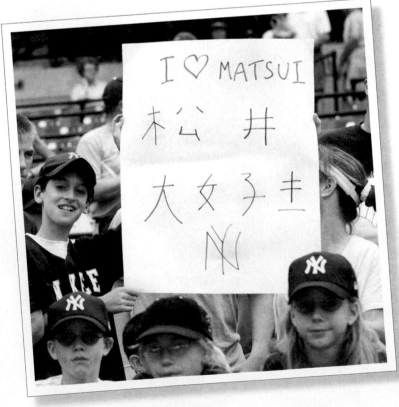

Helping People in Need

In a smaller world, global problems also connect the world's people. What happens in one part of the world affects the entire planet. Millions of people today suffer without life's necessities. In response to these problems, the global community tries to help as many people as possible.

Searching for Home One of the major global problems today are the 14 million people who seek refuge in other countries. These **refugees** require food, shelter, and help with finding jobs. Many international agencies help refugees start new lives. Unlike immigrants, however, refugees flee their countries because of persecution, war, or economic reasons. Some refugees even eventually become citizens in the country they settle in. For example, many Cuban refugees and their families are now United States citizens.

Hungry Planet A great shortage of food, or **famine**, affects millions of people throughout the world. International relief agencies provide **humanitarian aid** to famine areas. This aid includes medicine and millions of pounds of grain and other foods. These efforts, however, sometimes are not enough to relieve the problem. Today in Ethiopia more than 12 million people are at risk for starvation. The lack of rain, or **drought**, has prevented farmers from growing enough food to feed their country's population.

Movement In the late 1990s unrest in Kosovo, Yugoslavia, disrupted the lives of hundreds of thousands of ethnic Albanians. Many people were forced from their homes. Here, refugees in neighboring Macedonia wait to be transported to nearby transition camps.

✓ **READING CHECK:** (*Human Systems*) What are some reasons why refugees flee their homeland?

Section Review 3

Homework Practice Online Keyword: SK5 HP3

Define and explain: globalization, popular culture, refugees, famine, humanitarian aid, drought

Reading for the Main Idea

1. (*Human Systems*) What are some effects of globalization?
2. (*Human Systems*) How does humanitarian aid help people?

Critical Thinking

3. **Drawing Conclusions** How has globalization made the world smaller?

4. **Making Predictions** What will happen if the number of refugees continues to grow?

Organizing What You Know

5. **Contrasting** Copy the following graphic organizer. Use it to discuss two arguments about globalization.

Good results of globalization		Bad results of globalization
	⇦⇨	

CHAPTER 3 — Review and Practice

Define and Identify

Idenfify each of the following:

1. culture
2. ethnic groups
3. ethnocentrism
4. domestication
5. subsistence agriculture
6. civilization
7. gross national product
8. literacy rate
9. third-world countries
10. mixed economy
11. imports
12. birthrate
13. population density
14. migration
15. immigrant
16. globalization
17. popular culture
18. refugees
19. humanitarian aid

Review the Main Ideas

20. What is culture, and why should people study it?
21. How does diffusion occur?
22. What are two important factors that influence the way people meet basic needs?
23. What is the difference between subsistence and commercial agriculture?

24. How does gross national product differ from gross domestic product?
25. How do third-world countries differ from fourth-world nations?
26. Why do countries import products?
27. How has globalization affected how people communicate?
28. How do refugees differ from immigrants?

Think Critically

29. **Drawing Inferences and Conclusions** Why are ethnic groups sometimes confused with races?
30. **Identifying Cause and Effect** How did the development of agriculture affect the global population?
31. **Comparing and Contrasting** How do industrialized countries differ from developing countries?
32. **Summarizing** How have new technologies helped to create a global culture?
33. **Finding the Main Idea** How has globalization changed how countries trade with each other?

Map Activity

34. On a separate sheet of paper, match the letters on the map with their correct labels.
    Buddhism
    Christianity—Eastern Orthodox
    Christianity—Protestant
    Christianity—Roman Catholic
    Hinduism
    Islam

Writing Activity

Research the economy of your community. Has the economy grown or declined in the last 10 years? Why? What goods are exported from your community? What goods are imported to your community? Write about what you learn from your research. Then write about how you think your community might change in the future.

☑ internet connect

Internet Activity: go.hrw.com
KEYWORD: SK5 GT3

Choose a topic to explore online:
- Visit famous buildings and monuments around the world.
- Compare facts about life in different countries.
- Examine world population growth.

Social Studies Skills Practice

Interpreting Cartoons

Study the following cartoon. Then answer the questions.

MARTIN GUHL

1. What is the main idea of this cartoon?
2. Why is the Earth in the middle of a maze?
3. Does the cartoonist believe it is difficult or easy to connect with people around the world by using the Internet? Why?
4. How is this cartoon an example of globalization?

Analyzing Primary Sources

Read the following quote from French-American film director Jean-Marc Barr. Then answer the questions.

"We believe Europe is going to exist because the English language allows it to culturally. Never on this continent has there been a language that all the classes can speak, from a Polish man to a Spaniard to an Icelandic. My biggest and most rewarding events in my life have been because I have been able to speak English with people all over the world."

1. What advantage does Barr see for Europe as English is used more?
2. Why would a film director such as Barr be especially interested in language?
3. Based on your knowledge of culture, why might some Europeans resist the use of English?
4. How do you think Barr feels about globalization?

REGIONS

What is a Region?

Think about where you live, where you go to school, and where you shop. These places are all part of your neighborhood. In geographic terms, your neighborhood is a region. A region is an area that has common features that make it different from surrounding areas.

What regions do you live in? You live on a continent, in a country, and in a state. These are all regions that can be mapped.

Regions can be divided into smaller regions called subregions. For example, Africa is a major world region. Africa's subregions include North Africa, West Africa, East Africa, central Africa, and southern Africa. Each subregion can be divided into even smaller subregions.

Regional Characteristics Regions can be based on physical, political, economic, or cultural characteristics. Physical regions are based on Earth's natural features, such as continents, landforms, and climates. Political regions are based on countries and their subregions, such as states, provinces, and cities. Economic regions are based on money-making activities such as agriculture or industries. Cultural regions are based on features such as language, religion, or ethnicity.

▲

East Africa is a subregion of Africa. It is an area of plateaus, rolling hills, and savanna grasslands.

Major World Regions

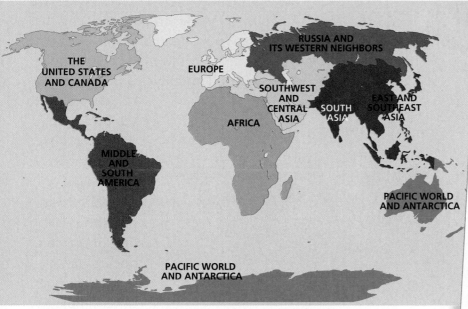

THE UNITED STATES AND CANADA

EUROPE

RUSSIA AND ITS WESTERN NEIGHBORS

SOUTHWEST AND CENTRAL ASIA

AFRICA

SOUTH ASIA

EAST AND SOUTHEAST ASIA

MIDDLE AND SOUTH AMERICA

PACIFIC WORLD AND ANTARCTICA

PACIFIC WORLD AND ANTARCTICA

The international border between Kenya and Tanzania is a clearly defined regional boundary.

Regional Boundaries All regions have boundaries, or borders. Boundaries are where the features of one region meet the features of a different region. Some boundaries, such as coastlines or country borders, can be shown as lines on a map. Other regional boundaries are less clear.

Transition zones are areas where the features of one region change gradually to the features of a different region. For example, when a city's suburbs expand into rural areas, a transition zone forms. In the transition zone, it may be hard to find the boundary between rural and urban areas.

Types of Regions There are three basic types of regions. The first is a formal region. Formal regions are based on one or more common features. For example, Japan is a formal region. Its people share a common government, language, and culture.

The second type of region is a functional region. Functional regions are based on movement and activities that connect different places. For example, Paris, France, is a functional region. It is based on the goods, services, and people that move throughout the city. A shopping center or an airport might also be a functional region.

The third type of region is a perceived region. Perceived regions are based on people's shared feelings and beliefs. For example, the neighborhood where you live may be a perceived region.

The three basic types of regions overlap to form complex world regions. The world can be divided into nine major world regions (see map above). Each has general features that make it different from the other major world regions. These differences include physical, cultural, economic, historical, and political features.

Understanding What You Read

1. Regions can be based on what types of characteristics?

2. What are the three basic types of regions?

Building Skills for Life: Drawing Mental Maps

We create maps in our heads of all kinds of places—our homes, schools, communities, country, and the world. Some of these places we know well. Others we have only heard about. These images we carry in our heads are shaped by what we see and experience. They are also influenced by what we learn from news reports or other sources. Geographers call the maps that we carry around in our heads mental maps.

We use mental maps to organize spatial information about people and places. For example, our mental maps help us move from classroom to classroom at school or get to a friend's home. A mental map of the United States helps us list the states we would pass through driving from New York City to Miami.

We use our mental maps of places when we draw sketch maps. A sketch map showing the relationship between places and the relative size of places can be drawn using very simple shapes. For example, triangles and rectangles could be used to sketch a map of the world. This quickly drawn map would show the relative size and position of the continents.

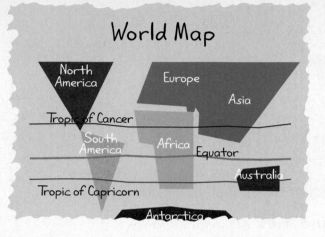

World Map

Think about some simple ways we could make our map of the world more detailed. Adding the equator, Tropic of Cancer, and Tropic of Capricorn would be one way. Look at a map of the world in your textbook's Atlas. Note that the bulge in the continent of Africa is north of the equator. Also note that all of Asia is north of the equator. Next note that the Indian subcontinent extends south from the Tropic of Cancer. About half of Australia is located north of the Tropic of Capricorn. As your knowledge of the world increases, your mental map will become even more detailed.

THE SKILL

1. Look at the maps in your textbook's Atlas. Where does the prime meridian fall in relation to the continents?

2. On a separate sheet of paper, sketch a simple map of the world from memory. First draw the equator, Tropic of Cancer, Tropic of Capricorn, and prime meridian. Then sketch in the continents. You can use circles, rectangles, and triangles.

3. Draw a second map of the world from memory. This time, draw the international date line in the center of your map. Add the equator, Tropic of Cancer, and Tropic of Capricorn. Now sketch in the continents. What do you notice?

HANDS on GEOGRAPHY

Mental maps are personal. They change as we learn more about the world and the places in it. For example, they can include details about places that are of interest only to you.

What is your mental map of your neighborhood like? Sketch your mental map of your neighborhood. Include the features that you think are important and that help you find your way around. These guidelines will help you get started.

1. Decide what your map will show. Choose boundaries so that you do not sketch more than you need to.

2. Determine how much space you will need for your map. Things that are the same size in reality should be about the same size on your map.

3. Decide on and note the orientation of your map. Most maps use a directional indicator. On most maps, north is at the top.

4. Label reference points so that others who look at your map can quickly and easily figure out what they are looking at. For example, a major street or your school might be a reference point.

5. Decide how much detail your map will show. The larger the area you want to represent, the less detail you will need.

6. Use circles, rectangles, and triangles if you do not know the exact shape of an area.

7. As you think of them, fill in more details, such as names of places or major land features.

Lab Report

1. What are the most important features on your map? Why did you include them?

2. Compare your sketch map to a published map of the area. How does it differ?

3. At the bottom, list three ways that you could make your sketch map more complete.

UNIT 2

Southwest and Central Asia

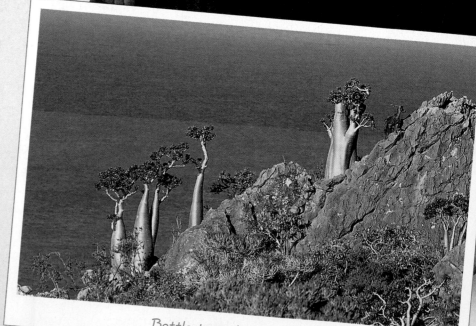

Bottle trees, Yemen

An Exchange Student in Turkey

Sara Lewis was an American exchange student in Turkey. Here she describes how teenagers live in Istanbul, Turkey's largest city, and the month-long fast of Ramadan. **WHAT DO YOU THINK?** *What would it be like to live in a place where you can see the remains of thousands of years of history?*

The people of Istanbul are very traditional and family-oriented, but today's Turk also has European-style tastes. Turkish teens go dancing and hang out in coffeehouses. All around them, though, are reminders of the past. There are many monuments left over from Greek, Roman, Byzantine, and Ottoman times.

Islam plays a big part in daily life. Five times every day I can hear the people being called to prayer. For more than a month, my host parents fasted during Ramadan. They didn't eat or drink anything while the sun was up. My host sister and I fasted for one day. By the time the sun went down we were starving! I'm glad we weren't expected to continue the fast. Then we shopped for new clothes. It is the custom to wear new clothes to the feast at the end of Ramadan. The fresh clothes seem to stand for the cleanliness one achieves during the month of fasting.

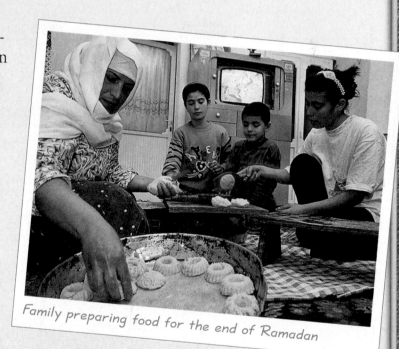

Family preparing food for the end of Ramadan

Jewish girls, Zefat, Israel

Understanding Primary Sources

1. What do modern Turkish teenagers do for fun?
2. How is Ramadan observed in Turkey?

Sooty falcon

Southwest and Central Asia

Elevation Profile

Profile at 30°N latitude

Zagros
Mountains

Arabian
Peninsula

Sinai
Peninsula

Persian
Gulf

Plateau of
Iran

10,000 ft. — 3,048 m
5,000 ft. — 1,524 m
4,000 ft. — 1,220 m
3,000 ft. — 914 m
2,000 ft. — 610 m
1,000 ft. — 305 m
Sea Level — Sea Level

Approximately 1,800 miles

The United States and Southwest and Central Asia:
Comparing Sizes

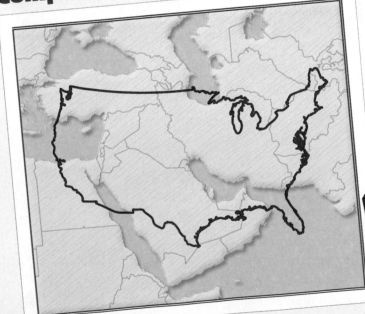

GEOSTATS:

🌐 World's lowest point on land: the Dead Sea, in Israel and Jordan—1,312 feet (400 m) below sea level

🌐 World's leading exporter of oil: Saudi Arabia

🛢 Approximate amount of proven oil reserves in Saudi Arabia: 261 billion barrels

🛢 Estimated number of barrels of oil that pass through the Strait of Hormuz every day: 15.4 million

1. (Place) Which rivers flow into the Aral Sea?

2. (Region) Where are the region's highest mountains? What are these mountains called?

3. (Place) Which country is partly in Europe and partly in Asia?

Critical Thinking

4. (Movement) How might one travel overland from Syria to Oman? Why?

5. (Interaction) Compare this map to the **population map**. What physical features contribute to Iraq's relatively high population density?

1. **Place** What is the region's largest country? the region's smallest?

2. **Location** Which capital lies near latitude 30°N and longitude 50°E?

Critical Thinking

3. **Region** Examine the **climate map**. Why do you think so many of the boundaries in this region are straight lines?

4. **Movement** Which countries lie along the Persian Gulf and the Gulf of Oman? Why might conflicts occur among these countries?

Southwest and Central Asia: Climate

CLIMATE
- Desert
- Steppe
- Mediterranean
- Humid subtropical
- Humid continental
- Highland

SCALE
0   250   500 Miles

0   250   500 Kilometers
Projection: Lambert Conformal Conic

1. (*Place*) What two climate types are most common in this region?

2. (*Place*) Compare this map to the **physical map.** What mountain ranges do not have a highland climate?

Critical Thinking

3. (*Interaction*) Compare this map to the **land use and resources map.** In which climate regions are nomadic herding most common?

4. (*Interaction*) Compare this map to the **population map.** How may climate influence the region's population patterns?

POPULATION DENSITY

Persons per sq. mile	Persons per sq. km
520	200
260	100
130	50
25	10
3	1
0	0

● Metropolitan areas with more than 2 million inhabitants

○ Metropolitan areas with 1 million to 2 million inhabitants

SCALE
0   250   500 Miles
0   250   500 Kilometers
Projection: Lambert Conformal Conic

1. (Region) Which country has an area of high population density but no large cities?

2. (Region) What is the largest city in the easternmost part of the region?

Critical Thinking

3. (Location) Look at Istanbul's location. Why is it good for a large city?

4. (Region) Compare this map to the **land use and resources map**. Why do you think the southwestern tip of the Arabian Pennisula has a high population density?

Legend:
- ● Major manufacturing and trade centers
- —— Oil pipelines
- —— Shipping lanes

LAND USE
- Nomadic herding
- Livestock raising
- Commercial farming
- Subsistence farming
- Forests
- Manufacturing
- Limited economic activity

RESOURCES
- 🚃 Coal
- 🜂 Natural gas
- ⚒ Oil
- ⚡ Hydroelectric power
- G Gold
- S Silver
- ◆ Other minerals
- 🐟 Seafood

SCALE
0   250   500 Miles
0   250   500 Kilometers
Projection: Lambert Conformal Conic

Map labels: RUSSIA, BLACK SEA, CASPIAN SEA, ARAL SEA, MEDITERRANEAN SEA, AEGEAN SEA, RED SEA, ARABIAN SEA, PERSIAN GULF, GULF OF OMAN, GULF OF ADEN, AFRICA, Istanbul, Ankara, Izmir, Almaty, Tashkent, Tehran, Kabul, Isfahan, Abadan, Bandar-e Abbas, Baghdad, Damascus, Haifa, Tel Aviv, Jubail, Yanbu, Jidda, Abu Dhabi, Aden, Suez Canal, Tropic of Cancer

1. (*Interaction*) Where are the region's gold mines located?

2. (*Interaction*) What two energy resources are often found together in the region?

3. (*Movement*) By what route would an oil tanker travel from Abadan to Mediterranean ports?

Critical Thinking

4. (*Place*) Why might fresh vegetables be costly in Kuwait?

5. (*Interaction*) Compare this map to the physical map. Which waterway might be used to transport minerals to Tashkent?

Southwest and Central Asia

AFGHANISTAN
CAPITAL:
Kabul

AREA:
250,000 sq. mi.
(647,500 sq km)

POPULATION:
28,717,213

MONEY:
afghani

LANGUAGES:
Pashtu,
Afghan Persian (Dari), Turkic
languages

UNEMPLOYMENT:
data not available

IRAQ
CAPITAL:
Baghdad

AREA:
168,753 sq. mi.
(437,072 sq km)

POPULATION: 24,683,313

MONEY:
Iraqi dinar

LANGUAGES:
Arabic, Kurdish

UNEMPLOYMENT:
70 percent

BAHRAIN
CAPITAL:
Manama

AREA:
239 sq. mi.
(620 sq km)

POPULATION:
667,238

MONEY:
Bahraini dollar

LANGUAGES:
Arabic, English, Farsi, Urdu

UNEMPLOYMENT:
15 percent

ISRAEL
CAPITAL:
Jerusalem

AREA:
8,019 sq. mi.
(20,770 sq km)

POPULATION:
6,116,533

MONEY:
Israeli shekel

LANGUAGES:
Hebrew (official), Arabic,
English

UNEMPLOYMENT:
10.4 percent

CYPRUS
CAPITAL:
Nicosia

AREA:
3,571 sq. mi. (9,250 sq km)

POPULATION:
771,657

MONEY:
Greek area: Cypriot pound;
Turkish area: Turkish lira

LANGUAGES:
Greek, Turkish, English

UNEMPLOYMENT:
Greek area: 3.3 percent;
Turkish area: 5.6 percent

Western Wall and Dome of the Rock, Jerusalem, Israel

IRAN
CAPITAL:
Tehran

AREA:
636,293 sq. mi.
(1,648,000 sq km)

POPULATION:
68,278,826

MONEY:
Iranian rial

LANGUAGES:
Persian, Turkic,
Kurdish

UNEMPLOYMENT:
16.3 percent

Jordanian boys with camel

KYRGYZSTAN

CAPITAL:
Bishkek

AREA:
76,641 sq. mi.
(198,500 sq km)

POPULATION:
4,892,808

MONEY:
Kyrgyzstani som

LANGUAGES:
Kirghiz, Russian

UNEMPLOYMENT:
7.2 percent

KUWAIT

CAPITAL:
Kuwait City

AREA:
6,880 sq. mi.
(17,820 sq km)

POPULATION:
2,183,161

MONEY:
Kuwaiti dinar

LANGUAGES:
Arabic, English

UNEMPLOYMENT:
7 percent

JORDAN

CAPITAL:
Amman

AREA:
35,637 sq. mi.
(92,300 sq km)

POPULATION:
5,460,265

MONEY:
Jordanian dinar

LANGUAGES:
Arabic, English

UNEMPLOYMENT:
30 percent

LEBANON

CAPITAL:
Beirut

AREA:
4,015 sq. mi.
(10,400 sq km)

POPULATION: 3,727,703

MONEY:
Lebanese pound

LANGUAGES:
Arabic (official), French

UNEMPLOYMENT:
18 percent

KAZAKHSTAN

CAPITAL:
Astana

AREA:
1,049,150 sq. mi.
(2,717,300 sq km)

POPULATION:
16,763,795

MONEY:
tenge

LANGUAGES:
Kazakh, Russian

UNEMPLOYMENT:
8.8 percent

*A warrior's armor
from Kazakhstan.*

Sources: Central Intelligence Agency, *The World Factbook 2003*, CPA and Labor Secretary, Iraqi Interim Government; population figures are 2003 estimates.

OMAN

CAPITAL:
Muscat

AREA:
82,031 sq. mi.
(212,460 sq km)

POPULATION: 2,807,125

MONEY:
Omani rial

LANGUAGES:
Arabic (official), English

UNEMPLOYMENT:
data not available

SYRIA

CAPITAL:
Damascus

AREA:
71,498 sq. mi.
(185,180 sq km)

POPULATION: 17,585,540

MONEY:
Syrian pound

LANGUAGES:
Arabic (official), Kurdish

UNEMPLOYMENT:
20 percent

QATAR

CAPITAL:
Doha

AREA:
4,416 sq. mi.
(11,437 sq km)

POPULATION:
817,052

MONEY:
Qatari rial

LANGUAGES:
Arabic (official),
English

UNEMPLOYMENT:
2.7 percent

TAJIKISTAN

CAPITAL:
Dushanbe

AREA:
55,251 sq. mi.
(143,100 sq km)

POPULATION:
6,863,752

MONEY:
somoni

LANGUAGES:
Tajik (official), Russian

UNEMPLOYMENT:
40 percent (and many underemployed)

SAUDI ARABIA

CAPITAL:
Riyadh

AREA:
756,981 sq. mi.
(1,960,582 sq km)

POPULATION:
24,293,844

MONEY:
Saudi riyal

LANGUAGES:
Arabic

UNEMPLOYMENT:
25 percent

Children learning Islam in Tajikistan

Mosque in Uzbekistan

UNITED ARAB EMIRATES

CAPITAL: Abu Dhabi

AREA:
32,000 sq. mi.
(82,880 sq km)

POPULATION: 2,484,818

MONEY:
Emirati dirham

LANGUAGES:
Arabic (official), Persian

UNEMPLOYMENT:
data not available

UZBEKISTAN

CAPITAL:
Tashkent

AREA:
172,741 sq. mi.
(447,400 sq km)

POPULATION:
25,981,647

MONEY:
Uzbekistani sum

LANGUAGES:
Uzbek, Russian, Tajik

UNEMPLOYMENT:
10 percent (and many underemployed)

TURKEY

CAPITAL: Ankara

AREA:
301,382 sq. mi.
(780,580 sq km)

POPULATION:
68,109,469

MONEY:
Turkish lira

LANGUAGES:
Turkish (official), Kurdish

UNEMPLOYMENT:
10.8 percent (6.1 percent underemployed)

YEMEN

CAPITAL:
Sanaa

AREA:
203,849 sq. mi.
(527,970 sq km)

POPULATION:
19,349,881

MONEY:
Yemeni rial

LANGUAGES:
Arabic

UNEMPLOYMENT:
30 percent

TURKMENISTAN

CAPITAL:
Ashgabat

AREA:
188,455 sq. mi.
(488,100 sq km)

POPULATION: 4,775,544

MONEY:
Turkmen manat

LANGUAGES:
Turkmen, Uzbek, Russian

UNEMPLOYMENT:
data not available

internet connect
COUNTRY STATISTICS
GO TO: go.hrw.com
KEYWORD: SK5 FactsU2
FOR: more facts about
Southwest and Central Asia

Sources: Central Intelligence Agency, *The World Factbook 2003*, CPA and Labor Secretary, Iraqi Interim Government; population figures are 2003 estimates.

The History of Southwest and Central Asia

We start our study of Southwest and Central Asia by going back to the beginnings of civilization, in a land called Sumer.

Statue of mythical Sumerian king Gilgamesh

The cities of Sumer were built about 5,000 years ago in what is now Iraq. Some Sumerian boys from rich families went to school. Their subjects included mathematics and writing. The teachers, known as "big brothers," sometimes punished the students harshly.

A story survives from Sumer about one student who was afraid to explain to his teacher why he was late for class. Too scared to speak, he entered the room and bowed deeply to the teacher. History doesn't tell us if the boy had to serve detention!

Cuneiform tablet

Sumerian mosaic, c. 2500 B.C.

Read to Discover

1. What discoveries have scientists made about prehistoric times?
2. What are the characteristics of civilization?
3. Where did the first civilizations develop?

Vocabulary

hominids
prehistory
nomads
land bridges

irrigation
division of labor
history

Reading Strategy

VISUALIZING INFORMATION Look at the photographs in this section. What information do they show about past civilizations? Write your answers on a sheet of paper. As you read, write what you learn about these civilizations.

Looking into the Past

Peoples of Southwest and Central Asia created some of the greatest civilizations the world has ever seen. However, for our study of the region's history, we need to start by looking further back into the past. In fact, we must start with the dawn of humanity. The story begins in Africa.

In the late 1970s in Tanzania, a country in East Africa, scientist Mary Leakey discovered fossilized footprints millions of years old. She concluded the footprints were those of **hominids**, early humanlike creatures. This find was one of many discoveries in the same region. Ancient skulls and skeletons, along with objects found near them, provide clues about hominid life. For example, scientists can tell that hominids walked upright and used primitive tools made of stone.

Archaeologists dig carefully through layers of soil and rubble to find clues about how people lived long ago.

Interpreting the Visual Record What kinds of objects may these archaeologists be hoping to find?

These stone ax heads date from the Stone Age. They were found in Italy. The ivory tool in the shape of a dagger was found in China.

The period during which hominids and early humans lived is called **prehistory**. This means that no written records exist for those times. The period of prehistory in which stone tools were used is called the Stone Age. It began about 2.5 million years ago and lasted until about 3500 B.C.

The First Humans Early humans that looked like modern people may have first appeared during the Stone Age between 200,000 and 100,000 years ago. These first humans, called *Homo sapiens*, lived in Africa. They were **nomads** who moved from place to place in search of food. They gathered seeds, fruits, and nuts from wild plants. In time they also began to hunt small animals. Dangerous times lay ahead, though.

Migration Within the last 1.8 million years, Earth has gone through several periods of very cold weather. Together these periods are known as the Ice Age. During each period, large parts of Earth's surface were covered with ice. Sea levels dropped, leaving strips of dry land called **land bridges** between continents. Humans walked over these land bridges to new regions. They may have been following the animals they hunted. Slowly, humans spread out to all parts of the world.

An important discovery helped people survive during the Ice Age. They learned how to control fire and use it for warmth and cooking.

Later Developments In time humans began to make more advanced tools, including spears. As a result, they could hunt larger animals. They made clothes from animal skins. Perhaps as early as 40,000 years ago, people began to create art. Carved ivory figures show that some groups had time for activities besides hunting, gathering, and tool making. Beautiful paintings on the walls of caves in France and Spain show animals such as lions, bulls, and horses in great detail.

Later, between 10,000 and 5,500 years ago, people learned to make sharper tools by grinding and polishing stone. People developed better hunting methods. They made bows and arrows, which meant that hunters could attack prey from a safer distance. The hunters shaped

Shown in beautiful detail, this cave painting in Lascaux, France, is an example of Stone Age art. People may have drawn on cave walls to express ideas.

Interpreting the Visual Record What kinds of animals did the Lascaux artists paint on this wall?

Emergence of Agriculture

fishhooks and harpoons from bones and antlers. People hollowed out logs to make canoes for fishing in deep water and crossing rivers. Also at about this time, people tamed dogs. Dogs helped locate prey and warned of wild animals or strangers approaching.

In the late Stone Age, people began to practice agriculture. We don't know exactly how people made the change from gathering plants to growing them. We do know that life changed drastically when they did. Instead of moving from place to place to hunt animals and gather wild plants, people began to stay in one place. They became farmers. People also domesticated animals such as cattle and sheep. That means people tamed animals that had been living wild.

The Importance of Agriculture Agriculture changed how people interacted with their surroundings. To grow food, people learned to control and change their environment. They created fields by clearing forested areas. People became farmers by gathering the seeds or pieces of wild plants and planting them in fields. They invented **irrigation** systems, digging ditches and canals to move water from rivers to fields where crops could be grown.

Agriculture also changed the ways people interacted with each other. Because people who farmed stayed in one area, they began to live in larger groups. In addition, some animals, such as pigs, couldn't be herded from place to place. By about 9000 B.C., people began to live in permanent villages. Because farming made food more plentiful, populations increased. Small villages eventually grew into cities.

The spread of agriculture meant that people no longer had to travel in search of food. As a result, civilization began to develop.

Interpreting the Map What crops were grown in Southwest and Central Asia?

The people of ancient Jericho may have worshipped their ancestors by preserving their skulls in plaster and decorating them like these.

In towns and cities, people shared new ideas and methods of doing things. Historians think that the first cities were built some 10,000 years ago. Jericho, the world's oldest known city, developed around 8000 B.C. on the Jordan River in Southwest Asia. About 3,000 people lived in Jericho at this time. The people of Jericho grew wheat and barley and built a massive stone wall around their city.

Because of the ways it changed people's lives, agriculture and the domestication of animals were enormously important. In fact, learning how to grow food prepared the way for a new chapter in the story of human life—the story of civilization.

✔ **READING CHECK:** (*Summarizing*) How did agriculture change how people lived?

The Beginnings of Civilization

Historians describe civilizations as having four basic features. First, a civilization is made up of people living in an organized society, not simply as a loosely connected group. Second, people are able to produce more food than they need to survive. Third, they live in towns or cities with some form of government. And fourth, there is a **division of labor**. This means that people perform specific, different jobs.

Agriculture and Civilization How did the development of agriculture affect the growth of civilization? Before agriculture, people spent almost all of their time finding food. When a group of people could produce more than it needed to survive, some people didn't have to grow food at all. They could develop other skills, such as making pottery or cloth. Then they could trade these goods or even services for food or other needs.

Trade and Cities Once people began to trade, they had to deal with each other in more complex ways. Disagreements arose, creating a need for laws. Governments developed to fill that need. Government officials made laws and made sure they were obeyed. In addition, religious leaders taught people what they should and shouldn't do. During this time in human history, religion and government were closely connected. In fact, leaders often had both political and religious power.

When people traded, they went where they could exchange goods with other people. Many of these places were along rivers or seacoasts because people often traveled by water. Some of these places grew into cities where people exchanged ideas along with products. Over time, city dwellers built palaces, temples, and other public buildings.

The Development of Writing Trade in ancient times, like business today, required record-keeping. Written languages may have developed from this need. The invention of writing dates back to about 3000 B.C. in Southwest Asia. Farmers also needed to keep track of seasonal cycles. They had to know when it was time to plant new crops and when they could expect rain. Over time, they developed calendars.

Once they had writing and calendars, people began to keep written records of events. **History**, which is the written record of human civilization, had begun.

✓ **READING CHECK:** (*Identifying Cause and Effect*) How did trade lead to the development of writing?

Human civilization began in four different river valleys. Each of these regions provided rich soil and access to water for crops.

▼

River Valley Civilizations

The people of the Indus Valley traded with other civilizations including Mesopotamia. These weights were used to weigh goods for sale such as wheat, rice, and cotton. **Interpreting the Visual Record How do you think a merchant used these weights?**

River Valley Civilizations

Now let's return to the history of Southwest and Central Asia. The earliest civilization in these areas arose along the Tigris and Euphrates (yooh-FRAY-teez) Rivers in Southwest Asia. Called Mesopotamia, which means "between the rivers," this area was in present-day Iraq. Civilizations also developed in three other places. All four were river valleys. In the Nile River valley, Egyptian civilization developed. The first civilization of India was centered on the Indus River. Early Chinese civilization began in the valley of the Huang, or Yellow, River. (See the map on the previous page.)

These four river valleys had fertile soil for farming and water for irrigation. Because the people there had to work together to build irrigation and flood control systems, government developed further. The valley dwellers also learned how to make metal tools and weapons. First they used bronze, then iron. Eventually, the valley peoples developed advanced civilizations. In addition, all of them wrote down information about themselves. Thus, these civilizations mark the beginning of human history.

✓ **READING CHECK:** (*Drawing Inferences*) How did physical geography influence the beginnings of civilization?

Homework Practice Online
Keyword: SK5 HP4

Section Review 1

Define and explain: hominids, prehistory, nomads, land bridges, irrigation, division of labor, history

Reading for the Main Idea

1. (*Human Systems*) What are some important discoveries that scientists have made about life in prehistoric times?

2. (*Human Systems*) How did the division of labor lead to the development of trade?

3. (*Environment and Society*) Why did early civilizations develop around river valleys?

Critical Thinking

4. **Identifying Cause and Effect** How did the needs of early civilizations lead to the development of government?

Organizing What You Know

5. **Summarizing** Copy the following graphic organizer. Use it to describe the traits of civilizations.

What Is Civilization?

Section 2 — Mesopotamia and the Fertile Crescent

Read to Discover

1. What skills did the Sumerians develop?
2. What were some features of other civilizations of Mesopotamia and the Fertile Crescent?
3. What was Persian rule like?

Vocabulary

Fertile Crescent
ziggurats
pictographs
cuneiform
Hanging Gardens
provinces

People

Sumerians
Babylonians
Hammurabi
Hittites
Persians
Darius I

Places

Babylon

Reading Strategy

READING ORGANIZER   Before you read, draw a circle in the center of a sheet of paper. Label the circle Fertile Crescent Groups. Draw six rays out from the circle and draw circles at the end of each ray. Label the outer circles Sumerians, Babylonians, Hittites, Assyrians, Chaldeans, and Persians. As you read, write what you learn about each group of people next to each circle.

The Fertile Crescent, c. 3000 B.C.

▲
The world's earliest civilizations began in the Fertile Crescent. The waters of the Tigris, Euphrates, and Jordan Rivers allowed these civilizations to thrive.

The Fertile Crescent

A strip of fertile land begins along the Jordan River and curves through Southwest Asia to the Persian Gulf. The Tigris and the Euphrates (yooh-FRAY-teez) Rivers flow through Mesopotamia, the eastern part of the region. Because the land is good for farming, the area is called the **Fertile Crescent**.

The Tigris-Euphrates valley lies on a wide, flat plain. As a result, the rivers often flooded in the past.

The Land   By 8000 B.C., farmers had begun to grow crops in the region. In time they learned to control river flooding and to irrigate their fields. Early residents worked together to build canals and dikes. They used these skills to irrigate their fields and return floodwaters to the rivers. A new civilization developed as a result of their cooperation.

Although the area's wide plain had good farmland, the flat topography allowed a problem to develop. No mountains or other natural barriers protected the area's borders from invasion. As a result, conquerors would often sweep in and take over the region.

The Sumerians Historians say that the Sumerians developed the first civilization in the Fertile Crescent. They lived in an area called Sumer, in the southern part of Mesopotamia. Most Sumerians were farmers. When they could grow extra food, some people could become artisans and traders.

The Sumerians developed many technical skills. They were probably the first people to use wheeled vehicles. They also used a machine called a potter's wheel, which allowed workers to make high-quality bowls and jars. Sumerian builders were very advanced. To worship their gods, they built great temples, known as **ziggurats**. The ziggurats were shaped like pyramids and set upon heavy bases. Because the surrounding land was flat, people could see the temples from miles around. The ziggurats were both religious and governmental centers.

The Sumerians' greatest achievement was the world's first writing system. At first, people sent messages using small pictures, called pictographs, drawn on clay tablets. However, drawing these **pictographs** took too much time. So, the Sumerians simplified the pictures, until the marks no longer looked like the objects they represented. Over time, some of these simplified pictures stood for sounds, not objects. In this way, the first letters were created. To form the letters, a Sumerian writer would press the end of a triangular stick into soft clay. The stick formed wedge-shaped marks on the clay. This form of writing became known as **cuneiform** (kyoo-NEE-uh-fawrm).

✔ **READING CHECK:** (*Finding the Main Idea*) What was the Sumerians' greatest achievement?

This ziggurat was built in about 2100 B.C. in what is now Iraq. When the ziggurat was first constructed, additional layers would have risen above those that remain. The Sumerians may have built ziggurats as bridges between heaven and Earth.

Interpreting the Visual Record How do you think visitors reacted when they first saw a ziggurat?

▼

A Flood of Invaders

Eventually, the Sumerians were conquered. Hundreds of years later the Babylonians (bab-l-LOHN-ee-uhnz) took over the same area. The culture is named for its beautiful city, Babylon, on the southern Euphrates River.

The Babylonians In some ways, the Babylonian and Sumerian civilizations were similar. The people were farmers, artisans, and traders. The Babylonians were even better merchants than the Sumerians. Babylonian traders went beyond the Fertile Crescent—all the way to Egypt and India.

The greatest Babylonian king was Hammurabi (ham-uh-RAHB-ee). In the 1790s B.C., he conquered most of the Tigris-Euphrates valley. Hammurabi was not only a powerful military leader but also an outstanding lawmaker. He put together a set of laws governing many aspects of daily life. The collection is known as the Code of Hammurabi. The code included the idea of "an eye for an eye." For example, if a poorly built house fell on and killed the owner, the builder was killed as a punishment. Penalties weren't equal, however. So, a slave may have suffered a worse punishment than a rich man for the same crime. Still, the code was an improvement on ancient customs. No longer could people take the law into their own hands.

The Hittites Babylon fell to invaders around 1600 B.C. The first of these conquerors were the Hittites (HIT-yts). They came from what is now southeastern Turkey.

The Hittites had two major skills that helped them conquer their enemies. They built chariots and used them well in battle. In addition, they were among the first people to make iron weapons. They learned to use heat to separate the metal from iron ore. Iron tools, such as a better plow, helped the Hittites in peacetime also.

BIOGRAPHY

Hammurabi
(died c. 1750 B.C.)

As king of Babylon in the 1700s B.C., Hammurabi collected 282 laws, known as the Code of Hammurabi. The code was one of the world's first sets of written laws. Hammurabi's laws dealt with family matters, trade, agriculture, and criminal acts.

The code ends with a blessing for people who obey the laws and curses for those who do not. Inscribed on a large plaque, the code survives today. It is in the Louvre Museum in Paris. *What activities did the Code of Hammurabi address?*

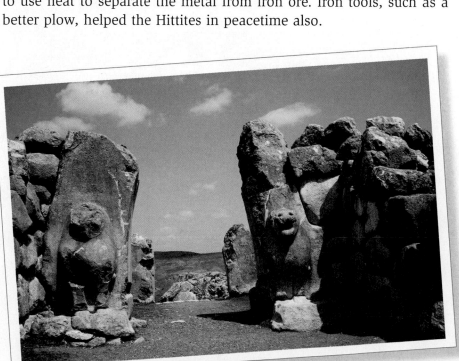

The ruins of an ancient Hittite city in present-day Turkey reflect the impressive building skills of the Hittites. This entrance is known as the Lion Gate for its sculptures of lions that guarded the city.

The Assyrians Next on the scene were the Assyrians, who swooped down from northern Mesopotamia. Their army was fearsome. It was organized into regular units, led by professional officers, and equipped with iron weapons. The Assyrian army was able to conquer an empire that stretched all the way to Egypt.

Assyrians ruled by terror. They used cruel punishments on those who dared to get in their way. Sometimes when they had conquered a people, they carried all of them off to a different land. These methods made many enemies, of course. In the 600s B.C. the Assyrians lost their empire.

The Chaldeans As the Assyrian Empire crumbled, the Chaldeans took over their lands. Under their king Nebuchadnezzar (neb-uh-kuhd-NEZ-uhr), Babylon again became a great city. Its most famous feature were its **Hanging Gardens**. These were actually lush gardens built on rooftops. Water pumped from the Euphrates River kept the gardens green. According to legend, the king ordered the gardens be planted for his wife. She missed the green hills of her homeland.

The Chaldeans were expert astronomers, making careful records of the movement of stars and planets. They also excelled at mathematics. The Chaldeans developed the idea of square roots along with many other basic mathematical concepts.

✓ **READING CHECK:** (*Summarizing*) What were the names of four other major Mesopotamian civilizations?

The Hanging Gardens of Babylon were included in the Seven Wonders of the World, but no traces of the gardens remain today. However, written accounts of the gardens describe the terraces irrigated by the Euphrates River. This painting shows one artist's idea about how the gardens may have looked.

The Persians

Another civilization, however, would outshine those that had come before it. A people called the Persians spread out from Iran. In 539 B.C. they conquered Babylon. Little by little, Persian rulers took over all the lands between India and southeastern Europe. Their empire became the largest the world had ever seen. King Darius I was one of its most powerful rulers.

Persian Rule The Persian Empire was divided into large areas called **provinces**. Darius named a governor to rule each one. Darius also used spies called "the king's eyes and ears" to report on the governors. He wanted to make sure they stayed loyal to him. The provinces had to pay heavy taxes to Darius and supply soldiers for his army.

A huge system of well-built roads made this system work. Spies, along with messengers, soldiers, and traders, could move around the empire easily. By changing horses at stations along the way, fast riders could cover about 1,700 miles in nine days.

Persian Law Because it was so large, many different peoples with different customs lived within the empire. In general, the Persians allowed people to keep their own religions, languages, and even local laws. For example, women of old Babylon had more rights than women in Iran. A system of Persian laws, however, applied to everybody. Government officials made sure the judges were fair and didn't take bribes. In fact, justice and fairness were very important to Persian society.

✓ **READING CHECK:** (*Analyzing Information*) Why was Persian rule successful?

A highly skilled army helped expand and maintain the Persian Empire. Archers like this one belonged to an elite unit called the "10,000 immortals."

Section Review 2

Define or identify: Fertile Crescent, Sumerians, ziggurats, pictographs, cuneiform, Babylonians, Hammurabi, Hittites, Hanging Gardens, Persians, Darius I, provinces

Reading for the Main Idea

1. (*Finding the Main Idea*) What were the Sumerians' main achievements?

2. (*Summarizing*) What are some lasting contributions made by the peoples of Southwest Asia?

go.hrw.com Homework Practice Online
Keyword: SK5 HP4

Critical Thinking

3. **Making Generalizations** How did Mesopotamia's physical geography affect its history?

4. **Comparing and Contrasting** How did Assyrian rule compare to Persian rule?

Organizing What You Know

5. **Time Line** Copy the following time line onto a large piece of paper. Fill in as many events as you can.

3000 B.C.   2000 B.C.   1000 B.C.   A.D. 1

2500 B.C.   1500 B.C.   500 B.C.

Section 3 Land of Three Faiths

Read to Discover

1. How did Judaism develop in Southwest Asia?
2. How did the life of Jesus lead to the development of Christianity?
3. Who was Muhammad, and what did he teach?

Vocabulary

Judaism
Exodus
Ten Commandments
monotheism
Torah
Gospels
disciples
Resurrection
Christianity
New Testament
Qur'an
Five Pillars of Islam

Places

Palestine
Jerusalem
Mecca

People

Hebrews
Abraham
Moses
Jesus
Saul of Tarsus
Muhammad
Muslims

Reading Strategy

FOLDNOTES: TRI-FOLD Create a **Tri-Fold** FoldNote described in the Appendix. Label one column Judaism, another Christianity, and the third Islam. As you read this section, write what you learn about each religion on the FoldNote.

Floor tiles from an ancient synagogue in Israel form an image of a Jewish menorah. This seven-branched candleholder is a symbol of Judaism and used during the celebration of Hanukkah.

Judaism

You have read how many civilizations developed in the Fertile Crescent and nearby lands in Southwest Asia. The region was also the birthplace of three religions—Judaism, Christianity, and Islam. All three grew into worldwide religions with many millions of followers.

Out of Sumer The oldest of the three faiths is **Judaism**. It developed among a people called the Hebrews, who lived in the grasslands of the Fertile Crescent. Much of what we know about the Hebrews comes from their own writings. These writings later were the basis for the Bible. According to these accounts, the founder of the Hebrews was a shepherd from Sumer named Abraham.

Perhaps in about 2000 B.C., Abraham led his family to the area called Palestine. The Bible tells that God commanded Abraham to move there. If Abraham obeyed this command, God promised him a new nation. This agreement would give birth to the nation of Israel. Abraham's descendants lived in Israel for many years. Eventually, the Hebrews went to Egypt. The Egyptians made them slaves. According to tradition, a leader named Moses led them out of Egypt. They went northeast in search of the "promised land." Today, Jews still celebrate the **Exodus**, the escape from slavery in Egypt.

Moses Character Trait: Responsibility

According to the Bible, Moses accepted the responsibility for getting the Hebrews released from slavery and bringing them to a faraway promised land. The task required that he lead them across the Red Sea and through a desert. Although the Hebrews found their promised land, Moses died before he could reach it.

Moses is an important figure in three of the world's great religions. The words of Moses lived on and helped shape the Jewish faith. He is also revered by Christians and Muslims. *How may a sense of responsibility have aided Moses throughout the journey?*

Judaism's Beginnings The Bible tells that during the journey, Moses brought the **Ten Commandments** to his people. These were laws given to him by the Hebrew god Yahweh (YAH-way). They stressed the importance of worshipping God. The commandments also taught people to honor their parents and how to live together in peace. For example, they shouldn't lie, steal, or kill. When the Hebrews agreed to follow the Ten Commandments, they accepted God's rule. The agreement to live by God's laws in return for his protection was called a covenant.

Over time, the Hebrews' basic ideas about God changed. At first, they thought of Yahweh as one god among other gods. Later they saw him as the only God. We call this idea **monotheism**. With the change to monotheism, the religion we know today as Judaism truly began.

The Torah and Mosaic Law The teachings of Moses were written down in five books, known as the **Torah**. The Hebrew word Torah means "to show the way," or "to teach." The law of Moses, or Mosaic law, included the Ten Commandments along with laws written later. Jewish synagogues keep a copy of the Torah on handwritten scrolls of parchment.

Mosaic law valued human life more than did older laws. Mosaic law also guided Hebrews' daily lives. The laws said that the Hebrews must not work on the Sabbath, the seventh day of each week. The Sabbath was considered a day of worship and rest. The laws set down other rules, such as which foods Jews could eat. Jews believe that keeping these laws is part of the covenant that the Hebrews made with God centuries ago. Belief in God and their covenant has helped the Jews endure through many hardships.

✓ **READING CHECK:** (*Analyzing Information*) How did Judaism change over time?

By the late 900s B.C., Israel was split in two. The northern kingdom remained Israel, with Samaria as its capital. The southern kingdom became Judah, with Jerusalem as its capital.

▼

The Founding of Israel, c. 900s B.C.

Christianity

To study the next religion, we look again to Judaism and a time about 2,000 years ago. Not all Jews held exactly the same beliefs. Some Jews wanted to rebel against the Romans, who had conquered their ancient land. Others believed a Messiah, or spiritual leader, would save them from all enemies. Long before, Jewish holy men called prophets had said that the Messiah would come some day.

Birth and Life of Jesus of Nazareth As you can see, these were troubled times. Into this setting a boy was born in Bethlehem to a poor young woman and her carpenter husband. The boy Jesus grew up in Nazareth as a faithful Jew.

Most of what we know about Jesus comes from the first four books of the New Testament in the Christian Bible. These books, known as the **Gospels**, tell that Jesus studied the writings of Jewish prophets. Eventually, Jesus began to preach. A small group of followers called **disciples** helped spread his message. Jesus told the people who gathered around him that God would judge humanity. Those who asked forgiveness for their sins and believed in God would live with God forever. In addition, Jesus had two basic teachings for his followers. They should love God above all else and love others as much as they loved themselves. He said that people should be humble and kind. His message of love and forgiveness drew large crowds.

Death and Resurrection The authorities didn't like the fact that Jesus was so popular. Some leaders thought that Jesus was putting himself above religious and civil law. Finally, the authorities in Jerusalem decided that Jesus was a serious problem and had to be executed.

According to the Gospels, the Romans crucified Jesus. That is, he was nailed to a wooden cross and left there to die. The Gospels report that after Jesus died on the cross he was buried, but rose from the dead three days later. This event was the **Resurrection**. After living

This mosaic above the entrance to an Italian mausoleum is an example of early Christian art. Jesus shown as a shepherd taking care of sheep is a common Christian symbol.

Interpreting the Visual Record What other symbols do you see in the picture?

The Spread of Christianity

From its beginnings in Judea, in some 300 years Christianity spread across the Roman Empire and beyond. Some of the Roman emperors persecuted Christians. Constantine was the first emperor to embrace the faith—in the early A.D. 300s.

Interpreting the Map What are some of the cities where Christianity was well established by the end of the A.D. 300s?

among his disciples for 40 days, Jesus rose into heaven. The disciples believed that these events showed that Jesus was indeed the Messiah. They called him Jesus Christ. Christos was the Greek word for Messiah. From this word we get the name for the new faith, **Christianity**.

A New Faith The early Christians taught that because Jesus died for them and conquered death, all people could be saved. That is, everyone's sins could be forgiven, and they could live again after death.

At first, the disciples preached only to other Jews. One Jew, Saul of Tarsus, preached the Christian message to non-Jews too. Saul, also called Paul, said that people didn't have to be Jews in order to be Christians. Paul traveled throughout the eastern Mediterranean area preaching. His encouraging letters to Christian communities make up a large portion of the **New Testament**. This part of the Bible tells the stories of Jesus, his followers, and later Christian ideas. Christians around the world base their faith on the message of the New Testament.

✓ **READING CHECK:** *Finding the Main Idea* On what event did early Christians base their preaching?

Islam

Both Judaism and Christianity teach that there is only one God. **Islam**, the third of the great religions that developed in Southwest Asia, is also monotheistic. It began farther to the southeast, in what is now Saudi Arabia.

A Voice in the Desert In the A.D. 600s, Arabia didn't have a central government. Instead, Arab clans often fought for wealth and power. Most Arabs worshipped many gods and goddesses. One of the places where they worshipped their gods was in the town of Mecca.

A young businessman named Muhammad often left Mecca's crowded streets to pray in a desert cave. One day, according to Islamic belief, Muhammad heard a voice cut through the cave's silence. The voice was that of an angel. It ordered Muhammad to tell about the glories of Allah—"God" in Arabic. Over the next 22 years, Muhammad received hundreds of messages. Muhammad and his early followers memorized or wrote down all of Allah's messages. After Muhammad's death, his followers put together all of these messages in one book called the **Qur'an**. This holy book of Islam is written in Arabic and contains 114 chapters.

Muhammad's Message Muhammad began with only two basic ideas. First, there was only one God. Second, everyone who believed in God had to follow his laws. Believers then formed a special community. Members of this community were supposed to help each other.

These ideas weren't popular. Merchants made money off of the people who came to Mecca to worship the old gods. They didn't want Arabs to believe in only one god. Clan leaders didn't like the idea of one big community. They feared they would lose power. Mecca's rulers started to threaten Muhammad. Finally, in 622, Muhammad and his followers fled about 200 miles to the town of Medina. This event is called the *hijrah* (hi-JY-ruh), or "flight." It came to mark the beginning of the Islamic calendar. After many years of fighting, Mecca finally welcomed Muhammad back to the city.

In this photo, Iraqi Muslims kneel to pray. Devout Muslims pray five times a day while facing Mecca, the holy city of Islam. At the proper times, a person called a muezzin calls the faithful to prayer from a high tower called a minaret.

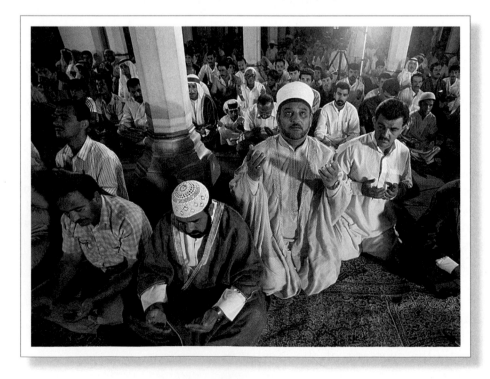

The Five Pillars At Muhammad's death, the basis for a new religion had been laid. Followers of Islam, called Muslims, were to follow five rules. They are called the **Five Pillars of Islam**. The Five Pillars order Muslims to: (1) Say that there is only one God, and that Muhammad is God's prophet; (2) Pray five times a day toward Mecca; (3) Help the poor; (4) Fast during the holy month of Ramadan; and (5) Go on a pilgrimage to Mecca.

Other rules apply also. Muslims are not supposed to drink alcohol or eat pork. Although Muslim men may have four wives, they must treat each wife with respect. Many other rules appear in the Qur'an. They include rules about inheriting property and the treatment of slaves.

Muslims believe that people who obey God's rules go to a paradise when they die. The Qur'an describes it as a beautiful garden full of wonderful things, like fine food. Those who did not obey God would burn in fire forever.

We have seen that three religions began in Southwest Asia. Of these, Islam became the most widespread in the region. In fact, within a hundred years of Muhammad's death, Islam stretched from the Atlantic Ocean to India. You will learn how that happened in the next section.

✓ **READING CHECK:** *Identifying Cause and Effect*
Why did Mecca's rulers reject Muhammad's message at first?

In the courtyard of the Great Mosque in Mecca stands a shrine called the Kaaba. Each year, millions of Muslims travel to Mecca during the hajj, or pilgrimage, and circle the Kaaba seven times. Muslims consider the site the most sacred place on Earth.

Section Review 3

Define or identify: Judaism, Hebrews, Abraham, Moses, Exodus, Ten Commandments, monotheism, Torah, Jesus, Gospels, disciples, Resurrection, Christianity, Saul of Tarsus, New Testament, Islam, Muhammad, Qur'an, Muslims, Five Pillars of Islam

Reading for the Main Idea

1. (*Places and Regions*) What role does Mosaic law play in Judaism?

2. (*Places and Regions*) How did Saul of Tarsus affect early Christianity?

Critical Thinking

3. **Drawing Inferences and Conclusions** Which of the Five Pillars of Islam is related to how Muslims should treat other people?

4. **Drawing Inferences and Conclusions** What are features that Judaism, Christianity, and Islam have in common?

Organizing What You Know

5. **Summarizing** Copy the graphic organizer below. Use it to describe the main beliefs of Judaism, Christianity, and Islam.

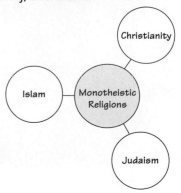

Christianity

Islam — Monotheistic Religions

Judaism

Empires in Southwest and Central Asia

Read to Discover

1. How did Islam spread to become a large empire?
2. What other rulers took over Southwest and Central Asia?

Vocabulary

caliph
mosques
shah

People

Abbasids
Caliph Harun ar-Rashid
Mongols
Genghis Khan
Ottoman Turks
Suleiman
Babur the Tiger

Places

Baghdad

Reading Strategy

TAKING NOTES Use the headings in this section to create an outline. As you read this section, write what you learn about Southwest and Central Asia under each heading.

The Muslim Empire

After the death of Muhammad, Abu Bakr became Islam's first caliph, or successor, in A.D. 632.

Muhammad's followers formed an army that fought for control of Arabia. By the time of his death in 632, they had taken over most of the peninsula. A new problem arose, however. Muhammad's followers couldn't agree on who should be the leader. They broke into two groups over who should be **caliph** (KAY-luhf), which means "deputy."

Muhammad had not named anyone to take over his leadership role. He did have a daughter, Fatima. Some of Muhammad's followers thought the caliph should be a descendant of Fatima and her husband Ali. Another group thought that any Muslim could become caliph. The first group eventually became known as the Shia. People in the second group were called the Sunni. This division still plays a big role in modern politics in Southwest Asia.

Spreading the Word Although the conflict was bitter and bloody, the division didn't slow the growth of Islam. One reason lay with a policy begun by 'Umar (oo-mahr), one of Muhammad's closest friends. People could get money if they or family members signed up to serve in the military. The armies grew huge and powerful as a result. Mighty Persia fell to them by 642. The armies pushed south and west. By 750, Muslim forces had conquered the Arabian Peninsula, North Africa, and Spain.

The Spread of Islam

Islamic lands at Muhammad's death, 632
Territory added, 633–661
Territory added, 662–750
✶ Battle site

Many of the conquered people chose to become Muslims. Others did not. The Qur'an had given special protection to Jews, Christians, and other people who had written religious texts. They were called People of the Book. These protected peoples had to pay higher taxes than Muslims. In general, though, the taxes weren't a heavy burden.

Abbasid Rule Meanwhile, conflict within the Muslim leadership continued. For a time, a clan that had fought against Muhammad in Mecca was in power. Later, a new group that claimed descent from Muhammad's uncle 'Abbas took over the leadership. They were called the Abbasids. Abbasid rule reached its height under Caliph Harun ar-Rashid (huh-ROON ahr-rah-SHEED). Under Harun's rule industries in metalwork, paper, and cloth developed. He supported musicians and poets. However, Harun had the power of life and death over his subjects and often used that power. Stories tell that Harun would leave his palace in disguise with his executioner at his side.

Baghdad, on the Tigris River, was Harun's capital. It became a center of learning, with a fine university. It was a beautiful busy city at the center of a vast trade network. Among the goods that flowed through Baghdad were carpets, silks, rubies, peacocks, horses, and medicines. By the middle of the 1000s, however, invasions by nomadic tribes and crop failures caused Baghdad to decline.

In the 100 years following Muhammad's death, Islam spread quickly. Muslim Arabs conquered many other peoples, uniting them within Islam.

Interpreting the Map How far west had Islam spread by A.D. 662?

The interior of the Great Mosque in Córdoba, Spain, shows the lasting beauty of Moorish architecture. A cathedral was built within the mosque after Christians took back the city.

Interpreting the Visual Record Why do you think arches are important in certain building designs?

Muslim Civilization The Muslim Empire grew rich from trade with other parts of the world. To help manage the huge empire's economy, banking developed. Banks had both central and branch offices. Bankers even worked with letters of credit, similar to today's checks.

The Muslim Empire had many accomplishments. Centers of learning like Córdoba and Toledo in Spain attracted scholars from around the world. Muslim doctors were highly skilled. They even performed eye surgery! Geographers drew remarkably accurate maps. Mathematicians introduced the number system we use today. Throughout the Islamic world, architects built beautiful houses of worship called **mosques**.

✓ **READING CHECK:** (*Finding the Main Idea*) How far did the Muslim Empire reach?

Later Empires

In the 1200s, a new threat faced Islam. From far to the east came the Mongols, a fierce non-Muslim tribe of nomads. The Mongols were skilled warriors who fought on horseback. Under Genghis Khan and his descendants, the Mongols conquered a huge empire. It reached from Korea in the east to what is now Hungary in Europe. The ancient lands of Mesopotamia and Persia fell into Mongol hands. In 1258 the Mongols killed the last Abbasid caliph and destroyed Baghdad. Later, the region's Mongol rulers converted to Islam. Fights between Mongols broke out, though. The Mongol Empire in Southwest and Central Asia fell apart.

This illustration from the 1200s shows a Mongol battle.

Interpreting the Visual Record What may this picture tell us about Mongol armor and weapons?

Over the centuries other peoples and rulers came to power in parts of Southwest and Central Asia. Although these rulers came from different ethnic groups, they were all Muslims.

The Ottomans During the 1300s, a group of Muslim warriors captured most of what is now Turkey. They were called the Ottoman Turks after their ancestor Osman. In 1453, the Ottomans took the Christian city of Constantinople and made it their capital. The Ottoman Empire continued to grow in the 1500s under the leadership of Suleiman (soo-lay-MAHN). Suleiman's people called him "the Lawgiver" because he improved the court system and issued new laws. He also built mosques, schools, hospitals, bridges, and other public works. Under Suleiman, the Ottomans ruled much of southeastern Europe, western Asia, and northern Africa. Although it slowly lost power, the empire lasted until 1922.

The Safavids Another Muslim empire, the Safavid Empire, included much of what is now Iran. It began about 1500 when a Shia Muslim ruler conquered Persia. He took the title **shah**, an ancient Persian word for "king." The Safavids built their wealth on trade. Their capital, Esfahan, was one of the world's most beautiful cities. The Safavid Empire collapsed by 1736.

The Mughals The Mughal Empire was founded in northern India in the 1500s. Its first leader was a Mongol leader called Babur the Tiger. One of the most famous Mughal rulers was Shah Jahan, who built the famous Taj Mahal in the mid-1600s. Soon after his reign, however, the Mughal Empire began to crumble. In the 1700s, Great Britain began taking over Mughal lands.

▲

The Safavids built this mosque in Persia in the 1600s. A mosque is a place for worship and a symbol of Islam.

Interpreting the Visual Record What material appears to decorate the dome of the mosque and the minarets alongside?

✔ **READING CHECK:** (**Summarizing**) What were the four empires that followed the Muslim Empire in Southwest and Central Asia?

Homework Practice Online

Keyword: SK5 HP4

Define or identify: caliph, Abbasids, Caliph Harun al-Rashid, mosques, Mongols, Genghis Khan, Ottoman Turks, Suleiman, shah, Babur the Tiger

Reading for the Main Idea

1. (*Places and Regions*) What caused the split between the Shia and the Sunni?

2. (*Places and Regions*) What areas did the Muslim Empire include?

Critical Thinking

3. **Summarizing** What were some accomplishments of the Muslim Empire?

4. **Analyzing Information** Why do you think the Muslims treated those they called People of the Book with some respect?

Organizing What You Know

5. **Categorizing** Copy the following graphic organizer. Use it to identify the people and features of these Southwest and Central Asian empires.

Empire	People	Features
Mongol		
Ottoman		
Safavid		
Mughal		

Review and Practice

Define and Identify

Identify each of the following:

1. hominid
2. land bridges
3. irrigation
4. Sumerians
5. Fertile Crescent
6. Persians
7. cuneiform
8. Judaism
9. Abraham
10. Christianity
11. Jesus
12. Muhammad
13. mosques
14. Genghis Khan
15. Ottoman Turks

Review the Main Ideas

16. What are the four characteristics of civilization?
17. How did the development of agriculture lead to the growth of villages and towns?
18. What were some of the Sumerians' achievements?
19. How did the Assyrians rule?
20. What do Judaism, Christianity, and Islam have in common?

21. What event convinced Jesus' followers that he was the Messiah?
22. What were some achievements of the Islamic Empire?
23. How were the Mongols able to conquer so much territory?

Think Critically

24. **Drawing Conclusions** Why is the ability to make and use tools an important step in human development?
25. **Drawing Inferences** Why are the developments of a calendar, a system of counting, and a system of writing so important to a civilization?
26. **Analyzing Information** According to tradition, how did the Jews escape slavery in Egypt?
27. **Contrasting** On what issue do the Sunni and the Shia disagree?
28. **Evaluating** How did the Muslim Empire become so powerful?

Map Activity

29. Identify the places marked on the map.
    Arabia
    Mesopotamia
    Sumer
    Baghdad
    Palestine

Writing Activity

Imagine that you are a merchant who comes to Mesopotamia to do business. Write a diary entry about what you see both in the cities and in the countryside. First, choose a time period in which to set your "visit." Then review which culture controlled the area at the time and what life was like during that time. You may want to pay particular attention to the technologies that you see demonstrated and how those technologies affect your business deals. For example, how might the Persian road system have affected your ability to bring goods to market? Use the illustrations in the chapter to help you add detail to your diary entry.

internet connect

Internet Activity: go.hrw.com
KEYWORD: SK5 GT4

Choose a topic to explore about the history of Southwest and Central Asia:

- Learn more about the development of writing.
- Explore the Persian Empire.
- Trace the spread of the Mongol Empire.

Social Studies Skills Practice

Interpreting Maps

Study the following map about trade routes from Mesopotamia. Then answer the questions.

1. What role did the Tigris and Euphrates play in trade?
2. According to this map, how far west did the trade routes from Mesopotamia extend?
3. Why do you think there were no routes through the Arabian Desert?
4. What major trade center was located in Sumer?

Analyzing Primary Sources

Read the following passage from the Code of Hammurabi. Then answer the questions.

"If any one open his ditches to water his crop, but is careless, and the water flood the field of his neighbor, then he shall pay his neighbor corn for his loss. . . . If a man let in the water, and the water overflow the plantation of his neighbor, he shall pay ten gur *of corn for every ten* gan *of land."*

1. What is the main purpose of this portion of the Code of Hammurabi?
2. Based on your knowledge of ancient civilizations, why would this issue be important?
3. Based on your understanding of this quote, what do you think a *gur* and a *gan* are?
4. Does the punishment in the code seem just and fair? Why or why not?

CHAPTER 5

The Eastern Mediterranean

The next student we will meet lives in Turkey, a country that lies partly in Europe, partly in Asia.

My name is Adalet, and I am in the tenth grade at Ted College, a private school in Ankara, the capital of Turkey. I live in an apartment a little outside the city with my mom and dad. We live on the twelfth floor, and have a view of the city, the distant mountains, and of course the parking lot. In the summers, my favorite time is when I can go to stay with my grandma and my grandpa in their summer house on the Aegean Sea, in Kusadasi near the ancient Greek city of Ephesus. I sleep until 11:00 A.M. or noon, then spend the day at the beach with my friends until the sun goes down.

On school days, from September to June, I get up at 8:00 A.M., put on my school uniform, and have breakfast of corn flakes or bread and cheese with milk or tea. At school we go directly to our classes. I am studying biology, physics, algebra, geometry, history, Turkish, and English. The English, science, and math classes are taught in English, the others in Turkish.

Türkiye'den selamlar!

Translation: Greetings from Turkey!

Section 1 Physical Geography

Read to Discover

1. What are the main physical features of the eastern Mediterranean?
2. What are the climate types of the region?
3. What natural resources are found in this area?

Vocabulary

phosphates
asphalt

Places

Dardanelles
Bosporus
Sea of Marmara
Jordan River
Dead Sea
Syrian Desert
Negev

Reading Strategy

BRAINSTORMING Write the letters of the alphabet down a sheet of paper. With a partner, brainstorm what you already know about the eastern Mediterranean region. List your ideas next to as many letters as possible.

The Eastern Mediterranean: Physical-Political

ELEVATION

	FEET	METERS
⊛ National capitals	13,120	4,000
	6,560	2,000
• Other cities	1,640	500
	656	200
	(Sea level) 0	0 (Sea level)
	Below sea level	Below sea level

Size comparison of the eastern Mediterranean to the contiguous United States

The status of the Gaza Strip and the West Bank is in transition.

Istanbul lies on both sides of the waterway known as the Bosporus. This waterway divides Europe from Asia.

Interpreting the Visual Record

(Movement) Why do you think the Bosporus would be an important crossroads of trade?

Physical Features

The countries of the eastern Mediterranean are Turkey, Lebanon, Syria, Jordan, and Israel. In addition to its own territory, Israel controls areas known as the Occupied Territories. These include the West Bank, the Gaza Strip, and the Golan Heights.

On Two Continents The eastern Mediterranean region straddles two continents. A small part of Turkey lies on Europe's Balkan Peninsula. This area consists of rolling plains and hills. A narrow waterway, made up of the Dardanelles (dahrd-uhn-ELZ), the Bosporus (BAHS-puh-ruhs), and the Sea of Marmara (MAHR-muh-ruh), separates Europe from Asia. The larger, Asian part of Turkey is mostly plateaus and highlands.

Hills, Valleys, and Plains Heading south from Turkey and into Syria, we cross a narrow plain. The Euphrates River, fed by precipitation in Turkey's eastern mountains, flows southeast through this plain. Farther south are more hills and plateaus. Two main ridges run north-south. One runs from southwestern Syria through western Jordan. The other, closer to the coast, runs through Lebanon, Israel, and the West Bank. The Jordan River valley separates these two ridges. A narrow coastal plain rims the region along its seacoasts. In western Turkey the coastal plain is wider.

River and Sea The Jordan River begins in Syria and flows south. Israel and the West Bank lie on the west side of the river. The country of Jordan lies on the east side. The Jordan River flows into the Dead Sea. This unusual body of water is the lowest point on any continent—1,312 feet (400 m) below sea level. It is so salty that swimmers cannot sink in it.

✓ **READING CHECK:** (*Places and Regions*) What are the region's main physical features?

Climate

Dry climates are the rule in most of this region. However, there are important variations. Turkey's Black Sea coast and the Mediterranean coast all the way to Israel have a Mediterranean climate. Central Syria and lands farther south have a desert climate. A small area of northeastern Turkey has a humid subtropical climate.

The Syrian Desert covers much of Syria and Jordan. It usually receives less than five inches (12.7 cm) of rainfall a year. Another desert, the Negev (NE-gev), lies in southern Israel.

✓ **READING CHECK:** (*Places and Regions*) What are the climates of the eastern Mediterranean?

Resources

Unlike nearby countries in Southwest Asia, the countries of the eastern Mediterranean do not have large oil reserves. The people of this region make their living from the land in other ways.

Limited Farming Commercial farming is possible only where rain or irrigation provides enough water. Subsistence farming and livestock herding are common in drier areas. Desert areas support a few nomadic herders.

Mineral Resources Many minerals, including sulfur, mercury, and copper, are found in the region. **Phosphates**—mineral salts containing the element phosphorus—are produced in Syria, Jordan, and Israel. Phosphates are used to make fertilizers. The area also exports **asphalt**—the dark tarlike material used to pave streets. The Dead Sea is a source of mineral salts.

✓ **READING CHECK:** (*Places and Regions*) What natural resources are found in this area?

A shepherd in eastern Turkey watches his sheep.
Interpreting the Visual Record
(*Human-Environment Interaction*) **Why is livestock herding common in many parts of the eastern Mediterranean region?**

▼

Define and explain: phosphates, asphalt

Working with Sketch Maps On a map of the eastern Mediterranean that you draw or that your teacher provides, label the following: Dardanelles, Bosporus, Sea of Marmara, Jordan River, Dead Sea, Syrian Desert, and the Negev.

Reading for the Main Idea

1. (*Places and Regions*) What country lies on two continents?

2. (*Places and Regions*) What are the most common climates of the region?

3. (*Places and Regions*) How do geographic factors affect the economic activities of the region?

go.hrw.com
Homework Practice Online
Keyword: SK5 HP5

Critical Thinking

4. Drawing Inferences and Conclusions How do you think the Dead Sea got its name?

Organizing What You Know

5. Categorizing Copy the following graphic organizer. Use it to list the major landforms and bodies of water of each region.

Country/ territory	Landforms and bodies of water

The Eastern Mediterranean • 109

Section 2 Turkey

Read to Discover

1. What is the history of the area that is now Turkey?
2. What kind of government and economy does Turkey have?
3. How is Turkish society divided?

Vocabulary

secular

Places

Ankara
Istanbul

People

Kemal Atatürk

Reading Strategy

FOLDNOTES: LAYERED BOOK Create the FoldNote titled **Layered Book** described in the Appendix. Label the book Turkey. Label the pages with these geography themes: Location and Place, Human-Environment Interaction, Movement, and Region. As you read, write what you learn about Turkey that supports the themes.

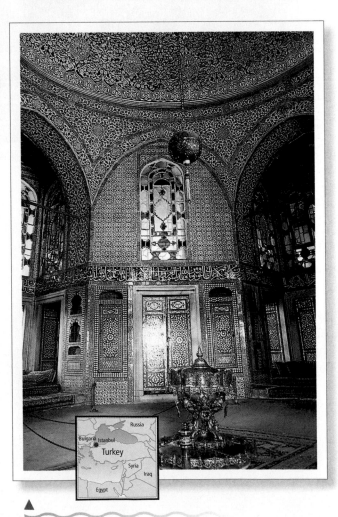

Place Ottoman monarchs lived in the Topkapi Palace built in 1462.

History

Turkey, except for the small part that lies in Europe, makes up a region called Asia Minor. In ancient times this area was part of the Hittite and Persian Empires. In the 330s B.C. Alexander the Great conquered Asia Minor. Later it became part of the Roman Empire. Byzantium, renamed Constantinople, was one of the most important cities of the empire. After the fall of Rome, Constantinople became the capital of the Byzantine Empire.

In the A.D. 1000s the Seljuk Turks invaded Asia Minor. The Seljuks were a nomadic people from Central Asia who had converted to Islam. In 1453 another Turkish people, the Ottoman Turks, captured the city of Constantinople. They made it the capital of their Islamic empire.

Ottoman Empire During the 1500s and 1600s the Ottoman Empire was very powerful. It controlled territory in North Africa, Southwest Asia, and southeastern Europe. In the 1700s and 1800s the empire gradually weakened.

In World War I the Ottoman Empire fought on the losing side. When the war ended, the Ottomans lost all their territory outside of what is now Turkey. Greece even invaded western Asia Minor in an attempt to take more land. However, the Turkish army pushed out the invaders. Military officers

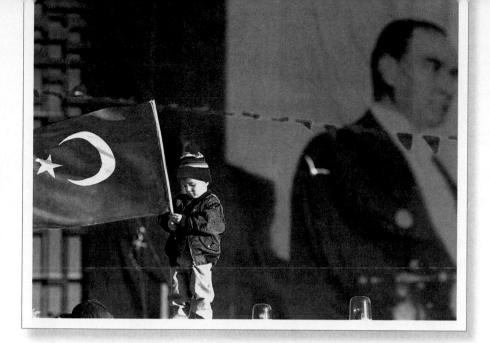

then took over the government. Their leader was a war hero, Mustafa Kemal. He later adopted the name Kemal Atatürk, which means "father of the Turks." He formally dissolved the Ottoman Empire and created the nation of Turkey. He made the new country a democracy and moved the capital to Ankara. Constantinople was renamed Istanbul in 1930.

Modern Turkey Atatürk wanted to modernize Turkey. He believed that to be strong Turkey had to westernize. He banned the fez, the traditional hat of Turkish men, and required that they wear European-style hats. The Latin alphabet replaced the Arabic one. The European calendar and metric system replaced Islamic ones. Women were encouraged to vote, work, and hold office. New laws made it illegal for women to wear veils.

✔ **READING CHECK:** (*Human Systems*) What is the history of what is now Turkey?

Turkish women harvest grapes.
Interpreting the Visual Record (*Place*)
What kind of climate do Turkey's coastal plains have?

Government and Economy

Today, Turkey has a legislature called the National Assembly. A president and a prime minister share executive power. The Turkish military has taken over the government three times. However, each time it has returned power to civilian hands.

Although most of its people are Muslim, Turkey is a **secular** state. This means that religion is kept separate from government. For example, the religion of Islam allows a man to have up to four wives. However, by Turkish law a man is permitted to have just one wife. In recent years Islamic political parties have attempted to increase Islam's role in Turkish society.

CONNECTING TO *Literature*

Statue of Gilgamesh

Gilgamesh is the hero of this ancient story that was popular all over Southwest Asia. In this passage Utnapishtim (oot-nuh-peesh-tuhm), whom the gods have given everlasting life, tells Gilgamesh about surviving a great flood.

Epic of Gilgamesh

"In those days . . . the people multiplied, the world bellowed like a wild bull, and the great god was aroused by the clamor[1]. Enlil (en-LIL) heard the clamor and he said to the gods in council, 'The uproar of mankind is intolerable[2] and sleep is no longer possible by reason of the babel[3].' So the gods agreed to exterminate[4] mankind. Enlil did this, but Ea (AY-uh) because of his oath warned me in a dream. . . . 'Tear down your house, I say, and build a boat. . . . then take up into the boat the seed of all living creatures.'

Utnapishtim does as he is told. He builds a boat and fills it with supplies, his family, and animals. Then terrible rains come and flood Earth.

"When the seventh day dawned the storm from the south subsided, the sea grew calm, the flood was stilled; I looked at the face of the world and there was silence, all mankind was turned to clay. . . . I opened a hatch and the light fell on my face. Then I bowed low, I sat down and I wept, . . . for on every side was the waste of water."

Analyzing Primary Sources
1. Why did the god bring the flood?
2. Why does Utnapishtim cry?

Vocabulary [1]clamor: noise   [2]intolerable: not bearable   [3]babel: confusing noise   [4]exterminate: kill off

---

Turkey's mixed economy includes modern factories as well as village farming and craft making. The most important industries are clothing, chemicals, and oil processing. About 40 percent of Turkey's labor force works in agriculture. Grains, cotton, sugar beets, and hazelnuts are major crops. The Turkish economy has grown rapidly in recent years, but inflation is a problem. Large numbers of Turks have left Turkey in search of better jobs. By 2001, an estimated 1.2 million Turks were working abroad to earn higher wages.

In the 1990s Turkey began building dams on the Tigris and Euphrates Rivers. These will provide electricity and irrigation water. However, the dams have caused concern for Syria and Iraq. They are disturbed that another country controls the sources of their water.

✓ **READING CHECK:** (*Human Systems*) What kind of government and economy does Turkey have?

People and Culture

Turkey has more than 68 million people. Ethnic Turks make up 80 percent of the population. Kurds are the largest minority. They are about 20 percent of the population. Since ancient times the Kurds have lived in what is today southeastern Turkey. Kurds also live in nearby parts of Iran, Iraq, and Syria. In the 1980s and 1990s some Kurds fought for independence from Turkey. The Turkish government has used military force against this rebellion.

Kemal Atatürk's changes created a cultural split between Turkey's urban middle class and rural villagers. The lifestyle and attitudes of middle-class Turks have much in common with those of middle-class Europeans. Most Turks, though, are more traditional. Islam influences their attitudes on matters such as the role of women. This cultural division is a factor in Turkish politics.

Turkish cooking is much like that of the rest of the Mediterranean region. It features olives, vegetables, cheese, yogurt, and bread. Shish kebab—grilled meat on a skewer—is a favorite Turkish dish.

✓ **READING CHECK:** (*Human Systems*) What are the divisions in Turkish society?

(Place) Crowds pass through a square near the University of Istanbul. Different styles of dress reflect the diverse attitudes that exist in Turkey today.

 Section Review 2

Define or identify: Kemal Atatürk, secular

Working with Sketch Maps On the map you created in Section 1, label Ankara and Istanbul. What are the advantages of Istanbul's location?

Reading for the Main Idea

1. (*Human Systems*) How did Atatürk try to modernize Turkey?

2. (*Human Systems*) What foods are popular in Turkish cooking?

go.hrw.com **Homework Practice Online** Keyword: SK5 HP5

Critical Thinking

3. **Finding the Main Idea** Why were some Turks unhappy with changes brought about by Atatürk?

4. **Analyzing Information** Why is the Turkish government building dams on the Tigris and Euphrates Rivers? How will this affect countries downriver?

Organizing What You Know

5. **Sequencing** Create a time line listing major events in Turkey's history. List major people, groups, invasions, empires, and changes in government.

400 B.C.   A.D. 2000

Section 3 Israel and the Occupied Territories

Read to Discover

1. What was the early history of Israel like?
2. What is modern Israel like?
3. What is the conflict over the Occupied Territories?

Vocabulary

Diaspora
Zionism

Places

Jerusalem
Gaza Strip
Golan Heights
West Bank
Tel Aviv

Reading Strategy

TAKING NOTES   Before you read, write the main ideas down the left side of a sheet of paper. As you read this section, write what you learn about Israel next to the main ideas.

Place The ancient port of Caesarea lies on the coast of Israel. It was the regional capital during the time of Roman control. Today the harbor structure is partly underwater.

Ancient Israel

The Hebrews, the ancestors of the Jews, first established the kingdom of Israel about 3,000 years ago. It covered roughly the same area as the modern State of Israel. In the 60s B.C. the Roman Empire conquered the region, which they called Palestine. After a series of Jewish revolts, the Romans forced most Jews to leave the region. This scattering of the Jewish population is known as the **Diaspora**.

During the era of Roman control, a Jewish man named Jesus began preaching. Jesus taught that faith and love were more important than Judaism's many laws. His teachings particularly appealed to the poor and powerless. Both Roman and Jewish rulers saw Jesus as dangerous. Jesus was tried and executed by the Roman authorities. His followers believe he rose from the dead. Christianity—Jesus's teachings and the belief in his resurrection—spread through the Roman Empire. In time, Christianity became the most common religion of the Mediterranean region.

Arabs conquered Palestine in the mid-600s. From the 1000s to the 1200s, European armies launched a series of invasions called the Crusades. Crusaders captured Jerusalem in 1099. In time the Crusaders were pushed out of the area altogether. From the 1500s to World War I, Palestine was part of the Ottoman Empire. At the end of the war, it came under British control.

✓ **READING CHECK:**   *Human Systems*   What significant events occurred in the early history of the area of Israel?

Dialing for Peace

"Hello Peace!" is the name of a popular phone service in Israel, the West Bank, and Gaza. This free service gives Israelis and Palestinians the rare chance to talk directly to each other. The service's organizers hope it will lead to a better understanding between the two cultures. For example, a 20-year-old Palestinian man named Sammy used the service to chat with an Israeli soldier. After the soldier explained to Sammy that he felt bad about guarding Palestinian neighborhoods, Sammy said, "Now I know they do care. And now I have hope that there can be peace." By keeping the lines of communication open, the "Hello Peace" organizers are bringing new hope to the region.

In what other ways could groups in conflict ease tensions?

Modern Israel

In the late 1800s a movement called **Zionism** began among European Jews. Zionism called for Jews to establish a country or community in Palestine. Tens of thousands of Jews moved to the area.

After World War II, the United Nations recommended dividing Palestine into Arab and Jewish states. Jewish leaders declared the independent state of Israel. Armies from surrounding Arab countries invaded Israel. The Israelis defeated the Arabs.

Many Palestinians fled to other Arab states, particularly to Jordan and Lebanon. Some used terrorist attacks to strike at Israel. Israel and its Arab neighbors also fought wars in 1956, 1967, and 1973.

▲
Thousands of devout Jews gather for prayer during Passover at the Western Wall. This wall is all that survives from an ancient temple complex.

Government and Economy Israel has a prime minister and a parliament, called the Knesset. There are two major political parties and many smaller parties.

Israel has built a strong military for protection from the Arab countries around it. Terrorist attacks have also occurred. At age 18 most Israeli men and women must serve in the military.

The West Bank in Transition

SCALE
0   5   10 Miles
0 5 10 Kilometers
Projection:
Transverse Cylindrical

Jabatiya

Tulkarm

Qalqilyah

Nablus

Jordan R.

West Bank

N

Ramallah

Jericho

Jerusalem

ISRAEL

Bethlehem

Dead
Sea

Hebron

Control of West Bank:

- Israeli
- Palestinian civil, Israeli security
- Palestinian before 2003
- Palestinian, 2003
- City of Jerusalem

The Gaza Strip is densely populated and has few natural resources. Israel captured this territory from Egypt in 1967.

▼

Israel has a modern mixed economy. Items like high-technology equipment and cut diamonds are important exports. Tourism is a major industry. Israel's lack of water limits farming. However, using highly efficient irrigation, Israel has successfully increased food production. It imports grain but exports citrus fruit and eggs.

Languages and Diversity Israel's population includes Jews from all parts of the world. Both Hebrew and Arabic are official languages. When they arrive in Israel, many Jews speak English, Russian, German, Hungarian, Yiddish, or Arabic. The government provides classes to help them learn Hebrew.

About 82 percent of Israel's population is Jewish. The rest of it is mostly Arab. About three fourths of these are Muslim. The rest are Christian. Israel's art, music, and literature reflect its great diversity.

Food and Festivals Israeli food is influenced by Jewish religious laws. Jews are forbidden to eat pork and shellfish. They also cannot eat meat and milk products at the same meal. The country's food is as diverse as the population. Eastern European dishes are popular, as are Southwest Asian foods.

For Jews, Saturday is a holy day. Yom Kippur, the most important Jewish holiday, is celebrated in October. Passover, in the spring, celebrates the Hebrews' escape from captivity in Egypt. During Passover, people eat matzo (MAHT-suh), a special bread without yeast.

✔ **READING CHECK:** (*Human Systems*) What are modern Israel's government, economy, and culture like?

The Occupied Territories

In 1967 Israel captured the Gaza Strip, the Golan Heights, and the West Bank. These are sometimes called the Occupied Territories.

Disputed Land The Gaza Strip is a small, crowded piece of coastal land. More than a million Palestinians live there. The area has almost no resources. The Golan Heights is a hilly area on the Syrian border. In 1981 Israel formally declared the Golan Heights part of Israel. Syria still claims this territory.

The West Bank is the largest of the occupied areas, with a population of about 2.2 million. Since Israel took control of the West Bank, more than 187,000 Jews have moved into settlements there. The Palestinians consider this an invasion of their land. This has caused tension and violence between Arabs and Israelis.

Israel annexed East Jerusalem in 1980. Even before this, the Israeli government had moved the capital from Tel Aviv to Jerusalem. Most foreign countries have chosen not to recognize this transfer. The Palestinians still claim East Jerusalem as their rightful capital.

Control of Jerusalem is a difficult and often emotional question for Jews, Muslims, and Christians. The city contains sites that are holy to all three religions.

The Future of the Territories In the 1990s Israel agreed to turn over parts of the Occupied Territories to the Palestinians. In return, the Palestinian leadership— the Palestinian Authority—agreed to work for peace. Parts of the Gaza Strip and West Bank have been transferred to the Palestinian Authority. More areas of the West Bank are expected to be handed over in the future.

The future of the peace process is uncertain. Some Palestinian groups have continued to commit acts of terrorism. Some Jewish groups believe for religious reasons that Israel must not give up the West Bank. Other Israelis fear they would be open to attack if they withdrew from the territories.

✓ **READING CHECK:** (*Human Systems*) Why have the Occupied Territories been a source of conflict?

Muslim women gather to pray at the Dome of the Rock in Jerusalem.
▼

Section Review 3

Homework Practice Online
Keyword: SK5 HP5

Define and explain: Diaspora, Zionism

Working with Sketch Maps On the map you created in Section 2, label Jerusalem, Gaza Strip, Golan Heights, West Bank, and Tel Aviv.

Reading for the Main Idea

1. (*Environment and Society*) How has technology allowed Israel to increase its food production?

2. (*Human Systems*) What historical factors helped create a culturally diverse region in Israel?

Critical Thinking

3. **Finding the Main Idea** How do political boundaries in Israel create conflicts?

4. **Summarizing** What are some difficult issues involved in the Israeli-Palestinian peace process?

Organizing What You Know

5. **Sequencing** Copy the following graphic organizer. Use it to list the sequence of events that led to the formation of modern Israel.

☐ ⇨ ☐ ⇨ ☐ ⇨ ☐ ⇨ ☐

The Eastern Mediterranean • 117

Section 4 — Syria, Lebanon, and Jordan

Read to Discover

1. What kind of government and economy does Syria have?
2. How is Lebanese society divided?
3. What events have shaped the history of Jordan?

Vocabulary

mandate

Places

Damascus
Beirut
Amman

People

Hafiz al-Hassad
King Hussein

Reading Strategy

FOLDNOTES: DOUBLE-DOOR Create a FoldNote titled **Double-Door** described in the Appendix. Write Syria, Lebanon, and Jordan on the upper flap. Label the three sections Syria, Lebanon, and Jordan. As you read, write what you learn about each country.

Syria

The capital of Syria, Damascus, is believed to be the oldest continuously inhabited city in the world. For centuries it was a leading regional trade center. Syria became part of the Ottoman Empire in the 1500s. After World War I, France controlled Syria as a **mandate**. Mandates were former territories of the defeated nations of World War I. They were placed under the control of the winning countries after the war. Syria finally became independent in the 1940s.

Politics and Economy From 1971 to 2000, the Syrian government was led by Hafiz al-Assad. Assad increased the size of Syria's military. He wanted to match Israel's military strength and protect his rule from his enemies within Syria. Assad's son, Bashar, was elected president after his father's death in 2000.

Syria's government owns the country's oil refineries, larger electrical plants, railroads, and some factories. Syria's key manufactured goods are textiles, food products, and chemicals. Agriculture remains important.

Place Roman columns still stand in the ancient city of Apamea, Syria.

Syria has only small deposits of oil and natural gas. It is rich in limestone, basalt, and phosphates.

People Syria's population of more than 17 million is about 90 percent Arab. The other 10 percent includes Kurds and Armenians. About 74 percent of Syrians are Sunni Muslim. Another 16 percent are Alawites and Druze, members of small branches of Islam. About 10 percent of Syrians are Christian. There are also small Jewish communities in some cities.

✔ **READING CHECK:** (*Places and Regions*) How is Syria's economy organized?

Lebanon

Lebanon is a small, mountainous country on the Mediterranean coast. It is home to several different groups of people. At times these different groups have fought each other.

History and People During the Ottoman period many religious and ethnic minority groups settled in Lebanon. After World War I Lebanon, along with Syria, became a French mandate. Lebanon finally gained independence in the 1940s.

The Lebanese are overwhelmingly Arab, but they are divided by religion. Most Lebanese are either Muslim or Christian. Each of those groups is divided into several smaller groups. Muslims are divided into Sunni, Shia, and Druze. The Maronites are the largest of the Christian groups in Lebanon. At the time of independence, there were slightly more Christians than Muslims. Over time, however, Muslims became the majority.

▲

People must drill for water in dry areas of Syria.

Interpreting the Visual Record

(*Human-Environment Interaction*)

Judging from this photo, how has technology affected the lifestyle of people in desert areas?

▲

This photograph from the early 1900s shows a tall cedar tree in the mountains of northern Lebanon. Lebanon's cedars have long been a symbol of the country.

A vendor in Beirut sells postcards of what the city looked like before it was scarred by war.

Interpreting the Visual Record What were the effects of the civil war in Lebanon?

Civil War For some decades after independence, Christian and Muslim politicians managed to share power. A complex system assigned certain government positions to different religious groups. For example, the president was always a Maronite. However, over time this cooperation broke down. The poorest group, the Shia, grew rapidly but were not given additional power. Tensions mounted. Adding to the divisions between Lebanese was the presence of hundreds of thousands of Palestinian refugees living in Lebanon. Ethnic and religious groups armed themselves, and in the 1970s fighting broke out. Warfare between Lebanese groups lasted until 1990. Tens of thousands of people died, and the capital, Beirut, was badly damaged.

During the 1990s Lebanon's economy slowly recovered from the civil war. The refining of crude oil brought in by pipeline is a leading industry. Other industries include food processing, textiles, cement, chemicals, and jewelry making. Lebanese farmers produce tobacco, fruit, grains, and vegetables.

✓ **READING CHECK:** (*Human Systems*) What is causing divisions in Lebanese society?

Jordan

Jordan's short history has been full of conflict. Great Britain drew its borders, and Jordan's royal family is actually from Arabia. The country has few resources and several powerful neighbors. In addition, most of its people think of another country as their homeland. Yet Jordan has survived.

History and Government The country of Jordan (called Transjordan until 1949) was created from Ottoman territory following World War I. The British controlled the area as a mandate. They established an Arabian prince named Abdullah as the monarch of the new country. Abdullah had helped the British in World War I, but he had been driven out of Saudi Arabia. In the 1940s the country became fully independent. After the creation of Israel and the war of 1948, Jordan annexed the Arab lands of the West Bank.

At the time of its independence, Jordan's population was small. Most Jordanians lived a nomadic or seminomadic life. After each of the Arab-Israeli wars of 1948 and 1967, hundreds of thousands of Palestinian Arab refugees came to live in Jordan. These immigrants strained Jordan's resources. In addition, a cultural division arose between the Palestinians and the "original" Jordanian Arabs. After 1967 Palestinians actually made up a majority of Jordan's people.

From 1952 to 1999 Jordan was ruled by King Hussein. Most observers, both inside and outside Jordan, considered him one of the

The city of Petra in Jordan dates back more than 2,000 years. This building was carved out of the sandstone cliff.

King Hussein (1935–1999) **Character Trait: Kindness**

On his 18th birthday, Hussein ibn Talal was crowned king of Jordan. King Hussein is known to Jordanians as "The Humane King" for the ways he improved living conditions in Jordan. He also developed economic opportunities for Jordanians and built new highways across the country. Throughout his reign, Hussein also made many attempts to bring about peace in the Middle East. In 1994, he signed a peace treaty with Israel.

Why is Hussein known as "The Humane King"?

best rulers in the region. Hussein's popularity allowed him to begin some democratic reforms in the 1980s and 1990s. Today, the division between Palestinian and Jordanian Arabs causes less conflict.

Economy and Resources Jordan is a poor country with limited resources. The country does produce phosphates, cement, and potash. Tourism and banking are becoming important industries. Jordan depends on economic aid from the oil-rich Arab nations and the United States. Amman, the capital, is Jordan's only large city.

Jordanian farmers raise fruits and vegetables in the Jordan River valley, using irrigation. Some highland areas receive enough winter rainfall to grow grains. Raising sheep and goats is an important source of income. However, overgrazing has caused soil erosion. A crucial resource issue for Jordan is its shortage of water.

✓ **READING CHECK:** (*Human Systems*) How did King Hussein affect Jordan's history?

Section Review 4

Homework Practice Online
Keyword: SK5 HP5

Define or identify: mandate, Hafiz al-Hassad, King Hussein

Working with Sketch Maps On the map you created in Section 3, label Damascus, Beirut, and Amman.

Reading for the Main Idea

1. (*Human Systems*) How did Hafiz al-Assad affect Syria?

2. (*Human Systems*) What divisions led to conflict in Lebanon?

3. (*Places and Regions*) Which of the countries discussed in this section does not border the Mediterranean Sea?

Critical Thinking

4. Finding the Main Idea How have foreign countries influenced Jordan?

Organizing What You Know

5. Categorizing Use the graphic organizer to gather information about Syria, Lebanon, and Jordan.

	Syria	Lebanon	Jordan
Major religion(s)			
Type of government			
Major problem(s)			
Greatest strength(s)			

Review and Practice

Define and Identify

Identify each of the following:

1. phosphates
2. asphalt
3. Kemal Atatürk
4. secular
5. Diaspora
6. Zionism
7. mandate
8. Hafiz al-Hassad
9. King Hussein

Review the Main Ideas

10. What are the region's main rivers? Where do they flow?
11. What makes the Dead Sea an unusual body of water? What are its commercial uses?
12. What mineral resources are located in the eastern Mediterranean?
13. People and customs from what three continents have influenced the eastern Mediterranean region?
14. How did the Ottoman Empire come to an end?
15. How has westernization changed Turkey's government, economy, and culture?
16. What three major religions have holy sites in Jerusalem?

17. What cultures have ruled the lands now called Israel and the Occupied Territories?
18. What is the conflict over the Occupied Territories?
19. What issue divides the Arabs of Lebanon?

Think Critically

20. **Drawing Inferences and Conclusions** Why do you think Atatürk moved Turkey's capital from Istanbul to Ankara?
21. **Finding the Main Idea** How has human migration to Israel affected its population?
22. **Analyzing Information** Why is conflict over dams in this region so important?
23. **Analyzing Information** How did refugees from Palestine affect Jordan?
24. **Drawing Inferences and Conclusions** Why did attempts to balance religious groups' participation in Lebanon's government fail?

Map Activity

25. On a separate sheet of paper, match the letters on the map with their correct labels.

Dardanelles, Bosporus, Sea of Marmara, Jordan River, Dead Sea, Negev, Istanbul, Tel Aviv, Jerusalem, Damascus

Writing Activity

Imagine that your family is about to travel to the eastern Mediterranean for a vacation. Your parents have asked you to help plan the trip. Write about the places you would like to visit and the reasons you would find them interesting. Be sure to use standard grammar, spelling, sentence structure, and punctuation.

internet connect

Internet Activity: go.hrw.com
KEYWORD: SK5 GT5

Choose a topic to explore about the eastern Mediterranean:
- Visit the Dead Sea.
- Compare Israeli and Arab foods.
- Travel to historic Jerusalem.

Social Studies Skills Practice

Interpreting Charts

Study the following chart and answer the questions.

Year	Total Population of Turkey (in millions)	Kurdish Population in Turkey (in millions)	Percentage of Turkish Population that is Kurdish
Projected Growth of Turkey's Kurdish Population			
1990	56.7	13.7	24.1
2000	65.9	18.7	28.4
2020	87.5	32.3	36.9
2050	105.8	47.0	44.4

Source: Mehrdad R. Izady, *The Kurds: A Concise Handbook,* 1992

1. In what year will the Kurds make up the greatest percentage of the Turkish population?

2. What prediction can you make about Kurdish population growth?

3. Which group appears to have a higher birthrate? the Kurds or the overall Turkish population?

4. Based on this chart and your knowledge of the region, what might result from the continued growth of the Kurdish population?

Analyzing Primary Sources

Read the following passage from a 2003 newspaper article about the Dead Sea. Then answer the questions.

"In less than 50 years, the lowest point on earth has dropped even lower—from 1,294 feet below sea level to 1,360 feet. . . . The Dead Sea's only sources of water are sparse rainfall—less than 3 inches a year—and the Jordan River. But Israel and Jordan have diverted so much of the river's flow for agricultural use that the Dead Sea gets just 10 percent of the water it once did. At the same time, the sea's own waters are being sucked out by Israeli and Arab companies that extract the potassium and other minerals . . . The result? The level of the Dead Sea is dropping by more than 3 feet per year."

1. By how many feet has the Dead Sea dropped in the past 50 years?

2. What is the Dead Sea's only source for water?

3. What two factors are causing the level of the Dead Sea to drop?

4. At the current rate, how much lower will the Dead Sea be in 10 years?

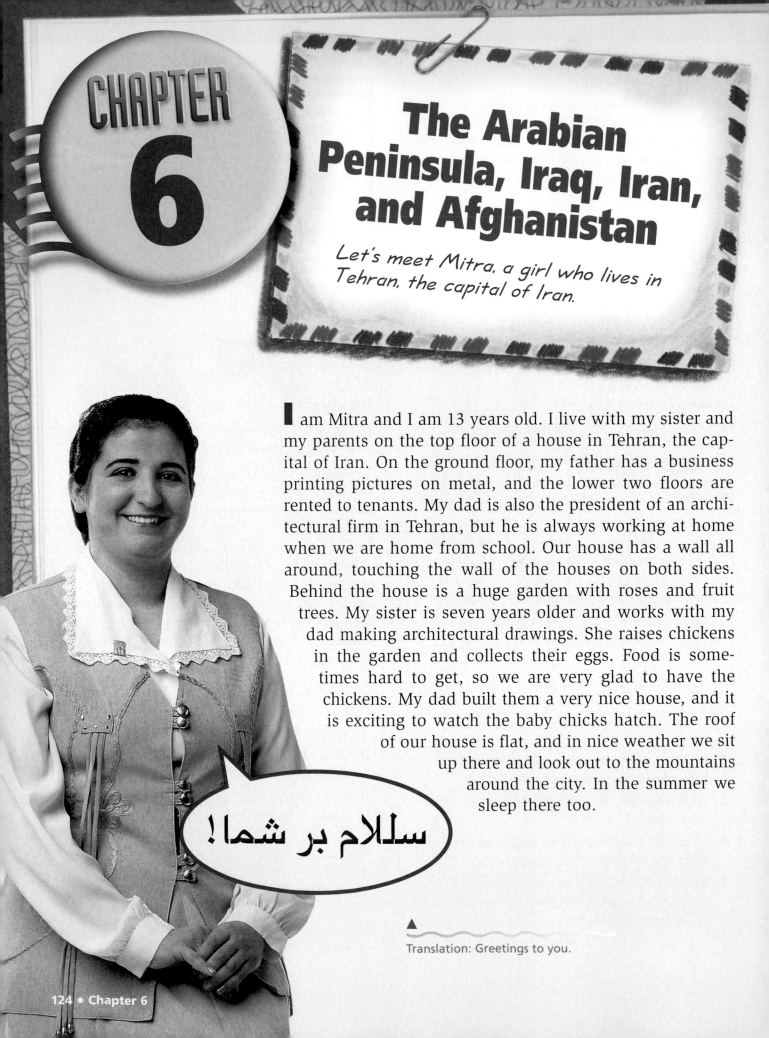

CHAPTER 6

The Arabian Peninsula, Iraq, Iran, and Afghanistan

Let's meet Mitra, a girl who lives in Tehran, the capital of Iran.

I am Mitra and I am 13 years old. I live with my sister and my parents on the top floor of a house in Tehran, the capital of Iran. On the ground floor, my father has a business printing pictures on metal, and the lower two floors are rented to tenants. My dad is also the president of an architectural firm in Tehran, but he is always working at home when we are home from school. Our house has a wall all around, touching the wall of the houses on both sides. Behind the house is a huge garden with roses and fruit trees. My sister is seven years older and works with my dad making architectural drawings. She raises chickens in the garden and collects their eggs. Food is sometimes hard to get, so we are very glad to have the chickens. My dad built them a very nice house, and it is exciting to watch the baby chicks hatch. The roof of our house is flat, and in nice weather we sit up there and look out to the mountains around the city. In the summer we sleep there too.

سلام بر شما!

Translation: Greetings to you.

Section 1 Physical Geography

Read to Discover

1. What are the major physical features of the region?
2. What climates are found in this region?
3. What are the region's important resources?

Vocabulary

exotic rivers
wadis
fossil water

Places

Persian Gulf
Arabian Peninsula
Red Sea
Arabian Sea
Tigris River

Euphrates River
Elburz Mountains
Zagros Mountains
Hindu Kush
Rub' al-Khali

Reading Strategy

READING ORGANIZER Create a three-column chart. Title the first column Arabian Peninsula, the second column Tigris-Euphrates plain, and the third column Mountains and Plateaus. As you read this section, list the countries and characteristics found in each region.

The Arabian Peninsula, Iraq, Iran, and Afghanistan: Physical-Political

ELEVATION

FEET	METERS
13,120	4,000
6,560	2,000
1,640	500
656	200
(Sea level) 0	0 (Sea level)
Below sea level	Below sea level

⊛ National capitals
• Other cities

Size comparison of the Arabian Peninsula, Iraq, Iran, and Afghanistan to the contiguous United States

SCALE
0   250   500 Miles
0   250   500 Kilometers
Projection: Lambert Conformal Conic

☑ internet connect

GO TO: go.hrw.com
KEYWORD: SK5 CH6
FOR: Web sites about the
Arabian Peninsula, Iraq,
Iran, and Afghanistan

Physical Features

The 10 countries of this region are laid out like a semicircle, with the Persian Gulf in the center. They are Saudi Arabia, Kuwait (koo-WAYT), Bahrain (bah-RAYN), Qatar (KAH-tuhr), the United Arab Emirates (E-muh-ruhts), Oman (oh-MAHN), Yemen (YE-muhn), Iraq (i-RAHK), Iran (i-RAN), and Afghanistan (af-GA-nuh-stan).

This area can be divided into three landform regions. The Arabian Peninsula is a large rectangular area. The Red Sea, Gulf of Aden, Arabian Sea, and Persian Gulf border the peninsula. North of the Arabian Peninsula is the plain of the Tigris (TY-gruhs) and Euphrates (yooh-FRAY-teez) Rivers. In ancient times, this area was called Mesopotamia (me-suh-puh-TAY-mee-uh), or the "land between the rivers." East of this plain is a region of mountains and plateaus. It stretches through Iran and Afghanistan.

The surface of the Arabian Peninsula rises gradually as one moves westward from the Persian Gulf. The highest point is in the southwest, in the mountains of Yemen.

North of the Arabian Peninsula is a low, flat plain. It runs from the Persian Gulf into northern Iraq. The Tigris and Euphrates Rivers flow across this plain. They are what are known as **exotic rivers**. Exotic rivers begin in humid regions and then flow through dry areas.

East of this low plain the land climbs sharply. Most of Iran is a plateau bordered by mountains. The Elburz (el-BOOHRZ) Mountains and Kopet-Dag range lie in the north. The Zagros (ZA-gruhs) Mountains lie in the southwest. Afghanistan includes many mountain ranges, such as the towering Hindu Kush range.

✓ **READING CHECK:** (*Places and Regions*) What are the major physical features of this area?

Cold nighttime temperatures and extremely hot days help break rock into sand in Saudi Arabia's Rubʻ al-Khali, or "empty quarter."

Interpreting the Visual Record How do you think deserts like the Rubʻ al-Khali affected trade and travel in the region?

Climate

Most of Southwest Asia has a desert climate. A nearly constant high-pressure system in the atmosphere causes this climate. Some areas—mostly high plateaus and the region's edges—do get winter rains or snow. These areas generally have steppe climates. Some mountain peaks receive more than 50 inches (130 cm) of rain per year.

The desert can be both very hot and very cold. In summer, afternoon temperatures can reach 129°F (54°C). During the night, however, the temperature may drop quickly. Temperatures sometimes dip below freezing during winter nights.

The Rub' al-Khali (ROOB ahl-KAH-lee), or "empty quarter," of southern Saudi Arabia is the largest sand desert in the world. In northern Saudi Arabia is the An Nafud (ahn nah-FOOD), another desert.

✓ **READING CHECK:** (*Places and Regions*) What are the climates of this region?

Resources

Water is an important resource everywhere, but in this region it is crucial. Many desert regions are visited only by nomads and their animal herds. In many places, springs or wells provide water. Nomads sometimes get water by digging shallow wells into dry streambeds called **wadis**. Wells built with modern technology can reach water deep underground. The groundwater in these wells is often **fossil water**. Fossil water is water that is not being replaced by rainfall. Wells that pump fossil water will eventually run dry.

Other than water, oil is the region's most important mineral resource. Most of the oilfields are located near the shores of the Persian Gulf. The countries of the region are not rich in resources other than oil. Iran is an exception, with deposits of many metals.

✓ **READING CHECK:** (*Places and Regions*) What are the region's important resources?

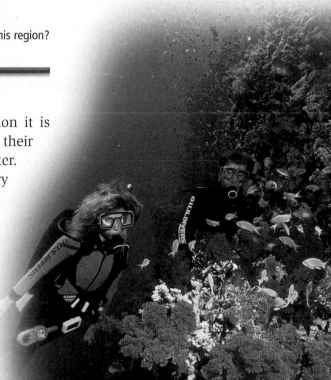

Human-Environment Interaction
Beneath the Red Sea lie many valuable resources, such as oil, sulfur, and metal deposits.

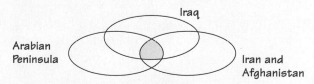
Homework Practice Online
Keyword: SK5 HP6

Section Review 1

Define and explain: exotic rivers, wadis, fossil water

Working with Sketch Maps On a map of the Arabian Peninsula, Iraq, Iran, and Afghanistan that you draw or that your teacher provides, label the following: Persian Gulf, Arabian Peninsula, Red Sea, Arabian Sea, Tigris River, Euphrates River, Elburz Mountains, Zagros Mountains, Hindu Kush, and Rub' al-Khali.

Reading for the Main Idea

1. (*Places and Regions*) Why do you think Mesopotamia was important in ancient times?

2. (*Places and Regions*) What is the region's climate?

Critical Thinking

3. **Drawing Inferences and Conclusions** Why do you think the Persian Gulf is important to international trade?

4. **Drawing Inferences and Conclusions** What settlement pattern might you find in this region?

Organizing What You Know

5. **Summarizing** Copy the following graphic organizer. Use it to list as many details of landforms, resources, and climate as you can. Place them in the correct part of the diagram.

Iraq

Arabian Peninsula

Iran and Afghanistan

The Arabian Peninsula, Iraq, Iran, and Afghanistan • 127

Read to Discover

1. What are Saudi Arabia's history, government, and people like?
2. What kinds of government and economy do the other countries of the Arabian Peninsula have?

Vocabulary

Muslims
caliph
Sunni
Shia
Qur'an
OPEC

Places

Mecca
Riyadh

People

Muhammad

Reading Strategy

FOLDNOTE: TRI-FOLD Create the FoldNote titled **Tri-Fold** described in the Appendix. Write what you know about the Arabian Peninsula in the column labeled "Know." Then write what you want to know in the column labeled "Want." As you read the section, write what you learn in the column labeled "Learn."

Saudi Arabia

Saudi Arabia is by far the largest country of the Arabian Peninsula. Although the kingdom of Saudi Arabia was not created until the 1930s, the region has long been an important cultural center.

Islam The history of the Arabian Peninsula is closely linked to Islam. This religion was founded by Muhammad, a merchant from the Arabian town of Mecca. Around A.D. 610 he had a vision that he had been named a prophet by Allah, or God. Arab armies and merchants carried Muhammad's teachings to new areas. Islam spread quickly across North Africa, much of Asia, and parts of Europe. Followers of Islam are called **Muslims**. Islam provides a set of rules to guide human behavior.

The Islamic world was originally ruled by a religious and political leader called a **caliph**. Gradually this area broke up into several empires. There are also religious divisions within Islam. Followers of the largest branch of Islam are called **Sunni**. Followers of the second-largest branch of Islam are called **Shia**. In the late 600s

Place Non-Muslims are not allowed to enter Mecca, Islam's holiest city.

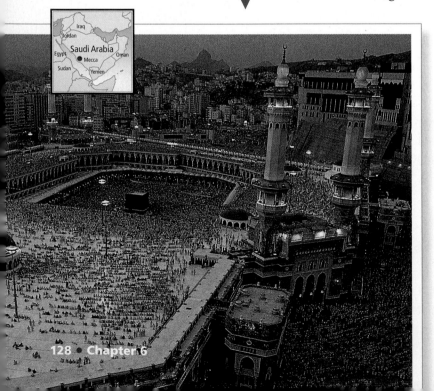

these two groups disagreed over who should lead the Islamic world. There are many smaller groups within Islam as well.

Islamic culture helps to unite Muslims around the world. For example, all Muslims learn Arabic to read the **Qur'an**, the holy book of Islam. Muslims are also expected to visit Mecca at least once. These practices and many others help make Muslims part of a global community.

Government and Economy In the 1920s a local ruler from the Saud family of central Arabia conquered his neighbors and in 1932 created the kingdom of Saudi Arabia. Members of the Saud family have ruled the country ever since. Riyadh, a city near the center of the country, became the capital.

Saudi Arabia is a monarchy with no written constitution or elected legislature. Most government officials are relatives of the king. The king may ask members of his family, Islamic scholars, and tribal leaders for advice on important decisions.

For some time, Saudi Arabia and the United States have had a close relationship. Both countries have strategic military and economic interests in the region. Saudi Arabia purchases U.S. weapons, such as fighter planes. In 1990, when Iraq invaded Kuwait, the Saudi government allowed U.S. military forces to operate from Saudi Arabia. However, the September 11 terrorist attacks strained the relationship because most of the hijackers were from Saudi Arabia.

Oil and related industries are central to Saudi Arabia's mixed economy. Saudi Arabia has the world's largest reserves of oil. It is also the world's leading exporter of oil. Saudi Arabia is a leader of the Organization of Petroleum Exporting Countries, or **OPEC**. The members of OPEC try to influence the price of oil on world markets.

Opened in 1986, this causeway links Saudi Arabia to Bahrain.
Interpreting the Visual Record Why are modern transportation systems important to a country's economy?

This aerial view shows how fossil water has converted desert land near Riyadh into farmers' fields. Each circular plot has a water source at its center.

Oil was discovered in Saudi Arabia in the 1930s. Before then farming and herding had been the main economic activities. Crops included barley, dates, fruits, millet, vegetables, and wheat. Nomads kept herds of sheep, goats, horses, and camels.

Like other oil-rich states in the region, Saudi Arabia has tried to increase its food production. Because freshwater is scarce, desalination plants remove the salt from seawater. This water is then used in farming. Income from oil allows the Saudi government to pay for this expensive process. Even so, Saudi Arabia imports much of its food.

People and Customs Nearly all Saudis are ethnic Arabs and speak Arabic. About 85 percent are Sunni. The rest are Shia. Most Saudis now live in cities, and a sizable middle class has developed. Bedouins, or traditional nomads, make up less than 10 percent of the population.

Some 65 percent of Saudi Arabia's workers are from other countries, including Yemen and Pakistan. Unemployment is very high among young Saudis. One reason is the very high population growth rate. More than 40 percent of Saudis are younger than 15. Another reason is that many young Saudis study religion instead of the technical subjects their economy requires.

Saudi laws and customs limit women's activities. For example, a woman rarely appears in public without her husband or a male relative. Women may not drive cars. However, women may make up two thirds of the country's Internet users.

Islam is an important part of Saudi Arabia's culture. Because Islam encourages modesty, Saudi clothing keeps arms and legs covered. Men traditionally wear a loose, ankle-length shirt. They often wear a cotton headdress held in place with a cord. These styles are practical in the desert, giving protection from sun, wind, and dust. Saudi women usually wear a black cloak and veil in public. Islam also has a great influence on Saudi art and music.

Saudi Arabia has several Islamic holidays. One of the most important is 'Id al-Fitr, a feast ending the month of Ramadan. During Ramadan, Muslims do not eat or drink anything between dawn and sunset. Saudis may attend huge dinner parties after sundown, however.

✓ **READING CHECK:** (*Human Systems*) What is significant about Saudi Arabia's history, government, and people?

Our Amazing Planet

A *sabchat* is a thick, slushy deposit of sand, silt, mud, and salt found in coastal Saudi Arabia. A *sabchat* can trap people and animals who do not see it in time.

Other Countries of the Arabian Peninsula

Six small coastal countries share the Arabian Peninsula with Saudi Arabia. All are heavily dependent on oil. All but Yemen are monarchies, and each is overwhelmingly Islamic. Oil is a major part of each country's economy. However, possession of differing amounts of oil has made some countries much richer than others.

CONNECTING TO Math

Muslim astronomers in the 1500s

Muslim Contributions to Mathematics

During the early centuries of the Middle Ages, European art, literature, and science declined. However, during this same period Islamic civilization, stretching from Spain to the borders of China, was flowering. Muslim scholars made important advances in art, literature, medicine, and mathematics.

The system of numerals we call Arabic, including the use of the zero, was first created in India. However, it was Muslim thinkers who introduced that system to Europe. They also developed algebra, geometry, and trigonometry. In fact, words like *algebra* and *algorithm* come from Arabic words.

Other Muslims advanced the study of astronomy and physics. Arab geographers calculated distances between cities, longitudes and latitudes, and the direction from one city to another. Muslims developed the first solution for cubic equations. They also defined ratios and used mathematics to explain the rainbow.

Understanding What You Read

1. Where did the Arabic system of numerals originate, and how did it get to Europe?
2. How did Muslim scholars contribute to our knowledge of geography?

Kuwait The country of Kuwait was established in the mid-1700s. Trade and fishing were once the main economic activities there. Oil, which was discovered in the 1930s, has made Kuwait very rich. The Iraqi invasion of 1990 caused massive destruction.

As in Saudi Arabia, a royal family dominates politics in Kuwait. In 1992, however, Kuwait held elections for a legislature. Less than 15 percent of Kuwait's population were given the right to vote. These people were all men from well-established families.

Bahrain and Qatar Bahrain is a group of small islands in the western Persian Gulf. It is a constitutional monarchy headed by a ruling royal family and a legislature. These islands have been a center for trade since ancient times. In 1986 a 15.5 mile (25 km) bridge was completed that connects Bahrain to Saudi Arabia, making movement between the two countries easier.

The Arabian Peninsula

Country	Population/ Growth Rate	Life Expectancy	Literacy Rate	Per Capita GDP
Bahrain	667,238 1.6%	71, male 76, female	89%	$14,000
Kuwait	2,183,161 3.3%	76, male 78, female	85%	$15,000
Oman	2,807,125 3.4%	70, male 74, female	76%	$8,300
Qatar	817,052 2.9%	71, male 76, female	83%	$21,500
Saudi Arabia	24,293,844 3.3%	67, male 71, female	79%	$10,500
United Arab Emirates	2,484,818 1.6%	72, male 77, female	78%	$22,000
Yemen	19,349,881 3.4%	59, male 63, female	50%	$840
United States	290,342,554 0.9%	74, male 80, female	97%	$37,600

Source: Central Intelligence Agency, *The World Factbook 2003*

Interpreting the Chart Which country has the lowest standard of living?

Oil was discovered in Bahrain in the 1930s, creating wealth for the country. However, by the 1990s this oil was starting to run out, and banking and tourism are now becoming important to the economy. Bahrain also refines crude oil imported from nearby Saudi Arabia.

Qatar occupies a small peninsula in the Persian Gulf. Like Bahrain, Qatar is ruled by a powerful monarch. In the 1990s, Qatar's ruler announced a plan to make the country more democratic. He also ended censorship of Qatari newspapers and television.

Qatar's economy used to be based on pearl fishing. Today Qatar relies on oil and huge natural gas reserves for its income.

The United Arab Emirates

The United Arab Emirates, or UAE, consists of seven tiny kingdoms. They are ruled by emirs. This country also has great reserves of oil and natural gas. Profits from these resources have created a modern, comfortable lifestyle for the people of the UAE. The government has also worked to build up other industries.

Like Saudi Arabia and many of the small Persian Gulf countries, the UAE depends on foreign workers. In the UAE, foreign workers outnumber citizens.

Oman

Oman is located just outside the mouth of the Persian Gulf. The country is slightly smaller than Kansas. In ancient times, Oman was a major trade center for merchants traveling the Indian Ocean. Today, Oman's economy is heavily dependent on oil. However, Oman does not have the oil wealth of Kuwait or the UAE. Therefore, the government, ruled by the Al Bu Sa'id family, is attempting to create new industries.

◄

Kindergarten students in the United Arab Emirates kneel to pray.

Interpreting the Visual Record *Place* For what cultural reason do you think these girls and boys are seated in separate rows?

Yemen Yemen is located on the southern corner of the Arabian Peninsula. It borders the Red Sea and the Gulf of Aden. Yemen was formed in 1990 by the joining of North Yemen and South Yemen. The country has an elected government and several political parties. However, political corruption and internal conflicts have threatened this young democracy.

In ancient times, farmers in this area used very advanced methods of irrigation and farming. Yemen was famous for its coffee. Today, Yemen is the poorest country on the Arabian Peninsula. Oil was not discovered there until the 1980s. It now generates a major part of the national income.

✓ **READING CHECK:** *Human Systems* How are the governments and economies of the countries of the Arabian Peninsula organized?

Place An important part of Yemen's culture is its distinctive architecture, which features tall buildings and carved wooden windows.

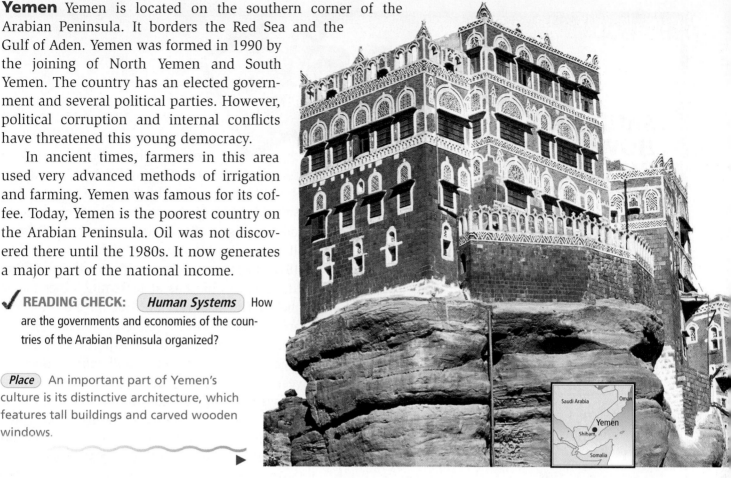

go.hrw.com
Homework Practice Online
Keyword: SK5 HP6

Section Review 2

Define and explain: Muhammad, Muslims, caliph, Sunni, Shia, Qur'an, OPEC

Working with Sketch Maps On the map you created in Section 1, label Mecca and Riyadh. Why is Riyadh's location more suitable than Mecca's to be the capital city of Saudi Arabia?

Reading for the Main Idea

1. *Places and Regions* What kind of government does Saudi Arabia have?

2. *Environment and Society* What role does oil play in the economies of small countries on the Arabian Peninsula?

Critical Thinking

3. **Drawing Inferences and Conclusions** How might trips to Mecca help create a sense of community among Muslims?

4. **Drawing Inferences and Conclusions** Why would a country like Saudi Arabia or the United Arab Emirates bring in large numbers of foreign workers?

Organizing What You Know

5. **Comparing** Copy the following graphic organizer. Use it to list these countries' locations, governments, and economies. Place them in the appropriate part of the chart.

	Location	Government	Economy
Saudi Arabia			
Kuwait			
Bahrain			
Qatar			
UAE			
Oman			
Yemen			

The Arabian Peninsula, Iraq, Iran, and Afghanistan • 133

CASE STUDY

SAUDI ARABIA: HOW OIL HAS CHANGED A COUNTRY

At the beginning of the 1900s, Saudi Arabia was a poor country. Most people followed traditional ways of life and lived by herding animals, farming, or fishing. There were few good roads or transportation systems, and health care was poor.

Major Oil Fields in Saudi Arabia

SCALE
0   200   400 Miles
0   200   400 Kilometers
Projection: Lambert Conformal Conic

▲

Place Saudi Arabia's huge oil fields contain about one quarter of the world's known oil reserves.

Then, in the mid-1930s, oil was discovered in Saudi Arabia. Soon, even larger oil reserves were found. Eventually it was learned that Saudi Arabia had the largest oil reserves in the world. Most of the country's oil reserves are located in eastern Saudi Arabia along the Persian Gulf coast. The Al-Ghawar oil field, discovered in 1948, is the largest in the world. In addition to this field, Saudi Arabia has at least nine other major oil fields. The discovery of these huge oil reserves changed Saudi Arabia's economy and society.

Rising income from oil exports gave Saudi Arabia's government more and more money to invest. New airports, apartments, communications systems, oil pipelines, and roads were built. In 1960 Saudi Arabia had about 1,000 miles (1,600 km) of roads. By 1997 it had about 91,000 miles (145,600 km). Saudi Arabia's cities grew as people left small villages. These changes helped modernize Saudi Arabia's economy.

Saudi society was also affected. The standard of living rose, and people had more money to spend on goods. Foreign companies began to open stores and restaurants in Saudi Arabia. New schools were built throughout the country, and education became available to all citizens. The literacy rate increased from about 3 percent to about 63 percent. Thousands of Saudis traveled to other countries, and many new universities were opened. Health care also improved.

As Saudi Arabia's economy grew, many foreign workers came to the country to work. In the early 2000s foreign workers made up about 25 percent of Saudi Arabia's population. These workers included people from Yemen, Egypt, Palestine, Syria, Iraq, South Korea, and the Philippines. Americans and Europeans also went to Saudi Arabia to work in the oil industry.

The development of the oil industry greatly increased Saudi Arabia's importance in the world. In 1960 Saudi Arabia was a founding member of

◄

Movement Oil is refined in eastern Saudi Arabia. Then it is pumped into ships and exported to countries around the world.

the Organization of Petroleum Exporting Countries (OPEC). Members of OPEC try to influence the price of oil on the world market. Saudi Arabia's huge oil reserves make it one of OPEC's most powerful member countries.

The Saudi government has also bought military equipment from the United States and other countries. This military strength has increased Saudi Arabia's importance in the Persian Gulf region. Since 1991, Saudi Arabia has given large sums to countries that sided with it against Iraq in the Persian Gulf War. Egypt, Turkey, and Syria have especially benefited from this aid.

Unfortunately, however, the oil industry has also damaged Saudi Arabia's environment. Leaks from oil pipelines and ships have spilled millions of gallons of oil into the sea, and oil refineries release chemicals into the air. The country is looking for ways to fight pollution without reducing its oil exports.

◄

Movement Since the mid-1960s Saudi Arabia has expanded its transportation network. A modern road system now connects many parts of the country.

Understanding What You Read

1. What was Saudi Arabia like before oil was discovered there?

2. How has oil changed Saudi Arabia's economy and society?

Read to Discover

1. What were the key events in Iraq's history?
2. What are Iraq's government and economy like?
3. What is the makeup of Iraq's population?

Vocabulary

embargo

Places

Baghdad

Reading Strategy

TAKING NOTES Draw a large triangle on a sheet of paper. Draw two lines across the triangle to create three sections. As you read, write details about Iraq's history in the lower part of the triangle. Write details about its government and economy in the middle of the triangle. Finally, write the details about its people in the top part of the triangle.

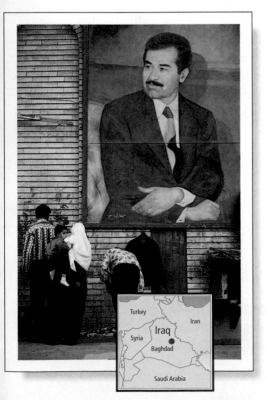

▲

Before March 2003, murals and posters of Saddam Hussein were found throughout Baghdad, Iraq's capital.

History

The history of Mesopotamia, an ancient region in Iraq, stretches back to some of the world's first civilizations. The Sumerian, Babylonian, and Assyrian cultures arose there. The Persians conquered Mesopotamia in the 500s B.C. Alexander the Great made it part of his empire in 331 B.C. In the A.D. 600s Arabs conquered Mesopotamia, and the people gradually converted to Islam.

Mesopotamia became part of the Ottoman Empire in the 1500s. During World War I Great Britain took over the region. The British set up a kingdom of Iraq in 1932 and placed a pro-British ruler in power. In the 1950s a group of Iraqi army officers overthrew this government.

After several more changes in government, the Ba'ath (BAH-ahth) Party took power in 1968. A Ba'ath leader named Saddam Hussein became the president and leader of the armed forces. He was a harsh ruler. Saddam controlled the press, restricted personal freedoms, and killed an unknown number of political enemies.

In 1980 Iraq invaded Iran. Saddam Hussein hoped to take advantage of the confusion following the Iranian Revolution. The Iranians fought back, however, and the Iran-Iraq War dragged on until 1988. Casualties were high on both sides. Both countries' economies were damaged.

In 1990, Iraq invaded Kuwait, a small oil-rich country. This event shocked Western leaders. They were also concerned that Iraq would control such a large share of the world's oil. In addition, Iraq had weapons of mass destruction (WMDs), including chemical and biological weapons. An alliance of countries, led by the United States and Great Britain, soon forced the Iraqis out of Kuwait. This 1991 event was called the Persian Gulf War. Saddam remained in power, however.

Because he would not accept all the UN's terms for peace, the UN placed an **embargo**, or limit on trade, on Iraq. As a result, Iraq's economy suffered.

✔ **READING CHECK:** (*Human Systems*) What are some key events in Iraq's history?

Iraq Today

Shortly after the fighting stopped, Saddam faced two rebellions. He brutally put down uprisings of Shia Muslims in the south and of Kurds in the north. The UN forced Saddam to end all military activity in the Kurdish area of northern Iraq. The UN also required that Iraq allow inspectors into the country to make sure he had destroyed the WMDs. Iraq failed to cooperate completely with the UN and armed conflict continued off and on.

In the meantime, the events of September 11, 2001 had created new tensions. The U.S. government believed Iraq aided terrorists. In March 2003, U.S. forces began attacking Iraqi targets. Within a few weeks Saddam's government fell. The United States then began the long, difficult process of rebuilding the country.

One of the main goals of U.S. officials was creating a stable, democratic country. Another was repairing Iraq's oil industry. Before the war with Iran, Iraq was the world's second-largest oil exporter. Time will tell if Iraq can again be a major oil producer.

Oil isn't Iraq's only resource. From earliest times its wide plains have produced many food crops. Irrigation from the Tigris and Euphrates Rivers allows farmers to grow barley, cotton, rice, vegetables, wheat, dates, and other fruits.

✔ **READING CHECK:** (*Environment and Society*) What happened to Iraq's oil industry?

Our Amazing Planet

Dust storms occur throughout Iraq and can rise to several thousand feet above the ground. These storms often happen during the summer. Five or six usually strike central Iraq in July, the worst month.

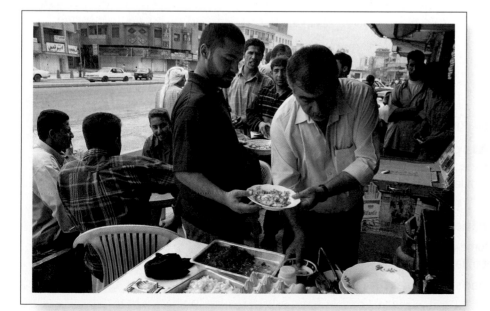

In March 2003, war left much of Baghdad without electricity and water. Some restaurants, however, stayed open by cooking with propane gas on the city's sidewalks.

◀

The Ma'dan are a minority people who live in Iraq's southern marshes. Saddam's government drained part of the marshes, putting the Ma'dan way of life in danger.

People

More than 75 percent of the population are Arabs. Some 15 to 20 percent are Kurds, and the rest belong to small minority groups. Nearly all Iraqis are Muslim. About two thirds of Iraqis are Shia. Saddam and his supporters, however, were Sunnis. Under Saddam, the government often conflicted with Shia leaders.

After decades of harsh government and warfare Iraq's future remains uncertain. Rebuilding schools, hospitals, roads, and other basic structures may take years. Many people hope that Iraqi entrepreneurs can help the country rebuild a free and prosperous society.

✓ **READING CHECK:** (*Human Systems*) What challenges face Iraqis?

 Homework Practice Online

Keyword: SK5 HP6

Section Review 3

Define and explain: embargo

Working with Sketch Maps On the map you created in Section 2, label Baghdad. Where would you expect most of Iraq's population to be concentrated? Why?

Reading for the Main Idea

1. (*Human Systems*) What are some different groups that have controlled Mesopotamia?

2. (*Human Systems*) What was Iraq's government like under Saddam Hussein?

Critical Thinking

3. **Finding the Main Idea** Why did several countries force Iraqi troops out of Kuwait?

4. **Analyzing Information** How have recent wars affected Iraq's economy?

Organizing What You Know

5. **Sequencing** Create a time line tracing the history of the area now known as Iraq. List events from the Arab conquest to 2003.

A.D. 600s ———————————————————— 2003

Read to Discover

1. What were some important events in Iran's history?
2. What are Iran's government and people like?
3. What problems does Afghanistan face today?

Vocabulary
shah
theocracy

Places
Tehran
Khyber Pass
Kabul

People
Shirin Ebadi

Reading Strategy

READING ORGANIZER Before you read, draw two large overlapping circles on a sheet of paper. As you read, write what you learn about Iran in one circle. Then write what you learn about Afghanistan in the other circle. Where the circles overlap, write the characteristics that the countries share.

Iran

Iran is a large country with a large population, rich history, and valuable natural resources. A revolution in 1979 made Islam the guiding force in Iran's government.

History The Persian Empire, established in the 500s B.C., was centered in what is now Iran. It was the greatest empire of its time and was an important center of learning. In the 300s B.C. Alexander the Great conquered the Persian Empire. In the A.D. 600s Arabs invaded the region and established Islam. Persian cultural and scientific contributions became elements of Islamic civilization. Later, different peoples ruled the region, including the Mongols and the Safavids.

Human-Environment Interaction In the dry climates of Iran and Afghanistan, some farmers use an ancient irrigation method. Runoff from mountains moves through tunnels, called *qanats* (kuh-NAHTS), to fields. The Taliban destroyed some *qanats* in Afganistan.

Qanat **Irrigation System**

Mountains

Water from mountains seeps into water table

Ventilation and access shafts

Water tunnel

Surface canal

Irrigated fields

BIOGRAPHY

Shirin Ebadi
(1947–)

Character Trait: Respect

Iranians hoping for more democratic reforms were encouraged in 2003 by Shirin Ebadi's receiving the Nobel Peace Prize. Ebadi is a lawyer, judge, and author. However, her work improving human rights in Iran has at times made her unpopular with the country's authorities. Ebadi's special interests include better conditions for women, children, and refugees.

How does Shirin Ebadi show respect towards others?

During New Year celebrations, Iranians grow or buy fresh grass to symbolize spring and life.

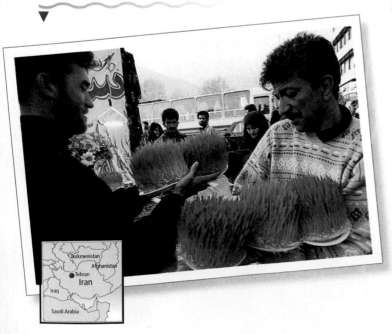

In 1921 an Iranian military officer took power and encouraged reform. He claimed the old Persian title of **shah**, or king. In 1941 the Shah's son took control. He was an ally of the United States and Britain and tried to modernize Iran. His programs were unpopular, however, and in 1979 he was overthrown.

Iran's new government set up an Islamic republic. Soon afterward, relations with the United States broke down. A mob of students attacked the U.S. Embassy in Iran's capital, Tehran, in November 1979. They took Americans hostage with the approval of Iran's government. More than 50 Americans were held by force for a year. The Iranian Revolution itself was soon followed by a long, destructive war with Iraq beginning in 1980.

Government and Economy Iran is a **theocracy**—a government ruled by religious leaders. The country has an elected president and legislature. An expert on Islamic law is the supreme leader, however.

Iran's government has supported many hard-line policies. For example, the country's government has called for the destruction of the state of Israel. Iran has also supported terrorist groups in other countries. However, in the 2000s some signs indicated that Iran was trying to make democratic reforms.

Iran has the fifth-largest oil reserves in the world. Oil is its main industry. Iran is a member of OPEC. Iran's other industries include construction, food processing, and the production of beautiful woven carpets. About one third of Iran's workforce is employed in agriculture.

People and Customs Iran has a population of about 68 million—one of the largest in Southwest Asia. It is also quite diverse. Ethnic Persians make up a slight majority. Other groups include ethnic Azerbaijanis, Kurds, Arabs, and Turkomans. Persian is the official language. Almost all Iranians speak Persian, although some speak it as a second language. The region's other languages include several Kurdish dialects, some Turkic languages, and Arabic.

The Shia branch of Islam is Iran's official religion. About 90 percent of Iranians are Shia. About 10 percent of Iran's residents are Sunni Muslim. The rest are Christian, Jewish, or practice other religions.

In addition to the Islamic holy days, Iranians celebrate Nauruz—the Persian New Year. They also recognize the anniversary of the Iranian Revolution on February 11. Iranian food features rice, bread, vegetables, fruits, and lamb. Strong tea is a popular drink among many Iranians.

✓ **READING CHECK:** (*Human Systems*) What are Iraq's government and people like?

Afghanistan

Afghanistan is a landlocked country of high mountains and fertile valleys. Merchants, warriors, and missionaries have long used the Khyber (KY-buhr) Pass to reach India. This narrow passage through the Hindu Kush lies between Afghanistan and Pakistan.

History and People In 1979 the Soviet Union sent troops into Afghanistan to help the communist government there in a civil war. This led to a long war between Soviet troops and Afghan rebels. The Soviets left in 1989, and an alliance of Afghan groups took power. Turmoil continued, and in the mid-1990s a radical Muslim group known as the Taliban arose. Its leaders took over most of the country, including the capital, Kabul. The Taliban ruled Afghanistan strictly. For example, they forced women to wear veils and to stop working outside the home.

In 2001 Taliban officials came into conflict with the United States. Investigation of terrorist attacks on September 11 on Washington, D.C., and New York City led to terrorist Osama bin Laden and his al Qaeda network, based in Afghanistan. U.S. and British forces then attacked Taliban and al Qaeda targets and toppled the Taliban government.

The long period of war has damaged Afghanistan's industry, trade, and transportation systems. Farming and herding are the most important economic activities now.

Afghans belong to many different ethnic groups. The most numerous are the Pashtun, Tajik, Hazara, and Uzbek. Almost all Afghans are Muslims, and about 84 percent are Sunni.

✓ **READING CHECK:** (*Human Systems*) What are some of the challenges Afghanistan faces today?

Iran and Afghanistan

COUNTRY	POPULATION/ GROWTH RATE	LIFE EXPECTANCY	LITERACY RATE	PER CAPITA GDP
Afghanistan	28,717,213 3.4%	47, male 46, female	36%	$700
Iran	68,278,826 1.1%	69, male 71, female	79%	$6,800
United States	290,342,554 0.9%	74, male 80, female	97%	$37,600

Source: Central Intelligence Agency, *The World Factbook 2003*

Interpreting the Chart How many times greater is the U.S. per capita GDP than Afghanistan's?

Homework Practice Online
Keyword: SK5 HP6

Section Review 4

Define or identify: Shirin Ebadi, shah, theocracy

Working with Sketch Maps On the map you created in Section 3, label Tehran, Khyber Pass, and Kabul. What physical features do Tehran and Kabul have in common?

Reading for the Main Idea

1. (*Places and Regions*) What ethnic and religious groups live in Iran?

2. (*Human Systems*) How have Afghanistan's recent wars affected the country?

Critical Thinking

3. Making Generalizations and Predictions What challenges might the Iranian government face in the future?

4. Drawing Inferences and Conclusions How might Afghanistan's political problems be affected by its rugged physical geography?

Organizing What You Know

5. Sequencing Copy the following graphic organizer. Use it to show the main events in Iran in recent decades.

Define and Identify

Identify each of the following:

1. exotic rivers
2. wadis
3. fossil water
4. Muslims
5. Muhammad
6. Sunni
7. Shia
8. Qur'an
9. OPEC
10. embargo
11. theocracy
12. Shirin Ebadi

Review the Main Ideas

13. What are the three landform regions that make up this part of Southwest Asia?
14. What is the climate in Southwest Asia like?
15. What is the most important resource of this region?
16. Which countries in this area have large reserves of oil?
17. Which small country has some of the largest natural gas reserves in the world?
18. What language is widely spoken in Iran?
19. Why were Western leaders concerned when Iraq invaded Kuwait?

20. What two groups in Iraq rebelled against Saddam Hussein's regime?
21. What ethnic group do most Iraqis belong to?
22. How have wars affected politics in this region?
23. What group ruled Afghanistan after the Soviets left the country?

Think Critically

24. **Drawing Inferences and Conclusions** Why might it be dangerous for these countries' economies to be almost entirely dependent on the sale of oil?
25. **Summarizing** Some of the countries of Southwest Asia are trying to increase crop production. What environmental factors might make this difficult?
26. **Drawing Inferences and Conclusions** How might Iran's recent history have been different if the 1979 revolution had not taken place?
27. **Finding the Main Idea** Why has the United States become involved in the politics of this region?
28. **Summarizing** What are the main goals to rebuilding Iraq?

Map Activity

29. On a separate sheet of paper, match the letters on the map with their correct labels.

Persian Gulf	Riyadh
Tigris River	Baghdad
Euphrates River	Tehran
Hindu Kush	Khyber Pass
Mecca	Kabul

Writing Activity

Imagine that you have been asked to write a description of travel conditions in one of the following countries: Afghanistan, Iran, Iraq, or Saudi Arabia. Use your textbook, the library, and the Internet to research your country. Then write a few paragraphs about its climate, attractions, and cultural events.

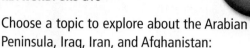

☑ internet connect

Internet Activity: go.hrw.com
KEYWORD: SK5 GT6

Choose a topic to explore about the Arabian Peninsula, Iraq, Iran, and Afghanistan:
- Visit Mesopotamia.
- Discover the importance of camels.
- See Arabian arts and crafts.

Social Studies Skills Practice

Interpreting Graphs

In the countries you learned about in this chapter, education for women is often limited. Study the following graph and answer the questions.

Literacy Rates

Percent

(Bar graph showing literacy rates by percent for Women and Men)

Afghanistan — Women ~20, Men ~50
Iraq — Women ~24, Men ~55
Iran — Women ~73, Men ~85
Kuwait — Women ~81, Men ~83
Saudi Arabia — Women ~70, Men ~83

■ Women ■ Men

Source: Central Intelligence Agency, *World Factbook 2003*

1. Which countries have the highest literacy rates for women?
2. What can you tell about the education of women in Afghanistan and Iraq?
3. Which country has nearly the same number of literate men and women?

Analyzing Primary Sources

In this chapter, you have learned that Iran is a theocracy. However, Iran's president Mohammad Khatami hopes to move the country towards democracy. Read the following quote from Khatami and answer the questions.

"Our constitution explicitly states that absolute power belongs to God and it is God that has made man the ruler of his fate. Nothing and no one can take this right away from humans. This is a view of Islam which results in a system based on the rule of the people, a free system, a democratic one, and a system based on the rule of laws which themselves have been accepted and approved by the people.

We believe our country has suffered . . . from dependence on foreigners. Therefore, the kind of Islam that we offer is the kind . . . that leads us to independence."

Source: *New York Times*, November 10, 2001

1. According to Iran's constitution, who has absolute power?
2. What does Khatami claim Iran has suffered from?
3. According to Khatami, what will lead Iran towards independence?

CHAPTER 7

Central Asia

Leila is a student from Central Asia, a region of grasslands, scorching deserts, and high mountains.

Salam! (Hi!)
Men Türkmenistanda
ýaşaýaryn.

Salam! (Hi!)—we also say "privyet," which is "hi" in Russian. My name is Leila, and I am 16. I live in Turkmenabat, the "city of Turkmen," with my parents, my three older brothers, and my younger sister. My oldest brother's wife also lives with us. My father is a professor of British studies at Turkmenabat University and my mother teaches cooking and sewing at the high school. Our house is on a canal with lots of trees. It is surrounded by a high wall, and has a balcony and an open roof where we can go if we want to be outdoors in privacy.

I am in the ninth and last year at School Number Five. The school has about 2,000 students in nine grades from kindergarten to high school. We go to school six days a week and study 18 different subjects. There is no choice of courses. I could have gone to a Russian school, but my parents chose a Turkmen one. At school, we line up by class and do 5 minutes of exercises before classes start. Each class has 25 boys and girls who stay together from kindergarten through high school. We are like a second family.

Translation: Hello, I live in Turkmenistan.

Section 1 Physical Geography

Read to Discover

1. What are the main landforms and climates of Central Asia?
2. What resources are important to Central Asia?

Vocabulary

landlocked
oasis

Places

Pamirs
Tian Shan
Aral Sea
Kara-Kum

Kyzyl Kum
Syr Dar'ya
Amu Dar'ya
Fergana Valley

Reading Strategy

FOLDNOTES: TWO-PANEL FLIP CHART Create the FoldNote titled **Two-Panel Flip Chart** described in the Appendix. Label one panel Landforms and Climates. Label the other panel Resources. As you read this section, write what you learn beneath each panel.

Central Asia: Physical-Political

Size comparison of Central Asia to the contiguous United States

Ismail Semani Peak
24,590 ft. (7495 m)

ELEVATION

	FEET		METERS
⊛ National capitals	13,120		4,000
	6,560		2,000
• Other cities	1,640		500
	656		200
	(Sea level) 0		0 (Sea level)
	Below sea level		Below sea level

SCALE

0 — 250 — 500 Miles

0 — 250 — 500 Kilometers

Projection: Two-Point Equidistant

Mountain climbers make camp before attempting to scale a peak in the Pamirs.

Our Amazing Planet

With temperatures above 122°F (50°C), it is not surprising that the creatures that live in the Kara-Kum are a tough group. Over a thousand species live there, including cobras, scorpions, tarantulas, and monitor lizards. These lizards can grow to more than 5 feet (1.5 m) long.

Lynxes can still be found in the mountains of Central Asia.

Interpreting the Visual Record How are these lynxes well suited to the environment in which they live?

Landforms and Climate

This huge, **landlocked** region is to the east of the Caspian Sea. Landlocked means the region does not border an ocean. The region lies north of the Pamirs (puh-MIRZ) and Tian Shan (TYEN SHAHN) mountain ranges.

Diverse Landforms As the name suggests, Central Asia lies in the middle of the largest continent. Plains and low plateaus cover much of this area. Around the Caspian Sea the land is as low as 95 feet (29 m) below sea level. However, the region includes high mountain ranges along the borders with China and Afghanistan.

Arid Lands Central Asia is a region of mainly steppe, desert, and highland climates. Summers are hot, with a short growing season. Winters are cold. Rainfall is sparse. However, north of the Aral (AR-uhl) Sea rainfall is heavy enough for steppe vegetation. Here farmers can grow crops using rain, rather than irrigation, as their water source. South and east of the Aral Sea lie two deserts. One is the Kara-Kum (kahr-uh-KOOM) in Turkmenistan. The other is the Kyzyl Kum (ki-ZIL KOOM) in Uzbekistan and Kazakhstan. Both deserts contain several **oasis** settlements where a spring or well provides water.

✔ **READING CHECK:** (*Places and Regions*) What are the landforms and climates of Central Asia?

Resources

The main water sources in southern Central Asia are the Syr Dar'ya (sir duhr-YAH) and Amu Dar'ya (uh-MOO duhr-YAH) rivers. These rivers flow down from the Pamirs and then across dry plains. Farmers have used them for irrigation for thousands of years. When it first flows down from the mountains, the Syr Dar'ya passes through the

Fergana Valley. This large valley is divided among Uzbekistan, Kyrgyzstan, and Tajikistan. As the river flows toward the Aral Sea, irrigated fields line its banks.

During the Soviet period, the region's population grew rapidly. Also, the Soviets encouraged farmers to grow cotton. This crop grows well in Central Asia's sunny climate. However, growing cotton uses a lot of water. Increased use of water has caused the Aral Sea to shrink.

A Dying Sea Today, almost no water from the Syr Dar'ya or Amu Dar'ya reaches the Aral Sea. The rivers' waters are used up by human activity. The effect on the Aral Sea has been devastating. It has lost more than 75 percent of its water since 1960. By 2003 it had shrunk to two smaller seas divided by a desert. Towns that were once fishing ports are now dozens of miles from the shore. Winds sweep the dry seafloor, blowing dust, salt, and pesticides hundreds of miles.

Mineral Resources The Central Asian countries' best economic opportunity is in their fossil fuels. Uzbekistan, Kazakhstan, and Turkmenistan all have huge oil and natural gas reserves. However, transporting the oil and gas to other countries is a problem. Economic and political turmoil in some surrounding countries has made it difficult to build pipelines.

Several Central Asian countries are also rich in other minerals. They have deposits of gold, copper, uranium, zinc, and lead. Kazakhstan has vast amounts of coal. Rivers in Kyrgyzstan and Tajikistan could be used to create hydroelectric power.

✓ **READING CHECK:** (*Environment and Society*) How has human activity affected the Aral Sea?

This boat sits rusting on what was once part of the Aral Sea. The sea's once thriving fishing industry has been destroyed.

▼

Section Review 1

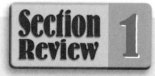

Define and explain: landlocked, oasis

Working with Sketch Maps On a map of Central Asia that you draw or that your teacher provides, label the following: Pamirs, Tian Shan, Aral Sea, Kara-Kum, Kyzyl Kum, Syr Dar'ya, Amu Dar'ya, and Fergana Valley.

Reading for the Main Idea

1. (*Environment and Society*) What has caused the drying up of the Aral Sea?

2. (*Places and Regions*) What mineral resources does Central Asia have?

Homework Practice Online
Keyword: SK5 HP7

Critical Thinking

3. Analyzing Information Why did the Soviets encourage Central Asian farmers to grow cotton?

4. Finding the Main Idea What factors make it hard for the Central Asian countries to export oil and gas?

Organizing What You Know

5. Sequencing Copy the following graphic organizer. Use it to describe the courses of the Syr Dar'ya and Amu Dar'ya, including human activities that use water.

| Melting snows in the Pamirs | ⇨ | | ⇨ | Aral Sea |

Read to Discover

1. How did trade and invasions affect the history of Central Asia?

2. What are political and economic conditions like in Central Asia today?

Vocabulary

nomads
caravans

Reading Strategy

READING ORGANIZER Before you read, draw three large boxes on a sheet of paper. Label the first box Trade. Label the second box Invasions and the Soviet Era. Finally, label the third box Today. As you read this section, write what you learn about the history and culture of Central Asia in the boxes.

Bukhara, in Uzbekistan, was once a powerful and wealthy trading center of Central Asia.

Interpreting the Visual Record _Place_
What architectural features can you see that distinguish Bukhara as an Islamic city?

History

For centuries, Central Asians have made a living by raising horses, cattle, sheep, and goats. Many of these herders lived as **nomads**, people who often move from place to place. Other people became farmers around rivers and oases.

Trade At one time, the best land route between China and the eastern Mediterranean ran through Central Asia. Merchants traveled in large groups, called **caravans**, for protection. The goods they carried included silk and spices. As a result, this route came to be called the Silk Road. Cities along the road became centers of wealth and culture.

Central Asia's situation changed after Europeans discovered they could sail to East Asia through the Indian Ocean. As a result, trade through Central Asia declined. The region became isolated and poor.

Silk processing in modern Uzbekistan

The *Silk Road*

The Silk Road stretched 5,000 miles (8,000 km) across Central Asia from China to the Mediterranean Sea. Along this route passed merchants, armies, and diplomats. These people forged links between East and West.

The facts of the Silk Road are still wrapped in mystery. Chinese trade and military expeditions probably began moving into Central Asia in the 100s B.C. Chinese trade goods soon were making their way to eastern Mediterranean ports.

Over the next several centuries, trade in silk, spices, jewels, and other luxury goods increased. Great caravans of camels and oxcarts traveled the Silk Road in both directions. They crossed the harsh deserts and mountains of Central Asia. Cities like Samarqand and Bukhara grew rich from the trade. In the process, ideas and technology also moved between Europe and Asia.

Travel along the Silk Road was hazardous. Bandits often robbed the caravans. Some travelers lost their way in the desert and died. In addition, religious and political turmoil occasionally disrupted travel.

Understanding What You Read
1. What was the Silk Road?
2. Why was the Silk Road important?

Invasions and the Soviet Era About A.D. 500, Turkic-speaking nomads from northern Asia spread through Central Asia. In the 700s Arab armies took over much of the region, bringing Islam. In the 1200s the armies of Mongol leaders conquered Central Asia. Later, another Turkic people, the Uzbeks, took over parts of the region. In the 1800s the Russian Empire conquered Central Asia.

After the Russian Revolution, the Soviet government set up five republics in Central Asia. The Soviets encouraged ethnic Russians to move to this area and made the nomads settle on collective ranches or farms. Religion was discouraged. Russian became the language of government and business. The government set up schools and hospitals. Women were allowed to work outside the home.

✔ **READING CHECK:** (*Human Systems*) What type of government system did the five republics set up by the Soviet Union have?

Central Asia Today

The five republics became independent countries when the Soviet Union broke up in 1991. All have strong economic ties to Russia. Ethnic Russians still live in every country in the region. However, all five countries are switching from the Cyrillic alphabet to the Latin alphabet. The Cyrillic alphabet had been imposed on them by the Soviet Union. The Latin alphabet is used in most Western European languages, including English, and in Turkey.

Government All of these new countries have declared themselves to be democracies. However, they are not very free or democratic. Each is ruled by a strong central government that limits opposition and criticism.

Economy Some of the Central Asian countries have oil and gas reserves that may someday make them rich. For now, though, all are suffering economic hardship. Causes of the hardships include outdated equipment, lack of funds, and poor transportation links.

Farming is important in the Central Asian economies. Crops include cotton, wheat, barley, fruits, vegetables, almonds, tobacco, and rice. Central Asians raise cattle, sheep, horses, goats, and camels. They also raise silkworms to make silk thread.

Industry in Central Asia includes food processing, wool textiles, mining, and oil drilling. Oil-rich Turkmenistan and Kazakhstan also process oil into other products. Kazakhstan and Uzbekistan make heavy equipment such as tractors.

READING CHECK: (*Human Systems*) How do political freedoms in the region compare to those of the United States?

A Kyrgyz teacher conducts class.

Interpreting the Visual Record How is this class similar to yours?

go.hrw.com

Homework Practice Online

Keyword: SK5 HP7

Section Review 2

Define and explain: nomads, caravans

Working with Sketch Maps On the map you created in Section 1, draw and label the five Central Asian countries.

Reading for the Main Idea

1. (*Environment and Society*) How have the people of Central Asia made a living over the centuries?

2. (*Human Systems*) What are four groups that invaded Central Asia?

3. (*Human Systems*) How did Soviet rule change Central Asia?

Critical Thinking

4. **Drawing Inferences and Conclusions** What does the switch to the Latin alphabet suggest about the Central Asian countries?

Organizing What You Know

5. **Categorizing** Copy the following graphic organizer. Use it to categorize economic activities in Central Asia. Place the following items in the chart: making cloth, growing crops, mining metals, making food products, raising livestock, making chemicals from oil, drilling for oil, and manufacturing tractors.

Primary industries	Secondary industries

The Countries of Central Asia

Read to Discover

1. What are some important aspects of culture in Kazakhstan?
2. How does Kyrgyz culture reflect nomadic traditions?
3. Why have politics in Tajikistan in recent years been marked by violence?
4. What are two important art forms in Turkmenistan?
5. How is Uzbekistan's population significant?

Vocabulary

yurt
mosques

Places

Tashkent
Samarqand

Reading Strategy

READING ORGANIZER   Draw a circle in the center of a sheet of paper. Label the circle Central Asian Countries. Draw five lines from the circle. Then, draw a small circle at the end of each line. Label the five circles Kazakhstan, Kyrgyzstan, Tajikistan, Turkmenistan, and Uzbekistan. As you read this section, write what you learn about each country next to each circle.

Kazakhstan

Of the Central Asian nations, Kazakhstan was the first to be conquered by Russia. Russian influence remains strong there. About one third of Kazakhstan's people are ethnic Russians. Kazakh and Russian are both official languages. Many ethnic Kazakhs grow up speaking Russian at home and have to learn Kazakh in school.

Kazakhstanis celebrate the New Year twice—on January 1 and again on Nauruz, the start of the Persian calendar's year. Nauruz falls on the spring equinox.

Food in Central Asia combines influences from Southwest Asia and China. Rice, yogurt, and grilled meat are common ingredients. One Kazakh specialty is smoked horsemeat sausage with cold noodles.

✓ **READING CHECK:** (*Human Systems*) How has Kazakhstan been influenced by Russia?

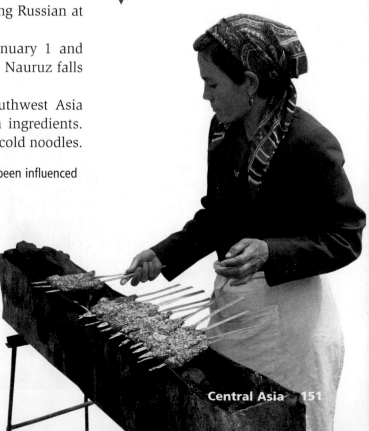

A woman in Uzbekistan grills meat on skewers.

▼

Kyrgyzstan

Kyrgyzstan has many mountains, and the people live mostly in valleys. People in the southern part of the country generally share cultural ties with Uzbekistan. People in northern areas are more linked to nomadic cultures and to Kazakhstan.

The word *kyrgyz* means "forty clans." Clan membership is still important in Krygyz social, political, and economic life. Many Kyrgyz men wear black and white felt hats that show their clan status.

Nomadic traditions are still important to many Kyrgyz. The **yurt** is a movable round house of wool felt mats over a wood frame. Today the yurt is a symbol of the nomadic heritage. Even people who live in cities may put up yurts for weddings and funerals.

✔ **READING CHECK:** (*Human Systems*) In what ways do the Kyrgyz continue traditions of their past?

Tajikistan

In the mid-1990s Tajikistan experienced a civil war. The Soviet-style government fought against a mixed group of reformers, some of whom demanded democracy. Others called for government by Islamic law. A peace agreement was signed in 1996, but tensions remain high.

The other major Central Asian languages are related to Turkish. However, the Tajik language is related to Persian. Tajiks consider the great literature written in Persian to be part of their cultural heritage.

✔ **READING CHECK:** (*Human Systems*) What has happened in politics in recent years in Tajikistan?

Turkmenistan

The major first language of Turkmenistan is Turkmen. In 1993 Turkmenistan adopted English, rather than Russian, as its second official language. However, some schools teach in Russian, Uzbek, or Kazakh.

Islam has experienced a revival in Central Asia since the breakup of the Soviet Union. Many new **mosques**, or Islamic houses of worship, are being built and old ones are being restored. Donations from other Islamic countries, such as Saudi Arabia and Iran, have helped

Turkoman women display carpets. Central Asian carpets are famous for their imaginative patterns, bright colors, and expert artistry.

Interpreting the Visual Record
(*Movement*) Why were carpets suited to the nomadic way of life?

these efforts. The government of Turkmenistan supports this revival and has ordered schools to teach Islamic principles. However, like the other states in the region, Turkmenistan's government views Islam with some caution. It does not want Islam to become a political movement.

Historically, the nomadic life required that all possessions be portable. Decorative carpets were the essential furniture of a nomad's home. They are still perhaps the most famous artistic craft of Turkmenistan. Like others in Central Asia, the people of Turkmenistan also have an ancient tradition of poetry.

✓ **READING CHECK:** (*Human Systems*) What are two forms of art in Turkmenistan, and how do they reflect its cultural traditions?

Central Asia				
COUNTRY	POPULATION/ GROWTH RATE	LIFE EXPECTANCY	LITERACY RATE	PER CAPITA GDP
Kazakhstan	16,763,795 .02%	58, male 69, female	98%	$7,200
Kyrgyzstan	4,892,808 1.5%	59, male 68, female	97%	$2,900
Tajikistan	6,863,752 2.1%	61, male 67, female	99%	$1,300
Turkmenistan	4,775,544 1.8%	57, male 65, female	98%	$6,700
Uzbekistan	25,981,647 1.6%	60, male 68, female	99%	$2,600
United States	290,342,554 0.9%	74, male 80, female	97%	$37,600

Source: Central Intelligence Agency, *The World Factbook 2003*

Interpreting the Chart Which country has the lowest per capita GDP in the region?

Uzbekistan

Uzbekistan has the largest population of the Central Asian countries—about 24 million people. Uzbek is the official language. People are required to study Uzbek to be eligible for citizenship.

Tashkent and Samarqand are ancient Silk Road cities in Uzbekistan. They are famous for their mosques and Islamic monuments. Uzbeks are also known for their art of embroidering fabric with gold.

✓ **READING CHECK:** (*Human Systems*) What is one of an Uzbekistan citizen's responsibilities?

Define and explain: yurt, mosques

Working with Sketch Maps On the map you created in Section 2, label Tashkent and Samarqand.

Reading for the Main Idea

1. (*Places and Regions*) In which Central Asian nation is the influence of Russia strongest? Why is this true?

2. (*Human Systems*) What were the two sides in Tajikistan's civil war fighting for?

3. (*Human Systems*) What is the role of Islam in the region today?

Critical Thinking

4. **Finding the Main Idea** What are two customs or artistic crafts of modern Central Asia that are connected to the nomadic lifestyle?

Organizing What You Know

5. **Contrasting** Copy the following graphic organizer. Use it to describe the conditions in Central Asia during the Soviet era and today.

	Soviet era	Today
Type of government		
Official language		
Alphabet		
Government attitude toward Islam		

CASE STUDY

KAZAKHS: PASTORAL NOMADS OF CENTRAL ASIA

Nomads are people who move around from place to place during the year. Nomads usually move when the seasons change so that they will have enough food to eat. Herding, hunting, gathering, and fishing are all ways that different nomadic groups get their food.

Nomads that herd animals are called pastoral nomads. Their way of life depends on the seasonal movement of their herds. Pastoral nomads may herd cattle, horses, sheep, goats, yaks, reindeer, camels, or other animals. Instead of keeping their animals inside fenced pastures, pastoral nomads let them graze on open fields. However, they must make sure the animals do not overgraze and damage the pastureland. To do this, they keep their animals moving throughout the year. Some pastoral nomads live in steppe or desert environments. These nomads often have to move their animals very long distances between winter and summer pastures.

The Kazakhs of Central Asia are an example of a pastoral nomadic group. They have herded horses, sheep, goats, and cattle for hundreds of years. Because they move so much, the Kazakhs do not have permanent homes. They bring their homes with them when they travel to new places.

A Kazakh nomad keeps a watchful eye over a herd of horses.

▼

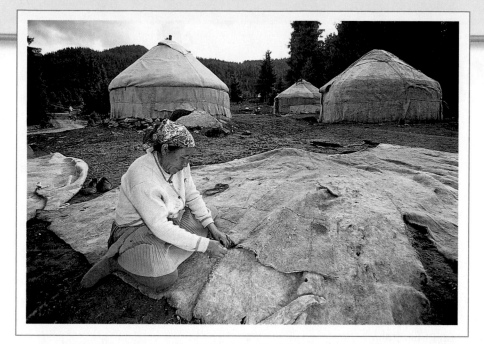

The Kazakhs live in tent-like structures called yurts. Yurts are circular structures made of bent poles covered with thick felt. Yurts can be easily taken apart and moved. They are perfect homes for the Kazakhs' nomadic lifestyle.

During the year, a Kazakh family may move its herds of sheep, horses, and cattle as far as 500 miles (805 km). For one Kazakh family, each year is divided into four different parts. The family spends the first part of the year in winter grazing areas. Then, in early spring, they move to areas with fresh grass shoots. When these spring grasses are gone, the family moves their animals to summer pastures. In the fall, the animals are kept for six weeks in autumn pastures. Finally, the herds are taken back to their winter pastures. Each year, the cycle is repeated.

The nomadic lifestyle of the Kazakhs has changed, however. In the early 1800s people from Russia and eastern Europe began to move into the region. These people were farmers. They started planting crops in areas that the Kazakhs used for pasture. This made it more difficult for the Kazakhs to move their animals during the year. Later, when Kazakhstan was part of the Soviet Union, government officials encouraged the Kazakhs to settle in villages and cities. Many Kazakhs still move their animals during the year. However, tending crops has also become an important way to get food.

Seasonal Movement of a Kazakh Family

During the year, a Kazakh family may move its herds to several different pasture areas as the seasons change.

Interpreting the Graph Why do you think animals are moved to higher elevations during the summer and to lower elevations during the winter?

Understanding What You Read

1. Why do some pastoral nomads have to travel such great distances?

2. How has the nomadic lifestyle of the Kazakhs changed during the last 100 years?

CHAPTER 7 Review and Practice

Define and Identify

Identify each of the following:

1. landlocked
2. oasis
3. nomads
4. caravans
5. yurt
6. mosques

Review the Main Ideas

7. What types of climates are most common in Central Asia?
8. What problems have resulted from the shrinking of the Aral Sea?
9. What was the Silk Road?
10. Why did trade through Central Asia decline?
11. How did Soviet rule change Central Asians' way of life?
12. What are the Central Asian governments like?
13. What are some of Central Asia's main crops and products?
14. Which of the Central Asian countries still has a strong Russian presence?
15. What happened in the mid-1990s in Tajikistan?

16. How has the government of Turkmenistan responded to the revival of Islam?
17. What are some of the languages spoken in Central Asia?
18. Which of the region's countries has the largest population?

Think Critically

19. **Summarizing** How have politics influenced language and the alphabet used in Central Asia?
20. **Finding the Main Idea** How do the artistic crafts of Central Asia reflect the nomadic lifestyle?
21. **Analyzing Information** Why did the Soviets encourage cotton farming in the region? What were the environmental consequences?
22. **Finding the Main Idea** What obstacles are making it hard for the Central Asian countries to export their oil?
23. **Summarizing** What are some reasons the Central Asian countries have experienced slow economic growth since independence? How are they trying to improve the situation?

Map Activity

24. On a separate sheet of paper, match the letters on the map with their correct labels.

   Caspian Sea
   Pamirs
   Tian Shan
   Aral Sea
   Kara-Kum
   Kyzyl Kum
   Tashkent
   Samarqand

Writing Activity

Imagine that you are a caravan trader traveling along the Silk Road during the 1200s. Write a journal entry describing your journey from the Mediterranean Sea through Central Asia. You may want to describe the landscape, other people that you meet, or dangers that you face. Be sure to use standard grammar, spelling, sentence structure, and punctuation.

⚡ internet connect

Internet Activity: go.hrw.com
KEYWORD: SK5 GT7

Choose a topic to explore about Central Asia:
• Study the climate of Central Asia.
• Travel along the historic Silk Road.
• Learn about nomads and caravans.

Social Studies Skills Practice

Interpreting Charts

Study the following chart and then answer the questions.

Rural and Urban Population in Central Asia, 1989–1992

Country	Urban Population	Rural Population
Kazakhstan	9,610,000	7,120,000
Kyrgyzstan	1,680,000	2,770,000
Tajikistan	1,660,000	3,440,000
Turkmenistan	1,590,000	1,930,000
Uzbekistan	8,040,000	11,770,000

Source: Federal Research Division, Library of Congress

1. Which country had the largest urban population? The smallest?
2. Which country had the largest rural population? The smallest?
3. Which country's urban population was larger than its rural population?
4. Which country had urban and rural populations that were roughly the same size?

Analyzing Primary Sources

Read the following quote from Mrs. B. Ospanova, a citizen of Kazakhstan. Then answer the questions.

"I am glad that the republic is independent. My husband and I feel more liberated. Earlier we lived from salary to salary, the flat [apartment] was small, we stood in turn for a car during 20 years. But another times came and my husband organized his own small-scale business. We bought a big flat, a car and gave education to our children. Is it bad? Work and you will have everything. I, for example, have no nostalgia for Soviet times."

1. What problems with the Soviet-era economy does Mrs. Ospanova discuss?
2. What new business opportunity became available after independence?
3. How has life changed for the Ospanova family since independence?
4. What does Mrs. Ospanova identify as the key to success in Kazakhstan?

FOCUS ON REGIONS

Differences and Connections

In this textbook the countries of Africa are grouped together. This has been done to emphasize the region's connections. Yet any region as large as Africa has important differences from place to place. East Africa is different from West Africa, and West Africa is different from North Africa. This is also true of other large regions. In South America, for example, Brazil is different from Argentina in many important ways.

North Africa and Southwest Asia One subregion of Africa that geographers often include in another region is North Africa. These geographers see more connections between North Africa and Southwest Asia than between North Africa and the rest of the continent. For example, in both areas Arabic is the main language. The major religion is Islam. Political issues also tie North Africa to its eastern neighbors, as does physical geography. The countries of North Africa and Southwest

The Muhammad Ali Mosque is one of many beautiful places of worship for Muslims in Cairo, Egypt. Although various religions, including Judaism and Christianity, are practiced in North Africa and Southwest Asia, most people in the two regions are Muslim.

Asia are part of a vast desert region. These countries face common issues such as water conservation and water management.

The African Continent There are also many reasons for placing North Africa in a region with the rest of Africa. People in Africa share some important historical, cultural, and economic ties. For example, ancient Egyptians had close contact with other peoples in Africa. In turn, cultures south of the Sahara contributed to the development of Egypt's great Nile Valley civilizations. Farther west, Mediterranean peoples have long traded with West African kingdoms south of the Sahara. Such contact helped spread

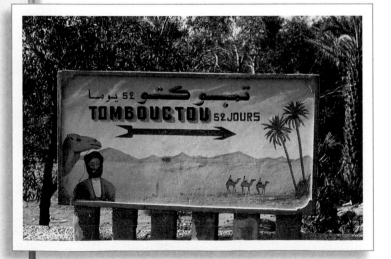

This sign in Morocco is in both Arabic and French. Arabic is spoken throughout North Africa and many parts of Southwest Asia.

Regional Links

Language, religion, and climate are some of the ties between North Africa and Southwest Asia. Arabic speakers, Muslims, and desert climates are dominant throughout much of the two regions and in parts of the surrounding transition zones.

Islam among the peoples of North Africa and the rest of the continent. Today, there are mosques as far south as Nigeria and Tanzania.

North Africa also has political connections to the rest of Africa. Many African countries face similar political and economic challenges. In part, these issues arise from their shared colonial history. To resolve some of these issues, the countries of North Africa are working with other African countries. They have formed associations such as the Organization of African Unity.

Transition Zones There are many differences and connections between North Africa and the rest of the continent. Perhaps they are most evident in a band of countries that lie just south of the Sahara. These countries stretch from Mauritania in the west to Ethiopia and Sudan in the east. They form a transition zone. In other words, they resemble both North Africa and Africa south of the

Sahara. In Chad and Sudan, for example, strong political and cultural differences separate north and south. The northern regions of these countries are tied closely to North Africa. The southern regions of these countries are tied closely to African countries to the south.

North Africa and the countries in the transition zone have important connections to two major world regions. Which region they are placed in depends on the geographer's point of view. Understanding the differences among countries and their connections to other areas of the world is important. It is more important than deciding where on a map a region begins or ends.

Understanding What You Read

1. What ties are there between North Africa and Southwest Asia?

2. What ties are there between North Africa and the rest of the African continent?

Building Skills for Life: Interpreting the Past

Both people and places are a product of the past. Therefore, understanding the geography of past times is important. It gives us a more complete understanding of the world today.

History and geography can hardly be separated. All historical events have to happen somewhere. These events are affected by local geography. For example, wheat and barley were domesticated in an area of Southwest Asia called the Fertile Crescent. This region received enough rainfall for these crops to grow.

Geographers who specialize in studying the past are called historical geographers. Historical geographers are interested in where things used to be and how they developed. They also try to understand how people's beliefs and values influenced historical events. In other words, why did people do what they did?

All geographers must be skilled at interpreting the past. Cultural geographers might study how old buildings and houses reflect earlier times. Physical geographers may need to reconstruct past landscapes. For example,

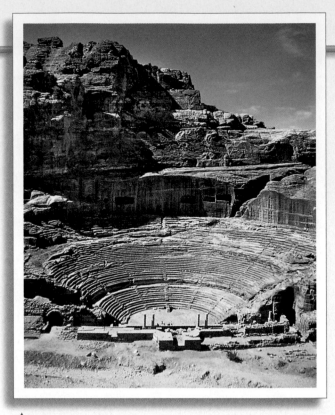

▲
Ancient ruins in Petra, Jordan, can provide clues to the region's past.

many rivers have changed their course. Understanding where a river used to flow could help explain its present course.

In your study of geography, think about how a place's history has shaped the way it is today. Look for clues that can tell you about its past. Ask yourself how people may have thought about a place in earlier times. No matter where you are, the evidence of the past is all around!

PRACTICING THE SKILL

1. Look at some of the buildings in your community. How old do you think they are? Do some look older than others? Can you describe how building styles in your community have changed over time? Why do you think styles have changed?

2. Analyze an important historical event that occurred in your state. What happened? Where did it happen? How was the event influenced by local geography?

3. Interpret the settlement history of your state or community. When was it settled? What attracted people to it? How do you think they felt about the place at the time?

HANDS on GEOGRAPHY

One way to interpret the past is by studying old travel accounts. They often have detailed information about the people, places, and daily life of past times.

One famous travel account describes the journeys of Ibn Battuta. Ibn Battuta was one of the greatest travelers in history. During the mid-1300s he traveled about 75,000 miles (120,700 km) throughout parts of Asia and Africa. Near the end of his travels, he gave a long account of the many places he visited. This account is a valuable historical document today.

The following passage is taken from Ibn Battuta's travel account. In this passage, Ibn Battuta is visiting the Sultan of Birgi, a town in what is now western Turkey. Read the passage, and then answer the Lab Report questions.

> **"** In the course of this audience the sultan asked me this question: "Have you ever seen a stone that fell from the sky?" I replied, "I have never seen one, nor ever heard tell of one." "Well," he said, "a stone did fall from the sky outside this town of ours," and then called some men and told them to bring the stone. They brought in a great black stone, very hard and with a glitter in it—I reckoned its weight to amount to a hundredweight. The sultan ordered the stonebreakers to be summoned, and four of them came and on his command to strike it they beat upon it as one man four times with iron hammers, but made no impression on it. I was astonished at this phenomenon, and he ordered it to be taken back to its place. **"**

▲ This painting shows Ibn Battuta during his travels in the mid-1300s.

Lab Report

1. What did the "stone that fell from the sky" look like? What do you think it was?

2. Why do you think Ibn Battuta was "astonished" by what he saw?

3. What can this story tell us about the historical geography of this region?

UNIT 3

Africa

Holding back the desert in Morocco

Cape Town, South Africa

A Physician in Sierra Leone

Dr. James Li went to Africa fresh out of medical school to work as a general practice physician. Here he describes what it was like to work at a hospital in Sierra Leone. **WHAT DO YOU THINK?** *What might Dr. Li's patients think about health care in the United States?*

Malaria, tuberculosis, and leprosy were widespread in our hospital population. We often saw patients who had walked over 100 miles for treatment. None of the patients in our area had access to clean water. Phone lines installed by the British had been cut down and the copper wires melted to make cooking pots. Our hospital was in the remote jungle, about six hours by dirt road from the nearest major city. It had 140 beds. In the clinic, we saw several hundred other patients each day. Food for the staff and patients was grown on the hospital grounds.

I came to love the people who were our patients, particularly the very young and the very old. In the midst of shortages, I met people who lived happily and suffered the tragedies of utter poverty with a dignity that would have failed me. These reflections fill me with a strange combination of awe, sadness, humility, and excitement.

Hospital in Butare, Rwanda

Masai dancers, Kenya

Understanding Primary Sources

1. What were conditions like at Dr. Li's hospital?

2. How does Dr. Li describe the culture of Sierra Leone?

Giraffe

Africa

Elevation Profile

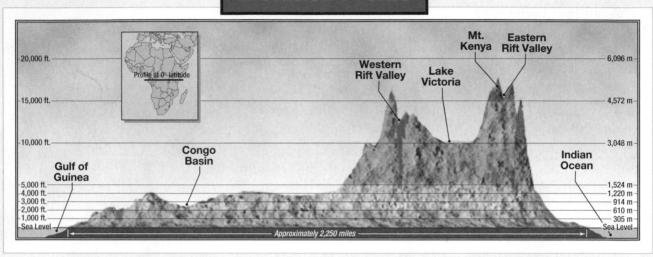

Profile at 0° latitude

20,000 ft. — 6,096 m
15,000 ft. — 4,572 m
10,000 ft. — 3,048 m
5,000 ft. — 1,524 m
4,000 ft. — 1,220 m
3,000 ft. — 914 m
2,000 ft. — 610 m
1,000 ft. — 305 m
Sea Level — Sea Level

Mt. Kenya
Eastern Rift Valley
Western Rift Valley
Lake Victoria
Congo Basin
Gulf of Guinea
Indian Ocean

Approximately 2,250 miles

The United States and Africa:
Comparing Sizes

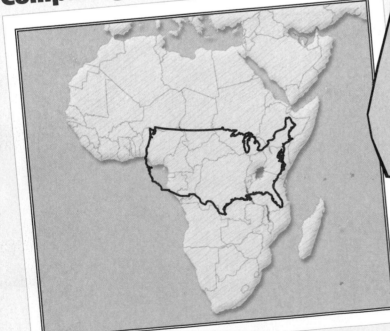

GEOSTATS:

World's longest river: Nile River—4,160 miles (6,693 km)

World's largest hot desert: Sahara—about 3,500,000 sq. mi. (9,065,000 sq km)

World's highest recorded temperature: 136°F (58°C) in Al Azizyah, Libya on September 13, 1992

ELEVATION

FEET	METERS
13,120	4,000
6,560	2,000
1,640	500
656	200
(Sea level) 0	0 (Sea level)
Below sea level	Below sea level

SCALE

Projection: Azimuthal Equal Area

1. (Region) Which region of Africa has the highest mountains? Which country appears to have the largest number of high mountains?

2. (Place) Which countries have areas that lie below sea level? Where is the highest point in Africa?

Critical Thinking

3. (Region) Which North African mountains might create a rain-shadow effect?

4. (Region) Compare this map to the **climate map** of the region. Which areas might have tropical rain forests?

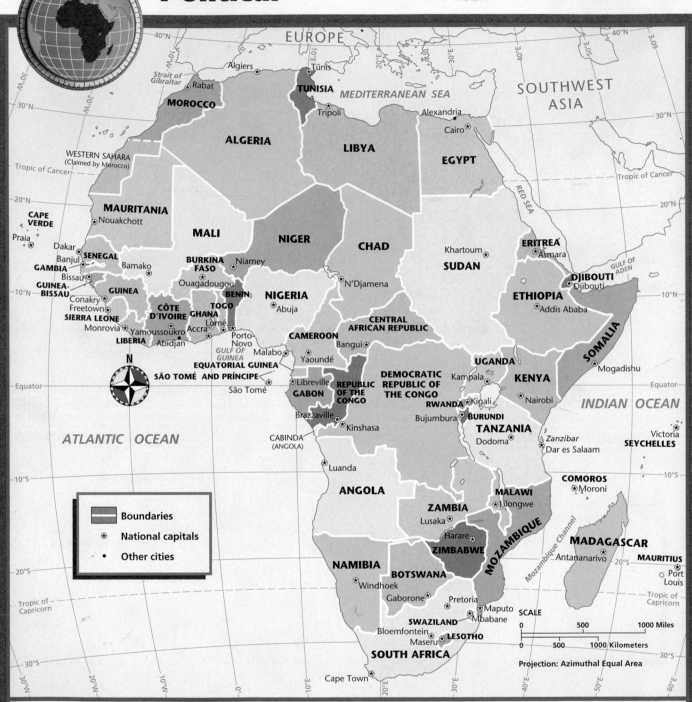

EUROPE

SOUTHWEST ASIA

MEDITERRANEAN SEA

Strait of Gibraltar

Algiers ⊛
Rabat •
Túnis ⊛
Tripoli •
Alexandria •
Cairo ⊛

MOROCCO

TUNISIA

ALGERIA

LIBYA

EGYPT

WESTERN SAHARA (Claimed by Morocco)

Tropic of Cancer

MAURITANIA
⊛ Nouakchott

CAPE VERDE
⊛ Praia

Dakar ⊛
Banjul ⊛
SENEGAL
GAMBIA
Bissau ⊛
GUINEA-BISSAU
Conakry ⊛
Freetown ⊛
SIERRA LEONE
Monrovia ⊛
LIBERIA
Abidjan •

MALI
Bamako •

BURKINA FASO
Ouagadougou ⊛

Niamey ⊛
NIGER

CHAD
N'Djamena ⊛

SUDAN
Khartoum ⊛

ERITREA
Asmara ⊛

DJIBOUTI
Djibouti ⊛

GULF OF ADEN

ETHIOPIA
Addis Ababa •

GUINEA

CÔTE D'IVOIRE
Yamoussoukro ⊛
GHANA
Accra ⊛
TOGO
Lomé ⊛
BENIN
Porto-Novo ⊛

NIGERIA
Abuja ⊛

CAMEROON
Yaoundé ⊛

CENTRAL AFRICAN REPUBLIC
Bangui ⊛

SOMALIA
Mogadishu •

UGANDA
Kampala ⊛
KENYA
Nairobi ⊛

GULF OF GUINEA
Malabo ⊛

EQUATORIAL GUINEA
SÃO TOMÉ AND PRÍNCIPE
São Tomé ⊛

Libreville ⊛
GABON

REPUBLIC OF THE CONGO
Brazzaville ⊛

DEMOCRATIC REPUBLIC OF THE CONGO
Kinshasa ⊛

RWANDA
Kigali ⊛
BURUNDI
Bujumbura ⊛

TANZANIA
Dodoma ⊛
Zanzibar •
Dar es Salaam •

Equator

INDIAN OCEAN

SEYCHELLES
Victoria •

ATLANTIC OCEAN

CABINDA (ANGOLA)

Luanda ⊛

ANGOLA

ZAMBIA
Lusaka ⊛

MALAWI
Lilongwe ⊛

COMOROS
Moroni ⊛

MADAGASCAR
Antananarivo ⊛

MAURITIUS
Port Louis ○

ZIMBABWE
Harare ⊛

MOZAMBIQUE

Mozambique Channel

NAMIBIA
Windhoek ⊛

BOTSWANA
Gaborone ⊛

Pretoria ⊛
Maputo ⊛
Mbabane ⊛
SWAZILAND

Bloemfontein •
Maseru ⊛
LESOTHO

SOUTH AFRICA

Cape Town ⊛

Legend:
- Boundaries
- ⊛ National capitals
- • Other cities

N

SCALE
0 — 500 — 1000 Miles
0 — 500 — 1000 Kilometers
Projection: Azimuthal Equal Area

---

1. (Place) Which country is completely surrounded by another country?

2. (Location) Which country lies mostly on the mainland but has its capital on an island?

3. (Place) What is the largest African island country? What are the other island countries?

Critical Thinking

4. (Human-Environment Interaction) Compare this map to the **climate map** of the region. Why do you think the capitals of Algeria, Tunisia, and Libya all lie on the Mediterranean Sea?

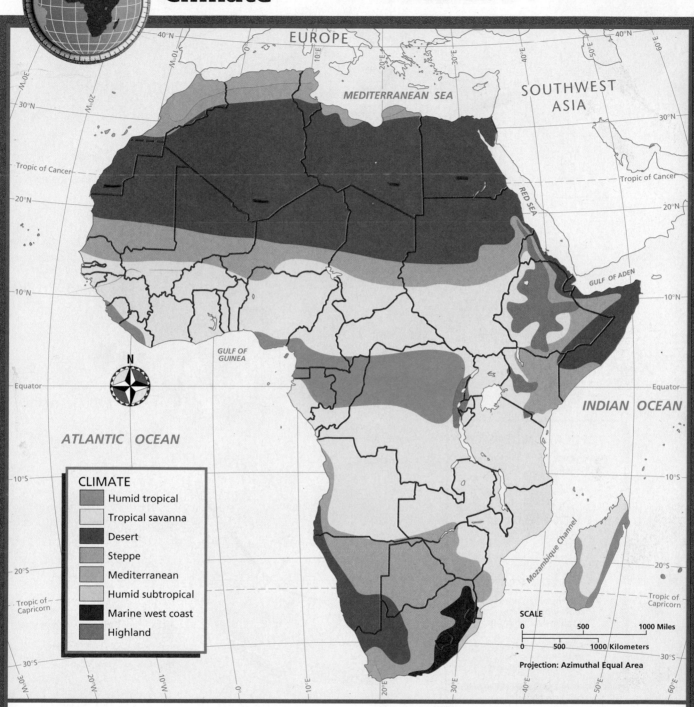

EUROPE

MEDITERRANEAN SEA

SOUTHWEST ASIA

40°N

30°N

Tropic of Cancer

20°N

RED SEA

GULF OF ADEN

10°N

GULF OF GUINEA

N

Equator

INDIAN OCEAN

ATLANTIC OCEAN

10°S

CLIMATE

- Humid tropical
- Tropical savanna
- Desert
- Steppe
- Mediterranean
- Humid subtropical
- Marine west coast
- Highland

20°S

Mozambique Channel

Tropic of Capricorn

SCALE

0   500   1000 Miles

0   500   1000 Kilometers

Projection: Azimuthal Equal Area

30°S

1. (*Region*) Where are humid tropical climates found in Africa?

2. (*Region*) Compare this map to the **land use and resources map** of the region. Which climate region in North Africa has limited economic activity?

Critical Thinking

3. (*Human-Environment Interaction*) Compare this map to the **land use and resources** and **population maps** of the region. Why might the eastern part of South Africa be more densely populated than the western part?

POPULATION DENSITY

Persons per sq. mile	Persons per sq. km
520	200
260	100
130	50
25	10
3	1
0	0

● Metropolitan areas with more than 2 million inhabitants

○ Metropolitan areas with 1 million to 2 million inhabitants

SCALE

0   500   1000 Miles

0   500   1000 Kilometers

Projection: Azimuthal Equal Area

1. (Place) Which country has the most cities with more than 2 million people? Compare this map to the **physical map** of the region. Which river flows through or near these cities?

2. (Place) What are the two largest African cities shown south of the equator?

Critical Thinking

3. (Human-Environment Interaction) Compare this map to the **climate map** of the region. Notice that both the humid tropical climate region in central Africa and the desert regions in the north and south are areas of low population density. What is one conclusion you might draw from this?

LAND USE

- Nomadic herding
- Livestock raising
- Commercial farming
- Subsistence farming
- Limited economic activity
- Manufacturing
- ● Major manufacturing and trade centers

RESOURCES

- Coal
- Natural gas
- Oil
- Hydroelectric power
- Gold
- Silver
- PL Platinum
- Diamonds
- U Uranium
- Other minerals
- Seafood

1. **Region** Which region of Africa seems to have the most mineral resources?

2. **Human-Environment Interaction** What type of farming is the most common in Africa?

3. **Human-Environment Interaction** Compare this map to the **physical map** of the region. Which rivers support commercial farming in dry areas? Which river in southeastern Africa provides hydroelectric power to the region?

Critical Thinking

4. **Human-Environment Interaction** Compare this map to the **physical map** of the region. Why might mining be the only major economic activity on Namibia's western coast?

Fast FACTS

Africa

ALGERIA

CAPITAL:
Algiers

AREA:
919,590 sq. mi.
(2,381,740 sq km)

POPULATION:
32,818,500

MONEY:
Algerian dinar

LANGUAGES:
Arabic (official), French,
Berber

PEOPLE PER DOCTOR:
1,066

BURKINA FASO

CAPITAL:
Ouagadougou

AREA:
105,869 sq. mi.
(274,200 sq km)

POPULATION:
13,228,460

MONEY:
CFAF*

LANGUAGES:
French (official),
ethnic languages

PEOPLE PER DOCTOR:
27,158

ANGOLA

CAPITAL:
Luanda

AREA:
481,351 sq. mi.
(1,246,700 sq km)

POPULATION:
10,766,471

MONEY:
kwanza

LANGUAGES:
Portuguese (official), Bantu
languages

PEOPLE PER DOCTOR:
data not available

BURUNDI

CAPITAL:
Bujumbura

AREA:
10,745 sq. mi.
(27,830 sq km)

POPULATION:
6,096,156

MONEY:
Burundi franc

LANGUAGES:
Kirundi (official), French
(official), Swahili

PEOPLE PER DOCTOR:
16,667

BENIN

CAPITAL:
Porto-Novo

AREA:
43,483 sq. mi.
(112,620 sq km)

POPULATION:
7,041,490

MONEY:
CFAF*

LANGUAGES:
French (official), Fon, Yoruba,
other ethnic languages

PEOPLE PER DOCTOR:
14,216

CAMEROON

CAPITAL:
Yaoundé

AREA:
183,567 sq. mi.
(475,440 sq km)

POPULATION:
15,746,179

MONEY:
CFAF*

LANGUAGES:
English (official), French (official), 24 ethnic language
groups

PEOPLE PER DOCTOR:
14,286

BOTSWANA

CAPITAL:
Gaborone

AREA:
231,803 sq. mi.
(600,370 sq km)

POPULATION:
1,573,267

MONEY:
pula

LANGUAGES:
English (official), Setswana

PEOPLE PER DOCTOR:
4,395

CAPE VERDE

CAPITAL:
Praia

AREA:
1,557 sq. mi. (4,033 sq km)

POPULATION:
412,137

MONEY:
Cape Verdean escudo

LANGUAGES:
Portuguese,
Crioulo

PEOPLE PER DOCTOR:
3,448

*Communaute Financiere Africaine franc

Countries not drawn to scale.

CENTRAL AFRICAN REPUBLIC

CAPITAL: Bangui

AREA:
240,534 sq. mi.
(622,984 sq km)

POPULATION: 3,683,538

MONEY: CFAF*

LANGUAGES: French (official), Sangho (national language), tribal languages

PEOPLE PER DOCTOR: 18,660

CHAD

CAPITAL:
N'Djamena

AREA:
495,752 sq. mi.
(1,284,000 sq km)

POPULATION:
9,253,493

MONEY:
CFAF*

LANGUAGES:
French (official), Arabic (official), Sara and Sango

PEOPLE PER DOCTOR: 27,765

COMOROS

CAPITAL:
Moroni

AREA:
838 sq. mi.
(2,170 sq km)

POPULATION:
632,948

MONEY:
Comoran franc

LANGUAGES:
Arabic (official), French (official), Comoran

PEOPLE PER DOCTOR:
10,000

CONGO, DEMOCRATIC REPUBLIC OF THE

CAPITAL:
Kinshasa

AREA:
905,563 sq. mi.
(2,345,410 sq km)

POPULATION:
56,625,039

MONEY:
Congolese franc

LANGUAGES:
French (official), Lingala, Kingwana, Kikongo, Tshiluba

PEOPLE PER DOCTOR:
data not available

CONGO, REPUBLIC OF THE

CAPITAL: Brazzaville

AREA:
132,046 sq. mi.
(342,000 sq km)

POPULATION: 2,954,258

MONEY: CFAF*

LANGUAGES:
French (official), Lingala, Monokutuba

PEOPLE PER DOCTOR: 3,704

CÔTE D'IVOIRE

CAPITAL:
Yamoussoukro

AREA:
124,502 sq. mi.
(322,460 sq km)

POPULATION: 16,962,491

MONEY: CFAF*

LANGUAGES:
French (official), Dioula, ethnic languages

PEOPLE PER DOCTOR:
data not available

DJIBOUTI

CAPITAL:
Djibouti

AREA:
8,494 sq. mi.
(22,000 sq km)

POPULATION:
457,130

MONEY:
Djiboutian franc

LANGUAGES:
French (official), Arabic (official), Somali, Afar

PEOPLE PER DOCTOR:
5,000

EGYPT

CAPITAL:
Cairo

AREA:
386,660 sq. mi.
(1,001,450 sq km)

POPULATION:
74,718,797

MONEY:
Egyptian pound

LANGUAGES:
Arabic (official), English, French

PEOPLE PER DOCTOR:
472

Sources: Central Intelligence Agency, *The World Factbook 2003*; United Nations Development Programme: *Health Profile*, pop. figures are 2003 estimates.

EQUATORIAL GUINEA

CAPITAL: Malabo

AREA:
10,830 sq. mi.
(28,051 sq km)

POPULATION: 510,473

MONEY: CFAF*

LANGUAGES:
Spanish (official), French
(official), Fang, Bubi, Ibo

PEOPLE PER DOCTOR: 4,762

ERITREA

CAPITAL: Asmara

AREA:
46,842 sq. mi.
(121,320 sq km)

POPULATION:
4,362,254

MONEY: nafka

LANGUAGES:
Afar, Amharic, Arabic, Tigre,
Kunama, Tigrinya

PEOPLE PER DOCTOR:
36,000

ETHIOPIA

CAPITAL: Addis Ababa

AREA:
435,184 sq. mi.
(1,127,127 sq km)

POPULATION:
66,557,553

MONEY: birr

LANGUAGES:
Amharic, Tigrinya, Orominga,
Guaraginga, Somali, Arabic

PEOPLE PER DOCTOR:
25,000

GABON

CAPITAL: Libreville

AREA:
103,346 sq. mi.
(267,667 sq km)

POPULATION:
1,321,560

MONEY: CFAF*

LANGUAGES:
French (official), Fang,
Myene, Nzebi,
Bapounou/Eschira, Bandjabi

PEOPLE PER DOCTOR: 5,263

GAMBIA

CAPITAL: Banjul

AREA:
4,363 sq. mi.
(11,300 sq km)

POPULATION:
1,501,050

MONEY: dalasi

LANGUAGES:
English (official), Mandinka,
Wolof, Fula

PEOPLE PER DOCTOR:
50,000

GHANA

CAPITAL: Accra

AREA:
92,100 sq. mi.
(238,540 sq km)

POPULATION:
20,467,747

MONEY: new cedi

LANGUAGES:
English (official), Akan,
Moshi-Dagomba, Ewe, Ga

PEOPLE PER DOCTOR:
22,970

GUINEA

CAPITAL: Conakry

AREA:
94,925 sq. mi.
(245,857 sq km)

POPULATION:
9,030,220

MONEY:
Guinean franc

LANGUAGES:
French (official),
ethnic languages

PEOPLE PER DOCTOR: 6,667

GUINEA-BISSAU

CAPITAL: Bissau

AREA:
13,946 sq. mi.
(36,120 sq km)

POPULATION: 1,360,827

MONEY: CFAF*

LANGUAGES:
Portuguese (official), Crioulo,
ethnic languages

PEOPLE PER DOCTOR: 5,556

KENYA

CAPITAL:
Nairobi

AREA:
224,961 sq. mi.
(582,650 sq km)

POPULATION: 31,639,091

MONEY:
Kenyan shilling

LANGUAGES:
English (official), Kiswahili
(official), ethnic languages

PEOPLE PER DOCTOR: 5,999

LESOTHO

CAPITAL: Maseru

AREA:
11,720 sq. mi.
(30,355 sq km)

POPULATION:
1,861,959

MONEY: loti

LANGUAGES:
English (official), Sesotho,
Zulu, Xhosa

PEOPLE PER DOCTOR:
14,306

*Communaute Financiere Africaine franc

Countries not drawn to scale.

LIBERIA

CAPITAL: Monrovia

AREA:
43,000 sq. mi.
(111,370 sq km)

POPULATION:
3,317,176

MONEY:
Liberian dollar

LANGUAGES:
English (official),
many ethnic languages

PEOPLE PER DOCTOR: 8,333

LIBYA

CAPITAL: Tripoli

AREA:
679,358 sq. mi.
(1,759,540 sq km)

POPULATION:
5,499,074

MONEY: Libyan dinar

LANGUAGES:
Arabic, Italian, English

PEOPLE PER DOCTOR:
data not available

MADAGASCAR

CAPITAL: Antananarivo

AREA:
226,656 sq. mi.
(587,040 sq km)

POPULATION:
16,979,744

MONEY:
Malagasy franc

LANGUAGES:
French (official),
Malagasy (official)

PEOPLE PER DOCTOR: 4,167

MALAWI

CAPITAL: Lilongwe

AREA:
45,745 sq. mi.
(118,480 sq km)

POPULATION:
11,651,239

MONEY:
Malawian kwacha

LANGUAGES: English (official),
Chichewa (official), many
ethnic languages

PEOPLE PER DOCTOR: 50,000

MALI

CAPITAL: Bamako

AREA:
478,764 sq. mi.
(1,240,000 sq km)

POPULATION: 11,626,219

MONEY: CFAF*

LANGUAGES:
French (official), Bambara,
many ethnic languages

PEOPLE PER DOCTOR: 25,000

MAURITANIA

CAPITAL: Nouakchott

AREA:
397,953 sq. mi.
(1,030,700 sq km)

POPULATION:
2,912,584

MONEY:
ouguiya

LANGUAGES:
Hassaniya Arabic (official),
Wolof (official), Pulaar,
Soninke, French

PEOPLE PER DOCTOR: 11,085

MAURITIUS

CAPITAL:
Port Louis

AREA:
718 sq. mi.
(1,860 sq km)

POPULATION:
1,210,447

MONEY:
Mauritian rupee

LANGUAGES:
English (official), Creole,
French, Hindi, Urdu, Hakka,
Bhojpuri

PEOPLE PER DOCTOR: 1,182

MOROCCO

CAPITAL:
Rabat

AREA:
172,413 sq. mi.
(446,550 sq km)

POPULATION:
31,689,265

MONEY:
Moroccan dirham

LANGUAGES:
Arabic (official), Berber,
French

PEOPLE PER DOCTOR: 2,923

MOZAMBIQUE

CAPITAL:
Maputo

AREA:
304,494 sq. mi.
(801,590 sq km)

POPULATION:
17,479,266

MONEY:
metical

LANGUAGES:
Portuguese (official), ethnic
languages

PEOPLE PER DOCTOR:
131,991

Sources: Central Intelligence Agency, *The World Factbook 2003*; United Nations Development Programme: *Health Profile*, pop. figures are 2003 estimates.

NAMIBIA

CAPITAL:
Windhoek

AREA:
318,694 sq. mi.
(825,418 sq km)

POPULATION:
1,927,447

MONEY:
Namibian dollar, South
African rand

LANGUAGES:
English (official), Afrikaans,
German, Oshivambo, Herero,
Nama

PEOPLE PER DOCTOR: 4,594

NIGER

CAPITAL: Niamey

AREA:
489,189 sq. mi.
(1,267,000 sq km)

POPULATION:
11,058,590

MONEY: CFAF*

LANGUAGES:
French (official), Hausa,
Djerma

PEOPLE PER DOCTOR:
35,141

NIGERIA

CAPITAL: Abuja

AREA:
356,667 sq. mi.
(923,768 sq km)

POPULATION:
133,881,703

MONEY:
naira

LANGUAGES:
English (official), Hausa,
Yoruba, Ibo, Fulani

PEOPLE PER DOCTOR: 4,496

RWANDA

CAPITAL:
Kigali

AREA:
10,169 sq. mi.
(26,338 sq km)

POPULATION:
7,810,056

MONEY:
Rwandan franc

LANGUAGES:
Kinyarwanda (official),
French (official), English (offi-
cial), Kiswahili

PEOPLE PER DOCTOR: 50,000

SÃO TOMÉ AND PRÍNCIPE

CAPITAL: São Tomé

AREA:
386 sq. mi. (1,001 sq km)

POPULATION:
175,883

MONEY:
dobra

LANGUAGES:
Portuguese (official)

PEOPLE PER DOCTOR: 3,125

SENEGAL

CAPITAL: Dakar

AREA:
75,749 sq. mi.
(196,190 sq km)

POPULATION: 10,580,307

MONEY: CFAF*

LANGUAGES:
French (official), Wolof,
Pulaar, Diola, Mandinka

PEOPLE PER DOCTOR: 14,285

SEYCHELLES

CAPITAL:
Victoria

AREA:
176 sq. mi. (455 sq km)

POPULATION: 80,469

MONEY:
Seychelles rupee

LANGUAGES: English (official),
French (official), Creole

PEOPLE PER DOCTOR: 906

SIERRA LEONE

CAPITAL: Freetown

AREA:
27,699 sq. mi. (71,740 sq km)

POPULATION: 5,732,681

MONEY: leone

LANGUAGES:
English (official), Mende,
Temne, Krio

PEOPLE PER DOCTOR: 10,832

SOMALIA

CAPITAL:
Mogadishu

AREA:
246,199 sq. mi.
(637,657 sq km)

POPULATION:
8,025,190

MONEY:
Somali shilling

LANGUAGES:
Somali (official),
Arabic, Italian, English

PEOPLE PER DOCTOR:
data not available

SOUTH AFRICA

CAPITALS: Pretoria,
Cape Town, Bloemfontein

AREA:
471,008 sq. mi.
(1,219,912 sq km)

POPULATION: 42,768,678

MONEY: rand

LANGUAGES: 11 official
languages, including Afrikaans,
English, Ndebele, Pedi, Sotho,
Swazi, Tsonga, Tswana, Venda,
Xhosa, Zulu

PEOPLE PER DOCTOR: 1,742

*Communaute Financiere Africaine franc

Countries not drawn to scale.

SUDAN

CAPITAL: Khartoum
AREA:
967,493 sq. mi.
(2,505,810 sq km)
POPULATION:
38,114,160

MONEY:
Sudanese dinar
LANGUAGES: Arabic (official),
Nubian, Ta Bedawie, English,
many ethnic languages
PEOPLE PER DOCTOR: 11,300

UGANDA

CAPITAL:
Kampala
AREA:
91,135 sq. mi.
(236,040 sq km)
POPULATION:
25,632,794

MONEY:
Ugandan shilling
LANGUAGES:
English (official), Luganda,
Swahili, Arabic
PEOPLE PER DOCTOR:
25,000

SWAZILAND

CAPITAL: Mbabane
AREA:
6,704 sq. mi. (17,363 sq km)
POPULATION:
1,161,219

MONEY: lilangeni
LANGUAGES:
English (official), siSwati
PEOPLE PER DOCTOR:
data not available

ZAMBIA

CAPITAL:
Lusaka
AREA:
290,584 sq. mi.
(752,614 sq km)
POPULATION:
10,307,333

MONEY:
Zambian kwacha
LANGUAGES:
English (official), Bemba,
Kaonda, Lozi, Lunda, Luvale,
many ethnic languages
PEOPLE PER DOCTOR: 10,917

TANZANIA

CAPITALS:
Dar es Salaam and Dodoma
AREA:
364,898 sq. mi.
(945,087 sq km)
POPULATION:
35,922,454

MONEY:
Tanzanian shilling
LANGUAGES:
Kiswahili (official),
English (official), Arabic,
many ethnic languages
PEOPLE PER DOCTOR: 20,511

ZIMBABWE

CAPITAL:
Harare
AREA:
150,803 sq. mi.
(390,580 sq km)
POPULATION: 12,576,742

MONEY:
Zimbabwean dollar
LANGUAGES:
English (official), Shona,
Sindebele
PEOPLE PER DOCTOR: 6,909

TOGO

CAPITAL: Lomé
AREA:
21,925 sq. mi.
(56,785 sq km)
POPULATION: 5,429,299

MONEY: CFAF*
LANGUAGES:
French (official), Ewe, Mina,
Kabye, Dagomba
PEOPLE PER DOCTOR: 16,667

internet connect

COUNTRY STATISTICS
GO TO: go.hrw.com
KEYWORD: SK5 FACTSU3
FOR: more facts about Africa

TUNISIA

CAPITAL:
Tunis
AREA:
63,170 sq. mi.
(163,610 sq km)
POPULATION: 9,924,742

MONEY:
Tunisian dinar
LANGUAGES:
Arabic (official), French
PEOPLE PER DOCTOR:
1,640

Sources: Central Intelligence Agency, *The World Factbook 2003*; United Nations Development *Programme: Health Profile*; pop. figures are 2003 estimates.

CHAPTER 8

Africa's History

In this chapter you will discover Africa's rich and fascinating history that includes sophisticated civilizations and courageous people. Your journey begins along the Nile River with the great achievements of the early Egyptians.

Wood carving of Tutankhamen

What would it be like to be a king at only nine years old? That's what happened to Tutankhamen, now often called King Tut. He became Egypt's pharaoh in about 1360 B.C. Much of what we know about this boy king's daily life we learned from the contents of his tomb. Buried with Tut were clothes decorated with gold and precious stones and pieces for board games. Scenes on Tut's casket showed that he enjoyed riding his chariot out into the countryside to hunt. Other objects show that Tut had kept some of his childhood things. There was a tiny chair, for example, and clothes that he had outgrown long before his death at the age of about 18.

King Tut's casket

Read to Discover

1. Why was the Nile an important river to the Egyptians?
2. What were some of the achievements of the Egyptians?
3. What was Egyptian religion based on?
4. What great kingdoms developed along the Nile south of Egypt?

Vocabulary

dynasty
pharaohs
hieroglyphics
papyrus
Rosetta Stone
pyramids
sphinxes
mummification

Places

Nile River
Red Sea
Giza
Kush
Aksum

People

Ramses II
Imhotep
Hatshepsut
King 'Ezana

Reading Strategy

FOLDNOTES: PYRAMID Create a **Pyramid** FoldNote as described in the Appendix. As you read, write what you learn about Egyptians on one triangle, Kush on another triangle, and Aksum on the third triangle.

The Nile Valley

Early Egyptians lived along the Nile River. At about 4,160 miles (6,693 km) long, the Nile is the world's longest river. As the Nile flooded each spring, the waters spread fine soil over the river's banks. This process supported plentiful crops of wheat and barley. It also created a very fertile area that cut right through the Sahara, the world's largest desert. Without the Nile and its annual flood, Egypt would not exist. As a result, Egypt is often called the Gift of the Nile.

The Nile Valley offered other advantages also. The river flows south to north, which made it possible for early residents to sail to the Mediterranean Sea. East and west of the Nile, deserts and the Red Sea provided early civilizations natural protection from invaders. The Isthmus of Suez, a land bridge between Africa and Asia, allowed trade between early Egyptians and their neighbors.

Government and Society Over hundreds of years, the rich Nile River valley supported the development of two kingdoms with distinct cultures. Around 3100 B.C., King Menes united them and founded a **dynasty**, a family line of rulers that passes power from one generation to the next. In later years, these rulers were called **pharaohs**. The pharaohs controlled the government completely. They also served as judges, high priests, and generals of the armies.

The Kingdom of Egypt around 1450 B.C.

Interpreting the Map Into which body of water does the Nile River flow?

Egyptian society was divided into two classes. Priests, scribes, and government officials formed the upper class. Peasants and farmers formed the lower class. Some also had to serve in the military. During the months that their fields were flooded, the farmers worked on building projects such as canals or the pyramids. You will read more about these projects on the following pages.

During the time of the pharaohs, Egypt's contact with other lands grew through conquest and trade. By about 1085 B.C., Egypt had expanded into what are now Syria, Israel, and Libya. The Egyptians traded with peoples throughout Southwest Asia and North Africa.

Egypt's Later History In the 1200s B.C., Ramses II, also known as Ramses the Great, ruled Egypt. Ramses was considered great for his military leadership and the massive monuments he had built during his reign. Ramses the Great was Egypt's last strong leader. After his rule, attacks from foreign peoples, including the Phoenicians, the Persians, and the Greeks, weakened Egypt. By the 500s B.C., Greeks, Romans and eastern Mediterranean peoples settled in the region. As a result, Egypt was no longer ruled by Egyptians.

✓ **READING CHECK:** (*Main Idea*) What role did the Nile play in the creation of early Egyptian civilization?

Along the west bank of the Nile at Giza, Egyptians built enormous pyramids to honor their kings. Each of the millions of limestone blocks that make up the pyramids weighs an average of 2.5 tons.

Egyptian Achievements

In addition to their architectural achievements, Egyptians developed a writing system that used pictures and symbols we call **hieroglyphics**. More than 600 signs, pictures, and symbols represented different words and sounds. The Egyptians wrote on stone or a paperlike material called **papyrus** made from the inner stalk of the reedlike papyrus plant. Egyptian officials recorded many important events and details about daily life on papyrus.

Scholars can read Egyptian hieroglyphics today because of a discovery in 1799. A French soldier found a large stone in the Egyptian village of Rosetta. Known as the **Rosetta Stone**, this stone had writings carved in Greek, hieroglyphics, and an Egyptian writing style called demotic. When scholars realized that the three passages were of the same text, they used the Greek text to translate the hieroglyphics. Now scholars can read and understand other hieroglyphic texts.

Egyptians also developed an accurate 365-day calendar similar to the one we use today. This calendar had 12 months of 30 days each. The remaining five days were holidays. To keep track of years, they counted the years of a pharaoh's reign. For example, they might refer to the first, second, or tenth years of the reign of a certain pharaoh. Egyptians also used a number system based on 10, and they understood both fractions and geometry.

Pyramids Built as tombs for the pharaohs over 4,000 years ago, the Egyptian **pyramids** are still some of the most magnificent structures in the world. Most of these huge stone monuments were built along the west bank of the Nile. The most famous Egyptian pyramids are located at Giza, near Cairo. Built around 2600 B.C., the Great Pyramid was the tomb of the pharaoh Khufu. See the Connecting to Technology feature in the next chapter for more information on how pyramids were built.

One of the most talented pyramid architects was Imhotep. He designed the famous step pyramid of King Djoser, an early Egyptian ruler. Imhotep was not only a brilliant architect but also a great healer and writer.

Egyptian Hieroglyphics

HIEROGLYPH	ENGLISH MEANING	HIEROGLYPH	ENGLISH MEANING
	heart		rain
	to cry		to make an offer
	to fly		to sail upstream
	tree		to go

The Egyptians developed one of the world's first writing systems. Hieroglyphic writing used pictures, or hieroglyphs, to represent objects and sounds.

Hatshepsut (ruled c. 1490–1468 B.C.)

One of Egypt's most remarkable pharaohs was a woman. Hatshepsut reigned during a time of peace and prosperity. She is perhaps best known for increasing Egyptian trade. Among the items she received from faraway lands were gold, precious woods, baboons, and living trees. In addition, Hatshepsut sponsored great building projects, several of which still stand. *What did Hatshepsut accomplish as pharoah?*

The Great Sphinx The Egyptians are also known for building sculptures called **sphinxes**. A sphinx is a monster that has a lion's body and a human head. The most famous Egyptian sphinx is the Great Sphinx, which stands near the pyramids at Giza. Carved from a solid block of bedrock in the 2500s B.C., the head of the Great Sphinx is probably a likeness of the pharaoh Khafre. His tomb lies in one of Giza's pyramids. The sphinx's body stretches about 170 feet long and stands 66 feet tall.

Temples Sphinxes also stood guard in front of temples. Egyptians built enormous temples to their gods. The interior of Egyptian temples housed large statues representing different gods. However, only the king and some priests were allowed inside the temples. Common people had to pray outside.

To honor the gods, priests cared for the temple's statues with offerings of food twice a day. The priests also dressed the statues in linen clothing and fine jewelry. At the main temple in Karnak, the public could only see the temple's statues during a festival held each year. At this time, priests escorted the statues of three gods down the Nile to the temple at Luxor. During the elaborate parade, people sang hymns and danced in celebration of the gods.

✔ **READING CHECK:** (*Summarizing*) What were some achievements of the early Egyptians?

┌─History Close-Up─

Karnak's Great Temple Sunlight reveals the brilliantly painted inner hall of Karnak's Great Temple in this illustrated re-creation. The temple's massive columns tower about 70 feet above a parade of priests and royal attendants leaving the temple during an annual festival. Royal attendants carry the sacred statues of the temple's gods in a miniature golden ship. The images and hieroglyphics on the walls and columns celebrate the lives of two kings—Ramses II and his father Seti I. **Does Karnak's Great Temple appear gloomy or cheerful? How might the temple's appearance reflect the Egyptian belief in life after death? Defend your answer.**

Egyptian Religion

Egyptian religion was based on the belief in an afterlife. Egyptians believed Osiris, the god of the underworld, met them in death. Death to them was simply the beginning of a new life in the next world. There were several obstacles, however, to eternal life.

The Egyptians believed their life force, or *ka,* left the body at death. A person's soul, or *ba,* did not leave the body until after burial. Then the *ba* had to pass through doorways of fire and cobras to get to the hall of judgment. There, the person's heart was weighed on a scale against a feather. The god Osiris then determined whether the person's heart was too heavy. If the heart wasn't balanced, a monster that was part lion, part hippopotamus, and part crocodile would eat the heart. On the other hand, if the person's heart was balanced, he or she earned an afterlife filled with all the pleasures they enjoyed in life.

Because the Egyptians believed the body was needed in an afterlife, they preserved their dead rulers through a process called **mummification**. To mummify a body, the Egyptians first removed the internal organs. The heart, however, was left in place. They then covered the body with substances to dry it out. The body was then rubbed with ointment and wrapped in linen. They placed a mask over the head and shoulders and placed the mummy in a coffin. Sometimes, this coffin was placed inside two other coffins. The mummy's internal organs were dried and placed inside four different jars.

In addition to the mummy, the tomb also housed many items that the person might need on the afterlife journey, including clothes, food, jewelry, tools, and weapons. Scenes of the dead ruler making offerings to the gods decorated the tomb's walls. To protect the body, sculpted or painted figures of servants also lined the walls. To help guide a person into the afterlife, a copy of the *Book of the Dead* was placed in the tomb. Written on rolls of papyrus, the book included maps and magic spells that provided protection for the person's soul.

No royal tomb in ancient Egypt was without a copy of the *Book of the Dead.* Egyptians believed the book was a necessary guide to the afterlife.

Interpreting the Visual Record What does this page of the book show?

 READING CHECK:

Finding the Main Idea Why did Egyptians mummify their dead rulers?

Kush and Aksum

Two great ancient kingdoms developed along the Nile River south of Egypt. The first was Kush. It was eventually conquered by Aksum, its neighbor to the southeast.

Kush Kush was probably founded around 2000 B.C. By about 1500 B.C., however, it was conquered by Egypt. Egypt ruled Kush for many years. The two countries were never completely unified, however, and Kush remained largely free from Egyptian control. In the 700s B.C., Kush invaded and conquered Egypt. The kings of Kush ruled Egypt for about 50 years. In the 600s B.C., invasions by groups from Southwest Asia weakened the kingdom. Kush survived, however, and became a powerful kingdom again.

The people of Kush were mostly traders. They traveled along the Nile to trade goods and ideas with Egypt. Because of this trade, Kush's culture was in many ways similar to Egypt's. Kush also lay along the trade routes between the Red Sea and the Nile. Caravans traveling between these two areas passed through Kush. This allowed the kingdom to become a rich trading center. The Kushites built huge pyramids and temples. They made beautiful pottery and jewelry. They also developed a written form of their language.

Kush and Aksum

Interpreting the Map **On what river would goods from Kush be sent to Egypt?**

The Lion Temple was built by the people of Kush.

Interpreting the Visual Record **What are some features that this temple shares with Karnak's Great Temple?**

The people of Aksum carved massive stelae like this one from solid blocks of stone. These monuments were erected on a royal burial ground and are thought to represent buildings as high as 13 stories.

Interpreting the Visual Record What is represented at the bottom of this stela?

Aksum Aksum lay in a hilly area called the Ethiopian Highlands. Like Kush, Aksum controlled trade routes between the Red Sea and the Nile. In addition, Aksum lay on trade routes between the Red Sea and central Africa. By the A.D. 100s, Aksum had grown into a major trading kingdom. Two hundred years later, it had also become a strong military power. In about A.D. 350, Aksum conquered Kush.

At the time of its conquest of Kush, Aksum was ruled by King 'Ezana. He was a strong leader who led other rulers in the area. While he was king, 'Ezana became a Christian. He made Christianity the official religion of Aksum. The form of Christianity that 'Ezana followed included some local traditions, customs, and beliefs. This practice made it popular with other people throughout the region. Christianity slowly became a powerful influence in East Africa.

From the A.D. 300s to the 600s, Aksum continued to grow rich from trade. By this time, it controlled nearly all the trade on the western shore of the Red Sea. In the late A.D. 500s, however, Aksum began to decline for several reasons. One reason may have been soil exhaustion. Farmers had been growing crops in this region for hundreds of years. Over time, it probably became more difficult for farmers to produce enough food to support the population.

Increased competition for trade also hurt Aksum. By the 700s, the Persian Empire had taken over much of the trade along the Red Sea. Muslim traders from the north also took business away from Aksum. Faced with these new trading empires, Aksum slowly lost most of its economic and political power.

✓ **READING CHECK:** (*Contrasting*) How was the form of Christianity practiced in Aksum different from Christianity as practiced elsewhere?

go.hrw.com **Homework Practice Online** Keyword: SK5 HP8

Section Review 1

Define or identify: dynasty, pharoahs, Ramses II, hieroglyphics, papyrus, Rosetta Stone, pyramids, Imhotep, Hatshepsut, sphinxes, mummification, King 'Ezana

Reading for the Main Idea

1. (*Environment and Society*) How was the Nile River important to the Egyptians?

2. (*Human Systems*) What are some of the achievements of Egyptian civilization?

Critical Thinking

3. **Making Generalizations** Why did the Egyptians bury dead rulers in tombs filled with material goods?

4. **Comparing and Contrasting** In what ways was civilization in Kush similar to and different from civilization in Aksum?

Organizing What You Know

5. **Sequencing** Copy the following time line. Fill in as many events as you can.

3000 B.C.	2000 B.C.	1000 B.C.	A.D. 1 A.D. 500
2500 B.C.	1500 B.C.	500 B.C.	

Early Sub-Saharan Africa

Read to Discover

1. How do historians study cultures that left no written records?
2. How did trade affect the growth of kingdoms in Sub-Saharan Africa?

Vocabulary

oral history

Places

Swahili States
Zimbabwe
Ghana
Mali
Timbuktu

People

Mansa Musa

Reading Strategy

FOLDNOTES: TRI-FOLD Create a **Tri-Fold** FoldNote as described in the Appendix. Label the columns East Africa, Zimbabwe, and West Africa. As you read, write what you learn about these trading states in each column.

Ancient Sub-Saharan Africa

Egypt was the first kingdom to develop in Africa, but it was not the only one. South of the vast desert called the Sahara, many different cultures developed. In time some of these groups established city-states, kingdoms, and even empires. It is sometimes difficult, however, for historians to study the earliest African civilizations.

Language One reason for this difficulty is the absence of written records. Historians therefore must find other ways to study early cultures. One common method is the study of **oral history**, spoken information passed from one generation to the next.

These oral traditions are often contained in stories or songs. Many of the stories tell about great kings and heroes from the past. Other stories included animals playing tricks on each other, which usually ended in an important lesson. Many cultures of ancient Sub-Saharan Africa had an official storyteller who memorized these stories. Storytellers used different voices and facial expressions to express emotion as they spoke. They entertained large audiences with their performances. In some parts of Africa storytellers are still performing today. Scholars today study these tales to learn about Africa's past.

The modern languages of Africa can also provide clues about the continent's history. Scholars have tried to figure out which African languages are related. This is often a clue that cultures have had

▲
The Yoruba were skilled artisans. This life-sized head of a king was sculpted from bronze. The vertical lines on the face may represent ritual scarring.

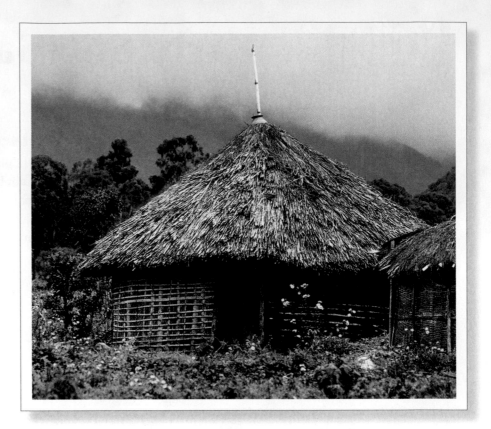

Many houses built in Africa today are similar to those built in ancient times. **Interpreting the Visual Record From what materials are traditional houses like this made?**

contact with each other in the past. Some African languages are related to languages spoken in other parts of the world. Scholars have learned from this that early Africans had contact with people from distant lands. Other evidence suggests the same thing. Bananas, for example, have been popular in Africa for a long time, but the banana tree is not native to Africa. Early traders must have brought the plant from Asia.

Life in Early Africa There is much historians do not know about life in ancient Sub-Saharan Africa. However, they have pieced together a picture of life in the region. Across most of the continent, life was centered around small villages. Usually, all of the people in a village were related to each other. These relationships helped tie the village together. Older members of a community were often its leaders. Everyone in the village respected and obeyed them. Women played many roles in early African societies. They were responsible for farming. In addition, people in some societies traced their family lines through their mothers.

Life was very similar in many villages across Africa. Most people were involved in farming, herding, or fishing. Basic agricultural practices did not vary much from place to place. Most people in early Africa also had similar religious beliefs. They believed that spirits, including the spirits of their ancestors, were all around. They also believed in many gods who controlled nature and human activities.

✔ **READING CHECK:** (*Summarizing*) What do historians study to learn about ancient Africa?

African Trading States, c. A.D. 1230–1591

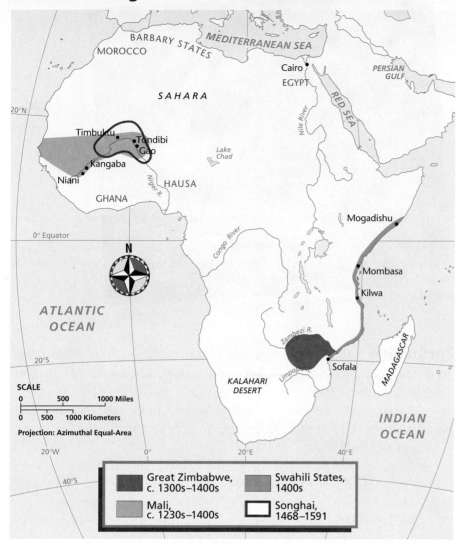

Great wealth from trade helped develop several powerful states throughout Africa. In the east, the Swahili States and Great Zimbabwe traded goods with peoples across the Indian Ocean. In the west, an almost endless supply of gold and salt gave rise to the kingdoms of Mali and Songhai.

Interpreting the Map What trading advantage did the Swahili States have in their location?

The Trading States

Egypt, Kush, and Aksum were the largest kingdoms in ancient Africa. Like these kingdoms, most of the civilizations of Sub-Saharan Africa were great traders. Across the continent, trade connected Africa with other civilizations.

East Africa Along the coast of East Africa, dozens of small city-states appeared. The earliest such city-states, like Mogadishu (moh-guh-DEE-shoo) and Mombasa, were located in the northern part of the region. Eventually city-states like these lined most of the eastern coast of Africa. They controlled trade in the Indian Ocean. They sold gold, ivory, hides, and tortoise shells to traders from around the world. They also sold slaves. In exchange, these traders brought weapons and porcelain to Africa.

Eventually a new culture arose out of this trade. A new language, called Swahili, developed. It was an African language, but it also included many words from Arabic. For this reason, the city-states of East Africa are sometimes called the Swahili States.

Sailing vessels called dhows were used by Swahili traders to cross the Indian Ocean. These vessels are still in use today.

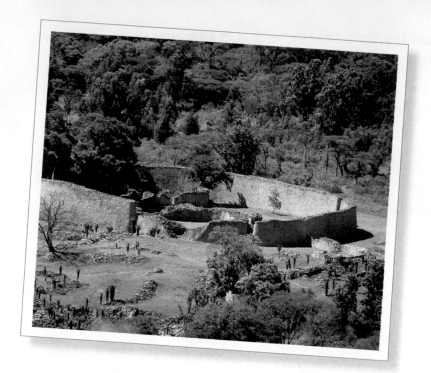

These ruins of the Great Zimbabwe fortress near Masvingo, Zimbabwe, reveal the past glory of a trading empire.

Interpreting the Visual Record What do these ruins reveal about the region's natural resources?

Zimbabwe Later traders built settlements farther south. By A.D. 900, gold had been discovered in the interior of southeastern Africa. This gold was shipped to the coast on the Zambezi River. The discovery of gold greatly increased trade along the Indian Ocean because many peoples wanted it. African kingdoms fought to control the sources of gold and the gold trade.

A group of people called the Shona gained control of the region in the 1200s. Their kingdom was centered around Great Zimbabwe, a huge stone city of perhaps 10,000 people or more. *Zimbabwe* is a Shona word that means "stone houses." From Great Zimbabwe, the Shona controlled the gold trade out of southeastern Africa. Great Zimbabwe's builders used local granite to create the rectangular blocks that formed the city's stone structures. A circular stone wall that reaches up to 36 feet in height is the largest structure at Great Zimbabwe. Within this stone enclosure, local traders exchanged gold for porcelain, glass beads, and other goods with traders from China and India. Great Zimbabwe was abandoned during the 1400s.

West Africa In West Africa, trade centered on the Atlantic Ocean. Many trading societies developed between the Atlantic and Lake Chad. The most powerful trading societies in this region were those that controlled trade routes across the Sahara. Traders from the north brought salt across the desert in exchange for gold from West Africa. Cities grew up along these trade routes.

The first of the great West African trading kingdoms was Ghana. It began as a trading village in what is now Mauritania. Gold trade made the kings of Ghana rich and powerful. They built strong armies and conquered new lands. Eventually, however, Ghana declined. In about A.D. 1235, a neighboring people conquered Ghana. They set up a new empire called Mali.

Mansa Musa (died 1332)

Mansa Musa was famous not just because he supported education and the arts. He was also very wealthy. When he went on a pilgrimage to Mecca, 500 slaves carrying gold rods walked in front of him. Mansa Musa gave away so much gold while in Egypt that the precious metal lost much of its value.

Why would gold go down in value when it is plentiful?

Mali covered all of the area that had been Ghana. It also included new lands to the north and west. Mali reached the height of its power in the early 1300s under a ruler named Mansa Musa. He was a strong supporter of education and the arts. During his reign, the city of Timbuktu became an important center of learning and trade. People came from as far away as Egypt and Arabia to study at the university there. After Mansa Musa died, Mali began to weaken. In 1468, rebels captured Timbuktu. They set up a new kingdom called Songhai.

Songhai was a powerful trading kingdom. It was centered on the city of Gao, a key trade center on the Niger River. By this time the Niger had become an important trade route. The kings of Songhai encouraged Islamic study at the university in Timbuktu. This helped Timbuktu remain an important cultural and trade center. Goods from Europe, India, and China were exchanged there. Timbuktu also remained a center of learning. Books sold for very high prices in the markets there. Songhai remained a powerful state until 1591. In that year, it was conquered by Morocco.

✓ **READING CHECK:** (*Identifying Cause and Effect*) What led to the development of strong kingdoms in West Africa?

Homework Practice Online
Keyword: SK5 HP8

Define or Identify: oral history, Mansa Musa

Reading for the Main Idea

1. (*Human Systems*) What do scholars study to learn about early African civilizations?

2. (*Human Systems*) What were some items traded by early African trading kingdoms?

3. (*Human Systems*) What East African culture developed as a result of trade?

Critical Thinking

4. **Drawing Inferences and Conclusions** Why were some of the civilizations of Sub-Saharan Africa located on or near the coast?

Organizing What You Know

5. **Comparing and Contrasting** Copy the following chart. Use it to name and describe the trading kingdoms of early Sub-Saharan Africa.

State	Location in Africa	Features

Read to Discover

1. Why did European nations want colonies in Africa?
2. What effects did imperialism have on Africa?

Vocabulary

imperialism
nationalism

People

Samory Touré

Reading Strategy

READING ORGANIZER Draw a circle in the center of a sheet of paper. Label the circle *Imperialism.* Draw three rays from the circle. Then draw a circle at the end of each ray. Label the three rays Nationalism in Europe, Modern Technology, and Partition of Africa. As you read this section, write what you learn about imperialism in each circle.

This cartoon was created after Cecil Rhodes, a British imperialist, announced he wanted to build a railroad from Egypt to South Africa. Rhodes believed a railroad would help Great Britain control more territory in Africa.

European Imperialism

Between 1870 and 1914, many European countries tried to control much of Africa. Using a practice called **imperialism**, they tried to dominate other countries' government, trade, and culture. Beginning in the early 1800s, most European nations ended their participation in the slave trade. Instead of slaves, they focused on trading products such as gold, ivory, and rubber. To get these goods, Europeans believed they needed to dominate regions of Africa rich in these natural resources.

Nationalism in Europe In addition to economic reasons, imperialism was also caused by the desire of European nations to expand their empires. In the 1800s, many small European states unified to form larger nations. In the process, a new sense of national pride called **nationalism** was created. These new nations fought for power and control of land and resources.

Modern Technology Imperialism in Africa would not have been possible without new weapons and advances in transportation and medicine. These changes were the result of the Industrial Revolution in Europe during the 1800s. Discovery of a treatment to control malaria, for example, made it possible for Europeans to live in tropical regions.

By the 1880s, steam replaced wind as a source of power for warships. However, ships could only carry about two weeks' worth of coal.

Africa in 1914

As a result, ports where ships could stop to resupply coal were needed. Along the African coast, such ports became so valuable that colonies grew around them. Settlers and the military provided some protection to the ships.

Partition of Africa The competition between European nations for land in Africa was fierce. To lessen this tension, countries held a conference in Berlin, Germany, in 1884–85. There European leaders came to an agreement that there had to be settlers living in each European colony. If a colony did not have any settlers, it could not exist. Second, they agreed that a nation had to get approval from other nations to claim new territory. Finally, they decided that nations had to end slavery in their colonies.

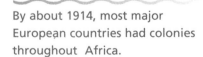

By about 1914, most major European countries had colonies throughout Africa.

Interpreting the Map Which African nations were not European colonies?

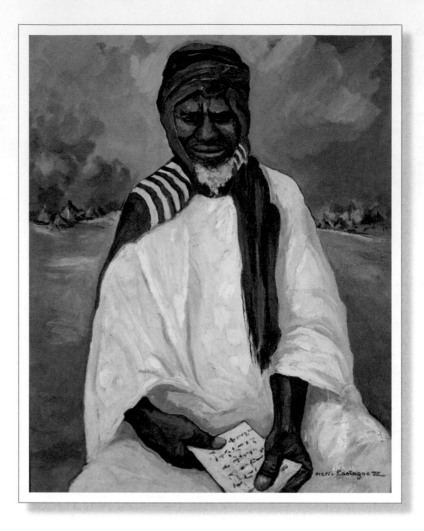

In the late 1800s, Samory Touré resisted French colonialism in his native Guinea by creating his own army. Touré also tried to create a kingdom in West Africa, but was later captured by the French. **Interpreting the Visual Record What emotion is Touré expressing in this portrait?**

Between 1885 and 1914, almost all of Africa was divided between Belgium, France, Great Britain, Germany, Spain, Italy, and Portugal. Only Ethiopia and Liberia remained independent. Former slaves from the United States went to Africa and settled in Liberia which became an independent nation in 1847. In drawing boundaries throughout Africa, Europeans did not consider the African peoples living there. Africans already had their own political and cultural boundaries. Many kingdoms and states that had already been established were divided by the Europeans.

✔ **READING CHECK:** (*Human Systems*) Why did European nations colonize Africa?

African Resistance

During the period of European imperialism, new roads and railroads were built throughout Africa. Europeans introduced new crops and new ways of farming. European medicine helped save and improve the lives of Africans. But even though European imperialism did benefit some Africans, most objected to European rule. Many Africans did not want Europeans telling them how to live. Ethnic groups throughout Africa resisted adopting European culture. Africans wanted to keep their own cultures and religions.

As Europeans continued to dominate Africans, wars erupted between Africans and Europeans. Even though Africans did not have rifles like the Europeans, they fought fiercely. In southern Africa, the Zulu fought against a British invasion of their land. The Zulu defeated the British in the first war in 1879. However, the British invaded Zululand again several months later and defeated the Zulu. A war correspondent described the Zulu's courage by writing, "Their noble ardour (determination) could not endure in the face of . . . civilized warfare."

A major resistance against European imperialism, however, came from a military leader in Guinea named Samory Touré. He fought the French for 15 years. Touré proclaimed himself king, and his empire was the largest in West Africa. In 1898, the French captured Touré and defeated his army.

Many Africans resisted the attempt by Europeans to change their way of life. Some African leaders, however, cooperated with the Europeans. For example, in 1892, a king in northern Ghana signed a free trade treaty with Great Britain. The French hoped Africans living in their colonies would adopt French culture. Most Europeans, however, did not think Africans should be treated equally.

✓ **READING CHECK:** (*Human Systems*) In what ways did Africans resist European imperialism?

▲
This drawing from about 1875 shows a Zulu warrior with shield, spears, and traditional dress.

Section Review 3

Define or identify: imperialism, nationalism, Samory Touré

Reading for the Main Idea

1. (Places and Regions) What regions of Africa were colonized by the British?

2. (Human Systems) In what ways did Africans resist European imperialism?

Critical Thinking

3. Finding the Main Idea Why did Africans resist European imperialism?

4. Analyzing Information Why did Europeans draw political boundaries in Africa?

Organizing What You Know

5. Summarizing Copy the following graphic organizer. Use it to list three causes of European imperialism in Africa.

Causes of European imperialism

Homework Practice Online
Keyword: SK5 HP8

Nationalist Movements

Read to Discover

1. How did World War I increase feelings of nationalism in Africa?
2. What made South Africa different from the rest of Africa?
3. What were some results of independence for African countries?

Vocabulary

boycotted
apartheid

People

Nelson Mandela
Wole Soyinka

Reading Strategy

TAKING NOTES Use the headings in this section to create an outline. As you read about nationalist movements in Africa, write what you learn beneath each heading.

▲
A French colonist directs African workers on a rubber plantation in French Equatorial Africa in the 1940s.

Interpreting the Visual Record Why did the French want to control this region of Africa?

Beginnings of Nationalism in Africa

Until the years following World War I, European countries controlled nearly all of Africa. Europe's African colonies gained access to better health care, more effective farming methods, and improved roads and railroads. The people who lived in these colonies, however, had few rights. They played little part in running their countries, and their cultures were usually not respected by the colonial rulers.

Around the end of the war, the people in these colonies began to express resentment over European control. Many Africans did not want to continue working for low wages on land owned by European colonists. As a result, many Africans moved to cities to find better work. There they organized workers' associations and protested unfair treatment by colonial governments. They developed more pride in their own cultures and national identities. These feelings of nationalism led to demands for self-rule. By the 1930s many colonies in Africa were calling for independence.

✓ **READING CHECK:** *Summarizing* Why did many colonies in Africa want to become independent?

African Nationalism

Most African countries did not actually become independent until after World War II. African soldiers who had fought in British and French armies during the war had been exposed to new ideas. They probably learned about European political systems from their fellow soldiers. When they returned home, they brought some new ideas with them. Some began to protest against racism and political oppression.

These protests were linked to a worldwide movement called Pan-Africanism. The movement was begun by people of African descent living in Britain, the United States, and the West Indies. They wanted cultural unity and equality for everyone of African heritage. Members of the Pan-African movement wanted two things. First, they sought to end European control over Africa. They also wanted Africa to become a homeland for all people of African descent. Despite these efforts, however, it took many years for most African colonies to gain independence. In some countries the people were able to achieve their goals peacefully. In others, however, the fight for independence became an armed struggle.

▲
The Organization of African Unity (OAU), whose flag is seen here, grew out of the Pan-African movement in the 1960s. In 2002, the OAU changed its name to the African Union.

Ghana gained independence from Great Britain in 1957.
Interpreting the Visual Record How are these women celebrating their independence from colonial rule?

▼

British Colonies The first British African colony to gain independence was the Gold Coast. Protestors staged demonstrations and **boycotted**, or refused to buy, British goods. Finally in 1957 the British agreed to let the people of the Gold Coast choose their own government. The people voted for independence. The Gold Coast became the independent nation of Ghana. Other British colonies followed this example. The colonies that became Kenya, Malawi, Nigeria, and Zambia all won their independence by the 1960s. Zimbabwe became independent in 1980.

Other Colonies By 1962 France had granted independence to nearly all of its African colonies. Other European countries were not as quick to give up their colonies. Belgium gave up any claim to its Congo colony—which later became the Democratic Republic of the Congo—after violence broke out in 1959. Portugal also refused to free its colonies until after bloody civil wars. Angola, the last Portuguese colony in Africa, won its independence in 1975.

South Africa The independent Union of South Africa was created in 1910. However, from the beginning, its government had been controlled by the descendants of British and Dutch settlers. White South Africans enforced a policy of **apartheid**. This was a system of laws that denied black South Africans any political rights. Many South Africans—both black and white—protested apartheid laws. Some protests turned violent, and others were violently put down. Many people were killed. Black leaders like Nelson Mandela were thrown into prison. Other countries around the world also disapproved of apartheid policies. Some of these countries refused to trade or have any dealings with South Africa.

Things changed in the 1990s. South Africa banned apartheid. Nelson Mandela was freed from prison and was elected president in 1994. Mandela and his government worked to establish a new government based on equality for all South Africans.

✔ **READING CHECK:** (*Contrasting*) How was South Africa different from other African countries?

◄

Nelson Mandela called on the people of South Africa to "heal the wounds of the past."

Interpreting the Visual Record What do you think the phrase "heal the wounds of the past" means?

Life in Independent Africa

Independence did not solve all of the problems of the former African colonies. In addition, new challenges faced the newly independent countries. At the same time, however, people around the world developed a new interest in Africa.

Challenges Many political leaders of the new African countries were inexperienced. If they were unable to improve conditions in their countries, military leaders sometimes took control. Many African countries were run by military dictatorships through the late 1900s. Civil wars broke out between ethnic groups in some countries. Thousands of people died. Many countries also fell into debt. Crops failed due to droughts and the overuse of land, and millions more people died. Diseases like malaria and AIDS have also killed many Africans. Together these factors prevented economic development in many countries, leaving much of Africa poor and unable to create new industries.

Cultural Revival As demands for independence in Africa grew, people around the world developed an interest in African culture. Writers like Nigeria's Wole Soyinka and Chinua Achebe won awards for their stories about African life. African music and art became popular worldwide. Also, African directors such as Senegal's Ousmane Sembene made movies that were seen in many countries.

✔ **READING CHECK:** (*Summarizing*) How did life in Africa change after independence?

▲ Beginning in the early 1900s, African art was recognized outside of Africa. The expressive style of African artists influenced artists throughout the world including Spanish painter Pablo Picasso.

go.hrw.com
Homework Practice Online
Keyword: SK5 HP8

Section Review 4

Define or Identify: boycotted, apartheid, Nelson Mandela, Wole Soyinka

Reading for the Main Idea

1. (*Human Systems*) How did World War I lead to the growth of nationalism in Africa?

2. (*Human Systems*) What were some features of life in independent Africa?

Critical Thinking

3. **Drawing Inferences and Conclusions** How did other countries influence South Africa's decision to end apartheid?

4. **Analyzing** How did boycotting British goods affect the Gold Coast's struggle for independence?

Organizing What You Know

5. **Identifying Cause and Effect** Copy the following graphic organizer. Use it to describe the process that led to the growth of nationalism in and independence for former African colonies.

Define and Identify

Identify each of the following:

1. pharaohs
2. pyramids
3. hieroglyphics
4. mummification
5. Imhotep
6. oral history
7. Mansa Musa
8. imperialism
9. nationalism
10. Samory Touré
11. apartheid
12. Nelson Mandela

Review the Main Ideas

13. Why did the Egyptians build pyramids?
14. Why did the kingdom of Aksum decline?
15. What language is a combination of an African language and Arabic?
16. What was a unique feature of Great Zimbabwe?
17. What factors made imperialism possible?
18. What was necessary before a European country could claim a colony in Africa?

19. What did supporters of Pan-Africanism want in Africa?
20. Which British colony in Africa was the first to achieve independence?

Thinking Critically

21. **Summarizing** Why did ancient Egyptians mummify their dead rulers?
22. **Analyzing Information** How do you think the location of the Swahili States affected the creation of a new culture in East Africa?
23. **Finding the Main Idea** What was life like in ancient Sub-Saharan Africa?
24. **Drawing Inferences and Conclusions** Why do you think Africans resisted European imperialism?
25. **Analyzing Information** What were some challenges African countries faced after independence?

Map Activity

26. Identify the places marked on the map.
    Red Sea
    Great Zimbabwe
    Egypt
    Kush
    Nile River
    Swahili States

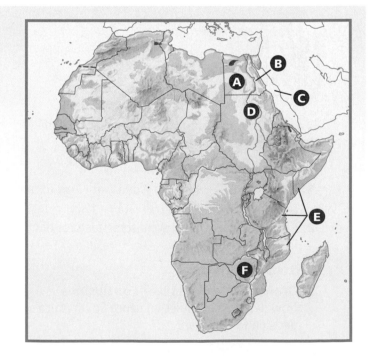

Writing Activities

Imagine that you are a reporter for a newspaper in South Africa in the 1990s. Write a news story about the protests you witness and what the protesters hope to achieve. Think about who you would interview and what questions you would ask. Be sure to use standard grammar, spelling, sentence structure, and punctuation.

internet connect

Internet Activity: go.hrw.com
KEYWORD: SK5 GT8

Choose a topic to explore about Africa's history:
- Learn more about ancient Egypt.
- Write a report about the trading states of Sub-Saharan Africa.
- Write a biography of a figure in Africa's history.

Social Studies Skills Practice

Interpreting Maps

Study the following map of Indian Ocean trade routes. Then answer the questions.

Indian Ocean Trade Routes

1. Based on your knowledge of physical geography, how did traders sail easily back and forth across the Indian Ocean?
2. What regions outside Africa did East Africans trade with?
3. How do you think trade influenced the lives of East Africans?

Analyzing Primary Sources

Read the following passage from "The Great Hymn to the Aten," an early Egyptian hymn to the sun god Aten. Then answer the questions.

Your rays nurse all fields.
When you shine they live, they grow for you;
You made the seasons to foster all that you made,
Winter to cool them, heat that they taste you.
You made the far sky to shine therein,
To behold all that you made;
You alone, shining in your form of living Aten,
Risen, radiant, distant, near.
You made millions of forms from yourself alone,
Towns, villages, fields, the river's course;
All eyes observe you upon them,
For you are the Aten of daytime on high . . .

1. What is the subject of this hymn?
2. Why do you think an early Egyptian wrote this hymn?
3. What did the early Egyptians believe the god Aten was responsible for making?
4. From reading this passage, do you think religion was a central part of Egyptian life? Why or why not?

CHAPTER 9

North Africa

The first region in Africa we will study is North Africa. Before we do that, we will meet Shaimaa. She and nearly all other Egyptians live along the Nile River or in the Nile Delta.

Ahlan! (Hi!) My name is Shaimaa, and I am 18. I live with my mother and my little sister in an apartment. We live about an hour from downtown Cairo. My father lives in the United States but visits us every year.

Every day but Friday, I get up at 7:00 A.M., drink a glass of milk, and then meet my friends. School is about 15 minutes away on the metro (subway). We go to an all-girls school. We all have religious education in school. I study Islam with the other Muslim girls. The Christian girls meet with their religious teacher. At about 3:00 P.M., I get home from school. I eat a big lunch of chicken and vegetables and sleep for a couple of hours. When I wake up, I have a lot of homework. At 10:00 P.M. we have a small meal of cheese, yogurt, or beans before bedtime.

On Fridays I usually go to movies with my girlfriends and walk along the Nile. Sometimes I stay home and listen to music.

أنا طالبة في القاهرة،
في شمال افريقيا.
أهلاً وسهلاً بكم

Translation: I am a student in Cairo, in North Africa. Welcome to all of you.

Section 1 Physical Geography

Read to Discover

1. What are the major physical features of North Africa?
2. What climates, plants, and wildlife are found in North Africa?
3. What are North Africa's major resources?

Vocabulary

ergs
regs
depressions
silt

Places

Red Sea
Mediterranean Sea
Sahara
Nile River
Sinai Peninsula
Ahaggar Mountains
Atlas Mountains
Qattara Depression
Nile Delta
Lake Nasser
Suez Canal

Reading Strategy

USING PRIOR KNOWLEDGE On a sheet of paper write the word Know on the left side. Write Learn on the right side. Look at the physical-political map of North Africa. What do you know about this region? Write your answers on the left side of the paper. As you read the section, write what you learn on the right side.

North Africa: Physical-Political

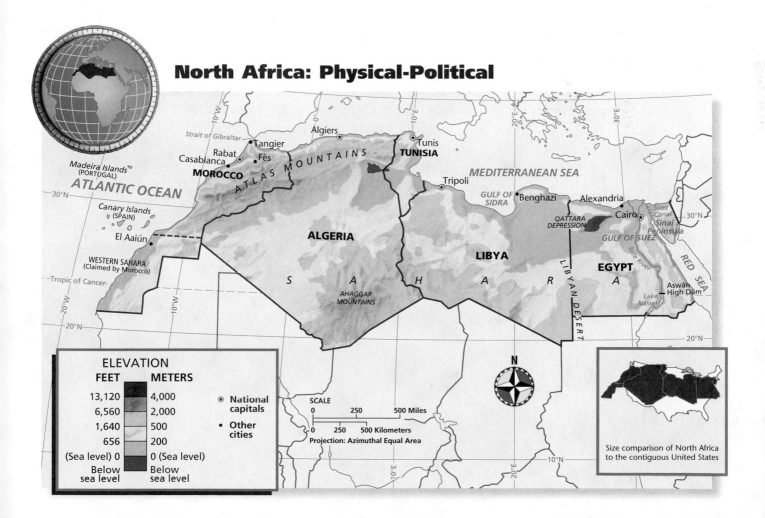

ELEVATION

FEET	METERS
13,120	4,000
6,560	2,000
1,640	500
656	200
(Sea level) 0	0 (Sea level)
Below sea level	Below sea level

⊛ National capitals
• Other cities

SCALE
0   250   500 Miles
0   250   500 Kilometers
Projection: Azimuthal Equal Area

Size comparison of North Africa to the contiguous United States

Physical Features

North Africa includes Morocco, Algeria, Tunisia, Libya, and Egypt. The region stretches from the Atlantic Ocean to the Red Sea. Off the northern coast is the Mediterranean Sea. In the south is the Sahara (suh-HAR-uh), a vast desert. The region also has mountains, the northern Nile River valley, and the Sinai (SY-ny) Peninsula.

The Sahara The huge Sahara covers most of North Africa and stretches southward. The name *Sahara* comes from the Arabic word for "desert." The Sahara is the largest desert in the world. It is so big that nearly all of the United States would fit into it.

Large areas of this very dry region have few people or none at all. Great "seas" of sand dunes called **ergs** cover about a quarter of the desert. Much of the rest of the Sahara is made up of broad, windswept gravel plains. These gravel plains are called **regs**.

Mountains Do you think of deserts as flat regions? Well, the Sahara is not flat. Some sand dunes and ridges rise as high as 1,000 feet (305 m). The Sahara also has mountain ranges. For example, the Ahaggar (uh-HAH-guhr) Mountains are located in the central Sahara. Their highest peak is 9,842 feet (3,000 m). The Atlas Mountains on the northwestern side of the Sahara are higher. Mountains there rise to 13,671 feet (4,167 m).

There also are very low areas in the Sahara. These low areas are called **depressions**. The Qattara (kuh-TAHR-uh) Depression in western Egypt is 440 feet (134 m) below sea level. Other low areas often have large, dry lake beds. Water from rare rain storms collects there.

Oases like this one in Algeria are scattered throughout the vast Sahara.

Interpreting the Visual Record How do these trees survive in the desert's harsh, dry climate?

▼

The Nile The world's longest river, the Nile, flows northward through the eastern Sahara. The Nile empties into the Mediterranean Sea. It is formed by the union of two rivers, the Blue Nile and the White Nile. They meet in Sudan, south of Egypt.

The Nile River valley is like a long oasis in the desert. Water from the Nile irrigates surrounding farmland. The Nile fans out near the Mediterranean Sea, forming a large river delta. About 99 percent of Egypt's population lives in the Nile River valley and the Nile Delta.

For centuries rain far to the south caused annual floods along the northern Nile that left rich **silt** in surrounding fields. Silt is finely ground soil good for growing crops. The Aswan High Dam, which was completed in 1971, was built to control flooding. Water trapped by the dam formed Lake Nasser in southern Egypt. However, the dam also traps silt, preventing it from being carried downriver. Today Egypt's farmers must use fertilizers to enrich the soil.

The Sinai and Suez Canal East of the Nile is the triangular Sinai Peninsula. Barren, rocky mountains and desert cover the Sinai. Between the Sinai and the rest of Egypt is the Suez Canal. The canal was built by the French in the 1860s. It is a strategic waterway that connects the Mediterranean Sea with the Red Sea.

✓ READING CHECK: (*Places and Regions*) What are the major physical features of North Africa?

Water from the Nile River irrigates rich farmlands along the river and in its delta. You can clearly see the Nile Delta in the satellite photograph. The irrigated farmlands of the delta are shown in red.

Interpreting the Visual Record
(*Human-Environment Interaction*)
Why do you think most Egyptians live near the Nile River?

The Arabian camel has long been used for transportation in the Sahara. It can store water in the fat of its hump. Camels have survived for more than two weeks without drinking.

Climate, Vegetation, and Animals

There are three main climates in North Africa. A desert climate covers most of the region. Temperatures range from mild to very hot. How hot can it get? Temperatures as high as 136°F (58°C) have been recorded in Libya! However, the humidity is very low. As a result, temperatures can drop quickly after sunset.

In some areas there has been no rain for many years. However, rare storms can cause flash floods. In places these floods as well as high winds have carved bare rock surfaces out of the land. Storms of sand and dust can also be severe.

Hardy plants and animals live in the desert. Grasses, small shrubs, and even trees grow where there is enough water. Usually this is in oases. Gazelles, hyenas, baboons, foxes, and weasels are among the region's mammals.

Much of the northern coast west of Egypt has a Mediterranean climate. Winters there are mild and moist. Summers are hot and dry. Plant life includes grasses, shrubs, and even a few forests in the Atlas Mountains. Areas between the Mediterranean climate and the Sahara have a steppe climate. Shrubs and grasses grow there.

✓ **READING CHECK:** (*Physical Systems*) How does climate affect the plants and wildlife of North Africa?

Olives like these in Morocco are an important agricultural product in North Africa. Olives and olive oil are common ingredients in many foods around the Mediterranean.

Resources

Good soils and rain or river water aid farming in coastal areas and the Nile River valley. Common crops are wheat, barley, olives, grapes, citrus fruits, and cotton. The region also has good fishing waters.

Oil and gas are important resources, particularly for Libya, Algeria, and Egypt. Morocco mines iron ore and minerals used to make fertilizers. The Sahara has minerals such as copper, gold, and silver.

✓ **READING CHECK:** (*Physical Systems*) What are North Africa's major resources?

go.hrw.com
Homework Practice Online
Keyword: SK5 HP9

Section Review 1

Define and explain: ergs, regs, depressions, silt

Working with Sketch Maps On a map of North Africa that you draw or that your teacher provides, label the following: Red Sea, Mediterranean Sea, Sahara, Nile River, Sinai Peninsula, Ahaggar Mountains, Atlas Mountains, Qattara Depression, Nile Delta, Lake Nasser, and the Suez Canal. In a box in the margin, identify the dam that created Lake Nasser.

Reading for the Main Idea

1. (*Places and Regions*) What two mountain ranges are found in North Africa?

2. (*Places and Regions*) What part of Egypt is east of the Suez Canal?

3. (*Environment and Society*) How did the Nile affect farming in the river valley?

Critical Thinking

4. Drawing Inferences and Conclusions Where would you expect to find most of North Africa's major cities?

Organizing What You Know

5. Summarizing Use this graphic organizer to describe the physical features of North Africa.

Climates	Plants and Animals	Resources

Read to Discover

1. What are the major events in the history of North Africa?
2. What are some important facts about the people and culture of North Africa?

Vocabulary

pharaohs
hieroglyphs
Bedouins

Places

Alexandria
Cairo
Fès
Western Sahara

People

Alexander the Great
Naguib Mahfouz

Reading Strategy

FOLDNOTES: TWO-PANEL FLIP CHART Create the FoldNote titled **Two-Panel Flip Chart** described in the Appendix. Label one flap History and the other flap Culture. As you read the section, write what you learn about each topic beneath its flap.

History

The Nile River valley was home to some of the world's oldest civilizations. Sometime after 3200 B.C. lands along the northern Nile were united into one Egyptian kingdom.

The early Egyptians used water from the Nile to grow wheat, barley, and other crops. They also built great stone pyramids and other monuments. Egyptian **pharaohs**, or kings, were buried in the pyramids. How did the Egyptians build these huge monuments? See Connecting to Technology on the next page.

The Egyptians also traded with people from other places. To identify themselves and their goods, the Egyptians used **hieroglyphs** (HY-ruh-glifs). Hieroglyphs are pictures and symbols that stand for ideas or words. They were the basis for Egypt's first writing system.

West of Egypt were people who spoke what are called Berber languages. These people herded sheep and other livestock. They also grew wheat and barley in the Atlas Mountains and along the coast.

Invaders Because of North Africa's long coastline, the region was open to invaders over the centuries. Those invaders included people from the eastern Mediterranean, Greeks, and Romans. For example, one invader was the Macedonian king Alexander the Great. He founded the city of Alexandria in Egypt in 332 B.C. This city became an important seaport and trading center on the Mediterranean coast.

Beginning in the A.D. 600s, Arab armies from Southwest Asia swept across North Africa. They brought the Arabic language and Islam to the

The tombs of early Egyptian pharoahs were decorated with paintings, crafts, and treasures. You can see hieroglyphs across the top of this wall painting.

BUILDING THE PYRAMIDS

The monuments of ancient Egypt are among the wonders of the world. They are thousands of years old. These pyramids, temples, and other structures reflect the power of Egyptian rulers and the skills of Egyptian engineers.

The most famous of Egypt's monuments are the huge stone pyramids at Giza near Cairo. The pyramids there were built more than 4,000 years ago as tombs for Egyptian pharaohs. The largest structure is the Great Pyramid. At its base the pyramid's sides are each about 755 feet (230 m) long. The pyramid rises nearly 500 feet (152 m) above the desert floor.

How did the Egyptians build the pyramids? Workers cut large blocks of stone far away and rolled them on logs to the Nile. From there the blocks were moved on barges. At the building site, the Egyptians finished carving the blocks. Then they built dirt and brick ramps alongside the pyramids. They hauled the blocks up the ramps.

The average weight of each of the 2.3 million blocks in the Great Pyramid is 2.5 tons (2.25 metric tons). Building the Great Pyramid probably required from 10,000 to 30,000 workers. They finished the job in about 20 years, but the pyramid still stands thousands of years later.

Understanding What You Read

1. What kinds of monuments did the Egyptians build?
2. How did the Egyptians make up for not having wheeled vehicles?

region. Today most North Africans are Muslim and speak Arabic. Under Muslim rule, North African cities became major centers of learning, trade, and craft making. These cities included Cairo in Egypt and Fès in Morocco.

European Control In the 1800s European countries began to take over the region. By 1912 they controlled all of North Africa. In that year Italy captured Libya from the Ottoman Empire. Spain already controlled northern Morocco. France ruled the rest of Morocco as well as Tunisia and Algeria. Egypt was under British control.

Egypt gained limited independence in 1922. The British kept military bases there and maintained control of the Suez Canal until 1956. During World War II the region was a major battleground. After the war, North Africans pushed for independence. Libya, Morocco, and Tunisia each won independence in the 1950s.

Algeria was the last North African country to win independence. Many French citizens had moved to the country. They considered Algeria part of France. Algeria finally won independence in 1962, after a long, bitter war. Most French residents of Algeria then moved to France.

Modern North Africa Since independence, the countries of North Africa have tried to build stronger ties with other Arab countries. For example, Egypt led other Arab countries in several wars against Israel. However, in 1979 Egypt signed a peace treaty with Israel.

In 1976 Morocco took over the former Spanish colony of Western Sahara. Western Saharan rebels have been trying to win independence from Morocco since then.

✔ **READING CHECK:** *Places and Regions* What were some major events in the history of North Africa?

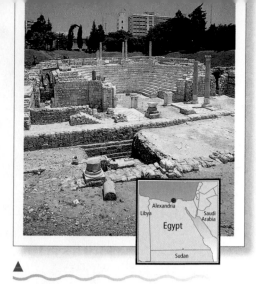

The ruins of an old Roman amphitheater remain in Alexandria, Egypt.

The inset photograph shows the beautiful doors of the royal palace in Fès, Morocco.

The floor of the beautiful Muhammad Ali mosque in Cairo is covered with carpet. Muslim men kneel and bow with their faces to the ground to pray.

Culture

As you have read, the histories of the North African countries have much in common. You will also find many cultural similarities among those countries.

Language and Religion Egyptians, Berbers, and **Bedouins** make up nearly all of Egypt's population. Bedouins are nomadic herders who travel throughout deserts of Egypt and Southwest Asia. Most people in the countries to the west are of mixed Arab and Berber ancestry. Arabic is the major language. Some people speak Berber languages.

Most ethnic Europeans left North Africa after the region's countries became independent. However, French, Italian, and English still are spoken in many areas.

Most North Africans are Muslims. Of the region's countries, Egypt has the largest number of non-Muslims. About 6 percent of Egyptians are Christians or practice other religions.

Food and Festivals What kind of food would you eat on a trip to North Africa? Grains, vegetables, fruits, and nuts are common there. Many meals include couscous (KOOS-koos). Couscous is made from wheat and looks like small pellets of pasta. It is steamed over boiling water or soup. Often it is served with vegetables or meat, butter, and olive oil. Some people mix their couscous with a fiery hot sauce called *harissa*.

A popular dish in Egypt is *fuul*. It is made from fava beans mashed with olive oil, salt, pepper, garlic, and lemons. The combination is then served with hard-boiled eggs and bread.

Important holidays in North Africa include the birthday of the prophet of Islam, Muhammad. The birthday is marked

A variety of vegetables and meat surround a large serving of couscous.

Interpreting the Visual Record What does this food tell you about agricultural products of the region?

with lights, parades, and special sweets of honey, nuts, and sugar. During the holy month of Ramadan, Muslims abstain from food and drink during the day.

Art and Literature North Africa has long been known for its beautiful architecture, wood carving, and other crafts. Women weave a variety of textiles. Among these are beautiful carpets that feature geometric designs and bright colors.

The region has also produced important writers and artists. For example, Egyptian poetry and other writing date back thousands of years. One of Egypt's most famous writers is Naguib Mahfouz. In 1988 he became the first Arab writer to win the Nobel Prize in literature. Egypt also has a growing movie industry. Egyptian films in Arabic have become popular throughout Southwest Asia and North Africa.

Many North Africans also enjoy popular music based on singing and poetry. The musical scale there has many more notes than are common in Western music. As a result, North African tunes seem to wail or waver. Musicians often use instruments such as the three-stringed *sintir* of Morocco.

▲

This Algerian woman and her daughter are using a loom to weave a rug. The loom allows a rug maker to weave horizontal and vertical threads together.

✓ **READING CHECK:** (*Human Systems*) What are some important facts about the people and culture of North Africa?

Homework Practice Online
Keyword: SK5 HP9

Define or identify: pharaohs, hieroglyphs, Alexander the Great, Bedouins, Naguib Mahfouz

Working with Sketch Maps On the map you drew in Section 1, label Alexandria, Cairo, Fès, and Western Sahara. In a box in the margin, identify the country that claims Western Sahara.

Reading for the Main Idea

1. (*Places and Regions*) What early civilization thrived along the northern Nile River about 3200 B.C.?

2. (*Human Systems*) How did Islam and the Arabic language come to North Africa?

3. (*Human Systems*) Which European countries controlled countries in North Africa by 1912?

Critical Thinking

4. **Drawing Inferences and Conclusions** Look at the world map in the textbook's Atlas. Why do you think the Suez Canal is an important waterway for world shipping?

Organizing What You Know

5. **Summarizing** Copy the following graphic organizer. Use it to identify at least six important facts about the languages, religions, food, festivals, art, and literature of North Africa.

Culture in North Africa

COULD YOU SURVIVE THE SAHARA?

ON-LINE EXPEDITIONS

GO TO: go.hrw.com
KEYWORD: SK5 CH9

A Land of Sun and Sand

Despite scorching heat, blinding sandstorms, scorpions, poisonous snakes, and death by starvation or thirst, people have traveled across the desert sands of the Sahara for centuries. Groups of merchants, or caravans, still travel together in the desert for protection. These merchants trade mostly in salt, or "white gold." However, water is the most important resource needed to survive the Sahara. Travelers must find a source of water every few days, or they will perish in temperatures of more than 130 degrees!

SURVIVAL CHALLENGE

You are an archaeologist working at a dig near Lake Chad. You want to find the ruins of Garama, the main city of an ancient warrior people known as the Garamantes. The city's location, in southern Libya, is not on your map. You do have a list of riddles that guided traders north during the height of the Garamantian Empire. Each riddle will lead you to the next source of water. A caravan is leaving soon for Tripoli, so jump on a camel and set out on your adventure! Remember—to survive today's environment, you'll have to solve riddles about the ancient environment. How may looking at the region's geography today shed light on its past?

Throughout the Sahara, traders travel great distances in camel caravans like this one.

Land of Change

The Sahara was not always a desert. About 8000 B.C. the region was a grassland. Stone age peoples who lived in this environment fished in large lakes and hunted giraffes, elephants, and zebras. Early peoples engraved pictures of these animals on rock walls.

By about 500 B.C. the Garamantes were powerful in the Sahara. Even though the Sahara was by this time much drier, the Garamantes grew crops. By digging miles of irrigation canals, the Garamantes tapped into billions of gallons of fossil water. From what you have learned about the importance of water in the desert, what may have caused the Garamantian civilization to decline? How do you think peoples today survive in dry environments? Can you predict what might happen to them in the future?

The Way to Garama

You are on the right path if you see the long necks who once grazed on green land not sand.

Cross the flowing waters three times but wait to drink at the well.

This lake will not quench your thirst. Gather some white gold from its edges.

Rest well in the shade of many trees. You do not have far to go.

Miles of fertile crops point you to a rich and powerful people.

You are here.

0 — 200 miles

Legend:
- ══ Trade route
- ⦿ Well
- ⊙ Salt flat
- ∿ Wadi
- 🦒 Rock art
- 🌴 Oasis
- ⬭ Erg
- ∞∞∞ Ancient irrigation

ALGERIA
LIBYA
SAHARA
NIGER
CHAD
Lake Chad

Section 3 Egypt Today

Read to Discover

1. What are the people and cities of Egypt like today?
2. What are Egypt's important economic activities?
3. What challenges does Egypt face today?

Vocabulary
fellahin

Places
Egypt
Cairo
Alexandria

People
Anwar Sadat

Reading Strategy

FOLDNOTES: LAYERED BOOK Create the FoldNote titled **Layered Book** described in the Appendix. Write Egypt Today on the top tab. Label the other tabs People and Cities, Economy, and Challenges. As you read this section, write what you learn about each topic above each label.

People and Cities

Egypt is North Africa's most populous country. More than 74 million people live there.

Rural Egypt More than half of all Egyptians live in small villages and other rural areas. Most rural Egyptians are farmers called **fellahin** (fel-uh-HEEN). They own very small plots of land. Most fellahin also work large farms owned by powerful families. Many also depend on money sent home by family members working abroad. Many Egyptians work in Europe or oil-rich countries in Southwest Asia.

Cities Egypt's capital and largest city is Cairo. More than 10 million people live there. Millions more live in surrounding cities.

Place A muezzin (moo-E-zuhn) calls Muslims to prayer in Cairo. A muezzin often makes his calls from the door or the minaret, or tower, of a mosque. His calls—or recordings played through speakers—can be heard throughout Islamic communities five times daily.

Place Tourist ships sit on the Nile River in Luxor. Tourists visit the ruins of a beautiful temple built there more than 2,300 years ago. These and other historical sites make tourism an important part of Egypt's economy.

Cairo was founded more than 1,000 years ago along the Nile. Its location at the southern end of the delta helped it grow. The city lies along old trading routes between Asia and Europe. Later it was connected by railroad to Mediterranean ports and the Suez Canal.

Today Cairo is a mixture of modern buildings and small, mud-brick houses. People continue to move there from rural areas. Many live in makeshift housing. Traffic and pollution are serious problems.

Alexandria has more than 4 million people. It is located in the Nile Delta along the Mediterranean coast. The city is a major seaport and home to many industries.

✔ **READING CHECK:** (*Places and Regions*) What are Egypt's people and cities like today?

Fish is an important food for people living along the Nile. One fish, the giant Nile perch, can grow to a weight of 300 pounds (136 kg).

Economy

To provide for its growing population, Egypt is working to expand its industries. Textiles, tourism, and oil are three of the most important industries. The Suez Canal is another source of income. Ships pay tolls to pass through it. Ships use the canal to avoid long trips around southern Africa. This makes the canal one of the world's busiest waterways.

About 30 percent of Egyptian workers are farmers. A warm, sunny climate and water for irrigation make the Nile Delta ideal for growing cotton. Farmlands along the Nile River are used for growing vegetables, grain, and fruit.

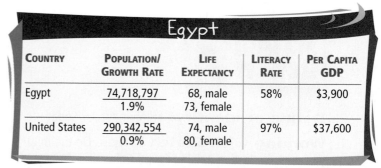

COUNTRY	POPULATION/ GROWTH RATE	LIFE EXPECTANCY	LITERACY RATE	PER CAPITA GDP
Egypt	74,718,797 1.9%	68, male 73, female	58%	$3,900
United States	290,342,554 0.9%	74, male 80, female	97%	$37,600

Source: Central Intelligence Agency, *The World Factbook 2003*

Interpreting the Chart **How does the growth rate of Egypt compare to that of the United States?**

✔ **READING CHECK:** (*Places and Regions*) How does the Suez Canal affect Egypt's economy?

Challenges

Egypt faces important challenges today. For example, the country's farmland is limited to the Nile River valley and delta. To keep the land productive, farmers must use more and more fertilizer. This can be expensive. In addition, overwatering has been a problem. It has brought to the surface salts that are harmful to crops. These problems and a rapidly growing population have forced Egypt to import much of its food.

In addition, Egyptians are divided over their country's role in the world. Many want their country to remain a leader among Arab countries. However, others want their government to focus more on improving life for Egyptians at home.

Many Egyptians live in severe poverty. Many do not have clean water for cooking or washing. The spread of disease in crowded cities is also a problem. In addition, about half of Egyptians cannot read and write. Still, Egypt's government has made progress. Today Egyptians live longer and are much healthier than 50 years ago.

Another challenge facing Egyptians is the debate over the role of Islam in the country. Some Muslims want to shape the country's government and society along Islamic principles. However, some Egyptians worry that such a change would mean fewer personal freedoms. Some supporters of an Islamic government have turned to violence to advance their cause. Attacks on tourists in the 1990s were particularly worrisome. A loss of tourism would hurt Egypt's economy.

✓ **READING CHECK:** *Places and Regions* What are some of the challenges Egypt faces today?

go. hrw .com **Homework Practice Online**
Keyword: SK5 HP9

Define or identify: fellahin, Anwar Sadat

Working with Sketch Maps On the map you drew in Section 2, label Egypt, Cairo, and Alexandria. Identify the capital of Egypt.

Reading for the Main Idea

1. *Human Systems* What is the relationship between religion and culture in Egypt today?

2. *Places and Regions* What industries and crops are important to Egypt's economy?

Critical Thinking

3. **Analyzing Information** Why do so many Egyptians live along the Nile and in the Nile Delta?

4. **Finding the Main Idea** How has Cairo's location shaped its development?

Organizing What You Know

5. **Summarizing** Copy the following graphic organizer. Use it to describe some of the challenges facing Egypt today.

Challenges

Read to Discover

1. What are the region's people and cities like today?
2. What are the countries' important economic activities?
3. What challenges do the countries face today?

Vocabulary

Casbah
souks
free port
dictator

Places

Libya
Tunisia
Algeria
Morocco
Tripoli
Benghazi
Algiers
Casablanca
Rabat
Tunis
Strait of Gibraltar

People

Mu 'ammar al-Gadhafi

Reading Strategy

READING ORGANIZER   Create a five-column chart on a sheet of paper. Label the columns Country, People, Cities, Economy, and Challenges. In the Country column, write Libya, Tunisia, Algeria, and Morocco, skipping several lines between them. As you read the section, write what you learn about each country in the appropriate column.

People and Cities

Western Libya, Tunisia, Algeria, and Morocco are often called the Maghreb (MUH-gruhb). This Arabic word means "west" or "the direction of the setting sun." Most of the Maghreb is covered by the Sahara. There you will find sandy plains and rocky uplands. Cities and farmland are located in narrow coastal strips of land. These strips lie between the Atlantic and Mediterranean coasts in the north and the Sahara and Atlas Mountains farther inland.

Libya is almost completely desert. Fertile land is limited to small areas along the coast. Cities and most of the population are found in those coastal areas. Libya is the most urbanized country in the region. More than 85 percent of Libya's more than 5 million people live in cities. The largest cities are Benghazi and the capital, Tripoli.

Algiers is a large city and is Algeria's capital. The central part of Algiers is a maze of winding alleys and tall walls. This old district is called the **Casbah**. The Casbah is basically an old fortress. **Souks**, or marketplaces, are found there today. The centers of other North African cities also have Casbahs.

Other large cities include Casablanca and Rabat in Morocco and Tunis in Tunisia. Another Moroccan city, Tangier, overlooks the Strait of Gibraltar. This beautiful city was once a Spanish territory. Today tourists can take a quick ferry ride from Spain across the strait to Tangier, a **free port**. A free port is a city in which almost no taxes are placed on goods sold there.

✓ **READING CHECK:**   *Places and Regions*   What geographic factors explain the region's population patterns?

▲
With a backdrop of brightly colored mosaics, Moroccan boys enjoy a day in Tangier's Casbah.

Libya, Tunisia, Algeria, and Morocco

COUNTRY	POPULATION/ GROWTH RATE	LIFE EXPECTANCY	LITERACY RATE	PER CAPITA GDP
Algeria	32,818,500 1.65%	69, male 72, female	70%	$5,300
Libya	5,499,074 2.4%	74, male 78, female	83%	$7,600
Morocco	31,689,265 1.6%	68, male 72, female	52%	$3,900
Tunisia	9,924,742 1.7%	74, male 76, female	74%	$6,500
United States	290,342,554 0.9%	74, male 80, female	97%	$37,600

Source: Central Intelligence Agency, *The World Factbook 2003*

Interpreting the Chart **Which country is the least economically developed?**

Place Marrakech (muh-RAH-kish) is a popular tourist resort in central Morocco. It sits in the foothills of the Atlas Mountains.

Economy

Oil, mining, and tourism are important industries in these countries. Oil is the most important resource, particularly in Libya and Algeria. Money from oil pays for schools, health care, other social programs, and military equipment. The region's countries also have large deposits of natural gas, iron ore, and lead.

Morocco is the only North African country with little oil. However, the country is an important producer and exporter of fertilizer.

About 20 percent of the workers in Libya, Tunisia, and Algeria are farmers. In Morocco farmers make up about half of the labor force. North Africa's farmers grow and export wheat, other grains, olives, fruits, and nuts. However, the region's desert climate and poor soils limit farming, particularly in Libya. Libya imports most of its food.

The Maghreb countries have close economic relationships with European countries. This is partly because of old colonial ties between North Africa and Europe. In addition, European countries are located nearby, lying just across the Mediterranean Sea. Formal agreements between North African countries and the European Union (EU) also have helped trade. Today about 80 percent of Tunisia's trade is with EU countries. The largest trade partners of Algeria, Libya, and Morocco are also EU members. Many European tourists visit North Africa.

✓ **READING CHECK:** *Places and Regions* How does the oil industry affect Libya's and Algeria's schools, health care, and other social programs?

Challenges

The countries of the Maghreb have made much progress in health and education. However, important challenges remain. Among these challenges is the need for more economic freedom. Each of these countries has had elements of a command economy, in which government owns and operates industry. However, in recent years the region's governments have moved to loosen that control.

Political freedoms are limited for many North Africans. Many have little say in their governments. For example, Morocco is officially ruled by a king and an elected parliament, but the parliament actually has little power. Since 1969 Libya has been ruled by a **dictator**, Mu'ammar al-Gadhafi. A dictator is someone who rules a country with complete power. Gadhafi has supported bombing, kidnapping, and other acts of violence against Israel and Israel's supporters. As a result, countries have limited their economic relationships with Libya.

As in Egypt, another challenge is conflict over the role of Islam in society. For example, in Algeria some groups want a government based on Islamic principles and laws. In 1992 the government canceled elections that many believed would be won by Islamic groups. Violence between Algeria's government and some Islamic groups has claimed thousands of lives since then.

✓ **READING CHECK:** (*Places and Regions*) What are some of the challenges the region's countries face today?

These Islamic students at a religious school in Libya are reciting verses from the Qur'an. Religious education is important in this mostly Islamic region.

▼

Section Review 4

go.hrw.com **Homework Practice Online**
Keyword: SK5 HP9

Define or identify: Casbah, souks, free port, dictator, Mu'ammar al-Gadhafi

Working with Sketch Maps On the map you created in Section 3, label Libya, Tunisia, Algeria, Morocco, Tripoli, Benghazi, Algiers, Casablanca, Rabat, Tunis, and the Strait of Gibraltar. In a box in the margin, identify the national capitals of the region's countries.

Reading for the Main Idea

1. (*Places and Regions*) What are the old, central districts of many North African cities like?

2. (*Places and Regions*) What type of economy have these nations had, and how is this changing?

Critical Thinking

3. Finding the Main Idea Where are the region's farms and most of its people found today? Why?

4. Analyzing Information How are the political rights of North Africans different from those of people in the United States?

Organizing What You Know

5. Summarizing Copy the following graphic organizer. Use it to list industries, resources, farm products, and trade partners of the Maghreb countries.

Industries	
Resources	
Farm products	
Trade partners	

Define and Identify

Identify each of the following:

1. ergs
2. regs
3. depressions
4. silt
5. pharaohs
6. hieroglyphs
7. Alexander the Great
8. Naguib Mahfouz
9. Bedouins
10. fellahin
11. Anwar Sadat
12. Casbah
13. souks
14. free port
15. dictator
16. Mu'ammar al-Gadhafi

Review the Main Ideas

17. How does geography affect settlement patterns in North Africa?
18. What are North Africa's main climates?
19. Why did many French citizens move to Algeria before 1962?
20. What are some important holidays in North Africa?
21. Which Egyptian city lies along old trading routes and was founded more than 1,000 years ago?
22. What are some important challenges facing Egypt today?

23. What are the most important industries in North Africa?
24. Which is the most urbanized country in North Africa?
25. Why do the Maghreb countries have close economic relationships with European countries?

Think Critically

26. **Finding the Main Idea** How do you think the Sahara has influenced settlement in the region?
27. **Finding the Main Idea** Why are most of North Africa's cities and population located in coastal areas?
28. **Analyzing Information** Why is the Suez Canal important to world trade?
29. **Finding the Main Idea** In what way has Islam influenced politics in North Africa?
30. **Making Generalizations and Predictions** Based on what you have read, what kinds of challenges do you think North Africans will face in coming decades? Explain your answer.

Map Activity

31. On a separate sheet of paper, match the letters on the map with their correct labels.

   Sinai Peninsula
   Ahaggar Mountains
   Atlas Mountains
   Nile Delta
   Cairo
   Western Sahara
   Tripoli
   Algiers
   Casablanca
   Strait of Gibraltar

Writing Activity

Imagine that you are a Bedouin teenager in the Sahara. Write a one-paragraph journal entry about a typical day in your life. How do you cope with the desert heat? What is it like living without a permanent home? What religion do you practice? What do you eat? Use the library and other resources to help you. Be sure to use standard grammar, spelling, sentence structure, and punctuation.

☑ internet connect ▇▇▇

Internet Activity: go.hrw.com
KEYWORD: SK5 GT9

Choose a topic to explore about North Africa:

- Journey through the Sahara.
- Examine the rich history of North Africa.
- Practice using Arabic calligraphy.

Social Studies Skills Practice

Analyzing Graphs

Arable land is land that is suitable for farming. Study the following chart of the percentages of arable land in North Africa. Then answer the questions.

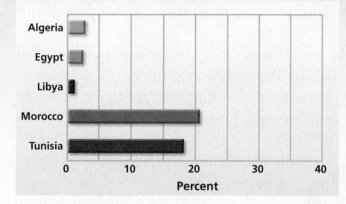

Arable Land in North Africa

1. Which country has the least land suitable for growing crops?
2. Which country has the most land suitable for growing crops?
3. Overall, do the countries of North Africa have good land for farming? Explain your answer.
4. What can you determine about the region's climate and soils from these numbers?

Analyzing Primary Sources

Read the following excerpt from Egyptian writer Naguib Mahfouz's acceptance speech after he was awarded the Nobel Prize for Literature. Then answer the questions.

"This man coming from the third world, how did he find the peace of mind to write stories? You are perfectly right. I come from a world labouring under the burden of debts whose paying back exposes it to starvation or very close to it. . . . Fortunately, art is generous and sympathetic. In the same way that it dwells with the happy ones it does not desert the wretched [unhappy]. It offers both alike the convenient means for expressing what swells up in their [heart]."

1. According to Mahfouz, what purpose does writing serve?
2. Does Mahfouz feel that everyone can become writers? Why?
3. What does Mahfouz mean when he says he comes from the third world?
4. According to Mahfouz, how are third-world countries burdened?

West Africa

We move south now to West Africa. The land becomes much wetter as we move southward. Before we continue, we meet Ousseina from Niger.

*I*na kwanna! (Good morning!) My name is Ousseina, and I am 11. I have an identical twin sister whose name is Hassana. I live in Niamey, the capital of Niger, with my sister, our grandmother, our parents, and many aunts and uncles. We have a large compound of many one- or two-room houses around a common courtyard. After breakfast, my sister and I go from door to door, greeting all the elders in our compound.

We have to walk many miles to school, but we meet all our friends along the way. Some of our friends speak Hausa like us. Others speak a different language of Niger. In the afternoon, we go home to sleep because it is so hot—more than 110°F (43°C)! Late in the afternoon we return to school for more classes.

After school, we help grandma pound spices for dinner, sweep the room, and wash the dishes. At bedtime, grandma tells us stories and sings.

Ni Ousseina ce. Gidana yana Nijar.

Translation: I am Ousseina.
My home is in Niger.

Section 1 Physical Geography

Read to Discover

1. What landforms and climates are found in West Africa?
2. Why is the Niger River important to the region?
3. What resources does West Africa have?

Vocabulary

zonal
Sahel
harmattan
tsetse fly
bauxite

Places

Sahara
Sahel
Niger River
Gulf of Guinea

Reading Strategy

READING ORGANIZER Create a spider map by drawing a circle on a sheet of paper. Label the circle West Africa. Create legs for Landforms, Climate, Niger River, and Resources. As you read the section, write what you learn beneath each leg.

West Africa: Physical-Political

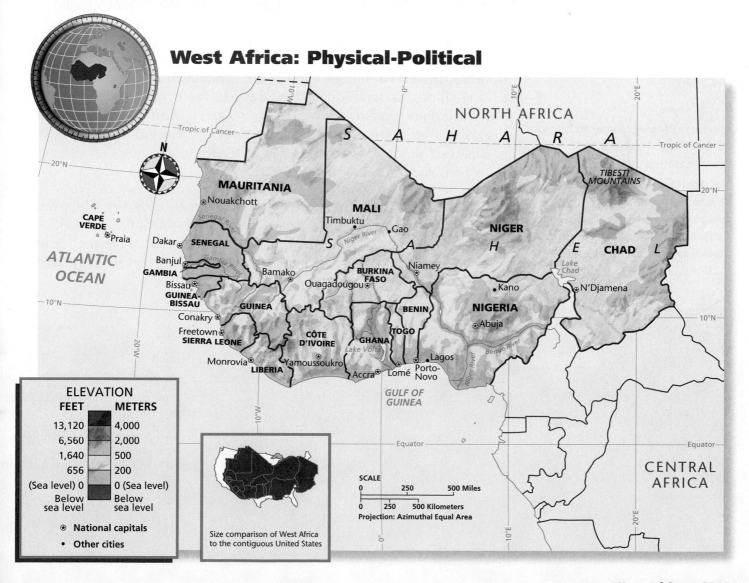

ELEVATION

FEET	METERS
13,120	4,000
6,560	2,000
1,640	500
656	200
(Sea level) 0	0 (Sea level)
Below sea level	Below sea level

⊛ National capitals
• Other cities

Size comparison of West Africa to the contiguous United States

SCALE
0   250   500 Miles
0   250   500 Kilometers
Projection: Azimuthal Equal Area

☑ internet connect

GO TO: go.hrw.com
KEYWORD: SK5 CH10
FOR: Web sites about
West Africa

Landforms and Climate

West Africa is largely a region of plains. There are low mountains in the southwest and high mountains in the northeast. Four major climate types stretch from east to west in bands or zones. Therefore, geographers say the region's climates are **zonal**.

The Sahara The northernmost parts of the region lie within the Sahara, the first climate zone. The Sahara is the world's largest desert. It stretches across northern Africa from the Atlantic Ocean to the Red Sea. Large areas of this dry climate zone have few or no people.

The Sahel South of the Sahara is a region of dry grasslands called the **Sahel** (sah-HEL). This second climate zone has a steppe climate. Rainfall varies greatly from year to year. In some years it never rains. During winter a dry, dusty wind called the **harmattan** (hahr-muh-TAN) blows south from the Sahara.

During the late 1960s a drought began in the Sahel. Crops failed for several years, and there was not enough grass for the herds. Animals overgrazed the land, and people cut the few large trees for firewood. Wind blew away fertile soil, and the Sahara expanded southward. Without plants for food, many animals and people died. Recent years have been rainier, and life has improved.

The Savanna Farther south is the savanna zone. It contains good soil, thick grass, and scattered tall trees. Farmers can do well when the rains come regularly. However, the region is home to a dangerous insect. The **tsetse** (TSET-see) **fly** carries sleeping sickness, a deadly disease. Although insecticides can help control the flies, they are too expensive for most people to buy.

The Coast and Forest The fourth climate zone lies along the Atlantic and Gulf of Guinea coasts. Many of West Africa's largest cities lie in this coastal zone. You will find a wet, humid tropical climate there. Plentiful rain supports tropical rain forests. However, many trees

Farmers use river water to irrigate onion fields in central Mali. Farming can be difficult in the dry Sahel.

Interpreting the Visual Record

Human-Environment Interaction How do you think economic factors have affected the use of technology in bringing water to the fields?

have been cut to make room for growing populations. As a result, environmental damage is a serious problem.

✓ **READING CHECK:** (*Places and Regions*) What are the region's landforms and climate zones?

The Niger River

The most important river in West Africa is the Niger (NY-juhr). The Niger River starts in low mountains just 150 miles (241 km) from the Atlantic Ocean. It flows eastward and southward for 2,600 miles (4,183 km) and empties into the Gulf of Guinea.

The Niger brings life-giving water to West Africa. In the Sahel it divides into a network of channels, swamps, and lakes. This network is known as the inland delta. The Niger's true delta on the Gulf of Guinea is very wide. Half of Nigeria's coastline consists of the delta.

✓ **READING CHECK:** (*Environment and Society*) Why is the Niger River important to West Africa?

▲

The hippopotamus is just one of the many animal species living in the Niger region. Hippopotamuses are good swimmers and can stay underwater for as long as six minutes.

Resources

West Africa's mineral riches include diamonds, gold, iron ore, manganese, and **bauxite**. Bauxite is the main source of aluminum. Nigeria is a major exporter of oil. In fact, oil and related products make up about 95 percent of that country's exports.

✓ **READING CHECK:** (*Places and Regions*) What are some of the region's resources?

Homework Practice Online
Keyword: SK5 HP10

Section Review 1

Define and explain: zonal, Sahel, harmattan, tsetse fly, bauxite

Working with Sketch Maps On a map of West Africa, label the following: Sahara, Niger River, and Gulf of Guinea.

Reading for the Main Idea

1. (*Physical Systems*) What effect has drought had on West Africa's vegetation?

2. (*Places and Regions*) What natural resources are found in West Africa?

3. (*Places and Regions*) What is West Africa's most important river? Describe its two delta regions.

Critical Thinking

4. **Making Generalizations and Predictions** Where in the region would you expect to find the densest populations? Why?

Organizing What You Know

5. **Summarizing** Copy the following graphic organizer. Use it to list and describe the region's climate zones.

Zones	Characteristics

Read to Discover

1. What great African kingdoms once ruled the region?
2. How did contact with Europeans affect West Africa?
3. What challenges do the region's governments face?
4. What are some features of West African culture?

Vocabulary

archaeology
oral history
animism

Places

Timbuktu

People

Mansa Musa

Reading Strategy

READING ORGANIZER Before you read, draw eight boxes down the center of a sheet of paper. As you read this section, write what you learn in the boxes to create a chain of events in the history of West Africa.

West Africa's History

Much of what we know about West Africa's early history is based on **archaeology**. Archaeology is the study of the remains and ruins of past cultures. **Oral history**—spoken information passed down from person to person through generations—offers other clues.

Great Kingdoms Ancient artifacts suggest that the earliest trading towns developed in the Niger's inland delta. Traders brought dates and salt from the desert. People from the Sahel sold animals and hides. Other trade goods were grains, fish, kola and other tropical nuts, and metals, such as gold. (Much later, kola nuts provided the flavor for cola drinks.) This trade helped African kingdoms grow. One of the earliest West African kingdoms, Ghana (GAH-nuh), had become rich and powerful by about A.D. 800.

Place These early West African cliff paintings illustrate features from a ceremonial ritual for young people.

Map: Algeria, Mauritania, Mali, Niger, Guinea, Burkina Faso, Côte d'Ivoire

Some 200 years later, North African merchants began crossing the Sahara to trade in Ghana. These merchants introduced Islam to West Africa. In time, Islam became the main religion practiced in the Sahel.

Later Ghana fell to Muslim warriors from Morocco. The Muslim empire of Mali (MAH-lee) replaced the kingdom of Ghana. Mali stretched from the Niger's inland delta to the Atlantic coast. Mansa Musa was king of Mali during the early 1300s. Famous for his wealth and wise rule, Mansa Musa supported artists, poets, and scholars.

The kingdom of Songhay (SAWNG-hy) came to power as Mali declined. With a university, mosques, and more than 100 schools, the Songhay city of Timbuktu was a cultural center. By about 1600, however, Moroccan invasions had weakened the kingdom.

Forested areas south of the Sahel were also home to great civilizations. In what is now Nigeria, wealthy kings were buried with brass sculptures and other treasures.

✓ **READING CHECK:** (*Human Systems*) What are some of the great African kingdoms that once ruled the region?

The Slave Trade During the 1440s Portuguese explorers began sailing along the west coast of Africa. The Europeans called it the Gold Coast for the gold they bought there. Once they could buy gold where it was mined, the Europeans stopped buying it from Arab traders. As a result, the trans-Sahara trade and the great trade cities faded.

For a while, both Europeans and Africans profited from trade with each other. However, by the 1600s the demand for labor in Europe's American colonies changed everything. European traders met this demand by selling enslaved Africans to colonists. The slave trade was very profitable for these traders.

The slave trade had devastating effects on West African communities. Families were broken up when members were kidnapped and enslaved. Many Africans died on the voyage to the Americas. Most who survived were sent to the West Indies or Brazil. The slave trade finally ended in the 1800s. By then millions of Africans had been forced from their homes.

Colonial Era and Independence In the late 1800s, many European countries competed for colonies in West Africa. France claimed most of the region's northwest. Britain, Germany, and Portugal seized the rest.

In all of West Africa only tiny Liberia remained independent. Americans had founded it in the 1820s as a home for freed slaves. Sierra Leone, a British colony, also became a home for freed slaves.

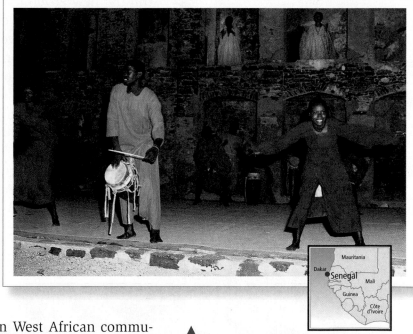

▲

(*Place*) There are many reminders of the slave trade and its effects on West Africans. Performers here reenact the treatment of enslaved Africans in an old slave house in Dakar, Senegal.

Some Europeans moved to West Africa to run the colonies. They built roads, bridges, and railroads. Teachers and missionaries set up Christian churches and schools. After World War II, Africans increasingly worked for independence. Most of the colonies gained independence during the 1950s and 1960s. Portugal, the last European country to give up its West African colonies, did so in 1974.

✔ **READING CHECK:** (*Human Systems*) What impact did contact with Europeans have on West Africa?

Challenges

Independence brought a new set of challenges to the region. The borders that the Europeans had drawn ignored human geography. Sometimes borders separated members of one ethnic group. Other borders grouped together peoples that did not get along. As a result, many West Africans were more loyal to their ethnic groups than to their new countries. In addition, too few people had been trained to run the new governments. Dictators took control in many countries. Unrest and military rulers still trouble the region. Some countries have made progress, however. For example, in 1996 Chad created its first democratic constitution.

The governments of West African countries have several difficult problems in common. Birthrates are high. As a result, more and more people must make a living from the small amount of fertile land. In addition, many people are moving to already crowded cities even though urban jobs are few. To fight these challenges and promote economic growth, countries formed the Economic Community of West African States (ECOWAS) in 1975.

✔ **READING CHECK:** (*Places and Regions*) What are three challenges the region faces?

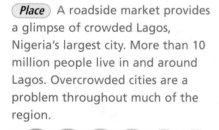

(*Place*) A roadside market provides a glimpse of crowded Lagos, Nigeria's largest city. More than 10 million people live in and around Lagos. Overcrowded cities are a problem throughout much of the region.

▼

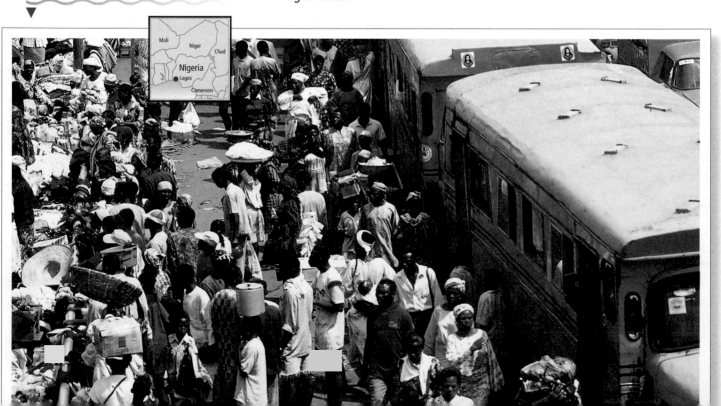

Marriage Is a Private Affair
by *Chinua Achebe*

Chinua Achebe was born in an Ibo village in Nigeria in 1930. Many of his writings explore the changes colonialism brought to Africa. They also look at the conflict between old and new ways. In this story, Achebe looks at different views a father and son have about marriage.

A Nigerian church carving

"Father," began Nnaemeka suddenly, "I have come to ask for forgiveness."

"Forgiveness? For what, my son?" he asked in amazement.

"It's about this marriage question."

"Which marriage question?"

"I can't—we must—I mean it is impossible for me to marry Nweke's daughter."

"Impossible? Why?" asked his father.

"I don't love her."

"Nobody said you did. Why should you?" he asked.

"Marriage today is different . . ."

"Look here, my son," interrupted his father, "nothing is different. What one looks for in a wife are a good character and a Christian background."

Nnaemeka saw there was no hope along the present line of argument.

"Moreover," he said. "I am engaged to marry another girl who has all of Ugoye's good qualities, and who . . ."

His father did not believe his ears. "What did you say?" he asked slowly and disconcertingly[1]. . . .

"Whose daughter is she, anyway?"

"She is Nene Atang."

"What!" All the mildness was gone again. "Did you say Neneataga, what does that mean?"

"Nene Atang from Calabar. She is the only girl I can marry." This was a very rash reply and Nnaemeka expected the storm to burst.

Analyzing Primary Sources

1. What universal theme does the passage illustrate?
2. Why do you think the father and son disagree about marriage?

Vocabulary [1]disconcertingly: disturbingly

Place These homes in Burkina Faso are made of a mixture of mud, water, and cow dung. Trees are scarce in the Sahel and savanna zones. As a result, there is little wood for construction. Women are responsible for painting and decorating the walls of the homes.

Culture

Hundreds of ethnic groups exist in West Africa today. Hundreds of languages are spoken in the region. In some areas, using the colonial languages of French or English helps people from different groups communicate. West African languages that many people share, such as Fula and Hausa, also aid communication.

Religion The traditional religions of West Africa have often been forms of **animism**. Animism is the belief that bodies of water, animals, trees, and other natural objects have spirits. Animists also honor the memories of ancestors. In some isolated areas animism still forms the basis of most religious practices. Today most people of the Sahel practice Islam. Farther south live many Christians.

Clothing and Homes Some West Africans, particularly in cities, wear Western-style clothing. Others wear traditional robes, pants, blouses, and skirts. These are often made from colorful patterned cotton fabric. Because of the warm climate, most clothing is loose and flowing. Many women wear beautiful folded and wrapped headdresses. In the desert men often wear turbans. Both men and women may use veils to protect their faces from blowing sand.

Rural homes are small and simple. Many homes in the Sahel and savanna zones are circular. Straw or tin roofs sit atop mud, mud-brick, or straw huts. However, in cities you will find some modern buildings.

✓ **READING CHECK:** (**Human Systems**) What are some features of West African culture?

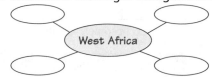
Homework Practice Online
Keyword: SK5 HP10

Section Review 2

Define or identify: archaeology, oral history, Mansa Musa, animism

Working with Sketch Maps On the map you created in Section 1, label Timbuktu. What made Timbuktu an important Songhay city?

Reading for the Main Idea

1. (**Human Systems**) How did European contact affect West Africa's people?

2. (**Human Systems**) Where in West Africa are Islam and Christianity practiced?

Critical Thinking

3. Drawing Inferences and Conclusions How might shared histories and challenges lead to more cooperation among the region's countries?

4. Drawing Inferences and Conclusions Why do you think mud bricks are used in West Africa?

Organizing What You Know

5. Summarizing Use the following graphic organizer to summarize challenges facing West Africa.

West Africa

Read to Discover

1. What are Mauritania, Mali, and Niger like today?
2. What challenges do Chad and Burkina Faso face?

Vocabulary

millet
sorghum
malaria
staple

Places

Nouakchott
Senegal River
Gao
Tibesti Mountains
Lake Chad
Ouagadougou

People

Moors

Reading Strategy

READING ORGANIZER Draw a three-column chart on a sheet of paper. Label the columns Country, Economic Activities, and Challenges. As you read this section, list each country and what you learn about their economic activities and challenges.

Mauritania, Mali, and Niger

Most of the people in these three large countries are Muslim. Mauritania, in fact, has laws based on Islam. These countries are also former French colonies, and French influence remains. In Mali and Niger, the official language is French. However, the people there speak more than 60 different local languages.

Today, drought and the expanding desert make feeding the people in these countries difficult. In the Sahel nomads depend on their herds of cattle, goats, and camels. In the savanna regions farmers grow **millet** and **sorghum**. These grain crops can usually survive drought.

Mauritania Many Mauritanians are Moors, people of mixed Arab and Berber origin. They speak Arabic. In the past, Moors enslaved some of the black Africans. Today, tension between the two groups continues.

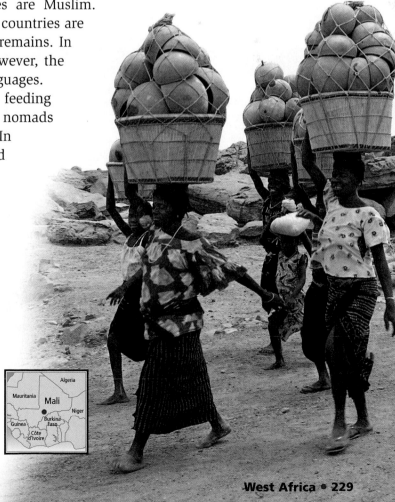

Women carry goods for sale in a market in central Mali. Much of Mali's economic activity takes place in the Niger River's inland delta.

Interpreting the Visual Record

Human-Environment Interaction Why is Mali's economic activity centered around the inland delta?

Region Mud and other local materials were used to build many mosques in the Sahel. This mosque is located in Djenné [je-NAY], Mali. The majority of people living in the Sahel are Muslims.

The Tuareg (TWAH-reg) people of the Sahara and Sahel pound powdered blue dye into their flowing robes. They do this rather than dip the fabric in precious water. The blue powder wears off onto the skin, where it may help hold in moisture.

Most Mauritanians were once nomadic herders. Today, the expanding Sahara has crowded more than half of the nomads into the cities. Just 40 years ago, Nouakchott (nooh-AHK-shaht), Mauritania's capital, was a small village. More than 700,000 people live there now. About half of the population lives in shacks at the city's edges.

Throughout the country, people are very poor. Only in the far south, near the Senegal River, can farmers raise crops. Fishing in the Atlantic Ocean is another source of income.

Mali To the east of Mauritania lies landlocked Mali. The Sahara covers much of northern Mali. In the south lies a wetter farming region. About 80 percent of Mali's people fish or farm along the Niger River. Cotton is the country's main export. Timbuktu and Gao (GOW), ancient trading cities, continue to attract tourists.

Health conditions in Mali are poor. **Malaria**, a disease spread by mosquitoes, is a major cause of death among children.

Niger The Niger River flows through just the southwestern corner of landlocked Niger. Only about 3 percent of Niger's land is good for farming. All of the country's farmland lies along the Niger River and near the Nigerian border. Much of the rest of Niger lies within the Sahara. Farmers raise cotton, peanuts, beans, peas, and rice. Millet and sorghum are two of the region's **staple**, or main, food crops. The grains are cooked like oatmeal. Nomads in the desert region depend on the dairy products they get from their herds for food.

✔ **READING CHECK:** *Places and Regions* What is it like to live in Mauritania, Mali, and Niger?

The Sahel Countries

Country	Population/Growth Rate	Life Expectancy	Literacy Rate	Per Capita GDP
Burkina Faso	13,228,460 2.6%	43, male 45, female	27%	$1,080
Chad	9,253,493 3.1%	46, male 50, female	48%	$1,100
Mali	11,626,219 3%	44, male 46, female	46%	$860
Mauritania	2,912,584 2.9%	49, male 54, female	41%	$1,900
Niger	11,058,590 2.7%	42, male 42, female	17%	$830
United States	290,342,554 0.9%	74, male 80, female	97%	$37,600

Source: Central Intelligence Agency, *The World Factbook 2003*

Interpreting the Chart Based on the numbers in the chart, which two countries in the region are the least economically developed?

Chad and Burkina Faso

Drought has also affected the former French colonies of Chad and Burkina Faso (boohr-KEE-nuh FAH-soh). These countries are among the world's poorest and least developed. Most people farm or raise cattle.

Chad Chad is located in the center of Africa. The Tibesti Mountains in northern Chad rise above the Sahara. Lake Chad is in the south. Not long ago, the lake had a healthy fishing industry. It even supplied water to several other countries. However, drought has evaporated much of the lake's water. At one time, Lake Chad had shrunk to just one third its size in 1950.

The future may be better for Chad. A civil war ended in the 1990s. Also, oil reserves now being explored may help the economy.

Burkina Faso This country's name means "land of the honest people." Most of its people follow traditional religions. The country has thin soil and few mineral resources. Few trees remain in or near the capital, Ouagadougou (wah-gah-DOO-goo). They have been cut for firewood and building material. Jobs in the city are also scarce. To support their families many young men work in other countries. However, foreign aid and investment are starting to help the economy.

✔ **READING CHECK:** *Places and Regions* What are the challenges facing Chad and Burkina Faso?

Major Religions of the Sahel Countries

Country	Animism	Islam	Christianity
Burkina Faso	40%	50%	10%
Chad	14%	51%	35%
Mali	9%	90%	1%
Mauritania		100%	
Niger	20%	80%	

■ Animism ■ Islam ■ Christianity

Source: Central Intelligence Agency, *The World Factbook 2003*

Although most people in the Sahel are Muslim, some practice forms of animism and Christianity.

Interpreting the Graph (*Place*) Which country's population is entirely Muslim? Which countries have significant numbers of Christians?

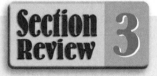

Section Review 3

Define or identify: millet, sorghum, Moors, malaria, staple

Working with Sketch Maps On the map you created in Section 2, draw the boundaries of Mauritania, Mali, Niger, Chad, and Burkina Faso. Then label Nouakchott, Senegal River, Gao, Tibesti Mountains, Lake Chad, and Ouagadougou. In a box in the margin, describe what has happened to Lake Chad in recent decades.

Reading for the Main Idea

1. (*Places and Regions*) Why has Nouakchott grown so rapidly?

2. (*Places and Regions*) Which European language is most common in the Sahel countries? Why?

Critical Thinking

3. **Drawing Inferences and Conclusions** How do the typical foods of Niger relate to the country's water resources?

4. **Comparing** What do Chad and Burkina Faso have in common with the other Sahel countries?

Organizing What You Know

5. **Comparing** Copy the following graphic organizer. Label each of the star's points with one of the Section 3 countries. In the center, list characteristics the countries share.

go.hrw.com

Homework Practice Online

Keyword: SK5 HP10

Read to Discover

1. What is life in Nigeria like today?
2. What economic challenges do the region's other countries face?

Vocabulary

secede
griots
cacao

Places

Abuja
Lagos
Dakar
Monrovia
Lake Volta

People

Wole Soyinka

Reading Strategy

FOLDNOTES: TRI-FOLD Create a **Tri-Fold** FoldNote as described in the Appendix. Write what you know about West Africa's coastal countries in the column labeled "Know." Then, write what you want to know in the column labeled "Want." As you read the chapter, write what you learn about each country in the column labeled "Learn."

The faces of Nigeria are very young. About 45 percent of all Nigerians are younger than 15 years old. Only about 22 percent of all Americans are that young.

Nigeria

The largest country along West Africa's coast is Nigeria. With more than 130 million people, it has Africa's largest population.

Nigeria's People Nigeria was once an important British colony. Like many other colonies, Nigeria's borders included many ethnic groups. Today, a great variety of ethnic groups live in Nigeria. The Yoruba, Fula, Hausa, and Ibo are four of the largest ethnic groups. More than 200 languages are spoken there.

Nigeria's ethnic groups have not always gotten along. In the 1960s the Ibo tried to **secede**. That is, they tried to break away from Nigeria and form their own country. They called it Biafra (bee-AF-ruh). However, the Ibo lost the bloody war that followed.

Avoiding ethnic conflicts has continued to be an issue in Nigeria. It was important in choosing a site for a new Nigerian capital in the late 1970s. Leaders chose Abuja (ah-BOO-jah) because it was centrally located in an area of low population density.

Nigeria's Economy Nigeria has some of the continent's richest natural resources. Oil is the country's most important resource. Major oil fields are located in the Niger River delta and just off the coast. Oil accounts for 95 percent of the country's export earnings. Nigeria also

Human-Environment Interaction
Oil drilling rigs like this one are common in areas of southern Nigeria. Oil accounts for about 20 percent of Nigeria's GDP.

Place The headdresses and patterned clothing worn by these women in Dakar are common in Senegal.

has good roads and railroads. Lagos (LAY-gahs), the former capital, is the country's largest city. The city is a busy seaport and trade center.

Although the country has rich resources, many Nigerians are poor. A major cause of the poverty there is a high birthrate. In addition, many Nigerians lack the education and training necessary to hold modern jobs. Another cause is the economy's dependence on oil. When prices are low, the whole country suffers. A third cause of Nigeria's poverty is a history of bad government. Corrupt government officials have used their positions to enrich themselves.

✔ **READING CHECK:** (*Places and Regions*) What are Nigeria's people and economy like today?

Other Coastal Countries

Several small West African countries lie along the Atlantic Ocean and the Gulf of Guinea. They are struggling to develop their economies.

Senegal and Gambia Senegal (se-ni-GAWL) wraps around Gambia (GAM-bee-uh). The odd border was created by French and British diplomats. Senegal, a former French colony, is larger and richer than Gambia, a former British colony. Dakar (dah-KAHR) is Senegal's capital and an important seaport and manufacturing center. Senegal and Gambia have many similarities. Peanuts are their most important crop. Common foods include chicken stew and fish with a peanut sauce. Tourism is growing slowly.

The Ashanti of Ghana

Festivals and ceremonies help the Ashanti people of Ghana keep their heritage of royal grandeur alive. The Ashanti observe the Akwasidae ceremony every six weeks. On this occasion, the Ashanti king emerges from his palace to receive the respect of his people. It is quite a sight. The king, wearing heavy gold ornaments, rides beneath immense colorful umbrellas. Drummers, dancers, musicians, and singers accompany the procession.

What does the king do during the Akwasidae ceremony?

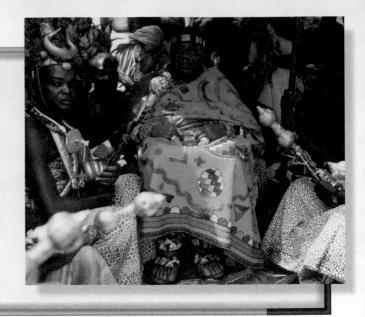

Many of the people speak a language called Wolof (WOH-lawf). **Griots** (GREE-ohz) are important to the Wolof-speakers and other West Africans. Griots are storytellers who pass on the oral histories of their tribes or peoples. Sometimes the griots combine music with their stories, which may take hours or days to tell. Wolof women wear complex hairstyles and gold jewelry.

Guinea, Guinea-Bissau, and Cape Verde Guinea's main natural resource is a huge supply of bauxite. Its small neighbor to the east, Guinea-Bissau (GI-nee bi-SOW), has undeveloped mineral resources. Cape Verde (KAYP VUHRD) is a group of volcanic islands in the Atlantic. It is West Africa's only island country. Farming and fishing bring in the most money there.

Liberia and Sierra Leone Liberia is Africa's oldest republic. Monrovia, Liberia's capital, was named for U.S. president James Monroe. The freed American slaves who settled Liberia and their

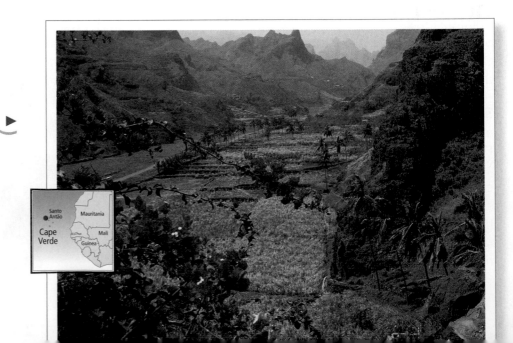

Flowers color the countryside on Santa Antão island in Cape Verde. However, farming can be difficult because droughts are common in the island country.

descendants lived in coastal towns. They often clashed with the Africans already living there. Those Africans and their descendants were usually poorer and lived in rural areas. In the 1980s conflicts led to a bitter civil war. Sierra Leone (lee-OHN) has also experienced violent civil war. The fighting has wrecked the country's economy. Now, both Liberia and Sierra Leone must rebuild. They do have natural resources on which to build stronger economies. Liberia produces rubber and iron ore. Sierra Leone exports diamonds.

Ghana and Côte d'Ivoire The countries of Ghana and Côte d'Ivoire (koht-dee-VWAHR) have rich natural resources. Those resources may help them build strong economies. Ghana is named for the ancient kingdom, although the kingdom was northwest of the modern country. Ghana has one of the largest human-made lakes in the world—Lake Volta. Gold, timber, and **cacao** (kuh-KOW) are major products. Cocoa and chocolate are made from the seeds of the cacao tree. The tree came originally from Mexico and Central America.

Côte d'Ivoire is a former French colony whose name means "Ivory Coast" in English. It is a world leader in cacao and coffee exports. Côte d'Ivoire also boasts Africa's largest Christian church building.

Togo and Benin Unstable governments have troubled both Togo and Benin (buh-NEEN) since independence. Both have experienced periods of military rule. Their fragile economies have contributed to their unstable and sometimes violent politics. These long, narrow countries are poor. The people depend on farming and herding for income. Palm tree products, cacao, and coffee are the main crops in Togo and Benin.

✔ **READING CHECK:** (*Places and Regions*) What are characteristics of the economies of the coastal countries?

go.hrw.com

Homework Practice Online

Keyword: SK5 HP10

Section Review 4

Define or identify: secede, griots, cacao, Wole Soyinka

Working with Sketch Maps On the map that you drew in Section 3, draw the boundaries for the coastal countries. Label Abuja, Lagos, Dakar, Monrovia, and Lake Volta. In a box in the margin, identify the largest and most populous country on West Africa's coast.

Reading for the Main Idea

1. (*Places and Regions*) How is Cape Verde different from the other countries in the region?

2. (*Places and Regions*) What is Nigeria's most important natural resource? Why?

Critical Thinking

3. **Finding the Main Idea** Why must Liberia and Sierra Leone rebuild their economies?

4. **Analyzing Information** Why was choosing a new capital important to Nigeria's future?

Organizing What You Know

5. **Summarizing** Copy the following graphic organizer. Use it to list three main causes of poverty in Nigeria today.

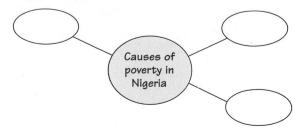

Causes of poverty in Nigeria

CHAPTER 10 — Review and Practice

Define and Identify

Identify each of the following:

1. zonal
2. Sahel
3. harmattan
4. tsetse fly
5. bauxite
6. archaeology
7. oral history
8. Mansa Musa
9. animism
10. millet
11. sorghum
12. malaria
13. staple
14. secede
15. griots
16. cacao
17. Wole Soyinka

Review the Main Ideas

18. What are the four climate zones of West Africa?
19. How do the Niger River's two delta regions differ?
20. How did Islam come to West Africa?
21. What were the effects of the slave trade on West African communities?
22. How has drought affected the countries of the Sahel?
23. What religion do most people in the Sahel practice?
24. On what natural resource does Nigeria's economy depend?
25. How did the United States influence the development of Liberia?

Think Critically

26. **Drawing Inferences and Conclusions** Why are many of West Africa's largest cities located in the coastal and forest zone?
27. **Finding the Main Idea** What role did trade play in the early West African kingdoms and later European colonies in the region?
28. **Analyzing Information** What are three cultural features of West Africa influenced by Europeans?
29. **Drawing Inferences and Conclusions** How have borders set by European colonial powers led to conflicts such as Nigeria's war in Biafra in the late 1960s?
30. **Contrasting** How is Liberia's history different from that of other West African countries?

Map Activity

31. On a separate sheet of paper, match the letters on the map with their correct labels.

    Niger River
    Gulf of Guinea
    Timbuktu
    Nouakchott
    Senegal River
    Tibesti Mountains
    Lake Chad
    Abuja
    Lagos
    Lake Volta

Writing Activity

Imagine that you are an economic adviser to a West African country of your choice. Use print resources to prepare a short economic report for your country's leader. Identify the country's important natural resources and what can be done with them. In addition, describe economic advantages or disadvantages of the country's climate, location, and physical features. Be sure to use standard grammar, spelling, sentence structure, and punctuation.

⚡ internet connect

Internet Activity: go.hrw.com
KEYWORD: SK5 GT10

Choose a topic to explore about West Africa:
- Find out about giant baobab trees.
- Meet the people of West Africa.
- Learn about the history of the slave trade.

Social Studies Skills Practice

Interpreting Graphs

Today, Nigeria relies on crude oil production for much of its wealth. However, during the 1980s the country's oil industry experienced many ups and downs. Study the graph and answer the questions.

Nigeria's Crude Oil Production, 1980–1990

Source: Energy Information Administration

1. In what year did Nigeria produce the least amount of oil?

2. In what years did Nigeria produce more than 1.5 million barrels per day?

3. By approximately how much did oil production decline between 1980 and 1981?

4. Did Nigeria's oil production between 1988 and 1990 increase or decrease?

Analyzing Primary Sources

Read the following description of the kingdom of Ghana in the 1060s by the Arab geographer Al Bakri. Then answer the questions.

"The city of Ghana consists of two towns lying in a plain. One of these towns is inhabited by Muslims. It is large and possesses twelve mosques in one of which the people assemble for the Friday prayer . . . Around the town are wells of sweet water from which they drink and near which they grow vegetables. The land between the two towns is covered with houses. The houses of the inhabitants are made of stone and acacia wood. The king has a palace and a number of dome-shaped dwellings, the whole surrounded by an enclosure like the defensive wall of a city."

1. What resource may have determined the location of the two towns?

2. Why do you think the houses were made of stone and acacia wood?

3. Why were mosques in only one town within the kingdom of Ghana?

4. What is a unique feature of the king's palace?

CHAPTER 11

East Africa

East Africa has been identified by historians as the cradle of the human race. It has made great contributions to the development of world civilization.

My name is Tsiyon. I am 13, and I live in Addis Ababa, the capital of Ethiopia. My house is very far from the city center. I live with my parents and my brothers. We have a servant who helps my mother with the housework. My mother stays at home. My father works for the game department, doing research on the wild animals of Ethiopia.

After a breakfast of bread and tea with milk, I ride to school in a city taxi—a small blue and white minibus—with my brother, Wondemagegn, who works in a garage. I am in the seventh grade at Freyhewat Number Two Junior Secondary School. There are 82 kids in my class! I am in school from 8:00 A.M. to 3:00 P.M. I am studying Amharic—an Ethiopian language—English, math, science, and sports. When I grow up, I want to be a doctor.

At noon, I eat a lunch I brought from home. When I get home, I help my mother sweep the house. Then I watch television. In the evenings, I do my homework.

Indemin adderu?

Translation: How did you pass the night?

Section 1 — Physical Geography

Read to Discover

1. What are the major landforms of East Africa?
2. Which rivers and lakes are important in this region?
3. What are East Africa's climate types and natural resources?

Vocabulary

rifts

Places

Great Rift Valley
Mount Kilimanjaro
Lake Victoria
White Nile
Blue Nile

Reading Strategy

FOLDNOTES: DOUBLE-DOOR Create the FoldNote titled **Double-Door** described in the Appendix. Label the top flap "Rivers and Lakes" and the bottom flap "Climate and Resources." Label the paper beneath the top flap "Rift Valleys" and the paper beneath the lower flap "Mountains and Plains." Then write what you learn about each topic under each label.

East Africa: Physical-Political

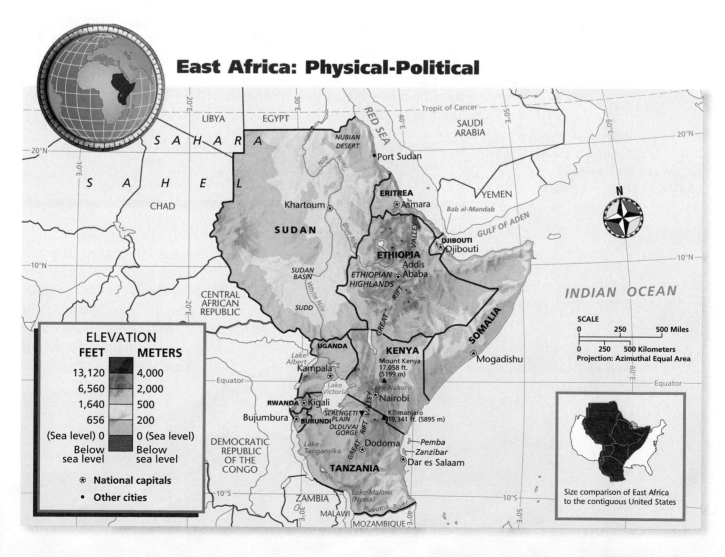

ELEVATION

FEET	METERS
13,120	4,000
6,560	2,000
1,640	500
656	200
(Sea level) 0	0 (Sea level)
Below sea level	Below sea level

⊛ National capitals

• Other cities

Size comparison of East Africa to the contiguous United States

This is a crater rim view of Mount Kilimanjaro. Another name for this volcano is Kilima Njaro— "shining mountain" in Swahili.

The Land

East Africa is a land of high plains and plateaus. In the north, deserts and dry grasslands define the landscape. In the southwest, large lakes dot the plateaus. In the east, sandy beaches and beautiful coral reefs run along the coast. East Africa's most striking features are its great **rifts**. They cut from north to south across the region. Rifts are long, deep valleys with mountains or plateaus on either side. Rifts form when Earth's tectonic plates move away from each other.

The Rift Valleys Deep beneath East Africa's surface, Earth's mantle is churning. This movement causes the land to arch and split along the rift valleys. If you look at the Great Rift Valley from the air, it looks like a giant scar. The Great Rift Valley is made up of two rifts—the eastern rift and the western rift. The rift walls are usually a series of steep cliffs. These cliffs drop an average of about 9,000 feet (2,743 m) to the valley floor. The eastern rift begins north of the Red Sea. The rift continues south through Eritrea (er-uh-TREE-uh) and Ethiopia (ee-thee-OH-pee-uh) into southern Tanzania (tan-zuh-NEE-uh). The western rift extends from Lake Albert in the north to Lake Malawi (mah-LAH-wee), also known as Lake Nyasa, in the south.

Mountains and Plains East Africa also has many volcanic mountains. Mount Kilimanjaro (ki-luh-muhn-JAHR-oh), at 19,341 feet (5,895 m), is Africa's tallest mountain. Although this part of Africa is along the equator, the mountain is so high that snow covers its two volcanic cones. Plains along the eastern rift in Tanzania and Kenya are home to famous national parks.

✓ **READING CHECK:** *Places and Regions* What are the major landforms of East Africa?

Rivers and Lakes

East Africa is the site of a number of rivers and large lakes. The Nile is the world's longest river. It begins in East Africa and flows north to the Mediterranean Sea. Water from small streams collects in Lake Victoria, the source of the White Nile. Waters from Ethiopia's highlands form the Blue Nile. These two rivers

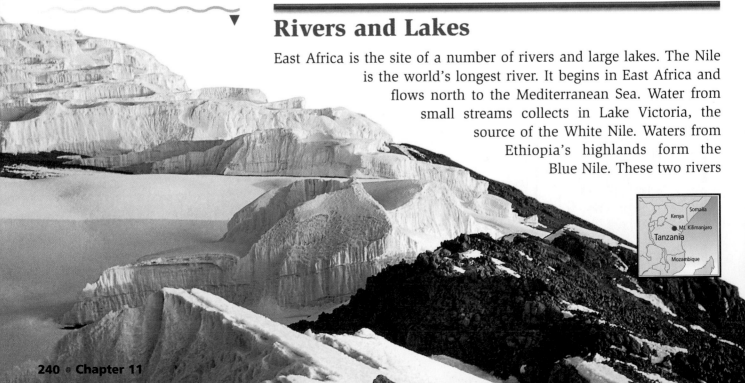

meet at Khartoum, Sudan, to create the mighty Nile. The Nile provides a narrow, fertile lifeline through Sudan by providing irrigation in the desert.

Lake Victoria is Africa's largest lake in area, but it is shallow. Along the western rift is a chain of great lakes. Many of the lakes along the drier eastern rift are quite different. Heat from Earth's interior makes some of these eastern lakes so hot that no human can swim in them. Others, like Lake Nakuru, are too salty for most fish. However, algae in Lake Nakuru provides food for more than a million flamingos.

✓ **READING CHECK:** *Places and Regions* Which rivers and lakes are most important in this region?

▲ Lake Nakuru is known in part for the many flamingos that gather there.

Climate and Resources

Northern Sudan and the northeast coast have desert and steppe climates. The climate changes to tropical savanna as you travel south. However, the greatest climate changes occur along the sides of the rift valleys. The rift floors are dry, with grasslands and thorn shrubs. In contrast, the surrounding plateaus and mountains have a humid highland climate and dense forests. Rain falls at the high elevations, but the valleys are in rain shadows.

Most East Africans are farmers or herders. However, the region does have mineral resources such as coal, copper, diamonds, gold, iron ore, and lead.

✓ **READING CHECK:** *Places and Regions* What are East Africa's climate types and natural resources?

Homework Practice Online
Keyword: SK5 HP11

Define and explain: rifts

Working with Sketch Maps On a map of East Africa that you draw or that your teacher provides, label the following: Great Rift Valley, Mount Kilimanjaro, Lake Victoria, White Nile, and Blue Nile. How do the mountains help support the river systems?

Reading for the Main Idea

1. (*Places and Regions*) What are the major landforms of East Africa?

2. (*Places and Regions*) Which rivers and lakes are located in this part of Africa?

3. (*Physical Systems*) Why are volcanic mountains found in parts of East Africa?

Critical Thinking

4. **Drawing Inferences and Conclusions** How do you think the climate types found in East Africa influence what grows there?

Organizing What You Know

5. **Summarizing** Copy the following graphic organizer. Use it to describe what you know about East Africa's physical geography.

	Vegetation	Climates
Coasts		
Rift Valleys		
Plateaus/mountains		

Read to Discover

1. What important events and developments influenced the history of East Africa?
2. What is the culture of East Africa like?

Vocabulary
Swahili

People
Amanirenus

Reading Strategy

TAKING NOTES   Use the headings in this section to create an outline. As you read the section, write what you learn about East Africa's history and culture beneath each heading.

History

Several early civilizations developed at the site known as Meroë, near where the branches of the Nile come together. These civilizations had their own forms of writing. Each controlled a major trade route. East Africans traded ivory and gold, among other things.

This statue depicts a prince from the early Nubian civilization of northern Sudan.

Christianity and Islam Like Egypt, Ethiopia was an early center of Christianity. In the A.D. 500s Christianity spread into neighboring Nubia, which is now part of Egypt and Sudan. In Nubia, Christian kingdoms lasted until about 1500. Ethiopia still has a large Christian population today.

Arab armies conquered Egypt and North Africa by about A.D. 700. However, these armies were not able to keep control of East Africa. Gradually, Arabic-speaking nomads spread into northern Sudan from Egypt. They brought their Islamic faith with them. At the same time, Islam spread to the coastal region of what is now Somalia. Christianity is believed to have been introduced in Ethiopia as early as the A.D. 300s. Christian kingdoms, particularly in Ethiopia, have fought wars with Muslim leaders. Religion continues to be a source of conflict in this East African region.

The Slave Trade The east coast slave trade dates back more than 1,000 years. Most slaves went to Islamic countries in Africa and Asia. The Portuguese had begun setting up forts and settlements on the East African coast by the early 1500s. At first, the Europeans made little

Kings and nobles of Meroë were buried in these pyramids.

effort to move into the interior. However, in the late 1700s the East African island of Zanzibar became an international slave-trading center. Later, plantations like those of the Americas were set up with slave labor to grow cloves and sugarcane.

Africa Divided In the mid-1800s European adventurers traveled into the African interior searching for the source of the Nile. Here they found rich lands well suited for agriculture. In the 1880s the European powers divided up most of the continent. Most of Africa's modern borders resulted from this process. Control over much of East Africa went to the British. Germany colonized Tanzania, Rwanda, and Burundi. After World War I, with the defeat of Germany, the British took over Tanzania. Belgium gained control of Rwanda and Burundi.

Conflict Within East Africa, just Kenya was settled by large numbers of Europeans. The colonial rulers usually controlled their countries through African deputies. Many of these deputies were traditional chiefs, who often favored their own peoples. This tended to strengthen ethnic rivalries. These ethnic divisions have made it hard for governments to create feelings of national identity.

Independence Ethiopia was never colonized. Its mountains provided natural protection, and its peoples and emperors resisted colonization. It was, however, annexed by Italy from 1936 to 1941. Most East African countries were granted independence by European colonizers in the early 1960s. More recently, East Africa has become headquarters for some international companies and organizations.

✓ **READING CHECK:** (*Human Systems*) Which European countries influenced the history of East Africa?

BIOGRAPHY

Amanirenus
(lived 20s B.C.)

Early in East Africa's history, women often ruled in the region. Those who ruled Kush used the title "Candace." Amanirenus was one of them. She led her army against invading Romans in 24 B.C. Both she and the Romans claimed that they won the fight. The Kushites were able to remove the head from a statue of Augustus Caesar. They put it under the temple stairs so everyone who entered could step on the foreigner who threatened their land.

What symbol did the Kushites use to express their pride in their land?

▲

Afar nomads stop for rest in a desert region of northern Ethiopia.

Culture

East Africa has the world's longest history of human settlement. Gradually, the region developed the continent's greatest diversity of people and ways of life. The **Swahili** language is widely spoken in East Africa. This Bantu language has been greatly influenced by Arabic. In fact, the word Swahili comes from the Arabic word meaning "on the coast."

East Africa shares many challenges with other African regions. One challenge is that populations are growing faster than the economies that support them. Many jobless people have crowded into the cities. Another challenge is religious and ethnic conflict. Such conflict and other political problems have slowed economic progress. Often a country's wealth is spent on weapons rather than helping people.

The ethnic conflicts have roots in the region's history. Colonial borders drawn by Europeans often lumped different ethnic groups into one country. Differences between groups have led to conflict in some countries since independence.

The worst ethnic conflict has been in Rwanda and Burundi. Thousands of Tutsi were killed by the Hutu in Rwanda in the 1990s. There also has been fighting between Muslims and Christians in the northern part of the region.

✓ **READING CHECK:** *Human Systems* What conflicts have occurred between groups in East Africa?

Homework Practice Online
Keyword: SK5 HP11

Section Review 2

Define or identify: Amanirenus, Swahili

Working with Sketch Maps On the map you created in Section 1, highlight the location of the bodies of water you labeled. Why do you think early civilizations settled near these bodies of water?

Reading for the Main Idea

1. *Human Systems* Which European countries influenced the history of this area?

2. *Human Systems* What are the main religions practiced in East Africa?

Critical Thinking

3. **Finding the Main Idea** What conflicts have occurred because of political boundary lines?

4. **Drawing Inferences and Conclusions** Why might Swahili be a particularly important language in East Africa?

Organizing What You Know

5. **Sequencing** Create a time line listing historical events in East Africa from the A.D. 400s to the 1990s. Be sure to include the adoption of Christianity, the slave trade, exploration, colonial rule, independence, and ethnic conflict.

A.D. 400   1990s

Section 3 The Countries of East Africa

Read to Discover

1. Why did settlers come to Kenya?
2. How was Tanzania created?
3. What are Rwanda and Burundi like?
4. What is Uganda like?
5. What are the physical features of Sudan?

Vocabulary

gorge

Places

Kenya
Tanzania
Rwanda
Burundi
Uganda
Sudan

People

Kikuyu
Tutsi
Hutu

Reading Strategy

READING ORGANIZER Before you read, draw a circle in the center of a sheet of paper. Label the circle East African Countries. Draw five rays from the circle. Draw a circle at the end of each ray. Label the circles Kenya, Tanzania, Rwanda and Burundi, Uganda, and Sudan. As you read the section, write what you learn about the countries beside each circle.

Kenya

Kenya's first cities were founded along the coast of the Indian Ocean by Arab traders. Beginning in the 1500s Portugal controlled this coast for about 200 years. Arabs then recaptured it.

During the 1800s British merchants began trading on the coast. They built a railway from Mombasa to Lake Victoria. British settlers then came to take advantage of the fertile highlands. People from India and Pakistan also came to work on the Europeans' farms. Many of the local people, particularly the Kikuyu, moved out of their traditional areas. They became farmworkers or took jobs in the cities. After World War II many Africans protested British colonial rule. There were peaceful demonstrations as well as violent ones.

One conflict was over land. The British and the Kikuyu viewed land differently. The British considered land a sign of personal wealth, power, and property. The Kikuyu saw land as a source of food. This caused conflict because the British wanted the land. Kenya gained independence from Britain in the 1960s, and its government—an elected democracy headed by a president—has been stable ever since.

Kenya is a popular tourist destination. Tourism is a major source of income for the country. Kenya's greatest challenges stem from its rapidly increasing population and a work force hindered by disease and little education. In addition to tourism, many

Movement As in the rest of Africa, Europeans once ruled colonies in East Africa. Fort Jesus, founded in 1593 by the Portuguese, is a national monument in Kenya.

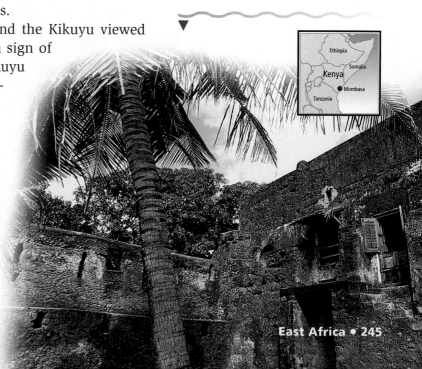

East Africa

COUNTRY	POPULATION/ GROWTH RATE	LIFE EXPECTANCY	LITERACY RATE	PER CAPITA GDP
Burundi	6,096,156 2.2%	42, male 44, female	52%	$600
Kenya	31,639,091 1.3%	45, male 45, female	85%	$1,020
Rwanda	7,810,056 1.8%	38, male 40, female	70%	$1,200
Sudan	38,114,160 2.7%	56, male 58, female	61%	$1,420
Tanzania	35,922,454 1.7%	43, male 46, female	78%	$630
Uganda	25,632,794 2.9%	43, male 46, female	70%	$1,260
United States	290,342,554 0.9%	74, male 80, female	97%	$37,600

Source: Central Intelligence Agency, *The World Factbook 2003*

Interpreting the Chart What relationship do you see between countries' literacy rates and their economic development?

These giraffe feed on the tree-studded grasslands of the Serengeti. This reserve was opened in 1974 and is Kenya's most famous and popular animal reserve.

Kenyans are creating other business opportunities. For example, some entrepreneurs own companies to provide marketing services to businesses in other countries.

✔ **READING CHECK:** (*Human Systems*) Why did settlers come to Kenya?

Tanzania

South of Kenya is the large country of Tanzania. It was created in the 1960s when Tanganyika and the island of Zanzibar united. Today many tourists come to explore numerous national parks and Mount Kilimanjaro. The mountain's southern slopes are a rich agricultural region that provides coffee and tea for exports. Also in Tanzania is the Serengeti Plain. On this plain, herds of antelope and zebras still migrate freely, following the rains. Nearby is a famous archaeological site, Olduvai Gorge. A **gorge** is a narrow, steep-walled canyon. Evidence of some of the earliest humanlike fossils have been found in Olduvai Gorge.

Tanzania is a country of mainly poor subsistence farmers. Poor soils and limited technology have restricted productivity. This country has minerals, particularly gold and diamonds. Although the Tanzanian government has tried to make the country more self-sufficient, it has not yet succeeded.

✔ **READING CHECK:** (*Places and Regions*) How was the country of Tanzania created?

CONNECTING TO *Science*

Olduvai Gorge, Tanzania

Many scientists believe the human species has its origins in Africa. Archaeologists there have discovered fossil remains of humans and humanlike animals several million years old. Some of the most important finds have occurred at a site known as Olduvai Gorge.

Located in Tanzania, Olduvai is a steep-sided canyon some 30 miles (48 km) long. It is up to 300 feet (90 m) deep. The exposed sides of this gorge contain fossil deposits estimated to be more than 4 million years old. Along with the fossils, scientists found stone tools and the remains of numerous humanlike animals.

Archaeologists Louis and Mary Leakey played a key role in uncovering Olduvai's secrets. In 1931 Louis Leakey found remains of ancient tools and bones in the gorge. Then in 1959 Mary Leakey found the skeleton of an *Australopithecus*, the first humanlike creature to walk upright. Several years later, the

OLDUVAI GORGE

Leakeys found the remains of a more advanced species. The new find was known as *Homo habilis*. The species could make stone tools.

These discoveries helped provide some of the missing links between humans and their ancestors. Today archaeological work at Olduvai Gorge continues to add to our understanding of human origins.

Understanding What You Read
1. What is Olduvai Gorge?
2. What part has Olduvai played in the search for human origins?

Rwanda and Burundi

These two countries in fertile highlands were once German colonies. After World War I the Belgians ruled them. In the 1960s, after they gained independence, they were divided into two countries. Both countries are mostly populated by two ethnic groups—the Tutsi and the Hutu. Violence between the groups has killed thousands. Rwanda and Burundi have the densest rural settlement in Africa. Foreign aid has helped improve farming and health care.

✓ **READING CHECK:** (*Human Systems*) Why did the creation of Rwanda and Burundi create conflict?

Our Amazing Planet

Red colobus monkeys of Zanzibar eat charcoal, which absorbs poisons in the fruit-tree leaves the monkeys sometimes eat.

Uganda

Uganda, another site of an ancient empire, is found on the plateau north and west of Lake Victoria. Economic progress has been slow. Foreign investment stopped as a result of a violent dictatorship. In the 1970s the country's economy collapsed. Limited peace and democracy were achieved in the late 1980s.

✓ **READING CHECK:** (*Human Systems*) What is Uganda like today?

Sudan

Sudan is Africa's largest country. It has three physical regions. The Sahara makes up the northern half of the country. Dry savannas extend across the country's center. Much of southern Sudan is taken up by a swamp called the Sudd. Sudan is mainly an agricultural country, but it is also developing some of its mineral resources. Oil reserves have not yet been developed.

Modern Sudanese culture shows influences of Arab and traditionally African cultures. Arab Muslims make up about 70 percent of the population and have political power. They dominate northern Sudan. Khartoum, the capital, is located in this area. During the last several decades there was a civil war between northern Muslims and southerners who practice Christianity or traditional African religions.

✓ **READING CHECK:** (*Human Systems*) What conflict has been occurring in Sudan?

Alfred Louis Sargent created this engraving of Khartoum, Sudan, in the 1800s.

go.hrw.com
Homework Practice Online
Keyword: SK5 HP11

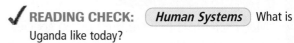

Section Review 3

Define or identify: Kikuyu, gorge, Tutsi, Hutu

Working with Sketch Maps On the map you created in Section 2, label Kenya, Tanzania, Rwanda, Burundi, Uganda, and Sudan. Why are some of the countries of this region agriculturally fertile while others are not?

Reading for the Main Idea

1. (*Places and Regions*) What makes the highlands of Kenya important?

2. (*Places and Regions*) Which areas of East Africa are tourist attractions?

Critical Thinking

3. **Making Generalizations and Predictions** How might irrigation help a region's economic development?

4. **Finding the Main Idea** How has unrest hurt Rwanda and some other East African countries?

Organizing What You Know

5. **Summarizing** Copy the following graphic organizer. Use it to list each country in this section. In one column list resources important to its development, and in the next column list obstacles that could prevent the country's economic success.

Country	Resources	Obstacles

Read to Discover

1. What are the main physical features of Ethiopia?
2. What is Eritrea like?
3. What is Somalia like?
4. What are the physical and cultural characteristics of Djibouti?

Vocabulary

droughts

Places

Ethiopia
Eritrea
Somalia
Djibouti
Bab al-Mandab

People

Somali

Reading Strategy

READING ORGANIZER Before you read, draw a large square on a sheet of paper. Draw a vertical line down the center of the square. Draw a horizontal line across the center of the square. Label the boxes Ethiopia, Eritrea, Somalia, and Djibouti. As you read the section write details about each country in its box.

Ethiopia

Ethiopia is one of the world's poorest countries. The rugged mountain slopes and upland plateaus have rich volcanic soil. Agriculture is Ethiopia's chief economic activity. It exports coffee, livestock, and oilseeds. However, during the last 30 years the region has experienced serious **droughts**. Droughts are periods when little rain falls and crops are damaged. Drought, combined with war and ineffective government policies, caused the starvation of several million people in the 1980s.

Except for a time when Ethiopia was at war with Italy, the Ethiopian highlands have never been under foreign rule. The mountains protected the interior of the country from invasion. Most of the highland people are Christian, while most of the lowland people are Muslim.

✓ **READING CHECK:** *Places and Regions* What physical features are found in Ethiopia?

As Afar nomads in Ethiopia move their encampment, they are continually challenged by the environment.

Interpreting the Visual Record

Movement How important are these camels for the Afar? What purpose do they serve?

The Horn of Africa

Country	Population/ Growth Rate	Life Expectancy	Literacy Rate	Per Capita GDP
Djibouti	457,130 2.1%	42, male 44, female	68%	$1,300
Eritrea	4,362,254 1.3%	51, male 55, female	59%	$740
Ethiopia	66,557,553 1.9%	40, male 42, female	43%	$750
Somalia	8,025,190 3.4%	45, male 49, female	38%	$550
United States	290,342,554 0.9%	74, male 80, female	97%	$37,600

Source: Central Intelligence Agency, *The World Factbook 2003*

Interpreting the Chart Which country in the region has the highest level of economic development, and why?

The main mosque, Khulafa el Rashidin, was built in 1937 with Italian Carrara marble in Asmara, Eritrea.

Interpreting the Visual Record What architectural elements of this building have you seen in other regions you have studied?

▼

Eritrea

Eritrea, located on the Red Sea, was once part of Ethiopia. In the late 1800s the Italians made this area a colony. In the 1960s it became an Ethiopian province. After years of war, Eritrea broke away from Ethiopia in 1993. The economy has slowly improved since then. The population is made up of Muslims and Christians.

✔ **READING CHECK:** *Places and Regions* What is Eritrea like today?

Somalia

Somalia is a land of deserts and dry savannas. Most Somalis are nomadic herders. Livestock and bananas are the main exports. Somalia is less diverse than most other African countries. Most residents of Somalia are members of the Somali people. Most Somali share the same culture, religion (Islam), language (Somali), and way of life (herding). Somalia has been troubled by civil war. In the 1990s widespread starvation caused by the war and a severe drought attracted international attention. The United Nations sent aid and troops to the country. U.S. troops were sent to Somalia to assist with this operation.

✔ **READING CHECK:** *Environment and Society* How have drought and conflict affected Somalia?

Djibouti's Lake Assal has one of the lowest surface levels on the planet. It lies 515 feet (157 m) below sea level. The only way to reach this area is by use of a four-wheel drive vehicle.

Djibouti

Djibouti is a small desert country. It lies on the Bab al-Mandab. This is the narrow strait that connects the Red Sea and the Indian Ocean. The strait lies along a major shipping route. This has helped Djibouti's economy. In the 1860s Djibouti came under French control. It gained independence in 1977. The French government still contributes economic and military support to the country. Its port, which serves landlocked Ethiopia, is a major source of income. Djibouti is heavily dependent on food imports.

The people of Djibouti include the Issa and the Afar. The Issa are closely tied to the people of Somalia. The Afar are related to the people of Ethiopia. Members of both groups are Muslim. Somalia and Ethiopia have both wanted to control Djibouti. So far the country has maintained its independence.

✓ **READING CHECK:** *Places and Regions* What are Djibouti's physical and cultural features?

Homework Practice Online

Keyword: SK5 HP11

Define or identify: droughts, Somali

Working with Sketch Maps On the map you created in Section 3, label Ethiopia, Eritrea, Somalia, Djibouti, and Bab al-Mandab. What physical features help the economies of the region?

Reading for the Main Idea

1. *Places and Regions* What physical features have helped protect Ethiopia from foreign invasion?

2. *Places and Regions* What country was part of Ethiopia until it broke away in 1993?

Critical Thinking

3. **Drawing Inferences and Conclusions** Why do you think France remains interested in Djibouti?

4. **Finding the Main Idea** Why have foreign aid agencies been involved in East Africa?

Organizing What You Know

5. **Analyzing Information** Copy the following graphic organizer. Use it to show the major religions of these countries. Add boxes as needed.

Country	Religion

CHAPTER 11 Review and Practice

Define and Identify

Identify each of the following:

1. rifts
2. Swahili
3. Kikuyu
4. gorge
5. droughts
6. Somali

Review the Main Ideas

7. What are East Africa's main natural resources?
8. What caused the formation of the Great Rift Valley of East Africa?
9. Why didn't Europeans ever colonize Ethiopia?
10. What is a major source of income for Kenya?
11. What was the island of Zanzibar known for in the late 1700s?
12. What factors have slowed Tanzania's economic growth?
13. How have Arabs, Portuguese, the British, and the Kikuyu affected Kenya?
14. How did the British and Kikuyu view land differently?
15. What two ethnic groups live mostly in Rwanda and Burundi?

16. How have droughts in the Horn of Africa affected its people and their relationship with the rest of the world?
17. What landform in Djibouti has helped the country's economy?

Think Critically

18. **Finding the Main Idea** What is the significance of the Nile River in this region's human history?
19. **Analyzing Information** Why are foreign investors hesitant to invest in many countries of this region?
20. **Summarizing** Why do most East Africans make their living by farming and herding?
21. **Making Generalizations and Predictions** What problems have resulted in part from the boundary lines drawn by European powers, and how might the countries of East Africa overcome these problems?
22. **Analyzing Information** How has Ethiopia avoided falling under foreign rule for most of its history?

Map Activity

23. On a separate sheet of paper, match the letters on the map with their correct labels.

Great Rift Valley
Mount Kilimanjaro
Lake Victoria
White Nile
Blue Nile
Bab al-Mandab

Writing Activity

Imagine that you have been awarded an all-expenses-paid vacation to East Africa. Write a letter to your travel agent explaining what you want to do on your trip. List and describe physical features you want to see and African wildlife and historical sites you would like to explore. Be sure to use standard grammar, spelling, sentence structure, and punctuation.

⚏ internet connect

Internet Activity: go.hrw.com
KEYWORD: SK5 GT11

Choose a topic to explore about East Africa:
- Hike Mount Kilimanjaro.
- Learn about cultural groups in East Africa.
- Travel back to ancient Nubian kingdoms.

Social Studies Skills Practice

Interpreting Charts

You have read about the role of religion in the history and culture of East Africa. Study the following chart and answer the questions below.

Religion in East Africa			
Country	**Christian**	**Muslim**	**Indigenous**
Burundi	67%	10%	23%
Kenya	78%	10%	10%
Rwanda	94%	5%	0.1%
Sudan	5%	70%	25%
Tanzania (mainland)	30%	35%	35%
Uganda	66%	16%	18%

Source: Central Intelligence Agency, *The World Factbook 2003*

1. Where is Christianity most heavily practiced?
2. Where is Islam most heavily practiced?
3. Indigenous religions are practiced the least in which country?
4. Which two countries have the most similar patterns of religious diversity?

Analyzing Primary Sources

In "The Snows of Kilimanjaro," a short story written by Ernest Hemingway in 1938, a couple travels on safari to East Africa. Read the following passage that describes their view of the region's landscape from a small airplane. Then answer the questions.

"Then they were over the first hills and the wildebeeste were trailing up them, and then they were over the mountains with sudden depths of green-rising forest and the solid bamboo slopes, and then the heavy forest again, sculptured into peaks and hollows until they crossed, and hills sloped down and then another plain, hot now, and purple brown, bumpy with heat . . ."

1. How does an aerial view give you a sense of the region's physical geography?
2. What types of landforms, vegetation, and wildlife are described?
3. From this passage, what can you tell about the climate of the region?
4. How does the landscape described in this passage differ from other areas of East Africa?

CHAPTER 12

Central Africa

The fourth region in Africa we will study includes the 10 countries of central Africa. Before we begin, meet Akalemwa Ngenda, a student living in Zambia.

Bwanji? (How are you?) This is how you say hi in Nyanja, a common language spoken by most people in my country, Zambia. At home, I would say "Mucwañi?" to my father in Lozi, my own language. My name is Akalemwa, and I am 18. *Akalemwa* means "the one you cannot outrun." I am in the twelfth grade at Choma Secondary School in Zambia's southern province. Choma is a small town. My family's house is near the hospital, about 2.5 kilometers (1.6 mi.) from town. My father is a medical assistant in charge of village health clinics for our region. My mother is a nurse. I have an older half sister, two older brothers, two younger sisters, and five younger brothers. Our house has three bedrooms and a vegetable garden.

I attend a Protestant missionary school. We sleep in a dormitory at school. Our school year has three three-month terms, starting in January. We have a month vacation after each one. I want to be a doctor, so I am studying math, physics, chemistry, biology, English, and geography.

Lumela, ni muituti mwa naha Zambia.

▲

Translation: Hi, I am a student in Zambia.

Section 1 Physical Geography

Read to Discover

1. What are the major physical features of central Africa?
2. What climates, plants, and animals are found in the region?
3. What major natural resources does central Africa have?

Vocabulary

basin
canopy
copper belt
periodic markets

Places

Congo Basin
Western Rift Valley
Lake Tanganyika
Lake Malawi
Congo River
Zambezi River

Reading Strategy

VISUALIZING INFORMATION Look at the pictures in this section. What do they show you about Central Africa? Write your answers on a sheet of paper. As you read this section, write down the new information you learn.

Central Africa: Physical-Political

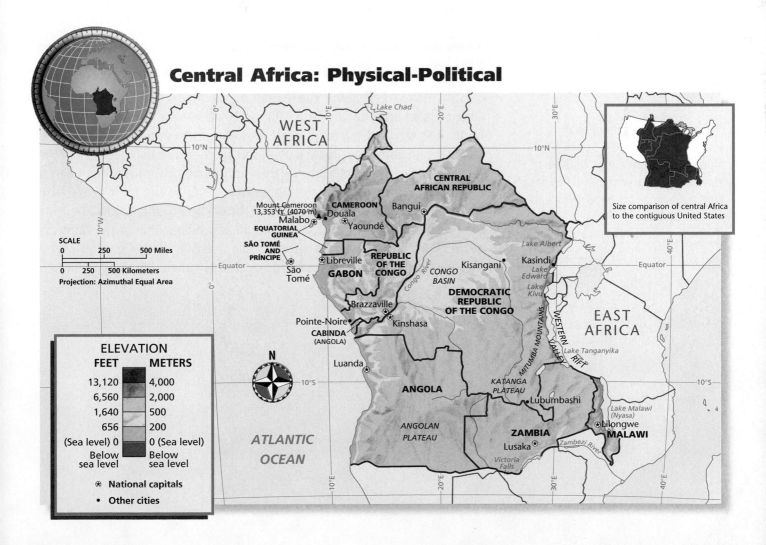

SCALE
0   250   500 Miles
0   250   500 Kilometers
Projection: Azimuthal Equal Area

Size comparison of central Africa to the contiguous United States

ELEVATION

FEET	METERS
13,120	4,000
6,560	2,000
1,640	500
656	200
(Sea level) 0	0 (Sea level)
Below sea level	Below sea level

⊛ National capitals
• Other cities

Our Amazing Planet

One of the Congo River's most common animals is the crocodile. This sharp-toothed reptile can grow to about 20 feet (6 m) in length. It swims by sweeping its long tail from side to side.

(Location) Local people call Victoria Falls *Mosi-oa-Tunya*, which means "the smoke that thunders." The Zambezi River plunges 355 feet (108 m) over a cliff between Zambia and Zimbabwe.

Physical Features

Central Africa stretches southward from Cameroon and the Central African Republic to Angola and Zambia. The Atlantic Ocean lies off the western coast.

Think of the region as a big soup bowl with a wide rim. Near the middle of the bowl is the Congo Basin. A **basin** is a generally flat region surrounded by higher land such as mountains and plateaus.

In northwestern Cameroon are volcanic mountains. The highest is 13,353 feet (4,070 m). Central Africa's highest mountains lie along the Western Rift Valley. Some of these snow-capped mountains rise to more than 16,700 feet (5,090 m). The Western Rift Valley stretches southeastward from the Democratic Republic of the Congo. Lake Tanganyika (tan-guhn-KEE-kuh) and Lake Malawi are found there.

Two major river systems drain the region. In the north the Congo River flows westward to the Atlantic Ocean. Hundreds of smaller rivers flow into the Congo. In the south the Zambezi (zam-BEE-zee) River flows eastward to the Indian Ocean. The Zambezi is famous for its great falls, hydroelectric dams, and lakes.

✓ **READING CHECK:** (*Places and Regions*) What are the major physical features of central Africa?

Climates, Plants, and Animals

Central Africa lies along the equator and in the low latitudes. The Congo Basin and much of the Atlantic coast have a humid tropical climate. It is wet and warm all year. This climate supports a large, dense tropical rain forest but makes overland travel difficult.

The many different kinds of trees in the tropical rain forest form a complete **canopy**. This is the uppermost layer of the trees where the limbs spread out. Leaves block sunlight to the ground below.

Small antelopes, hyenas, elephants, and okapis live in the rain forest region. The okapi is a short-legged relative of the giraffe. Many insects also live in the forest. However, few other plants or creatures live on the forest floor. This is because little sunlight shines through the canopy. Many animals live in the trees. They include birds, monkeys, bats, and snakes. Large areas of the tropical rain forest are being cleared rapidly for farming and timber. This threatens the plants, animals, and people who live there.

North and south of the Congo Basin are large areas with a tropical savanna climate. Those areas are warm all year, but they have distinct dry and wet seasons. There are grasslands, scattered trees, and shrubs. Only in the high eastern mountains is there a highland climate. Dry steppe and even desert climates are found in the far south.

✓ **READING CHECK:** *Places and Regions* What are the region's climates, plants, and animals?

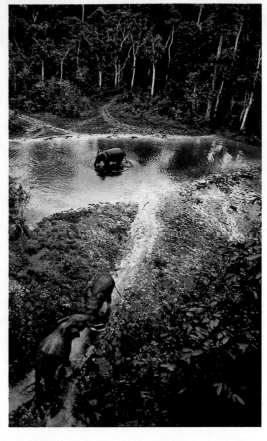

Resources

Central Africa's rivers are among the region's most important natural resources. They are used for travel, trade, and producing hydroelectricity. Other energy resources are oil, natural gas, and coal.

Central Africa has many minerals, including copper, uranium, tin, zinc, diamonds, gold, and cobalt. Most of Africa's copper is found in an area called the **copper belt**, which includes northern Zambia and the southern Democratic Republic of the Congo.

Central African countries have mostly traditional economies. Most people in central Africa are subsistence farmers. However, an increasing number of farmers are growing crops for sale. Common crops include coffee, bananas, and corn. In rural areas, people trade their products in **periodic markets**. A periodic market is an open-air trading market. It is set up regularly at a crossroads or in a town.

▲

Elephants have created a network of trails and clearings throughout the tropical rain forest. Many animals will gather at forest clearings.

✓ **READING CHECK:** *Places and Regions* What is central Africa's most important natural resource, and why?

Homework Practice Online
Keyword: SK5 HP12

Define and explain: basin, canopy, copper belt, periodic markets

Working with Sketch Maps
On a map of central Africa that you draw or that your teacher provides, label the following: Congo Basin, Western Rift Valley, Lake Tanganyika, Lake Malawi, Congo River, and Zambezi River. In a box in the margin, describe the location of the highest mountains.

Reading for the Main Idea

1. *Places and Regions* What major landforms and rivers are found in the region?

2. *Physical Systems* Why do few plants and animals live on the floor of the tropical rain forest?

3. *Places and Regions* For the most part, what type of economy do central African countries have?

Critical Thinking

4. **Making Generalizations and Predictions** How might central Africa become a rich region?

Organizing What You Know

5. **Summarizing** Copy the following graphic organizer. Use it to describe the region's climates, plants and animals, and major resources.

Climates	Plants and Animals	Resources

Central Africa • 257

Read to Discover

1. What is the history of central Africa, and what challenges do the people there face today?

2. What are the people and cultures of central Africa like?

Vocabulary

ivory
dialects

Places

Brazzaville
Kinshasa

Reading Strategy

READING ORGANIZER Before you read, create a spider map. Draw a circle. Label the circle History and Culture. Draw seven legs and label them Early History, Modern Central Africa, Challenges, Peoples and Languages, Religion, Food, and The Arts. As you read the section, write what you learn about these topics next to each leg.

History

Early humans lived in central Africa many thousands of years ago. They had different languages and cultures. About 2,000 years ago new peoples began to move into the region from western Africa. Those new peoples spoke what are called Bantu languages. Today, Bantu languages are common in most of the region.

Early History Several early Bantu-speaking kingdoms formed in central Africa. Among the most important was the Kongo Kingdom. It was located around the mouth of the Congo River. The Kongo and other central Africans traded with peoples in western and eastern Africa.

Some of the early kingdoms used slaves. In the late 1400s, Europeans came to the region. They began to trade with some African kingdoms for slaves. The Europeans took many enslaved Africans to the Americas. Europeans also wanted the region's forest products and other resources, such as **ivory**. Ivory is a cream-colored material that comes from elephant tusks. It is used in making fine furniture, jewelry, and crafts.

Some African kingdoms became richer by trading with Europeans. However, all were gradually weakened or destroyed by the Europeans. European countries divided all of central Africa into colonies in the late 1800s. The colonial powers were France, the United Kingdom, Belgium, Germany, Spain, and Portugal.

The Europeans drew colonial borders that ignored the homelands of central Africa's ethnic groups. Many groups were lumped together in colonies. These groups spoke different languages and had different

This carved mask was created by a Bantu-speaking people called the Fang. Most live in Cameroon, Equatorial Guinea, and Gabon. Their ancestors moved there in the 1800s.

ways of life. These differences resulted in conflicts, particularly after the colonies won independence.

Modern Central Africa African colonies did not gain independence until after World War II. The largest central African colony was the Belgian Congo. It is now the Democratic Republic of the Congo. That country won independence in 1960. Angola won independence from Portugal in 1975. It was the last European colony in central Africa.

Independence for some African countries came after bloody wars. After independence, fighting between some ethnic groups continued within the new countries. The region also became a battleground in the Cold War. The United States and the Soviet Union supported their allies in small wars throughout Africa. The region's wars killed many people and caused great damage. Some fighting continues off and on in the region.

Challenges Today Ending these wars is one of central Africa's many challenges today. The region's countries must also develop their natural resources more effectively. This would help the many poor people who live there. Another great challenge is stopping the spread of diseases such as malaria and AIDS. These diseases are killing millions of people and leaving many orphans.

✔ **READING CHECK:** (*Human Systems*) What role did Europeans play in central Africa's history?

Culture

Today, about 100 million people live in central Africa. They belong to many different ethnic groups with varying customs.

Zambian women are grinding wheat to prepare it for cooking. They are using rods called pestles. The container is called a mortar. This technique is used for grinding many ingredients.

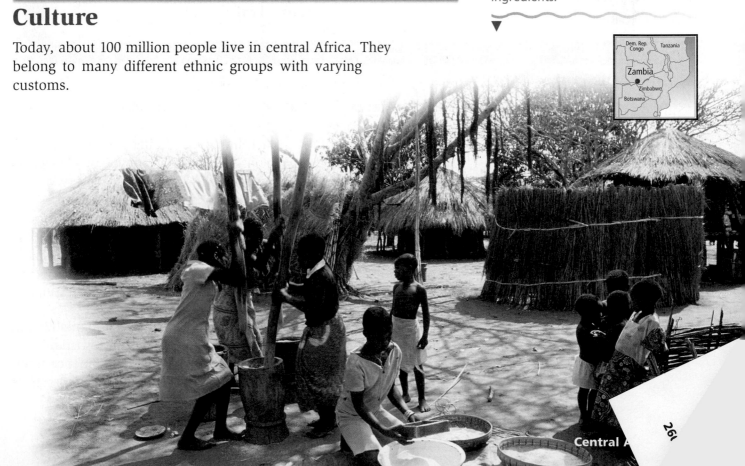

Central A

CONNECTING TO *History*

A headrest from early Luanda, a Bantu kingdom

BANTU LANGUAGES

About 2,000 years ago, the movement of groups of people began to change Africa. Traders, farmers, and other people moved across the southern third of Africa. Experts believe these people came from areas that are now part of Nigeria and Cameroon. Their movement across Africa lasted many centuries. During this period new languages developed. We call them Bantu languages. The grammar and root sounds of the different Bantu languages remain similar.

Some Bantu speakers moved southward along the Atlantic coast. Others moved eastward to Kenya and then turned southward. Over time they reached the tip of southern Africa. The Bantu speakers mixed with peoples who already lived in these lands.

The migration of Bantu speakers had important effects on African life. They brought new ways for growing food. They used tools made of iron, which others also began to use. The Bantu-speakers of course brought their languages. Today, many Africans speak Swahili, Zulu, and other Bantu languages.

Understanding What You Read
1. (*Movement*) From where did the Bantu peoples come?
2. (*Movement*) How did their movement shape Africa?

Peoples and Languages As you have read, many central Africans speak Bantu languages. However, those languages can be very different from each other. In fact, hundreds of different languages and **dialects** are spoken in the region. A dialect is a variation of a language.

Many people in the region speak African languages in everyday life. However, the official languages of the central African countries are European. French is the official language of the former French colonies in the north. It is also the official language of the Democratic Republic of the Congo. English is the official language in Zambia and Malawi. Portuguese is spoken in Angola and the island country of São Tomé and Príncipe. Spanish and French are the official languages of tiny Equatorial Guinea.

Religion Many people in the former French, Spanish, and Portuguese colonies are Roman Catholic. Protestant Christianity is most common in former British colonies. Many people practice traditional African religions. In some cases Christian and African practices have been combined.

Many Muslims live near the mostly Muslim countries of the Sahel in the north. Zambia also has many Muslims as well as Hindus. The Hindus are the descendants of immigrants from southern Asia.

Food In most central African countries, corn, rice, grains, and fish are common foods. In the tropical rain forest, plantains, cassava, and various roots are important foods. For example, in Cameroon you might eat a dish called *fufu*. *Fufu*, a thick, pasty ball of mashed cassava, yams, or plantains, is served with chicken, fish, or a beef gravy.

The Arts *Makossa* dance music from Cameroon has become popular throughout Africa. It can be played with various instruments, including guitars and electric keyboards. The cities of Brazzaville and Kinshasa on the Congo River are the home of *soukous* music.

The region is also famous for carved masks, sculpture, and beautiful cotton gowns. The gowns are dyed in bright colors. They often show pictures that represent things important to the wearer.

Region The *likembe*, or thumb piano, was invented in the lower Congo region. Today its music is heard in many African countries.

✔ **READING CHECK:** (*Human Systems*) What are some characteristics of the people and culture of central Africa?

Section Review 2

Define and explain: ivory, dialects

Working with Sketch Maps On the map you created in Section 1, label Brazzaville and Kinshasa.

Reading for the Main Idea

1. (*Human Systems*) Why are many languages that are spoken today in central Africa related?

2. (*Human Systems*) What have been some of the causes of wars in central Africa?

3. (*Human Systems*) What arts are popular in the region?

Critical Thinking

4. **Finding the Main Idea** How did Europeans influence the culture of the region?

Organizing What You Know

5. **Summarizing** Copy the following graphic organizer. Use it to identify central Africa's challenges.

Challenges

Central Africa • 261

The Democratic Republic of the Congo

Read to Discover

1. What is the history of the Democratic Republic of the Congo?
2. What are the people and culture of the country like?
3. What is the economy of the country like?

Vocabulary
civil war

Places
Lubumbashi

People
Mobutu Sese Seko

Reading Strategy

READING ORGANIZER Before you read, draw a circle in the center of a sheet of paper. Label the circle Democratic Republic of the Congo. Draw three rays from the circle. Draw a circle at the end of each ray. Label the circles History, People, and Economy. As you read this section, write what you learn about these topics next to each circle.

History

Portuguese sailors made contact with the Kongo Kingdom in 1482. Over time the slave trade and other problems weakened the Kongo and other African kingdoms.

A Belgian Colony In the 1870s King Leopold II of Belgium took control of the Congo Basin. The king ruled the Congo Free State as his personal colony until 1908. His soldiers treated the Africans harshly. They forced people to work in mines and on plantations. These policies brought international criticism.

The Belgian government took control of the colony from the king in 1908. Many Belgian businesses and people moved there. They mined copper and other resources. The giant colony won independence from tiny Belgium in 1960.

A New Country Many Belgians fled the country after 1960. There were few teachers, doctors, and other professionals left in the former colony. In addition, people from different areas and ethnic groups fought each other. These problems were partly to blame for keeping the country poor.

A dictator, who later changed his name to Mobutu Sese Seko, came to power in 1965. He was an ally of the United States during the Cold War. Mobutu changed the country's name to Zaire in 1971. During his rule, the country suffered from economic problems and government corruption.

A dancer performs in a coming-of-age ceremony for young people. Many such African traditions have survived the period of colonial rule by Europeans.

A new government took over in 1997 after a **civil war**. A civil war is a war between two or more groups within a country. The new government changed the country's name to the Democratic Republic of the Congo. However, fighting between ethnic groups has continued.

✓ **READING CHECK:** (*Human Systems*) What has the history of the Democratic Republic of the Congo been like?

The Democratic Republic of the Congo

Country	Population/ Growth Rate	Life Expectancy	Literacy Rate	Per Capita GDP
Democratic Republic of the Congo	53,625,039 2.9%	47, male 51, female	65%	$600
United States	290,342,554 0.9%	74, male 80, female	97%	$37,600

Source: Central Intelligence Agency, *The World Factbook 2003*

The People

More than 50 million people live in the Democratic Republic of the Congo today. The population is very diverse. It is divided among more than 200 ethnic groups. The Kongo people are among the largest groups. These groups speak many different languages, but the official language is French. About half of the country's people are Roman Catholic. Protestant Christians, Muslims, and people who practice traditional African religions also live in the country.

More than 4 million people live in Kinshasa, the capital and largest city. Kinshasa is a river port located along the Congo River near the Atlantic coast. The crowded city has some modern buildings. However, most of the city consists of poor slums.

✓ **READING CHECK:** (*Human Systems*) What are the people and culture of the Democratic Republic of the Congo like?

Human-Environment Interaction

A family sells charcoal along a road in the northern Democratic Republic of the Congo. Charcoal is a major fuel source. In many rural areas there is no electricity.

The Congo River lies in the distance in this photograph of Kinshasa.

The Economy

The Democratic Republic of the Congo is a treasure chest of minerals and tropical resources. For example, the south is part of central Africa's rich copper belt. Much of the copper from the area is shipped through the city of Lubumbashi (loo-boom-BAH-shee). The country also has gold, diamonds, and cobalt. The country's tropical rain forest also supplies wood, food, rubber, and other products.

However, the country's people are very poor. Most people live in rural areas. They must farm and trade for food. Civil war, bad government, and crime have scared many foreign businesses away. As a result, the country's rich resources have helped few of its people.

For the economy to improve, the country needs peace and a stable government. Schools must be improved and better health care provided. The country also must repair and expand roads and railways. If its challenges are met, the country's resources can make the future brighter.

✓ **READING CHECK:** (**Environment and Society**) How might the economy of the country improve?

Homework Practice Online
Keyword: SK5 HP12

Section Review 3

Define or identify: Mobutu Sese Seko, civil war

Working with Sketch Maps On the map you created in Section 2, label the Democratic Republic of the Congo and Lubumbashi. Why is Lubumbashi economically important?

Reading for the Main Idea

1. (**Places and Regions**) What European country ruled what is now the Democratic Republic of the Congo as a colony until 1960?

2. (**Places and Regions**) What were some problems the country faced after independence?

Critical Thinking

3. **Finding the Main Idea** In what ways is the Democractic Republic of the Congo a culturally diverse country? What ethnic group is among the largest?

4. **Drawing Inferences and Conclusions** How might better schools and transportation help the country's economy?

Organizing What You Know

5. **Sequencing** Copy the following time line. Use it to identify important groups and individuals in the history of the present-day Democratic Republic of the Congo.

1482 ——————————————— 2000

Read to Discover

1. What are the people and economies of the northern central African countries like?
2. What are the people and economies of the southern central African countries like?

Vocabulary

exclave

Places

Douala
Yaoundé
Luanda

Reading Strategy

FOLDNOTES: TWO-PANEL FLIP CHART Create the FoldNote **Two-Panel Flip Chart.** Label one flap Northern Central Africa and the other flap Southern Central Africa. As you read this section, write what you learn about these regions beneath each flap.

Northern Central Africa

Six countries make up northern central Africa. Four are Cameroon, the Central African Republic, Gabon, and the Republic of the Congo. They gained independence from France in 1960. Cameroon had been a German colony until after World War I. Tiny Equatorial Guinea gained independence from Spain in 1968. The island country of São Tomé and Príncipe won independence from Portugal in 1975.

The People Cameroon is by far the most populous country in this region. About 15.8 million people live there. The Central African Republic has the second-largest population, with 3.5 million. Tiny São Tomé and Príncipe has only about 165,000 people.

A large variety of ethnic groups are found in northern central Africa. Many people are moving from rural areas to cities to search for jobs. Governments are struggling to provide basic services in those crowded cities.

Douala (doo-AH-lah) and Yaoundé (yown-DAY) in Cameroon are the largest cities. Each has more than 1 million people. Douala is an important seaport on the Atlantic coast. Yaoundé is Cameroon's capital. Brazzaville, the capital of the Republic of the Congo, also has 1 million people. The city is a major Congo River port.

The Economy Most of the area's countries are very poor. Most people are farmers. Gabon has the strongest economy in central

Region Although the region's cities are growing rapidly, most people still live in rural areas. This small village is located in northern Cameroon. As in much of rural Africa, several buildings make up a family's home.
▼

Northern Central Africa

COUNTRY	POPULATION/ GROWTH RATE	LIFE EXPECTANCY	LITERACY RATE	PER CAPITA GDP
Cameroon	15,746,179 2.0%	47, male 49, female	79%	$1,700
Central African Republic	3,683,538 1.6%	40, male 43, female	51%	$1,300
Congo, Republic of the	2,954,258 1.5%	49, male 51, female	84%	$900
Equatorial Guinea	510,473 2.5%	53, male 57, female	86%	$2,700
Gabon	1,321,560 2.5%	55, male 58, female	63%	$5,700
São Tomé and Príncipe	175,883 3.2%	64, male 67, female	79%	$1,200
United States	290,342,554 0.9%	74, male 80, female	97%	$37,600

Source: Central Intelligence Agency, *The World Factbook 2003*

Interpreting the Chart Which country in the region has the smallest population? the largest?

Africa. More than half of the value of its economy comes from the oil industry. Oil is important in Cameroon as well as in the Republic of the Congo.

The mighty Congo River is also a vital trade and transportation route. As a result, it plays a major role in the region's economy. Many of the region's goods and farm products are shipped down river to Brazzaville. Brazzaville lies across the Congo River from Kinshasa. From Brazzaville, goods are shipped by railroad to a port on the Atlantic coast.

✓ **READING CHECK:** (*Human Systems*) What are the people and economies of northern central Africa like?

Southern Central Africa

Zambia, Malawi, and Angola make up the southern part of central Africa. The British gave Zambia and Malawi independence in 1964. Angola won independence from Portugal in 1975.

The People The populations of the three southern countries are nearly the same size. They range from about 10 million in Zambia to more than 11 million in Malawi. Angola and Zambia are much larger in area than Malawi. Large parts of Angola and Zambia have few people. Most people in the region live in rural areas. They grow crops and herd cattle and goats.

(Movement) Riverboats carry the king of Zambia's Lozi people to a dryland home during the flooding season. This event is an annual ritual for the Lozi, who live in western Zambia. As in other central African countries, many different ethnic groups live in Zambia.

Angola's capital, Luanda, is the southern region's largest city. More than 2 million people live there. Seen from the sea, Luanda looks like a modern city. The city has many high-rise buildings and factories. Unfortunately, Luanda and its people have suffered from poverty and years of war. Rebels fought the Portuguese in the 1960s and early 1970s. After independence, the country plunged into civil war. Fighting continued off and on until 2002. Many people have been killed or injured by land mines.

The Economy In peacetime, the future of Angola could be bright. There are many places with fertile soils. The country has large deposits of diamonds and oil. The oil is found offshore north of Luanda and in the exclave of Cabinda. An **exclave** is part of a country that is separated by territory of other countries. Cabinda is separated from the rest of Angola by the Democratic Republic of the Congo.

Much of Zambia's income comes from rich copper mines. However, 85 percent of Zambia's workers are farmers. Most of the country's energy comes from hydroelectric dams and power plants along rivers.

About 75 percent of Malawi's people live in rural areas. Nearly all of them are farmers. The building of factories and industries has been slow. Aid from other countries and religious missionaries has been important to the economy.

Southern Central Africa

COUNTRY	POPULATION/ GROWTH RATE	LIFE EXPECTANCY	LITERACY RATE	PER CAPITA GDP
Angola	10,766,471 1.2%	36, male 38, female	42%	$1,600
Malawi	11,651,239 2.2%	37, male 38, female	62%	$670
Zambia	10,307,333 1.5%	37, male 38, female	80%	$890
United States	290,342,554 0.9%	74, male 80, female	97%	$37,600

Source: Central Intelligence Agency, *The World Factbook 2003*

Interpreting the Chart Which country in the region has the highest literacy rate?

✔ **READING CHECK:** (*Human Systems*) What are the people and economies of the southern central African countries like?

Homework Practice Online
Keyword: SK5 HP12

Section Review 4

Define and explain: exclave

Working with Sketch Maps On the map you created in Section 3, label the countries of northern and southern central Africa, and Douala, Yaoundé, and Luanda. In a box in the margin, describe Luanda.

Reading for the Main Idea

1. (*Places and Regions*) Which country has the strongest economy in central Africa?

2. (*Environment and Society*) What significance does oil have in the economies of many countries in the region?

3. (*Human Systems*) What has happened in Angola since that country won its independence?

Critical Thinking

4. Analyzing Information Why is Brazzaville important to the region's economy?

Organizing What You Know

5. Summarizing Copy the following graphic organizer. Divide it into nine rows below the headings. Use it to list the countries discussed in this section. Then identify the European country that colonized each central African country. Finally, list the date each country won independence.

Country	European colonial ruler	Year of independence

Review and Practice

Define and Identify

Identify each of the following:

1. basin
2. canopy
3. copper belt
4. periodic markets
5. ivory
6. dialects
7. civil war
8. Mobutu Sese Seko
9. exclave

Review the Main Ideas

10. What two river systems are most important in central Africa?

11. Where are central Africa's highest mountains found?

12. What types of economies do central African countries practice?

13. How were the Bantu languages introduced to central Africa?

14. What challenges are the countries of central Africa facing today?

15. What religions are practiced by people in the Democratic Republic of the Congo?

16. What European countries once colonized central Africa?

17. How important has oil been to Gabon's economy?

18. How does Zambia get its energy?

Think Critically

19. **Drawing Inferences and Conclusions** Why do few large animals live on the floor of central Africa's tropical rain forests?

20. **Finding the Main Idea** How have borders drawn by European colonial powers contributed to ethnic conflicts in central Africa?

21. **Analyzing Information** How have their locations on major rivers or near important natural resources aided the growth of cities such as Brazzaville and Lubumbashi?

22. **Drawing Inferences and Conclusions** Why do you think European languages are still the official languages in the countries of central Africa?

23. **Finding the Main Idea** How did the Cold War contribute to problems in central Africa?

Map Activity

24. On a separate sheet of paper, match the letters on the map with their correct labels.

Congo Basin	Zambezi River
Western Rift Valley	Kinshasa
Lake Tanganyika	Lubumbashi
Lake Malawi	Douala
Congo River	Luanda

Writing Activity

Imagine that you have been hired to write a magazine article describing challenges facing central Africans. Write a descriptive headline and a brief summary for your proposed article. The article should cover the region's economic, political, and health challenges. Be sure to use standard grammar, spelling, sentence structure, and punctuation.

☑ **internet** connect

Internet Activity: go.hrw.com
KEYWORD: SK5 GT12

Choose a topic to explore about central Africa:
- Identify threats to the Congo Basin.
- Visit the people of central Africa.
- Learn the importance of African cloth.

Social Studies Skills Practice

Interpreting Maps

Study the map of the Democratic Republic of Congo below. Then answer the questions.

Civil War in the Democratic Republic of Congo, 1998

1. What is the main idea of this map?
2. Which group controlled most of eastern Democratic Republic of Congo?
3. Which group controlled the Democratic Republic of Congo's capital?
4. Based on what you know about the region, why would control of Kinshasa be important?

Analyzing Primary Sources

Read the following quote from Werner Vansant, a humanitarian aid worker in the Democratic Republic of Congo during the 1998–2002 civil war. Then answer the questions.

"This is not a war of troops fighting against troops. It's a war against civil society, where infrastructures are destroyed and looted, all medicines stolen from health posts, key people like nurses are killed in villages, and agricultural fields are destroyed. So people have no food, no medical care, they don't get treated . . . They hide in the jungle for weeks and get malnourished, sick, weaker and weaker. Sometimes you see people coming out of the bush in terrible, terrible conditions, without clothes and without anything. Those are the victims of this war."

1. Why does Vansant think this civil war is different from other wars?
2. What goods and services do people in the Democratic Republic of Congo lack because of the war?
3. How did ordinary people respond to the crisis caused by the war?
4. Why does Vansant call people who are not fighting "the victims of the war"?

CHAPTER 13

Southern Africa

Southern Africa is a region going through many changes. Some people in the area have a comfortable lifestyle, but others live in severe poverty.

Abatsu! (Good morning!) My name is Kha//'an[1] and I am a San person from Namibia. I am in ninth grade at the Tsumkwe[2] Secondary School. We do not have a house, only a small shelter to store our things. We live near the gate in the fence at M'Kata. If you turn east when you arrive there, you will see our blankets under the tree. When we are seeking shade or shelter, we go and sit under the tree.

My mother and father passed away when I was five years old, and my elder brother took care of me. I live with my brother, and the government helps us survive by giving us food rations.

At school I live in a hostel. We wake up at five in the morning and have breakfast at six. Breakfast is only bread. We have maize meal, tea, and milk at noon. My favorite subjects are English, history, physical science, and mathematics. When I grow up, I want to be a doctor.

=Xai-o![3] Mi o Kha//'an.

Translation: Greetings! I am Kha//'an.

[1] The "//" is a click made by clucking the tongue at the sides of the mouth.
[2] The "k" in Tsumkwe is another kind of click. It is made by placing the tongue on the roof of the mouth and bringing it down with a "pop."
[3] The = is a click made by placing the tip of the tongue on the ridge behind the upper front teeth and bringing it down with a "pop."

Section 1 — Physical Geography

Read to Discover

1. What are the major physical features and climates of southern Africa?
2. What resources are found in the region?

Vocabulary

enclaves
the veld
pans

Places

Drakensberg
Inyanga Mountains
Cape of Good Hope
Kalahari Desert

Namib Desert
Orange River
Aughrabies Falls
Limpopo River

Reading Strategy

FOLDNOTES: LAYERED BOOK Create the FoldNote titled **Layered Book** described in the Appendix. Label the layers of the book Countries, Landforms, Climates, and Resources. As you read this section, write what you learn about each topic in the appropriate layer of the book.

Southern Africa: Physical-Political

SEYCHELLES
Victoria

DEMOCRATIC REPUBLIC OF THE CONGO

TANZANIA

ATLANTIC OCEAN

ANGOLA

ZAMBIA

MALAWI

Lake Malawi (Nyasa)

COMOROS
Moroni

INDIAN OCEAN

SCALE
0   250   500 Miles
0   250   500 Kilometers
Projection: Azimuthal Equal Area

Okavango R.

NAMIBIA

OKAVANGO BASIN

Victoria Falls

Zambezi R.

Cabora Bassa Dam

Kariba Dam

Harare

ZIMBABWE

Bulawayo

INYANGA MTS.

MOZAMBIQUE

Beira

Nampula

Mozambique Channel

Toamasina

Antananarivo

MADAGASCAR

MAURITIUS
Réunion (FRANCE)   Port Louis

BOTSWANA

NAMIB DESERT

Windhoek

Mahalapye

KALAHARI DESERT

Gaborone

Limpopo R.

Tropic of Capricorn

ELEVATION

FEET	METERS
13,120	4,000
6,560	2,000
1,640	500
656	200
(Sea level) 0	0 (Sea level)
Below sea level	Below sea level

⊛ National capitals
• Other cities

Johannesburg

Soweto

WITWATERSRAND

Pretoria

Maputo

Mbabane

SWAZILAND

Aughrabies Falls

Orange River

Vaal R.

Kimberley

Bloemfontein

Maseru

LESOTHO

Durban

SOUTH AFRICA

DRAKENSBERG

Cape Town

Cape of Good Hope

Port Elizabeth

Size comparison of southern Africa to the contiguous United States

The Drakensberg range rises sharply in eastern South Africa.

Drakensberg means "dragon mountain" in the Afrikaans language. The Zulu, one of the peoples of the region, call it Kwathlamba, meaning "barrier of pointed spears" or "piled-up rocks."

Countries of the Region

Lining southern Africa's coasts are Namibia (nuh-MI-bee-uh), South Africa, and Mozambique (moh-zahm-BEEK). Botswana (bawt-SWAH-nah), Zimbabwe (zim-BAH-bway), and the two tiny countries of Lesotho (luh-SOH-toh) and Swaziland (SWAH-zee-land) are all land-locked. Lesotho and Swaziland are **enclaves**—countries surrounded or almost surrounded by another country. Madagascar (ma-duh-GAS-kuhr), off the east coast, is the world's fourth-largest island.

Physical Features and Climate

The surface of southern Africa is dominated by a large plateau. The southeastern edge of this plateau is a mountain range called the Drakensberg (DRAH-kuhnz-buhrk). The steep peaks rise as high as 11,425 feet (3,482 m) from the plains along the coast. Farther north, another mountain range, the Inyanga (in-YANG-guh) Mountains, forms the plateau's eastern edge.

The open grassland areas of South Africa are known as **the veld** (VELT). Kruger National Park covers 7,523 square miles (19,485 sq km) of the veld. The park contains lions, leopards, elephants, rhinoceroses, hippos, baboons, and antelope.

Climate The region's climates range from desert to cool uplands. Winds carry moisture from the Indian Ocean. These winds are forced upward by the Drakensberg and Inyanga Mountains. The eastern slopes are rainy, but climates are drier farther inland and westward. Most of the interior of southern Africa is semiarid and has steppe and savanna vegetation.

Near the Cape of Good Hope, winter rains and summer drought create a Mediterranean climate. Off the Cape, storms and rough seas are common.

Deserts and Rivers In the central and western parts of the region, savanna and steppe give way to two major deserts. The Kalahari (ka-luh-hahr-ee) occupies most of Botswana. Here ancient streams have drained into low, flat areas, or **pans**. Minerals left behind when the water evaporated form a glittering white layer.

The Namib (NAH-mib) Desert lies along the Atlantic coast. Inland, the Namib blends into the Kalahari and steppe. Almost no rain falls, but at night fog rolls in from the ocean. Some plants and animals survive by using the fog as a source of water.

Southern Africa has some of the world's most spectacular rivers and waterfalls. The Orange River passes through the Aughrabies (oh-KRAH-bees) Falls as it flows to the Atlantic. When the water is highest, the Aughrabies Falls are several miles wide. The water tumbles down 19 separate waterfalls. The Limpopo (lim-POH-poh) River is the region's other major river. It flows into the Indian Ocean.

✔ **READING CHECK:** (*Places and Regions*) What are southern Africa's physical features and climate?

Resources

Southern Africa is very rich in mineral resources. Gold, diamonds, platinum, copper, uranium, coal, and iron ore are all found in the region. Where rain is plentiful or irrigation is possible, farmers can grow a wide range of crops. Ranchers raise livestock on the high plains. Some nomadic herders still live in desert areas.

✔ **READING CHECK:** (*Places and Regions*) What are the main resources of southern Africa?

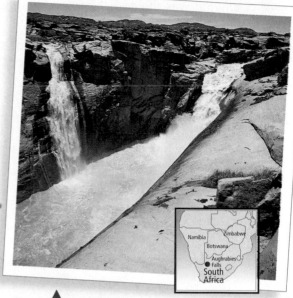

▲
The Orange River flows down the spectacular Aughrabies Falls. The falls are near the Namibian border in northwestern South Africa.

Section Review 1

Define and explain: enclaves, the veld, pans

Working with Sketch Maps On a map of southern Africa that you draw or that your teacher provides, label the following: Drakensberg, Inyanga Mountains, Cape of Good Hope, Kalahari Desert, Namib Desert, Orange River, Aughrabies Falls, and Limpopo River. The Orange River forms part of the border between what two countries?

Reading for the Main Idea

1. (*Places and Regions*) What are the major landforms of southern Africa?

2. (*Places and Regions*) What are the main natural resources of the region?

3. (*Physical Systems*) How do physical processes affect southern Africa's climate?

Critical Thinking

4. **Drawing Inferences and Conclusions** How do you think the climate off the Cape of Good Hope has affected shipping in the area?

Organizing What You Know

5. **Summarizing** Copy the following graphic organizer. Use it to list the landforms, climates, and resources of southern Africa.

Climates

Landforms

Resources

Southern Africa

Southern Africa's History and Culture

Read to Discover

1. What was the early history of southern Africa like?
2. How did Europeans gain control of southern Africa, and what changes did this cause?

Reading Strategy

TAKING NOTES Use the headings in this section to create an outline. As you read the section, write what you learn beneath each heading.

Vocabulary

Boers

Places

Cape Town

▲
Ancient rock art of southern Africa often includes hunters and animals.

Interpreting the Visual Record What do these images suggest about the people who made them?

Early History

Southern Africa's landscape and climate have influenced the region's history. For example, monsoon winds blow from the Indian Ocean to southern Africa from November to February. From May to September the wind blows the other way, from Africa to Asia. Ancient ships used these winds to make regular trading voyages between the two continents.

The Khoisan Some of the oldest human fossils have been found in southern Africa. By about 18,000 B.C., groups of hunter-gatherers were living throughout the mainland region. They left distinctive paintings of people and animals on rock surfaces. Some descendants of these people, including the Khoikhoi and the San, still live in certain desert regions. They speak languages of the Khoisan language family, which share unusual "click" sounds. However, most Khoisan people were absorbed into groups that moved into the region later.

Bantu Migrations Some 1,500–2,000 years ago a different group of people spread from central Africa into southern Africa. They spoke another family of languages known as Bantu. Today, most southern Africans speak one of the more than 200 Bantu languages. Scholars believe the early Bantu people introduced the use of iron and cattle herding to the region.

Shona and Swahili By about A.D. 1000 one Bantu group, the Shona, had built an empire. It included much of what is now Zimbabwe and Mozambique. They farmed, raised cattle, and traded gold with other groups on the coast. They also constructed stone-walled towns called zimbabwe. The largest town, now called Great Zimbabwe, may have had 10,000 to 20,000 residents. Great Zimbabwe was abandoned in the 1400s.

Among Great Zimbabwe's trading partners were the Swahili-speaking people of the east coast. These were Africans who had adopted Islam and many Arab customs by the A.D. 1100s. The Swahili-speakers were sailors and traders. Archaeologists have found Chinese porcelain at Great Zimbabwe. This suggests that Africa and East Asia were connected by an Indian Ocean trade network.

Madagascar Madagascar's early history is quite different from the rest of southern Africa. Madagascar's first settlers came from Asia, rather than Africa, about A.D. 700. The island's culture shows the influence of both Africa and Asia. Malagasy, Madagascar's official language, is related to languages spoken in Indonesia. Malagasy also includes many words from the Bantu language family.

Mozambique In the early 1500s the Portuguese set up forts in Mozambique. They hoped to take over the region's gold trade from the Swahili-speakers and Arabs. The Portuguese also established large estates along the Zambezi River that used slave labor. In the 1700s and 1800s Mozambique became an important part of the slave trade. Africans were captured there and sent as slaves to Brazil and other parts of the world.

▲

People fish with nets in the Indian Ocean. Fishing is an important industry in Mozambique and Madagascar.

The Portuguese built this prison in Mozambique in the 1800s.

Interpreting the Visual Record
(*Movement*) **How might this architecture reflect European influences?**

◄

✓ **READING CHECK:** (*Human Systems*) What were some key events in the early history of southern Africa?

In this painting, British ships sail past the Cape of Good Hope. The distinctively shaped Table Mountain is visible in the distance. ▶

Our Amazing Planet

Much of southern Africa was a malaria zone. Quinine, a medicine made from a South American tree, could combat malaria. Using this medicine, Europeans were able to move into lowland areas where malaria was common.

In this 1935 photograph, elephant tusks and rhino horns are inspected in a London warehouse. ▼

The Dutch, British, and Portuguese in South Africa

The land around the Cape of Good Hope lacked the gold and copper of the Zambezi Valley. However, it had a Mediterranean climate. It also was free of the mosquitoes and tsetse flies that spread tropical diseases. In 1652 the Dutch set up a trade station at a natural harbor near the Cape. This small colony would eventually become known as Cape Town. It provided supplies to Dutch ships sailing between the Dutch East Indies and Europe. The Dutch brought in slaves to work in the colony. Some were Malays from Southeast Asia. Others were Africans bought at slave markets in other parts of Africa.

Afrikaners and Afrikaans The main language spoken in the colony was Dutch. Over time, a new language called Afrikaans emerged. Khoison, Bantu, and Malay words were added to the Dutch, together with some English vocabulary. White descendants of the original colonists are called Afrikaners. Some European men married Khoisan or Malay women. People descended from Malays, Khoisan, or a mixture of these with Europeans are called Coloureds.

A British Colony Afrikaner frontier farmers called **Boers** gradually spread out from the original colony. Then, in the early 1800s, Great Britain took over the area of the Cape. The Boers resisted the British colonial government. Many Boers packed all their belongings into wagons and moved farther east and north. This movement was called the Great Trek.

At about the same time, a Bantu-speaking group, the Zulu, became a powerful fighting force. They conquered the surrounding African peoples, creating their own empire. When the Boers moved into the northern plains, they entered Zulu territory. The two sides clashed. Eventually the Zulu were challenged by the British and defeated after a series of battles.

Trade in Slaves and Ivory The British banned slavery in their empire in 1833. The Portuguese colonies of Angola and Mozambique remained as Africa's main slave markets. The slave trade eventually ended in the late 1800s. African trade began to focus on ivory—the tusks of elephants. Hunters wiped out the entire elephant population in some parts of southern Africa.

Diamonds, Gold, and Colonies In the 1860s diamonds were discovered in the northern part of the Cape Colony. In 1886 gold was discovered in the Transvaal, an area controlled by the Boers. Thousands of British and others came to South Africa. Railroads were built to connect the interior with the coast.

As the British moved north from the Cape Colony, some Boers moved into what is now Botswana. Afraid that the Boers would take over his country, Botswana's ruler asked for British protection. In 1885 Botswana (then known as Bechuanaland) came under British control. What is now Namibia became German Southwest Africa—a German colony. In 1889 what is now Zimbabwe came under control of the British South Africa Company as part of Rhodesia. It became a self-governing British colony in 1923.

South Africa In 1899 tensions over land and mineral wealth led to war between the Boers and the British. The Boers were greatly outnumbered, but held off the British army for three years. In the end the Boers were defeated. Their territory was added to the British colony of South Africa. In 1920, following Germany's defeat in World War I, Namibia was placed under South Africa's control.

✓ **READING CHECK:** (*Human Systems*) How did Europeans gain control of southern Africa, and what changes did this cause?

▲
This old steam train still operates in South Africa. The British built this and other railroads during the colonial period.

Interpreting the Visual Record
(*Movement*) **Why did the Europeans connect the interior with the coast?**

Section Review 2

Define and explain: Boers

Working with Sketch Maps On the map you created in Section 1, label Cape Town. What were the advantages of Cape Town's location?

Reading for the Main Idea

1. (*Human Systems*) How did the Bantu affect the history of southern Africa?

2. (*Human Systems*) How do archaeologists believe Chinese porcelain came to Great Zimbabwe?

Homework Practice Online
Keyword: SK5 HP13

Critical Thinking

3. **Finding the Main Idea** How did the slave trade affect southern Africa?

4. **Analyzing Information** What European groups settled in southern Africa? How did these groups interact with each other?

Organizing What You Know

5. **Sequencing** Copy the following time line. Use it to mark important events in the history of southern Africa from 18,000 B.C. to 1920.

18,000 B.C.   1920

Read to Discover

1. What was South Africa's policy of apartheid?
2. What factors led to the end of apartheid?
3. What is South Africa's economy like?
4. What are South Africa's prospects for the future?

Vocabulary

apartheid
townships
sanctions

Places

Witwatersrand
Johannesburg
Durban
Port Elizabeth

People

Nelson Mandela
Desmond Tutu

Reading Strategy

READING ORGANIZER Before you read this section, draw a large circle on a sheet of paper. Draw a vertical line and a horizontal line across the center of the circle. Label the parts Racial Divisions, Pressure against South Africa, Economy, and Future. As you read this section, write what you learn in each part of the circle.

BIOGRAPHY

Nelson Mandela
(1918–   )

Character Trait: Citizenship

Because he protested against apartheid, Nelson Mandela was imprisoned for 26 years. In 1990, however, South Africa's President de Klerk released Mandela from prison. Mandela and de Klerk shared the Nobel Peace Prize in 1993. One year later, Mandela became South Africa's first black president. He wrote a new constitution and worked to improve the living conditions of black South Africans.

How did Nelson Mandela show citizenship?

Racial Divisions

In the early 1900s South Africa's government, which was dominated by Afrikaners, became increasingly racist. Some black South Africans opposed the government. They formed the African National Congress (ANC) in 1912 to defend their rights. However, the trend toward racial division and inequality continued.

After World War II South Africa became an independent country. The South African government set up a policy of separation for its different peoples. This policy was called **apartheid**, meaning "apartness." The government divided people into three groups: whites, coloureds and Asians, and blacks—the overwhelming majority. Coloureds and Asians were only allowed to live in certain areas. Each African tribe or group was given its own rural "homeland."

The whites owned most of the good farmland. They also owned the mines and other natural resources. Black Africans had no rights in white areas. Blacks' land, housing, and health care were poor compared to those for whites. Education for blacks was limited, and classes were often taught in Afrikaans. Coloureds' facilities were poor but slightly better than those for blacks. People who protested these rules were sent to prison. One of those imprisoned was a lawyer named Nelson Mandela, a leader of the ANC.

Many blacks found work in white-owned industries, mines, shops, and farms. They had to live in separate areas called **townships**. These were often crowded clusters of tiny homes. They were far from the jobs in the cities and mines.

✔ **READING CHECK:** (*Human Systems*) What was apartheid?

In townships like Kayalitsha, black workers lived in crude shacks.

Interpreting the Visual Record How did the apartheid system affect the roles and responsibilities of South Africans?

Pressure against South Africa

Many people around the world objected to South Africa's apartheid laws. Some countries banned trade with South Africa. Some companies in the United States and Europe refused to invest their money in South Africa. Many international scientific and sports organizations refused to include South Africans in their meetings and competitions. These penalties, called **sanctions**, were intended to force South Africa to end apartheid.

South Africa and Its Neighbors During the 1960s, 1970s, and 1980s other countries in southern Africa gained their independence from colonial rule. British colonists in Rhodesia protested Britain's decision to grant independence. They declared their own white-dominated republic in 1970. This break resulted in years of violence and civil war. Finally the white government agreed to hold elections. They turned the country over to the black majority. The new government renamed the country Zimbabwe.

Mozambique was granted independence in 1975 after 10 years of war against Portuguese rule. However, rebels backed by Rhodesia and South Africa plunged Mozambique into another long war. Despite violent resistance, Namibia continued to be ruled by South Africa until independence in 1990.

The End of Apartheid As other countries in southern Africa gained independence, South Africa became more and more isolated. Protest within the country increased. The government outlawed the ANC. Many ANC members were jailed or forced to leave the country.

Writers and artists also spoke out against apartheid. One of the most vocal was South African novelist Nadine Gordimer. Her tales about the evils of apartheid captured the attention of readers around the world.

Finally, South Africa, led by F. W. deKlerk, began to move away from the apartheid system in the late 1980s. In 1990 the government released Nelson Mandela from prison. Mandela was elected president in 1994 after all South Africans were given the right to vote.

Today all races have equal rights in South Africa. Public schools and universities are open to all, as are hospitals and transportation. However, economic equality has been slow in coming. White South Africans are still wealthier than the vast majority of black South Africans. Also, divisions between different black ethnic groups have caused new tensions. Still, South Africans now hope for a better future.

✓ **READING CHECK:** (*Human Systems*) Why and how did South Africa do away with apartheid?

South Africa's Economy

South Africa's government is trying to create jobs and better conditions for black workers and farmers. However, South Africa's mineral wealth and industries are still mostly owned by white people. Even officials who favor reform are afraid that too-rapid change will weaken the economy. They fear it will drive educated and wealthy whites to leave the country. The government has avoided taking white-owned farmland to divide among black farmers.

South Africa's energy resources include coal and hydroelectric power. Rich uranium mines provide fuel for nuclear power plants. In addition to gold and diamonds, mineral resources include copper, platinum, iron ore, and chromium.

The Witwatersrand region around Johannesburg is the continent's largest industrial area. South African and foreign companies build computers, cars, televisions, and many other products needed for modern life. The major port is Durban on the Indian Ocean coast. Cape Town and Port Elizabeth are other important ports.

✓ **READING CHECK:** (*Human Systems*) How has apartheid continued to affect South Africa's economy today?

These are uncut, or rough, diamonds. Diamonds are the hardest mineral. This makes them useful for certain types of cutting and drilling.

South Africa's Future

South Africa has more resources and industry than most African countries but faces severe problems. It must begin to deliver equal education and economic opportunities to the entire population.

Place Cape Town has grown into a large industrial city. In this photograph, the harbor is visible beyond the tall buildings of the business district.

New problems have arisen since the end of apartheid. Crime has increased in the large cities. Also, South Africa, like the rest of the region, is facing a terrible AIDS epidemic.

There are 11 official languages in South Africa, although English is used in most areas. South Africa produces fine wines from the region around Cape Town. It has a unique cooking style combining Dutch, Malay, and African foods. The country also has a lively tradition of literature and the arts. Today, traditional ethnic designs are used in clothing, lamps, linens, and other products. These are sold to tourists and locals alike.

✓ **READING CHECK:** (*Places and Regions*) What are the challenges faced by South Africa?

South Africa

COUNTRY	POPULATION/ GROWTH RATE	LIFE EXPECTANCY	LITERACY RATE	PER CAPITA GDP
South Africa	42,768,678 0.3%	47, male 46, female	86%	$10,000
United States	290,342,554 0.9%	74, male 80, female	97%	$37,600

Source: Central Intelligence Agency, *The World Factbook 2003*

Interpreting the Chart What is South Africa's per capita GDP?

Section Review 3

go.hrw.com **Homework Practice Online** Keyword: SK5 HP13

Define or identify: apartheid, Nelson Mandela, townships, sanctions, Desmond Tutu

Working with Sketch Maps On the map you created in Section 2, label Witwatersrand, Johannesburg, Durban, and Port Elizabeth.

Reading for the Main Idea

1. (*Human Systems*) What was the system of apartheid, and how did it affect the roles and responsibilities of South Africans?

2. (*Human Systems*) How did people around the world protest apartheid?

3. (*Places and Regions*) What challenges remain for South Africa?

Critical Thinking

4. Analyzing Information Why is South Africa the continent's most economically developed country?

Organizing What You Know

5. Summarizing Use this graphic organizer to list information about life in South Africa during apartheid and since the system ended.

During apartheid	Since apartheid ended

Read to Discover

1. What groups have influenced Namibia's culture?
2. What factors have helped Botswana's economy?
3. What is Zimbabwe's economy like?
4. Why has Mozambique remained so poor?
5. What events have marked Madagascar's recent history?

Vocabulary

Organization of African Unity (OAU)

Places

Windhoek
Gaborone
Harare
Maputo

Reading Strategy

READING ORGANIZER Before you read, create a three-column chart on a sheet of paper. Label the columns Country, Resources, and Challenges. Then list each country covered in this section in the Country column. As you read this section, write what you learn about the resources and challenges of each country.

Namibia

Most Namibians live in the savannas of the north or in the cooler central highlands. Windhoek, the capital, is located in these highlands. About 6 percent of the population is white, mainly of German descent. The rest of the population is divided among several different ethnic groups. Most Namibians are Christian. English is the official language. However, schooling was in Afrikaans until recently.

At independence in 1990, white farmers held most of the productive land. Most of Namibia's income comes from the mining of diamonds, copper, lead, zinc, and uranium. Fishing in the Atlantic Ocean and sheep ranching are also important sources of income.

Namibian culture shows many different influences. In many rocky areas, ancient rock engravings and paintings of the Khoisan are preserved. Beer and pastries reflect the period of German colonization.

✔ READING CHECK: (Human Systems) What are Namibia's cultural influences?

A San grandmother and child drink water from an ostrich egg. The San people traditionally lived by hunting and gathering. However, just a few live this way today.

Interpreting the Visual Record

(Human-Environment Interaction) What factors do you think might lead many San people to give up their traditional way of life?

Botswana

Botswana is a large, landlocked, semiarid country. Thanks to mineral resources and stable political conditions, Botswana is one of Africa's success stories. Cattle ranching and mining of copper and diamonds are the principal economic activities. Recently, international companies have set up factories here. A new capital,

Gaborone, was built after independence. Like the other countries of the region, Botswana belongs to the **Organization of African Unity (OAU)**. The OAU, founded in 1963, tries to promote cooperation between African countries. Botswana also belongs to the South African Development Community (SADC), a group of countries working toward economic development in southern Africa.

Botswana's population is less than 1.6 million. About 79 percent belong to a single ethnic group, the Tswana. Most people live in the east and south. The San and other minority groups mostly live in the northern swamps and the Kalahari Desert. About 15 percent of Botswana's people are Christian. The rest follow traditional African religions.

Botswana's major river, the Okavango, flows from Angola into a huge basin. The swamps of this basin are home to elephants, crocodiles, antelope, lions, hyenas, and other animals. Many tourists travel to Botswana to see these wild animals.

Traditional crafts of Botswana include ostrich-eggshell beadwork and woven baskets with complex designs. People there also produce colorful wool tapestries and rugs.

✔ **READING CHECK:** (*Places and Regions*) Why might Botswana be considered a success story?

▲
The Okavango River spreads out to form a large swampy area. Dense vegetation allows only small boats to move through the narrow channels.

Zimbabwe

Zimbabwe's capital is Harare. Zimbabwe gained independence in 1980. Since then, the country has struggled to create a more equal distribution of land and wealth. White residents make up less than 1 percent of the population. However, they still own most of the large farms and ranches.

Zimbabwe exports tobacco, corn, sugar, and beef. It now manufactures many everyday items, including shoes, batteries, and radios. Exports of gold, copper, chrome, nickel, and tin are also important to Zimbabwe's economy.

The AIDS epidemic threatens to kill hundreds of thousands of Zimbabwe's people, leaving many orphans behind. These effects will make economic growth harder. Other diseases such as malaria and tuberculosis are often deadly. There are also tensions between the majority Shona people and the minority Ndebele.

Artists in Zimbabwe have revived the tradition of stone sculpture found at Great Zimbabwe. Some of the larger pieces are among the most striking examples of modern art in the world.

✔ **READING CHECK:** (*Places and Regions*) What is Zimbabwe's economy like?

Other Southern African Countries

COUNTRY	POPULATION/ GROWTH RATE	LIFE EXPECTANCY	LITERACY RATE	PER CAPITA GDP
Botswana	1,573,267 0.5%	32, male 32, female	79%	$9,500
Madagascar	16,979,744 3%	53, male 58, female	69%	$760
Mozambique	17,479,266 0.8%	31, male 32, female	48%	$1,000
Namibia	1,927,447 1.4%	44, male 41, female	84%	$6,900
Zimbabwe	12,576,742 0.2%	40, male 38, female	90%	$2,400
United States	290,342,554 0.9%	74, male 80, female	97%	$37,600

Source: Central Intelligence Agency, *The World Factbook 2003*

Interpreting the Chart Which countries are the least economically developed in the region?

CONNECTING TO *History*

In 1884–85, representatives of Europe's colonial countries met in Berlin. These countries included Belgium, France, Germany, Great Britain, Italy, Portugal, and Spain. Each was conquering areas in Africa. Their claims to territory were beginning to overlap. Leaders began to worry that a rivalry in Africa might trigger a war in Europe.

The Granger Collection, New York

Cartoon of France and Britain dividing Africa

AFRICA'S BORDERS

The Berlin conference was called to agree to boundaries for these African colonies. No Africans were invited to the conference. The European representatives divided up Africa among themselves. The new borders sometimes followed physical features, such as lakes and mountains. Many simply followed straight lines of latitude or longitude. Often people from the same ethnic group were separated by the new borders. In other places, ethnic groups hostile to each other were grouped together.

Most of the European colonies in Africa became independent after 1960. However, the leaders of the new African countries have mostly avoided drawing new boundary lines. So these countries still struggle with the borders they inherited from the Berlin Conference. These borders have made it hard for many African countries to build national loyalty among their citizens.

Understanding What You Read

1. How were Africa's borders established?
2. What consequences have these borders had for modern Africa?

Mozambique

Mozambique is one of the world's poorest countries. Its economy was badly damaged by civil war after independence from Portugal. Today, Mozambique's ports of Maputo—the capital—and Beira once again ship many products from interior Africa. The taxes collected on these shipments are an important source of revenue. Energy sources include coal and new hydroelectric dams on the Zambezi River. Plantations grow cotton, cashews, sugar, and tea.

Most of Mozambique's people belong to various Bantu ethnic groups. Each group has its own language. However, the country's official language is Portuguese. About 30 percent of the people are Christian, and 20 percent are Muslim.

Mozambique is famous for its fiery pepper or *peri-perri* sauces. They are often served on shrimp and rice.

✓ **READING CHECK:** (*Places and Regions*) What factor limited Mozambique's economic development?

Madagascar

Madagascar is a former French colony. It was ruled by a socialist dictator until the early 1990s. At that point the people demanded a new political system. The optimism that came with democracy faded as the new leaders struggled with poverty. Surprisingly, in 1996 the people voted the former dictator back into power.

Nearly all of Madagascar's people are still very poor. There is little industry. Most of the country's income comes from exports of coffee, sugar, vanilla, and cloves. Most of the people depend on subsistence farming.

Madagascar has many animals found nowhere else. This is because the island has been separated from the African mainland for millions of years. Some 40 species of lemurs, relatives of apes, live only on this island. However, destruction of the rain forests threatens many of Madagascar's animals with extinction.

Malagasy and French are spoken throughout Madagascar. About 52 percent of the people follow traditional African religions. Some 41 percent are Christian, and about 7 percent are Muslim.

✓ **READING CHECK:** (*Places and Regions*) What has Madagascar's recent history been like?

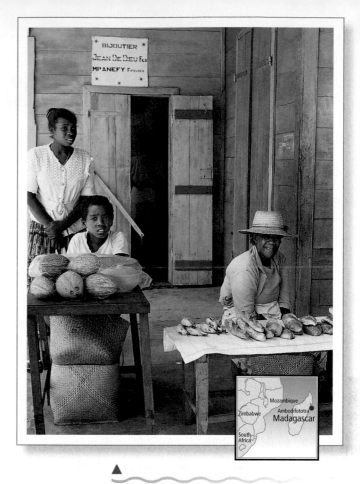

▲

Remnants of French culture can still be seen in Madagascar.

Interpreting the Visual Record
(*Movement*) **Which of these vendors' foods suggests a connection to French culture?**

 Homework Practice Online
Keyword: SK5 HP13

Define and explain: Organization of African Unity (OAU)

Working with Sketch Maps On the map you created in Section 3, label Windhoek, Gaborone, Harare, and Maputo. Which cities are located on the plateau of the southern African interior?

Reading for the Main Idea

1. (*Human Systems*) How have diseases affected Zimbabwe's people and economy?

2. (*Human Systems*) How did civil war affect Mozambique?

3. (*Environment and Society*) What minerals does Namibia have, and how do they affect its economy?

Critical Thinking

4. **Drawing Inferences and Conclusions** How do you think the fact that Botswana's population is almost entirely of a single ethnic group has affected its politics?

Organizing What You Know

5. **Summarizing** Copy the following graphic organizer. Use it to list information about southern African cultures.

Country	Culture
Namibia	
Botswana	
Zimbabwe	
Mozambique	
Madagascar	

Define and Identify

Identify each of the following:

1. enclaves
2. the veld
3. pans
4. Boers
5. apartheid
6. Nelson Mandela
7. townships
8. sanctions
9. Desmond Tutu
10. Organization of African Unity (OAU)

Review the Main Ideas

11. What two South African countries are enclaves?
12. What are southern Africa's two deserts like?
13. What natural resources are very plentiful in southern Africa?
14. How did traders travel between Africa and Asia?
15. What did the original Bantu migrants bring to southern Africa?
16. How have mineral resources affected South Africa?
17. What form of art have artists in Zimbabwe revived?
18. Why are some animals found only in Madagascar?
19. What three racial groups were defined and separated by apartheid? Which group made up the majority of the population?

Think Critically

20. **Drawing Inferences and Conclusions** In what parts of southern Africa do you think most farming takes place? Why?
21. **Analyzing Information** What finally motivated the South African government to end the apartheid system?
22. **Summarizing** Who were the Afrikaners, and what role did they play in the history of southern Africa?
23. **Summarizing** What factors have slowed the economic development of the countries in this region?
24. **Finding the Main Idea** How did the discovery of diamonds and gold affect the settlement of Europeans in southern Africa?

Map Activity

25. On a separate sheet of paper, match the letters on the map with their correct labels.

Drakensberg	Kalahari Desert
Inyanga Mountains	Namib Desert
	Orange River
Cape of Good Hope	Limpopo River
	Harare

Writing Activity

Write a brief essay in which you compare and contrast Botswana and Mozambique. How are the physical features of these two countries similar or different? How do these features affect the economies of Botswana and Mozambique? What are the major industries? Be sure to use standard grammar, spelling, sentence structure, and punctuation.

internet connect

Internet Activity: go.hrw.com
KEYWORD: SK5 GT13

Choose a topic to explore about southern Africa:
- Explore the Namib Desert.
- Go on a South African safari.
- Investigate apartheid.

Social Studies Skills Practice

Analyzing Charts

Many people in southern Africa carry the HIV virus that causes the disease called AIDS. Study the following chart and then answer the questions.

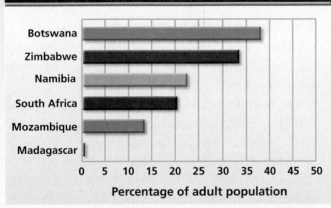

Adult Rate of HIV/AIDS

Percentage of adult population

Source: Central Intelligence Agency, *The World Factbook 2003*

1. What percentage of South Africa's adult population has HIV/AIDS?
2. Which country has the highest adult rate of HIV/AIDS?
3. Which country has the lowest adult rate of HIV/AIDS?
4. Based on the information in this chart, is AIDS a significant problem in most of southern Africa? Explain your answer.

Analyzing Primary Sources

On April 20, 1964, Nelson Mandela spoke at the opening of his trial. Read the following excerpt from his speech. Then answer the questions.

"I have fought against white domination [control], and I have fought against black domination. I have cherished the ideal of a democratic and free society in which all persons live together in harmony and with equal opportunities. It is an ideal which I hope to live for and to achieve. But if needs be, it is an ideal for which I am prepared to die."

1. What South African policy was Nelson Mandela fighting to abolish?
2. What type of government does Nelson Mandela cherish?
3. What are Nelson Mandela's goals?
4. Why might Mandela feel he must be prepared to die for his beliefs?

Kenya's Tree Planters

Twenty million young trees scattered throughout Kenya offer new hope to farmers and families. The trees were planted by women who farm these lands. "We are planting trees to ensure our own survival," says Wangari Maathai. She is the founder of Kenya's Green Belt Movement.

Deforestation

Like many other developing countries, Kenya is a country of farmers and herders. The most productive farmlands are in the highlands. This area was once green with trees and plants. Over the past century, however, much of this land has been cleared. Today, less than 10 percent of the original forests remain. Many trees were cut for firewood, which people use for cooking.

Without tree roots to hold the soil in place, the land eroded. The land was losing its fertility.

Farmers moved to the savannas in search of better land.

Wangari Maathai recognized what was happening. "When I would visit the village where I was born," she says, "I saw whole forests had been cleared for cultivation and timber. People were moving onto hilly slopes and riverbeds and marginal areas that were only bush when I was a child." Maathai was shocked to find children suffering from malnutrition. People were no longer eating foods such as beans and corn. Instead, they were eating refined foods such as rice. They were doing this because these foods need less cooking—and thus less firewood.

The Green Belt Movement

On June 5, 1977, in honor of World Environment Day, Maathai and a few supporters planted seven trees in Nairobi, Kenya's capital. Thus began the Green Belt Movement. This movement then spread through the Kenyan highlands and captured people's attention around the world.

From the beginning, Maathai knew that the success of her efforts depended mainly on women. In Kenya, men tend cash crops such as coffee and cotton. Women collect firewood and grow corn, beans, and other food crops. It is the women who grow the food their families eat. The women were the first to see the connection between poor soil and famine.

◀ ～～～

Human-Environment Interaction   Many of the trees in Kenya's highlands have been cleared for crops.

The movement's workers encouraged women in Kenya to plant trees. They pointed out that women would not have to walk miles to collect firewood. They would have wood available nearby for fires, fences, and buildings. If the tree seedlings survived, the women would also be paid a small sum of money.

First, a few small nurseries were started to give out free seedlings. The nurseries are staffed by local women who are paid for their work. Nurseries also train and pay local people known as Green Belt Rangers. The Rangers visit farms, check on seedlings, and offer advice.

Before long, nurseries were appearing in communities throughout the highlands. Kenyan women talked to friends and neighbors about the benefits of planting trees. Neighbors encouraged Esther Wairimu to plant seedlings. Five years later, her fields were surrounded by mango, blue gum, and other trees. "I have learned that a tree… is life," she says.

Today, the advantages of planting trees are clear. Farmers now have fuel and shade. Even more important, the soil is being protected from

▲ (*Human-Environment Interaction*) Workers from the Green Belt Movement teach schoolchildren in Kenya how to care for tree seedlings.

erosion. The number of Green Belt nurseries has grown to about 5,000. Most are run by women.

Expanding the Movement

Maathai believes that local people must work together to protect the environment. She stresses that the Green Belt Movement relies on farmers. The movement receives little government support. Most of the money comes from small personal donations.

Now Maathai dreams of spreading her movement to other African countries. "We must never lose hope…," she says. "One person *can* make a difference."

Wangari Maathai (right) has encouraged Kenyan women to plant millions of trees. Women are paid for the seedlings they plant that survive.

▼

Your Turn

Working in small groups, think of an environmental issue facing your community or state.

1. Develop a plan that demonstrates how "one person can make a difference."

2. Present your group's plan to the rest of the class.

Building Skills for Life: Understanding Ecosystems

The plants and animals in an area, together with the nonliving parts of their environment, form an ecosystem. An important thing to remember about ecosystems is that each part is interconnected.

Life on Earth depends on the energy and nutrients flowing through ecosystems. Energy and nutrients move between plants, animals, and soils through food chains and food webs.

Most ecosystems involve three groups of organisms: producers, consumers, and decomposers. Producers make their own food. Plants are producers. They make food by combining carbon dioxide, nutrients from the soil, sunlight, and water. Consumers are unable to make food. They have to get food from producers or from other consumers. Humans are consumers. We eat plants (producers) and animals (consumers). Decomposers get food from dead organisms and wastes. Bacteria and fungi are decomposers.

Elephants have adapted to the ecosystem of Africa's Namib Desert.

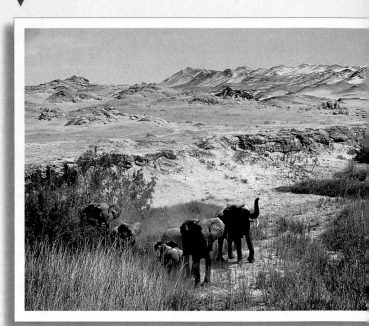

Like all forms of life, humans depend on ecosystems for survival. Knowing how ecosystems work helps us understand how we are connected to both living and nonliving things. It can also help us manage, protect, and use our environments wisely.

THE SKILL

1. Describe an ecosystem in the region where you live. What plants and animals live there? How are they connected?

2. Make a table showing some of the producers, consumers, and decomposers in an ecosystem. What do you think would happen if one of these groups suddenly disappeared?

3. Try to identify some ways that human activities have changed ecosystems in your community. Have some plants or animals disappeared?

HANDS on
GEOGRAPHY

Like all organisms, lions are part of an ecosystem. Lions survive by killing and eating other animals, such as zebras and gazelles. After lions have killed an animal, they eat their fill. Then other animals such as vultures and hyenas eat what is left.

The lion itself is food for other organisms. Small animals like ticks, fleas, and mosquitoes drink the lion's blood. The lion's waste serves as food for organisms that live in the soil. When the lion dies, it will be eaten by other animals.

How does the lion fit into its ecosystem? You can answer this question by drawing a connections web. These guidelines will help you get started.

1. Draw a picture of a lion.

2. Think of interactions that lions have with other parts of their environment.

3. Include these interactions in your drawing. For example, lions eat zebras, so you could add a zebra to your drawing.

4. Draw lines connecting the lion to other parts of its environment. For example, you could draw a line connecting the lion and the zebra.

5. Be sure to extend the connections to include nonliving parts of the environment as well. For example, lions eat

zebras, zebras eat grass, and grass depends on sunlight.

6. Continue making connections on your diagram. When you are done, answer the Lab Report questions.

Lab Report

1. Label the producers, consumers, and decomposers on your connections web. To which group do lions belong?

2. How are lions dependent on nonliving parts of their environment?

3. Imagine there are no more lions. How do you think the ecosystem shown in your connections web would be affected?

UNIT 4

South Asia

CHAPTER 14
India

CHAPTER 15
India's Neighbors

Swayambhunath Stupa, Kathmandu, Nepal

Karakoram Range, Pakistan

A Scholar in India

Emily K. Bloch coordinates educational programs at the South Asia Outreach center at the University of Chicago. Her special area of interest is South Asian children's literature. Here she describes the many types of transportation she has used in India. **WHAT DO YOU THINK?** *Which type of transportation would you enjoy the most?*

In my travels throughout India, I've had the good fortune to ride on a variety of vehicles. I've ridden in buses and cycle-rickshaws, taxis and three-wheeled scooters, on a motorcycle through Calcutta and on the crossbar of a bicycle. I rode in a howdah [seat] on the back of an elephant in a wildlife sanctuary. I even had an uncomfortable, but very welcome, lift in a bullock cart.

But my favorite mode of travel is also one of the most popular in India—riding the great trains. The railway, with more than 1.5 million employees, is the largest employer in the world. It has nearly 40,000 miles of track. Eleven thousand trains, connecting more than 7,000 stations, carry about 12 million people daily. Though the luxury of the princely rail lines beckons, and the first-class cars provide food and bed-linens, I love the crowded, second-class, wooden-benches experience and look forward to my next journey side by side with my fellow Indian and foreign travelers.

Polo players at elephant festival, Jaipur, India

Women in festival dress, Rajasthan, India

Understanding Primary Sources

1. What do Emily Bloch's transportation experiences illustrate about the use of technology in India?

2. Which method of travel does Emily Bloch prefer? Why?

White Bengal tiger

South Asia

Elevation Profile

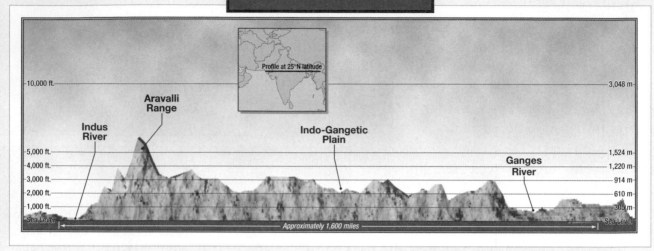

Profile at 25°N latitude

10,000 ft. — 3,048 m

Aravalli Range

Indus River

Indo-Gangetic Plain

Ganges River

5,000 ft. — 1,524 m
4,000 ft. — 1,220 m
3,000 ft. — 914 m
2,000 ft. — 610 m
1,000 ft. — 305 m
Sea Level — Sea Level

Approximately 1,600 miles

The United States and South Asia:
Comparing Sizes

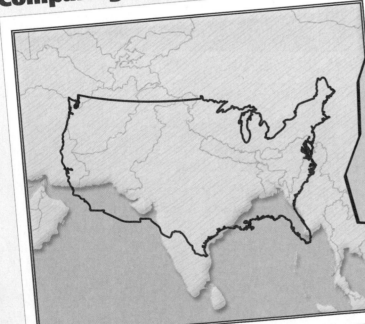

GEOSTATS:

India

World's second-largest population: 1,049,700,118 (July 2003 estimate)

Predicted population in 2025: 1,415,274,000

World's most populous democracy

World's greatest recorded total rainfall in one month: 366 in. (930 cm) in Cherrapunji, in July 1861

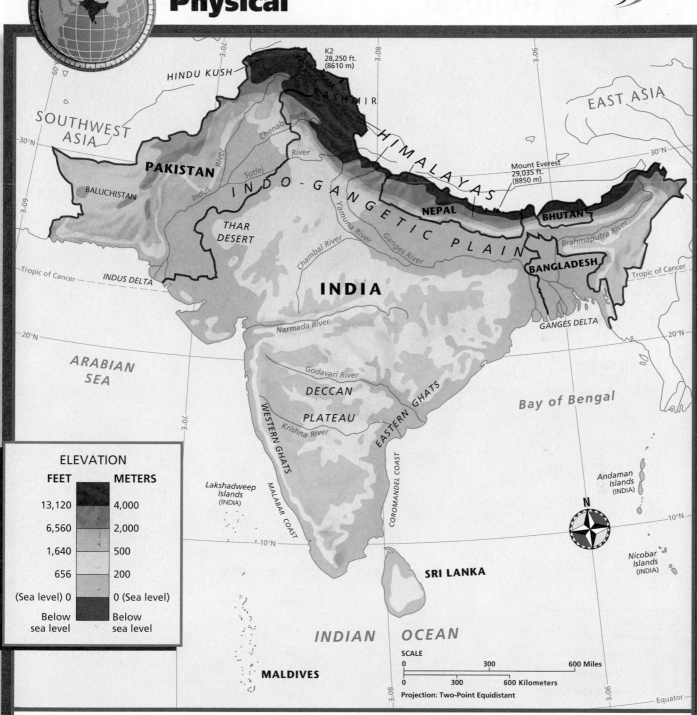

ELEVATION

FEET	METERS
13,120	4,000
6,560	2,000
1,640	500
656	200
(Sea level) 0	0 (Sea level)
Below sea level	Below sea level

SCALE

0   300   600 Miles

0   300   600 Kilometers

Projection: Two-Point Equidistant

1. (Region) Which country has the lowest overall elevation? Which countries have mountains that stretch from their western to eastern borders?

2. (Region) Which two rivers that drain the Deccan Plateau flow directly into the Bay of Bengal?

Critical Thinking

3. (Movement) Based on the map, do you think it would be easier for travelers or invaders to come to northern India by land or by sea? Why might this be the case?

KASHMIR

SOUTHWEST ASIA

EAST ASIA

Islamabad ⊛

PAKISTAN

Lahore •

PUNJAB

BALUCHISTAN

Delhi •
New Delhi ⊛

NEPAL ⊛ Kathmandu

BHUTAN
⊛ Thimphu

Karachi •

BANGLADESH
⊛ Dhaka

Tropic of Cancer

Tropic of Cancer

INDIA

• Ahmadabad

Kolkata •

ARABIAN SEA

Mumbai (Bombay) •

• Hyderabad

Bay of Bengal

Lakshadweep Islands (INDIA)

Bangalore •

Chennai (Madras) •

Andaman Islands (INDIA)

N

SRI LANKA

Nicobar Islands (INDIA)

⊛ Colombo

INDIAN OCEAN

| Boundaries |
| ⊛ National capitals |
| • Other cities |

SCALE

0   300   600 Miles

0   300   600 Kilometers

Projection: Two-Point Equidistant

• Male
MALDIVES

Equator

1. *Place* What are the region's two island countries? Which is larger?

2. *Location* Which country is almost completely surrounded by India?

3. *Region* Compare this map to the **physical map**. Which small countries might be called the "Mountain Kingdoms?"

Critical Thinking

4. *Location* Bangladesh was once part of Pakistan. What role do you think Bangladesh's location may have played in its drive for independence?

CLIMATE

- Humid tropical
- Tropical savanna
- Desert
- Steppe
- Humid subtropical
- Highland
- Wet monsoon air flow
- Dry monsoon air flow

SOUTHWEST ASIA

EAST ASIA

ARABIAN SEA

Bay of Bengal

INDIAN OCEAN

Tropic of Cancer

Equator

SCALE

| 0 | 300 | 600 Miles |

| 0 | 300 | 600 Kilometers |

Projection: Two-Point Equidistant

---

1. (Region) Compare this map to the **physical map.** Which landform in south central India has a steppe climate?

2. (Human-Environment Interaction) Compare this map to the **land use and resources map** of the region. Which climate regions have the least economic activity?

Critical Thinking

3. (Region) Compare this map to the **political map** of the region. Other than those with mainly highland climates, which country appears to be least affected by monsoons?

South Asia:
Population

POPULATION DENSITY

Persons per sq. mile		Persons per sq. km
520		200
260		100
130		50
25		10
3		1
0		0

● Metropolitan areas with more than 2 million inhabitants

○ Metropolitan areas with 1 million to 2 million inhabitants

SCALE
0   300   600 Miles
0   300   600 Kilometers
Projection: Two-Point Equidistant

1. *Location* Compare this map to the **physical map**. Which large Indian city is located on the Ganges Delta?

2. *Region* Compare this map to the **physical map** of the region. What is the name of the large densely populated area in the northeastern part of the region?

Critical Thinking

3. *Human-Environment Interaction* Compare this map to the **climate** and **land use and resources maps**. Why do you think few people live along the western and eastern edges of Pakistan?

LAND USE

- Nomadic herding
- Livestock raising
- Commercial farming
- Subsistence farming
- Manufacturing
- Forests
- Limited economic activity
- ● Major manufacturing and trade centers

RESOURCES

- Coal
- Natural gas
- Oil
- Hydroelectric power
- Nuclear power
- G Gold
- S Silver
- U Uranium
- Other minerals
- Timber
- Seafood

SCALE

0   300   600 Miles

0   300   600 Kilometers

Projection: Two-Point Equidistant

1. (Region) Which country has the largest area used for nomadic herding?

2. (Place) Which country has the largest area used for manufacturing?

3. (Location) Which city is near the region's gold, silver, and uranium mines?

4. (Human-Environment Interaction) Which country does not produce hydroelectric power?

Critical Thinking

5. (Human-Environment Interaction) Compare this map to the **climate map** of the region. Why do you think one of Bangladesh's major crops is rice?

Fast FACTS

South Asia

BANGLADESH

CAPITAL:
Dhaka

AREA:
55,598 sq. mi.
(144,000 sq km)

POPULATION:
138,448,210

MONEY:
taka

LANGUAGES:
Bangla (official),
English

ARABLE LAND:
73 percent

BHUTAN

CAPITAL:
Thimphu

AREA:
18,147 sq. mi.
(47,000 sq km)

POPULATION:
2,139,549

MONEY:
ngultrum, Indian rupee

LANGUAGES:
Dzongkha

ARABLE LAND:
2 percent

Crystal clear waters in the Maldives

INDIA

CAPITAL:
New Delhi

AREA:
1,269,338 sq. mi.
(3,287,590 sq km)

POPULATION:
1,049,700,118

MONEY: Indian rupee

LANGUAGES:
Hindi (official), English (associate official), 14 other official languages, many ethnic languages

ARABLE LAND: 56 percent

MALDIVES

CAPITAL:
Male

AREA:
116 sq. mi.
(300 sq km)

POPULATION:
329,684

MONEY:
rufiyaa

LANGUAGES:
Maldivian Dhivehi, English

ARABLE LAND:
10 percent

Countries not drawn to scale.

Buddhist monks in Kandy, Sri Lanka

NEPAL

CAPITAL:
Kathmandu

AREA:
54,363 sq. mi.
(140,800 sq km)

POPULATION:
26,469,569

MONEY:
Nepalese rupee

LANGUAGES:
Nepali (official), other ethnic languages

ARABLE LAND:
17 percent

SRI LANKA

CAPITAL: Colombo

AREA:
25,332 sq. mi.
(65,610 sq km)

POPULATION:
19,742,439

MONEY:
Sri Lankan rupee

LANGUAGES:
Sinhala, Tamil, English

ARABLE LAND:
14 percent

internet connect

COUNTRY STATISTICS
GO TO: go.hrw.com
KEYWORD: SK5 FactsU4
FOR: more facts about South Asia

PAKISTAN

CAPITAL:
Islamabad

AREA:
310,401 sq. mi.
(803,940 sq km)

POPULATION:
150,694,740

MONEY:
Pakistani rupee

LANGUAGES:
Punjabi, Sindhi, Siraiki, Pashtu, Urdu (official), Balochi, Hindko, Brahui, English, many ethnic languages

ARABLE LAND:
27 percent

Sources: Central Intelligence Agency, *The World Factbook 2003*; *The World Almanac and Book of Facts 2003*; pop. figures are 2003 estimates.

CHAPTER 14

India

India is a huge country with an ancient culture and a population of a billion people. However, you might find you have quite a bit in common with a student from India.

Hi! My name is Rojo, and I am 16. I live with my mother, father, and dog, Jacki. I live in Vaduthala, a small town outside the city of Cochin on the southern tip of India. I live in a one-floor house, with three bedrooms, two bathrooms, living area, dining area, kitchen, cooking terrace, front yard with lots of plants, and a road down to the lake. To cook, my mom usually goes outside to the cooking terrace and makes fish curry. That way, the whole house does not smell like the food.

I am a senior at the State Bank Officers Association High School. This term I am studying math, physics, chemistry, and computer science. My favorite subject is math, because I can use it in so many different ways. The computer language I am studying is based on math. We speak in English in school. At home or with friends, we speak Malayalam, the most common language of the state of Kerala.

Entha vishaisham?

◄
Translation: What's new?

Section 1 Physical Geography

Read to Discover

1. What are the three main landform regions of India?
2. What are the major rivers in India?
3. What climate types does India have?
4. What natural resources does India have?

Vocabulary

teak

Places

Gangetic Plain
Deccan
Eastern Ghats
Western Ghats

Ganges River
Bay of Bengal
Brahmaputra River
Thar Desert

Reading Strategy

READING ORGANIZER Before you read, create a spider map. Draw a circle in the center of a sheet of paper. Create four legs that you label Landforms, Rivers, Climate, and Resources. As you read this section, list what you learn about each topic beneath each leg.

India: Physical-Political

Size comparison of India to the contiguous United States

ELEVATION

FEET	METERS
13,120	4,000
6,560	2,000
1,640	500
656	200
(Sea level) 0	0 (Sea level)
Below sea level	Below sea level

⊛ National capital
• Other cities

Landforms

India has three main landform regions: the Himalayas, the Gangetic (gan-JE-tik) Plain, and the Deccan (DE-kuhn). The Himalayas run along the country's northern border and were created when two tectonic plates collided and pushed Earth's crust up.

The vast Gangetic Plain lies to the south of the Himalayas. It stretches about 1,500 miles (2,415 km) across northern India. About half of India's population lives there.

South of the Gangetic Plain is the triangular peninsula known as the Deccan. Most of its area is a plateau, which is divided by many hills and valleys. The plateau's edges are defined by the Eastern Ghats (GAWTS) and Western Ghats. These low mountain ranges separate the plateau's eastern and western edges from narrow coastal plains.

✓ **READING CHECK:** (*Places and Regions*) What are the three main landform regions of India?

Rivers

India's most important river, the Ganges (GAN-jeez), begins on the southern slopes of the Himalayas. It then flows southeastward across northern India. It spreads into a huge delta before flowing into the Bay of Bengal. Although it is now polluted, Hindus call the Ganges the "Mother River" and consider it sacred. Rich silt left by the Ganges has made the Gangetic Plain India's farming heartland.

The Brahmaputra (brahm-uh-POO-truh) River starts in the Plateau of Tibet. It flows through the far northeastern corner of India. From there the Brahmaputra flows southward through Bangladesh, where it empties into the Ganges Delta. The Narmada (nuhr-MUH-duh), Godavari (go-DAH-vuh-ree), and Krishna (KRISH-nuh) Rivers drain the Deccan. A large irrigation project along the Narmada River is under construction. It will include more than 40 branch canals.

✓ **READING CHECK:** (*Places and Regions*) What are India's most important rivers?

A farmer plows rice fields in northern India. The Himalayas rise in the distance.

Interpreting the Visual Record

(*Human-Environment Interaction*) Why do so many of India's people live on the Gangetic Plain?

Climate

India has a variety of climate types. Areas in the Himalayas have highland climates with snow and glaciers. The Thar Desert near the border with Pakistan is hot and dry year-round. The Gangetic Plain has a humid tropical climate. Farther south in the Deccan there are tropical savanna and steppe climates.

Seasonal winds—monsoons—bring moist air from the Indian Ocean in summer. In winter the wind brings dry air from the Asian interior. The timing of the monsoons is very important to farmers in India. If the summer rains come too soon or too late, food production suffers.

✔ **READING CHECK:** (*Places and Regions*) What are India's climates?

The city of Cherrapunji (cher-uh-POOHN-jee), in northeastern India, holds the world's record for rainfall in one year: almost 87 feet (26.5 m)!

Resources

India's fertile farmlands are important to its economy. Most of India's people work in agriculture. The country also produces cash crops for export. These include cashew nuts, cotton, jute, spices, sugarcane, tea, and tobacco.

Large deposits of iron ore, bauxite, uranium, and coal are among India's mineral resources. There are some oil reserves, but not enough to meet the country's needs. Gemstones are a valuable export.

India's forests are an important resource, as well as home to wildlife. **Teak**, one of the most valuable types of wood, grows in India and Southeast Asia. Teak is very strong and durable and is used to make ships and furniture.

✔ **READING CHECK:** (*Places and Regions*) What are India's natural resources?

Homework Practice Online
Keyword: SK5 HP14

Section Review 1

Define and explain: teak

Working with Sketch Maps On a map of India that you draw or that your teacher provides, label the following: Gangetic Plain, Deccan, Eastern Ghats, Western Ghats, Ganges River, Bay of Bengal, Brahmaputra River, and Thar Desert. How would you describe the relative location of India?

Reading for the Main Idea

1. (*Places and Regions*) What is the main mountain range of India?

2. (*Places and Regions*) What are some of India's most important cash crops? What type of wood is a valuable forest product?

Critical Thinking

3. **Making Generalizations and Predictions** What do you think happens to India's crops if the monsoon rains come too soon? too late?

4. **Summarizing** How does the Ganges affect economic activities in India?

Organizing What You Know

5. **Summarizing** Copy the following graphic organizer. Use it to list the landforms, climates, and resources of India.

Section 2 India's History

Read to Discover

1. What outside groups affected India's history?
2. What was the Mughal Empire like?
3. How did Great Britain gain control of India?
4. Why was India divided when it became independent?

Vocabulary
Sanskrit
sepoys
boycott

Places
Delhi
Kolkata
Mumbai

People
Harappans
Akbar
Mohandas Gandhi

Reading Strategy

READING ORGANIZER Before you read, draw four large boxes down a sheet of paper. As you read this section, write what you learn in the boxes to create a chain of events in India's history.

Mohenjo Daro was one of the largest cities of the Harappan civilization.

Interpreting the Visual Record How might you tell from this photo that Harappan cities were well planned?

▼

Early Indian Civilizations

The first urban civilization on the Indian Subcontinent was centered around the Indus River valley. Its territory was mainly in present-day Pakistan but also extended into India. Scholars call this the Harappan civilization after one of its cities, Harappa. By about 2500 B.C. the people of this civilization were living in large, well-planned cities. Scholars believe the Harappans traded by sea with the peoples of Mesopotamia. The Harappans had a system of writing, but scholars have not been able to read it. As a result, very little is known about Harappan religion and customs.

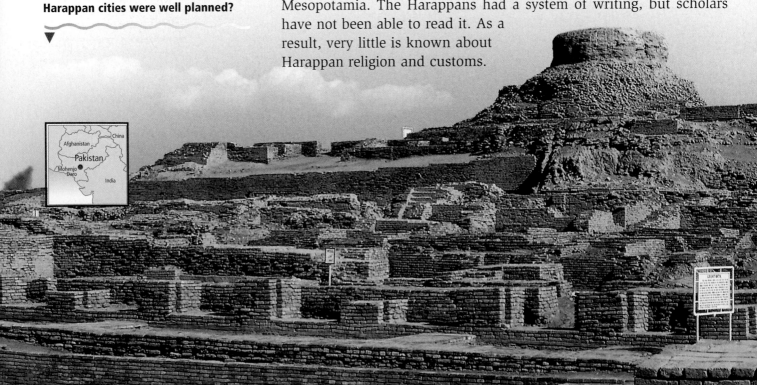

The Indo-Aryans By about 1500 B.C. a new group of people had come into northern India. Scholars call these people Indo-Aryans. Their language was an early form of **Sanskrit**. Sanskrit is still used in India in religious ceremonies.

The Indo-Aryans took control of northern India. These new arrivals mixed with Indian groups that were already living there. Their religious beliefs and customs mixed as well, forming the beginnings of the Hindu religion. Other Indo-Aryan developments are still in use today. For example, they created cotton fabric, the game of chess, and the system of numbers that we still use.

The Coming of Islam About A.D. 1000, Muslim armies began raiding northwestern India. In the early 1200s a Muslim kingdom was established at Delhi. Because the monarch was known as a sultan, this kingdom was called the Delhi sultanate. The Delhi sultanate eventually gained control over most of northern India. It also became a leading center of Islamic art, culture, and science. Most Indians, however, kept their own religions and did not convert to Islam.

Over the next two centuries the Delhi sultanate expanded into the Deccan. However, in the early 1500s a new invasion from Central Asia swept into India. This new conquest marked the beginning of the Mughal (MOO-guhl) Empire.

✔ **READING CHECK:** (*Human Systems*) How did outside groups affect early Indian history?

Place This carved-lion pillar comes from Sarnath, an ancient city in northern India. The pillar was created in the 200s B.C. and is now the state emblem of India.

The Mughal Empire

The founder of the Mughal Empire was Babur, whose name meant "the Tiger." Babur was descended from Mongol emperor Genghis Khan. He was not only a brilliant general, but also a gifted poet. Babur defeated the last sultan of Delhi and took over most of northern India. After his death, however, Babur's lands were divided among his sons. They fought each other for years.

Babur's grandson, Akbar, finally emerged to reunite the Mughal Empire. He recaptured northern India and then expanded his empire into central India. Akbar was a good ruler as well as a successful conqueror. He reorganized the government and the tax system to make them more efficient. The fertile farmland and large population of the Gangetic Plain made the Mughal Empire rich. It quickly became one of the most powerful states in the world. The reign of Akbar and his successors was a golden age of architecture, painting, and poetry.

This illustration is from a book of the life of Babur, the first Mughal emperor. It shows Babur surrounded by servants and nobles.

CONNECTING TO Literature

Indian writer R.K. Narayan's My Days: A Memoir *describes the author's childhood in the early 1900s. In the following passage Narayan recalls traveling from boarding school to his parents' new home. At that time, travel was complicated and sometimes dangerous.*

My Days: A Memoir

At the proper time, I was awakened and put into a huge mat-covered wagon drawn by a pair of bullocks; I sat on a bed of straw covered over with a carpet; a stalwart[1] peon[2] from Hassan high school was seated beside the driver. Manja was his name . . . Part of the way as we traveled along, Manja got off and walked ahead of the caravan, carrying a staff menacingly. Some spots in that jungle and mountain country were well-known retreats of highway robbers; one form of protection was to travel in a closely moving caravan with Manja waving a staff at the head of the column, uttering blood-curdling challenges. That was enough to keep off robbers in those days.

We passed along miles and miles of tree-shaded highway, gigantic mango and blueberry trees and lantana[3] shrubs in multicolored bloom stretching away endlessly. A couple of times the bullocks were rested beside a pond or a well. The road wound up and down steep slopes—the sort of country I had never known before. . . . The overpowering smell of straw in the wagon and the slow pace of the bullocks with their bells jingling made me drowsy . . . After hours of tossing on straw, we came to a bungalow[4] set in a ten-acre field. [It was my parents' new home.] . . . The moment I was received into the fold at the trellised ivy-covered porch, I totally ignored Manja, and never looked in his direction, while he carried my baggage in.

A bullock cart and a double-decker bus in India

Analyzing Primary Sources

1. What are some of the words the author uses to describe the countryside?
2. How do you think Manja's description of this journey might be different from the author's?

Vocabulary   [1]stalwart: strong and reliable   [2]peon: a menial laborer   [3]lantana: shrub with colorful flowers
[4]bungalow: one-story house with low roof that originated in Bengal, India

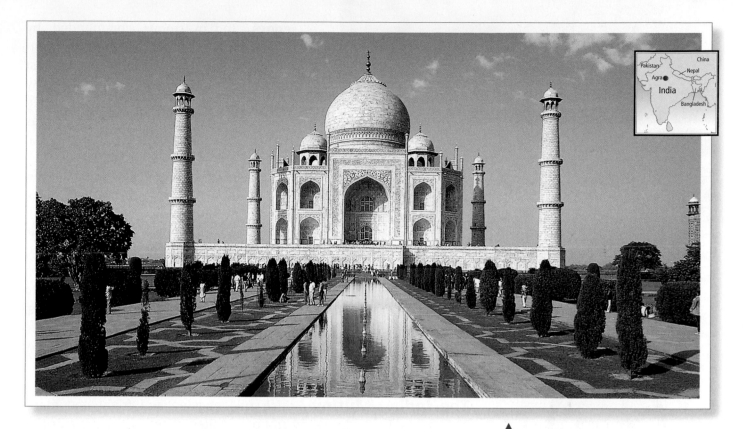

The ruling Mughals were Muslim, but Islam remained a minority religion in India. Most people continued to practice Hinduism. Akbar himself was tolerant and curious about other religions. He invited religious scholars and priests—including Christians, Hindus, Jains, and Muslims—to his court. He even watched them debate.

Akbar's grandson, Shah Jahan, is remembered for the impressive buildings and monuments he had built. These include the famous Taj Mahal. This grand building contains the tomb of Shah Jahan's beloved wife, Mumtaz Mahal.

In the 1600s and 1700s the Mughal Empire slowly grew weaker. Wars in the Deccan and revolts in many parts of the empire drained Mughal resources. At about this time, Europeans became an important force in Indian history.

✓ **READING CHECK:** (*Human Systems*) What was the Mughal Empire like?

(*Place*) The Taj Mahal is one of the most famous buildings in the world.

Construction of the Taj Mahal began in 1631 and was not completed until 1653. Almost 20,000 people worked on the building.

The British

During the 1700s and 1800s the British slowly took control of India. At first this was done by the English East India Company. This company won rights to trade in the Mughal Empire in the 1600s. The East India Company first took control of small trading posts. Later the British gained more Indian territory.

Company Rule As the Mughal Empire grew weaker, the British East India Company expanded its political power. The company also built up its own military force. This army was made up mostly of

In September 1857, British and loyal Sikh troops stormed the gate of Delhi, defended by rebel sepoys.

BIOGRAPHY

Mohandas Gandhi
(1869–1948)

Character Trait: Integrity

Gandhi practiced nonviolence in his struggle for Indian independence and the rights of India's lowest classes. Civil rights leaders in the United States and other countries have adopted Gandhi's nonviolent methods.

Among Gandhi's campaigns was a protest on the salt tax. To avoid having to buy salt and pay the tax, Gandhi and thousands of followers walked 200 miles to make salt from seawater.

Although he lived peacefully, violence took Gandhi's life. A radical Hindu who thought Gandhi was too kind to Muslims assassinated him.

How did Gandhi show integrity?

sepoys, Indian troops commanded by British officers. The British used the strategy of backing one Indian ruler against another in exchange for cooperation. By the mid-1800s the company controlled more than half of India. The rest was divided into small states ruled by local princes.

The British changed the Indian economy to benefit British industry. India produced raw materials, including cotton, indigo—a natural dye—and jute. These materials were then shipped to Britain for use in British factories. Spices, sugar, tea, and wheat were also grown in India for export. Railroads were built to ship the raw materials to Calcutta (now Kolkata), Bombay (now Mumbai), and other port cities. India also became a market for British manufactured goods. Indians, who had woven cotton cloth for centuries, were now forced to buy British cloth.

The Indian Mutiny British rule angered and frightened many Indians. In 1857, the sepoy troops revolted. They killed their British officers and other British residents. The violence spread across northern India. Large numbers of British troops were rushed to India. In the end the British crushed the rebellion.

The Indian Mutiny convinced the British government to abolish the British East India Company. The British government began to rule India directly, and India became a British colony.

Anti-British Protest During the late 1800s Indian nationalism took a different form. Educated, middle-class Indians led this movement. In 1885 these Indian nationalists created the Indian National Congress to organize their protests. At first they did not demand independence. Instead, they asked only for fairer treatment, such as a greater share of government jobs. The British refused even these moderate demands.

After World War I more and more Indians began demanding the end of British rule. A lawyer named Mohandas K. Gandhi became the most important leader of this Indian independence movement.

Gandhi and Nonviolence Gandhi reached out to the millions of Indian peasants. He used a strategy of nonviolent mass protest. He called for Indians to peacefully refuse to cooperate with the British. Gandhi led protest marches and urged Indians to **boycott**, or refuse to buy, British goods. Many times the police used violence against marchers. When the British jailed Gandhi, he went on hunger strikes. Gandhi's determination and self-sacrifice attracted many followers. Pressure grew on Britain to leave India.

✓ **READING CHECK:** (*Human Systems*) What role did the British play in India?

Independence and Division

After World War II the British government decided to give India independence. The British government and the Indian National Congress wanted India to become one country. However, India's Muslims demanded a separate Muslim state. Anger and fear grew between Hindus and Muslims. India seemed on the verge of civil war.

Finally, in 1947 the British divided their Indian colony into two independent countries, India and Pakistan. India was mostly Hindu. Pakistan, which then included what is today Bangladesh, was mostly Muslim. However, the new boundary left millions of Hindus in Pakistan and millions of Muslims in India. Masses of people rushed to cross the border. Hundreds of thousands were killed in rioting and panic.

Movement In the chaotic days of August 1947, millions of people left their homes to cross the new border between India and Pakistan. These Muslims are preparing to leave New Delhi by train.

✔ **READING CHECK:** *Places and Regions* Why was India divided when it became independent?

go.hrw.com
Homework Practice Online
Keyword: SK5 HP14

Section Review 2

Define or identify: Harappans, Sanskrit, Akbar, sepoys, Mohandas Gandhi, boycott

Working with Sketch Maps On the map you created in Section 1, label Delhi, Kolkata, and Mumbai. What bodies of water are important to each of these cities?

Reading for the Main Idea

1. *Human Systems* What made the Mughal Empire one of the most powerful states in the world?

2. *Human Systems* How did the British East India Company gain control of most of India?

3. *Human Systems* Who was the most important leader of the Indian independence movement, and what was his strategy?

Critical Thinking

4. **Finding the Main Idea** Why was the British colony of India divided into two countries?

Organizing What You Know

5. **Sequencing** Copy the following time line. Use it to mark important events in Indian history from 2500 B.C. to A.D. 1947.

2500 B.C.   A.D. 1947

Read to Discover

1. What four major religions originated in India?
2. What is the caste system?
3. What languages are important in India?
4. What kind of government does India have, and what is India's economy like?

Vocabulary

reincarnation
dharma
karma
nirvana
caste system
Dalits
green revolution

Places

Kashmir

People

Siddhartha Gautama
Mother Teresa

Reading Strategy

FOLDNOTES: FOUR-CORNER FOLD | Create the FoldNote titled **Four-Corner Fold** described in the Appendix. Label the flaps Religions, Castes, Languages, and Government and Economy. As you read this section, write what you learn beneath each flap.

Religions of India

Religion is an important part of Indian culture. Four major religions—Hinduism, Buddhism, Jainism, and Sikhism—originated in India. Christianity and Islam, both of which originated elsewhere, also have millions of followers in India. About 81 percent of India's people are Hindu. About 12 percent of Indians are Muslim, and 2.3 percent are Christian. Around 2 percent are Sikh, and 2.5 percent are Buddhist, Jain, Parsi, or followers of another religion. Remember that 1 percent of India's population is about 10 million people!

Hinduism Hinduism is one of the oldest religions in the world. It is a combination of the beliefs of the Indo-Aryans, who arrived in India in around 1750 B.C., and those of earlier Indian peoples. Hindus worship many gods. Hinduism teaches that all gods and all living beings are part of a single spirit called Brahma.

According to Hinduism, when people die their souls are reborn in new bodies. This process is called **reincarnation**. Every time a person is reborn, he or she must fulfill a moral duty, called **dharma**. A person's dharma depends upon the position he or she is born into. Hindus believe that people's actions during their lifetime have moral consequences, or **karma**, that affect how they will be reborn the next time. A person with good karma may be reborn as a person of higher status. A person with bad karma may be reborn with lower status, or as an animal or insect. People who in

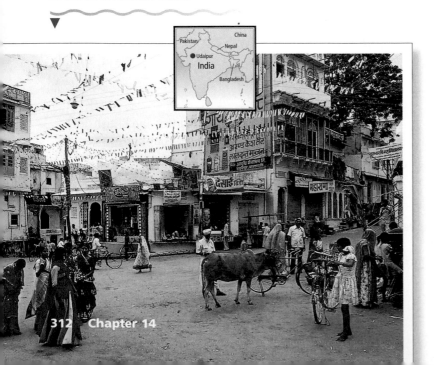

Place Cows mingle with pedestrians and bicyclists in the street of an Indian town.

each of their lifetimes fulfill their dharma may eventually break the cycle of birth and rebirth. They become one with Brahma.

Hinduism also teaches a special respect for certain plants and animals. Cows are considered sacred and are protected. Hindus do not eat beef. Even today, cows can be seen roaming cities and villages. Monkeys and some snakes are also sacred. The most sacred river is the Ganges, where millions of Hindus make a religious pilgrimage every year.

Hindus build temples for their gods and honor them with festivals at least once a year. Festivals may involve religious ceremonies, dance, and music. During the annual new year celebration, called Diwali, Hindus exchange gifts and set off fireworks.

Buddhism The founder of Buddhism, Siddhartha Gautama (sid-DAHR-tuh GOW-tuh-muh), was born a Hindu about 563 B.C. As a son of a prince, he lived a luxurious life. At age 29, Gautama left his palace and set out to learn about hunger, disease, and death.

For six years he searched for the truth. One day Gautama suddenly had a feeling of enlightenment—a state of calm and understanding. He then developed the main principles of Buddhism—the Four Noble Truths. Among these was the belief that all human life contains suffering and sadness and that desire causes suffering. By rejecting desire, people could achieve **nirvana**, or perfect peace.

Gautama rejected many of the beliefs of Hinduism, particularly that goodness and one's position in life were inherited. He also believed that priests should practice good conduct, nonviolence, and poverty.

Gautama spread his philosophy far and wide until his death about 483 B.C. His followers call him the Buddha, or "the Enlightened One." Eventually, Buddhism spread to many other parts of Asia. Buddhism is no longer widely practice in India. However, the religion is very important in Sri Lanka, China, Japan, and Southeast Asia.

▲
The Buddha is often depicted in poses of meditation.

FOCUS ON CULTURE

An Elephant-Headed God

One of the most beloved Hindu gods is Ganesh, who has the head of an elephant. Ganesh is called the Remover of Obstacles. To ensure their success, important events, such as weddings, begin with the worship of Ganesh. During Ganesh Chaturthi, a festival that honors him, Indians bring statues of Ganesh into their homes and later dip them in the sea or a river.

How do Hindus honor Ganesh?

Jainism Jainism was founded at about the same time as Buddhism. It teaches that all things in nature—animals, plants, and stones—have souls. Jains reject all forms of violence against any living thing. They are strict vegetarians. Some even cover their noses with cloth to avoid breathing in insects and thus killing them.

Jains make up only a small minority. However, they have made many contributions to Indian art, mathematics, and literature.

Sikhism Sikhism was founded in the late 1400s. It combines elements of Hinduism and Islam. Members of this religion are called Sikhs. Traditionally, many Sikh men have become soldiers. They continue to play an important role in India's army.

Most Sikhs live in the state of Punjab in northern India. Some Sikhs want to break away from India and form an independent country. The Indian government has refused to allow this, and violent clashes have resulted.

✔ **READING CHECK:** (*Human Systems*) What four religions originated in India?

A Sikh guards the Golden Temple, the center of the Sikh religion, in Amritsar, India. Sikh men can be recognized by their beards and special turbans.

Interpreting the Visual Record (*Place*)
Do you know of any other religious or cultural groups whose members have a distinctive way of dressing?

Castes

Another key feature of Indian society is the **caste system**. Castes are groups of people whose birth determines their position in society. The castes are ranked in status, from highest to lowest. People from a

Many Dalits, like this woman in Goa, still perform jobs that Indians consider dirty or impure.

higher caste cannot marry or even touch people of lower castes. The people at the bottom, called **Dalits**, do work that higher castes consider unclean. They wash and cremate dead bodies, process cow hides into leather goods, and sweep up trash.

Gandhi tried to improve people's attitudes toward the Dalits. He called them "Children of God." After independence, the Indian government officially ended the caste system. However, it is still a strong force in Indian society. The government also tried to improve economic conditions for the Dalits. Today some Dalits are educated and have good jobs. The majority, though, are still poor.

✓ **READING CHECK:** (*Human Systems*) How does the caste system create conflict in Indian society?

Languages

India's people speak an amazing number of different languages. There are 24 languages with a million or more speakers, plus hundreds of other languages. Hindi is the main language of about 30 percent of the people, mostly in northern India. In 1965 it became the official national language. However, the states of southern India have resisted the push to adopt Hindi. English is still commonly used in government, business, and higher education throughout India.

✓ **READING CHECK:** (*Human Systems*) What languages are important in India?

Government and Economy

India has made a great deal of economic progress since gaining independence, but the country remains poor. Rapid population growth strains the country's resources, and the divisions among India's people make it difficult to govern. Devastation on the coast caused by the December 26, 2004, tsunami further taxed the Indian economy.

Government India is ruled by a democratic government. With more than 1 billion people, the country is the world's largest democracy. The structure of the government is based on Britain's parliamentary system. India's constitution guarantees Indian citizens certain fundamental rights, such as the protection of freedom of speech. It also lists the fundamental duties of a citizen, including defending the country and protecting the natural environment. India's central government shares power with state governments.

Indian politics have sometimes been marked by violence and assassinations. The government used force to defeat Sikh rebels in 1984. There have also been outbreaks of violence between Hindus and Muslims. In 1992 a mob of Hindus tore down a mosque that stood on a Hindu holy site. Riots broke out in many parts of India as a result.

BIOGRAPHY

Mother Teresa
(1910–1997)

Character Trait: Kindness

Mother Teresa dedicated her life to helping people. She is best known for founding a mission for the sick and homeless in Kolkata. In 1979, Mother Teresa accepted the Nobel Peace Prize in honor of the millions of people she dedicated her life to caring for. Today, Mother Teresa's example of kindness toward the needy continues around the world at 4,500 missions she created.

How did Mother Teresa show kindness to others?

🔌 internet connect

GO TO: go.hrw.com
KEYWORD: SS Tsunami
FOR: Web sites about the tsunami of December 26, 2004, and its aftermath

▲ *Place* Parliament House, New Delhi, is the home of India's legislative branch.

Education is an important factor for the economic growth of countries.

India's Economy

India's economy has grown tremendously since its independence from Great Britain. Though much of the country is still poor, rich resources, a culture that rewards economic success, and innovative business leaders have all helped move India toward economic prosperity.

To encourage economic growth many countries invest in human capital—the knowledge and skills that workers bring to the work place—by providing the institutions that help people become good workers and creative members of society. By investing in good schools and health care, countries make sure that they have capable workers. Because of its investment in education, particularly in the fields of math and science, India has some of the most productive workers in the world.

Capital goods are another important source of economic growth. Capital goods include those goods that are necessary for economic growth such as factories, machinery, and new technology. India has rapidly industrialized by building railroads, offices, and wiring the country for the Internet. Natural resources, such as the fertile farmlands, forests, and minerals found in India, are also important for economic growth.

Entrepreneurs, or business leaders, are one of the most often overlooked ingredients for economic prosperity. In India, business leaders such as Dr. Gururaj Deshpande, co-founder and chairman of Sycamore Networks, have helped to grow India's technology industry by investing in Indian companies. His and other entrepreneurs' efforts will continue to push the economy forward.

Understanding What You Read
1. What factors lead to economic growth?
2. Why are entrepreneurs important?

India's border with Pakistan has been in dispute since 1947. Both countries claim a mountainous region called Kashmir. Before India gained independence, Kashmir was ruled by a Hindu prince. Most of its people were Muslim, however. India and Pakistan have fought over Kashmir several times. Today, both countries have nuclear weapons, making the prospect of a future war even more frightening.

Economy India's economy is a mixture of the traditional and the modern. In villages, farmers work the fields just as they have for centuries. At the same time, modern factories and high-tech service industries demonstrate India's potential for wealth. However, the country suffers from poor roads and telecommunications systems and from a low literacy rate.

Close to 60 percent of India's workforce are farmers. Farming makes up 25 percent of India's GDP. Most farmers work on small farms less than 2.5 acres (1 hectare) in size. They often have to burn forested areas to clear land for farming. Smoke from these fires contributes to air pollution. Many farmers grow barely enough to feed themselves and their families. India's leading crops include rice, wheat, cotton, tea, and jute. Cattle and water buffalo are raised to pull plows and to provide milk.

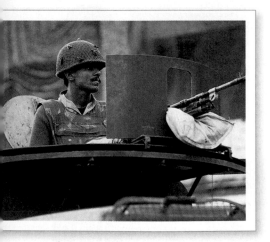

India has stationed large numbers of troops in Kashmir.

Beginning in the 1960s, the Indian government started agricultural programs known as the **green revolution**. This effort encouraged farmers to adopt more modern methods. It promoted greater use of fertilizers, pesticides, and new varieties of wheat and rice. Crop yields increased. In years with good weather, India exports farm products.

India is considered a developing country. However, its economy is large enough to rank among the world's top 10 industrial countries. India's industries include textiles, jewelry, cars, chemicals, and electronics. Bangalore is the center of India's electronics industry. The pleasant climate there draws many people to the city, and they make up a productive workforce.

The visual arts, including painting and sculpture, have been an important part of Indian heritage for thousands of years. Today artists such as M. F. Hussain blend artistic traditions from India's early history with modern global influences. Musical traditions vary from region to region. In the countryside, music plays a role not only in entertainment but also in religious rituals. Much of today's popular music is associated with India's highly successful film industry. More than 800 movies are made in India each year.

India now has a large, well-educated middle class. These people have enough money for luxuries like cable television and personal computers. Some Indians are very rich, but most are still poor.

▲
The steel industry provides jobs for Kolkata's workers. However, industries like this one also pollute the air and rivers.

Interpreting the Visual Record Which of India's industries might use the steel produced here?

✓ **READING CHECK:** (*Places and Regions*) What is India's economy like?

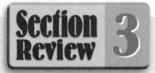

Section Review 3

Define or identify: reincarnation, dharma, karma, Siddhartha Gautama, nirvana, caste system, Dalits, Mother Teresa, green revolution

Working with Sketch Maps On the map that you created in Section 2, label the Kashmir region of India. What other country claims Kashmir?

Reading for the Main Idea

1. (*Human Systems*) What are the main religions practiced in India? Which religion has the largest number of followers?

2. (*Environment and Society*) How did India's government increase agricultural output in the 1960s?

go. hrw .com **Homework Practice Online** Keyword: SK5 HP14

Critical Thinking

3. Drawing Inferences and Conclusions Why might India's government find it difficult to improve the economic situation of the Dalits?

4. Finding the Main Idea What are some of the industries in India?

Organizing What You Know

5. Categorizing Copy the following graphic organizer. Use it to list the leading crops and industries of India.

Leading crops	Leading industries

Review and Practice

Define and Identify

Identify each of the following:

1. teak
2. Sanskrit
3. sepoys
4. boycott
5. reincarnation
6. karma
7. nirvana
8. caste system
9. Dalits
10. green revolution
11. Harappans
12. Mohandas Gandhi
13. Siddhartha Gautama
14. Mother Teresa

Review the Main Ideas

15. How were the Himalayas formed?
16. What is unique about the Ganges River?
17. Why are monsoons important to Indian farmers?
18. What was the first urban civilization on the Indian Subcontinent?
19. Who brought Sanskrit to India?
20. Who slowly took control of India after the Mughal Empire weakened?
21. What caused the Indian Mutiny of 1857?
22. What are the Hindu ideas of reincarnation and karma?
23. What factors divide Indian society?
24. How many languages are spoken in India?

Think Critically

25. **Drawing Inferences and Conclusions** Why do you think Hindi has not become the language of all of India?
26. **Summarizing** How do India's natural resources affect its economy?
27. **Finding the Main Idea** How did the Indian government's promotion of new farming technology affect India's farming culture?
28. **Drawing Inferences and Conclusions** Why do you think the Mughal Empire under Akbar and his successors was considered a "golden age"?
29. **Drawing Inferences and Conclusions** How might the growth of a well-educated, high-tech workforce affect India's economy?

Map Activity

30. On a separate sheet of paper, match the letters on the map with their correct labels.

    Himalayas
    Gangetic Plain
    Deccan
    Eastern Ghats
    Western Ghats
    Ganges River
    Brahmaputra River
    Thar Desert

Writing Activity

Write a one- to two-page report about how religion influences life in India. List and describe India's major religions, then write about how they relate to politics, border disputes, social classes, daily life, languages, the economy, and so on. Be sure to use standard grammar, spelling, sentence structure, and punctuation.

internet connect

Internet Activity: go.hrw.com
KEYWORD: SK5 GT14

Choose a topic to explore about India:
- Tour the regions of India.
- Study the Asian brown cloud.
- Learn about Mohandas Gandhi.

Social Studies Skills Practice

Interpreting Maps

India is divided into 28 states and 7 territories. Study the map and then answer the questions.

The States and Territories of India

1. In which state is Mumbai located?
2. If you were traveling from Kolkata to Chennai, which states would you travel through?
3. Which state or territory shares the same name as a major city in India?
4. Which states and territories border Nepal?

Analyzing Primary Sources

Using what you have learned about Gandhi, read the following quotes. Then answer the questions.

"I object to violence because when it appears to do good, the good is only temporary; the evil it does is permanent."

"An eye for an eye makes the whole world blind."

"Whether humanity will consciously follow the law of love, I do not know. But that need not disturb me. The law will work just as the law of gravitation works, whether we accept it or not."

1. What is the main idea of these statements?
2. What can you learn about Gandhi by reading these quotes?
3. How do these statements relate to Gandhi's role in achieving independence for India?
4. What is Gandhi's opinion about the "law of love"?

CHAPTER 15

India's Neighbors

The countries of this region, along with the Himalayas, help create India's border. After you meet Rehan you will learn that this land is one of majestic beauty with a rich heritage.

I am Rehan, and I am 14. I am an only child and live with my parents in Karachi, a big sprawling city like Los Angeles. On one side is the sea, on the other is the desert.

If you came to visit me in Pakistan, I would take you to the beach to watch the beautiful sunsets and ride on a camel. My parents used to take me there for camel rides when I was very little. Next I would take you to see the old colonial architecture in the city center. Then we would go and have a meal in a roadside cafe—grilled beef or lamb kabobs on a stick. I usually get up very early for school. By 7:10 A.M. I have breakfast—cereal and toast—and leave for school with my father. He is a doctor with an office near my school. I am in the second year (equivalent to grade 10) of a boys' private school styled after the British public school system.

Next year, I am going to America with my mother. My parents want me to have a chance to go to a world-class university.

السلام عليكم!

Translation: God's peace be upon you!

Read to Discover

1. What major physical features are located in India's Neighbors?
2. What climates and natural resources are found in this region?
3. What are the physical features of the island countries?

Vocabulary

cyclones
storm surges

Places

Brahmaputra River
Ganges River
Himalayas
Mount Everest
Tarai
Karakoram Range

Hindu Kush
Khyber Pass
Indus River
Thar Desert

Reading Strategy

VISUALIZING INFORMATION Before you read, look at the map and pictures in this section. What environmental challenges do you think the people living in this region could face? Write your answers on a sheet of paper under the name of each country: Pakistan, Bangladesh, Bhutan, and Nepal.

India's Neighbors: Physical-Political

Mount Godwin Austen (K2) 28,250 ft. (8611 m)

SCALE
0 — 250 — 500 Miles
0 — 250 — 500 Kilometers
Projection: Two-Point Equidistant

Size comparison of the Indian Perimeter to the contiguous United States

HINDU KUSH
Khyber Pass
KARAKORAM RANGE
KASHMIR
AFGHANISTAN
Islamabad
Indus River
Chenab River
Sutlej River
PAKISTAN
BALUCHISTAN
IRAN
INDUS VALLEY
THAR DESERT
Karachi
Hyderabad
Tropic of Cancer
ARABIAN SEA
GULF OF KUTCH
HIMALAYAS
CHINA
NEPAL
TARAI
Kathmandu
Mount Everest 29,035 ft. (8850 m)
BHUTAN
Thimphu
Brahmaputra River
Jamuna River
INDIA
Ganges River
Rajshahi
BANGLADESH
Khulna
Dhaka
Chittagong
Tropic of Cancer
MYANMAR (BURMA)
Bay of Bengal

Same scale as main map
Palk Strait
Jaffna
GULF OF MANNAR
SRI LANKA
Colombo
MALDIVES
INDIAN OCEAN
Male
To understand the relative locations of the Maldives and Sri Lanka as well as the distance separating them from the rest of the India's neighbors, see the Atlas map.
Equator

ELEVATION

FEET	METERS
13,120	4,000
6,560	2,000
1,640	500
656	200
(Sea level) 0	0 (Sea level)
Below sea level	Below sea level

⊛ National capitals
• Other cities

Physical Features

The broad delta formed by the Brahmaputra (brahm-uh-POO-truh) and Ganges (GAN-jeez) Rivers covers most of Bangladesh. Some 200 rivers and streams crisscross this eastern part of the Indian Subcontinent. These numerous waterways, the low elevation of the land, and heavy monsoon rains combine to bring frequent floods to Bangladesh. Although these floods cause great damage, they leave behind a layer of fertile soil.

North of Bangladesh is Bhutan. This tiny country lies high in the mountain range known as the Himalayas (hi-muh-LAY-uhz). To the west is Nepal. The Himalayas occupy some 75 percent of Nepal's land area. Mount Everest, Earth's highest mountain, is located on Nepal's border with China. The Tarai (tuh-RY) is a low plain along Nepal's southern border. It is the country's main farming area. West of the Himalayas is the Karakoram (kah-rah-KOHR-oohm) Range. To the west the Karakorams merge into another mountain range, the Hindu Kush.

On Pakistan's western border is the Khyber (KY-buhr) Pass. For centuries, invaders and traders have traveled through this high mountain pass to India. East of the Khyber Pass is the Indus River. The Indus Valley lies mostly to the east of the river. This valley is Pakistan's main farming region and its most heavily populated area. East of these fertile lands is the Thar (TAHR) Desert, or the Great Indian Desert. A barren, hilly, and dry plateau in western Pakistan joins the plateaus of Iran.

✔ **READING CHECK:** *Places and Regions* What are the major physical features of this region?

internet connect

GO TO: go.hrw.com
KEYWORD: SK5 CH15
FOR: Web sites about
India's Neighbors

Terraced fields in the mountains of Nepal allow farmers to increase their production of millet and corn.

Interpreting the Visual Record

Human-Environment Interaction **How can terracing lead to increased crop production?**

▼

Climate and Resources

Bangladesh has one of the world's wettest climates. Rainfall is generally more than 60 inches (127 to 152 cm) each year. Most of the rain falls from June to October, during the wet summer monsoon. In the early and late weeks of the monsoon, **cyclones** sweep in from the Bay of Bengal. These violent storms resemble the hurricanes of the Caribbean. They bring high winds and heavy rain. Cyclones are often accompanied by **storm surges**. These are huge waves of water that are whipped up by fierce winds. The summer monsoon brings hot, wet weather to the lowland areas of Bhutan and Nepal. In the mountains, climates are generally much cooler. Much of Pakistan has a desert climate, receiving less than 10 inches (25 cm) of rain each year. Summer temperatures can reach as high as 120°F (49°C).

Bangladesh's most important resource is its fertile farmland. About 15 percent of Bangladesh is forested, so it has some timber supplies. However, severe deforestation and soil erosion have plagued the region, particularly in Nepal. Bhutan and Nepal have farmland in low-land areas. Both countries have some minerals, but few are mined. Pakistan has large natural gas reserves but limited oil supplies. It has to import oil to meet its energy needs. Pakistan's other natural resources include coal, limestone, and salt.

✓ **READING CHECK:** (*Places and Regions*) What are the natural resources of the region?

The Island Countries

India's neighbors also include Sri Lanka and the Maldives. Sri Lanka is a large island located just off the southeastern tip of India. Plains cover most of the island's northern half and coastal areas. Mountains and hills rise in the south-central part of the island.

About 1,200 tiny tropical islands in the Indian Ocean make up the Maldives. The island group stretches from south of India to the equator. Only about 200 of the islands are inhabited. None rises more than 6 feet (1.8 m) above sea level.

✓ **READING CHECK:** (*Places and Regions*) What are the physical features of the island countries?

In May 1997 a cyclone and storm surges devastated Bangladesh. More than 1.5 million people were left homeless.

Section Review 1

Define and explain: cyclones, storm surges

Working with Sketch Maps On a map of India and India's Neighbors that you draw or that your teacher provides, label the following: Brahmaputra River, Ganges River, Himalayas, Mount Everest, Tarai, Karakoram Range, Hindu Kush, Khyber Pass, Indus River, and Thar Desert. Where is Earth's highest mountain located? What plains area is Nepal's main farming region?

Reading for the Main Idea

1. (*Places and Regions*) Why has the Khyber Pass been important in the history of Pakistan and India?

2. (*Places and Regions*) How have erosion and defor-estation affected the region? Which country has been most affected by these problems?

3. (*Places and Regions*) What island countries are found in the region? How are they different from each other?

Critical Thinking

4. **Drawing Inferences and Conclusions** How do you think climate affects life in Pakistan and Bangladesh?

Organizing What You Know

5. **Summarizing** Copy the following graphic orga-nizer. Use it to describe the landforms, climates, and resources of the region.

	Major Landforms	Climates	Resources
Pakistan			
Bangladesh			
Bhutan			
Nepal			

India's Neighbors • 323

Section 2 Pakistan and Bangladesh

Read to Discover

1. What is the history of Pakistan?
2. What are some features of Pakistan's culture?
3. What is the history of Bangladesh?
4. What challenges face Bangladesh today?

Vocabulary

cholera

Places

Pakistan
Bangladesh
Karachi
Lahore
Islamabad
Dhaka

People

Muhammad Yunus

Reading Strategy

READING ORGANIZER Create a four-column chart. Label the columns Country, History, Population, and Culture. As you read this section, write what you learn about Pakistan and Bangladesh on your chart.

These tombs in Pakistan were built in the 1500s–1700s. Women's graves had floral carvings. Horses and swords decorated men's tombs.

Pakistan's History

An ancient civilization developed in the Indus River valley about 2500 B.C. Ruins of cities show that this was a large and well-organized society. The cause of the disappearance of this civilization about 1500 B.C. remains a mystery.

Over time the fertile Indus River valley was inhabited and conquered by many different groups. It has been part of the empires of Persia, Alexander the Great, and the Mughals. About A.D. 1000 Turkish invaders established Islam in the area. Islam has been the main religion there ever since.

In the early 1600s merchants from England formed the English East India Company to increase the spice trade. It later became known as the British East India Company. Although trade was only moderately successful, the company established England's power in India. It was not until 1947 that India gained independence.

Upon independence, India became two countries. The division into two countries was based on religion. India was mostly Hindu. East and West Pakistan were inhabited mainly by Muslims. Although East Pakistan and West Pakistan were mostly Muslim, they had other cultural differences. These differences led East Pakistan to break away in 1971. It became known as Bangladesh.

✓ **READING CHECK:** *Human Systems* What was Pakistan's early history like?

Pakistan Today

Pakistan's population is 97 percent Muslim. The country has many different languages and ethnic groups. Urdu is the official language, but few people speak it as their main language.

Economy and People Pakistan's government owns and operates many of the businesses in the country. For this reason, the government invests a great deal of revenue in the country's factories, machinery, and new technology. Through its regulations and licensing requirements, the state also controls new private entrepreneurial investment. Though the economy has grown at a rapid rate in the past 25 years, the population has grown quickly as well. This has slowed the growth of the per capita income level of Pakistan's people. However, the number of people living in extreme poverty is one of the lowest in the region.

Pakistan's natural resources help support its large population. Irrigation of the fertile soil in the Indus River valley allows the country to grow enough food for the large population. In addition, many different types of minerals have been discovered in Pakistan. Limestone is used for the country's cement plants. Cement is the largest manufacturing industry in the country. Because much of the mineral resources remain undeveloped, they hold great promise for the future.

In spite of its economic successes, the country's healthcare and education systems struggle with providing quality services. Many people do not receive adequate medical care. Also, Pakistani children are not required to go to school. Literacy levels are low—as much as three-fourths of the population cannot read or write. Those students who complete education at the lower level may go on to college or job-training programs.

In Pakistan a woman joins her husband's family at marriage, which is usually arranged. Pakistani families celebrate many Islamic festivals, and celebrations include large meals featuring grilled meats, rice, and delicious breads. Pakistani foods feature strong spices and flavors.

✓ **READING CHECK:** *Human Systems*
What is the culture of Pakistan like?

Pakistan and Bangladesh

Country	Population/ Growth Rate	Life Expectancy	Literacy Rate	Per Capita GDP
Bangladesh	138,448,210 2.1%	61, male 61, female	43%	$1,700
Pakistan	150,694,740 2.1%	61, male 63, female	45%	$2,100
United States	290,342,554 0.9%	74, male 80, female	97%	$37,600

Source: Central Intelligence Agency, *The World Factbook 2003*

Interpreting the Chart Which country in the region has a larger population?

Place Pakistan's flag symbolizes the country's commitment to Islam and the Islamic world. The crescent and star are symbols of Islam. The vertical white stripe represents religious minorities.

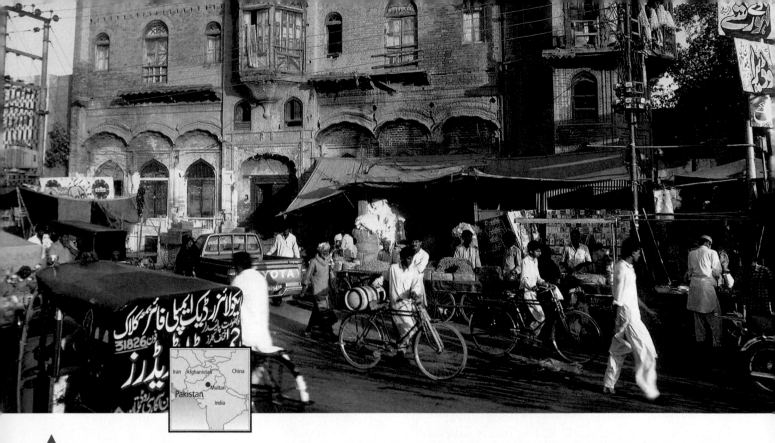

Place Multan is a commercial and industrial center with several colleges and a university. The city came under Muslim control in the A.D. 700s.

Bangladesh's History

Bangladesh is part of a region known as Bengal. Bengal's many rivers are used for transporting goods. This is one reason why the area was important to Europeans in the 1500s. From the 1500s through the 1700s, the Mughal Empire combined Islam and regional Indian traditions to create a distinctive culture in this region. Eventually, the Mughal Empire weakened. The British East India Company then expanded its control over the area.

Because the British East India Company was so powerful, it could control what was traded. Therefore, British goods came into the region, but few goods other than rice and jute were exported. With a decline in trade, industry suffered. As a result, the region's economy became more agricultural in the 1800s. As you learned earlier, East Pakistan became the independent country of Bangladesh in 1971.

✔ READING CHECK: (*Places and Regions*) What has Bangladesh's history been like?

Bangladesh Today

Unlike other South Asian countries, Bangladesh has only one main ethnic group—the Bengalis. They make up 98 percent of the population. Social standing is based mostly on wealth and influence rather than on heredity or caste. Muslims may move up or down in status. Even among the country's Hindus, caste has much less importance than it does in India.

Population Bangladesh is about the same size as Wisconsin. However, it has a population nearly half the size of the entire U.S. population. Only 24 percent of Bangladesh's population lives in cities. The country's capital and largest city is Dhaka (DA-kuh). Cities and rural areas are densely populated. On average in Bangladesh there are 2,580 people per square mile (670/sq km).

Flooding and disease are two of the country's biggest challenges. Occasional violent tropical cyclones bring huge storm surges on shore. In addition, runoff from heavy rains in the distant Himalayas causes extensive flooding. When the land is flooded, sewage often washes into the water. As a result, Bangladesh has often suffered from epidemics of diseases like **cholera**. Cholera is a severe intestinal infection.

Culture Family life in Bangladesh is different from that in Pakistan. For example, many Bangladeshi women keep close ties to their own families after marriage. However, as in other South Asian countries, marriages are arranged by parents. Most couples typically do not know each other prior to their wedding.

More girls are going to secondary schools and universities than ever. Even so, the literacy rate for women remains just about half that of men. Bangladesh's official language, Bengali (Bangla), is the language spoken in schools. The country celebrates Islam's main festivals with feasts that feature fish and rice.

✓ **READING CHECK:** (*Places and Regions*) What are some challenges that Bangladesh faces today?

BIOGRAPHY

Muhammad Yunus
(1940–   )

Character Trait: Fairness

With a dream to eliminate world poverty, Muhammad Yunus founded a bank in his native Bangladesh. Since then, Yunus' Grameen Bank has lent over 3 billion dollars to poor Bangladeshis. In addition to giving out loans, Grameen Bank also teaches people how to use their money effectively. Through his fair treatment of the poor, Yunus continues to give millions an opportunity for a better future.

How does Muhammad Yunus show fairness towards poor people?

go.hrw.com **Homework Practice Online**
Keyword: SK5 HP15

Section Review 2

Define or identify: cholera, Muhammad Yunus

Working with Sketch Maps On the map you created in Section 1, label Pakistan, Bangladesh, Karachi, Lahore, Islamabad, and Dhaka. What does the name of Pakistan's capital indicate about the country's dominant religion?

Reading for the Main Idea

1. (*Places and Regions*) Why were East and West Pakistan separated from India in 1947? When did East and West Pakistan split into two independent countries?

2. (*Environment and Society*) What technology allows Pakistan to grow enough food for its large population? How?

3. (*Environment and Society*) What climatic condition contributes to the high disease rate in Bangladesh? How?

Critical Thinking

4. **Contrasting/Comparing** How are marriage and married life in Pakistan different from marriage and married life in Bangladesh? How are they similar?

Organizing What You Know

5. **Comparing/Contrasting** Copy the following graphic organizer. Use it to compare and contrast Pakistan and Bangladesh.

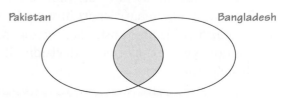

Pakistan   Bangladesh

COULD YOU SURVIVE THE FLOODS OF BANGLADESH?

ON-LINE EXPEDITIONS

GO TO: go.hrw.com
KEYWORD: SK5 CH15

A Land of Floods and Cyclones

Bangladesh is a very wet place! Some parts of the country get more than 100 inches of rain every year. Melting snow from the Himalayas combines with the heavy rain to cause disastrous floods. In addition, a cyclone can drive a wall of water, called a storm surge, inland from the ocean. People and livestock trying to escape the floods can get stranded on housetops or in trees. To make matters worse, rising waters drive poisonous snakes to the same crowded spots.

SURVIVAL CHALLENGE

What if you were a Bangladeshi farmer who lived at the location marked on the map? Your land has been flooded more than once, and your livestock have drowned. Should you abandon your farm and move to Dhaka, the capital? First, examine the chart and the map to assess the risks. Would you face the same dangers in Dhaka? Then consider what your life would be like in the city. For example, could you get a job in the city? What effect would the size of your family have on your decision?

With a partner, create a chart in which you balance the costs of remaining on the farm with the costs of moving to Dhaka. Do you have enough information yet to make your decision? If not, what kinds of information would help you?

Bangladeshis find temporary safety from floodwaters on the wreckage of houses.

Some Major Floods of Bangladesh

Year	Details
1970	Cyclones killed from 300,000 to 500,000 people.
1974	Floods ruined the grain crop, leading to 28,000 deaths. Some 2 million were left homeless.
1988	Water covered up to three-fourths of the country, and 28 million were homeless.
1991	A cyclone with 145-mile-per-hour winds hit the southeast coast with a 20-foot storm surge. Some 139,000 people and half a million animals died.
1998	Three-fourths of the country was flooded, including Dhaka.

Brahmaputra River
INDIA

Ganges R.

BANGLADESH

Dhaka

Meghna R.

Your farm is here.

INDIA

Normal flood depths during the wet season
- High or seldom flooded land
- Less than 3 feet
- 3 to 6 feet
- Greater than 6 feet
- Subject to salt buildup
- Mangrove forest
- River or major stream

Bay of Bengal

0   100 miles

On the Brighter Side

You may be wondering how Bangladesh maintains such a large population— more than 138,440,000 people in 2004. Moreover, the country usually produces enough rice to feed its population. How can this be? Here's a clue: The answer lies in the same floodwaters that cause such suffering. How may Bangladesh's floods be both a blessing and a curse?

The Himalayan and Island Countries

Read to Discover

1. What are some important features of Nepal?
2. How has Bhutan developed over time?
3. What is Sri Lanka like?
4. What are some economic activities of the Maldives?

Vocabulary

stupas
graphite
atolls

Places

Nepal
Kathmandu
Bhutan
Thimphu
Sri Lanka
Colombo
Maldives
Male

People

Tenzing Norgay

Reading Strategy

FOLDNOTES: LAYERED BOOK Create the FoldNote titled **Layered Book** described in the Appendix. Label the top layer Nepal. Label the other layers Bhutan, Sri Lanka, and the Maldives. As you read this section, write what you learn about each country above its label.

▲
(*Place*) A temple to the Hindu god Krishna can be seen from Durban Square in Patan, near Kathmandu, Nepal. The pillar in the square honors Krishna's companion, Garuda.

Nepal

Nepal's history is linked to the early civilizations of northern India. Nepal shared its languages, culture, and economic base with peoples to the south. It was probably in Nepal that Gautama, the Buddha, was born about 563 B.C. Some of the oldest monuments to the Buddha are **stupas** in Nepal. They date back to before 300 B.C. Stupas are mounds of earth or stones covering the ashes of the Buddha or relics of Buddhist saints. Like India, Nepal adopted Buddhism at first but was mostly Hindu by A.D. 1200. About 90 percent of Nepal's people are now Hindus.

The British never formally ruled Nepal. Their army did defeat the Nepalese army in the early 1800s. As a result, the British took away the territories claimed by Nepal and sent an official to maintain indirect control. The British later recognized Nepal's independence. Nepal now is a constitutional monarchy with a king and elected parliament.

One of Nepal's ethnic groups is the Sherpa. The Sherpa guide and serve as porters for Himalayan expeditions. Tenzing Norgay, a Sherpa, and Sir Edmund Hillary, an explorer from New Zealand, climbed Mount Everest in 1953. They were the first to reach the summit.

✓ **READING CHECK:** (*Places and Regions*) What has the history of Nepal been like?

CONNECTING TO *Technology*

CLIMBING MOUNT EVEREST

The world's highest peak, Mount Everest, sits on the border between China and Nepal. At 29,035 feet (8,850 m), it is one of the world's greatest mountaineering challenges.

After many failed attempts, two climbers—Edmund Hillary and Tenzing Norgay—finally reached the summit in 1953. One factor in their success was the use of advanced equipment. This equipment included special boots, oxygen bottles, and radio gear. Since then, technology has continued to play a key role in efforts to scale the Himalayas.

Today's climbers use a wide range of sophisticated gear. This gear includes everything from space-age mountaineering clothes to remote sensors and satellite-tracking devices. Even so, climbing Everest remains very dangerous. In the 1990s more than 50 climbers lost their lives trying to scale the peak. Now scientists are testing new medical technologies on Mount Everest in hopes of preventing such tragedies in the future.

A joint project of the National Aeronautics and Space Administration (NASA) and Yale University has been analyzing the effects of high-altitude climbing on the human body. In 1998 this project sent a team of climbers up Mount Everest wearing "bio-packs." These packs included high-tech devices to monitor heart rate, blood oxygen, and other vital signs.

This data was transmitted instantly to a base camp on Everest. There doctors could analyze the results. Scientists believe that this kind of "telemedicine" will help save lives in other extreme environments, including outer space.

Understanding What You Read

1. How do climbers use technology on Mount Everest?
2. How might climbers benefit from the use of new medical technology?

Sir Edmund Hillary (left) and Tenzing Norgay (right)

Nepal Today

Like other countries of the region, Nepal's economy is based on agriculture. More than 80 percent of the people make a living from farming. Most are subsistence farmers. The best farmland is found on the Tarai—Nepal's "breadbasket." Farmers there grow such crops as rice, other grains, and sugarcane. In the hills north of the Tarai, farmers grow fruits, grains, and vegetables. Kathmandu (kat-man-DOO), Nepal's capital and largest city, is located in this central region. For the most part, the Himalayan region is not good for

Human-Environment Interaction
Nepalese women are experts at winnowing grain. Winnowing is the process of separating chaff from grain by fanning.

farming. Farmers graze cattle, goats, sheep, and yaks on the lower slopes. Yaks are large, longhaired oxen. In addition, some farmers grow grain and fruit trees on terraces cut into mountainsides.

With few resources and limited access to world trade routes, Nepal has developed few industries. Most of its industries are based on farm products, such as jute. Jute is a plant fiber that is used in making twine. Tourism is one of the fastest-growing and most important industries in Nepal. Tourists like to hike and climb in the mountains.

Tourism brings in much-needed income to Nepal. However, the constant stream of hikers and climbers threatens the country's environment. How? Many visitors leave behind trash. Also, their need for firewood contributes to deforestation and soil erosion. This problem is worsened as Nepalese clear woodland for farming and for wood for fuel. In response, Nepal's government has restricted access by visitors to some of the most affected areas.

READING CHECK: *Places and Regions* What is Nepal like?

Place Folk dancers in traditional dress perform near Thimphu, Bhutan.

Bhutan

Little is known about the early history of Bhutan. Buddhism was practiced there as early as the A.D. 600s. Most of the people are of Tibetan origin and are Buddhist. In the 1600s a Tibetan monk helped organize Bhutan as a unified state. Then in the late 1700s the East India Company's business dealings increased British influence.

Bhutan, although very isolated, was under Indian control during British rule over that country.

Bhutan's ruler, or maharaja, declared a constitutional monarchy in 1969.

✓ READING CHECK: (Places and Regions) What has the history of Bhutan been like?

Bhutan Today

Until the mid-1970s, the government of Bhutan followed a policy of near total isolation. Even today, the country's international ties are somewhat limited.

Much of Bhutan's economy is traditional. More than 90 percent of the people make a living as subsistence farmers. Most grow rice, wheat, corn, and potatoes in fertile valleys and on mountainside terraces. A few grow fruits and spices for export. On mountain pastures, farmers raise cattle, goats, sheep, and yaks. Thimphu (thim-POO) is Bhutan's capital.

Timber and hydroelectricity are among Bhutan's most important resources. The country sells both to India, its main trading partner. Tourism is also a source of income for Bhutan. However, the government limits the number of visitors. By restricting tourism, the government hopes to protect Bhutan's way of life from outside influences and environmental damage.

✓ READING CHECK: (Places and Regions) What is Bhutan like today?

Himalayan and Island Countries

COUNTRY	POPULATION/ GROWTH RATE	LIFE EXPECTANCY	LITERACY RATE	PER CAPITA GDP
Bhutan	2,139,549 2.1%	53, male 53, female	42%	$1,300
Maldives	329,684 3.0%	62, male 64, female	97%	$3,900
Nepal	26,469,569 2.3%	59, male 58, female	45%	$1,400
Sri Lanka	19,742,439 0.9%	70, male 75, female	90%	$3,700
United States	290,342,554 0.9%	74, male 80, female	97%	$37,600

Source: Central Intelligence Agency, *The World Factbook 2003*

Interpreting the Chart Which country has the lowest literacy rate?

Sri Lanka

When Buddhism swept over India between the 400s and 200s B.C., Buddhist missionaries came to Sri Lanka. From Sri Lanka, traders spread Buddhism eastward to what are now Thailand and Indonesia. About 74 percent of Sri Lankans today belong to the Sinhalese ethnic group, and most are Buddhists. Sri Lanka has many dome-shaped stupas honoring the Buddha. Many are shaded by trees said to have been grown from cuttings of the original bo tree. It is believed the Buddha achieved enlightenment under this tree.

Throughout its history, Sri Lanka has been largely independent from India. In the 1500s the Portuguese established a trading post on the island. They were overthrown by the Dutch. The Dutch turned over Sri Lanka, then known as Ceylon, to the British in the late 1700s. The British granted independence in 1948. The new government made Sinhalese the official language and promoted Buddhism. An Indian and Hindu minority group, the Tamils, protested. Fighting between Tamils and the government has killed many people.

✓ READING CHECK: (Places and Regions) How have Europeans played a role in Sri Lanka's history?

▲ (Place) Buddhist monks prepare to pray at the top of Adam's Peak. The "yellow" robe is a symbol of Buddhism. The color of the robe varies according to the dye used.

India's Neighbors • 333

▲

Place The Dalada Maligawa (Temple of the Tooth) houses the sacred tooth of Buddha. Pilgrims come to pay respect to the Tooth Relic during daily ceremonies.

Human-Environment Interaction Semiprecious stones such as the sapphire, ruby, cat's eye, topaz, and garnet are mined in Sri Lanka.

▼

Sri Lanka Today

Caste determines how Sri Lankans behave toward one another. As in India, many Sri Lankans believe associating with a member of a lower caste brings bad karma. Bad karma forces a person to undergo endless reincarnations, or rebirths. It also prevents him or her from finding nirvana, or spiritual release.

Sri Lanka has several features in common with the countries of the mainland. First, it is a mainly rural country. Less than 25 percent of Sri Lankans live in cities. Second, about 38 percent of Sri Lankans make a living from farming. They grow rice, fruits, and vegetables. Sri Lankan farmers also grow coconuts, rubber, and tea for export. Sri Lanka has a number of industries. They include food processing, textiles and apparel, telecommunications, insurance, and banking.

Mining is another important economic activity in Sri Lanka. The main resources mined are graphite and precious gems. Sri Lanka leads the world in **graphite** exports. Graphite is a form of carbon used in pencils and many other products. Recently, manufacturing—particularly of textiles and clothing—has grown in importance. Many textile and clothing factories are found in Colombo, the capital of Sri Lanka. Located on the west coast, Colombo is the country's largest city. It is also its most important commercial center and seaport. Sri Lanka's economy has grown in recent years. However, continuing ethnic conflicts between the Sinhalese majority and the Tamil minority threaten the country's progress.

✔ **READING CHECK:** *Places and Regions* What is Sri Lanka like today?

The Maldives

The Maldives were originally settled by Buddhists from Sri Lanka. Today the main religion is Islam. Education includes traditional teachings of the Qur'an. However, there are no colleges or universities.

The Maldives consists of 19 **atolls**. An atoll is a ring of coral surrounding a body of water called a lagoon. These atolls sit atop an ancient submerged volcanic plateau. Altogether, the islands cover about 115 square miles (298 sq km). The largest island, Male (MAH-lay), is home to about one fourth of the population. A city by the same name serves as the country's capital. Only about 25 percent of the people live in cities.

Tourism is the Maldives largest industry. Fishing, particularly of tuna, is another of the country's chief economic activities. Exports of fresh, dried, frozen, and canned fish account for about half the country's income. Breadfruit—a fruit that resembles bread when baked—and coconuts are the Maldives' main food crops. Most other food must be imported. A small clothing industry and boatbuilding and repair are other sources of income for this island country.

▲
These fishers are working together to corral fish in large nets.

Interpreting the Visual Record

Human-Environment Interaction **Why must so many people be involved in catching fish in this way?**

✔ **READING CHECK:** *Environment and Society* What geographic factors affect the economic activities of the Maldives?

Section Review 3

Homework Practice Online
Keyword: SK5 HP15

Define or identify: stupas, Tenzing Norgay, graphite, atolls

Working with Sketch Maps On the map you created in Section 2, label Nepal, Kathmandu, Bhutan, Thimphu, Sri Lanka, Colombo, Maldives, and Male.

Reading for the Main Idea

1. *Environment and Society* How have the people of Nepal used the lower slopes of the Himalayas?

2. *Human Systems* How does the caste system affect social interaction in Sri Lanka?

3. *Places and Regions* What are the major economic activities of the Maldives?

Critical Thinking

4. **Comparing** In what ways have the cultures, people, and histories of India and the countries in this section been linked?

Organizing What You Know

5. **Categorizing** Copy the following graphic organizer. Use it to list the benefits and drawbacks of tourism in Nepal and Bhutan.

Tourism in Nepal and Bhutan

Benefits	Drawbacks

CHAPTER 15 Review and Practice

Define and Identify

Identify each of the following:

1. cyclones
2. storm surges
3. cholera
4. Muhammad Yunus
5. stupas
6. Tenzing Norgay
7. graphite
8. atolls

Review the Main Ideas

9. What two rivers are important to Bangladesh?
10. What mountain is located on Nepal's border with China?
11. What brings so much rain to Bangladesh?
12. Which three of India's Neighbors are dominated by Islam? Which two are primarily Buddhist? Which one is populated mostly by Hindus?
13. How is married life for women in Bangladesh different from married life in Pakistan?
14. What are some important resources of India's Neighbors?
15. Why have so few industries developed in Nepal? What are some of Nepal's industries?

16. Why does the government of Bhutan limit tourism?
17. Why is Colombo, Sri Lanka an important commercial center?
18. What kinds of islands make up the Maldives?

Think Critically

19. **Drawing Inferences and Conclusions** What role do you think the Khyber Pass might have played in the history of this region?
20. **Finding the Main Idea** How has tourism benefited countries in the region? What problems has it caused?
21. **Analyzing Information** How did the British East India Company affect the history of this region?
22. **Analyzing Information** Is the population of India's Neighbors mostly rural or mostly urban? Explain your answer.
23. **Drawing Inferences and Conclusions** How has religion played a role in shaping the region's borders?

Map Activity

24. On a separate sheet of paper, match the letters on the map with their correct labels.

Brahmaputra River	Hindu Kush
Ganges River	Khyber Pass
Himalayas	Indus River
Tarai	Thar Desert

Writing Activity

Imagine that you are moving to one of India's Neighbors. In which country would you choose to live? State your choice and explain your reasons in two or three paragraphs. Explain how landforms, climate, culture, and economy influenced your decision. Be sure to use standard grammar, spelling, sentence structure, and punctuation.

☑ internet connect ▤▤▤

Internet Activity: go.hrw.com
KEYWORD: SK5 GT15

Choose a topic to explore about India's Neighbors.
- Climb the Himalayas.
- Learn about Sri Lanka's history.
- Visit the regions of Pakistan.

Social Studies Skills Practice

Interpreting Cartoons

Study the cartoon about Mount Everest below. Then answer the questions.

WHY ARE WE PICKING ALL THIS TRASH UP?

BECAUSE IT'S THERE.

©2000 Paul Dlugokencky (www.aDailyCartoon.com) for APS News

Source: ©2000 Paul Dlugokencky

1. What problem does this cartoon highlight?
2. How does this cartoonist show that the problem is a major one?
3. Why do you think there is trash on Mount Everest?
4. Who does the cartoonist believe should be responsible for responding to the trash problem?

Analyzing Primary Sources

Read the following quote from Sheika Hasina, who was the prime minister of Bangladesh at the time of this 2000 interview. Then answer the questions.

"We're trying to create an environment that will help us participate in globalization. . . . In 1996, Bangladesh, a country with 120 million people, had only 200,000 phones. We've undertaken major expansion and introduced cellular phones. We've withdrawn taxes on computers, all of which we import. . . . We've started computer schools to create more skilled workers. We now have more than 50 Internet service providers."

Source: *Los Angeles Times*

1. What issue does this quote focus on?
2. What is Bangladesh doing to create skilled workers?
3. What changes does Sheika Hasina see as the key to improving Bangladesh?
4. How might withdrawing taxes on computers promote economic development?

Saving Tigers

The Tiger

In the early 1800s India's tiger population was very large. By 1900, hunters had reduced the tiger population to about 40,000. To protect these tigers, India's British rulers placed strict limits on hunting them. Laws against illegal hunting were strictly enforced. After India won its independence in 1947, the hunting laws were often ignored, however. As a result, fewer than 2,000 tigers remained in India by 1972.

Why Are Tigers Endangered?

Unfortunately, laws have not kept people from hunting tigers. Tiger bones are used in traditional Chinese medicines. The bones are in high demand. International treaties now make it illegal to sell any part of an endangered species. However, the international trade in tiger bones continues.

Loss of habitat also threatens tiger survival. India's population has about doubled in the last 50 years. More land is now farmed to feed these additional people. As a result, many forests where tigers lived have been cleared for farming. As tiger habitat has decreased, so has the number of tigers.

International Efforts to Save the Tiger

Many people realized that tigers would not survive in the wild without protection. As a result, several international organizations and governments are working to ensure the tiger's future.

India's Project Tiger

In 1973 the Indian government took steps to try to save its remaining tigers. With support from the World Wildlife Fund, nine tiger reserves were created as part of Project Tiger. By 2003, 27 reserves had been set up throughout India.

Each reserve has a core area. No one can enter this area without a park ranger. The core area is surrounded by a buffer zone. People can use land in these zones in ways that do not harm the environment.

Once on the verge of extinction, tigers have rebounded in India due largely to Project Tiger.

▼

Realm of the Tiger

REALM OF THE TIGER
- ● Project Tiger reserves
- ▩ Tiger roaming areas

SCALE
0   2000 Miles

0   3500 Kilometers
Projection: Miller Cylindrical

ASIA

CHINA

AFRICA

ARABIAN SEA

INDIA

BAY OF BENGAL

SOUTH CHINA SEA

— Tropic of Cancer —

INDIAN OCEAN

◀
Some rare Bengal tigers, such as this cub, are white. In the last 100 years, only about a dozen white tigers have been seen in the wild.

Some conservationists are reaching out to nearby villagers. Villagers have often felt that tigers are being protected at their expense. The conservationists want to show that tiger reserves can also help villagers. One organization has introduced new types of water buffalo that need very little grazing land. To boost the local economy, it has helped women sell their handicrafts in urban areas. The Global Environment Facility and the World Bank also helped. They spent about $10 million to aid villages around India's Ranthambhore National Park.

China's Year of the Tiger Despite these efforts, the number of tigers remains low. In 1998, the Chinese Year of the Tiger, conservationists in Hong Kong tried a new approach. They started an advertising campaign to remind people how important tigers are in traditional Chinese culture. The advertisements showed children dressed in clothes with popular tiger designs. The advertise-

ments read, "They protect your children; who will protect them?" Chinese conservationists hope their campaign will encourage people to stop using medicines made with tiger bones. They also hope it will encourage people to join the fight to save the world's tigers.

Your Turn

Imagine you are planning a worldwide campaign to save tigers in the wild. Write a short report that explains your plan and answers the following questions:

1. How would the Project Tiger reserves and the Chinese advertising campaign fit into your plan?

2. Do you think it is more important to save tiger habitat or to keep people from hunting them? why?

Building Skills for Life: Drawing Diagrams

Diagrams are drawings that explain how things work or fit together. They can be helpful in many different situations. For example, suppose you bought a bicycle and had to put it together. How would you do it? The easiest way would be to follow a diagram.

The goal of a diagram is to explain something. Diagrams are not intended to show exactly how something looks in real life. Diagrams should be easy to understand, neat, and simple.

In geography, diagrams are often used to show how different things are related. Physical geographers use diagrams to explain how sea and land breezes develop or how volcanoes form. Cultural geographers use diagrams to show settlement patterns and housing styles.

You can draw diagrams too. To draw a diagram, first decide exactly what you want it to show. Choose a short, descriptive title. Plan your diagram by making a quick sketch. How many drawings will you need? How will you arrange them? Then carefully draw your diagram. Label the important features. Use colors, patterns, and symbols if you need to. Use a ruler for straight lines and write the title at the top. Then add a short caption at the bottom that explains your diagram.

Sea and Land Breezes

Warm air

As warm air rises, it creates an area of low pressure over the land.

The cool air moves toward the land, producing a sea breeze.

Cool air

Air over the water is cooler and creates an area of high pressure.

Cool air

Air over land is cooler and creates an area of high pressure.

The cool air moves toward the water, producing a land breeze.

Warm air

Air over the water is warmer and creates an area of low pressure.

Breezes from the ocean cool the warmer land surface during the day. At night, cooler land surface breezes blow toward the ocean.

THE SKILL

1. Choose a diagram from a book, magazine, or newspaper. Write a short paragraph about the diagram. What does it show? Is it clear and easy to understand? why or why not?

2. Draw a diagram that shows how wind moves a sailboat through water.

3. Draw a diagram that shows how rocks can break off a mountain and cause a landslide.

HANDS on

The Himalayas are the highest mountains on Earth. Nine of the ten highest peaks in the world are located there. The Himalayas have 110 peaks that rise above 24,000 feet (7,315 m).

How did the Himalayas get to be so high? When were they formed? Drawing a diagram is one way to show how the Himalayas became the world's highest mountains.

Read the paragraph below. It describes how and when the Himalayas formed. Use this information to draw a diagram showing how the Himalayas became the world's highest mountains.

The Himalayas were formed long ago by the movement of Earth's tectonic plates. About 180 million years ago, the Indo-Australian plate broke off from the ancient supercontinent Gondwana and began moving north. This plate included what is now the Indian Subcontinent. About 50 million years ago, the Indo-Australian plate collided with the Eurasian plate and was forced under it. As the Indo-Australian plate was pulled under the Eurasian plate, the Himalayas began to rise. They grew slowly at first. Then, about 30 million years ago, the Himalayas began rising faster. However, they did not become the highest mountains in the world until about 500,000 years ago. The Himalayas are still rising today.

► Mountain peaks rise above the clouds in the world's highest mountains.

Lab Report

1. Is your diagram clear and easy to understand? Show your diagram to another person to see if he or she can easily understand it.

2. Did you use colors or symbols in your diagram? why or why not?

3. By drawing a diagram of the Himalayas, did you learn something about diagrams in general? What did you learn?

UNIT 5

East and Southeast Asia

Shwedagon Pagoda, Yangon, Myanmar

Rice paddies near Guilin, China

A Peace Corps Volunteer in Mongolia

Matt Heller served as a Peace Corps volunteer in Mongolia. He worked as an English teacher and coordinated a greenhouse reconstruction project. **WHAT DO YOU THINK?** *What kinds of changes would you have to make in your life to live in Mongolia?*

I've been a Peace Corps volunteer in Mongolia for eighteen months. I live in a *ger*, a tent with a small wood stove in the center. It is strong and practical, perfect for a nomadic herder. I, however, am an English teacher in a small school in rural Mongolia. *Ger* life is hard. It makes twenty-year-olds look thirty-five. It makes your soul hard.

Mongolians are very proud of their history. Once, while sitting on the train going from Ulaanbaatar to my own town, Bor-Undur, a Mongolian pointed to his arm and said, "In here is the blood of Genghis Khan. Beware." There is no argument to that statement. I responded, "Yes, older brother (a respectful title addressed to elders), your country is beautiful. Mongolians are lucky."

Along with many other things, I'm learning how Mongolians live. In the steppe there is very little snow, only biting wind and dust. It gets as cold as −50 degrees, not counting the wind chill factor. If I leave tea in a mug, it will freeze by morning. I've broken three mugs that way.

A Mongolian outside his home

Festival of Ages parade, Kyoto, Japan

Understanding Primary Sources

1. What conclusion does Matt Heller make about Mongolians and their past?

2. How does Matt Heller describe the climate in Mongolia?

Giant panda

East and Southeast Asia

Elevation Profile

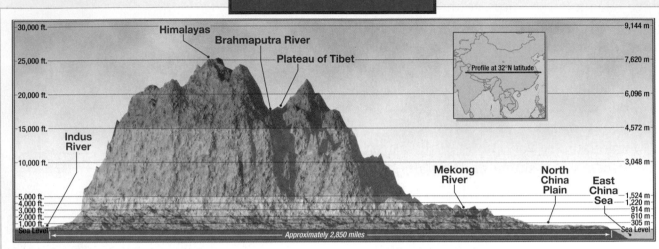

30,000 ft. — 9,144 m

Himalayas

Brahmaputra River

25,000 ft. — 7,620 m

Plateau of Tibet

Profile at 32°N latitude

20,000 ft. — 6,096 m

15,000 ft. — 4,572 m

Indus River

10,000 ft. — 3,048 m

Mekong River

North China Plain

East China Sea

5,000 ft.
4,000 ft.
3,000 ft.
2,000 ft.
1,000 ft.
Sea Level

1,524 m
1,220 m
914 m
610 m
305 m
Sea Level

Approximately 2,850 miles

The United States and East and Southeast Asia: Comparing Sizes

GEOSTATS:

China

🌐 World's largest population: 1,286,975,468 (2003 estimate)

👥 Population growth rate: 0.6% (2003 estimate)

⛰ Highest point: Mount Everest—29,035 ft. (8,850 m)

🏔 Lowest point: Turpan Depression—505 ft. (154 m) below sea level

ELEVATION

FEET	METERS
13,120	4,000
6,560	2,000
1,640	500
656	200
(Sea level) 0	0 (Sea level)
Below sea level	Below sea level

SCALE

0 — 500 — 1000 Miles

0 — 500 — 1000 Kilometers

Projection: Two-Point Equidistant

1. (Movement) Which of the region's physical features could make travel and trade difficult?

2. (Region) What are the region's three largest island countries?

3. (Location) Which countries have territory on the mainland and on islands?

Critical Thinking

4. (Place) Compare this map to the **population map**. What physical features might prevent western China from becoming densely populated? Why might eastern China be so densely populated?

1. **Region** Which country entirely on the main-land shares a border with just one of the region's other countries?

2. **Location** What is the only landlocked country in Southeast Asia? Which country in East Asia is landlocked?

Critical Thinking

3. **Region** Compare this map to the **physical map** of the region. Which physical feature forms the border of southwestern China? Which other physical features form natural borders in the region?

CLIMATE
- Humid tropical
- Tropical savanna
- Desert
- Steppe
- Humid subtropical
- Humid continental
- Subarctic
- Highland
- ← Wet monsoon airflow
- ← Dry monsoon airflow

NORTH ASIA

SOUTH ASIA

Tropic of Cancer

Bay of Bengal

INDIAN OCEAN

Equator

SEA OF JAPAN

PACIFIC OCEAN

SOUTH CHINA SEA

SCALE
0   500   1000 Miles
0   500   1000 Kilometers
Projection: Two-Point Equidistant

1. *Place* Compare this map to the **political map** of the region. What kind of climate does most of Mongolia have?

2. *Location* Study the monsoon airflow patterns shown on this map. In which directions do the wet and dry monsoons flow?

Critical Thinking

3. *Region* Why might this region have such a variety of climate types?

4. *Region* Why might the South China Sea be stormy?

East and Southeast Asia: Population

POPULATION DENSITY

Persons per sq. mile	Persons per sq. km
520	200
260	100
130	50
25	10
3	1
0	0

● Metropolitan areas with more than 2 million inhabitants

○ Metropolitan areas with 1 million to 2 million inhabitants

SCALE
0 — 500 — 1000 Miles
0 — 500 — 1000 Kilometers
Projection: Two-Point Equidistant

1. (Place) What is the population density in the area between Shanghai and Beijing?

2. (Region) Compare this map to the **physical map** of the region. Which physical features help explain the low population density in western China?

Critical Thinking

3. (Human-Environment Interaction) Compare this map to the **physical map** of the region. Which physical features help explain the high population densities near Bangkok, Ho Chi Minh City, and Yangon (Rangoon)?

NORTH ASIA

Ürümqi

Shenyang

Beijing   Tianjin
SEA OF
JAPAN
Pusan   Tokyo–Yokohama
Seoul   Nagoya
YELLOW   Osaka–Kobe–
SEA   Kyoto

Lhasa

**SOUTH
ASIA**

Nanjing
Shanghai

Wuhan

Tropic of Cancer

Chongqing

Taipei

Kaohsiung

Tropic of Cancer

PACIFIC OCEAN

Guangzhou
Macao
Hanoi   Hong Kong

Yangon (Rangoon)

**PHILIPPINE
SEA**

Bay of
Bengal

Bangkok

**SOUTH
CHINA
SEA**
Manila

Ho Chi Minh City

N

Equator

Singapore

Jakarta

RESOURCES

	Coal
	Natural gas
	Oil
	Nuclear power
	Hydroelectric power
G	Gold
S	Silver
	Other minerals
	Seafood

LAND USE

Commercial farming

Subsistence farming

Forest

Nomadic herding

Limited economic
activity

Manufacturing

• Major manufacturing
and trade centers

SCALE
0   500   1000 Miles
0   500   1000 Kilometers
Projection: Two-Point Equidistant

1. (Region) Which two countries have large
areas where nomadic herding is common?

2. (Region) Where in China is most commercial
farming found? In which countries is subsistence farming common?

Critical Thinking

3. (Human-Environment Interaction) Compare this
map to the **physical** and **climate maps** of
the region. Why do you think western
China and much of Mongolia have limited
economic activity?

Fast FACTS

East and Southeast Asia

BRUNEI

CAPITAL:
Bandar Seri Begawan

AREA:
2,228 sq. mi. (5,770 sq km)

POPULATION:
358,098

MONEY:
Bruneian dollar

LANGUAGES:
Malay (official), English, Chinese

NUMBER OF INTERNET USERS: 35,000

JAPAN

CAPITAL:
Tokyo

AREA:
145,882 sq. mi. (377,835 sq km)

POPULATION:
127,214,499

MONEY:
yen

LANGUAGES:
Japanese

NUMBER OF INTERNET USERS:
56,000,000

CAMBODIA

CAPITAL:
Phnom Penh

AREA:
69,900 sq. mi. (181,040 sq km)

POPULATION:
13,124,764

MONEY:
riel

LANGUAGES:
Khmer (official), French

NUMBER OF INTERNET USERS: 10,000

LAOS

CAPITAL:
Vientiane

AREA:
91,428 sq. mi. (236,800 sq km)

POPULATION:
5,921,545

MONEY:
kip

LANGUAGES:
Lao (official), French, English, ethnic languages

NUMBER OF INTERNET USERS: 10,000

CHINA

CAPITAL:
Beijing

AREA:
3,705,386 sq. mi. (9,596,960 sq km)

POPULATION:
1,286,975,468

MONEY:
yuan

LANGUAGES:
Mandarin, Yue, other forms of Chinese

NUMBER OF INTERNET USERS: 45,800,000

MALAYSIA

CAPITAL:
Kuala Lumpur

AREA:
127,316 sq. mi. (329,750 sq km)

POPULATION:
23,092,940

MONEY:
ringgit

LANGUAGES: Bahasa Melayu (official), English, Chinese dialects, ethnic languages

NUMBER OF INTERNET USERS: 5,700,000

INDONESIA

CAPITAL:
Jakarta

AREA:
741,096 sq. mi. (1,919,440 sq km)

POPULATION:
234,893,453

MONEY:
Indonesian rupiah

LANGUAGES:
Bahasa Indonesia (official), English, Dutch, Javanese

NUMBER OF INTERNET USERS: 4,400,000

MONGOLIA

CAPITAL:
Ulaanbaatar

AREA:
604,247 sq. mi. (1,565,000 sq km)

POPULATION:
2,712,315

MONEY:
togrog/tugrik

LANGUAGES:
Khalkha Mongol, Turkic, Russian

NUMBER OF INTERNET USERS: 40,000

Countries not drawn to scale.

MYANMAR (Burma)

CAPITAL:
Yangon (Rangoon)

AREA:
261,969 sq. mi.
(678,500 sq km)

POPULATION:
42,510,537

MONEY:
kyat

LANGUAGES:
Burmese, many
ethnic languages

NUMBER OF INTERNET USERS: 10,000

NORTH KOREA

CAPITAL:
P'yŏngyang

AREA:
46,540 sq. mi.
(120,540 sq km)

POPULATION:
22,466,481

MONEY:
North Korean won

LANGUAGES:
Korean

NUMBER OF INTERNET USERS: not available

PHILIPPINES

CAPITAL:
Manila

AREA:
115,830 sq. mi.
(300,000 sq km)

POPULATION:
84,619,974

MONEY:
Philippine peso

LANGUAGES:
Filipino, English

NUMBER OF INTERNET USERS: 4,500,000

SINGAPORE

CAPITAL:
Singapore

AREA:
250 sq. mi. (648 sq km)

POPULATION:
4,608,595

MONEY:
Singapore dollar

LANGUAGES:
Chinese, Malay, Tamil,
English

NUMBER OF INTERNET USERS: 2,310,000

SOUTH KOREA

CAPITAL:
Seoul

AREA:
38,023 sq. mi.
(98,480 sq km)

POPULATION: 48,289,037

MONEY:
South Korean won

LANGUAGES:
Korean, English

NUMBER OF INTERNET USERS: 25,600,000

TAIWAN

CAPITAL:
Taipei

AREA:
13,892 sq. mi.
(35,980 sq km)

POPULATION:
22,548,000

MONEY:
New Taiwan
dollar

LANGUAGES: Mandarin,
Taiwanese (Min), Hakka
dialects

NUMBER OF INTERNET USERS: 10,100,000

THAILAND

CAPITAL:
Bangkok

AREA:
198,455 sq. mi.
(514,000 sq km)

POPULATION: 64,265,276

MONEY:
baht

LANGUAGES: Thai, English,
ethnic languages

NUMBER OF INTERNET USERS: 1,200,000

VIETNAM

CAPITAL:
Hanoi

AREA:
127,243 sq. mi.
(329,560 sq km)

POPULATION:
81,624,716

MONEY:
dong

LANGUAGES: Vietnamese
(official), Chinese,
English, French,
Khmer, ethnic languages

NUMBER OF INTERNET USERS: 409,000

internet connect

COUNTRY STATISTICS
GO TO: go.hrw.com
KEYWORD: SK5 FactsU5
FOR: more facts about East
and Southeast Asia

Sources: Central Intelligence Agency, *The World Factbook 2003*; Taipei Economic and Cultural Representative Office, figures are 2003 estimates.

China, Mongolia, and Taiwan

This region of Asia with its varied landscape and cultures is home to one of the world's oldest living civilizations.

Hello! My name is Lu Hua. Lu is my family name, and Hua is my given name. In China the family name comes first. I am 16 and live in Jin Shan County, outside of Shanghai, with my parents and my brother. My father is a clerk in a Volkswagen factory. My ancestors have lived in this village for hundreds of years. All 200 people in this village are named Lu.

I am in my last year at Jin Shan County High School. To get into this school, which is the best in the county, I had to pass a very difficult exam when I was 11. I had the best score that year. The school goes from seventh to twelfth grade. Each grade has four classes with 50 kids in each class. Now I am hoping to go on to a university. In China only one or two out of a hundred kids can go to college.

Most of my friends want to be scientists. I think I would like to be a diplomat, to travel, and have adventures. My family are common people, though, not Chinese Communist Party members, so I may not get into the diplomatic college.

你好嗎?

Translation: How are you?

Section 1 Physical Geography

Read to Discover

1. What are the physical features of China, Mongolia, and Taiwan?
2. What types of climate are found in China, Mongolia, and Taiwan?
3. What natural resources do China, Mongolia, and Taiwan have?

Vocabulary

dikes
arable

Places

Himalayas
Mount Everest
Kunlun Mountains
Tian Shan
Plateau of Tibet
Taklimakan Desert
Tarim Basin

Gobi
North China Plain
Huang River
Chang River
Sichuan (Red) Basin
Xi River

Reading Strategy

USING VISUAL INFORMATION Look at the map and photographs in this section. Where do you think most of China's population lives? What challenges do the people of Mongolia and Taiwan face? Write your answers on a sheet of paper. As you read this section, correct your predictions and add more details.

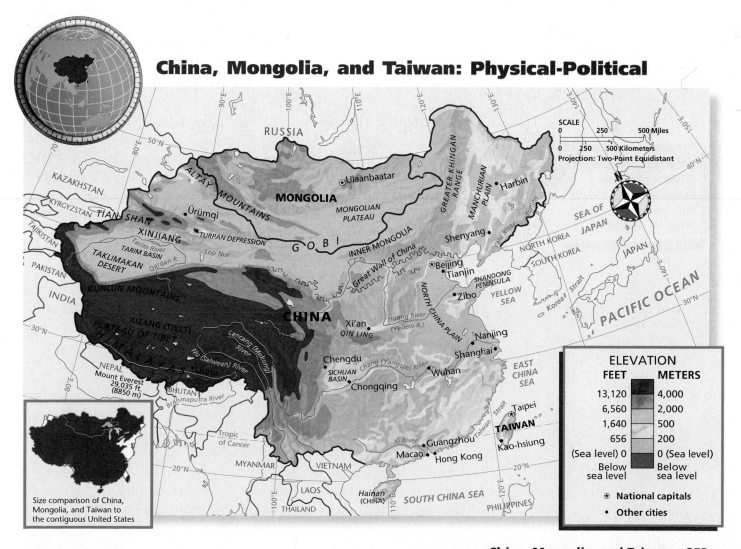

China, Mongolia, and Taiwan: Physical-Political

Size comparison of China, Mongolia, and Taiwan to the contiguous United States

SCALE
0 250 500 Miles
0 250 500 Kilometers
Projection: Two-Point Equidistant

ELEVATION

FEET		METERS
13,120		4,000
6,560		2,000
1,640		500
656		200
(Sea level) 0		0 (Sea level)
Below sea level		Below sea level

⊛ National capitals
• Other cities

These snow-covered mountains are in the Wolong Nature Reserve in central China.

Interpreting the Visual Record

 (Region) **What climate types would you expect to find in this area of the reserve?**

🔲 internet connect

GO TO: go.hrw.com
KEYWORD: SK5 CH16
FOR: Web sites about China, Mongolia, and Taiwan

Physical Features

China has some of the world's tallest mountains, driest deserts, and longest rivers. Mongolia (mahn-GOHL-yuh) is China's neighbor to the north. It is a large, rugged, landlocked country. Burning hot summers and bitter cold winters are common there. In contrast, Taiwan (TY-WAHN) is a green tropical island just off the coast of mainland China.

Mountains The towering Himalayas (hi-muh-LAY-uhz), the world's tallest mountain range, run along China's southwestern border. Mount Everest lies in the Himalayas on China's border with Nepal. At 29,035 feet (8,850 m), it is the world's tallest mountain. If you move north from the Himalayas, you will find several other mountain ranges. These are the Kunlun Mountains (KOON-LOON), the Tian Shan (TYEN SHAHN), and the Altay Mountains (al-TY). To the east, on Mongolia's eastern border with China, you will see the Greater Khingan (KING-AHN) Range.

Mountains stretch the length of Taiwan and cover the eastern half of the island. In some places, the mountains end in steep cliffs at the edge of the Pacific Ocean. To the west of the mountains is a fertile coastal plain.

Plateaus, Basins, and Deserts Isolated plateaus and basins separate the region's mountain ranges. The huge Plateau of Tibet lies between the Himalayas and the Kunlun Mountains. With an average elevation of 16,000 feet (4,877 m), it is the world's highest plateau. The Taklimakan (tah-kluh-muh-KAHN) Desert is a huge expanse of sand. It occupies the central part of the Tarim (DAH-REEM) Basin in western China. In the northeastern corner of the basin, the Turpan (toohr-PAHN) Depression drops about 505 feet (154 m) below sea level.

The Mongolian Plateau covers most of the country of Mongolia. The Gobi (GOH-bee) takes up much of the central and southeastern sections of the plateau. The Gobi is the coldest desert in the world and covers more than 500,000 square miles (1,295,000 sq km). Much of the Gobi is gravel and bare rock.

Plains China and Mongolia have few areas of lowlands made up of coastal and river floodplains. However, these fertile plains support the major population centers. Millions of people live in the North China Plain. It is the largest plain in China and is crossed by major rivers.

Rivers The river known as the Huang (HWAHNG) rises on the eastern edge of the Plateau of Tibet. It flows eastward through the North China Plain and empties into the Yellow Sea. It takes its name, which means "yellow river," from the yellowish mud it carries. Winds carry loess, a yellowish-brown soil, from the Gobi to northern China. The Huang picks up the loess as the river flows through the region. On its way to the sea the river dumps the loess, raising the river bottom. This can lead to flooding. Floodwaters deposit a layer of rich silt that is good for farming but also cause great damage and loss of life. As a result, the Huang has long been known as China's Sorrow. The Chinese have tried to control the Huang by building **dikes**. These high banks of earth or concrete help reduce flooding.

The Chang (CHAHNG), or Yangtze (YAHNG-TSE), River also rises in the Plateau of Tibet. It flows eastward for 3,434 miles (5,525 km) across central China through the fertile Sichuan (SEE-CHWAHN), or Red, Basin. The Chang is China's—and Asia's—longest river. In fact, its name means "long river." The Chang is one of China's most important transportation routes. It is connected to the Huang by the world's oldest and longest canal system, the Grand Canal. The Xi (SHEE) River is southern China's most important river and transportation route.

✓ **READING CHECK:** (*Places and Regions*) What are the major physical features of this region?

Climate

China, Mongolia, and Taiwan are part of a huge region with several different climates. China's precipitation varies. The southeastern coastal region is the country's most humid area. As you move northwestward the climate becomes steadily drier. The extreme northwest has a true desert climate.

Seasonal monsoon winds greatly affect the climate of the region's southern and eastern parts. In winter, winds from Central Asia bring dry, cool-to-cold weather to eastern

Our Amazing Planet

China has greater potential for hydroelectric power than any other country in the world. When completed in 2009, the Three Gorges Dam on the Chang River will be the world's largest dam.

The Gobi is the world's third-largest desert. Herders ride Bactrian camels.
Interpreting the Visual Record (*Place*)
What characteristics of a desert environment can be seen in this photo?

China, Mongolia, and Taiwan

Country	Population/ Growth Rate	Life Expectancy	Literacy Rate	Per Capita GDP
China	1,286,975,468 0.6%	70, male 74, female	86%	$4,400
Mongolia	2,712,315 1.4%	61, male 66, female	99%	$1,840
Taiwan	22,548,000 0.8%	74, male 80, female	94%	$17,400
United States	281,421,906 0.9%	74, male 80, female	97%	$36,200

Source: Central Intelligence Agency, *The World Factbook 2003*

Interpreting the Chart Which country has the fastest rate of population growth?

This bronze vessel dates to the A.D. 1000s. Found in a tomb, it is just over a foot long (30 cm) and is covered with detailed animal designs.

Asia. In summer, winds from the Pacific bring warm, wet air. This creates hot, rainy summers. Typhoons sometimes hit the coastal areas during the summer and fall. Typhoons are violent storms with high winds and heavy rains similar to hurricanes. They often bring flooding and cause a great deal of damage.

✔ **READING CHECK:** (*Places and Regions*) What are the climates of China, Mongolia, and Taiwan like?

Resources

China has a wide range of mineral resources. These include gold, iron ore, lead, salt, uranium, and zinc, as well as energy resources such as coal and oil. China has greater coal reserves than any other country. At the present rate of use, these reserves will last another 1,000 years. China also produces enough oil to meet most of its own needs.

Mongolia has deposits of coal, copper, gold, iron ore, and oil. Taiwan's most important natural resource is its **arable** land, or land that is suitable for growing crops.

✔ **READING CHECK:** (*Places and Regions*) What are the region's resources?

go.hrw.com **Homework Practice Online**
Keyword: SK5 HP16

Section Review 1

Define and explain: dikes, arable

Working with Sketch Maps On a map of China, Mongolia, and Taiwan that you draw or that your teacher provides, label the following: the Himalayas, Mount Everest, Kunlun Mountains, Tian Shan, Plateau of Tibet, Taklimakan Desert, Tarim Basin, Gobi, North China Plain, Huang River, Chang River, Sichuan Basin, and Xi River. Where do you think the most fertile areas of the region are located?

Reading for the Main Idea

1. (*Places and Regions*) What and where is the world's largest plateau? What is the world's tallest mountain? Where is it located?

2. (*Environment and Society*) What are three major rivers in eastern and southern China? How does the Huang affect China's people?

3. (*Places and Regions*) What is the region's driest area?

Critical Thinking

4. Drawing Inferences and Conclusions What do you think might be the major factors that influence this region's climate?

Organizing What You Know

5. Summarizing Summarize the natural environments of China, Mongolia, and Taiwan.

Country	Physical Features	Climates	Resources

China's History and Culture

Read to Discover

1. What are some of the major events in the history of China?
2. What are some features of China's culture?

Vocabulary

emperor
dynasty
porcelain
martial law
pagodas

Places

China
Great Wall

People

Confucius
Genghis Khan
Sun Yat-sen
Mao Zedong
Dalai Lama

Reading Strategy

USING PRIOR KNOWLEDGE Before you read this section, list information you already know about China's history and culture. Compare your list with a partner. As you read this section, add more information to your list. Then compare your completed list with your partner's list.

History

Farmers have cultivated rice in southern China for some 7,000 years. Warm, wet weather made the region ideal for growing rice. Rice remains one of the region's main sources of food. Farmers in drier northern China grew a grain called millet and other crops. The early Chinese also grew hemp for fiber for clothing and spun silk from the cocoons of silkworms. Various cultures developed, particularly along the region's rivers.

The Qin Dynasty and the Great Wall Beginning about 2000 B.C. northern Chinese living in the Huang valley formed kingdoms. As Chinese civilization began to develop, peoples from various regions organized into large states. Each state was governed by an **emperor**—a ruler of a large empire. An emperor is often a member of a **dynasty**. A dynasty is a ruling family that passes power from one generation to the next. Beginning in about 500 B.C., the Chinese began building earthen

(*Place*) The Great Wall of China, including its branches and curves, stretches more than 2,000 miles (3,218 km).

Archaeologists have discovered 6,000 of these uniquely crafted soldiers near Xi'an.

BIOGRAPHY

Confucius
(c. 551 B.C.–479? B.C.)

The philosopher's real name was K'ung Ch'iu or K'ung Fu-tzu ("Master K'ung"). We know him by the Latin version of his name—Confucius.

Few details about the life of Confucius are certain. We do know he was born about 551 B.C. in eastern China. It was a time troubled by warfare and wicked rulers. In response, Confucius argued for a different system of behavior and government. His ideas have shaped Chinese society for centuries.

How did Confucius influence Chinese society?

walls hundreds of miles long. These walls separated the kingdoms from the northern nomads and from each other. Records show that the first emperor of the Qin, also spelled Ch'in (CHIN), dynasty ordered the building of the Great Wall along China's northern border. People began to connect the sections of walls about 200 B.C.

The Qin dynasty is well known for its contributions to China's culture. It left behind many historical artifacts. For example, when the first emperor died, he was buried with thousands of life-sized warriors and horses made of clay. You might wonder why someone would want their tomb filled with clay figures. It was an ancient Chinese funeral tradition to bury masters with clay soldiers for protection. Since the Qin emperor had made many enemies during his life, he wanted protection after his death.

During the Qin dynasty the Chinese used a writing system to record their history. This system was similar to the one used in China today. China's name also dates from this time period. In Chinese, China means "Qin kingdom" or "middle kingdom." This name may refer to the Chinese belief that China was the center, or middle, of the world.

The Han Dynasty The Han dynasty came after the Qin dynasty. From the 200s B.C. to the A.D. 200s, the Han dynasty expanded its kingdom southward. The Han also extended the Great Wall westward to protect the Silk Road. This road was originally used by trading caravans taking silk and other Chinese goods to regions west of China. During the Han dynasty the Chinese invented the compass, which aided travel. The dynasties that followed the Han made China even more powerful. The Chinese continued to make important contributions to society. Later contributions include paper and **porcelain** (POHR-suh-luhn), a type of very fine pottery.

Mongols, Ming Dynasty, and the Manchu In the 1200s Mongol armies led by Genghis Khan conquered China. *Khan* is a title that means "ruler." The Mongols were feared and known for spreading terror throughout the region. Their use of horses added to their military advantage.

Within 100 years the Ming dynasty seized control of China. After several battles with the Mongols, the Ming emperors closed China to outsiders. These emperors strengthened the Great Wall and focused on the development of their own culture.

In the 1600s a group called the Manchu began expanding from their home in Manchuria. Manchuria is located in far northeastern China. The Manchus conquered Inner Mongolia, Korea, and all of northern China. Led by the Qing (CHING) dynasty, the Manchu controlled China for more than 260 years. The dynasty's strong government slowly weakened, however, and was overthrown in the early 1900s.

Outside Influences Marco Polo was one of the few Europeans to visit China before the 1500s. Europeans reached China by following the Silk Road. None came by sea before the 1500s. In the 1500s Portuguese sailors established a trade colony at Macao (muh-KOW) in south China. French and British sailors and traders followed. The Chinese believed that foreigners had little to offer other than silver in return for Chinese porcelain, silk, and tea. Even so, Europeans introduced crops like corn, hot chili peppers, peanuts, potatoes, sweet potatoes, and tobacco. By the 1800s the European countries wanted to control China's trade. A series of conflicts caused China to lose some of its independence. For example, during this period the British acquired Hong Kong. The British, Germans, and French also forced China to open additional ports. China did not regain total independence until the mid-1900s.

The Republics of China In 1912 a revolutionary group led by Sun Yat-sen (SOOHN YAHT-SUHN) forced the last emperor to abdicate, or give up power. This group formed the first Republic of China. Mongolia and Tibet each declared their independence.

After Sun Yat-sen's death the revolutionaries split into two groups, the Nationalists and the Communists. A military leader named Chiang Kai-shek (chang ky-SHEK) united China under a Nationalist government. The Communists opposed him, and a civil war began. During

The Catalan Atlas from the 1300s shows Marco Polo's family traveling by camel caravan.

Interpreting the Visual Record

(*Movement*) **What kind of information might this atlas provide?**

This time line reviews major events in China's rich history. The last Chinese dynasty was overthrown in 1912.

Interpreting the Time Line
What events have shaped China's government in the 1900s?

Historical China: A Time Line

Qin becomes China's first dynasty
200s B.C.

Rise of Ming dynasty
1368

People's Republic of China is formed under Mao Zedong
1949

The Cultural Revolution
1966–1976

| 5000 B.C. | A.D. 1 | 1000 | 1200 | 1400 | 1600 | 1800 | 2000 |

5000 B.C.
First rice farmers cultivate the area near the Chang River

206 B.C. – A.D. 220
Han dynasty dominates China

1200s
Mongols invade China

1912
Republic is established with the overthrow of the Manchu dynasty

1937
Japanese invade China

1989
Government troops crush protesters in Tiananmen Square

Mao Zedong
(1893–1976)

Mao Zedong founded a new country—the People's Republic of China. His policies, however, created disasters for his country's people.

Early in his career, Mao and 90,000 followers set off on a 6,000-mile walk to establish a new headquarters. Half of the group didn't survive the trip. Later, his economic program, The Great Leap Forward, brought widespread starvation. Some 20 million died. Mao's Cultural Revolution was supposed to make China an ideal Communist society. Instead, the country was damaged and many people were killed.

What was the result of Mao's Great Leap Forward?

World War II both groups fought the Japanese. The Communists finally defeated the Nationalists in 1949. Led by Mao Zedong (MOW ZUH-DOOHNG), the Communists set up the People's Republic of China. Mao's version of communism is known as Maoism. Only one political party—the Communist Party—was allowed.

Chiang Kai-shek and his Nationalists retreated to Taiwan. There they created a government for what they called the Republic of China. This government maintained its control through **martial law**, or military rule, for many years.

Mao's China Under Mao the government took over the country's economy. His government seized private land and organized it into large, government-run farms. Factories were also put under state control. The central government decided the amount and type of food grown on a farm. It also regulated the production of factory goods, owned all housing, and decided where people should live. Sometimes families were separated or forced to relocate. Women were given equal status and assigned equal work duties. Religious worship was prohibited. Despite the efforts to organize the economy, there were planning errors. In the 1960s a famine killed about 30 million people.

In 1966 Mao began a movement called the Cultural Revolution. The Revolution was an attempt to make everyone live a peasant way of life. Followers of Mao were known as Red Guards. They closed schools and universities. Millions of people were sent to the countryside to work in the fields. Opponents were imprisoned or executed.

(Place) The Potala Palace in Tibet was built in the A.D. 600s. Today, it has more than 1,000 rooms and is used for religious and political events.

Tibet Bordering the Himalayas in southwest China, the territory of Tibet is sometimes called the "Roof of the World." About two million people live in Tibet today. Tibetans see themselves as a separate nation and consider Lhasa their capital. However, Tibet is officially a part of China. The Chinese government wants Tibetans to be Chinese. In addition, China does not want Tibetans to practice their traditional Buddhist culture. For example, during China's Cultural Revolution, Chinese troops destroyed thousands of Buddhist monasteries. Many religious writings and art were demolished.

Tibetans trace their history back to the A.D. 500s when Tibet began as a Buddhist nation. In the 1400s, a religious leader called the Dalai Lama ruled Tibet. Since then 14 men have served as Dalai Lama. After a violent uprising against China in 1959, the 14th Dalai Lama sought exile in India where he lives today. In 1989, the Dalai Lama received the Nobel Peace Prize for his nonviolent protest against Chinese occupation of Tibet.

✓ **READING CHECK:** (*Human Systems*) What are some major events in China's history?

Culture

About 92 percent of China's population consider themselves Han Chinese. Almost everyone can speak one of the seven major Chinese dialects. Mandarin Chinese is the official language and the most common.

Values and Beliefs Several philosophies and religions began in China. Taoism (TOW-i-zuhm), or Daoism (DOW-i-zuhm), is an ancient Chinese religion. Taoists believe that humans should try to follow a path that agrees with nature and avoids everyday concerns. The word *dào* means "the path." Each object or natural feature is thought to have its own god or spirit that may reward good deeds or bring bad luck.

The teachings of Confucius also have been important to Chinese culture. Confucius was a philosopher who lived from 551 to 479 B.C. His teachings stressed the importance of family. Confucius believed that children should

The Chinese New Year is also called the Lunar New Year. This is because the cycles of the moon are the basis for the Chinese calendar.

Interpreting the Visual Record

(*Place*) What object are parade participants carrying? What does it resemble?

CONNECTING TO Literature

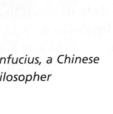

Confucius, a Chinese philosopher

This Chinese tale comes from the Hsiao Ching, or Book of Filial Piety—which means "devotion to parents." A student of a follower of Confucius is believed to have written it about 400 B.C. This story encourages children to protect their parents.

A Loving Son

Wu Meng was eight years old and very dutiful to his parents. His family was so poor that they could not afford to furnish their beds with mosquito-curtains. Every summer night thousands of mosquitoes attacked them, feasting upon their flesh and blood.

Wu Meng looked at his tired parents asleep on their bed as thousands of mosquitoes fiercely attacked them. Wu saw them sucking his parents' blood, which caused his heart to grieve.

To protect his parents, Wu decided that he would not drive the mosquitoes away from himself. Lying on the bed, he threw off his clothes, and soon feeling the pain of the mosquito attacks, he cried: "I have no fear of you, nor have you any reason to fear me. Although I have a fan, I will not use it, nor will I strike you with my hand. I will lie very quietly and let you gorge to the full." Such was his love for his parents!

Analyzing Primary Sources

1. How does this tale reflect traditional Chinese philosophical beliefs?
2. Why do you think the author of the *Hsiao Ching* wrote this story?

respect their parents and subjects should respect their ruler. He believed people should treat those under their control justly and argued that state power should be used to improve people's lives.

The religion called Buddhism also has been important in China. It was founded by an Indian prince, Siddhartha Gautama. Gautama was born in Nepal about 563 B.C. He decided to search for truth and knowledge. Enlightenment—peace and a sense of being one with the universe—came to him while he was sitting under a Bo or Bodhi tree. As a result, he was given the name Buddha, which means "awakened or enlightened one." Buddhism reached China from India about A.D. 100. It became the country's main religion between the 300s and 500s. Indian architecture also became popular in China. Chinese **pagodas**, or Buddhist temples, are based on Indian designs. Pagodas have an upward-curving roof. Some pagodas are 15 stories tall.

Lifeways Chinese culture highly values education. Chinese children are required to attend nine years of school. However, just 1 to 2 percent of students pass the difficult entrance exams to get into a university.

The Chinese government tries to control many aspects of everyday life. For example, parents are allowed to have just one child. This is because the government is trying to slow population growth.

The government also controls the newspapers and telephone system. This allows it to limit the flow of information and ideas. Satellite TV, the Internet, and e-mail are becoming more widespread, however. This makes it more difficult for the government to control communication between individuals.

Chinese food varies widely from region to region. Food in Beijing is heavily salted and flavored with garlic and cilantro. Sichuan-style cooking features hot pepper sauces. Cantonese cooking was introduced to the United States by immigrants from Guangzhou (GWAHNG-JOH).

Traditional Chinese medicine stresses herbal products and harmony with the universe. People around the world have used acupuncture. This therapy involves inserting fine needles into specific parts of the body for pain relief. Many Chinese herbal remedies have been used by American drug companies as the basis for modern medicines.

China has rich literary traditions. Painting, porcelain, sculpture, and carving of ivory, stone, and wood are also popular. Performing arts emphasize traditional folktales and stories shown in dances or operas with elaborate costumes.

✔ **READING CHECK:** *(Human Systems)* What is China's culture like?

▲

For more than 200 years the Beijing Opera, or Peking Opera, has been recognized worldwide for its artistic contributions. Originally performed for the royal family, it is now viewed by the public and is aired on Chinese television and radio stations.

Section Review 2

Homework Practice Online
Keyword: SK5 HP16

Define or identify: emperor, dynasty, Confucius, porcelain, Genghis Khan, Sun Yat-sen, Mao Zedong, martial law, Dalai Lama, pagodas

Working with Sketch Maps On the map you created in Section 1, label China and the Great Wall. Why do you think the Chinese chose to build the Great Wall where they did?

Reading for the Main Idea

1. *(Human Systems)* What contributions did the Qin and Han dynasties make to Chinese history?

2. *(Human Systems)* How did Mao's rule change China?

3. *(Human Systems)* How has China changed since Mao's death in 1976?

Critical Thinking

4. Summarizing What are three philosophies or religions that have been important in China? Describe them.

Organizing What You Know

5. Summarizing Copy the following graphic organizer. Use it to describe the Ming and the Manchu.

Ming Dynasty	Manchu

Read to Discover

1. Where do most of China's people live?
2. What are the major cities in China, and what are they like?
3. What is China's economy like?
4. What challenges does China face?

Vocabulary

command economy
multiple cropping
most-favored-nation
   status

Places

Shanghai
Nanjing
Wuhan
Chongqing

Beijing
Hong Kong
Macao

Reading Strategy

READING ORGANIZER Before you read this section, create a concept map. Draw a circle in the center of a sheet of paper. Label the circle China Today. Draw four lines coming out of the circle. Then draw a circle at the end of each line. Label the circles Population, Cities, Economy, and Challenges. As you read, write what you learn about each topic beside its circle.

China's Population

China has the largest population in the world—some 1.28 billion people. That number is equal to about 20 percent of the world's population. More people live in China than in all of Europe, Russia, and the United States combined. China's population is growing rapidly—by about 11 million each year. Some years ago, China's leaders took steps to bring the growth rate under control. They encouraged people to delay getting married and starting families. The government also tried to limit couples to one child.

China's population is not evenly distributed across the land. The western half of the country, which is mostly desert and mountain ranges, is almost empty. Just 10 percent of China's people live there. The rest are crowded into the country's eastern half. In fact, more people live in the North China Plain than in the entire United States. However, this region is only about the size of Texas. Most Chinese live in the countryside. Even so, China has 40 cities with populations greater than 1 million.

✓ **READING CHECK:** (*Human Systems*) Where do most of China's people live?

COMPARING POPULATIONS

China and the United States

China

United States

= 150,000,000 people

Source: Central Intelligence Agency, *The World Factbook 2003*

Interpreting the Chart How many people does one figure on the chart represent?

China's Cities

Studying China's physical features helps explain why its residents live where they do. By locating rivers and river valleys, we can see where millions of people could best survive.

Several of China's most important cities are located on the Chang River. Shanghai, the country's largest city, lies on the Chang Delta. It serves as China's leading industrial center and is the major seaport.

Using the map in Section 1, follow the course of the Chang River inland. Locate the cities of Nanjing and Wuhan (WOO-HAHN). These two industrial centers were built around iron-ore and coal mines. If you continue to follow the river upstream, you will reach Chongqing (CHOOHNG-CHING), located in the Sichuan Basin. It is one of the few large cities in China's interior. Guangzhou, located at the mouth of the Xi River, is southern China's largest city. Long famous as a trading center, it was known in the West as Canton. Today Guangzhou is one of China's major industrial cities.

Beijing, also known as Peking, is China's capital. It was built more than 3,000 years ago as a trading center. Beijing is the largest city in northern China and is well known for its cultural heritage.

Southeast of Guangzhou is Hong Kong. With a population of 6.5 million, Hong Kong is one of the world's most densely populated places. It is only half as large as Rhode Island, but has more than seven times as many people. Hong Kong is China's major southern seaport and is a center for banking, international trade, and tourism.

The British occupied the island of Hong Kong in the 1830s. In the late 1800s Hong Kong was leased to the British for 99 years. The lease ran out in 1997, and the British left. Hong Kong then became a special administrative region of China. Hong Kong has some political independence and is allowed to maintain its free-market economy. Macao, a nearby port city, was once a Portuguese colony. At the end of 1999, it was returned to China.

✔ **READING CHECK:** (*Places and Regions*) What are the major cities of China?

Towering skyscrapers mark Shanghai's constantly changing skyline.

Interpreting the Visual Record (*Place*)
How can you tell this city is growing rapidly?

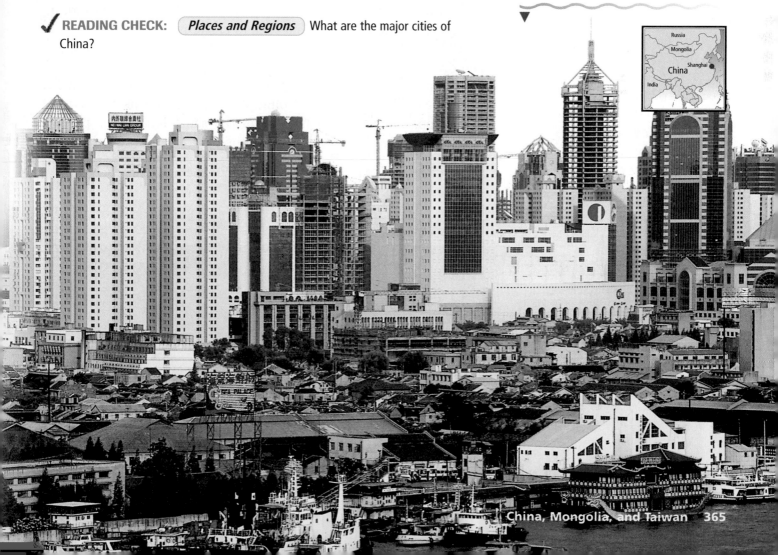

China's Economy

When the Chinese Communists took power in 1949 they set up a **command economy**. In this type of economy, the government owns most industries and makes most economic decisions. It set almost all production goals, prices, and wages.

Industry The Communists took over an economy that was based almost entirely on farming. Soon the Communist government introduced programs to increase literacy and build industry. Today, China produces everything from satellites and rockets to toys.

In the late 1970s the government began to introduce elements of free enterprise. Now farmers can grow and market their own crops on part of their rented land. Many state-run factories are being closed or turned over to private industries. Millions of Chinese have started small businesses. A few Chinese have become wealthy. Some business owners can afford to build private homes and to buy cars and computers. However, most Chinese are poor.

Agriculture Only about 10 percent of China's land is good for farming. Nevertheless, China is a world leader in the production of many crops and can meet most of its food needs. China's huge workforce makes this possible. More than 50 percent of Chinese workers are farmers. Having many farmers means the land can be intensively worked to produce high yields. Farmers have also increased production by cutting terraces into hillsides to create new farmland.

China is divided between rice-growing and wheat-growing regions. The divide lies midway between the Huang and the Chang River. To the south, rice is the main crop. Here the warm wet weather makes **multiple cropping** possible. Multiple cropping means that two or three crops are raised each year on the same land. This practice makes southern China more prosperous than northern China.

✔ **READING CHECK:** (*Human Systems*) What kind of economy does China have?

Models of rice fields like these have been found in Han dynasty tombs.

Interpreting the Visual Record

(*Human-Environment Interaction*) **What resources appear to be necessary for growing rice in this region?**

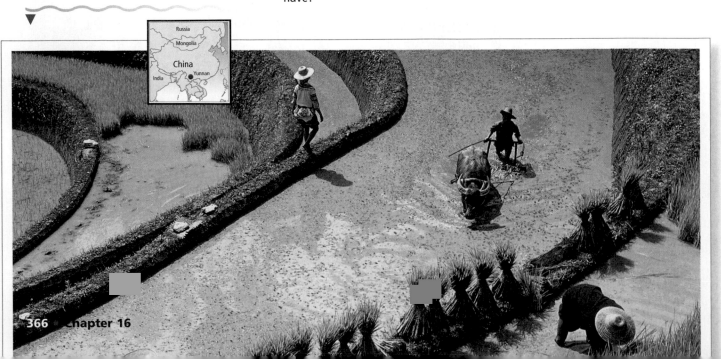

China's Government

After Mao's death in 1976, the new Chinese communist leadership admitted some past mistakes. It tried to modernize the government.

Although the government has allowed individuals some economic freedom, it restricts political and religious freedom. In 1989 the Chinese army was called in to attack pro-democracy student demonstrators in Tiananmen Square in Beijing (BAY-JING). Many students were injured or killed. Other rebellions among China's ethnic minorities, particularly in Tibet, have been crushed.

✓ **READING CHECK:** (*Human Systems*) What freedoms does China's government restrict?

Future Challenges

China has enjoyed remarkable economic success in recent years. China's drive to industrialize has caused major problems. For example, the air and water are badly polluted by factory wastes.

Another challenge involves the government's unwillingness to match the new economic freedoms with political reforms. China's human rights record has affected its economic relations with other countries. The U.S. government has considered canceling China's **most-favored-nation status** several times. Countries with this status get special trade advantages from the United States. China's economic future might depend on its government's willingness to accept political reforms.

✓ **READING CHECK:** (*Human Systems*) What challenges does China face?

By the mid-1990s clothing, electrical equipment, footwear, textiles, and other consumer goods were among China's leading exports. Employees of the Bei Bei Shoe Factory glue soles on by hand on an assembly line in Shanghai.

Homework Practice Online
Keyword: SK5 HP16

Section Review 3

Define and explain: command economy, multiple cropping, most-favored-nation status

Working with Sketch Maps On the map you created in Section 2, label Shanghai, Nanjing, Wuhan, Chongqing, Beijing, Hong Kong, and Macao. In the margin of your map, draw a box for each city. List the characteristics of each city in its box.

Reading for the Main Idea

1. (*Places and Regions*) Where do most people in China live? Why?

2. (*Places and Regions*) Along which rivers are several of China's most important cities located? Why?

3. (*Environment and Society*) What farming practices have allowed the Chinese to increase production?

Critical Thinking

4. **Finding the Main Idea** How has the Chinese government changed its economic policies since the late 1970s? What has been the impact of these changes?

Organizing What You Know

5. **Summarizing** Copy the following graphic organizer. Use it to describe the kinds of challenges facing China today. Identify specific environmental, political, and economic challenges.

Challenges

Read to Discover

1. How has Mongolia's culture developed?
2. What is Taiwan's culture like?

Vocabulary

gers

Places

Mongolia
Ulaanbaatar
Taiwan
Kao-hsiung
Taipei

People

Chiang Kai-shek

Reading Strategy

FOLDNOTES: TWO-PANEL FLIP CHART Create a **Two-Panel Flip Chart** as described in the Appendix. Label one of the flaps Mongolia and the other flap Taiwan. As you read this section, write what you learn about each country beneath its flap.

Mongolia

Mongolia is home to the Mongol people and has a fascinating history. You will learn of invaders and conquests and a culture that prizes horses.

Mongolia's History Today when people discuss the world's leading countries, they do not mention Mongolia. However, 700 years ago Mongolia was perhaps the greatest power in the world. Led by Genghis Khan, the Mongols conquered much of Asia, including China. Later leaders continued the conquests, building the greatest empire the world had seen. The Mongol Empire reached its height in the late 1200s.

It stretched from Europe's Danube River in the west to the Pacific Ocean in the east. Over time, however, the empire declined. In the late 1600s Mongolia fell under the rule of China.

In 1911, with Russian support, Mongolia declared its independence from China. Communists took control of the country 13 years later and established the Mongolian People's Republic. The country then came under the influence of the Soviet Union. Mongolia became particularly dependent on the Soviet Union for economic aid. This aid ended when the Soviet Union collapsed

This engraving shows early Mongolian soldiers.

Movement Nomads of Mongolia live in *gers* like those shown here.

in the early 1990s. Since then, Mongolians have struggled to build a democratic government and a free-market economy.

Mongolia's Culture Despite years of Communist rule and recent Western influence, the Mongolian way of life remains quite traditional. Many people still follow a nomadic lifestyle. They live as herders, driving their animals across Mongolia's vast grasslands. They make their homes in **gers** (GUHRZ). These are large, circular felt tents that are easy to raise, dismantle, and move.

Since most people live as herders, horses play an important role in Mongolian life. Mongolian children learn to ride when they are very young—often before they are even five years old. In Mongolia, the most powerful piece in the game of chess is the horse, not the queen.

Mongolia Today Mongolia is a large country—slightly larger than Alaska. Its population numbers just over 2.7 million. Some 25 percent of Mongolians live in Ulaanbaatar (oo-lahn-BAH-tawr), the capital city. Ulaanbaatar is also Mongolia's main industrial and commercial center. Mongolia's other cities are quite small. Not one has a population greater than 100,000.

✔ **READING CHECK:** (*Human Systems*) What are some elements of Mongolian culture?

Our Amazing Planet

In the Gobi, temperatures can range from -40°F (-40°C) in January to 113°F (45°C) in July. Some areas of this desert receive little more than 2 inches (5 cm) of rain each year.

Taiwan

For many years the island of Taiwan was known in the West as Formosa. This name came from Portuguese sailors who visited the island in the late 1500s. They thought the island was so lovely that they called it *Ilha Formosa*, or "beautiful island."

Chiang Kai-shek served in the Japanese army before returning to China to help overthrow the Manchu dynasty. He was head of the Nationalist government in China for 20 years, then moved with his followers to Taiwan.

Region Taiwan has good farmlands, but the island's eastern half is mountainous.

Taiwan's History The Chinese began settling Taiwan in the A.D. 600s. Some 600 years later the Japanese took control of eastern Taiwan. The search for spices brought European traders to Taiwan. The Dutch, Portuguese, and Spanish all tried to set up bases there. However, raiders from mainland China drove out these Europeans in the mid-1600s.

The struggle among the Chinese, Japanese, and Europeans for control of Taiwan continued until the late 1800s. In 1895 a treaty between the Chinese and the Japanese gave Taiwan to Japan. The Japanese then tried to force their way of life on the people of Taiwan. The Taiwanese rebelled against these efforts, but their revolts were crushed by the Japanese military.

After Japan's surrender at the end of World War II in 1945, China once again took command of Taiwan. In 1949 Mao Zedong established the People's Republic of China in mainland China. Chiang Kai-shek and the Nationalist Chinese government fled to Taiwan. The Nationalist government controlled Taiwan through martial law for decades. In recent years, however, the government has expanded democratic rights. China still claims that Taiwan is a province of China—not an independent country.

Taiwan's Culture Taiwan's history is reflected in its culture. Its population is about 85 percent native Taiwanese. They are descendants of people who migrated from China to Taiwan over hundreds of years. Chinese ways dominate Taiwan's culture. However, some building styles and certain foods reflect Japanese influences. European and American practices and customs have strongly influenced Taiwan's way of life in recent years. This is particularly true in the cities.

Taiwan Today Taiwan has a modern, industrial economy and a population of about 22 million. These people live on an island the size of Delaware and Maryland combined. Most people live on the western coastal plain of Taiwan. Population densities there can reach higher than 2,700 per square mile (1,042 per sq km). Taiwan's two largest cities, Kao-hsiung (KOW-SHYOOHNG) and Taipei (TY-PAY), are located on the coastal plain. Taipei is the capital city. It faces serious overcrowding and environmental problems. The thousands of cars, motorcycles, and trucks that clog Taipei's streets each day cause severe air pollution.

In the early 1950s Taiwan's economy was still largely based on agriculture. Today, however, only about 8 percent of workers make a living as farmers. Even so, Taiwan still produces enough rice—the country's chief food crop—to feed all of its people. Taiwan's farmers also grow fruits, sugarcane, tea, and vegetables.

Taiwan now has one of Asia's most successful economies. It is a world leader in the production and export of computers and sports equipment.

Taipei, Taiwan, was founded in the 1700s and has developed into an important city for overseas trade.

✓ **READING CHECK:** (*Human Systems*) What are some elements of the culture of Taiwan?

Section Review 4

Define or identify: *gers,* Chiang Kai-shek

Working with Sketch Maps On the map you created in Section 3, label Mongolia, Ulaanbaatar, Taiwan, Kao-hsiung, and Taipei. In the border of your map, draw a box for each city. Describe each city in its box. How has the history of each city played a part in its growth?

Reading for the Main Idea

1. (*Human Systems*) How do most people earn a living in Mongolia?

2. (*Human Systems*) Write a brief outline of the significant individuals or groups that have influenced Taiwan's history.

3. (*Human Systems*) How has Taiwan's economy changed since the early 1950s?

Critical Thinking

4. **Analyzing Information** What are some problems Taiwan faces today?

Organizing What You Know

5. **Summarizing** Copy the following graphic organizer. Use it to design and write two postcards to a friend describing life in Mongolia. In your postcards, note how life follows traditional patterns yet is also undergoing changes.

China, Mongolia, and Taiwan • 371

Review and Practice

Define and Identify

Identify each of the following:

1. dikes
2. arable
3. emperor
4. Confucius
5. dynasty
6. porcelain
7. Genghis Khan
8. Sun Yat-sen
9. martial law
10. Mao Zedong
11. Dalai Lama
12. pagodas
13. command economy
14. multiple cropping
15. most-favored-nation status
16. *gers*
17. Chiang Kai-shek

Review the Main Ideas

18. What physical features separate this region's mountain ranges?
19. Why is the Huang called the Yellow River?
20. What idea did the first emperor of the Qin dynasty have that greatly affected the landscape of China?
21. What was the purpose of the Cultural Revolution in China?
22. How does Hong Kong differ from the rest of China?

23. What do more than 50 percent of China's workers do for a living?
24. What country discussed in this chapter once ruled a vast empire that stretched into Europe?
25. What are Taiwan's leading exports?

Think Critically

26. **Drawing Inferences and Conclusions** Why do you think so few Europeans reached China before the 1500s?
27. **Drawing Inferences and Conclusions** How might Chinese history have been different if Europeans had not forced trade upon the Chinese?
28. **Finding the Main Idea** What was the Cultural Revolution and how did it affect life in China?
29. **Making Generalizations and Predictions** In what ways does modern technology threaten the Chinese government's ability to control the flow of information in the country? What changes might the free flow of information bring to China?
30. **Analyzing Information** How is Taiwan's history reflected in the island's culture today?

Map Activity

31. On a separate sheet of paper, match the letters on the map with their correct labels.

Mount Everest	Chang River
Plateau of Tibet	Great Wall
North China Plain	Shanghai
Huang River	Hong Kong
	Ulaanbaatar

Writing Activity

Imagine that you are a Chinese university professor. Using the time line in section 2, the text, and other sources, write a brief lesson plan on China's history. You may want to include some visuals, such as photographs of artifacts, in your lesson plan. Be sure to use standard grammar, spelling, sentence structure, and punctuation.

☐ **internet** connect

Internet Activity: go.hrw.com
KEYWORD: SK5 GT16

Choose a topic to explore about China, Mongolia, and Taiwan:
- Follow the Great Wall of China.
- Visit the land of Genghis Khan.
- See the artistic treasures of China.

Social Studies Skills Practice

Interpreting Graphs

Study the following graph and answer the questions.

Total Population of China, 1949–1989

Source: *The Cambridge Handbook of Contemporary China*, 1991

1. What was the total population of China in 1950?
2. During what period did the population decline?
3. In what year did the population reach one billion?
4. How much did the population grow between 1965 and 1985?

Analyzing Primary Sources

Read the following passage from a 1993 U.S. State Department publication on Mongolia. Then answer the questions.

"As a result of rapid urbanization and industrial growth policies under the communist regime, Mongolia's deteriorating environment has become a major concern. The burning of soft coal coupled with thousands of factories in Ulaanbaatar has resulted in severely polluted air. Deforestation, overgrazed pastures, and . . . by plowing up more virgin land has increased soil erosion. The government responded by . . . increasing publicity on environmental issues."

1. What are the two main causes of environmental problems in Mongolia?
2. What is the result of burning coal in Mongolia?
3. How has agricultural development affected the environment?
4. How might publicity help solve the problem of environmental damage?

Japan and the Koreas

Now we continue east to North and South Korea and the island nation of Japan. First we meet Akiko, a Japanese student whose school day may be very different from yours.

Konichiwa! (Good afternoon!) I'm Akiko, and I'm in the seventh grade at Yamate school. Every morning except Sunday I put on my school uniform and eat rice soup and pickles before I leave for school. The train I take is so crowded I can't move. At school, I study reading, math, English, science, and writing. I know 1,800 Japanese characters, but I need to know about 3,000 to pass the ninth grade exams. For lunch, I eat rice and cold fish my mom packed for me. Before we can go home, we clean the school floors, desks, and windows. My dad usually isn't home until after 11:00 P.M., so my mom helps me with my homework in the "big" (8 feet by 8 feet) room of our three-room apartment. In the evenings, I go to a *juku* school to study for the ninth grade exams. If I do not do well, I will not go to a good high school, and my whole family will be ashamed. On Sundays, I sometimes go with my parents to visit my grandparents, who are rice farmers. I like rock music a lot, especially U2.

こんにちは.
私は東京に
住んでいます.

Translation: Good afternoon. I live in Tokyo.

Section 1 Physical Geography

Read to Discover

1. What are the physical features of Japan and the Koreas?
2. What natural resources does the region have?
3. Which climate types are found in the region?

Vocabulary

tsunamis
Oyashio Current
Japan Current

Places

Korean Peninsula
Sea of Japan
Hokkaido

Honshu
Shikoku
Kyushu

Reading Strategy

FOLDNOTES: DOUBLE-DOOR Create a **Double-Door** FoldNote as described in the Appendix. Label the outer flaps Japan and the Koreas. As you read this section, write what you learn about the physical features, resources, and climate of Japan in the center section, North Korea in the top section, and South Korea in the bottom section.

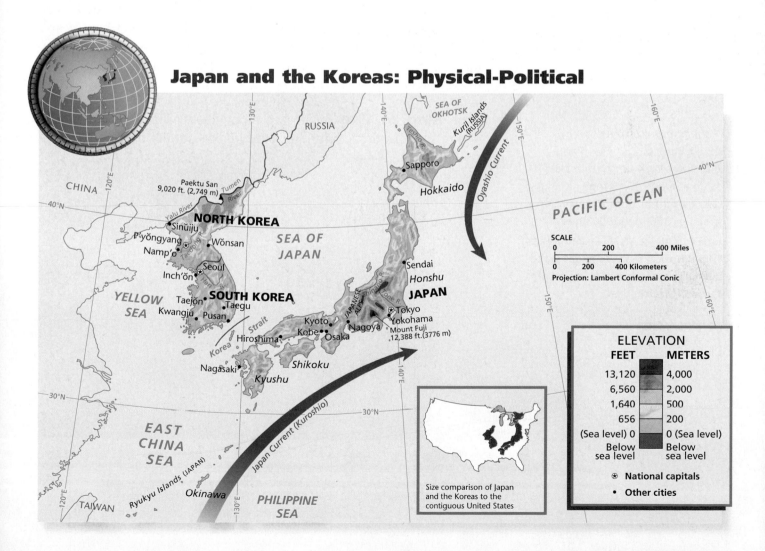

Japan and the Koreas: Physical-Political

Physical Features

The Korean Peninsula extends southward about 600 miles (965 km) from mainland Asia. The peninsula is relatively close to southern Japan.

The Korean Peninsula is about the same size as Utah. It contains two countries, North Korea and South Korea. The Yalu and Tumen Rivers separate North Korea from China. The Tumen River also forms a short border with Russia. Off the coast of the Korean Peninsula lie more than 3,500 islands.

The Sea of Japan separates Japan from the Eurasian mainland. The narrow Korea Strait lies between South Korea and the island country of Japan. No place in Japan is more than 90 miles (145 km) from the sea. Japan is about the size of California. It is made up of four large islands called the home islands. The country also includes more than 3,000 smaller islands. The home islands from north to south are Hokkaido (hoh-KY-doh), Honshu (HAWN-shoo), Shikoku (shee-KOH-koo), and Kyushu (KYOO-shoo). South of the home islands are Japan's Ryukyu (ree-YOO-kyoo) Islands. Okinawa is the largest of these islands. Fewer than half of the Ryukyus are inhabited.

Mountains Rugged and heavily forested mountains are a common sight in the landscape of this region. Mountains cover about 75 percent of Japan. Many of Japan's mountains were formed by volcanic activity. The country's longest mountain range, the Japanese Alps, forms a volcanic spine through Honshu. The small amount of plains in these countries is found along the coasts and river valleys.

The Ring of Fire Japan lies along the Pacific Ring of Fire—a region of volcanic activity and earthquakes. Under Japan the dense

Our Amazing Planet

The world's largest crab lives off the southeastern coast of Japan. The giant spider crab can grow larger than 12 feet (3.6 m) across (from claw to claw). It can also weigh more than 40 pounds (18 kg)!

A *shinkansen*, or bullet train, speeds past Mount Fuji. This Hiroshima-to-Kokura train travels at an average 162.3 mph (261.8 kmh) but has a maximum speed of 186 mph (300 kmh).

Interpreting the Visual Record (Place)
What physical features might make building railroads in this region of Japan difficult?

Pacific plate dives beneath the lighter Eurasian and Philippine plates. This subduction zone borders the Pacific side of the Japanese islands, forming the Japan Trench. This is one of the deepest places on the ocean floor. The movement of one tectonic plate below another builds up tension in Earth's crust. The Eurasian plate buckles and pushes up, creating mountains and fractures in the crust. Magma flows up through these fractures. Where magma rises to the surface, it forms volcanoes. Today, Japan has about 40 active volcanoes. Mount Fuji (FOO-jee), Japan's highest peak, is an inactive volcano.

Because Japan lies along a subduction zone, earthquakes are also common. As many as 1,500 occur every year. Most are minor quakes. In 1995, however, an earthquake killed more than 5,000 people in Kobe.

Underwater earthquakes sometimes create huge waves called **tsunamis** (tsoo-NAH-mees). These dangerous waves can travel hundreds of miles per hour. They can also be as tall as a 10-story building when they reach shore. In 1993 a tsunami caused terrible destruction when it struck the coast of Hokkaido.

Unlike Japan, the Korean Peninsula is not located in a subduction zone. As a result, it has no active volcanoes and is dominated by eroded mountains. Earthquakes are quite rare.

✔ **READING CHECK:** (*Places and Regions*) What are the physical features of Japan and the Koreas?

Natural Resources

Except for North Korea, the region is not rich in natural resources. It has no oil or natural gas. The Korean Peninsula's mountainous terrain and rivers, however, are good for producing hydroelectric power. North Korea also has iron ore, copper, zinc, lead, and coal.

Japan lies near one of the world's best fisheries. East of Japan the cool **Oyashio** (oh-YAH-shee-oh) **Current** dives beneath the warm, less dense **Japan Current**. The cool water scours the bottom, bringing nutrients to the surface. Fish can find plentiful food to eat in this rich marine environment.

✔ **READING CHECK:**
(*Places and Regions*) What are the region's natural resources?

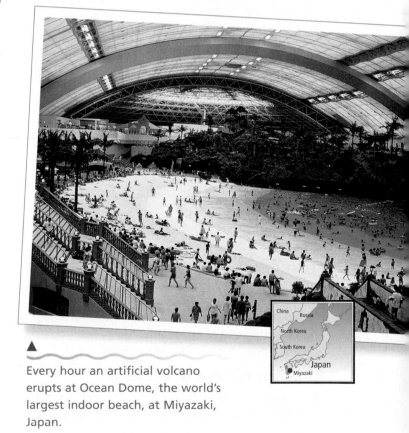

▲ Every hour an artificial volcano erupts at Ocean Dome, the world's largest indoor beach, at Miyazaki, Japan.

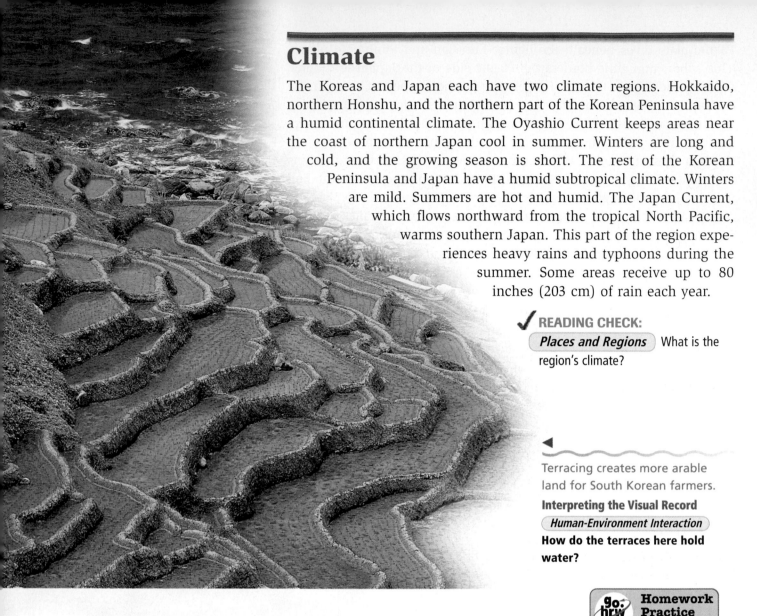

Climate

The Koreas and Japan each have two climate regions. Hokkaido, northern Honshu, and the northern part of the Korean Peninsula have a humid continental climate. The Oyashio Current keeps areas near the coast of northern Japan cool in summer. Winters are long and cold, and the growing season is short. The rest of the Korean Peninsula and Japan have a humid subtropical climate. Winters are mild. Summers are hot and humid. The Japan Current, which flows northward from the tropical North Pacific, warms southern Japan. This part of the region experiences heavy rains and typhoons during the summer. Some areas receive up to 80 inches (203 cm) of rain each year.

✓ **READING CHECK:**
Places and Regions What is the region's climate?

◀ Terracing creates more arable land for South Korean farmers.

Interpreting the Visual Record
Human-Environment Interaction
How do the terraces here hold water?

 Homework Practice Online
Keyword: SK5 HP17

Section Review 1

Define and explain: tsunamis, Oyashio Current, Japan Current

Working with Sketch Maps On a map of Japan and the Koreas that you draw or that your teacher provides, label the following: the Korean Peninsula, Sea of Japan, Hokkaido, Honshu, Shikoku, and Kyushu. On what physical features might Japan and the Koreas depend for their economies?

Reading for the Main Idea

1. (*Physical Systems*) How has Japan's location in a subduction zone made it different from the Koreas?

2. (*Physical Systems*) How do ocean currents affect the climates of Japan?

Critical Thinking

3. **Drawing Inferences and Conclusions** How do you think residents are affected by this region's mountainous terrain and the nearness of the sea?

4. **Making Generalizations and Predictions** What can you predict about South Korea's and Japan's economies?

Organizing What You Know

5. **Summarizing** List the landforms, natural resources, and climates of Japan, North Korea, and South Korea.

	Landforms	Resources	Climate
Japan			
South Korea			
North Korea			

Section 2 The History and Culture of Japan

Read to Discover

1. What was Japan's early history and culture like?
2. How did the modernization of Japan take place?

Vocabulary

Shintoism
shamans
samurai
shogun
Diet

People

Murasaki Shikibu

Reading Strategy

FOLDNOTES: KEY-TERM FOLD Create a **Key-Term Fold** FoldNote as described in the Appendix. Then write a vocabulary term from the section on each tab. Under each tab, write the definition of the term.

Early Japan

Japan's first inhabitants came from central Asia thousands of years ago. Rice farming was introduced to Japan from China and Korea about 300 B.C. As the population increased, farmers irrigated new land for growing rice. They also built dikes and canals to channel water into the rice paddies. Local chieftains organized the workers and controlled the flow of water. This control allowed the chieftains to extend their political power over larger areas.

Religion The earliest known religion of Japan, **Shintoism**, centers around the *kami*. *Kami* are spirits of natural places, sacred animals, and ancestors. Many of Japan's mountains and rivers are sacred in Shintoism. **Shamans**, or priests who communicated with the spirits, made the *kami*'s wishes known.

Buddhism and Confucianism were later introduced from China. Buddhist shrines were often located next to older *kami* shrines. Today, as in the past, most Japanese practice Shintoism and Buddhism. As you learned in an earlier chapter, the principles of Confucianism include respect for elders, parents, and rulers.

Todaiji Temple in Nara, Japan, contains the largest wooden hall in the world and a statue of Buddha that is more than 48 feet (15 m) tall.

Interpreting the Visual Record *Place*
What interesting features do you see in this building's architecture?

CONNECTING TO Art

A Japanese scroll painting showing a scene from The Tale of Genji.

Japanese Scroll Paintings

Beginning in the 1100s and 1200s Japanese artists created beautifully detailed ink paintings on paper scrolls. This form of art originated in China where artists painted mostly mountain landscapes. In Japan, however, scroll paintings told stories. The themes of many scroll paintings included Buddhist teachings and historical subjects.

Many Japanese scrolls were as long as 30 feet and included text. In these paintings, artists purposely left the roofs off of buildings so they could show the interiors.

Understanding What You Read
1. Where did scroll painting originate?
2. How did Japanese artists show the interior of buildings?

Murasaki Shikibu
(c. 978–c. 1026)

The women who lived at a Japanese emperor's court were educated in many areas. One of the women, Murasaki Shikibu, wrote the world's first novel—*The Tale of Genji*. The book describes court life in about A.D. 1000.

How might Murasaki Shikibu's life have compared with that of most Japanese women?

The Shoguns In the A.D. 700s Japan began to develop a political system of its own. Many small feudal domains were each ruled by a lord. **Samurai** (SA-muh-ry) were warriors who served the lords. Rivalries were put aside when a foreign threat appeared. For example, the feudal domains united against the Mongols in the 1200s. Later, power shifted from the emperor to a **shogun**. The word *shogun* means "great general" and is the highest rank for a warrior.

In the mid-1500s, Portuguese traders arrived in Japan. Spanish missionaries followed, introducing Christianity to Japan. Europeans were later forced to leave. Japanese leaders feared that foreign ideas might undermine Japanese society. Japan remained cut off from the Western world until the mid-1850s.

✓ **READING CHECK:** (*Human Systems*) What was early Japan like?

Modern Japan

In 1853 U.S. commodore Matthew Perry's warships sailed into Tokyo Bay. Perry displayed U.S. naval power and brought gifts that showed the wonders of American technology. Perry's arrival convinced the Japanese that they needed to become as politically strong as the Americans and Europeans. In the 1860s Japan began to industrialize and modernize its educational, legal, and governmental systems.

An Imperial Power Japan needed resources in order to industrialize. As a result, it began to expand its empire around 1900. Japan annexed, or took control of, Korea in 1910. Japan also took over northeastern China and its supply of coal and iron ore. Japan continued to expand in Asia during the late 1930s.

World War II During World War II Japan was an ally of Germany and Italy. Japan brought the United States into the war in 1941 by attacking the U.S. naval base at Pearl Harbor, Hawaii. Japan conquered much of Southeast Asia and many Pacific islands before being defeated by U.S. and Allied forces in 1945. With the end of World War II Japan lost its empire.

Government After World War II the United States occupied Japan until 1952. With U.S. aid, Japan began to rebuild into a major world industrial power. Japan also established a democratic government. Today, Japan is a constitutional monarchy with several political parties. The government is made up of the **Diet** (DY-uht)—an elected legislature—and a prime minister. Japan's emperor remains a symbol of the nation, but he has no political power.

▲

(*Movement*) Commodore Matthew Perry arrives in Japan in 1853.

✔ **READING CHECK:** (*Places and Regions*) How did Japan modernize?

Homework Practice Online
Keyword: SK5 HP17

Define or identify: Shintoism, shamans, Murasaki Shikibu, samurai, shogun, Diet

Working with Sketch Maps On the map you created in Section 1, label China and Korea. In a box in the margin, identify the body of water that separates Korea from Japan. Why do you think China and Korea had a strong influence on Japan's culture and history?

Reading for the Main Idea

1. (*Human Systems*) What religions have been practiced in Japan, and from where did they come?

2. (*Places and Regions*) Why did Japan decide to trade with the United States and Europe?

Critical Thinking

3. **Finding the Main Idea** How and why did rice farming develop in Japan?

4. **Analyzing Information** What influences do the principles of Confucianism have on the Japanese?

Organizing What You Know

5. **Sequencing** Copy the following graphic organizer. Use it to show important developments in modern Japanese history from the 1850s to today.

☐ ⇨ ☐ ⇨ ☐ ⇨ ☐ ⇨ ☐

Section 3 | Japan Today

Read to Discover

1. Where do most Japanese live?
2. What are the major Japanese cities like?
3. What is life in Japan like?
4. How has the Japanese economy developed?

Vocabulary

megalopolis
kimonos
futon
intensive cultivation
work ethic
protectionism
trade surplus

Places

Inland Sea
Osaka
Tokyo
Kobe
Kyoto

Reading Strategy

FOLDNOTES: TRI-FOLD Create a **Tri-Fold** FoldNote as described in the Appendix. Write what you know about Japan in the column labeled "Know." Then write what you want to know in the column labeled "Want." As you read the section, write what you learn about Japan in the column labeled "Learn."

▲ Beyond Tokyo's Nijubashi Bridge is the Imperial Palace, the home of the emperor.

Where People Live

Japan is one of the world's most densely populated countries. It is slightly smaller than California but has nearly four times as many people! There are an average of 863 people per square mile (333/sq km). However, Japan is very mountainous. Within its area of livable land, population density averages 7,680 people per square mile (2,964/sq km).

Most people live on the small coastal plains, particularly along the Pacific and the Inland Sea. Japan's major cities and farms compete for space on these narrow coastal plains. Only about 11 percent of Japan's land is arable, or fit for growing crops.

The Japanese have reclaimed land from the sea and rivers. In some places, they have built dikes to block off the water. They have drained the land behind the dikes so it could be used for farming or housing. They have even built artificial islands. The airport near Osaka, for example, was built on an artificial island in the early 1990s.

✓ **READING CHECK:** (*Human Systems*) Where do most people in Japan live?

Japan's Cities

Japan's cities, like major cities everywhere, are busy, noisy, and very crowded. Almost 30 million people live within 20 miles of the Imperial Palace in Tokyo. This densely populated area forms a **megalopolis**. A megalopolis is a giant urban area that often includes more than one city as well as the surrounding suburban areas. Yokohama is Japan's major seaport.

Most of Tokyo was built recently. An earthquake in 1923 and bombings during World War II destroyed most of the old buildings.

Tokyo is the capital and the center of government. Japan's banking, communications, and education are also centered here. Tokyo is densely populated, and land is scarce. As a result, Tokyo's real estate prices are among the world's highest.

Tokyo's Ginza shopping district is the largest in the world. Some department stores sell houses and cars and provide dental care. They also offer classes on how to properly wear **kimonos**—traditional robes—and to arrange flowers.

High rents in Ginza and elsewhere in Tokyo encourage the creative use of space. Tall buildings line the streets. However, shops are also found below the streets in the subway stations. Another way the Japanese have found to maximize space is the "capsule hotel." The guests in these hotels sleep in compartments too small to stand in upright. Businesspeople often stay in these hotels rather than commuting the long distances to their homes.

So many people commute to and from Tokyo that space on the trains must also be maximized. During peak travel periods, commuters are crammed into cars. They are helped by workers hired to push as many people into the trains as possible.

Another megalopolis in Japan is located in the Kansai region. It has three major cities: Osaka (oh-SAH-kah), Kobe (KOH-bay), and Kyoto (KYOH-toh). Industrial Osaka has been a trading center for centuries. Kobe is an important seaport. Kyoto was Japan's capital for more than 1,000 years.

✓ **READING CHECK:**

Places and Regions What is life like in Japan's major cities?

COUNTRY	POPULATION/ GROWTH RATE	LIFE EXPECTANCY	LITERACY RATE	PER CAPITA GDP
Japan	127,214,499 0.1%	78, male 84, female	99%	$28,000
United States	290,342,554 0.9%	74, male 80, female	97%	$37,600

Japan

Source: Central Intelligence Agency, *The World Factbook 2003*

Interpreting the Chart (*Place*) How does life expectancy in Japan compare to that of the United States?

Japanese workers stay focused on their responsibilities on an electronics production line.

▼

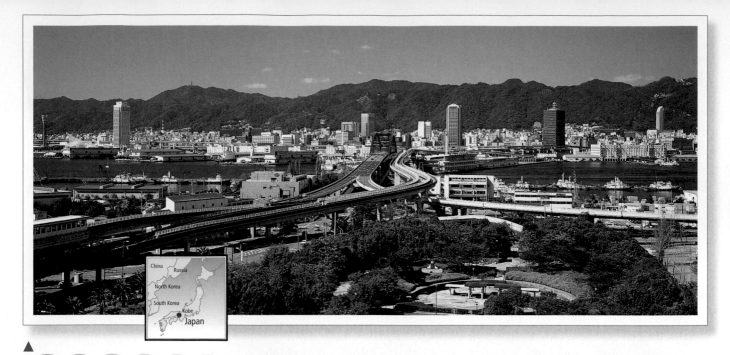

Location The port of Kobe is located in the central part of the Japanese islands.

Japanese and American all-star baseball teams compete in Yokohama.

Interpreting the Visual Record *Place*
How is this scoreboard different from one in the United States?

Life in Japan

Japan is a very homogeneous nation. In other words, almost everyone—more than 99 percent of the population—is ethnically Japanese and shares a common language and culture. Japanese society has traditionally been dominated by men, but this is changing. More Japanese women have jobs today than in the past, but most women are still expected to be dutiful wives and mothers. Many quit their jobs when they marry.

Many Japanese families live in suburbs, where housing is cheaper. As a result, many Japanese spend as much as three hours commuting to and from work.

Because land is so scarce, most Japanese homes do not have large yards. Most homes are also smaller than typical American homes. Rooms are usually used for more than one purpose. For example, a living room may also serve as a bedroom. During the day, people sit on cushions at low tables. At night, they sleep on the floor on a **futon** (FOO-tahn)—a lightweight cotton mattress. In the morning they put the mattress away, and the bedroom becomes a living room again.

For most occasions, people wear Western-style clothing. Many Japanese wear kimonos at festivals and weddings. Listening to music and playing video games are popular leisure activities. Baseball, golf, and skiing are also popular. On festival days, families may gather to enjoy the cherry blossoms or visit a local shrine or temple. They might also watch the ancient sport of sumo wrestling or traditional dramas on television. Many Japanese enjoy traditional arts such as the tea ceremony, flower arranging, growing dwarf potted trees called bonsai, and kite flying.

✔ READING CHECK: (*Human Systems*) What is life like in Japan?

Japan's Economy

Japan has few natural resources. It therefore imports many of the raw materials it uses to run its industries. Oil is one key material that Japan must import. The country produces about one third of its energy through nuclear power.

The sea is an important source of food. Japan has the world's largest fishing industry. It also imports fish from all over the world. Fish is a major part of the Japanese diet. In fact, Tokyo's largest fish market sells about 5 million pounds of seafood each day. The average Japanese eats more than 100 pounds of fish each year. In contrast, the average American eats less than 5 pounds each year.

Agriculture Most Japanese farms are located on Honshu. Many farmers own their land and live in small villages. Farms in Japan are much smaller than those in the United States. The average Japanese farm is about 2.5 acres (1 hectare). Most American farms are about 150 times larger. Japan's shortage of land means that there is little pastureland for livestock. Meat is a luxury. The Japanese get most of their protein from fish and soybeans.

Farmers make the most of their land by terracing the hillsides. This means cutting the hillside into a series of small flat fields. The terraces look like broad stair steps. The terraces give farmers more room to grow crops. Japanese farmers use **intensive cultivation**—the practice of growing food on every bit of available land. Even so, Japan must import about two thirds of its food.

Farmers are encouraged to stay on the land and to grow as much rice as possible. However, many farms are too small to be profitable. To solve this problem, the Japanese government buys the rice crop. The price is set high enough to allow farmers to support their families. The government then resells it at the same price. Because this price is much higher than the world market price, the government restricts rice imports.

Seeds of the tea plant were first brought to Japan about A.D. 800. Tea is now an important product of southern Japan. Top-quality teas are harvested by hand only. Workers pick just the tender young leaves at the plant's tip.

Interpreting the Visual Record

(*Human-Environment Interaction*)

How might using machines for harvesting leaves affect the quality of the tea?

Currency and Trade

Trading between Japan and other nations would not be possible without currency, or money. Because countries around the world use different currencies, nations have created an exchange rate that tells them how much one currency is worth in another. Japanese currency is based on the yen. If a U.S. company wanted to buy computers made in Japan, the U.S. company would need to convert the price of the computers from yens to dollars to figure out the value. This system of conversion allows nations to trade with each other.

Japanese currency is based on the yen.

Industry Japan imports most of its raw resources. These resources are then used to make goods for export. For example, Japan is known for its high-quality automobiles. Japan also makes televisions, cameras, and compact disc players.

Japan's economic success is due in part to a high literacy rate and the people's strong **work ethic**. Most Japanese work for large companies and respect their leaders. In return, employers look after workers' needs by offering job security, exercise classes, and other benefits.

The Japanese have also benefited from investments in other countries. For example, some Japanese companies have built automobile factories in the United States. Other Japanese companies have invested in the American entertainment and real estate industries.

Japan and the Global Market Japan's market economy depends on trade, particularly with countries in the Pacific Rim. In the past the government set up trade barriers to protect Japan's industries from foreign competition. This practice is called **protectionism**. This has helped Japan build up a huge **trade surplus**. Some countries have objected to Japan's trade practices and set up barriers against Japanese goods. As a result, Japan has eased trade barriers.

Japan has other economic problems, too. Some Asian countries that pay lower wages are able to produce goods more cheaply than Japan. Japan faced an economic slowdown during the 1990s. It is now in a recovery and slow-growth period.

✔ **READING CHECK:** (**Human Systems**) How have Japan's leaders tried to protect the nation's economy?

Section Review 3

Define and explain: megalopolis, kimonos, futon, intensive cultivation, work ethic, protectionism, trade surplus

Working with Sketch Maps On the map you created in Section 2, label Inland Sea, Osaka, Tokyo, Kobe, and Kyoto. Draw a box in the margin of your map. What do the cities have in common? Write your answer in the margin box.

Reading for the Main Idea

1. (**Environment and Society**) How does Japan's physical geography affect farming?

2. (**Human Systems**) How has Japan developed its industries without plentiful raw materials?

Critical Thinking

3. **Drawing Inferences and Conclusions** In what ways do the daily lives of the Japanese reflect influences of Western culture?

4. **Drawing Inferences and Conclusions** Why do you suppose other countries might be concerned about Japan's surplus?

Organizing What You Know

5. **Summarizing** Copy the following graphic organizer. Use it to list the activities and services available in Tokyo.

Tokyo

Read to Discover

1. What was Korea's ancient history like?

2. What were the major events of Korea's early modern period?

3. Why was Korea divided after World War II, and what were the effects of the division?

Vocabulary

demilitarized zone

Places

North Korea
South Korea

Reading Strategy

TAKING NOTES Use the headings in this section to create an outline. As you read, write what you learn about the history and culture of the Koreas under each heading.

Ancient Korea

Korea's earliest inhabitants were nomadic hunters from north and central Asia. About 1500 B.C. they adopted rice farming, which had been introduced from China. Then, in 108 B.C., the Chinese invaded Korea. This invasion marked the beginning of a long period of Chinese influence on Korean culture. The Chinese introduced their system of writing and their system of examinations for government jobs. They also introduced Buddhism and Confucianism to Korea.

Korea's original religion—shamanism—continued to be practiced, along with the newer traditions introduced from China. According to shamanism, natural places and ancestors have spirits. Many mountains are particularly sacred to Koreans. Shamanism is still practiced in South Korea.

Over the centuries, Korean tribes eventually recaptured most of the peninsula. In the A.D. 600s the kingdom of Silla (SI-luh) united the peninsula. Korea's golden age began. Korea became known in Asia for its architecture, painting, ceramics, and fine jewelry.

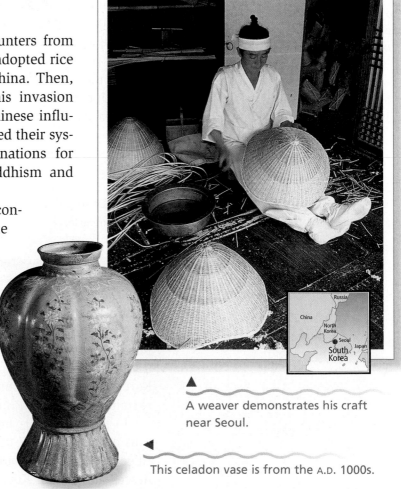

A weaver demonstrates his craft near Seoul.

This celadon vase is from the A.D. 1000s.

Heavy fencing and explosives have kept people out of the demilitarized zone for decades. As a result, this land has provided a safe home for rare animal and plant species. Some scientists hope that in the future the DMZ can be set aside as a nature preserve, which would attract tourists while protecting the wildlife.

During the Silla period Korea began using the results of examinations to award government jobs. Generally only boys who were sons of noblemen could take the examinations. People from the lower classes could not rise to important positions by studying and passing the examinations, as they could in China.

By the early 900s a new kingdom had taken power. The modern name of Korea comes from this kingdom's name, Koryo. During the Koryo dynasty, Korean artisans invented the first movable metal type. During the following dynasty, scholars developed the Hangul (HAHN-gool) alphabet, which was officially adopted in 1446. Hangul was much easier to use with the Korean language than Chinese characters had been. Because Hangul had only 24 symbols, it was easier to learn. It had previously been necessary to memorize about 20,000 Chinese characters to read the Buddhist scriptures.

✓ **READING CHECK:** (*Human Systems*) How did the Chinese influence Korea's ancient history?

Early Modern Korea

By the early 1600s China again controlled Korea. For 300 years Korea remained under Chinese control. Closed off to most other outsiders, Korea became known as the Hermit Kingdom. During this period, Catholicism was introduced into Korea through missionaries in China. Korea's Christian community was sometimes persecuted and remained small until the mid-1900s.

In the mid-1890s Japan defeated China in the Sino-Japanese War. This cleared the way for Japan to annex Korea in 1910. The Japanese ruled harshly. They took over the Korean government and many businesses and farms. Koreans were forced to take Japanese names, and

Japanese was taught in the schools. Japan ruled Korea until the end of World War II.

✔ **READING CHECK:** (*Places and Regions*) What were some major events in Korea's early modern period?

A Divided Korea

At the end of World War II, U.S. and Soviet troops oversaw the Japanese departure from Korea. Because the Soviets wanted communism to spread to other countries, they helped Communist leaders take power in the north. The United States backed a democratic government in the south. The United Nations hoped that the Koreas would reunite. However, the United States and the Soviet Union could not agree on a plan. In 1948 South Korea officially became the Republic of Korea. North Korea became the Democratic People's Republic of Korea led by Korean Communist dictator Kim Il Sung.

In 1950 North Korea tried to unify the country by invading South Korea, resulting in the Korean War. The United Nations sent troops—mostly U.S.—to defend South Korea. Communist China sent forces to North Korea. A truce was declared in 1953, but Korea remains divided. The border between North Korea and South Korea is a strip of land roughly 2.4 miles (4 km) wide called the **demilitarized zone** (DMZ). This buffer zone separates the two countries. A total of about 1 million U.S., South Korean, and North Korean soldiers patrol the DMZ. It is the world's most heavily guarded border.

In 2000, the leaders of both Koreas met to discuss the future. Also, families that had been separated for decades were briefly reunited. However, the two Koreas have not agreed on terms of reunification.

✔ **READING CHECK:** (*Places and Regions*) What were some events in Korea's history after World War II?

Our Amazing Planet

Casting bronze bells is an ancient Korean craft. The largest bell in South Korea, completed in A.D. 771, is more than 12 feet (3.6 m) tall and weighs about 25 tons (110,000 kg). When struck, it is said that the bell's tone can be heard 40 miles (64 km) away.

Section Review 4

go.hrw.com **Homework Practice Online**
Keyword: SK5 HP17

Define and explain: demilitarized zone

Working with Sketch Maps On the map you created in Section 3, label North Korea and South Korea. In the margin, draw a box and include in it information that explains the significance of the DMZ. When was it established?

Reading for the Main Idea

1. (*Human Systems*) What were some of the accomplishments of the early Koreans before about 1600? What dynasty gave Korea its name?

2. (*Human Systems*) What long-lasting effect did the Korean War have on the Korean Peninsula?

Critical Thinking

3. **Analyzing Information** How has the Korean Peninsula been influenced by other countries?

4. **Making Generalizations and Predictions** What might be preventing North Korea and South Korea from reuniting?

Organizing What You Know

5. **Sequencing** Copy the following time line. Use it to list the important events of Korean history from 1500 B.C. through the 1500s.

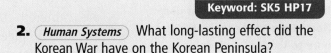

1500 B.C.   1500s

South and North Korea Today

Read to Discover

1. What are South Korea's government and society like?
2. What is South Korea's economy like?
3. What is North Korea like?
4. How has North Korea's government affected the country's development?

Vocabulary
entrepreneurs
chaebol
kimchi
famine

Places
Seoul
Pusan
P'yŏngyang

People
Kim Il Sung

Reading Strategy

READING ORGANIZER Create a spider map by drawing a circle on a sheet of paper. Label the circle South and North Korea Today. Create legs for People and Government, Society, and Economy. As you read the section, write what you learn about each country beneath each leg.

South Korea's People and Government

South Korea is densely populated. There are 1,197 people per square mile (462/sq km). Most people live in the narrow, fertile plain along the western coast of the Korean Peninsula. Travel in the peninsula's mountainous interior is difficult, so few people live there. South Korea's population is growing slowly, at about the same rate as in most industrialized countries.

South Korea's Cities Because South Korea is densely populated, space is a luxury—just as it is in Japan. Most South Koreans live in small apartments in crowded cities. Seoul (SOHL) is the country's capital and largest city. The government, the economy, and the educational system are centered there. After the Korean War, the population exploded because refugees flocked to Seoul seeking work and housing. By 1994 the city had nearly 11 million residents. Today, Seoul is one of the world's most densely populated cities. It has some 7,000 people per square mile (2,703/sq km).

South Korea's second-largest city is Pusan (POO-sahn). This major seaport and industrial center lies on the southern coast. Pusan also has an important fishing industry.

The rapid growth of South Korea's cities has brought problems. Housing is expensive. The many factories, cars, and coal-fired heating systems sometimes cause dangerous levels of air pollution. Industrial waste has also polluted the water.

Interpreting the Chart How does North Korea's per capita GDP compare to that of South Korea?

North Korea and South Korea

Country	Population/ Growth Rate	Life Expectancy	Literacy Rate	Per Capita GDP
North Korea	22,466,481 1.1%	68, male 74, female	99%	$1,000
South Korea	48,289,037 0.7%	72, male 79, female	98%	$19,400
United States	290,342,554 0.9%	74, male 80, female	97%	$37,600

Source: Central Intelligence Agency, *The World Factbook 2003*

Postwar Government South Korea is technically a democracy, but it was run by military dictators until the late 1980s. More recently, South Korea introduced a multiparty democratic government. The government controls economic development but does not own businesses and property.

✔ **READING CHECK:** (*Human Systems*) What kind of government does South Korea have?

South Korean Society

Like Japan's, South Korea's population is homogeneous. Most Koreans complete high school. About half go on to some form of higher education. Women are beginning to hold important jobs.

Traditional Families Most Koreans marry someone they meet through their parents. Most families still value sons. This is because only a son can take over the family name. Only a son can lead the ceremonies to honor the family's ancestors. Some couples who do not have a son adopt a boy with the same family name. This is not too difficult because there are few family names in Korea.

Religion Today, Christianity is the most common religion, followed closely by Buddhism. Whatever their religion, most Koreans take part in ceremonies to honor their ancestors. Most also follow Confucian values. Many Koreans still ask shamans for personal advice.

✔ **READING CHECK:** (*Human Systems*) What is South Korea's society like?

This view looks out over the busy harbor of Pusan. Travelers can take a ferry from Pusan across the Korean Strait to Japan.

Interpreting the Visual Record
(*Movement*) **How does this photo show the importance of shipping to this region's economy?**

This is one of many statues of Kim Il Sung in P'yŏngyang. He led North Korea from the end of World War II until his death in 1994. Although dead, Kim Il Sung was declared the "Eternal President" of North Korea in 1998.

South Korea's Economy

After the war, South Korea industrialized quickly, and its market economy grew. By the 1990s it had become one of the strongest economies in Asia.

Industry Koreans' strong sense of family often carries over into work. Large groups of relatives may become **entrepreneurs**. This means they use their money and talents to start and manage a business. Businesses are sometimes linked through family and personal ties into huge industrial groups called **chaebol**.

The government has encouraged the use of nuclear power. It also has encouraged the growth of high-technology industries. These industries make electronic goods for export. Other important industries are steel, shipbuilding, automobiles, and textiles. In the late 1990s South Korea, like many other Asian countries, experienced an economic slowdown. It is now making a rapid recovery.

Agriculture South Korea has the peninsula's richest agricultural land. However, less than 20 percent of the land can be farmed. The shortage of land means that South Korea must import about half of its food.

Most South Korean farms are small and lie along the western and southern coasts. The rugged terrain makes using heavy machinery difficult. As a result, farmers must do much of their work by hand and with small tractors. Since the late 1980s there has been a shortage of farmworkers.

Farmers grow rice on about half their land. Other important crops are Chinese cabbage and soybeans. Soybeans are used to make soy sauce and tofu, or bean curd. Chinese cabbage that has been spiced and pickled is called **kimchi**. This is Korea's national dish.

✓ **READING CHECK:** (*Places and Regions*) What is South Korea's economy like?

North Korea's People and Government

North Korea's Communist Party controls the government. Kim Il Sung's son, Kim Jong Il, took over leadership in 1998 and continued his father's strict policies.

For years, North Korea had ties mostly with other Communist countries. Since the Soviet Union's breakup, North Korea has been largely isolated from the rest of the world. In addition, many countries are worried about North Korea's ability to make nuclear weapons. In 2002 North Korea announced plans to restart a nuclear reactor. Just a year later, the government said it had enough materials to build six nuclear bombs. Negotiations have not solved the crisis.

Like South Korea and Japan, North Korea has a homogeneous population. However, North Korea is not as densely populated as South Korea.

Russia
China
North Korea
P'yŏngyang
South Korea
Japan

The capital of North Korea is P'yoŏgyang (pyuhng-YANG). More than 3 million people live there. North Korea's only university is in P'yoŏgyang. Few private cars are on the city streets. Most residents use buses or the subway system to get around. At night, many streets are dark because the city frequently experiences shortages of electricity.

✔ **READING CHECK:** (*Places and Regions*) What is North Korea like?

North Korea's Economy

North Korea has a command economy. This means that the central government plans the economy and controls what is produced. The government also owns all the land and housing and controls access to jobs.

North Korea's best farmland is along the west coast. Only 14 percent of North Korea's land can be farmed. Most of this land is owned by the state. It is farmed by cooperatives—groups of farmers who work the land together. Some people have small gardens to grow food for themselves or to sell at local markets.

North Korea does not produce enough food to feed its people. It lost its main source of food and fertilizer when the Soviet Union collapsed. Poor harvests in the mid-1990s made the situation worse. **Famine**, or severe food shortages, resulted. The government's hostility toward the West made getting aid difficult. Thousands starved.

North Korea is rich in mineral resources. It has also developed a nuclear power industry. North Korea makes machinery, iron, and steel. However, its factories use outdated technology.

✔ **READING CHECK:** (*Human Systems*) How has North Korea's government affected the country's economic development?

▲ Rice farming requires large amounts of human energy for transplanting, weeding, and harvesting. These farmers are planting seedlings.

go.hrw.com **Homework Practice Online** **Keyword: SK5 HP17**

Section Review 5

Define or identify: entrepreneurs, *chaebol*, Kim Il Sung, kimchi, famine

Working with Sketch Maps On the map you created in Section 4, label Seoul, Pusan, and P'yoŏgyang. Why do you think these cities remain important? Write your answer in a box in the margin.

Reading for the Main Idea

1. (*Places and Regions*) How did South Korea's cities change after the Korean War?

2. (*Environment and Society*) How does North Korea's physical geography affect its farmers?

3. (*Places and Regions*) What kind of economies do North and South Korea have, and how are they different?

Critical Thinking

4. **Finding the Main Idea** How have entrepreneurs affected South Korea's economy?

Organizing What You Know

5. **Sequencing** List characteristics of the government, industry, and agriculture of North and South Korea since World War II. Where the circles overlap, list things the countries share.

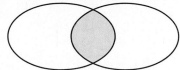

Japan and the Koreas • 393

CHAPTER 17 Review and Practice

Define and Identify

Identify each of the following:

1. tsunamis
2. shamans
3. Murasaki Shikibu
4. samurai
5. shogun
6. Diet
7. kimonos
8. intensive cultivation
9. work ethic
10. protectionism
11. trade surplus
12. entrepreneurs
13. *chaebol*
14. Kim Il Sung
15. kimchi
16. famine

Review the Main Ideas

17. What are the main geographic features of Japan and the Koreas?
18. How are the climates of Japan and South Korea similar?
19. What kind of political system did Japan have early in its history?
20. Why did the United States go to war against Japan in 1941?
21. Japan leads the world in which industry? What key material must it import?
22. Why have other countries objected to Japan's trade practices?
23. What contributions did the Chinese make to ancient Korea?
24. What purpose does the demilitarized zone serve? What makes it unique?
25. Why are sons valued in South Korean families?
26. What are some problems that face North Koreans?

Think Critically

27. **Analyzing Information** How have geographic features affected where people live in Japan and the Korean Peninsula?
28. **Contrasting** What physical features make Japan different from the Koreas? Create a chart to organize your answer.
29. **Finding the Main Idea** How have the Japanese changed the physical landscape to meet their needs?
30. **Analyzing Information** How has Tokyo developed into a megalopolis?
31. **Contrasting** How do the economies and governments of North and South Korea differ?

Map Activity

32. On a separate sheet of paper, match the letters on the map with their correct labels.

    Hokkaido
    Honshu
    Shikoku
    Kyushu

    Tokyo
    Seoul
    P'yŏngyang

Writing Activity

Imagine that you are traveling in Japan, North Korea, or South Korea. Write a one-page letter to a friend describing the places you have visited and an adventure you have had during your stay. Be sure to use standard grammar, spelling, sentence structure, and punctuation.

internet connect

Internet Activity: **go.hrw.com**
KEYWORD: SK5 GT17

Choose a topic to explore Japan and the Koreas:
- Investigate volcanoes.
- Visit Japan and the Koreas.
- Compare your school to a Japanese school.

Social Studies Skills Practice

Interpreting Political Cartoons

In this chapter you have learned that North Korea caused concern among many countries with its nuclear weapons program. Study the following political cartoon that addresses the relationship between President Bush and Kim Jong Il. Then answer the questions.

Source: Daryl Cagle, Slate.com

1. What is the main idea of this cartoon?
2. Which character represents President Bush?
3. What is Kim Jong Il's character holding?
4. What is Kim Jong Il preventing President Bush from doing?

Analyzing Primary Sources

Read the following passage about young samurai warriors from *Bushido, the Warrior's Code* by Inazo Nitobe. Then answer the questions.

"The stereotype of Spartan courage and of ignoring pain was indoctrinated [taught] into the children from the time of their birth. The fledgling samurai with an empty stomach knew it was a disgrace to feel the pangs [pains] of hunger. During training they were subjected to periods of deprivation [withholding] of food and exposure to extreme cold. Endurance was the hallmark of a successful novice [beginner]."

1. When did samurai training begin for future warriors?
2. What was life like for a young samurai?
3. Why would it be a disgrace to feel hungry?
4. How might this kind of training aid a warrior in battle?

Southeast Asia

Our study of the world now takes us to Southeast Asia. This vast region stretches from Myanmar eastward to New Guinea in the Pacific Ocean.

***S**awaddee!* (May you have good fortune!) I am Chosita, and I am 14 years old. I live in Bangkok with my parents and my older sister. We get up early for school because traffic in Bangkok is very heavy. By 6:00 A.M. we are on the road. My school has an eatery where street vendors sell all kinds of food—noodles in broth with beef, stir-fried noodles with meat and greens, dessert cakes of taro, pumpkin, and sticky rice, and fruits like rambutan, mangosteen, durian, and mango.

We go to school from June to September and from November to February. Our big vacation is March through May.

Our school has 38 students and two teachers in each class. I will not learn to use the computer until next year because we are the last class under the old school policy. The new policy has all students begin learning the computer in fourth grade.

สวัสดีค่ะ ดิฉันชื่อ โชสิตา
ดิฉันอยู่ที่กรุงเทพฯ
ซึ่งเป็นเมืองหลวงของประเทศไทยค่ะ

Translation: Hi! My name is Chosita. I live in Bangkok, the capital of Thailand.

Section 1 Physical Geography

Read to Discover

1. What are the major physical features of Southeast Asia?
2. What climates, vegetation, and wildlife are found in the region?
3. What resources does Southeast Asia have?

Vocabulary

mainland
archipelagos

Places

Indochina Peninsula
Malay Peninsula
New Guinea
Malay Archipelago
Philippines

Irian Jaya
Borneo
Java
Sumatra
Mekong River

Reading Strategy

MNEMONIC DEVICE Write the letters to the words Tropical down a sheet of paper. As you read this section, use each letter to write what you learn about the physical geography of Southeast Asia.

Southeast Asia: Physical-Political

Size comparison of Southeast Asia to the contiguous United States

internet connect

GO TO: go.hrw.com
KEYWORD: SK5 CH18
FOR: Web sites about
Southeast Asia

Physical Features

Southeast Asia is made up of two peninsulas and two large island groups. The Indochina and Malay (muh-LAY) Peninsulas lie on the Asian **mainland**. A mainland is a region's main landmass. The two large groups of islands, or **archipelagos** (ahr-kuh-PE-luh-gohs), lie between the mainland and New Guinea. They are the Malay Archipelago—made up mostly of Indonesia—and the Philippines. The Philippines are sometimes considered part of the Malay Archipelago. Western New Guinea is called Irian Jaya. It is part of Indonesia.

Landforms Southeast Asia's highest mountains are on the mainland in northern Myanmar (MYAHN-mahr). Mountain ranges fan out southward into Thailand (TY-land), Laos (LOWS), and Vietnam (vee-ET-NAHM). Between the mountains are low plateaus and river floodplains. The floodplains are rich farmlands.

Some of the large islands also have high mountains. Those islands include Borneo, Java, Sumatra, New Guinea, and some in the Philippines. They are part of the Pacific Ring of Fire. Earthquakes and volcanic eruptions often shake this part of the world.

Rivers Five major river systems drain the mainland. Many people and the largest cities are found near these rivers. The greatest river is the Mekong (MAY-KAWNG). The Mekong River flows southeast from China to southern Vietnam. You will read about the other rivers later in this chapter.

✔ READING CHECK: *Places and Regions* What are Southeast Asia's major physical features?

Climate Vegetation, and Wildlife

The warm temperatures of this tropical region generally do not change much during the year. However, northern and mountain areas tend to be cooler.

The Mekong River flows through a floodplain along the border between Thailand and Laos.

Interpreting the Visual Record What might happen to low islands and surrounding areas during the wet monsoon?

Much of the rainfall on the mainland is seasonal. Wet monsoon winds from nearby warm oceans bring heavy rains in the summer. Dry monsoons from the northeast bring drier weather in winter. Most of the islands are wet all year. Typhoons bring heavy rains and powerful winds to the island countries.

The region's tropical rain forests are home to many kinds of plants and animals. About 40,000 kinds of flowering plants grow in Indonesia alone. Rhinoceroses, orangutans, tigers, and elephants also live in the region. However, many of these plants and animals are endangered. Southeast Asia's rain forests are being cleared for farmland, tropical wood, and mining.

Orangutan is a Malaysian word for "man of the forest." These apes once lived in jungles throughout much of Southeast Asia. Hunting by humans has thinned the orangutan population in much of the region. Most orangutans today live on Borneo and Sumatra.

✓ **READING CHECK:** (*Places and Regions*) What are the region's climates, vegetation, and wildlife like?

Resources

Southeast Asia's rain forests produce valuable wood and other products. Thailand, Indonesia, and Malaysia (muh-LAY-zhuh) are the world's largest producers of natural rubber. The rubber tree is native to South America. However, it grows well in Southeast Asia's tropical climates.

Rich volcanic soils, floodplains, and tropical climates are good for farming. Abundant water and good soils in river deltas are ideal for growing rice. Coconuts, palm oil, sugarcane, coffee, and spices are also key products. Countries here also mine tin, iron ore, oil, and gas.

✓ **READING CHECK:** (*Places and Regions*) What are the region's important resources?

Homework Practice Online
Keyword: SK5 HP18

Define and explain: mainland, archipelagos

Working with Sketch Maps On a map of Southeast Asia that your teacher provides or that you draw, label the following: Indochina Peninsula, Malay Peninsula, New Guinea, Malay Archipelago, Philippines, Irian Jaya, Borneo, Java, Sumatra, and the Mekong River. In a box in the margin, describe the Mekong River.

Reading for the Main Idea

1. (*Places and Regions*) Where are the region's highest mountains?

2. (*Places and Regions*) Where are large cities found?

3. (*Places and Regions*) Which countries are the world's largest producers of natural rubber?

Critical Thinking

4. **Making Generalizations and Predictions** What do you think might happen to the region's wildlife if much of the tropical rain forests continue to be destroyed?

Organizing What You Know

5. **Summarizing** Copy the following graphic organizer. Use it to describe the region's climates, vegetation and wildlife, and resources.

Climates	Vegetation and wildlife	Resources

Read to Discover

1. What are some important events in the history of Southeast Asia?
2. What are the people and culture of Southeast Asia like today?

Vocabulary

refugees

Places

Angkor	Indonesia
Cambodia	Malaysia
Thailand	Timor
Vietnam	Myanmar
Laos	Singapore

Reading Strategy

TAKING NOTES Use the headings in this section to create an outline. As you read, write what you learn about the history and culture of Southeast Asia beneath each heading.

History Close-Up

Angkor Wat The magnificent stone towers of Angkor Wat rise from the Southeast Asian rain forest in this illustrated re-creation set in the early A.D. 1100s. Hindu priests are shown entering the temple where they will make offerings to statues of Hindu gods. To the Khmer, Angkor Wat was the center of the universe. The temple's towers symbolized mythical mountains. Reservoirs of water surrounding the temple represented the oceans. **What do you think this illustration says about Khmer society?**

History

Southeast Asia was home to some of the world's earliest human settlements. Over time many peoples moved there from China and India. The Khmer (kuh-MER) developed the most advanced of the region's early societies. The Khmer Empire was based in Angkor in what is now Cambodia (kam-BOH-dee-uh). It controlled a large area from the early A.D. 800s to the mid-1200s.

Colonial Era Europeans began to establish colonies in Southeast Asia in the 1500s. By the end of the 1800s, the Portuguese, British, Dutch, French, and Spanish controlled most of the region. The United States won control of the Philippines from Spain after the Spanish-American War in 1898. Just Siam (sy-AM), now called Thailand, remained independent.

Japan invaded and occupied most of Southeast Asia during World War II. After Japan was defeated in 1945, the United States granted the Philippines independence a year later. European countries tried to regain control of their colonies in the region. Some Southeast Asians decided to fight for independence. One of the bloodiest wars was in French Indochina. The French finally left in 1954. Their former colonies of Vietnam, Laos, and Cambodia became independent. By the mid-1960s, European rule had ended in most of the region.

Modern Era Unfortunately, fighting did not end in some countries when the Europeans left. Vietnam split into two countries. In the 1960s the United States sent troops to defend South Vietnam against communist North Vietnam. Civil wars also raged in Laos and Cambodia. In 1975, communist forces took power in all the countries. As communism continued to spread throughout the region, North and South Vietnam were then united into one country.

The region's wars caused terrible destruction. Millions died, including more than 50,000 Americans. About 1 million Vietnamese **refugees** tried to escape the communist takeover in South Vietnam. Refugees are people who flee their own country, usually for economic or political reasons. Many refugees from the region came to the United States.

In Cambodia more than 1 million people died under a cruel communist government. That government ruled from 1975 to 1978. Then Vietnam invaded Cambodia in 1978, sparking another conflict. That war continued off and on until the mid-1990s. Many Cambodian refugees fled to Thailand.

Communists and other groups also fought against governments in the Philippines, Indonesia, and Malaysia. In 1975 Indonesia invaded the former Portuguese against

GO TO: go.hrw.com
KEYWORD: SS Tsunami
FOR: Web sites about the tsunami of December 26, 2004, and its aftermath

colony of East Timor. The East Timorese demanded independence. However, the Indonesian military kept a tight grip on the region. The people of East Timor voted for independence in 1999. East Timor then plunged again into violence. The United Nations sent troops to restore peace and manage the area before independence was achieved.

In December 2004, a tsunami triggered by a massive earthquake in the Indian Ocean caused major damage to the region. At least 150,000 people were killed, and many more lost their homes, family members, and livelihoods. Most of those killed were in Indonesia and Sri Lanka, which were nearest to the epicenter of the earthquake. People around the world donated money to help the victims, and the United Nations pledged to send $1 billion in relief as the countries struggled with the aftermath of the disaster.

Governments The region's countries have had different kinds of governments. Many have been ruled by dictators. Some countries, such as the Philippines and Indonesia, now have governments elected by the people.

In other countries, the people still have little say in their government. For example, Myanmar is ruled by a military government. That government has jailed and even killed its opponents. Vietnam and Laos are still ruled by Communist governments. Only recently have Indonesians been allowed to vote in free elections. In some countries, such as Singapore, the same party always wins elections.

✔ **READING CHECK:** *Places and Regions* What were some key events in Southeast Asian history?

Culture

The populations of most countries in Southeast Asia are very diverse. This is because many different peoples have moved to the area over time. Today, for example, nearly 70 percent of the people in Myanmar are Burmese. However, Chinese, Asian Indians, and many other ethnic groups also live there.

Place The Shwedagon Pagoda is a beautiful Buddhist shrine in Yangon, Myanmar. Pagodas are important parts of a Buddhist temple complex.

Many ethnic Chinese live in the largest cities of most Southeast Asian countries. In Singapore they are a majority of the population—more than 75 percent. Singapore is a tiny country at the tip of the Malay Peninsula.

Languages and Religions The peoples of Southeast Asia speak many different languages. For example, in the former Dutch colony of Indonesia, most people speak Bahasa Indonesia. However, Javanese, other local dialects, English, and Dutch are also spoken there. European and Chinese languages are spoken in many other countries.

In addition, Indians, Chinese, Arab traders, and Europeans brought different religions to the region. For example, Hinduism is practiced in the region's Indian communities. However, Buddhism is the most common religion in the mainland countries today. Islam is the major religion in Malaysia, Brunei, and Indonesia. In fact, Indonesia has the largest Islamic population in the world. Nearly 90 percent of its more than 234 million people are Muslim.

Christians are a minority in most of the former European colonies. However, more than 80 percent of people in the Philippines, a former Spanish colony, are Roman Catholic.

Food Southeast Asian foods have been influenced by Chinese, South Asian, and European cooking styles. There are many spicy, mild, and sweet varieties. Rice is the most important food in nearly all of the countries. It is served with many other foods and spices, such as curries and chili peppers. Coconut is also important. It is served as a separate dish or used as an ingredient in other foods.

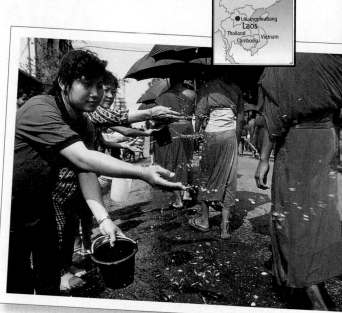

Women in Laos sprinkle water on Buddhist monks during a New Year festival. This custom symbolizes the washing away of the old year.

Interpreting the Visual Record What kinds of clothes are the monks wearing?

✓ **READING CHECK:** (*Human Systems*) How have migration and cultural borrowing influenced the region's culture?

go. hrw .com **Homework Practice Online**
Keyword: SK5 HP18

Section Review 2

Define and explain: refugees

Working with Sketch Maps On the map you created in Section 1, label the region's countries, Angkor, and Timor. In a box in the margin, describe the recent history of East Timor.

Reading for the Main Idea

1. (*Places and Regions*) What was the Khmer Empire?

2. (*Human Systems*) How did Europeans influence the region's history and culture?

Critical Thinking

3. **Drawing Inferences and Conclusions** Why do you think European countries wanted to regain their Southeast Asian colonies following World War II?

4. **Finding the Main Idea** What religion is most common in the mainland countries? in the island countries?

Organizing What You Know

5. **Sequencing** Copy the following time line. Use it to identify important people, years, periods, and events in Southeast Asia's history.

A.D. 800   2000

Mainland Southeast Asia Today

Read to Discover
1. Where do people in the mainland countries live today?
2. What are the economies of the mainland countries like?

Vocabulary
klongs

Places
Bangkok
Yangon
Hanoi
Ho Chi Minh City
Chao Phraya River
Irrawaddy River
Hong (Red) River
Vientiane
Phnom Penh

People
Aung San Suu Kyi

Reading Strategy

READING ORGANIZER Before you read this section, draw a large five-pointed star on a sheet of paper. As you read, write what you learn about Vietnam, Laos, Cambodia, Thailand, and Myanmar in the space created by the points. In the center, write the characteristics all the countries share.

People and Cities

Most mainland Southeast Asians today live in rural areas. Many are farmers in fertile river valleys and deltas. Fewer people live in remote hill and mountain villages.

However, the region's cities have been growing rapidly. People are moving to urban areas to look for work. The cities have many businesses, services, and opportunities that are not found in rural areas. Many of the cities today are crowded, smoggy, and noisy.

Look at the chapter map. You will find that the largest cities are located along major rivers. Location near rivers places these cities near important rice-growing areas. Access to rivers also makes them key

A Vietnamese man sells incense sticks in Ho Chi Minh City.

shipping centers for farm and factory products. The largest cities are Bangkok, Yangon, Hanoi, and Ho Chi Minh City.

Bangkok The mainland's largest city is Bangkok, Thailand's capital. Bangkok lies near the mouth of the Chao Phraya (chow PRY-uh) River. More than 7 million people live there. Much of Bangkok is connected by **klongs**, or canals. The klongs are used for transportation and for selling and shipping goods. They also drain water from the city.

Other Cities The region's second-largest city is Yangon, formerly known as Rangoon. It is Myanmar's capital and major seaport. The city is located in the Irrawaddy River delta on the coast of the Andaman Sea. To the east, Vietnam's largest cities are also located in major river deltas. The capital, Hanoi (ha-NOY), is located in the Hong (Red) River delta in the north. Ho Chi Minh City is located in the Mekong River delta in the south. Ho Chi Minh City was once known as Saigon and was South Vietnam's capital. Today it is an important seaport and business center with more than 4.6 million people.

✓ **READING CHECK:** (*Places and Regions*) Where do most people in mainland Southeast Asia live today and why?

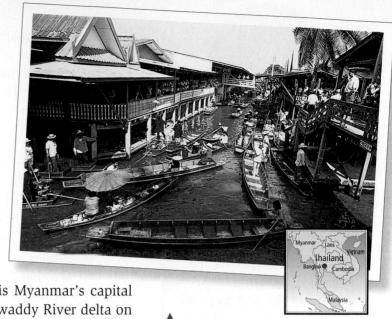

▲

(*Movement*) Boat traffic can be heavy along Bangkok's *klongs*. These canals have been part of the city's transportation system for centuries.

Economy

War, bad governments, and other problems have slowed progress in most of the mainland countries. However, rich resources could make the future brighter for the people there.

Vietnam Vietnam's economy has been slowly recovering since the end of the war in 1975. In recent years, the Communist government has begun moving from a command economy to a more market-oriented one. Some people are now allowed to own private businesses. Most Vietnamese remain farmers.

Most of Vietnam's factories, coal, oil, and other resources are in the north. The Hong and Mekong River deltas are major farming areas. Rice is the most important crop and food. In many places it is planted twice each year.

Mainland Southeast Asia

COUNTRY	POPULATION/ GROWTH RATE	LIFE EXPECTANCY	LITERACY RATE	PER CAPITA GDP
Cambodia	13,124,764 1.8%	55, male 60, female	70%	$1,500
Laos	9,921,545 2.5%	52, male 66, female	53%	$1,700
Myanmar	42,510,537 0.5%	54, male 57, female	83%	$1,500
Thailand	64,265,276 0.9%	71, male 73, female	96%	$6,900
Vietnam	81,624,716 1.3%	67, male 72, female	94%	$2,250
United States	290,342,554 0.9%	74, male 80, female	97%	$37,600

Source: Central Intelligence Agency, *The World Factbook 2003*

Interpreting the Chart According to the data in the chart, which country in the region is the most economically developed?

Laos This mountainous, landlocked country has few good roads, no railroads, and few telephones and televisions. Only some cities have electricity. The economy is mostly traditional—most people are subsistence farmers. They produce just enough food for themselves and their families. The Communist government in Vientiane (vyen-TYAHN), the capital, has also recently begun allowing more economic freedom.

Cambodia Economic progress in Cambodia has been particularly slow because of war and political problems. Agriculture is the most important part of the economy. The capital and largest city, Phnom Penh (puh-NAWM PEN), is located along the Mekong River. It lies in Cambodia's southern rice-growing area.

Thailand Thailand's economy has struggled but is the strongest of the mainland countries, partly because of rich resources. These resources include timber, natural rubber, seafood, rice, minerals, and gems. Factories produce computers and electronics. Many Thai operate small businesses. Tourism is also important. The tourism business was hurt in December 2004 when a tsunami devastated many coastal resorts.

Myanmar This former British colony is also called Burma. It gained independence in 1948 and was officially renamed Myanmar in 1989. It has rich resources, including copper, tin, iron ore, timber, rubber, and oil. However, a harsh military government has limited political freedom. This has slowed economic progress.

✔ **READING CHECK:** (*Places and Regions*) What are the mainland economies like?

go.hrw.com **Homework Practice Online**
Keyword: SK5 HP18

Section Review 3

Define or identify: *klongs*, Aung San Suu Kyi

Working with Sketch Maps On the map you created in Section 2, label Bangkok, Yangon, Hanoi, Ho Chi Minh City, Chao Phraya River, Irrawaddy River, Hong (Red) River, Vientiane, and Phnom Penh. Describe the mainland's largest city.

Reading for the Main Idea

1. (*Places and Regions*) Where do most mainland Southeast Asians live and why?

2. (*Human Systems*) Why are many people moving to cities?

3. (*Places and Regions*) Which country has the strongest economy and why?

Critical Thinking

4. **Finding the Main Idea** What kinds of problems appear to have slowed economic progress in the region?

Organizing What You Know

5. **Summarizing** Copy the following graphic organizer. Use it to describe the mainland's major cities. In each of its six circles, write the name of a city. In the circles, write important facts about the cities.

Cities

Section 4 Island Southeast Asia Today

Read to Discover

1. What are the major cities of the island countries?
2. What are the economies of the island countries like?

Vocabulary

kampongs
sultan

Places

Jakarta   Luzon
Manila   Bali
Kuala Lumpur

Reading Strategy

READING ORGANIZER Before you read, create a chart with three columns. Label the columns Country, Major City, and Resources. As you read this section, write what you learn about Indonesia, the Philippines, Singapore, Malaysia, and Brunei on your chart.

People and Cities

Indonesia is the largest of the island countries and the world's fourth-most-populous country. The country's more than 17,000 islands were known as the Dutch East Indies until 1949. Malaysia, Singapore, and Brunei were British colonies. The British granted independence to Malaysia in 1963. Singapore split from Malaysia in 1965. In 1984 Brunei became the region's last European colony to gain independence. As you have read, the Philippines gained independence from the United States in 1946. More than 7,000 islands make up that country.

Many people live in rural areas in the island countries. However, the island countries are more urbanized than the mainland countries. As on the mainland, many people are moving to cities in search of jobs. One country, Singapore, is simply a large city on a small island.

Modern skyscrapers tower over colonial-era buildings in Singapore. The city has one of the world's busiest ports.

Interpreting the Visual Record (Place)
What does Singapore's architecture tell you about its economy and culture?

CONNECTING TO Art

Wayang *puppets*

Puppetry is an art form with roots in ancient civilizations, including Greece, Rome, China, and India. On the Indonesian island of Java, one of the world's great puppet traditions is known as *wayang*. This shadow puppet theater still entertains audiences.

Shadow Puppets

Wayang puppets are beautiful works of art. The puppets are made from thin sheets of painted leather. They are pierced with holes so that light can shine through them. Then they are mounted on sticks. The performance takes place behind a screen. A light source is placed behind the puppets. The puppet's shadows fall on the screen and are visible to the audience on the other side.

Wayang performances tell stories from the *Ramayana* and the *Mahabharata*. These are two long poems of the Hindu religion. Hinduism came to Java from India hundreds of years ago. The puppets play the parts of gods, heroes, and villains. A performance usually lasts all night and includes the traditional music of Java. The music is played by an orchestra that includes gongs and other traditional instruments.

Over the years, *wayang* artists have developed other types of puppets. Some puppets are wooden forms. A new generation of artists is even creating computerized stories for *wayang* theater.

Understanding What You Read

1. Where did puppetry originate?
2. What is a *wayang* performance like?

Jakarta The region's largest city is Jakarta, Indonesia's capital. More than 11 million people live there. It is located on Java, which is by far Indonesia's most populous island. Many Indonesians live in **kampongs** around Jakarta. A kampong is a traditional village. It has also become the term for the crowded slums around large cities.

Singapore If you traveled from Jakarta to Singapore, you would find two very different cities. Singapore is one of the most modern and cleanest cities in the world. Crime rates also are very low. How has Singapore accomplished this?

Its government is very strict. For example, fines for littering are stiff. People caught transporting illegal drugs can be executed. The government even bans chewing gum and certain movies and music.

Is the lack of some individual freedoms a good trade-off for less crime, a clean city, and a strong economy? Some people in Singapore say yes. Others believe Singapore can be just as successful with less government control.

Other Cities The region's other large cities include Manila and Kuala Lumpur. More than 10 million people live in Manila, the capital of the Philippines. The city is a major seaport and industrial center on Luzon. Luzon is the country's largest and most populated island.

Kuala Lumpur is Malaysia's capital as well as its cultural, business, and transportation center. It is a modern city with two of the world's tallest buildings, the twin Petronas Towers.

✓ **READING CHECK:** *Places and Regions* What are some of the major cities of the island countries?

Island Southeast Asia

Country	Population/ Growth Rate	Life Expectancy	Literacy Rate	Per Capita GDP
Brunei	358,098 2.1%	71, male 76, female	92%	$18,600
Indonesia	234,893,453 1.5%	66, male 71, female	88%	$3,100
Malaysia	23,092,940 1.8%	69, male 74, female	89%	$9,300
Philippines	84,619,974 1.9%	66, male 72, female	96%	$4,200
Singapore	4,608,595 1.7%	77, male 83, female	93%	$24,000
United States	290,342,554 0.9%	74, male 80, female	97%	$37,600

Source: Central Intelligence Agency, *The World Factbook 2003*

Interpreting the Chart According to the chart, which country's economic development is closest to that of the United States?

Economy

The economies of the island countries grew rapidly until the mid-1990s. Then economic and political problems slowed growth for a while. However, rich resources are helping the economies there to recover. In addition, wages and labor costs are low in many of the countries. This means that companies there can manufacture many products more cheaply for export.

Indonesia Europeans once called Indonesia the Spice Islands because of its cinnamon, pepper, and nutmeg. Today, its rich resources include natural rubber, oil, natural gas, and timber. Indonesia also has good farmlands for rice and other crops. Busy factories turn out clothing, electronics, and furniture. Some islands, such as Bali, are popular with tourists.

(*Human-Environment Interaction*)
Farming is an important economic activity in the Philippines. In mountain areas, farmers plant rice and other crops in terraced fields. These flat terraces hold water and slow erosion along mountainsides.

▼

Dancers attract tourists to the island of Bali. Indonesia has many different dance styles. This *Barong* dancer uses her hands, arms, and eyes to tell a traditional story.

Large areas of Indonesia's tropical rain forests are often burned for farming. Smoke from the fires can spread for hundreds of miles. The smoke mixes with chemicals in the air, causing air pollution and smothering cities in haze.

The Philippines The Philippines is mostly an agricultural country today. A big problem is the gap between rich and poor Filipinos. A few very rich Filipinos control most of the land and industries. Most farmers are poor and own no land.

The economy has improved in recent years. Companies sell many electronics and clothing products to overseas customers, particularly in the United States. The country also has rich resources, including tropical forests, copper, gold, silver, and oil. Farmers grow sugarcane, rice, corn, coconuts, and tropical fruits.

Singapore Singapore is by far the most economically developed country in all of Southeast Asia. The British founded the city at the tip of the Malay Peninsula in 1819. This location along major shipping routes helped make Singapore rich. Goods are stored there before they are shipped to their final stop. In addition, many foreign companies have opened banks, offices, and high-technology industries there.

Malaysia Malaysia is made up of two parts. The largest part lies on the southern Malay Peninsula. The second part lies on the northern portion of Borneo. Well-educated workers and rich resources make Malaysia's future look bright. The country produces natural rubber, electronics, automobiles, oil, and timber. The government is trying to attract more high-technology companies to the country. Malaysia is also the world's leading producer of palm oil.

Electronics and technology products are increasingly important to the region's economies. This Filipino is working at a semiconductor manufacturing plant.

This beautiful mosque in Brunei's capital reflects the country's oil wealth. Money from oil and natural gas production pays for many social services there.

Brunei Large deposits of oil have made Brunei rich. This small country on the island of Borneo is ruled by a **sultan**. A sultan is the supreme ruler of a Muslim country. Brunei shares the island of Borneo with Indonesia and Malaysia.

✓ **READING CHECK:** (*Places and Regions*) How do rich resources affect the economies of the island countries?

Section Review 4

Define and explain: kampongs, sultan

Working with Sketch Maps On the map you created in Section 3, label Jakarta, Manila, Kuala Lumpur, Luzon, and Bali. In a box in the margin, identify the most heavily populated islands in Indonesia and the Philippines.

Reading for the Main Idea

1. (*Places and Regions*) What is the region's largest city? What is the importance of Manila and Kuala Lumpur to their countries?

2. (*Places and Regions*) Why was Indonesia once called the Spice Islands? What European country once controlled nearly all of Indonesia?

Homework Practice Online
Keyword: SK5 HP18

Critical Thinking

3. **Analyzing Information** Some Singaporeans say that limiting some individual freedoms is a good trade-off for less crime and a better economy. Do you agree? Why or why not?

4. **Comparing/Contrasting** How have Singapore and Brunei become rich countries?

Organizing What You Know

5. **Summarizing** Copy the following graphic organizer. Use it to list the nine Southeast Asian countries that are former European colonies. Next to each country's name, write the name of the European country that once controlled it.

Southeast Asian country	European colonial power

CASE STUDY

MULTIETHNIC INDONESIA

Indonesia is a multiethnic country—a country with many different ethnic groups. The national motto of Indonesia is *Bhinneka Tunggal Ika,* which means "the many are one." This motto comes from the many different ethnic groups that live there.

More than 300 different ethnic groups live in Indonesia. Most of these groups speak their own language and have their own way of life. No single ethnic group holds a majority. The largest are the Javanese, Sundanese, Madurese, and Coastal Malays. The country also has many smaller ethnic groups, such as the Dayaks and the Balinese. Why does Indonesia have so many different ethnic groups? Part of the answer lies in the country's diverse physical geography.

Indonesia is a very large country. It is made up of more than 17,000 islands. About 228 million people live on these islands. Indonesia's islands, mountains, and dense rain forests have served as boundaries between different ethnic groups. Many small ethnic groups lived in isolation and had very little contact with other peoples. Over time, these groups developed their own cultures, languages, and ways of life.

The modern country of Indonesia has its roots in the early 1600s. About this time, Dutch traders built forts in the area. They wanted to protect the trade routes used by Dutch ships to transport spices and other goods. The Dutch remained an important force in the region until Indonesia became independent in 1949. The long history of

Movement Most Indonesians are related to the peoples of East Asia. However, in the eastern islands, most people are of Melanesian origin. Over the centuries, many Arabs, Indians, and Europeans have added to the country's ethnic diversity.

Ethnic Groups in Indonesia

- Acehnese
- Balinese
- Batak
- Bonfia
- Coastal Malays
- Javanese
- Kupangese
- Land Dayak group
- Larantuka
- Loinang group
- Madurese
- Mori Laki group
- Redjang Lampong group
- Sundanese

◄ **Place** The Balinese are one of Indonesia's many ethnic groups. Unlike most other Indonesians, Hinduism is their main religion.

Dutch control helped unify the islands into the modern country of Indonesia.

In addition to this shared past, several other factors have helped unify Indonesia. For example, Indonesia's government has promoted the country's official language, Bahasa Indonesia. Although most Indonesians speak more than one language, Bahasa Indonesia is used in schools and government. The use of this language has been an important force in uniting the country. The government has also tried to develop a common Indonesian culture. It has promoted national holiday celebrations, education, popular art, and television and radio programs.

A shared history, a common education system, and an official language help give isolated ethnic groups an Indonesian identity. However, the country's multiethnic society still faces some important challenges. In certain parts of Indonesia, people want independence. For example, in 1999 people in East Timor voted for independence from Indonesia. This caused a great deal of unrest. Most people there supported the vote, but others did not. When some groups rioted, many Timorese left the area for their own safety. The Acehnese, an ethnic group on the island of Sumatra, have also been seeking independence.

Ethnic Groups in Indonesia

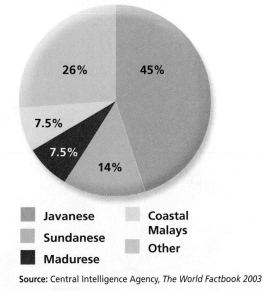

26% 45%

7.5%

7.5%

14%

- Javanese
- Sundanese
- Madurese
- Coastal Malays
- Other

Source: Central Intelligence Agency, *The World Factbook 2003*

Understanding What You Read

1. How diverse is Indonesia's society? What has helped to promote cooperation among the different ethnic groups that live in the country?

2. What are some important challenges facing Indonesia today?

Define and Identify

Identify each of the following:

1. mainland
2. archipelagos
3. refugees
4. *klongs*
5. Aung San Suu Kyi
6. kampongs
7. sultan

Review the Main Ideas

8. What peninsulas and archipelagos make up Southeast Asia?
9. Where will you find the highest mountains in Southeast Asia?
10. What mineral resources are found in Southeast Asia?
11. Which early society in Southeast Asia was based in Angkor?
12. What factors have slowed economic progress in mainland Southeast Asia?
13. What resources are important to the economy of Vietnam?
14. How did European countries influence Southeast Asia?

15. What is a common feature of the island countries in Southeast Asia?
16. Why do you think so many languages are spoken in Southeast Asia?

Think Critically

17. **Drawing Inferences and Conclusions** Why are some cities located near river deltas so large?
18. **Finding the Main Idea** What outside cultures have strongly influenced the development of Southeast Asian culture?
19. **Analyzing Information** How did the Philippines and Vietnam gain independence?
20. **Finding the Main Idea** How do the climates of mainland countries differ from those in the island countries? What natural disasters are a danger in the region?
21. **Analyzing Information** How do labor costs affect the island countries' economies?

Map Activity

22. On a separate sheet of paper, match the letters on the map with their correct labels.

Indochina Peninsula	Mekong River
Malay Peninsula	Timor
Malay Archipelago and the Philippines	Bangkok
Irian Jaya	Jakarta
Borneo	Manila

Writing Activity

Imagine that you are an economic adviser for a poor Southeast Asian country. Write a one-paragraph summary explaining how some countries in the region built stronger economies. Use the report to suggest policies your chosen country might adopt to build its economy. Be sure to use standard grammar, spelling, sentence structure, and punctuation.

internet connect

Internet Activity: go.hrw.com
KEYWORD: SK5 GT18

Choose a topic to explore about Southeast Asia:

- Explore an Indonesian rain forest.
- Learn about shadow puppets.
- See buildings of Southeast Asia.

Social Studies Skills Practice

Interpreting Graphs

Study the graph below. Then answer the questions.

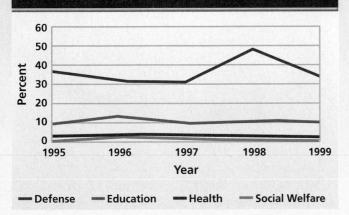

Government Spending in Myanmar

Defense — Education — Health — Social Welfare

Source: International Monetary Fund

1. What four areas of government spending are shown in the graph?

2. In what two areas did government spending stay about the same?

3. In what area did the government spend the most? the least?

4. What percentage of government spending was devoted to defense during the period 1998–99?

Analyzing Primary Sources

Read the following quote by Cristina Pantoja-Hidalgo, a Filipino journalist who lived in Myanmar in the 1980s. Then answer the questions.

"Everything was available through the black market . . . But all these were underground. For example, if you owned a video shop, it was quite possible that the army would swoop upon you and would confiscate all your tapes. Burma is not as isolated as North Korea where the government is really efficient about keeping controls. The Burmese government cannot control the black market because of the common borders between India and Thailand . . . Thus, there's a great deal of smuggling."

1. What does Pantoja-Hidalgo mean by the term "black market"?

2. How did the government try to stop the black market?

3. Why was the government unable to control smuggling?

4. What country does Pantoja-Hidalgo say is more isolated than Burma?

ENVIRONMENT

Indonesia's Threatened Rain Forests

Why Are Rain Forests Important?

Do you know where bananas, pineapples, and oranges originally came from? Each of these plants first grew in a tropical rain forest.

Tropical rain forests are considered by many to be the most important forests in the world. It is estimated that about half of all species of plants, animals, and insects on Earth live in tropical rain forests. Rain forest trees and plants help maintain global temperatures. They also help hold rain-drenched soil in place. This prevents it from washing away and clogging rivers. About one fourth of all medicines currently found in drugstores come from tropical rain forests.

Tropical rain forests can be found in many countries along the equator and between about 20° north and south latitude. One of the largest rain forests is in Brazil's Amazon Basin. In Africa, rain forests are found in many countries, such as Gabon and the Democratic Republic of the Congo. In Southeast Asia, rain forests are found in countries such as Thailand, Vietnam, and Indonesia.

Deforestation in Indonesia

Indonesia has large areas of tropical rain forest in Borneo, Sumatra, and Irian Jaya. These areas are home to many unusual species of plants and animals. For example, the largest flower in the world, the *Rafflesia arnoldii*, is found there.

Indonesia's tropical rain forests are being rapidly cut down. About 4,700 square miles (12,170 sq km) of rain forest are lost each year. This rate of deforestation is second only to Brazil's. Some people have predicted that much of Indonesia's

▲
Found in the rain forests of Sumatra, the *Rafflesia arnoldii* is the largest known flower in the world. It can weigh up to 24 pounds (11 kg) and can measure about 3 feet (1 meter) across.

rain forests will be gone in just 10 years. When the rain forests are cleared, animals such as the endangered orangutan do not have a home.

There are many reasons that Indonesia's tropical rain forests are being cleared. Trees from tropical rain forests produce beautiful woods. They are used to make furniture, boats, and houses. The demand for special trees and wood has made logging a profitable business. Much of the logging is done by large corporations that do not replant the areas that are cut.

Deforestation in Indonesia also occurs because people need land to farm and raise animals. They also need wood for fuel. People clear the land using a method called slash-and-burn. Large trees are cut, or slashed, and left on the ground. Then the land is burned during the dry season. This clears the land of vegetation and prepares it for farming. In 1997 large areas of land in Indonesia were cleared. Huge fires burned out of control. The fires burned an area roughly the size of Denmark. Smoke filled the sky and caused some airplanes and ships to crash.

Protecting Indonesia's Rain Forests

Some people in Indonesia are trying to protect the rain forests. Parks and nature reserves have been set up that are off-limits to logging companies. Some groups are finding ways to earn money without cutting down trees. Selling fruits and nuts from the rain forest is one way. Also, international organizations such as the Rainforest Action Network are helping to protect the forests. Some environmental groups are even pressuring countries to stop buying trees that come from tropical rain forests.

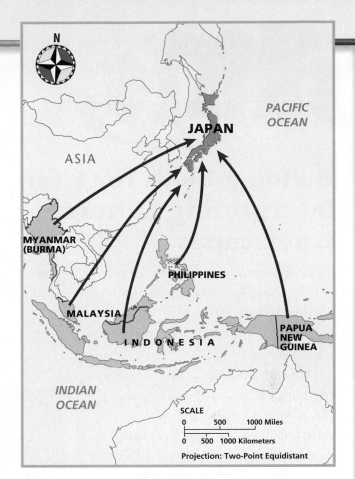

▲
Much of the timber cut in Indonesia and other Southeast Asian countries is exported to Japan. Indonesia exports about 2 million tons of plywood and 145,000 tons of lumber to Japan each year.

◀
Orangutans live in the tropical rain forests of Borneo and Sumatra. Deforestation has seriously reduced their habitat. The word *orangutan* means "man of the forest."

Understanding What You Read

1. (*Human-Environment Interaction*) Why are Indonesia's tropical rain forests being cut down?

2. (*Human-Environment Interaction*) What is being done to protect Indonesia's tropical rain forests?

Building Skills for Life: Interpreting Cultural Landscapes

Cultural landscapes are the forms put on the land by people. For example, buildings, field patterns, and roads are all a part of cultural landscapes. Cultural landscapes show a people's way of life.

Different cultures create distinctive cultural landscapes. For example, a village in China looks very different from a village in France. By comparing how the two villages look, we can begin to see how their cultures are different.

Geographers interpret cultural landscapes. They observe a landscape, describe what they see, and try to explain how it reflects the culture of the place. This is called reading the cultural landscape.

You can read cultural landscapes too. To read a cultural landscape, start by describing what you see. What kinds of buildings are there? What are they used for? What kinds of clothing are people wearing? Then, think about how what you see relates to the place's culture. What would it be like to live there? What do people there do for fun?

Cultural landscapes tell a story. By reading and interpreting these stories, you can learn a lot about people and geography.

Place Architecture is an important part of the cultural landscape at the Black Dragon Pool in southern China.

▼

THE SKILL

1. Try to read the cultural landscapes of your community. What forms have people put on the land? What do they tell you about the daily life of the people who live there?

2. Watch a television show or movie and interpret the cultural landscapes you see. What is distinctive about them? How are they different from the cultural landscapes you are used to? Can you guess where the program was filmed?

3. Look carefully at the pictures in a newspaper or magazine without reading the captions. Do the pictures tell a story? Is culture a part of this story?

HANDS on
GEOGRAPHY

The photographs below show two very different cultural landscapes. What can these photographs tell us about each place's culture and way of life? Look closely at each photograph and then answer the Lab Report questions.

◀ A cultural landscape in East Asia

▲ A cultural landscape in Southeast Asia

Lab Report

1. What do these two photographs show? On a separate sheet of paper, write a short description of each photograph.

2. Do these two photographs tell you something about each place's culture and way of life? On a separate sheet of paper, describe what you think the culture of these two places is like.

3. Are there some things about a place's culture that you cannot learn from just looking at a photograph? What are they? If you took a trip to these two places, what else could you learn about their cultures?

UNIT 6

The Pacific World and Antarctica

CHAPTER 19
Australia and New Zealand

CHAPTER 20
The Pacific Islands and Antarctica

King penguins watching photographer, Antarctica

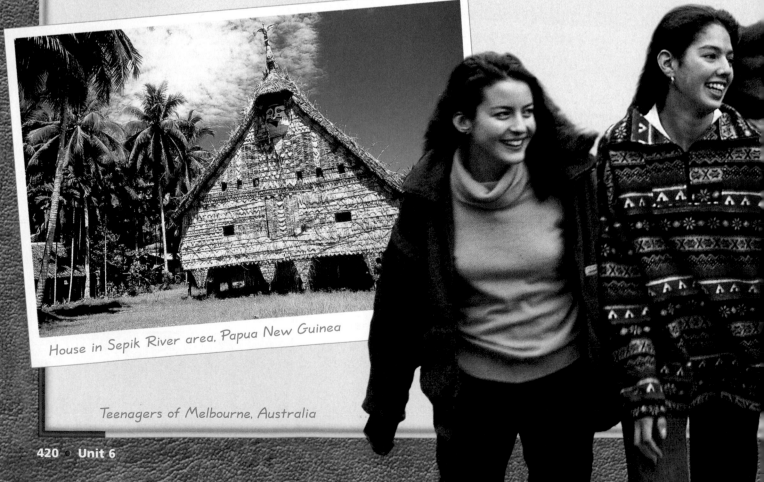

House in Sepik River area, Papua New Guinea

Teenagers of Melbourne, Australia

A Film Critic in New Zealand

David Gerstner is a film critic and lecturer from New York City. In 1999 he moved to New Zealand. He found the country was very different than he thought it would be. **WHAT DO YOU THINK?** *What do you know about New Zealand?*

Wellington, New Zealand

First I was surprised that New Zealand has such lively cities. I had thought it was all mountains and bush. I was also surprised by the laid-back New Zealand approach to personal interaction. Celebrities, politicians, and the "common folk" have an easier time getting together. For example, I have become friends with some of New Zealand's well-known filmmakers, writers, and fashion designers—all within a year. The social playing field is more level than in the United States.

In fact, a friend and I literally ran into Jenny Shipley, who was then New Zealand's Prime Minister, on a busy street in the capital, Wellington. She was with her daughter. There were no secret service guards with them—like there would be with the U.S. president. We even had our picture taken with her! The easy-going Kiwi style of security is refreshing. However, for a New Yorker it is sometimes unsettling.

Understanding Primary Sources

1. Why was David Gerstner surprised by New Zealand's cities?

2. What does this passage illustrate about New Zealand's culture?

Koalas

The Pacific World and Antarctica

Elevation Profile

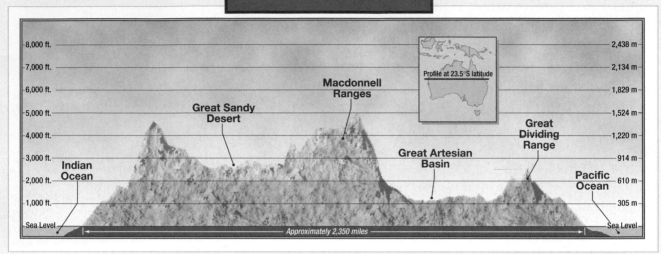

8,000 ft. — 2,438 m
7,000 ft. — 2,134 m
6,000 ft. — 1,829 m
5,000 ft. — 1,524 m
4,000 ft. — 1,220 m
3,000 ft. — 914 m
2,000 ft. — 610 m
1,000 ft. — 305 m
Sea Level — Sea Level

Profile at 23.5°S latitude

Macdonnell Ranges

Great Sandy Desert

Great Artesian Basin

Great Dividing Range

Indian Ocean

Pacific Ocean

Approximately 2,350 miles

The United States and the Pacific World and Antarctica: Comparing Sizes

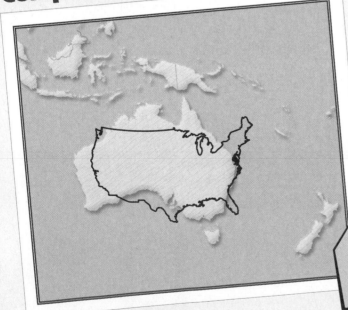

GEOSTATS:

Antarctica

World's highest, driest, coldest, and windiest continent

World's lowest recorded temperature: -129°F (-89.2°C) on July 21, 1983

Amount of the world's fresh-water stored as ice in Antarctica: about 70 percent

Average thickness of ice: over 1 mile (1.6 km)

Highest mountain in Antarctica: Vinson Massif—16,066 ft. (4,897 m)

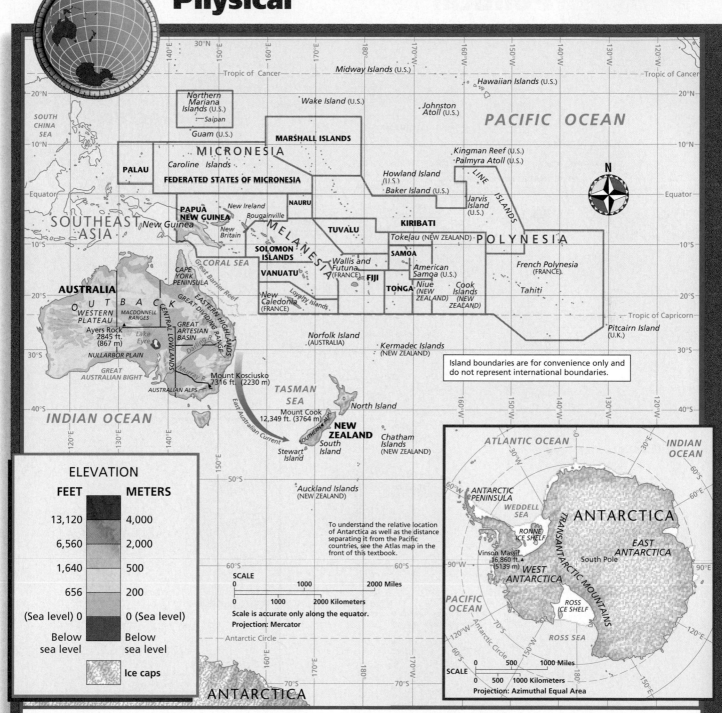

ELEVATION

FEET	METERS
13,120	4,000
6,560	2,000
1,640	500
656	200
(Sea level) 0	0 (Sea level)
Below sea level	Below sea level
	Ice caps

SCALE
0   1000   2000 Miles
0   1000   2000 Kilometers
Scale is accurate only along the equator.
Projection: Mercator

Island boundaries are for convenience only and do not represent international boundaries.

To understand the relative location of Antarctica as well as the distance separating it from the Pacific countries, see the Atlas map in the front of this textbook.

SCALE
0   500   1000 Miles
0   500   1000 Kilometers
Projection: Azimuthal Equal Area

1. (Place) What is the highest point in Australia? in the region?

2. (Location) About how far apart are Guam and Tahiti? New Zealand and Australia?

3. (Region) What physical features cover most of Australia?

Critical Thinking

4. (Region) Which country is more mountainous, Australia or New Zealand?

5. (Region) Compare this map to the **climate map** of the region. Which Australian mountain range seems to cause a rain-shadow effect?

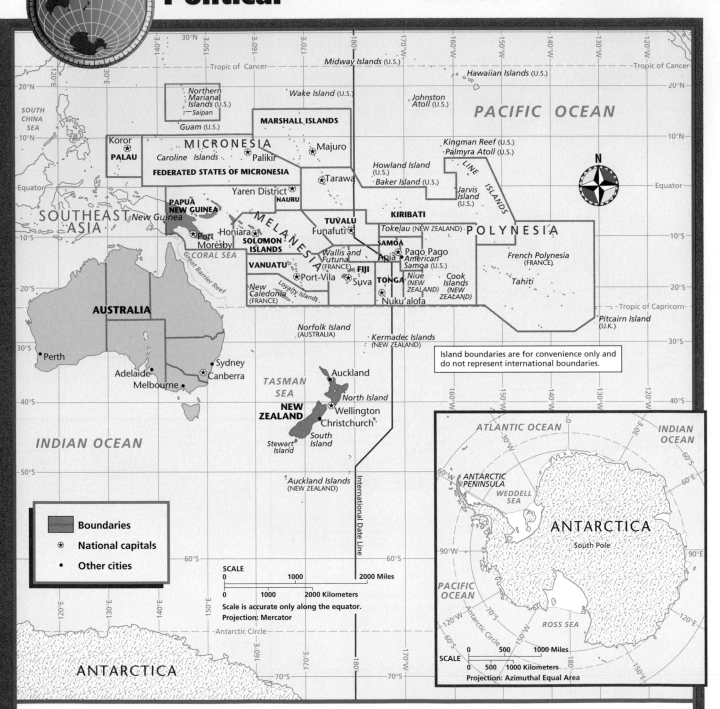

Northern Mariana Islands (U.S.)
Saipan
Guam (U.S.)
MARSHALL ISLANDS
Wake Island (U.S.)
Midway Islands (U.S.)
Hawaiian Islands (U.S.)
Tropic of Cancer
PACIFIC OCEAN
Johnston Atoll (U.S.)
Koror
PALAU
MICRONESIA
Caroline Islands
Palikir
Majuro
FEDERATED STATES OF MICRONESIA
Kingman Reef (U.S.)
Palmyra Atoll (U.S.)
Howland Island (U.S.)
Baker Island (U.S.)
Jarvis Island (U.S.)
Tarawa
Yaren District
NAURU
LINE ISLANDS
SOUTHEAST ASIA
PAPUA NEW GUINEA
New Guinea
MELANESIA
TUVALU
Funafuti
KIRIBATI
Tokelau (NEW ZEALAND)
POLYNESIA
Port Moresby
Honiara
SOLOMON ISLANDS
CORAL SEA
Great Barrier Reef
VANUATU
Wallis and Futuna (FRANCE)
SAMOA
Apia
FIJI
Port-Vila
Suva
TONGA
Pago Pago
American Samoa (U.S.)
Niue (NEW ZEALAND)
Cook Islands (NEW ZEALAND)
French Polynesia (FRANCE)
Tahiti
AUSTRALIA
New Caledonia (FRANCE)
Loyalty Islands
Nuku'alofa
Island boundaries are for convenience only and do not represent international boundaries.
Pitcairn Island (U.K.)
Tropic of Capricorn
Perth
Adelaide
Melbourne
Sydney
Canberra
Norfolk Island (AUSTRALIA)
Kermadec Islands (NEW ZEALAND)
TASMAN SEA
Auckland
North Island
Wellington
Christchurch
NEW ZEALAND
Stewart Island
South Island
INDIAN OCEAN
Auckland Islands (NEW ZEALAND)
International Date Line

Boundaries
⊛ **National capitals**
• **Other cities**

SCALE
0 .... 1000 .... 2000 Miles
0 .... 1000 .... 2000 Kilometers
Scale is accurate only along the equator.
Projection: Mercator
Antarctic Circle

ATLANTIC OCEAN
ANTARCTIC PENINSULA
WEDDELL SEA
INDIAN OCEAN
ANTARCTICA
South Pole
PACIFIC OCEAN
ROSS SEA
Antarctic Circle
SCALE
0 .... 500 .... 1000 Miles
0 .... 500 .... 1000 Kilometers
Projection: Azimuthal Equal Area

ANTARCTICA

1. _Location_ Which country occupies half of a large island? Which country occupies two large islands?

2. _Location_ What is the only country in the region that has a land boundary with another country?

Critical Thinking

3. _Region_ What is one thing you can tell about governments in the region just by looking at the map?

4. _Region_ Why do you think the international date line is not a straight line?

CLIMATE
- Humid tropical
- Tropical savanna
- Desert
- Steppe
- Mediterranean
- Humid subtropical
- Marine west coast
- Highland

Island boundaries are for convenience only and do not represent international boundaries.

SCALE
0   1000   2000 Miles
0   1000   2000 Kilometers
Scale is accurate only along the equator.
Projection: Mercator

SCALE
0   500   1000 Miles
0   500   1000 Kilometers
Projection: Azimuthal Equal Area

1. *Place* What type of climate does New Zealand have?

2. *Region* Which country has the greatest variety of climate types?

3. *Place* Compare this map to the **population map** of the region. What type of climate does Perth have?

Critical Thinking

4. *Region* Compare this map to the **physical map**. How might the East Australian Current affect New Zealand's weather?

5. *Human-Environment Interaction* How might climate affect Papua New Guinea's population patterns?

POPULATION DENSITY

Persons per sq. mile		Persons per sq. km
520		200
260		100
130		50
25		10
3		1
0		0

● Metropolitan areas with more than 2 million inhabitants

○ Metropolitan areas with 1 million to 2 million inhabitants

SCALE
0   1000   2000 Miles
0   1000   2000 Kilometers
Scale is accurate only along the equator.
Projection: Mercator

SCALE
0   500   1000 Miles
0   500   1000 Kilometers
Projection: Azimuthal Equal Area

1. *Place* What is the only country with cities of over 2 million people?

2. *Region* What region of Australia has the highest population density?

3. *Location* Compare this map to the **physical map**. What is the densely populated island northwest of New Zealand?

Critical Thinking

4. *Region* What large landmass has no permanent population? Why?

5. *Region* From looking at this map, what is one thing that Australia and Antarctica have in common?

The Pacific World and Antarctica: Land Use and Resources

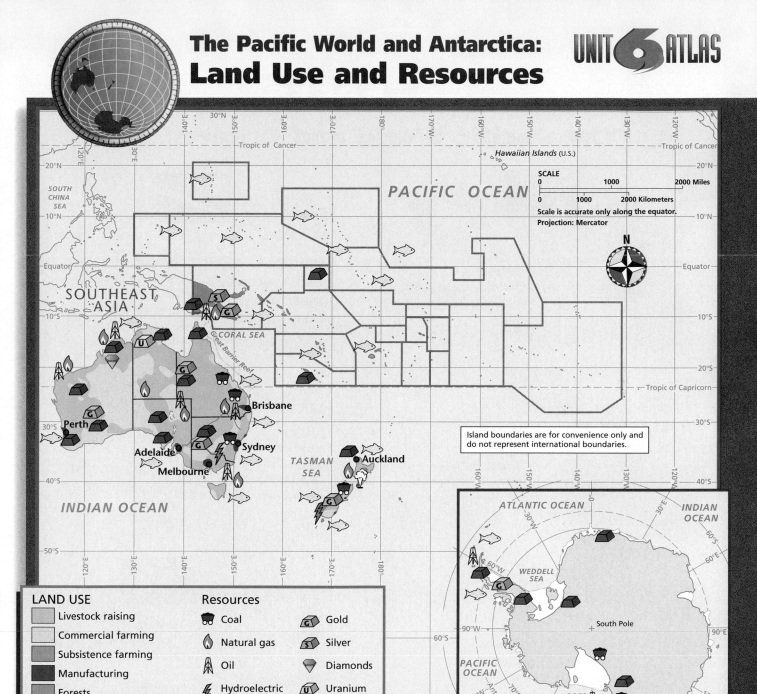

LAND USE

- Livestock raising
- Commercial farming
- Subsistence farming
- Manufacturing
- Forests
- Limited economic activity
- • Major manufacturing and trade centers

Resources

- Coal
- Natural gas
- Oil
- Hydroelectric power
- Geothermal power
- Gold
- Silver
- Diamonds
- Uranium
- Other minerals
- Seafood

Island boundaries are for convenience only and do not represent international boundaries.

SCALE
0   1000   2000 Miles
0   1000   2000 Kilometers
Scale is accurate only along the equator.
Projection: Mercator

---

1. (*Place*) What cities are part of Australia's major manufacturing and trade centers?

2. (*Human-Environment Interaction*) What resources are available in Papua New Guinea but not in Australia?

3. (*Human-Environment Interaction*) What is the main resource of most of the small Pacific islands?

Critical Thinking

4. (*Human-Environment Interaction*) Compare this map to the **physical** and **climate maps** of the region. Why would it be difficult to mine the mineral resources of Antarctica?

Fast FACTS

The Pacific World and Antarctica

AUSTRALIA

CAPITAL:
Canberra

AREA:
2,967,893 sq. mi.
(7,686,850 sq km)

POPULATION:
19,731,984

MONEY:
Australian dollar

LANGUAGES:
English, ethnic languages

POPULATION AGED 0-14 YEARS:
20 percent

MARSHALL ISLANDS

CAPITAL: Majuro

AREA: 70 sq. mi. (181.3 sq km)

POPULATION: 56,429

MONEY: United States dollar

LANGUAGES:
English (official), Marshallese dialects, Japanese

POPULATION AGED 0-14 YEARS: 39 percent

FEDERATED STATES OF MICRONESIA

CAPITAL: Palikir

AREA: 271 sq. mi. (702 sq km)

POPULATION: 108,143

MONEY:
United States dollar

LANGUAGES:
English (official), Trukese, Pohnpeian, Yapese, Kosrean

POPULATION AGED 0-14 YEARS: 38 percent

NAURU

CAPITAL:
no official capital

AREA:
8 sq. mi. (21 sq km)

POPULATION:
12,570

MONEY:
Australian dollar

LANGUAGES:
Nauruan (official), English

POPULATION AGED 0-14 YEARS:
40 percent

FIJI

CAPITAL:
Suva

AREA:
7,054 sq. mi.
(18,270 sq km)

POPULATION:
868,531

MONEY:
Fijian dollar

LANGUAGES:
English (official), Fijian, Hindustani

POPULATION AGED 0-14 YEARS:
32 percent

NEW ZEALAND

CAPITAL:
Wellington

AREA:
103,737 sq. mi.
(268,680 sq km)

POPULATION:
3,951,307

MONEY:
New Zealand dollar

LANGUAGES:
English (official), Maori

POPULATION AGED 0-14 YEARS:
22 percent

KIRIBATI

CAPITAL:
Tarawa

AREA:
277 sq. mi. (717 sq km)

POPULATION:
98,549

MONEY:
Australian dollar

LANGUAGES:
English (official), I-Kiribati

POPULATION AGED 0-14 YEARS:
40 percent

PALAU

CAPITAL:
Koror

AREA:
177 sq. mi. (458 sq km)

POPULATION:
19,717

MONEY:
United States dollar

LANGUAGES:
English (official), Sonsorolese, Angaur, Japanese, Tobi, Palauan

POPULATION AGED 0-14 YEARS:
27 percent

Countries not drawn to scale.

PAPUA NEW GUINEA

CAPITAL:
Port Moresby

AREA:
178,703 sq. mi.
(462,840 sq km)

POPULATION: 5,295,816

MONEY: kina

LANGUAGES:
715 ethnic languages, pidgin English, English

POPULATION AGED 0-14 YEARS: 38 percent

SAMOA

CAPITAL:
Apia

AREA:
1,104 sq. mi. (2,860 sq km)

POPULATION:
178,173

MONEY:
tala

LANGUAGES:
Samoan (Polynesian), English

POPULATION AGED 0-14 YEARS:
29 percent

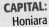

SOLOMON ISLANDS

CAPITAL:
Honiara

AREA:
10,985 sq. mi.
(28,450 sq km)

POPULATION:
509,190

MONEY:
Solomon Islands dollar

LANGUAGES:
Melanesian pidgin, 120 ethnic languages, English

POPULATION AGED 0-14 YEARS: 43 percent

TONGA

CAPITAL:
Nuku'alofa

AREA:
289 sq. mi.
(748 sq km)

POPULATION:
108,141

MONEY:
pa'anga

LANGUAGES:
Tongan, English

POPULATION AGED 0-14 YEARS:
38 percent

TUVALU

CAPITAL:
Funafuti

AREA:
10 sq. mi. (26 sq km)

POPULATION:
11,305

MONEY:
Tuvaluan dollar or Australian dollar

LANGUAGES:
Tuvaluan, English

POPULATION AGED 0-14 YEARS: 32 percent

VANUATU

CAPITAL:
Port-Vila

AREA:
4,710 sq. mi. (12,200 sq km)

POPULATION:
199,414

MONEY:
vatu

LANGUAGES:
English (official), French (official), pidgin (known as Bislama or Bichelama)

POPULATION AGED 0-14 YEARS: 35 percent

internet connect

COUNTRY STATISTICS
GO TO: go.hrw.com
KEYWORD: SK5 FactsU6
FOR: more facts about the Pacific World and Antarctica

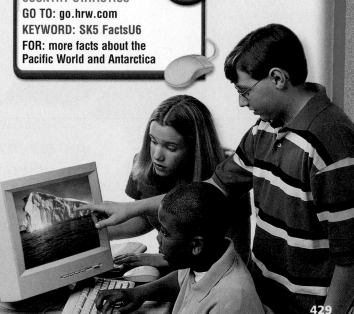

Source: Central Intelligence Agency, *The World Factbook 2003;* pop. figures are 2003 estimates.

CHAPTER 19

Australia and New Zealand

In this chapter we will study Australia and nearby New Zealand. First we meet Jared and Ashleigh. Their ancestors lived in Australia long before Europeans arrived.

Hi! My name is Jared. I have a twin sister, Ashleigh. We are 14 years old and live in Cooroy, Australia, which is about two hours north of Brisbane. We live with our mother in a three-bedroom house on a hill. Our land has a big creek with a dam on it. The dam forms a big pond, or a billabong. We can jump into it from the trees along the edge. Our father lives up north in the traditional lands of our people, the Djabugayndgi.

We used to speak our native language, but we've forgotten lots of it since we've been going to school. My totem, or special animal protector, is the *Ngumba*, or platypus. My sister's is the *Badgigal*, or freshwater turtle.

Since we were three years old, we have been singing and dancing in an Aboriginal dance group called *Bibayungen*. At Christmas, the whole family gathers with about 1,000 people in our traditional lands for a big dance and music festival (*warrima* in our language).

Nyurramba garran, bulmba nganydjin ngunda!

▲
Translation: Come and see our country!

Read to Discover

1. What are Australia's natural features and resources?
2. What is the history of Australia?
3. What is Australia like today?

Vocabulary

artesian wells
coral reef
endemic species
marsupials
outback
rugby
bush

Places

Eastern Highlands
Central Lowlands
Western Plateau
Great Dividing Range
Tasmania
Murray-Darling Rivers
Great Artesian Basin
Great Barrier Reef
Sydney
Melbourne
Brisbane
Perth

Reading Strategy

ANTICIPATING INFORMATION Before reading, predict whether you think the following statements are true or false.

• Australia is a mountainous continent with a cool climate.
• The seasons in Australia occur at the same time of year as those in the United States.
• Australia has a very mixed population.

Check your answers while reading. Then explain why each statement is true or false.

Australia and New Zealand: Physical-Political

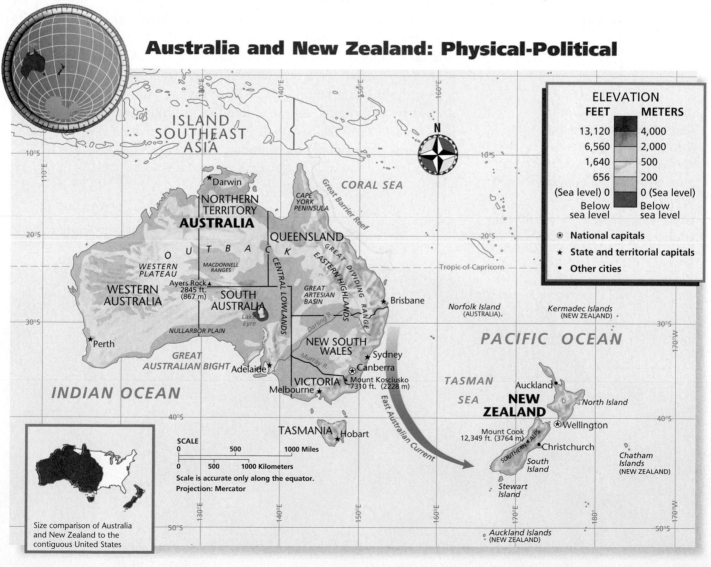

ELEVATION

FEET	METERS
13,120	4,000
6,560	2,000
1,640	500
656	200
(Sea level) 0	0 (Sea level)
Below sea level	Below sea level

⊛ National capitals
★ State and territorial capitals
• Other cities

SCALE
0   500   1000 Miles
0   500   1000 Kilometers
Scale is accurate only along the equator.
Projection: Mercator

Size comparison of Australia and New Zealand to the contiguous United States

Natural Features

Australia is the world's smallest, flattest, and lowest continent. In addition, it is the only country that is also a continent. The country sometimes is called the Land Down Under because it lies south of the equator. Seasons there are reversed from those north of the equator. For example, when it is winter in the United States, it is summer in Australia.

Land Australia has three main landform regions. These are the Eastern Highlands, the Central Lowlands, and the Western Plateau.

The Eastern Highlands are a system of ridges, plateaus, and valleys in the eastern part of Australia. They include the Great Dividing Range. This range stretches along the eastern coast and includes the island of Tasmania. It divides Australia's rivers into those that flow eastward and those that flow westward. Australia's one major river system, the Murray-Darling, flows westward from the range.

Australia's highest mountain is in the Great Dividing Range. It rises to just 7,310 feet (2,228 m). This tells us that Australia is very old. Erosion from wind and water has lowered the continent's mountains over millions of years.

The Central Lowlands are flatter and lower than the Eastern Highlands. The Central Lowlands include the Great Artesian Basin, Australia's largest source of underground water. **Artesian wells** dot this area. Artesian wells are those in which water rises toward the surface without being pumped. The groundwater comes from rain falling on nearby mountains. As the amount of groundwater increases, some is pushed to the surface. Much of the well water here is of poor quality, so it is used mostly for watering sheep.

Our Amazing Planet

Ayers Rock in central Australia is composed of sandstone with bits of reflective minerals. The sandstone changes color as the Sun moves across the sky. At sunset Ayers Rock turns a fiery orange-red.

Ayers Rock, called Uluru by Aborigines, rises more than 1,100 feet (335 m) above the surrounding Western Plateau. It is all that is left after erosion wore away an ancient mountain.

Interpreting the Visual Record How has erosion affected Ayers Rock?

Australia
● Ayers Rock

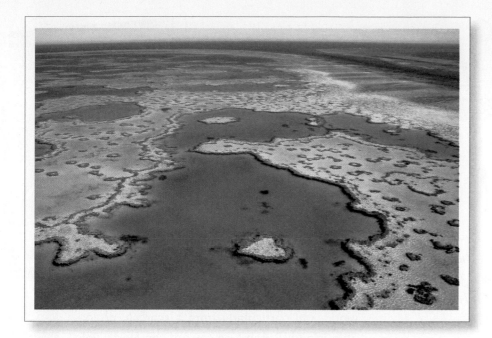

The Great Barrier Reef is really thousands of small reefs and tiny islands. Some rise barely above water level when the tide is low.

Farther west is the Western Plateau, which covers more than half of the continent. The treeless Nullarbor Plain stretches along the southern edge of the plateau. This plain is the flattest large area on any continent.

The Great Barrier Reef Off the northeastern coast of Australia is the Great Barrier Reef. It is the world's largest **coral reef**, stretching more than 1,250 miles (2,000 km). A coral reef is a ridge found close to shore in warm, tropical waters. It is made of rocky limestone material formed by the skeletons of tiny sea animals. You will read more about coral reefs in the next chapter.

The Great Barrier Reef and its shallow waters are home to many kinds of marine animals. They include fish, shellfish, and sea birds. Australia's government has made most of the reef a national park.

Climate Australia has been described as a desert with green edges. Dry desert and steppe climates cover most of the country. The eastern and southeastern edges and Tasmania have humid climates. Two coastal areas in the south and southwest have a Mediterranean climate. Summers there are long, dry, and sunny. Winters are mild and wet. The north has a tropical savanna climate. There monsoons bring strong wet and dry seasons.

Plants and Animals Australia has many **endemic species**. Endemic species are plants and animals that developed in one particular region of the world. Why does Australia have many endemic species? Australia has been separated from other continents for millions of years. However, over time many nonnative plants and animals have been brought to Australia. See the Case Study in this chapter.

The shallow ocean waters along Australia's northern coast are home to the deadly sea wasp jellyfish. Each jellyfish has as many as 60 tentacles that hang down six and a half feet (2 m). The venom from its sting can kill a human in less than five minutes.

Christmas on an Australian beach

THE LAND DOWN UNDER

Europeans began settling in Australia in the late 1700s. The following selection describes what settlers found in the Land Down Under. The selection comes from Christina Stead's For Love Alone, *published in 1944.*

In the part of the world Teresa came from, winter is in July, spring brides marry in September, and Christmas is consummated[1] with roast beef [and] suckling[2] pig . . . at 100 degrees in the shade, near the tall pine tree loaded with gifts and tinsel as in the old country, and old carols have rung out all through the night.

   This island continent lies in the water hemisphere. On the eastern coast, the neighboring nation is Chile, though it is far, far east, Valparaiso being more than six thousand miles away in a straight line; her northern neighbors are those of the Timor Sea, the Yellow Sea; to the south is that cold, stormy sea full of earth-wide rollers, which stretches from there without land, south to the Pole.

   The other world—the old world, the land [Northern] hemisphere—is far above her as it is shown on maps drawn upside-down by old-world cartographers. From that world and particularly from a scarcely noticeable island [Britain] up toward the North Pole the people came, all by steam; or their parents, all by sail. . . . Inside, over the Blue Mountains, are the plains heavy with wheat, then the endless dust, and after outcrops of silver, opal, and gold, Sahara, the salt-crusted bed of a prehistoric sea, and leafless mountain ranges. There is nothing in the interior; so people look toward the water, and above to the fixed stars and constellations which first guided men there.

Analyzing Primary Sources

1. How does life differ from that in the "old world" in Teresa's land?
2. How does the writer give the reader a sense of Australia's isolation?

[1]consummated: completed, marked, or celebrated; [2]suckling: a young mammal that is still nursing

Two of Australia's most famous native animals are the kangaroo and the koala. Both animals are **marsupials** (mahr-SOO-pee-uhls). Marsupials are animals that carry their young in pouches. Eucalyptus (yoo-kuh-LIP-tuhs) is Australia's most common tree.

Minerals Australia's **outback**, or inland region, has many mineral resources such as gold, iron ore, and bauxite. Australia also has coal, natural gas, oil, and gemstones such as opals and diamonds.

✔ **READING CHECK:** (*Places and Regions*) What are the natural features of Australia?

A bark painting provides a glimpse of some Aborigines' spiritual beliefs. The painting shows the path taken by a soul on its journey to another world. Traditional Aboriginal culture almost disappeared after Europeans arrived in Australia.

History

The first humans to live in Australia were the Aborigines (a-buh-RIJ-uh-nees). They came from Southeast Asia at least 40,000 years ago. Early Aborigines hunted animals and gathered food from wild plants. They had many different languages, traditions, and customs. The arrival of Europeans changed life for the Aborigines.

European Settlers The British began settling colonies in Australia in 1788. Many of the first settlers were British prisoners, but other British settlers came, too. As the settlers built farms and ranches, they took over the Aborigines' lands. In addition, many Aborigines died of diseases brought unintentionally by the Europeans.

Independence The British granted independence to the Australian colonies in 1901. The colonies were united into one country within the British Commonwealth of Nations. Australia fought on the side of the British and other Allied forces in World Wars I and II.

Today Australia has six states and one large territory. The national capital is Canberra. Because Australia is part of the Commonwealth, the British monarch also is Australia's monarch. However, a prime minister and parliament make Australia's laws. Some Australians want their country to leave the Commonwealth and replace the monarch with an Australian president or other official.

✓ **READING CHECK:** (*Movement*) How has migration affected Australia's history?

States and Territories of Australia

State	Capital
New South Wales	Sydney
Victoria	Melbourne
Queensland	Brisbane
Western Australia	Perth
South Australia	Adelaide
Tasmania	Hobart

Territory	Capital
Northern Territory	Darwin
Australian Capital Territory	Canberra

Interpreting the Chart What is the capital of Tasmania?

Culture

More than 90 percent of Australians today are of British or other European ancestry. Since the 1970s Asians have been moving to

The Sydney Opera House opened on the city's harbor front in 1973. It is one of Australia's most well-known buildings.

Australia in growing numbers. As a result, about 7 percent of Australia's population today is ethnic Asian. Only about 1 percent of the country's people are Aborigines. Nearly all Australians speak English, but some Aborigines also speak native languages.

Religion and Holidays Most Australians are Christians. They celebrate many of the same holidays as people in the United States. However, their traditions may be different. For example, December falls during summer in Australia. Christmas there is time for a beach party, picnic, or some other outdoor activity.

Outdoor activities are popular in sunny Australia. Many people enjoy picnics, swimming, and sports. Popular sports include the British game of cricket, sailing, horse racing, surfing, and Australian Rules football. Many Australians also enjoy **rugby**. Rugby is a British game similar to football and soccer.

The Arts Music and other arts are also popular in Australia. In fact, art by Aborigines has become popular around the world. The Australian government is an important source of money for the arts. For example, the government has built many public performance halls. One of the most famous is the Opera House in Australia's largest city, Sydney.

Australia

COUNTRY	POPULATION/ GROWTH RATE	LIFE EXPECTANCY	LITERACY RATE	PER CAPITA GDP
Australia	19,731,984 0.9%	77, male 83, female	100%	$27,000
United States	290,342,554 0.9%	74, male 80, female	97%	$37,600

Source: Central Intelligence Agency, *The World Factbook 2003*

Interpreting the Chart How does Australia's literacy rate compare to that of the United States?

✓ **READING CHECK:** (*Human Systems*) What are some characteristics of Australia's people?

Australia Today

About 85 percent of Australians live in and around cities. The rest live in the **bush**, or lightly populated wilderness areas. The largest cities are Sydney and Melbourne in the southeast. Brisbane, on the eastern coast, enjoys a warm, tropical climate that attracts tourists. Towns have grown around mining and ranching areas in parts of the dry, rugged outback. Large parts of the interior have few people. The seaport of Perth is the largest city in the west.

Economy Australia is a rich, economically developed country. It is a leading producer of agricultural goods such as wool, meat, and wheat. Australia supplies nearly half of the world's wool used in clothing. One of the country's most important industries is mining, particularly in the outback. Other industries include steel, heavy machines, and computers.

Challenges Australia faces important challenges. Among these is improving the economic and political status of the Aborigines. They have only recently gained back some of the rights they lost after Europeans colonized Australia. The country also must continue to build ties with Asian and Pacific countries. At one time Australia's strongest ties were with Britain. Today, its most important trading partners are much closer Asian countries and the United States. In addition, Australia must deal with the rapid growth of its cities. It also must protect native animals and the environment.

✓ **READING CHECK:** (**Places and Regions**) What is Australia's economy like?

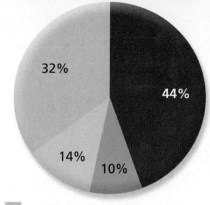

Major Producers of Wool

- Australia
- New Zealand
- China
- Rest of the world

Source: Based on data from The Woolmark Company

▲ Wool is produced from sheep's hair. Australia has one of the world's largest flocks of sheep.

Interpreting the Chart What nearby country is the world's second-largest wool producer?

Homework Practice Online
Keyword: SK5 HP19

Define and explain: artesian wells, coral reef, endemic species, marsupials, outback, rugby, bush

Working with Sketch Maps On a map of Australia and New Zealand that you draw or that your teacher provides, label the following: Eastern Highlands, Central Lowlands, Western Plateau, Great Dividing Range, Tasmania, Murray-Darling Rivers, Great Artesian Basin, Great Barrier Reef, Sydney, Melbourne, Brisbane, and Perth. In a box in the margin, describe why the Great Artesian Basin is important to a dry country like Australia.

Reading for the Main Idea

1. (**Human Systems**) How has migration affected Australia's population? Which ethnic group is the largest?

2. (**Places and Regions**) What are two of Australia's most famous native marsupials?

3. (**Human Systems**) Who were the first humans to live in Australia? When did Europeans start settling there?

Critical Thinking

4. Drawing Inferences and Conclusions Why is building ties with Asian countries important for Australia today?

Organizing What You Know

5. Categorizing Copy the following graphic organizer. Use it to list Australia's climates, plants and animals, and mineral resources.

Climates	Plants and Animals	Resources

CASE STUDY

NONNATIVE SPECIES IN AUSTRALIA

For about the last 35 million years, Australia has been separated from the other continents by oceans. During this time Australia's plants and animals developed in isolation from the rest of the world. Eventually, a unique Australian ecosystem developed. Many interesting species of plants and animals existed only in Australia. For example, kangaroos, koalas, and eucalyptus trees were all native to Australia. They were not found anywhere else in the world.

Europeans arrived in Australia in the late 1700s. They dramatically changed the natural balance that had developed over millions of years.

Europeans brought with them many new species of plants and animals. These nonnative species have had a major impact on the environment in Australia.

European settlers turned large areas of grasslands into fields for agriculture. They set up huge wheat farms in the south and southwest. They planted sugarcane fields in the northeast. These crops had never been grown in Australia. Farmers also brought nonnative animals, such as sheep, cows, and goats, into Australia. In less than 100 years, Australia had more than 100 million sheep and 8 million cows.

Cattle are herded on the island of Tasmania in Australia.

Interpreting the Visual Record Can you see how these animals are changing the environment?

▼

Introduced into Australia from Southeast Asia, water buffalo now eat food that Australia's native animals need to survive.

Many of the nonnative species that were brought into Australia spread across the continent. Some are now considered pests. These plants and animals are seriously damaging Australia's environment. For example, camels were introduced into Australia as pack animals. Now they run wild in the desert interior. Water buffalo were introduced from Southeast Asia. They trample riverbanks, killing grasses and eroding the soil. The prickly pear cactus was introduced into Australia from the United States as a garden plant. It spread across much of the country and has been very hard to control. Cane toads were introduced in the 1930s to protect Australia's sugarcane fields from cane beetles. However, they release toxic chemicals when attacked and are now threatening native species and household pets.

Of the nonnative animals introduced into Australia, rabbits have probably been the most destructive. Brought in by hunters in the 1800s, rabbits multiplied and spread quickly. With no natural predators and lots of food, their numbers increased to about 500 million. Rabbits overgrazed Australia's grasslands and caused major soil erosion.

The introduction of nonnative species into Australia has damaged the environment in several ways. Some native species have become extinct because they could not compete with nonnative species. About 13 species of mammals and one species of bird have become extinct in Australia since the late 1700s. Many more are endangered. Nonnative species such as cows, sheep, and rabbits have caused soil erosion. These animals also consume food and water that Australia's native plants and animals need to survive. As the case of Australia shows, the introduction of nonnative species into a new environment can cause serious environmental problems.

Understanding What You Read

1. How did isolation affect Australia's ecosystem?

2. What are some of the species that Europeans brought with them to Australia? How does Australia's environment now reflect their influence?

Discover

1. What are the natural features of New Zealand?
2. What are the history and culture of New Zealand?
3. What are New Zealand's cities and economy like today?

Vocabulary

kiwi

Places

Tasman Sea
South Island
North Island
Southern Alps

Wellington
Auckland
Christchurch

Reading Strategy

TAKING NOTES Taking notes while you read will help you understand and remember the information in this section. Write down the headings in the section. As you read, fill in notes under each heading. What are the most important details under each?

The Southern Alps stretch across much of New Zealand's South Island. New Zealand's government has established large national parks throughout the mountains.

▼

Natural Features

New Zealand lies southeast of Australia across the Tasman Sea. It includes two large islands—South Island and North Island. Put together, the islands are about the size of the U.S. state of Colorado.

Land The highest mountains are the Southern Alps on South Island. These rugged, glacier-capped mountains cover the western half of the island. The highest peak reaches 12,349 feet (3,764 m). A narrow coastal plain stretches along South Island's eastern side.

North Island has three major volcanic peaks separated by a volcanic plateau. Volcanic eruptions are common. Most of the rest of North Island is covered by hills and coastal plains.

Climate, Wildlife, and Resources Unlike mostly dry Australia, New Zealand is humid. It has a mild marine west coast climate. Rain falls throughout the year. Winds from the west bring very heavy rain or snow to South Island's western side. The grassy plains of the drier eastern side are in a rain shadow. The north of North Island, in the lower latitudes, has a warmer, more tropical climate.

Much of New Zealand was once forested. Today, more than half is covered by pastures and farms. Sheep and other livestock graze in New Zealand's pastures. Sheep and their wool have long been important to the country's economy.

As in Australia, many animals in New Zealand are endemic species. The country's endemic species include different kinds of bats and flightless birds such as the **kiwi** (KEE-wee). The kiwi has hairlike feathers and sharp senses of smell and hearing. This bird is so linked with the country that New Zealanders are sometimes called Kiwis.

Many other species have been brought to New Zealand over time. For example, deer and trout have been introduced to provide sport for hunters and fishers.

New Zealand has fewer mineral resources than Australia. Its natural resources include gold, iron ore, natural gas, and coal.

✓ **READING CHECK:** (*Place*) What are the natural features of New Zealand?

History and Culture

New Zealand's first settlers came from other Pacific islands more than 1,000 years ago. Their descendants, the Maori (MOWR-ee), still live in New Zealand. The early settlers' main source of food was the moa—a giant, flightless bird. However, overhunting by New Zealand's early peoples wiped out the moa. The bird was extinct by the time Europeans arrived in New Zealand.

Maori traditional art, like this carved entrance arch, survived New Zealand's colonial period.

Interpreting the Visual Record **What role does art play in Maori culture?**

New Zealand's All Black Rugby Union team performs a version of the Haka (HAH-kah) before international games. The Haka is a traditional Maori dance.

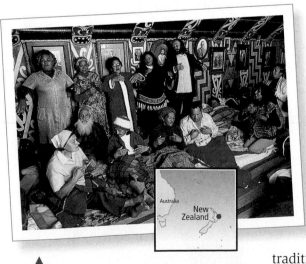

Mourners attend a funeral in a Maori-carved meeting house.

European Settlers A Dutch explorer in 1642 was the first European to sight New Zealand. British explorer Captain James Cook visited New Zealand in 1769. Many British settlers started to arrive after the British signed a treaty with the Maori in 1840. However, fighting broke out as British settlers took over Maori lands.

Independence The British granted New Zealand independence in 1907. Like Australia, New Zealand became a member of the British Commonwealth of Nations. New Zealanders fought alongside the British in World Wars I and II.

The government of New Zealand is led by a prime minister. An elected parliament makes the country's laws. The capital, Wellington, is located at the southern tip of North Island.

Culture Like Australia, most of New Zealand's 3.9 million people are of European ancestry. A growing number of ethnic Asians also live in the country. The Maori make up nearly 10 percent of the population. People from other Pacific islands have also come to New Zealand.

Most New Zealanders speak English. Some Maori also speak the Maori language. Most New Zealanders also are Christian. Sports, particularly rugby, are popular.

Maori culture has not disappeared. Traditional art, music, and dance remain important in Maori culture. Many Maori weddings, funerals, and other special events still are held in traditional carved houses. The Maori call these meetinghouses *whare whakairo*. Many meetinghouses are beautifully carved and decorated.

✓ **READING CHECK:** (*Human Systems*) How have conflict and cooperation affected the history of New Zealand?

New Zealand Today

Today about 75 percent of New Zealanders, including most Maori, live on North Island. Most of the country's industries and agriculture are also located there.

Cities About 85 percent of New Zealanders live in urban areas. The country's largest city and seaport, Auckland, is located in the northern part of North Island. Christchurch is South Island's largest city.

Economy New Zealand is a rich, modern country with a market economy. Its mild, moist climate helped make agriculture an important part of the economy. The country is a major producer of wool, meat, dairy products, wheat, kiwifruit, and apples.

New Zealand has become more industrialized in recent years. Factories turn out processed food, wood, paper products, clothing, and machinery. Banking, insurance, and tourism are also important industries. Australia, the United States, Japan, and the United Kingdom are the country's main trade partners.

✓ **READING CHECK:** (*Place*) What are some of New Zealand's cities, and what is its economy like?

Cable cars provide transportation for residents and visitors in Wellington.

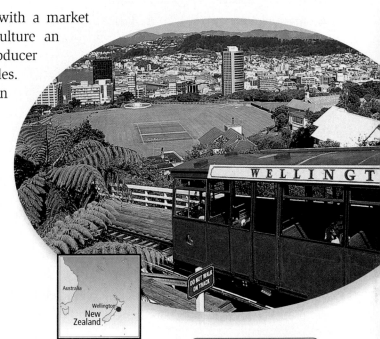

COUNTRY	POPULATION/ GROWTH RATE	LIFE EXPECTANCY	LITERACY RATE	PER CAPITA GDP
New Zealand	3,951,307 1.1%	75, male 81, female	99%	$20,200
United States	290,342,554 0.9%	74, male 80, female	97%	$37,600

New Zealand

Source: Central Intelligence Agency, *The World Factbook 2003*

Australia

Wellington
New Zealand

go. hrw .com **Homework Practice Online**
Keyword: SK5 HP19

Section Review 2

Define and explain: kiwi

Working with Sketch Maps On the map you created in Section 1, label the Tasman Sea, South Island, North Island, Southern Alps, Wellington, Auckland, and Christchurch. In a box in the margin, identify New Zealand's capital and the country's largest city.

Reading for the Main Idea

1. (*Human Systems*) From where did the ancestors of the Maori come?

2. (*Human Systems*) Describe New Zealand's economy. How has it changed in recent years?

Critical Thinking

3. **Contrasting** How is the physical geography of North Island different from that of South Island? Describe the physical geography of each island.

4. **Drawing Inferences and Conclusions** Why do you think most New Zealanders live on North Island?

Organizing What You Know

5. **Summarizing** Copy the following graphic organizer. Use it to list the climates, plants and animals, and resources of New Zealand.

Climates	Plants and Animals	Resources

Define and Identify

Identify each of the following:

1. artesian wells
2. coral reef
3. endemic species
4. marsupials
5. outback
6. rugby
7. bush
8. kiwi

Review the Main Ideas

9. What are the three main landform regions of Australia?
10. What are the climates of the interior and the "edges" of Australia like?
11. New Zealand's North Island is known for what type of landform?
12. When did Europeans begin to settle in Australia and New Zealand?
13. What native peoples lived in Australia and New Zealand before the arrival of Europeans?
14. Australia and New Zealand are the world's two top producers of what agricultural product?
15. What country is a major trading partner with both Australia and New Zealand?

Think Critically

16. **Drawing Inferences and Conclusions** Why do you think the Great Barrier Reef would interest tourists?
17. **Drawing Inferences and Conclusions** Why do you think Australia's interior is lightly populated?
18. **Finding the Main Idea** How have humans changed the natural environments of Australia and New Zealand since the arrival of Europeans?
19. **Contrasting** How is New Zealand's climate different from Australia's? Identify the main climates in each country.
20. **Analyzing Information** What role have the arts played in Australian society?
21. **Drawing Inferences and Conclusions** How have the Maori in New Zealand kept their traditional culture?

Map Activity

22. On a separate sheet of paper, match the letters on the map with their correct labels.

Central Lowlands	Sydney
Western Plateau	Melbourne
Tasmania	Perth
Great Barrier Reef	Auckland

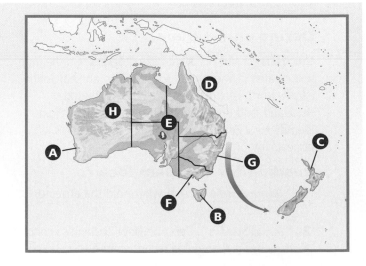

Writing Activity

Imagine that you are a European journalist in the late 1700s writing about the peoples and unique plants and animals in Australia and New Zealand. Write two paragraphs describing those peoples and endemic species. Include details that might surprise your European readers. Be sure to use standard grammar, spelling, sentence structure, and punctuation.

☑ internet connect

Internet Activity: go.hrw.com
KEYWORD: SK5 GT19

Choose a topic to explore about Australia and New Zealand:

- Explore the Great Barrier Reef.
- Learn about the Aborigines of Australia.
- Tour New Zealand.

Social Studies Skills Practice

Interpreting Maps

Study the following map of some of Australia's cities. Then answer the questions.

1. What is the capital city of Australia?
2. What key characteristic can you determine about most of the cities in Australia?
3. Which city is located near the Great Barrier Reef?
4. Which city is far from a water source?

Analyzing Primary Sources

Read the following excerpt from the 1840 treaty between the Maori and the British government. Then answer the questions.

"Victoria, the Queen of England, in her concern to protect the chiefs and the subtribes of New Zealand and in her desire to preserve their chieftainship [trusteeship] and their lands and to maintain peace and good order considers it just to appoint [select] an administrator—one who will negotiate with the people of New Zealand to the end that their chiefs will agree to the Queen's government being established over all parts of this land . . ."

1. Does the treaty promise that the Maori will have an equal say in their government?
2. What will be the main role of the administrator?
3. Does the Queen express a desire to protect the Maori under her leadership? How?
4. What is the final goal of the treaty?

CHAPTER 20

The Pacific Islands and Antarctica

In this chapter we will study the Pacific Islands and Antarctica, two very different regions.

My name is Jean Vanessa, and I am 13 years old. I live in Vabukori, a village in Port Moresby, the capital of Papua New Guinea. My mother is a journalist. My grandmother bakes our bread in a drum oven. Sometimes we sell the bread.

My house is built on stilts. It is near the village square where we have meetings and play sports. After breakfast, I take a bus to Port Moresby Grammar School. I make my own sandwiches to take for lunch.

In my society, when you are an eldest child and a girl, and if you have younger brothers and sisters, you are your mother's helper. You have to learn to cook, clean, and take care of younger children.

My favorite holidays are Christmas and New Year's. We celebrate with feasting and singing. The villagers are divided into two groups. On Christmas Day one group cooks for the other group. They sing prophet songs about Bible stories from dawn to dusk. On New Year's Day the groups exchange roles.

Daba namona!

Translation: Good morning!

Read to Discover

1. What are the physical features and resources of the Pacific Islands?
2. What are the physical features and resources of Antarctica?

Vocabulary

ice shelf
icebergs
polar desert
krill

Places

Melanesia
Micronesia
Polynesia
Tahiti
New Guinea
Papua New Guinea
Marshall Islands

New Caledonia
Transantarctic
   Mountains
Vinson Massif
Antarctic
   Peninsula

Reading Strategy

VISUALIZING INFORMATION Previewing the visuals in this section will help you understand the material you are about to read. What do the visuals on this page and the next two pages tell you about the regions you are studying? Write your answers on a sheet of paper.

The Formation of an Atoll

A A coral reef forms along the edges of a volcanic island.

Reef

A

B As the island sinks into the ocean, the reef continues to grow upward. It forms a barrier reef.

Barrier reef

B

C When the island is completely underwater, the reef forms an atoll. In the middle of the ring of islands is a lagoon.

Lagoon   Atoll

C

D A coral polyp builds a limestone skeleton that bonds it to a reef. When the coral polyp dies, it leaves behind its skeleton. The reef is made up of the skeletons of many dead coral polyps.

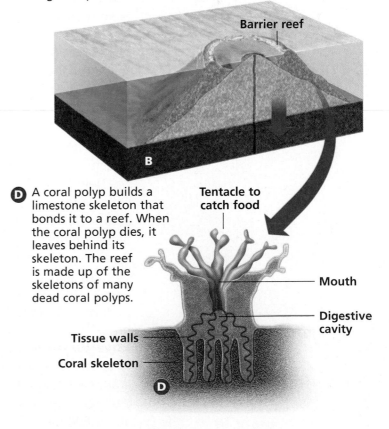

Tentacle to catch food

Mouth

Digestive cavity

Tissue walls

Coral skeleton

D

Place The airport on the left supports a healthy tourism industry in Bora-Bora, French Polynesia

The Pacific Islands

The Pacific Ocean covers more than one third of Earth's surface. East of Indonesia and the Philippines are thousands of large and small islands. These islands are divided into three regions: Melanesia, Micronesia, and Polynesia. These regions have high and low islands. Now we will look at these islands, their climates, and their resources.

High Islands There are two kinds of high islands: oceanic and continental. Oceanic high islands were formed by volcanoes rising from the sea floor. The Polynesian islands of Tahiti and Hawaii are examples of oceanic high islands. Many continental high islands also have volcanoes. However, these large islands were formed from continental rock. They lie on Australia's continental shelf. New Guinea, which is in Melanesia, is a continental high island.

New Guinea is the world's second-largest island. Only Greenland is larger. A long mountain chain stretches across the central part of New Guinea. The range's highest mountain lies in the western half of the island. It reaches an elevation of 16,535 feet (5,040 m). The western part of New Guinea is called Irian Jaya and is part of Indonesia. Papua New Guinea occupies the eastern half of the island.

Low Islands Most of the low islands are made of coral. They barely rise above sea level. Many are atolls. For example, the Marshall Islands include two parallel chains of coral atolls. The two chains are about 800 miles (1,287 km) long. The highest point is just 33 feet (10 m) above sea level. Measured from the ground to their roofs, many buildings in your town are probably higher!

Climates and Plants Most of the Pacific Islands lie in the tropics and have a humid tropical climate. The temperatures are warm, and rain is common all year. New Guinea's central highland regions are cooler. Rainfall there is heavy, particularly on the southern slopes of the highlands. In some years more than 300 inches (762 cm) of rain fall there. Some islands, such as New Caledonia, have a tropical savanna climate. Rain there falls mostly in the summer.

The low islands have thin soils. These islands support few trees other than the coconut palm. However, the high islands have dense tropical rain forests. In fact, Papua New Guinea is one of the world's most densely forested countries. Many peoples living in the forests and rugged mountains of the central highlands were isolated for centuries.

Resources The islands' natural beauty and pleasant climates attract many tourists. In addition, the high islands have freshwater, good soils, and forest resources. Continental high islands also have many minerals. For example, New Guinea has copper, gold, silver, and oil. However, mining these resources is difficult in the rugged highlands and dense tropical forests.

Low islands have few resources. There is little freshwater, and thin soils limit farming. Partly because of this, low islands have smaller populations than high islands. Coconut palms and the sea are important sources of food.

✔ **READING CHECK:** (*Places and Regions*) What are the physical features and resources of the Pacific Islands?

🔲 **internet** connect

GO TO: go.hrw.com
KEYWORD: SK5 CH20
FOR: Web sites about the Pacific Islands and Antarctica

(*Place*) Miners search for gold along a river in Papua New Guinea. They gently wash river water over pans to separate gold particles from less dense sand.

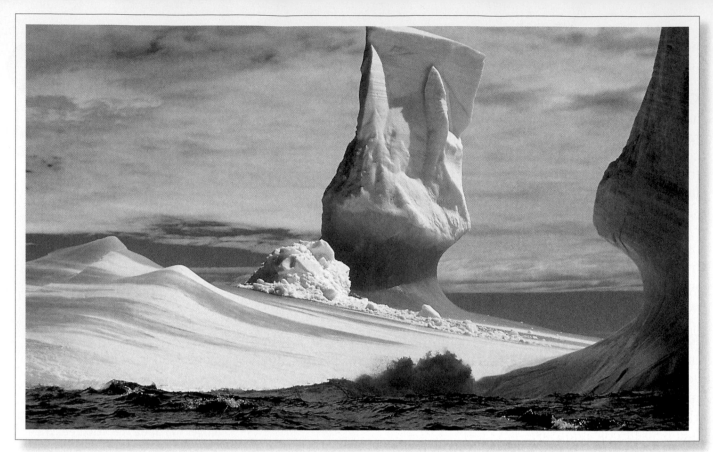

Huge icebergs like this one are found in the ocean waters around Antarctica. Icebergs are most numerous in the spring and summer. The warmer weather causes more ice to break away from ice sheets and glaciers.

Interpreting the Visual Record What forces do you think shaped this iceberg?

Antarctica

In the southernmost part of the world is the continent of Antarctica. This frozen land is very different from the tropical Pacific Islands.

The Land Antarctica is larger than the United States and Mexico combined. Ice covers about 98 percent of Antarctica's 5.4 million square miles (14 mil sq km). This ice sheet contains more than 90 percent of the world's ice. On average the ice sheet is more than one mile (1.6 km) thick.

The Transantarctic Mountains divide the continent into East Antarctica and West Antarctica. Antarctica's highest mountain peak is Vinson Massif. It rises to 16,864 feet (5,140 m). The continent also includes a few dry coastal valleys and the Antarctic Peninsula. (See the map of Antarctica in Focus On Environment at the end of this chapter.)

The weight of Antarctica's ice sheet causes the ice to flow slowly off the continent. When the ice reaches the coast, it forms a ledge over the water. This ledge is called an **ice shelf**. Sometimes huge chunks of ice, called **icebergs**, break away and drift into the ocean. Some of these icebergs are larger than the state of Rhode Island.

Climate and Wildlife Antarctica is the planet's coldest, driest, highest, and windiest continent. During the Southern Hemisphere's winter, the continent is hidden from the Sun. It remains in total darkness. During Antarctica's short summer, the Sun never sets.

Antarctica's temperatures can drop below -120°F (-84°C). Less precipitation falls in this polar desert than in the Sahara in Africa. A **polar desert** is a high-latitude region that receives little precipitation. However, there is almost no evaporation or melting of ice. As a result, Antarctica's ice has built up over thousands of years.

The continent's warmest temperatures are found on the Antarctic Peninsula, which has a tundra climate. In January, during Antarctica's summer, temperatures on the coast average just below freezing.

Only tundra plant life survives in the rare ice-free areas. A few insects are the frozen land's only land animals. Antarctica has never had a permanent human population. Marine animals live in the icy waters around the continent. These animals include penguins, seals, and whales. They depend on tiny shrimplike creatures called **krill** for food.

The emperor penguin is one of the most common marine animals found in Antarctica. Penguins are flightless birds and are awkward on land. However, they are very good swimmers and are able to live in the icy climate.

Resources Antarctica has many mineral resources, including iron ore, gold, copper, and coal. However, there is debate over whether these resources should be mined. Some people worry that mining would harm the continent's environment. Others question whether mining in Antarctica would even be worthwhile for businesses.

✓ **READING CHECK:** (*Places and Regions*) What are the physical features and resources of Antarctica?

Homework Practice Online
Keyword: SK5 HP20

Section Review 1

Define and explain: ice shelf, icebergs, polar desert, krill

Working with Sketch Maps On maps of the Pacific Islands and Antarctica that you draw or that your teacher provides, label the following: Melanesia, Micronesia, Polynesia, Tahiti, New Guinea, Papua New Guinea, Marshall Islands, New Caledonia, Transantarctic Mountains, Vinson Massif, and Antarctic Peninsula.

Reading for the Main Idea

1. (*Places and Regions*) What kinds of islands are found in the Pacific? How were they formed?

2. (*Places and Regions*) What animal life is found in Antarctica?

3. (*Places and Regions*) Which of the Pacific Islands is the second-largest island in the world?

Critical Thinking

4. **Making Generalizations and Predictions** What might happen if people were to begin mining Antarctica's mineral deposits on a large scale?

Organizing What You Know

5. **Summarizing** Copy the following graphic organizer. Use it to list physical features, climates, and resources of the Pacific Islands and Antarctica.

	Pacific Islands	Antarctica
Physical features		
Climates		
Resources		

Read to Discover

1. What is the history of the Pacific Islands?
2. What are the people and culture of the Pacific Islands like?
3. What are some challenges that Pacific Islanders face today?

Vocabulary

trust territories
Exclusive Economic Zones

Places

Guam
Northern Mariana Islands
Wake Island
French Polynesia

People

James Cook

Reading Strategy

DEVELOPING VOCABULARY Find unfamiliar words in this section. On a sheet of paper, write down what you think they might mean. Then look the words up in a dictionary. How do the words relate to the section's topics?

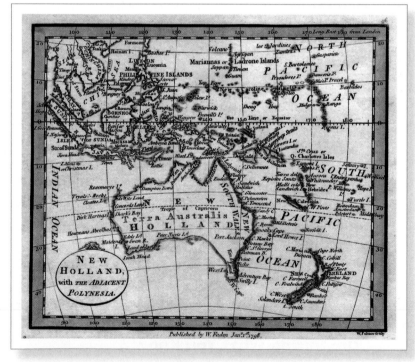

▲

This map of the South Pacific was made by a European cartographer in 1798.

Interpreting the Visual Record
Compare this map to the unit map. How accurate was this 1798 map?

History

Scholars believe that people began settling the Pacific Islands at least 40,000 years ago. Most early settlers came from Southeast Asia. The large islands of Melanesia were the first islands in the region settled. Over time, people moved to the islands of Micronesia and Polynesia.

Europeans in the Pacific In the early 1500s Ferdinand Magellan became the first European to explore the Pacific. In the late 1700s British captain James Cook explored the region. He visited all the main island regions of the Pacific. By the late 1800s European countries controlled most of the Pacific Islands. These European countries included France, Germany, the Netherlands, Spain, and the United Kingdom.

Modern History The Pacific Islands were battlegrounds during several wars in the colonial era. For example, the Spanish-American War of 1898 cost Spain the Philippines and Guam. They became U.S. territories after the war. Spain then sold other island territories to Germany. After World War I ended in 1918, Japan took over Germany's territories in the Pacific.

Japan conquered many other islands in World War II. The United States and its allies eventually won them back and defeated Japan. The United Nations then made some islands **trust territories**. Trust territories are areas placed under the temporary control of another country. When the territory later sets up its own government, it gains independence. U.S. trust territories included much of Micronesia.

Most of the island countries won independence in the last half of the 1900s. Australia, France, New Zealand, the United Kingdom, and the United States still have Pacific territories. U.S. territories include the Northern Mariana Islands, Guam, and Wake Island.

✓ **READING CHECK:** (*Places and Regions*) What are some events in the history of the Pacific Islands?

Culture

About 7 million people live in Melanesia, Micronesia, and Polynesia today. Check the unit map as we look more closely at each region and its people.

Melanesia Melanesia stretches from New Guinea to Fiji. It is the most populous of the three Pacific Island regions. Papua New Guinea and Fiji have the largest populations. Nearly two thirds of all Pacific Islanders live in Papua New Guinea.

Most Melanesians live in rural areas. Many homes in Melanesia and the other regions are made of timber and thatch, or straw. Papua New Guinea's capital, Port Moresby, is Melanesia's largest city. Nearly 260,000 people live there.

Melanesia's population includes ethnic Europeans and Asians, particularly Indians and Chinese. Many ethnic Asians are descended from people brought to the islands to work on colonial plantations. In Fiji, Indians make up nearly half of the population.

Either English or French is the official language on nearly all of the islands. This is a reflection of the region's colonial history. However, hundreds of local languages also are spoken there. In fact, about 700 languages are spoken in New Guinea alone. Many Papua New Guineans live in rugged, forested areas. They have had little contact with people from other areas. These isolated peoples developed their own languages.

Europeans brought Christianity to Melanesia and the other island regions. Today, most Pacific Islanders are Christian. However, some Melanesians still practice traditional local religions.

Micronesia and Polynesia Micronesia includes more than 2,000 tiny islands north of Melanesia. It stretches from Palau in the west to Kiribati in the east. Polynesia is the largest Pacific region. Its

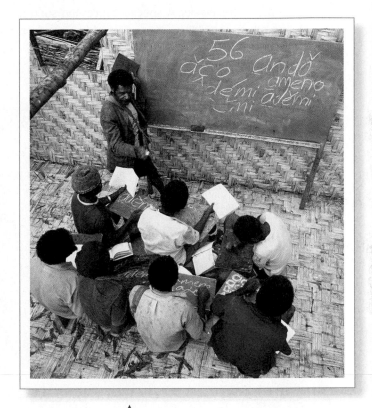

▲ Students learn the day's lessons at a school in Papua New Guinea. Papua New Guinea's government has struggled to make education available for all students. Many countries in Micronesia and Polynesia offer schooling for students through high school.

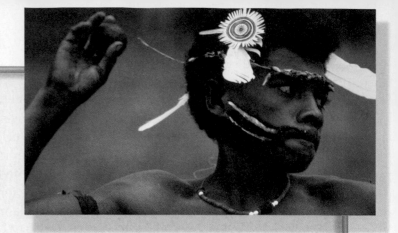

Playing with the Rules

People of the South Pacific have made interesting changes to some European sports. Missionaries brought cricket, an English bat-and-ball game, to the Trobriand Islands east of New Guinea. The islanders changed cricket into more of a ritual. They added costumes, chants, and dances. They also changed almost all the rules. Up to 60 men play on a team. A regular cricket team has only 11 members. These huge matches may go on for weeks. A special dance and song celebrates each point. Even the game's basic movements are different. Players throw the ball as if they are throwing spears.

Pacific Islanders also enjoy other unusual sports. Outrigger canoe racing, underwater spearfishing, and coconut tree climbing are all popular sporting events.

Why do you think the Trobriand Islanders changed the rules for playing cricket?

corners at New Zealand, Hawaii, and Easter Island form a huge triangle.

The populations of most Micronesian and Polynesian islands are much smaller than those of Melanesia. However, towns on these small islands can be very crowded. Micronesia is the most urban of the Pacific Island regions. Most Polynesians live in rural areas.

As in Melanesia, ethnic Europeans and Asians live in Micronesia and Polynesia. Most people in these regions are Christian and speak either English or French. Some speak local languages or Japanese.

✓ **READING CHECK:** (*Human Systems*) What are some characteristics of the people and cultures of Melanesia, Micronesia, and Polynesia?

The Pacific Islands Today

Many people imagine sunny beaches and tourists when they think of the Pacific Islands today. The islands do attract many tourists. For example, Tahiti, in French Polynesia, is a popular vacation spot. Many vacationers from South Korea and Japan enjoy visiting Guam, in Micronesia. Despite the region's healthy tourism industry, however, the Pacific countries face important challenges.

Economy The Pacific Islands are trying to build stronger economies. Tourism, agriculture, and fishing are already important there. Some countries, particularly Papua New Guinea, export valuable minerals and forest products.

Each Pacific country claims control of the fishing and seabed minerals around its islands. The 200-nautical-mile (370 km) zones they claim are called **Exclusive Economic Zones** (EEZs). Most of the world's countries also claim EEZs. A country must pay fees to fish or mine in another country's EEZ.

Natural resources should help the island economies grow. However, many Pacific countries import more products from abroad than they export. Many countries rely on the United Nations, the European Union, Great Britain, Australia, and Japan for economic aid.

Environment Many Pacific Islanders are concerned about their region's environment. Many have been angered by nuclear weapons tests conducted in the region by other countries. The United States held such tests in the islands from the 1940s to the 1960s. Radiation left some islands unsafe for people for many years. France held nuclear tests in the region until the mid-1990s.

Pacific Islands

COUNTRY	POPULATION/ GROWTH RATE	LIFE EXPECTANCY	LITERACY RATE	PER CAPITA GDP
Fiji	868,531 / 1.4%	66, male 71, female	93%	$5,500
Kiribati	98,549 / 2.3%	57, male 64, female	Not available	$840
Marshall Islands	56,429 / 2.3%	67, male 71, female	93%	$1,600
Micronesia, Federated States of	108,143 / 0.4%	67, male 70, female	89%	$2,000
Nauru	12,570 / 2.0%	58, male 65, female	Not available	$5,000
Palau	19,717 / 1.7%	66, male 72, female	92%	$9,000
Papua New Guinea	5,295,816 / 2.3%	62, male 66, female	66%	$2,300
Samoa	178,173 / −0.2%	67, male 73, female	99%	$5,600
Solomon Islands	509,190 / 3.0%	69, male 74, female	Not available	$1,700
Tonga	108,141 / 1.9%	66, male 71, female	99%	$2,200
Tuvalu	11,305 / 1.4%	65, male 69, female	Not available	$1,100
Vanuatu	199,413 / 1.6%	60, male 63, female	53%	$2,900
United States	290,342,554 / 0.9%	74, male 80, female	97%	$37,600

Source: Central Intelligence Agency, *The World Factbook 2003*

Interpreting the Chart What is the literacy rate like in most of the Pacific Islands?

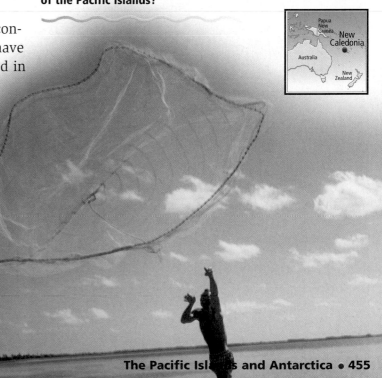

A fisher casts his net along the coast of New Caledonia.

Place This Fijian chief's home has many traditional handicrafts. Fiji's Great Council of Chiefs has influence in the country's political system and culture.

Some people who live on islands still controlled by foreign countries want independence, which has led to outbreaks of violence. This happened in the 1980s in the French territory of New Caledonia. France has agreed to give New Caledonians more control over their local government.

Culture Many Pacific Islanders are also concerned about the loss of traditional customs and beliefs. Modern travel and communications have introduced influences from other regions. Islanders worry about the cultural effects of tourism, television, processed food, and alcohol.

✓ **READING CHECK:** (*Human Systems*) What are some challenges Pacific Islanders face today?

go.hrw.com **Homework Practice Online**
Keyword: SK5 HP20

Section Review 2

Define or identify: James Cook, trust territories, Exclusive Economic Zones

Working with Sketch Maps On the map of the Pacific Islands that you created in Section 1, label the region's countries. Then label the territories of Guam, Northern Mariana Islands, Wake Island, and French Polynesia.

Reading for the Main Idea

1. (*Human Systems*) From where did the Pacific Islands' first settlers come? Which Pacific Island region was settled first?

2. (*Human Systems*) What colonial powers once controlled most of the Pacific Islands?

Critical Thinking

3. **Finding the Main Idea** In what ways did Europeans influence the islands' cultures?

4. **Finding the Main Idea** What are some of the challenges facing Pacific Islanders today?

Organizing What You Know

5. **Sequencing** Use this time line to explain important people and events in the region's history.

1500   2000

Read to Discover

1. How was Antarctica explored?
2. What can research in Antarctica tell us about our planet?
3. What problems threaten Antarctica's environment?

Vocabulary

antifreeze

Places

South Pole
Ross Ice Shelf

People

Ernest Shackleton

Reading Strategy

BRAINSTORMING Brainstorm about the following topics: traveling to Antarctica, climate and conditions in Antarctica, and environmental threats to Antarctica. After brainstorming, read the section. How does your brainstorming relate to the topic? Were your thoughts about Antarctica accurate?

Early Explorers

Can you imagine a time when a large continent like Antarctica was a complete mystery? Today, orbiting satellites give us views of all of Earth's surface. Jet airliners and modern ships take people to all points on the globe. However, all of this has become possible only in the last century. For a long time, stormy ocean waters hid Antarctica from explorers. In the 1770s British explorer James Cook sighted icebergs in the waters around Antarctica. These icebergs suggested the existence of the vast, icy continent.

Other explorers followed. Some died in Antarctica's dangerous conditions while attempting to reach the South Pole and return. The huts of famous Antarctic explorers are still scattered across the continent. The first human expedition reached the South Pole in 1911.

Some countries have claimed parts of Antarctica. These countries and others agreed in 1959 to preserve the continent "for science and peace." The Antarctic Treaty of 1959 prevented more claims to the continent. It banned military activity there and set aside the whole continent for research.

✓ **READING CHECK:** (*Environment and Society*) How did the physical environment affect early efforts to explore Antarctica?

BIOGRAPHY

Sir Ernest Shackleton
(1874–1922)

Character Trait: Responsibility

In 1914, Ernest Shackleton and his crew of 27 men set out to be the first to cross the entire Antarctic continent. But their ship, *Endurance*, became completely frozen in ice. Using their ship's rescue boats, Shackleton and his crew sailed to a nearby deserted island. Shackleton then decided to sail another 800 miles to reach help on South Georgia Island. After surviving the dangerous journey, Shackleton then led four expeditions to rescue the rest of his crew.

What actions did Shackleton take to demonstrate responsibility?

Some of Antarctica's rocks contain bacteria and other tiny forms of life. They live in small spaces that can only be seen with a microscope. These tough survivors may be thousands of years old!

Researchers are conducting experiments in icy waters off the coast of Antarctica.

Interpreting the Visual Record What might these underwater researchers be trying to learn?

Research in Antarctica

Today, researchers are the only people who live in Antarctica. They live in a number of bases or stations. U.S. stations include Palmer, on the Antarctic Peninsula, and McMurdo, on the Ross Ice Shelf. The United States also maintains a base at the South Pole. Researchers at these bases are looking for clues to Earth's past and future.

Air Pollution The researchers have made important discoveries. For example, some have studied gases trapped in old Antarctic ice. They have compared these gases with gases in Earth's atmosphere today. Their studies have shown that carbon dioxide levels in the air have risen over time. Some scientists believe high levels of carbon dioxide are responsible for global warming.

Scientists are also looking for evidence that air pollution is damaging Earth's ozone layer. The ozone layer protects living things from the harmful effects of the Sun's ultraviolet rays. Scientists have found a thinning in the ozone layer above Antarctica.

Life Other research helps us understand mysteries of life on Earth. For example, researchers have studied a kind of fish that produces a natural **antifreeze**. Antifreeze is a substance added to liquid to keep the liquid from turning to ice. Natural antifreeze in their blood protects the fish in the icy waters around Antarctica. These fish may help us understand how some animals adapt to harsh environments.

✔ **READING CHECK:** (*Environment and Society*) What can research in Antarctica tell us about our planet?

Cruise ships allow tourists to witness the icy beauty of Antarctica. About 10,000 tourists visit Antarctica during the summer months. A typical tourist trip lasts about two weeks. The only other economic activity in the region involves offshore fishing.

Interpreting the Visual Record

(*Movement*) What potential hazards do you see for ships?

Environmental Threats

Antarctica's environment is an excellent place for research. This is because humans have disturbed little of the continent. That is changing, however. As you have read, there is already debate about whether to allow mining in Antarctica. In addition, tourists and even researchers have left behind trash, polluting the local environment. Oil spills have also caused problems.

Some people fear that mining Antarctica's resources will result in other spills and problems. To prevent this, a new international agreement was reached in 1991. This agreement forbids most activities in Antarctica that do not have a scientific purpose. It bans mining and drilling and limits tourism.

✓ **READING CHECK:** (*Environment and Society*) What are some of the problems threatening Antarctica's environment?

Homework Practice Online

Keyword: SK5 HP20

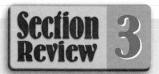

Define or identify: Ernest Shackleton, antifreeze

Working with Sketch Maps On the map of Antarctica you created in Section 1, label the South Pole and Ross Ice Shelf.

Reading for the Main Idea

1. (*Human Systems*) Who were the first Antarctic explorers to reach the South Pole, and when did they do so?

2. (*Environment and Society*) What did the 1959 Antarctic Treaty do? Why do you think this kind of agreement has not been made about other places on Earth?

Critical Thinking

3. **Making Generalizations and Predictions** How might future scientific discoveries in Antarctica affect the world?

4. **Finding the Main Idea** Why did many countries in 1991 agree to ban mining and to limit tourism in Antarctica?

Organizing What You Know

5. **Summarizing** Copy the following graphic organizer. Use it to describe research in Antarctica.

Research	Purpose

Define and Identify

Identify each of the following:

1. ice shelf
2. icebergs
3. polar desert
4. krill
5. James Cook
6. trust territories
7. Exclusive Economic Zones
8. Ernest Shackleton
9. antifreeze

Review the Main Ideas

10. What are the three Pacific Island regions?
11. How are oceanic high islands and low islands formed?
12. Why is Antarctica covered in ice and snow even though it receives little precipitation?
13. Where are dense tropical forests found in the Pacific Islands? What trees grow on low islands?
14. Who were the first Europeans to explore the Pacific region?
15. What happened in the Pacific Islands during World War II?
16. Why are so many languages spoken by the people of Papua New Guinea?

17. Which of the Pacific Islands regions is the most urban?
18. What agreements have been made to protect Antarctica's environment?

Think Critically

19. **Drawing Inferences and Conclusions** Why would the Pacific Island countries want to keep their 200-nautical-mile Exclusive Economic Zones?
20. **Finding the Main Idea** How have Europeans influenced the languages and religions of the Pacific Islands?
21. **Understanding Cause and Effect** What could happen to the economies of the Pacific Islands countries if there is a sharp increase in the cost of airline tickets?
22. **Drawing Inferences and Conclusions** Why do you think some Pacific Islanders would not welcome the construction of a new resort even though it creates many new jobs?
23. **Making Generalizations and Predictions** Why would pollution threaten the value of research done in Antarctica?

Map Activity

24. Identify the places marked on the map.

Papua New Guinea	Guam
Fiji	French Polynesia
Marshall Islands	Palau
New Caledonia	Solomon Islands

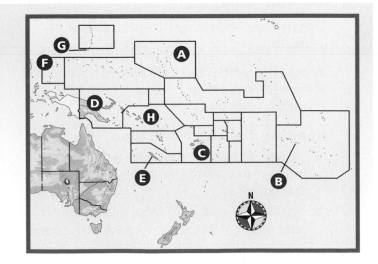

Writing Activity

Imagine that you are one of the first explorers trying to reach the South Pole. Write journal entries in which you describe what you have seen. Describe the conditions you have endured and the strategies you have used to survive. Use your textbook, the library, and the Internet to help you write your journal entries. Be sure to use standard grammar, spelling, sentence structure, and punctuation.

internet connect

Internet Activity: go.hrw.com
KEYWORD: SK5 GT20

Choose a topic to explore about the Pacific Islands and Antarctica.
- Tour the Pacific Islands.
- Explore Antarctica.
- Learn about native traditions.

Social Studies Skills Practice

Interpreting Charts

Study the chart below. Then answer the questions.

Tourism in the Pacific Islands

Country	Visitors in 2000	Visitors in 2001
Fiji	294,070	348,014
Palau	57,732	54,111
Papua New Guinea	63,448	54,235
Samoa	87,666	88,263
Solomon Islands	5,965	3,418
Tonga	34,694	32,386
Vanuatu	57,364	53,203

Source: *The Travel Industry World Yearbook 2002*

1. Which country received the most visitors in 2000? Which received the fewest?

2. Which countries experienced an increase in visitors in 2001? Which had a decrease?

3. Which country experienced more than a 40 percent decline in the number of visitors between 2000 and 2001?

4. What event took place in 2001 that might have caused many people to stay at home rather than visit another country?

Analyzing Primary Sources

Read the following quote by explorer Captain James Cook, who described the South Pacific islands that he visited. Then answer the questions.

"... they struck into a road leading into the Country ... several other Roads from different parts joined into this, some equally as broad and others narrower, the most of them shaded from the Scorching Sun by fruit trees. I thought I was transported into one of the most fertile plains in Europe, here was not an inch of waste ground, the roads occupied no more space than was absolutely necessary and each fence did not take up above 4 inches and even this was not wholly lost for in many of the fences were planted fruit trees and the Cloth plant, these served as support for them ..."

1. What can you learn about the climate from Cook's account?

2. Based on your knowledge of Cook, why do you think he compared this island to Europe?

3. What conclusions can you draw about the island's economy at the time of Cook's visit?

4. What aspect of the islanders' farms impressed Cook the most?

Preserving Antarctica

In 1912 a search party in Antarctica found the body of explorer Robert Falcon Scott. Scott had written in his diary, "Great God, what an awful place this is." He had dreamed of being the first person to reach the South Pole. However, when Scott's party arrived they found the tent and flag of Norwegian explorer Roald Amundsen. Amundsen had arrived five weeks earlier.

Almost a century later, Antarctica's modern-day explorers are research scientists. Antarctica has provided a location for international scientific research and cooperation.

A Scientific Laboratory

A wasteland to many, Antarctica is a scientific laboratory to some. Studying the continent helps scientists understand our planet. For example, the icy waters around Antarctica move north, cooling warmer waters. This movement affects ocean currents, clouds, and weather patterns. The world's climate is also affected by Antarctic sea ice. The ice acts as a shield. It keeps Earth cool by reflecting the Sun's heat energy.

Antarctic ice also provides information about the past. Buried deep within the ice are gas bubbles that are a record of Earth's air. Scientists have compared atmospheric gases trapped in Antarctic ice with atmospheric gases of today. They learned that the use of fossil fuels has raised the amount of carbon dioxide in the air. Carbon dioxide levels are now the highest in human history.

Eyes on Antarctica

Antarctica is not owned by any single country. Some countries claim parts of Antarctica, but these claims are not recognized. In 1959 the Antarctic Treaty established Antarctica as a continent for

How Antarctic Ice Affects Climate

A Freezing seawater squeezes out salt

B Water below becomes heavier with added salt and sinks

C Dense, cold Antarctic water moves north toward equator

D Warmer water moves south toward Antarctica

E Heat escapes into the air

science and peace. The treaty was originally signed by 12 countries and was later agreed to by more than a dozen others. The Antarctic Treaty banned military activity in the region. It also made Antarctica a nuclear-free zone and encouraged scientific research.

However, the Antarctic Treaty did not cover mining rights on the continent. When Antarctica's mineral riches were discovered, some countries wanted rights to this new source of wealth. Geographers, scientists, and environmentalists also took notice. They feared that if mining took place, Antarctica's environment would suffer. In particular, they feared that a practical method of obtaining the offshore oil would be found. Antarctica's coastline and marine life could then be threatened by oil spills.

At the same time, evidence of environmental neglect at some of Antarctica's research stations appeared. Environmentalists voiced concern about scientists' careless disposal of trash and sewage. A U.S. Coast Guard captain who worked on icebreakers described pollution at McMurdo, a U.S. research station. "Trash was just rolled down the hill. . . . One of the jobs of the icebreakers was to break up the ice where the

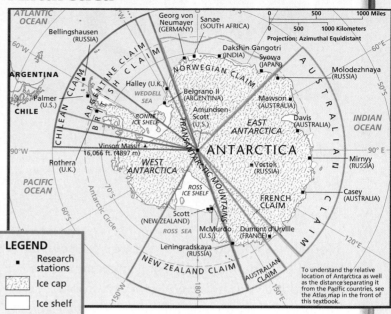

Antarctica

trash was and push it out to sea." In 1989, an Argentine ship ran aground in Antarctica, spilling thousands of gallons of oil. As a result, environmental concerns for the region increased.

Protecting Antarctica

In 1991, the countries that had signed the original Antarctic Treaty signed a new agreement called the Madrid Protocol. It forbids most activities on Antarctica that do not have a scientific purpose. It also bans mining and drilling and sets limits on tourism. Pollution concerns are addressed specifically.

In 50 years the agreement can be changed if enough of the signing countries agree. Then it becomes the responsibility of another generation to preserve Antarctica.

▲
Many countries have set up research stations and bases in Antarctica, such as Argentina's Camara Base on Half Moon Island.

Your Turn

Imagine you are helping to develop the Madrid Protocol.

1. Write a short description of the provisions you want included in the treaty.

2. Be sure to explain why you think these provisions are important.

Geo SKILLS

Building Skills for Life: Making Decisions about Local Environmental Problems

Florida has named the manatee, or sea cow, its official marine mammal. The state's manatees are endangered, however. Sometimes boats hit or cut the slow-moving animals. Other dangers are pollution and fishing nets. The air-breathing animals can get tangled in the nets and drown. Some manatees get caught in underwater gates.

Imagine that you are on a committee that must decide how to protect the manatees of a coastal Florida town. How will your committee make a decision?

PRACTICING THE SKILL

1. **Define the problem.** First, gather information. Read printed and Internet reports. Interview environmental experts. Then narrow down the problem. For example, you may find that all the local manatee deaths were caused by boats leaving a marina.

2. **List alternatives.** Now that you have defined the problem, create possible solutions for it. Would it help to put up more signs warning boaters about the manatees? Are there ways to keep the manatees away from the marina's entrance?

3. **State the criteria.** Decide on the criteria you will use to evaluate the alternatives. For example, will you choose a plan that offers a quick solution? Is low cost more important? Maybe neither cost nor speed is as important as the solution's total success.

4. **Evaluate alternatives.** Now, evaluate your alternatives in terms of these criteria. Perhaps the committee members think that speed—doing something now!—is more important than anything else. You may find that only one plan can be started quickly.

5. **Make the decision.** Put your plan into action! Follow through and keep track of your progress. What you learn could be useful in the future.

Everglades National Park in southern Florida is a beautiful wilderness with many rare plants and animals. Many of those species are now threatened with extinction. Why is this happening?

Almost 1,000 people move to Florida every day! Almost 40 million people vacation in the state every year. With more people come more roads, shopping malls, and houses. Open land has also been turned into ranches, vegetable farms, and orange groves. Developments like these take away land from wilderness areas, including the Everglades. However, rare animals that live in the Everglades, such as the Florida panther, need plenty of room to survive.

Imagine that you are an expert on the Florida panther. A town at the edge of the Everglades has asked for your help in deciding whether to allow construction of a new mall there because panthers have been seen in the area. Use the decision-making process to outline a plan for your recommendation.

Lab Report

1. What kinds of information will you need to have before you can list alternatives to solve the problem?
2. Which criteria will you use?
3. How do the alternatives fit the criteria?

FOLDNOTES APPENDIX

FoldNote Instructions

Have you ever tried to study for a test or quiz but didn't know where to start? Or have you read a chapter and found that you can remember only a few ideas? Well, FoldNotes are a fun and exciting way to help you learn and remember the ideas you encounter as you read!

FoldNotes are tools that you can use to organize concepts. By focusing on a few main concepts, FoldNotes help you learn and remember how the concepts fit together. They can help you see the "big picture." Below you will find instructions for building 10 different FoldNotes.

Pyramid

1. Place a sheet of paper in front of you. Fold the lower left-hand corner of the paper diagonally to the opposite edge of the paper.

2. Cut off the tab of paper created by the fold (at the top).

3. Open the paper so that it is a square. Fold the lower right-hand corner of the paper diagonally to the opposite corner to form a triangle.

4. Open the paper. The creases of the two folds will have created an X.

5. Using scissors, cut along one of the creases. Start from any corner, and stop at the center point to create two flaps. Use tape or glue to attach one of the flaps on top of the other flap.

Double Door

1. Fold a sheet of paper in half from the top to the bottom. Then, unfold the paper.

2. Fold the top and bottom edges of the paper to the crease.

Booklet

1. Fold a sheet of paper in half from left to right. Then, unfold the paper.
2. Fold the sheet of paper in half again from the top to the bottom. Then, unfold the paper.
3. Refold the sheet of paper in half from left to right.
4. Fold the top and bottom edges to the center crease.
5. Completely unfold the paper.
6. Refold the paper from top to bottom.
7. Using scissors, cut a slit along the center crease of the sheet from the folded edge to the creases made in step 4. Do not cut the entire sheet in half.
8. Fold the sheet of paper in half from left to right. While holding the bottom and top edges of the paper, push the bottom and top edges together so that the center collapses at the center slit. Fold the four flaps to form a four-page book.

Layered Book

1. Lay one sheet of paper on top of another sheet. Slide the top sheet up so that 2 cm of the bottom sheet is showing.
2. Hold the two sheets together, fold down the top of the two sheets so that you see four 2 cm tabs along the bottom.
3. Using a stapler, staple the top of the FoldNote.

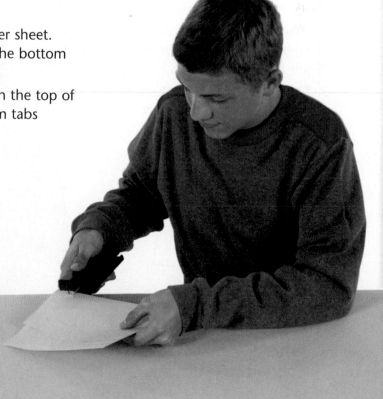

Key-Term Fold

1. Fold a sheet of lined notebook paper in half from left to right.

2. Using scissors, cut along every third line from the right edge of the paper to the center fold to make tabs.

Four-Corner Fold

1. Fold a sheet of paper in half from left to right. Then, unfold the paper.

2. Fold each side of the paper to the crease in the center of the paper.

3. Fold the paper in half from the top to the bottom. Then, unfold the paper.

4. Using scissors, cut the top flap creases made in step 3 to form four flaps.

Three-Panel Flip Chart

1. Fold a piece of paper in half from the top to the bottom.

2. Fold the paper in thirds from side to side. Then, unfold the paper so that you can see the three sections.

3. From the top of the paper, cut along each of the vertical fold lines to the fold in the middle of the paper. You will now have three flaps.

Table Fold

1. Fold a piece of paper in half from the top to the bottom. Then, fold the paper in half again.
2. Fold the paper in thirds from side to side.
3. Unfold the paper completely. Carefully trace the fold lines by using a pen or pencil.

Two-Panel Flip Chart

1. Fold a piece of paper in half from the top to the bottom.
2. Fold the paper in half from side to side. Then, unfold the paper so that you can see the two sections.
3. From the top of the paper, cut along the vertical fold line to the fold in the middle of the paper. You will now have two flaps.

Tri-Fold

1. Fold a piece a paper in thirds from the top to the bottom.
2. Unfold the paper so that you can see the three sections. Then, turn the paper sideways so that the three sections form vertical columns.
3. Trace the fold lines by using a pen or pencil. Label the columns "Know," "Want," and "Learn."

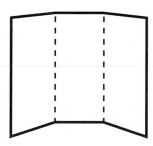

GAZETTEER

Phonetic Respelling and Pronunciation Guide

Many of the key terms in this textbook have been respelled to help you pronounce them. The letter combinations used in the respelling throughout the narrative are explained in this phonetic respelling and pronunciation guide. The guide is adapted from *Merriam-Webster's Collegiate Dictionary, Tenth Edition, Merriam-Webster's Geographical Dictionary,* and *Merriam-Webster's Biographical Dictionary.*

MARK	AS IN	RESPELLING	EXAMPLE
a	alphabet	a	*AL-fuh-bet
ā	Asia	ay	AY-zhuh
ä	cart, top	ah	KAHRT, TAHP
e	let, ten	e	LET, TEN
ē	even, leaf	ee	EE-vuhn, LEEF
i	it, tip, British	i	IT, TIP, BRIT-ish
ī	site, buy, Ohio	y	SYT, BY, oh-HY-oh
	iris	eye	EYE-ris
k	card	k	KAHRD
ō	over, rainbow	oh	OH-vuhr, RAYN-boh
ů	book, wood	ooh	BOOHK, WOOHD
ȯ	all, orchid	aw	AWL, AWR-kid
ȯi	foil, coin	oy	FOYL, KOYN
aů	out	ow	OWT
ə	cup, butter	uh	KUHP, BUHT-uhr
ü	rule, food	oo	ROOL, FOOD
yü	few	yoo	FYOO
zh	vision	zh	VIZH-uhn

*A syllable printed in small capital letters receives heavier emphasis than the other syllable(s) in a word.

Abu Dhabi (24°N 54°E) capital of the United Arab Emirates, 125

Abuja (ah-BOO-jah) (9°N 7°E) capital of Nigeria, 221

Accra (6°N 0°W) capital of Ghana, 221

Addis Ababa (9°N 39°E) capital of Ethiopia, 239

Afghanistan landlocked country in central Asia, 125

Africa second-largest continent; surrounded by the Atlantic Ocean, Indian Ocean, and Mediterranean Sea, A2–A3

Ahaggar Mountains mountain range in southern Algeria, 201

Alexandria (31°N 30°E) city in northern Egypt, 201

Algeria country in North Africa located between Morocco and Libya, 201

Algiers (37°N 3°E) capital of Algeria, 201

Amman (32°N 36°E) capital of Jordan, 107

Amu Dar'ya (uh-MOO duhr-YAH) river in Central Asia that drains into the Aral Sea, 145

Angkor ancient capital of the Khmer Empire in Cambodia, 397

Angola country in central Africa, 255

Ankara (40°N 33°E) capital of Turkey, 107

Antananarivo (19°S 48°E) capital of Madagascar, 271

Antarctic Circle line of latitude located at 66.5° south of the equator; parallel beyond which no sunlight shines on the June solstice (first day of winter in the Southern Hemisphere), A4–A5

Antarctic Peninsula peninsula stretching toward South America from Antarctica, A22

Antarctica continent around the South Pole, A22, 423

Apia (14°S 172°W) capital of Western Samoa, 424

Arabian Peninsula peninsula in Southwest Asia between the Red Sea and Persian Gulf, 125

Arabian Sea sea between India and the Arabian Peninsula, 125

Aral (AR-uhl) **Sea** inland sea between Kazakhstan and Uzbekistan, 145

Arctic Circle line of latitude located at 66.5° north of the equator; the parallel beyond which no sunlight shines on the December solstice (first day of winter in the Northern Hemisphere), A4–A5

Arctic Ocean ocean north of the Arctic Circle; world's fourth-largest ocean, A2–A3

Ashgabat (formerly Ashkhabad) (40°N 58°E) capital of Turkmenistan, 145

Asia world's largest continent; located between Europe and the Pacific Ocean, A3

Asmara (15°N 39°E) capital of Eritrea, 239

Astana (51°N 71°E) capital of Kazakhstan, 145

Atlantic Ocean ocean between the continents of North and South America and the continents of Europe and Africa; world's second-largest ocean, A2

Atlas Mountains African mountain range north of the Sahara, 201

Auckland (37°S 175°E) New Zealand's largest city and main seaport, 431

Aughrabies (oh-KRAH-bees) **Falls** waterfalls on the Orange River in South Africa, 271

Australia only country occupying an entire continent (also called Australia); located between the Indian Ocean and the Pacific Ocean, A3, 431

Bab al-Mandab narrow strait that connects the Red Sea with the Indian Ocean, 239

Baghdad (33°N 44°E) capital of Iraq, 101, 125

Bahrain country on the Persian Gulf in Southwest Asia, 125

Bali island in Indonesia east of Java, 397

Bamako (13°N 8°W) capital of Mali, 221

Bandar Seri Begawan (5°N 115°E) capital of Brunei, 397

Bangkok (14°N 100°E) capital and largest city of Thailand, 397

Bangladesh country in South Asia, 321

Bangui (4°N 19°E) capital of the Central African Republic, 255

Banjul (13°N 17°W) capital of Gambia, 221

Bay of Bengal body of water between India and the western coasts of Myanmar (Burma) and the Malay Peninsula, 303

Beijing (40°N 116°E) capital of China, 353

Beirut (34°N 36°E) capital of Lebanon, 107

Benghazi (32°N 20°E) major coastal city in Libya, 201

Benin (buh-NEEN) country in West Africa between Togo and Nigeria, 221

Bhutan South Asian country in the Himalayas located north of India and Bangladesh, 321

Bishkek (43°N 75°E) capital of Kyrgyzstan, 145

Bissau (12°N 16°W) capital of Guinea-Bissau, 221

Black Sea sea between Europe and Asia, A14, 107, 122

Bloemfontein judicial capital of South Africa, 271

Blue Nile East African river that flows into the Nile River in Sudan, 239

Bombay see Mumbai.

Borneo island in the Malay Archipelago in Southeast Asia, 397

Bosporus a narrow strait separating European and Asian Turkey, 107

Botswana country in southern Africa, 271

Brahmaputra River major river of South Asia that begins in the Himalayas of Tibet and merges with the Ganges River in Bangladesh, 303

Brazzaville (4°S 15°E) capital of the Republic of the Congo, 255

Brisbane (28°S 153°E) seaport and capital of Queensland, Australia, 431

Brunei (brooh-NY) country on the northern coast of Borneo in Southeast Asia, 397

Bujumbura (3°S 29°E) capital of Burundi, 239

Burkina Faso (boor-KEE-nuh FAH-soh) landlocked country in West Africa, 221

Burma see Myanmar.

Burundi landlocked country in East Africa, 239

Cairo (30°N 31°E) capital of Egypt, 201

Calcutta see Kolkata.

Cambodia country in Southeast Asia west of Vietnam, 397

Cameroon country in central Africa, p39, 255

Canberra (35°S 149°E) capital of Australia, 431

Cape of Good Hope cape of the southwest coast of South Africa, 271

Cape Town (34°S 18°E) major seaport city and legislative capital of South Africa, 271

Cape Verde island country in the Atlantic Ocean off the coast of West Africa, 221

Casablanca (34°N 8°W) seaport city on the western coast of Morocco, 201

Caspian Sea large inland salt lake between Europe and Asia, A16

Central African Republic landlocked country in central Africa located south of Chad, 255

Central Lowlands area of Australia between the Western Plateau and the Great Dividing Range, 431

Chad landlocked country in northern Africa, 221

Chang River major river in Central China, 353

Chao Phraya (chow-PRY-uh) **River** major river in Thailand, 397

China country in East Asia; most populous country in the world, 151, 353

Chongqing (30°N 108°E) city in southern China along the Chang River, 353

Christchurch (44°S 173°E) city on the eastern coast of South Island, New Zealand, 431

Colombo (7°N 80°E) capital city and important seaport of Sri Lanka, 321

Comoros island country in the Indian Ocean off the coast of Africa, 271

Conakry (10°N 14°W) capital of Guinea, 221

Congo Basin region in central Africa, 255

Congo River major navigable river in central Africa that flows into the Atlantic Ocean, 255

Congo, Democratic Republic of the largest and most populous country in central Africa, 255

Congo, Republic of the central African country located along the Congo River, 255

Constantinople (now called Istanbul) (41°N 29°E) former city in Turkey, 107

Côte d'Ivoire (KOHT-dee-VWAHR) (Ivory Coast) country in West Africa, 221

Cyprus island republic in the eastern Mediterranean Sea, 107

Dakar (15°N 17°W) capital of Senegal, 221

Damascus (34°N 36°E) capital of Syria and one of the world's oldest cities, 107

Dar es Salaam (7°S 39°E) capital and major seaport of Tanzania, 239

Dardanelles narrow strait separating European and Asian Turkey, 107

Dead Sea salt lake on the boundary between Israel and Jordan in southwestern Asia, 107

Deccan the southern part of the Indian subcontinent, 303

Delhi (29°N 77°E) city in India, 303

Dhaka (24°N 90°E) capital and largest city of Bangladesh, 321

Djibouti (12°N 43°E) capital of Djibouti, 239

Djibouti country located in the Horn of Africa, 239

Dodoma (6°S 36°E) legislative capital of Tanzania, 239

Doha (25°N 51°E) capital of Qatar, 125

Drakensberg mountain range in southern Africa, 271

Durban (30°S 31°E) port city in South Africa, 271

Dushanbe (39°N 69°E) capital of Tajikistan, 145

East Timor country in Southeast Asia; former province of Indonesia, 397

Eastern Ghats mountains on the eastern side of the Deccan Plateau in southern India, 303

Eastern Highlands mountain ranges in eastern Australia, 431

Egypt country in North Africa located east of Libya, 107, 112, 201

Elburz Mountains mountain range in northern Iran, 125

equator the imaginary line of latitude that lies halfway between the North and South Poles and circles the globe, A4–A5

Equatorial Guinea central African country, 255

Eritrea (er-uh-TREE-uh) East African country located north of Ethiopia, 239

Ethiopia East African country in the Horn of Africa, 239

Euphrates River major river in Iraq in southwestern Asia, 125

Europe continent between the Ural Mountains and the Atlantic Ocean, A3

Fergana Valley fertile valley in Uzbekistan, Kyrgyzstan, and Tajikistan, 145

Fertile Crescent rich farmland region in southwestern Asia, 89

Fès (34°N 5°W) city in north-central Morocco, 201

Fiji South Pacific island country in Melanesia, 423

Freetown (9°N 13°W) capital of Sierra Leone, 221

Funafuti (9°S 179°E) capital of Tuvalu, 424

Gabon country in central Africa located between Cameroon and the Republic of the Congo, 255

Gaborone (24°S 26°E) capital of Botswana, 271

Gambia country along the Gambia River in West Africa, 221

Ganges River major river in India flowing from the Himalayas southeastward to the Bay of Bengal, 303

Gangetic (gan-JE-tik) **Plain** vast plain in northern India, 303

Gao (GOW) (16°N 0°) city in Mali on the Niger River, 221

Gaza Strip area occupied by Israel from 1967 to 1994; under Palestinian self-rule since 1994, 107

Ghana country in West Africa, 188

Giza (30°N 31°E) Egyptian city on the west bank of the Nile, 179

Gobi desert that makes up part of the Mongolian plateau in East Africa, 353

Golan Heights hilly region in southwestern Syria occupied by Israel, 107

Great Artesian Basin Australia's largest source of underground well water; located in interior Queensland, 431

Great Barrier Reef world's largest coral reef; located off the northeastern coast of Australia, 431

Great Dividing Range mountain range of the Eastern Highlands in Australia, 431

Great Rift Valley valley system extending from eastern Africa to Southwest Asia, 239

Guam (14°N 143°E) South Pacific island and U.S. territory in Micronesia, 423

Guinea country in West Africa, 221

Guinea-Bissau (GI-nee bi-SOW) country in West Africa, 221

Gulf of Guinea part of the Atlantic Ocean south of the West African countries, 221

Hanoi (ha-NOY) (21°N 106°E) capital of Vietnam, 397

Harappa early city of the Indus River Valley, civilization of India and Pakistan, 306

Harare (18°S 31°E) capital of Zimbabwe, 271

Himalayas mountain system in Asia; world's highest mountains, 353

Hindu Kush high mountain range in northern Afghanistan, 125

Ho Chi Minh City (formerly Saigon) (11°N 107°E) major city in southern Vietnam; former capital of South Vietnam, 397

Hokkaido (hoh-KY-doh) major island in northern Japan, 377

Hong (Red) River major river that flows into the Gulf of Tonkin in Vietnam, 397

Hong Kong (22°N 115°E) former British colony in East Asia; now part of China, 353

Honiara (9°S 160°E) capital of the Solomon Islands, 424

Honshu (HAWN-shoo) largest of the four major islands of Japan, 377

Huang River (Yellow River) one of the world's longest rivers; located in northern China, 115, 353

India country in South Asia, 303

Indian Ocean world's third-largest ocean; located east of Africa, south of Asia, west of Australia, and north of Antarctica, A3

Indochina Peninsula peninsula in southeastern Asia that includes the region from Myanmar (Burma) to Vietnam, 397

Indonesia largest country in Southeast Asia; made up of more than 17,000 islands, 397

Indus River major river in Pakistan, 321

Inland Sea body of water in southern Japan between Honshu, Shikoku, and Kyushu, 377

Inyanga Mountains mountain region of Zimbabwe and Mozambique, 271

Iran country in southwestern Asia; formerly called Persia, 125

Iraq (i-RAHK) country located between Iran and Saudi Arabia, 125

Irian Jaya western part of the island of New Guinea and part of Indonesia, 397

Irrawaddy River important river in Myanmar (Burma), 397

Islamabad (34°N 73°E) capital of Pakistan, 321

Israel country in southwestern Asia, 107

Istanbul (formerly Constantinople) (41°N 29°E) largest city and leading seaport in Turkey, 107

Jakarta (6°S 107°E) capital of Indonesia, 397

Japan country in East Asia consisting of four major islands and more than 3,000 smaller islands, 377

Java major island in Indonesia, 397

Jerusalem (32°N 35°E) capital of Israel, 107

Johannesburg (26°S 28°E) city in South Africa, 271

Jordan River river in southwestern Asia that separates Israel from Syria and Jordan, 107

Jordan Southwest Asian country stretching east from the Dead Sea and Jordan River into the Arabian Desert, 107

Kabul (35°N 69°E) capital and largest city of Afghanistan, 125

Kalahari Desert dry plateau region in southern Africa, 271

Kampala (0° 32°E) capital of Uganda, 239

Kao-hsiung (23°N 120°E) Taiwan's second-largest city and major seaport, 353

Manila (15°N 121°E) capital of the Philippines, 397

Maputo (27°S 33°E) capital of Mozambique, 271

Marshall Islands Pacific island country in Indonesia, 424

Maseru (29°S 27°E) capital of Lesotho, 271

Masqat (Muscat) (23°N 59°E) capital of Oman, 125

Mauritania African country stretching east from the Atlantic coast into the Sahara, 221

Mauritius island country located off the coast of Africa in the Indian Ocean, 271

Mbabane (26°S 31°E) capital of Swaziland, 271

Mecca (21°N 40°E) important Islamic city in western Saudi Arabia, 98

Medina (Al Madinah) (24°N 39°E) important Islamic city north of Mecca, 125

Mediterranean Sea sea surrounded by Europe, Asia, and Africa, *m377*

Mekong River important river in Southeast Asia, 397

Melanesia island region in the South Pacific that stretches from New Guinea to Fiji, 423

Melbourne (38°S 145°E) capital of Victoria, Australia, 431

Micronesia island region in the South Pacific that includes the Mariana, Caroline, Marshall, and Gilbert island groups, 423

Micronesia, Federated States of island country in the western Pacific, 423

Mogadishu (2°N 45°E) capital and port city of Somalia, 239

Mongolia landlocked country in East Asia, 353

Monrovia (6°N 11°W) capital of Liberia, 221

Morocco country in North Africa south of Spain, 201

Moroni (12°S 43°E) capital of Comoros, 271

Mount Everest (28°N 87°E) world's highest peak (29,035 ft.; 8,850 m); located in the Himalayas, 353

Mount Kilimanjaro (3°S 37°E) (ki-luh-muhn-JAHR-oh) highest point in Africa (19,341 ft.; 5,895 m); located in northeast Tanzania, near Kenya border, 239

Mozambique (moh-zahm-BEEK) country in southern Africa, 271

Mumbai (Bombay) (19°S 73°E) India's largest city, 303

Murray-Darling Rivers major river system in southeastern Australia, 431

Muscat See Masqat.

Myanmar (MYAHN-mahr) (Burma) country in Southeast Asia between India, China, and Thailand, 397

N'Djamena (12°N 15°E) capital of Chad, 221

Nairobi (1°S 37°E) capital of Kenya, 239

Namib Desert Atlantic coast desert in southern Africa, 271

Namibia (nuh-MI-bee-uh) country on the Atlantic coast in southern Africa, 271

Nanjing (32°N 119°E) city along the upper Chang River in China, 353

Nauru South Pacific island country in Micronesia, 423

Negev desert region in southern Israel, 107

Nepal South Asian country located in the Himalayas, 321

New Caledonia French territory of Melanesia in the South Pacific Ocean east of Queensland, Australia, 423

New Delhi (29°N 77°E) capital of India, 303

New Guinea large island in the South Pacific Ocean north of Australia, 397

New Zealand island country located southeast of Australia, 431

Niamey (14°N 2°E) capital of Niger, 221

Nicosia (35°N 33°E) capital of Cyprus, 107

Niger (NY-juhr) country in West Africa, 221

Niger River river in West Africa, 107, 221

Nigeria country in West Africa, 221

Nile Delta region in northern Egypt where the Nile River flows into the Mediterranean Sea, 201

Nile River world's longest river (4,187 miles; 6,737 km); flows into the Mediterranean Sea in Egypt, 177, 201

Nile Valley area around the Nile River where distinct cultures developed, 177

North America continent including Canada, the United States, Mexico, Central America, and the Caribbean Islands, A2

North China Plain region of northeastern China, 353

North Island northernmost of two large continental islands of New Zealand, 431

North Korea country on the northern part of the Korean Peninsula in East Asia, 377

North Pole the northern point of Earth's axis, A22

Northern Mariana Islands U.S. commonwealth in the South Pacific, 424

Nouakchott (nooh-AHK-shaht) (18°N 16°W) capital of Mauritania, 221

Nuku'alofa capital of Tonga, 424

Oman country in the Arabian Peninsula; formerly known as Muscat, 125

Orange River river in southern Africa, 271

Osaka (oh-SAH-kuh) (35°N 135°E) major industrial center on Japan's southwestern Honshu island, 377

Ouagadougou (wah-gah-DOO-GOO) (12°N 2°W) capital of Burkina Faso, 221

P'yŏngyang (pyuhng-YANG) (39°N 126°E) capital of North Korea, 377

Pacific Ocean Earth's largest ocean; located between North and South America and Asia and Australia, A2–A3

Pakistan South Asian country located northwest of India, 321

Palau South Pacific island country in Micronesia, 424

Palikir capital of the Federated States of Micronesia, 424

Pamirs mountain area mainly in Tajikistan in Central Asia, 145

Papua New Guinea country on the eastern half of the island of New Guinea, 424

Persian Gulf body of water between Iran and the Arabian Peninsula, 125

Perth (32°S 116°E) capital of Western Australia, 431

Philippines Southeast Asian island country located north of Indonesia, 397

Phnom Penh (12°N 105°E) capital of Cambodia, 397

Plateau of Tibet high, barren plateau of western China, 353

Polynesia island region of the South Pacific that includes the Hawaiian and Line island groups, Samoa, French Polynesia, and Easter Island, 423

Port Elizabeth (34°S 26°E) seaport city in South Africa, 271

Port Louis (20°S 58°E) capital of Mauritius, 271

Port Moresby (10°S 147°E) seaport and capital of Papua New Guinea, 424

Porto-Novo (6°N 3°E) capital of Benin, 221

Port-Vila (18°S 169°E) capital of Vanuatu, 424

Praia (PRIE-uh) (15°N 24°W) capital of Cape Verde, 221

Pretoria (26°S 28°E) administrative capital of South Africa, 271

Pusan (35°N 129°E) major seaport city in southeastern South Korea, 377

Qatar Persian Gulf country located on the Arabian Peninsula, 125

Qattara Depression lowland region (436 feet below sea level; 133 m) in western Egypt, 201

Rabat (34°N 7°W) capital of Morocco, 201

Rangoon See Yangon.

Red Sea sea between the Arabian Peninsula and northeastern Africa, 177, 125

Riyadh (25°N 47°E) capital of Saudi Arabia, 125

Ross Ice Shelf ice shelf of Antarctica, 423

Rub' al-Khali uninhabited desert area in southeastern Saudi Arabia, 125

Rwanda country in East Africa, 239

Sahara desert region in northern Africa, 201

Samarqand (40°N 67°E) city in southeastern Uzbekistan, 145

Samoa South Pacific island country in Polynesia, 423

Sanaa (15°N 44°E) capital of Yemen, 125

São Tomé (1°N 6°E) capital of São Tomé and Príncipe, 255

São Tomé and Príncipe island country located off the Atlantic coast of central Africa, 255

Saudi Arabia country occupying much of the Arabian Peninsula in southwestern Asia, 125

Sea of Japan body of water separating Japan from mainland Asia, 535

Sea of Marmara sea between European Turkey and the Asian peninsula of Anatolia, 107

Senegal country in West Africa, 221

Senegal River river in West Africa, 221

Seoul (38°N 127°E) capital of South Korea, 377

Seychelles island country located east of Africa in the Indian Ocean, 271

Shanghai (31°N 121°E) major seaport city in eastern China, 353

Shikoku (shee-KOH-koo) smallest of the four main islands of Japan, 377

Sichuan Basin rich agriculture and mining area along the Chang (Yangtze) River in central China, 353

Sierra Leone West African country located northwest of Liberia, 221

Sinai (SY-ny) **Peninsula** peninsula in northeastern Egypt, 201

Singapore island country located at the tip of the Malay Peninsula in Southeast Asia, 397

Solomon Islands South Pacific island country in Melanesia, 424

Somalia East African country located in the Horn of Africa, 239

South Africa country in southern Africa, 271

South Island the southern island of two main islands of New Zealand, 431

South Korea country occupying the southern half of the Korean Peninsula, 377

South Pole the southern point of Earth's axis, A22

Southern Alps mountain range in South Island, New Zealand, 431

Sri Lanka island country located south of India; formerly known as Ceylon, 321

Strait of Gibraltar (juh-BRAWL-tuhr) strait between the Iberian Peninsula and North Africa that links the Mediterranean Sea to the Atlantic Ocean, 165

Sudan East African country; largest country in Africa, 239

Suez Canal canal linking the Red Sea to the Mediterranean Sea in northeastern Egypt, 201

Sumatra large island of Indonesia, 397

Suva (19°S 178°E) capital of Fiji, 424

Swaziland country in southern Africa, 271

Sydney (34°S 151°E) largest urban area and leading seaport in Australia, 431

Syr Dar'ya (sir duhr-YAH) river draining the Pamirs in Central Asia, 145

Syria Southwest Asian country located between the Mediterranean Sea and Iraq, 107

Syrian Desert desert region covering parts of Syria, Jordan, Iraq, and northern Saudi Arabia, 107

T

Tahiti French South Pacific island in Polynesia, 423

Taipei (25°N 122°E) capital of Taiwan, 353

Taiwan (TY-WAHN) island country located off the southeastern coast of China, 353

Tajikistan (tah-ji-ki-STAN) country in Central Asia; former Soviet republic, 145

Taklimakan Desert desert region in western China, 353

Tanzania East African country located south of Kenya, 239

Tarai (tuh-RY) region in Nepal along the border with India, 321

Tarawa capital of Kiribati, 424

Tarim Basin arid region in western China, 353

Tashkent (41°N 69°E) capital of Uzbekistan, 145

Tasman Sea part of South Pacific Ocean between Australia and New Zealand, 431

Tasmania island state of Australia, 431

Tehran (36°N 52°E) capital of Iran, 125

Tel Aviv (tehl uh-VEEV) (32°N 35°E) largest city in Israel, 107

Thailand (TY-land) country in Southeast Asia, 397

Thar (TAHR) **Desert** sandy desert of northwestern India and eastern Pakistan; also called the Great Indian Desert, 303

Thimphu (28°N 90°E) capital of Bhutan, 321

Tian Shan (TIEN SHAHN) high mountain range separating northwestern China from Russia and some Central Asian republics, 145

Tibesti Mountains mountain group in northwest Chad, 221

Tigris River major river in southwestern Asia, 107, 125

Timbuktu (17°N 3°W) city in Mali and an ancient trading center in West Africa, 189

Togo West African country located between Ghana and Benin, 221

Tokyo (36°N 140°E) capital of Japan, 377

Tonga South Pacific island country in Polynesia, 424

Transantarctic Mountains major mountain range that divides Antarctica into East and West, 423

Tripoli (33°N 13°E) capital of Libya, 201

Tropic of Cancer parallel 23.5° north of the equator; parallel on the globe at which the Sun's most direct rays strike Earth during the June solstice (first day of summer in the Northern Hemisphere), A4–A5

Tropic of Capricorn parallel 23.5° south of the equator; parallel on the globe at which the Sun's most direct rays strike Earth during the December solstice (first day of summer in the Southern Hemisphere), A4–A5

Tunis (37°N 10°E) capital of Tunisia, 201

Tunisia country in North Africa located on the Mediterranean coast between Algeria and Libya, 201

Turkey country of the eastern Mediterranean occupying Anatolia and a corner of southeastern Europe, 107

Turkmenistan country in Central Asia; former Soviet republic, 145

Tuvalu South Pacific island country of Polynesia, 423

Uganda country in East Africa, 239

Ulaanbaatar (oo-lahn-BAH-tawr) (48°N 107°E) capital of Mongolia, 353

United Arab Emirates country located on the Arabian Peninsula, 125

Uzbekistan country in Central Asia; former Soviet republic, 145

Vanuatu South Pacific island country in Melanesia, 423

Victoria (1°S 33°E) capital of the Seychelles, 271

Vientiane (18°N 103°E) capital of Laos, 397

Vietnam country in Southeast Asia, 397

Vinson Massif (78°S 87°W) highest mountain (16,066 ft.; 4,897 m) in Antarctica, 423

Wake Island (19°N 167°E) U.S. South Pacific island territory north of the Marshall Islands, 423

Wellington (41°S 175°E) capital of New Zealand, 431

West Bank area of Palestine west of the Jordan River; occupied by Israel in 1967; political status is in transition, 107

Western Ghats (GAWTS) hills facing the Arabian Sea on the western side of the Deccan Plateau, India, 303

Western Plateau large, flat plain covering more than half of Australia, 431

Western Rift Valley westernmost of two deep troughs beginning near Lake Malawi (Lake Nyasa) in eastern Africa and continuing north into the Red Sea and then into Syria, 255

Western Sahara disputed territory in northwestern Africa; claimed by Morocco, 201

White Nile part of the Nile River system in eastern Africa, 239

Windhoek (22°S 17°E) capital of Namibia, 271

Witwatersrand (WIT-wawt-uhrz-rahnd) a range of low hills in north central South Africa, 271

Wuhan (31°N 114°E) city in south central China, 353

Xi River river in southeastern China, 353

Yamoussoukro (7°N 5°W) capital of Côte d'Ivoire, 221

Yangon (Rangoon) (17°N 96°E) capital of Myanmar (Burma), 397

Yaoundé (4°N 12°E) capital of Cameroon, 255

Yemen country located in the southwestern corner of the Arabian Peninsula, 125

Zagros Mountains mountain range of southwestern Iran, 125

Zambezi (zam-BEE-zee) **River** major river in central and southern Africa, 255

Zambia country in central Africa, 255

Zimbabwe (zim-BAH-bway) country in southern Africa, 188

GLOSSARY

A

absolute location The exact spot on Earth where something is found, often stated in latitude and longitude, **7**

acculturation The process of cultural changes that result from long-term contact with another society, **49**

acid rain A type of polluted rain, produced when pollution combines with water vapor, **30**

alluvial fan A fan-shaped landform created by deposits of sediment at the base of a mountain, **21**

animism A religious belief that bodies of water, animals, trees, and other natural objects have spirits, **228**

antifreeze A substance added to liquid to keep the liquid from turning to ice, **458**

apartheid The South African government policy of separation of races, which began to disappear in the 1980s, **196, 278**

aquifers Underground, water-bearing layers of rock, sand, or gravel, **26**

arable Land suitable for growing crops, **356**

archaeology The study of the remains and ruins of past cultures, **224**

archipelago (ahr-kuh-PE-luh-goh) A large group of islands, **398**

artesian wells Wells in which water rises toward the surface without being pumped, **432**

asphalt The tar-like material used to pave streets, **109**

atmosphere Layer of gasses that surrounds Earth, **31**

atolls Rings of coral surrounding lagoons, **335**

B

basins Regions surrounded by mountains or other higher land, **256**

bauxite The most important aluminum ore, **223**

Bedouins Nomadic herders in the deserts of Egypt and Southwest Asia, **208**

birthrate Number of births per 1,000 people in a year, **59**

Boers Afrikaner frontier farmers, white descendents of South Africa's original European colonists, **276**

boycott Refuse to buy, **196, 310**

bush Lightly populated wilderness areas, such as parts of Australia, **437**

C

cacao (kuh-KOW) A small tree on which cocoa beans grow, **235**

caliph A religious and political ruler in the Muslim world, a title which means "successor to the Prophet Muhammad," **100, 128**

canopy The uppermost layer of a forest's trees where limbs spread out and block out sunlight, **256**

caravans Groups of people who travel together for protection, **148**

cartography The art and science of mapmaking, **13**

Casbah The old fortress and central part of some North African cities, **215**

caste system A system in which people's position in society is determined by their birth into a particular caste or group, **314**

chaebol Huge industrial groups of South Korean companies, banks, and other businesses, **392**

cholera A life-threatening intestinal infection, **327**

Christianity Religion based on the teachings of Jesus, **97**

city-states Self-governing cities, such as those of ancient Africa, **187**

civil war A conflict between two or more groups within a country, **263**

civilization A highly complex culture with growing cities and economic activity, **52**

climate Weather conditions in an area over a long period of time, **32**

climatology The field of tracking Earth's larger atmospheric systems, **13**

command economy An economy in which the government owns most of the industries and makes most of the economic decisions, **56, 366**

commercial agriculture A type of farming in which farmers produce food for sale, **52**

condensation The process by which water changes from a gas into tiny liquid droplets, **27**

copper belt A major copper-mining region of central Africa, **257**

coral reef A ridge made up of the skeletal remains of tiny sea animals and found close to shore in warm, tropical waters, **433**

Crusades A long series of battles starting in 1096 between the Christians of Europe and the Muslims to gain control of Palestine, **114**

culture A learned system of shared beliefs and ways of doing things that guide a person's daily behavior, **47**

culture region Area of the world in which people share certain culture traits, **47**

culture traits Elements of culture such as dress, food, or religious beliefs, **47**

cuneiform Writing system using wedge-shaped marks on clay, **90**

currents Giant streams of ocean water that move from warm to cold or from cold to warm areas, **34**

cyclones Violent storms with high winds and heavy rain in South Asia, similar to hurricanes in the Caribbean, **322**

D

Dalits People at the bottom of the Indian caste system who do the work that is considered unclean, **315**

death rate Number of deaths per 1,000 people in a year, **59**

deforestation Destruction or loss of forest area, **39**

delta Landform created by the deposit of sediment at the mouth of a river, **21**

demilitarized zone A buffer zone that serves as a barrier separating two countries, such as North and South Korea, **389**

depressions Low areas, **202**

developing countries Countries in different stages of moving toward development, **55**

dharma In Hinduism, a moral duty, **312**

dialect A variation of a language, **260**

Diaspora The scattering of the Jewish population from Palestine under Roman rule, **114**

dictator One who rules a country with complete authority, **217**

Diet (DY-uht) Japan's elected legislature, **381**

diffusion The movement of ideas or behaviors from one cultural region to another, **9**

dikes High banks of earth or concrete built along waterfronts to help reduce flooding, **355**

disciples Small group of followers, **96**

division of labor Organization of society in which each person performs a specific job, **86**

domestication The growing of a plant or taming of an animal by a people for their own use, **51**

droughts Periods when little rain falls and crops are damaged, **63, 249**

dynasty A ruling family that passes power from one generation to the next, **177, 357**

E

earthquakes Sudden, violent movements along a fracture in the Earth's crust, **20**

embargo A limit on trade, **137**

emigrant Person who leaves one place for another, **59**

emperor A ruler of a large empire, **357**

enclaves Countries surrounded or almost surrounded by another country, **272**

endemic species Plants and animals that developed in one particular region of the world, **433**

entrepreneurs People who use their money and talents to start a business, **392**

ergs Great "seas" of sand dunes in the Sahara, **202**

erosion The movement by water, ice, or wind of rocky materials to another location, **21**

ethnic groups Cultural groups of people who share learned beliefs and practices, **47**

ethnocentrism Seeing differences in another culture as inferior, **49**

evaporation The process by which heated water becomes water vapor and rises into the air, **27**

exclave A part of a country that is separated by territory of other countries, **267**

Exclusive Economic Zones Areas off a country's coast within which the country claims and controls all resources, **455**

Exodus Hebrews' escape from ancient Egypt, **94**

exotic rivers Rivers that begin in humid regions and then flow through dry areas, **126**

exports Products a country sells to other countries, **57**

famine A great shortage of food, **63, 393**

fault A fractured surface in Earth's crust where a mass of rock is in motion, **20**

fellahin (fel-uh-HEEN) Egyptian farmers who own very small plots of land, **212**

Fertile Crescent An area of fertile land in Southwest Asia curving from the Jordan River along the Tigris and Euphrates Rivers to the Persian Gulf, **89**

Five Pillars of Islam Rules Muslims follow, **99**

floodplain A landform of level ground built by sediment deposited by a river or stream, **21**

fossil fuels Nonrenewable resources formed from the remains of ancient plants and animals, **40**

fossil water Water that is not being replaced by rainfall, **127**

free enterprise An economic system in which people, not government, decide what to make, sell, or buy, **56**

free port A city in which almost no taxes are placed on goods sold there, **215**

futon (FOO-tahn) A lightweight cotton mattress, often used in Japan, **384**

geography The study of Earth's physical and cultural features, **3**

geothermal energy A renewable energy resource produced from the heat of Earth's interior, **41**

gers (GURHZ) Large, circular tents that are easy to raise, dismantle, and move; used by nomadic herders in Mongolia, **369**

glaciers Large, slow-moving sheets or rivers of ice, **22**

global warming A slow increase in Earth's average temperature, **30**

globalization Process in which connections around the world increase and cultures around the world share similar practices, **60**

gorge A narrow, steep-walled canyon, **246**

Gospels First four books of the Christian Bible that tell about Jesus' life, **96**

graphite A form of carbon used in pencils and many other products, **334**

greenhouse effect Process by which Earth's atmosphere traps heat, **30**

green revolution A program, begun by the Indian government in the 1960s, that encouraged farmers to modernize their methods to produce more food, **317**

griots (GREE-ohz) West African storytellers who pass on the oral histories of their tribes or people, **234**

gross domestic product Value of all goods and services produced within a country, **53**

gross national product Value of all goods and services that a country produces in one year within or outside the country, **53**

groundwater Water from rainfall, rivers, lakes, and melting snow that seeps into the ground, **26**

Hanging Gardens Lush rooftop gardens built in Babylon by King Nebuchadnezzar, **92**

harmattan (HAR-muh-TAN) Dry, dusty wind that blows south from the Sahara during winter, **222**

hieroglyphics (HY-ruh-glifs) Pictures and symbols used to record information in ancient Egypt, **179**

hieroglyphs Pictures and symbols that stand for ideas or words, **205**

history A written record of human civilization, **87**

hominid An early humanlike creature, **83**

human geography The study of people, past or present, **11**

mainland A region or country's main landmass, **398**

malaria A deadly disease spread by mosquitoes, **230**

mandate Former territories of defeated World War I countries that were placed under the control of winning countries after the war, **118**

market economy An economy in which business owners and consumers make decisions about what to make, sell, and buy, **56**

marsupials (mahr-SOO-pee-uhls) Animals that carry their young in pouches, **434**

martial law Military rule, **360**

megalopolis A giant urban area that includes a string of cities that have grown together, **383**

Mesopotamia Ancient land between the Tigris and Euphrates Rivers, **126**

meteorology The field of forecasting and reporting rainfall, temperatures, and other atmospheric conditions, **13**

migration Movement of people, **59**

millet A grain crop that can survive drought, **229**

mixed economy An exchange of goods and services based on at least two other types of economic systems, **57**

monotheism Belief in only one god, **95**

mosques Islamic houses of worship, **102, 152**

most-favored-nation status A status that grants special trade advantages from the United States, **367**

movement People and ideas moving from place to place, **9**

multicultural A mixture of different cultures within the same country or community, **47**

multiple cropping A type of agriculture in which two or three crops are raised each year on the same land, **366**

mummification Process of preserving dead bodies, **182**

Muslims Followers of Islam, **128**

nationalism The demand for self-rule and a strong feeling of loyalty to one's nation, **190**

New Testament Part of the Bible containing stories of Jesus, his followers, and later Christian ideas, **97**

nirvana Among Buddhists, the escape from the suffering of life, **313**

nomads People who often move from place to place, **84, 148**

nonrenewable resources Resources, such as coal and oil, that cannot be replaced by Earth's natural processes, **38**

oasis A place in the desert where a spring or well provides water, **146**

one-crop economy Economy based on a single crop, such as bananas, sugarcane, or cacao, **57**

OPEC Organization of Petroleum Exporting Countries, which tries to influence the price of oil on world markets, **129**

oral history Spoken information passed from one generation to the next, **185, 224**

Organization of African Unity (OAU) An organization, founded in 1963, that tries to promote cooperation among African countries, **283**

outback Australia's inland region, **434**

overpopulation More people than a region or country can self-support, **58**

Oyashio (oh-YAH-shee-oh) **Current** A cool ocean current east of Japan, **377**

ozone layer A form of oxygen in the atmosphere that helps protect Earth from harmful solar radiation, **30**

Rosetta Stone Ancient rock tablet carved in Greek, Egyptian hieroglyphics, and demotic writing, **179**

rugby A game with British origins; similar to football and soccer, **436**

rural An area of open land that is often used for farming, **4**

S

Sahel (sah-HEL) A dry grasslands region with a steppe climate south of the Sahara, **222**

samurai (SA-muh-ry) Warriors who served Japanese lords, **380**

sanctions An economic or political penalty, such as an embargo, used by one or more countries to force another country to cease an illegal or immoral act, **279**

Sanskrit An early language form in South Asia; used as a sacred language in India today, **307**

secede To break away from a country to form another, **232**

secular Kept separate from religion, as in a secular government or state, **111**

sepoys Indian troops commanded by British officers during the colonial era in India, **310**

shah An ancient Persian word for king, **103, 140**

shamans Shinto priests, **379**

Shia The second-largest branch of Islam, **128**

Shintoism The earliest known religion of Japan, **379**

shogun "Great General," the highest Japanese warrior rank, **380**

silt Finely ground soil, **203**

solar power Heat and light from the Sun, **41**

sorghum A grain crop that can survive drought, **229**

souks Marketplaces in North Africa, **215**

spatial perspective Point of view based on looking at where something is and why it is there, **3**

sphinxes Sculptures of monsters with a lion's body and a human head, **180**

staple A region or country's main food crop, **230**

storm surges Huge waves of water that are whipped up by fierce winds, particularly from cyclones, hurricanes, and other tropical storms, **322**

stupas Mounds of earth or stones covering the ashes of the Buddha or relics of Buddhist saints, **330**

subduction The movement of one of Earth's heavier tectonic plates underneath a lighter tectonic plate, **20**

subsistence agriculture A type of farming in which farmers grow just enough food to provide for themselves and their own families, **52**

sultan The supreme ruler of a Muslim country, **411**

Sunni The largest branch of Islam, **128**

Swahili A Bantu language that is widely spoken in areas of Africa, **244**

symbol A word, shape, color, flag, or other sign that stands for something else, **49**

T

teak A valuable type of wood; grown in India and Southeast Asia, **305**

Ten Commandments Basic laws given to Moses, **95**

terraces Horizontal ridges built into the slopes of steep hillsides to prevent soil loss and aid farming, **22**

theocracy A government ruled by religious leaders, **140**

third-world countries Developing countries that lack economic opportunities, **55**

topography Shape, height, and arrangement of landforms in a certain place, **19**

Torah Five books of Moses that Jews follow, **95**

townships Special areas of crowded clusters of tiny homes for black South Africans living outside cities, **278**

trade surplus The value of exports is greater than the value of imports, **386**

tradition-based economy Exchange of goods or services based on custom and tradition, **56**

tributary Any smaller stream or river that flows into a larger stream or river, **26**

trust territories Areas placed under the temporary control of another country until they set up their own government, **453**

tsetse (TSET-see) **fly** A fly in Africa south of the Sahara that spreads sleeping sickness, a deadly disease, **222**

tsunamis (tsooh-NAH-mees) Huge waves created by undersea tectonic activity, such as earthquakes, **377**

urban An area that contains a city, **4**

veld, the (VELT) Open grasslands areas of South Africa, **272**

wadis Dry streambeds in Southwest Asia and Africa, **127**

water cycle The circulation of water from Earth's surface to the atmosphere and back, **27**

water vapor The gaseous form of water, **27**

weather The condition of the atmosphere at a given place and time, **32**

weathering The process of breaking rocks into smaller pieces through heat, water, or other means, **21**

work ethic The belief that work in itself is worthwhile, **386**

yurt A movable round house of wool felt mats over a wood frame, **152**

ziggurats Pyramid-shaped temples built by Sumerians, **90**

Zionism The movement to establish a Jewish country or community in Palestine, **115**

zonal How climates in Africa stretch east to west in bands, **222**

SPANISH GLOSSARY

A

absolute location/posición exacta Lugar exacto de la tierra donde se localiza un punto, por lo general definido en términos de latitud y longitud, **7**

acculturation/aculturación Proceso de asimilación de una cultura a largo plazo por el contacto con otra sociedad, **49**

acid rain/lluvia ácida Tipo de lluvia contaminada que se produce cuando partículas de contaminación del aire se combinan con el vapor de agua de la atmósfera, **30**

alluvial fan/abanico aluvial Accidente geográfico en forma de abanico que se origina por la acumulación de sedimentos en la base de una montaña, **21**

animism/animismo Creencia religiosa que explica que los cuerpos de agua, los animales, los árboles y otros objetos de la naturaleza tienen un espíritu, **228**

antifreeze/anticongelante Sustancia que se agrega a un líquido para evitar que se congele, **458**

apartheid The South African government policy of separation of races, which began to disappear in the 1980s, **196, 278**

aquifers/acuíferos Capas subterráneas de roca, arena y grava en las que se almacena el agua, **26**

arable/cultivable Tierra con características que favorecen el cultivo, **356**

archaeology/arqueología Estudio de los restos de culturas pasadas, **224**

archipelago/archpiélago Grupo grande de islas, **398**

artesian wells/pozos artesianos Pozos en los que el agua sube a la superficie de la tierra sin ser impulsada por medios artificiales, **432**

asphalt/asfalto Material oscuro usado para pavimentar calles, **109**

atmosphere/atmósfera Capa de gases que rodea a la tierra, **31**

atolls/atolones Anillos de coral que se forman alrededor de las lagunas, **335**

B

basins/cuencas Regiones rodeadas por montañas u otras tierras altas, **256**

bauxite/bauxita El mineral con contenido de aluminio más importante, **223**

Bedouins/beduinos Ganaderos nómadas del desierto de Egipto y el sudoeste de Asia, **208**

birthrate/índice de natalidad número de nacimientos por 1,000 personas en un año, **59**

Boers/boers agricultores africanos de raza blanca, descendientes de los primeros colonizadores europeos de Sudáfrica, **276**

boycott/boicot Rechazo de compra, **196, 310**

bush Zonas salvajes de escasa población, como ciertas regiones de Australia, **437**

C

cacao/cacas Árbol pequeño que produce los granos de cacao, **235**

caliph/califa Líder político y religioso del mundo musulmán, **100, 128**

canopy/dosel Capa superior de un bosque espeso en el que las ramas se entrelazan, bloqueando el paso de la luz solar, **256**

caravans/caravanas Grupos de personas que viajan juntas por razones de seguridad, **148**

cartography/cartografía Arte y ciencia de la elaboración de mapas, **13**

Casbah/casbah Antigua fortaleza y centro de las ciudades del norte de África, **215**

caste system/sistema de castas Sistema en el que la posición de una persona en la sociedad es determinada por el nivel social del grupo en el que nace, **314**

chaebol/chaebol Enormes grupos industriales formados por compañías, bancos y otros negocias en Corea del Sur, **392**

cholera/cólera Infección intestinal seria que puede provocar a muerta, **327**

Christianity/cristianismo religión basada en las enseñadas de Jesus, **97**

city-states/ciudades estado Ciudades con un sistema de autogobierno, como en la antigua África, **187**

civil war/guerra civil conflicto entre dos o más grupos dentro de un país, **263**

civilization/civilización Cultura altamente compleja con grandes ciudades y abundante actividad económica, **52**

climate/clima condiciones meteorológicas registradas en un periodo largo, **32**

climatology/climatología Registro de los sistemas atmosféricos de la Tierra, **13**

command economy/economía autoritaria Economía en la que el gobierno es propietario de la mayor parte de las industrias y toma la mayoría de las decisiones en materia de economía, **56, 366**

commercial agriculture/agricultura comercial Tipo de agricultura cuya producción es exclusiva para la venta, **52**

condensation/condensación Proceso mediante el cual el agua cambia de estado gaseoso y forma pequeñas gotas, **27**

copper belt/región del cobre Importante región minera de producción de cobre localizada en la parte central de África, **257**

coral reef/arrecife coralino Formaciones creadas por la acumulación de los restos de animales marinos diminutos cerca de las costas en las aguas templadas de las regiones tropicales, **433**

Crusades/Cruzadas Expediciones hecas por los cristianos para recuperar la Tierra Santa de los musulmanes, **114**

culture/cultura Sistema de creencias y costumbres comunes que guía la conducta cotidiana de las personas, **47**

culture region/región cultural Región del mundo en la que se comparten ciertos rasgos culturales, **47**

culture traits/rasgos culturales Características de una cultura, como la ropa, la comida o las creencias religiosas, **47**

cuneiform/cuneiforme Sistema de escritura en el que se usan signos de forma triangular sobre barro, **90**

currents/corrientes Enormes corrientes del océano que transportan agua tibia a las regiones frías y viceversa, **34**

cyclones/ciclones Tormentas violentas con fuertes lluvias, paracidas a los huracanes del Caribe, comunes en el sur de Asia, **322**

D

Dalits/dalits Personas de la clase social más baja de la India, cuyas actividades son consideradas poco salubres, **315**

death rate/índice de mortalidad número de muertes por 1,000 personas en un año, **59**

deforestation/deforestación Destrucción o pérdida de un área boscosa, **39**

deltas/deltas Formaciones creadas por la acumulación de sedimentos en las desembocadura de los ríos, **21**

demilitarized zone/zona desmilitarizada Zona de protección que sirve como barrera entre dos países en conflicto, como Corea del Norte y Corea del Sur, **389**

depressions/cavidades Zonas de elevación muy baja, **202**

developing countries/países en vaís de desarrollo países que se encuentran en alguna etapa de su proceso de desarrollo, **55**

dharma/dharma En el hinduismo, un deber moral, **312**

dialect/dialecto Variación de un idioma, **260**

Diaspora/Diáspora Dispersión de la población judía que emigró de territorio palestino durante el imperio romano, **114**

dictator/dictadore Persona que ejercen total autoridad sobre un gobierno, **217**

Diet/Dieta Legislatura electa de Japón, **381**

diffusion/difusión Extensión de ideas o conducta de una región cultura a otra, **9**

dikes/diques Grandes muros de tierra o concreto construidos para contener a un cuerpo de agua y evitar inundaciones, **355**

disciples/discípulos grupo pequeño de partidarios, **96**

division of labor/división de labores Característa de las civilizaciones en la cual diferentes personas realizan diferentes trabajos, **86**

domestication/domesticación Cuidado de una planta o animal para uso personal, **51**

droughts/sequías Periodos en los que los cultivos sufren daños debido a la escasez de lluvia, **63, 249**

dynasty/dinastía Familia que gobierna y hereda el podor de generación en generación, **177, 357**

E

earthquakes/terremotos Movimientos repentinos y fuertes que se producen en las fisuras de la superficie de la tierra, **20**

embargo/embargo Límite impuesto a las relaciones comerciales, **137**

emigrant/emigrante persona que sale de un lugar para otro, **59**

emperor/emperador Gobernante supremo de vastos territorios, **357**

enclaves/enclaves Países rodeados en su mayor parte o en su totalidad por otro país, **272**

endemic species/especies endémicas Plantas y animales que se desarrollan en una región particular del planeta, **433**

entrepreneurs/empresarios Personas que usan su dinero y su talento para iniciar un negocio, **392**

ergs/ergs Grandes "mares" de arena formados por las dunas del desierto del Sahara, **202**

erosion/erosión Desplazamiento de agua, hielo, viento o minerales a otro lugar, **21**

ethnic groups/grupos étnicos Grupos culturales que comparten creencias y prácticas comunes, **47**

ethnocentrism/etnocentrismo ver diferencias en otra cultura como inferior, **49**

evaporation/evaporación Proceso mediante el cual el agua se convierte en vapor y se eleva en el aire, **27**

exclave/exclave Parte de un país separada por el territorio de uno o más países, **267**

Exclusive Economic Zones/zonas de exclusividad económica Zonas costeras de un país en las que éste tiene derecho a extraer y controlar los recursos existentes, **455**

Exodus/éxodo el escape de los judios de Egipto antigua, **94**

exotic rivers/ríos exóticos Ríos originados en regiones húmedas que fluyen a zonas más secas, **126**

exports/exportaciones productos que un país vende a otros paises, **57**

famine/hambruna Gran escasez de alimeno, **63, 393**

fault/falla Fractura de la superficie de la tierra que causa el movimiento de grandes masas de rocas, **20**

fellahin/fellahin agricultores egipcios dueños de pequeñas porciones de terreno, **212**

Fertile Crescent/Creciente fértil Área de tierra fértil en Asia del suroeste que hace una curva desde el río Jordán a lo largo de los ríos Tigris y Eufrates hasta el Gulfo Pérsico, **89**

Five Pillars of Islam/cinco pilares de islam reglas que los musulmanes siguen, **99**

floodplain/llanura aluvial Especie de plataforma a nivel de la tierra, formada por la acumulación de los sedimentos de una corriente de agua, **21**

fossil fuels/combustibles fósiles Recursos no renovables formados por restos muy antiguos de plantas y animales, **40**

fossil water/aguas fósiles Agua que no es reemplazada por el agua de lluvia, **127**

free enterprise/libre empresa Sistema económico en el que las personas, y no el gobierno, deciden qué productos fabrican, venden y compran, **56**

free port/puerto libre Cuidad en la que casi no se aplican impuestos a los productos que allí se adquieren, **215**

futon/futón Especie de sofá ligero, también usado como cama, muy común en Japón, **384**

geography/geografía Estudio de las características físicas y culturales de la Tierra, **3**

geothermal energy/energía geotérmica Fuente energética no removable producida por el calor del interior de la tierra, **41**

gers/gers Grandes tiendas circulares que son fáciles de armar, desarmar y transportar; usadas por los ganaderos nómades de Mongolia, **369**

glaciers/glaciares Grandes bloques de hielo que se desplazan con lenitud sobre el agua, **22**

global warming/calentamiento global Aumento lento y constante de la temperatura de la Tierra, **30**

globalization/globalización Proceso mediante el que as comunicaciones alrededor del mundo se han incrementado haciendo a las culturas más parecidas, **60**

gorge/garganta Cañón estrecho y muy profundo, **246**

Gospels/Evangelios primeros cuatro libros de la Biblia cristiana que cuenta de la vida de Jesus, **96**

graphite/grafito Tipo de carbón usado para fabricar puntas de lápices y muchos otros productos, **334**

greenhouse effect/efecto invernadero Proceso mediante el cual la atmósfera terrestre atrapa el calor de su superficie, **30**

green revolution/revolución verde Programa iniciado por el gobierno de la India en la década de 1960 para modernizar los métodos y producir mayor cantidad de alimento, **317**

griots/griots Narradores de historias de África Occidental que pasan sus tradiciones tribales de manera oral, **234**

gross domestic product/producto interno bruto Valor de todos los bienes y servicios producidos en un país, **53**

gross national product/producto nacional bruto Valor de todos los bienes y servicios producidos en un año por un país, dentro o fuera de sus límites, **53**

groundwater/agua subterránea Agua de lluvia, ríos, lagos y nieve derretida que se filtra al subsuelo, **26**

Hanging Gardens/Jardines colgantes Jardines de tejado abundantes construidos en Babilonia por el rey Nabucodonosor, **92**

harmattan/harmattan Viento seco y polvoso que sopla con fuerza hacia el sur durante el envierno en el desierto del Sahara, **222**

hieroglyphics/jeroglíficos Forma antigua de escritura con imágenes y símbolos usados para registrar información, **179**

hieroglyphs/jeroglíficos Dibujos y símbolos que representan ideas o palabras, **205**

history/historia Registro escrito de la civilización humana, **87**

hominid/homínido Primera criatura similares al hombre, **83**

human geography/geografía humana estudio del pasado y presente de la humanidad, **11**

human-environment interaction/interacción humano-ambiente relación entre personas y el medio ambiente, **9**

humanitarian aid/ayuda humanitaria medicina, comida, y cobertizo que las agencias de ayuda internacional dan a las personas con necesidades, **63**

hurricanes/huracanes Tormentas tropicales con intensos vientos, fuertes lluvias y altas mareas, **14**

hydroelectric power/energía hidroeléctrica Fuente energética renovable producida en generadores impulsados por caídas de agua, **41**

icebergs/icebergs Grandes bloques de hielo que se separan de los glaciales y flotan a la deriva en el océano, **450**

ice shelf/capa de hielo Cubierta de hielo que se forma en aguas costeras, **450**

immigrant/inmigrante persona que llega de otro país, **59**

imperialism/imperialismo control por un país sobre el gobierno, comercio, y cultura de otro país, **190**

imports/importaciones productos que un país compra de otros paises, **57**

industrialized countries/paises industrializados paises que depende más en la industria que en la agricultura, **54**

intensive cultivation/cultivo intenso Cultivo de productos en cualquier terreno disponible, **385**

interdependence/interdependencia depender en otro país para recursos o productos y servicios, **57**

irrigation/riego Proceso mediante el cual el agua se hace llegar a los cultivos de manera artificial, **85**

Islam/Islam Religión monoteísta basada en el Corán y en las enseñanzas de Mahoma y que se desarrolló en la Arabia Saudí actual, **98**

ivory/marfil Material de color crema extraído de los colmillos de los elefantes que se usa para fabricar joyería y artículos decorativos, **258**

Japan Current/Corriente de Japón corriente oceánica de aguas tibias que fluye al este de Japón, **377**

Judaism/judaismo religón monoteística que se desarrolló entre los hebreos en semicírculo fértil, **94**

kampongs/kampongs Aldea tradicional de Indonesía; el término también se usa para referirse a las grandes poblaciones humanas establecidas en los alrededores de las ciudades de Indonesia, **408**

karma/karma Para los hinduistas y budistas, es la fuerza positiva o negativa generada por las acciones de una persona, **312**

kimchi/kimchi Especie de col china aderezada y avinagrada que se sirve como plato tradicional en Corea, **392**

kimonos/kimonos vestidos tradicionales japoneses, **383**

kiwi/kiwi Ave que no vuela, originaria de Nueva Zelanda; a veces, este término se usa para referirse a los neozelandeses, **441**

klongs/klongs Canales de Bangkok, una ciudad de Tailandia, **405**

krill/krill Animales marinos diminutos que son una importante fuente alimenticia para otras especies marinas del Océano Atlántico, **451**

land bridges/puentes de terreno Franjas de terreno seco que conecta grandes masas de tierra, **84**

landforms/accidentes geográficos Forma de la tierra en differentes partes de la superficie, **19**

landlocked/sin salida al mar Zona rodeada de agua por completo y sin acceso directo al océano, **146**

lava/lava Magma que emerge del interior de la tierra por un orificio de la corteza, **20**

literacy rate/índice de alfabetismo porcentaje de personas que pueden leer y escribir, **54**

mainland/región continental Región donde se localiza la mayor porción de terreno de un país, **398**

malaria/malaria Enfermedad mortal que se difunde por medio de los mosquitos, **230**

mandate/mandato Territorios que formaban parte de los países derrotados en la Primera Guerra Mundial, y que pasaron a control de los países vencedores, **118**

market economy/economía de mercado Tipo de economía en la qué los consumidores ayudan a determinar qué productos se fabrican al comprar o rechazar ciertos bienes y servicios, **56**

marsupials/marsupiales Animales que transportan a sus crías en un saco, **434**

martial law/ley marcial Ley militar, **360**

megalopolis/megalópolis Enorme zona urbana que abarca una serie de ciudades que se han desarrollado juntas, **383**

Mesopotamia/Mesopotamia Tierra antigua entre los ríos Tigris y Eufrates, **126**

meteorology/meteorología Predicción y registro de lluvias, temperaturas y otras condiciones atmosféricas, **13**

migration/migración movimiento de personas, **59**

millet/mijo Tipo de cultivo resistente a las sequías, **229**

mixed economy/economía mixta Intercambio de bienes y servicios basado en al menos dos otros sistemas, **57**

monotheism/monoteísmo creencia en un solo dios, **95**

mosques/mezquitas Casas de adoración islámica, **102, 152**

most-favored-nation status/estatus de nación favorecida Estatus que otorga privilegios de intercambio comercial entre Estados Unidos y otros países, **367**

movement/movimiento El ir y venir de gente e ideas, **9**

multicultural/multicultural Mezcla de culturas en un mismo país o comunidad, **47**

multiple cropping/cultivo múltiple Tipo de agricultura en la que se producen dos o tres cultivos cada año en las mismas tierras, **366**

mummification/momificación proceso de preservar los cuerpos de los muertos, **182**

Muslims/Musulmanes Seguidores del Islam, **128**

nationalism/nacionalismo Demanda de autogo-bierno y fuerte sentimiento de lealtad hacia una nación, **190**

New Testament/Testamento Nuevo parte de la Biblia que contiene historias de Jesus, sus partidarios, y ideas cristianas posteriores, **97**

nirvana/nirvana Para los budistas, es el escape de los sufrimientos de la vida, **313**

nomads/nómadas Personas que se mudan frecuentemente de un lugar a otro, **84, 148**

nonrenewable resources/recursos no renovables Recursos, como el carbón mineral y petróleo, que no pueden reemplazarse a corto plazo por medios naturales, **38**

oasis/oasis Lugar del desierto donde un manantial proporciona una fuente natural de agua, **146**

one-crop economy/economía de un cultivo Economía basada en un solo cultivo, como las bananas, la caña de azúcar o el cacao, **57**

OPEC/OPEP Organización de países exportadores de petróleo; grupo formado para ejercer influencia en el precio de los mercados petroleros mundiales, **129**

oral history/historia oral Información oral transmitida de una persona a otra y de generación en generación, **185, 224**

Organization of African Unity (OAU)/Organización Africa Unida (OAU) Grupo fundado en 1963 para promover la cooperación entre los países africanos, **283**

outback/*Outback* (Interior) Región interior de Australia, **434**

overpopulation/superpoblación más personas que una región o un país puede mantener por sus propios medios, **58**

Oyashio Current/Corriente Oyashio Corriente de aguas frías que fluye al este de Japón, **377**

ozone layer/ozonosfera Forma del oxígeno en la atmósfera que ayuda a proteger a la Tierra de los daños que produce la radiación solar, **30**

pagodas/pagodas Templos budistas, **362**

pans/pans Regiones desérticas del sur de África, de terreno bajo y plano, en las que desaguaban corrientes antiguas, **273**

papyrus/papiro una materia como papel hecho de la parte interna de los tallos de la planta papiro, **179**

periodic markets/mercados periódicos Mercados al aire libre en el África central, **257**

perspective/perspectiva Punto de vista basado en la experiencia y la comprensión de una persona, **3**

petroleum/petróleo Líquido graso que al refinarse produce gasolina y otros combustibles y aceites, **40**

pharaohs/faraones Reyes del antiguo Egipto, **177, 205**

phosphates/fosfatos Sales minerales que contienen el elemento fósforo; se usa para hacer fertilizantes, **109**

physical geography/geografía física Estudio del paisaje natural y los sistemas físicos de la Tierra, entre ellos la atmósfera, **11**

pictographs/pictografías sistema de escribir que usa dibujos pequeños para mostrar información, **90**

place/lugar Rasgos físicos y humanos de una ubicación específica, **7**

plain/planicie Área casi plana de la superficie terrestre, **21**

plate tectonics/tectónica de placas Teoría de que la superficie terrestre está dividida en varias placas enormes que se mueven lentamente, **19**

polar desert/desierto polar Región de latitudes altas donde cae muy poca precipitación, **451**

popular culture/cultura popular Creencias, gustos, metas y practicas generalmente compartidos, **60**

population density/densidad de población Número promedio de personas que viven en una milla cuadrada o un kilómetro cuadrado, **58**

porcelain/porcelana Tipo de vajilla muy fina, **358**

precipitation/precipitación Proceso por el que el agua vuelve de regreso a la Tierra, **27**

prehistory/prehistoria Tiempo antiguo del que no se conservan registros escritos, **84**

prevailing winds/vientos predominantes brisas que sopla consistentemente en la misma dirección sobre grandes regiones de la Tierra, **33**

protectionism/proteccionismo Práctica de poner barreras comerciales para proteger a las industrias nacionales de la competencia de las industrias extranjeras, **386**

provinces/provincias Divisiones administrativas de un país, **93**

pyramids/pirámides Enormes monumentos de piedra cuadrados y con cuatro lados triangulares, **179**

Qur'an/Corán El libro sagra do del Islam, **98, 129**

R

race/raza Grupo de personas que comparten características físicas o biológicas heredades, **48**

rain shadow/barrera montañosa Área seca en el sotavento de una montaña o de una cordillera, **35**

reforestation/reforestación Plantación de árboles donde los bosques han sido talados, **39**

refugees/refugiados Personas que han escapado a otro país, generalmente por razones económicas o políticas, **63, 401**

region/región Área de la superficie de la Tierra con una o más características compartidas, **8**

regs/regs Extensas planicies de grava azotadas por el viento, en el Sahara, **202**

reincarnation/reencarnación Creencia de que el alma humana vuelva a nacer una y otro vez en diferentes cuerpos, **312**

relative location/ubicación relativa Posición de un lugar en relación con otro, **7**

renewable resources/recursos renovables Recursos, como el suelo y los bosques, que pueden reemplazarse por medio de procesos naturales de la Tierra, **38**

Resurrection/Resurrección creencia cristiana que Jesus se levantó del muerto, **96**

rifts/hendeduras Valles largos y profundos con montañas o mesetas a cada lado, **240**

Rosetta Stone/piedra roseta tableta antigua de roca tallada en griego, jeroglíficos egipcios, y escritura demotica, **179**

rugby/rugby Juego de origen británico similar a fútbol, **436**

rural/rural Área de terreno abierto que se usa para la agricultura, **4**

S

Sahel/sahel Región de pastizales secos con clima estepario del Sur del Sahara, **222**

samurai/samurai Guerreros al servicio de señores japoneses, **380**

sanctions/sanciones Penalidad económica o política, como un embargo, que uno o más países usan para obligar a otro país a dejar de cometer un acto ilegal o inmoral, **279**

Sanskrit/sánscrito Idioma antiguo del Sur de Asia; en la actualidad se usa en la India como lengua sagrada en la, **307**

secede/separar Dividir un país para formar otro, **232**

secular/seglar Que está separado de la religión, como un gobierno o estado secular, **111**

sepoys/cipayos Tropas indias dirigidas por oficiales británicos durante el periodo colonial de la India, **310**

shah/sha Rey de Irán, **103, 140**

shamans/shaman Monje sintoísta, **379**

Shia/Shia La segunda más grande rama del Islam, **128**

Shintoism/shintoismo Religión más antigua conocida de Japón, **379**

shogun/shogún "Gran General" el más alto rango entre los guerreros japoneses, **380**

silt/cieno Tierra de granos muy finos, **203**

solar power/energía solar calor y luz del sol, **41**

sorghum/sorgo Grano de cultivo que puede sobrevivir a las sequías, **229**

souks/souks Mercados del norte de África, **215**

spatial perspective/perspectiva espacial Punto de vista basado o visto en relación con el lugar en que se encuentra un objeto, así como la razón por la que está ahí, **3**

sphinxes/esfinges esculturas de monstruos con cuerpo de leon y cabeza de humano, **180**

staple/producto básico Cultivo principal de una región o un país, **230**

storm surges/mareas de tormenta Grandes ondas de agua que se elevan por la fuerza del viento, en particular de los ciclones, huracanes y otras tormentas tropicales, **322**

stupas/stupas Montículos de tierra o piedras que cubren las cenizas del Buda o las reliquias de los santos budistas, **330**

subduction/subducción Movimiento en el que una placa tectónica terrestre más gruesa se sumerge debajo de una más delgada, **20**

subsistence agriculture/agricultura de subsistencia Tipo de agricultura en que los campesinos siembran sólo lo necesario para mantenerse a ellos mismos y a sus familias, **52**

sultan/sultán Gobernante supremo de un país musulmán, **411**

Sunni/sunita La rama más grande del Islam, **128**

Swahili/suahili Idioma bantú que se habla extensamente en África, **244**

symbol/símbolo Palabra, forma, color, estadarte o cualquier otra cosa que se use en representación de algo, **49**

teak/teca Tipo de madera preciosa que crece en la India y al sudeste de Asia, **305**

Ten Commandments/diez mandamientos reglas básicas dado a Moisés, **95**

terraces/terrazas Crestas horizontales que se construyen sobre las laderas de las colinas para prevenir la pérdida de suelo y favorecer la agricultura, **22**

theocracy/teocracia Gobierno regido por líderes religiosos, **140**

third-world countries/paises del tercer mundo paises en desarrollo que faltan oportunidades económicas, **55**

topography/topografía forma, altura y arreglo de la tierra en un cierto lugar, **19**

Torah/Tora los cinco libros de Moises que los judeos siguen, **95**

townships/municipios Regiones de multitudes de pequeñas casas apiñadas que habitan los sudafricanos de raza negra en las afueras de las ciudades, **278**

trade surplus/excedente comercial Ocurre cuando el valor de las imporaciones es mayor que el de las importaciones, **386**

tradition-based economy/economía tradicional Economía basada en las costumbres y las tradiciones, **56**

tributary/tributario Cualquier corriente pequeña o río que fluye hacia un río o una corriente más grande, **26**

trust territories/territorios bajo administración fiduciaria Regiones que están bajo el control temporal de otro país hasta que establezca su propio gobierno, **453**

tsetse fly/mosca tse tse Mosca africana del sur del Sahara que transmite el mal del sueño, una enfermedad mortal, **222**

tsunamis/tsunamis Olas muy grandes que se forman por la actividad submarina de las placas tectónicas, tales como los terremotos, **377**

urban/urbano Área en que se encuentra una ciudad, **4**

veld, the/el veld regiones de pastos altos en el sur de África, **272**

wadis/wadis Lechos secos de corrientes en el sudoeste de Asia y África, **127**

water cycle/ciclo del agua Circulación del agua del la superficie de la Tierra a la atmósfera y su regreso, **27**

water vapor/vapor de agua Estado gaseoso del agua, **27**

weather/tiempo Condiciones de la atmósfera en un tiempo y un lugar determinados, **32**

weathering/desgaste Proceso de desintegración de las rocas en pedazos pequeños por la acción del calor, el agua y otros medios, **21**

work ethic/ética laboral Creencia de que el trabajo es un mérito en sí mismo, **386**

yurt/yurta Tienda redonda y portátil de lana tejida que se coloca sobre una armazón de madera, **152**

ziggurats/zigurates templos en forma de pirámide construidos por los sumerios, **90**

Zionism/sionismo Movimiento que trata de establecer un país o comunidad judía en Palestina, **115**

zonal/zonal Clima del este de África que se extiende en franjas de este a oeste, **222**

INDEX

Dakar, Senegal, *m221, p225,* 233, *p233*

Dalits, *p314,* 315

Damascus, Syria, *m107,* 118

Dardanelles, *m107,* 108

Darius I, 93

Darwin, Australia, *g435*

Dead Sea, *m107,* 108

death rate, 59

Deccan, *m303,* 304

deforestation, 39; Indonesia and, 416–18, *m417;* Kenya and, 288, *p288;* Nepal, 329

degrees, S2

Delhi, India, *m303,* 307

delta, 21

demilitarized zone, 389, *p388*

demotic writing, 179

desalinization, 130

deserts, as dry climates, *m36–37*

developing countries, 55, *g55*

Dhaka, Bangladesh, *m321,* 327, *p327*

dhow, *p187*

diagrams, S10–S11, 340, 341

dialects, 260

Diaspora, 114

dictator, 217

Diet, 381

diffusion, 9

dikes, 355

disciples, 96

division of labor, 85

Djibouti, *m239,* 251, *p251;* climate, 241; culture, 244; economy, 251; ethnic groups, 252; government, 251; history, 242–43; landforms, 240; resources, 241; rivers and lakes, 240–41, *p251;* statistics, 171, *g250*

Djoser, King, 179

Dodoma, *m239*

Doha, Qatar, *m125*

Dome of the Rock (Jerusalem), *p117*

domestication, 51

Douala, Cameroon, *m255,* 265

Drakensberg, *m271,* 272, *p272*

droughts, 63, 249

Druze, 119

Durban, South Africa, *m271,* 280

Dushanbe, Tajikistan, *m145*

Dutch East Indies. *See* Indonesia

dynasty, 177, 357

Earth: climate and vegetation, 32–37, *g36, m37;* energy resources, 40–41; landforms, 19; minerals, 42; forests, 39; plate tectonics, 19, *m19*

earthquakes, 20, 376–77

East Africa, 120, *m239,* 238–51; climate, 241; countries of, 245–48, 249–51; culture, 244, *g253;* history, 242–43; Horn of Africa region, 249–51; landforms, 240; religion, *g255;* resources, 241; rivers and lakes, 240–41; statistics, *g246, g250, g253;* student profile, 238, *p238. See also* specific countries

East Asia, *m353, m375;* cities, 364–66; climate, *m347,* 355–56, 238; culture, 361–63, 369, 370; economy, 366–67, 369, 371; elevation profile, *g344;* geostats, *g344;* history, 357–61, 368, 370; land use, *m349;* physical features, 354–55, 345; physical geography, *m345, m345;* political geography, *m346;* population, *m348,* 364; resources, *mS9, m349,* 355, 377; statistics, 350–51, *g355, g383, g390. See also* specific countries

East Timor, *m397,* 102, 113

Eastern Ghats, *m303,* 304

Eastern Hemisphere, S3, *gS3*

Eastern Highlands (Australia), *m431,* 432

Eastern Mediterranean, 106, *m107;* climate, 108–09; Israel, *m95,* 114–17; physical features, 108; resources, 109; Turkey, 110–131. *See also* specific countries

Ebadi, Shirin, 140, *p140*

Economic Community of West African States (ECOWAS), 226

economic geography *See* human geography

economy: command economy, 56, 393; definition of, 53; global population and, 54–55; gross domestic product, 53; gross national product, 53

ecosystem, 290, 291, 438

Egypt, ancient, *m177;* history, 177–78; *Book of the Dead, p182;* hieroglyphics, 179, *g179,* 205; Nile River valley, 177, *m177;* papyrus, 179; pharoahs, 177, 205, *p205;* pyramids, *p6, p178,* 206; temples, 180, *p180–81*

Egypt, *m201;* climate, 203–04; European control, 207; culture, *p208;* economy, 213; history 205–07, *p205, p206, p207;* modern challenges, 214; people and cities, 212–13, *m212, p212, p213;* Nile River valley, 203, *p203;* physical features, 202–03; resources, 204; statistics, 171, *g213;* student profile, 200, *p200;* Suez Canal and Sinai, *m201,* 203, 207, 213

Elburz Mountains, *m125,* 126

embargo, 137

emigrant, 59

emperor, 357

enclaves, 272

endangered species: tigers, 338–39, *p338, m339, p339;* orangutans, 416, *p417*

endemic species, 433

energy resources: coal, 40; fossil fuels, 40; geothermal energy, 41; hydroelectric power, 40; natural gas, 40; nonrenewable resources, 38; nuclear energy, 41; petroleum, 40; renewable resources, 38; solar energy, 41; wind, 41, *p40*

entrepreneurs, 392

environment: forests, 39; soil, 38; making decisions about local environmental problems, 464–65

equator, A4–A5, S2, *gS2*

ACKNOWLEDGMENTS

For permission to reproduce copyrighted material, grateful acknowledgment is made to the following sources:

Doubleday, a division of Random House, Inc.; electronic format by permission of Harold Ober Associates Incorporated: From "Marriage Is a Private Affair" from *Girls at War and Other Stories* by Chinua Achebe. Copyright © 1972, 1973 by Chinua Achebe.

FocalPoint f/8: From "October 5—Galtai" from "Daily Chronicles" and from "Buddhist Prayer Ceremony" from "Road Stories" by Gary Matoso and Lisa Dickey from *The Russian Chronicles* from *FocalPoint f/8*, accessed October 14, 1999, at http://www.f8.com/FP/Russia.

HarperCollins Publishers, Inc.; electronic format by permission of Wallace Literary Agency: From *My Days* by R. K. Narayan. Copyright © 1973, 1974 by R. K. Narayan.

International Rescue Committee: From "IRC Staff Members Talk About 'The Biggest Humanitarian Crisis on the Planet'" by Werner Vansant from *International Rescue Committee* Web site, accessed October 19, 2003, at http://www.theirc.org/index.cfm?section = where& wwwID = 1708. Copyright © 2003 by International Rescue Committee.

Professor Hugh Kawharu: From "Treaty of Waitangi, 1840," translated by Prof. Sir Hugh Kawharu from *Government of New Zealand* Web site, accessed October 30, 2003, at http://www.govt.nz/en/ aboutnz/?id = a32f7d70e71e9632aad1016cb343f900.

James Li, M.D.: From "Africa" by James Li, M.D from *eMedicine*, accessed October 11, 1999, at http://www.emedicine.com/emerg/topic726.htm. Copyright © 1999 by James Li.

Ms. Magazine: From "Foresters Without Diplomas" by Wangari Maathai from *Ms.*, vol. 1, no. 5, March/April 1991. Copyright © 1991 by *Ms.* Magazine.

Penguin Books Ltd.: From *The Epic of Gilgamesh*, translated by N. K. Sandars (Penguin Classics 1960, Third Edition, 1972). Copyright © 1960, 1964, 1972 by N. K. Sandars.

Taylor & Francis, Inc.: "Kurdish Present and Near Future Demographic Trends" (table) from *The Kurds: A Concise Handbook* by Mehrad R. Izady. Copyright © 1992 by Taylor & Francis. All rights reserved.

University of California Press: From pp. 96–99 from *Ancient Egyptian Literature*, Three Volumes, translated by Miriam Lichtheim. Copyright © 1973, 1980 by the Regents of the University of California.

Writer's House, Inc. c/o The Permissions Company: From *For Love Alone* by Christina Stead. Copyright © 1944 by Harcourt, Inc.; copyright renewed © 1972 by Christina Stead.

Sources Cited:

"B. Ospanova, a citizen of Almaty, 50 years old, December 1998" from *President of the Republic of Kazakhstan* Web site, accessed December 2, 2003, at http://www.president.kz/articles/Sover_Kaz.asp?lng = en&art = kazakh_10. Published by the Analysis and Strategic Research Center of the Administration of the President of the Republic of Kazakhstan, 1998.

From "Weekender: Woman of Courage (Tales of the Century: A Filipino writer recalls an interview with Aung San Suu Kyi)" from *Businessworld*, Manila, March 5, 1999, pg.1.

From "President Khatami's Interview with the NY Times" from *The New York Times*, November 9, 2001.

From "Courage, the Spirit of Daring" from *Bushido: The Warrior's Code* by Inazo Nitobe. Published by Ohara Publications, Inc., Burbank, CA, 1979.

From "Ancient Ghana and the Customs of Its Inhabitants" by Al Bakri from *Africa in the Days of Exploration*, edited by Roland Oliver and Caroline Oliver. Published by Prentice-Hall, Inc., Englewood Cliffs, NJ, 1965.

ART CREDITS

Abbreviated as follows: (t) top, (b) bottom, (l) left, (r) right, (c) center.

Unit flags of United States created by One Mile Up, Inc. Unit flags of Canadian provinces created by EyeWire, Inc. Other flags, country silhouettes, feature maps and atlas maps created by MapQuest.com., Inc. All other illustrations, unless otherwise noted, contributed by Holt, Rinehart and Winston.

Table of Contents: Page VII, Nick Rotondo; XVI, Dave Henderson.

Atlas: Page A2, MapQuest.com, Inc.; A4, MapQuest.com, Inc.; A6, MapQuest.com, Inc.; A8, MapQuest.com, Inc.; A10, MapQuest.com, Inc.; A11, MapQuest.com, Inc.; A12, MapQuest.com, Inc.; A13, MapQuest.com, Inc.; A14, MapQuest.com, Inc.; A15, MapQuest.com, Inc.; A16, MapQuest.com, Inc.; A17, MapQuest.com, Inc.; A18, MapQuest.com, Inc.; A19, MapQuest.com, Inc.; A20, MapQuest.com, Inc.; A21, MapQuest.com, Inc.; A22, MapQuest.com, Inc.

Geography and Map Skills Handbook: Page S2, MapQuest.com, Inc.; S3, MapQuest.com, Inc.; S4 (cl, bl), MapQuest.com, Inc.; S5, MapQuest.com, Inc.; S6, MapQuest.com, Inc.; S7, MapQuest.com, Inc.; S8, MapQuest.com, Inc.; S9, MapQuest.com, Inc.; S10 (t, br), Leslie Kell; S11 (t), Leslie Kell; S11 (b), Ortelius Design; S12 (b), Leslie Kell; S13, Uhl Studios, Inc.; S14, MapQuest.com, Inc.; S16, Robert Hynes.

Chapter 1: Page 5 (cl), MapQuest.com, Inc.; 6 (bl), MapQuest.com, Inc.; 8 (l, bc), MapQuest.com, Inc.; 9 (tr), MapQuest.com, Inc.; 10 (tc), MapQuest.com, Inc.; 11 (bc), MapQuest.com, Inc.; 14 (b), MapQuest.com, Inc.; 16 (b), MapQuest.com, Inc.

Chapter 2: Page 19, MapQuest.com, Inc.; 27, Uhl Studios, Inc.; 28 HRW Art; 31, Uhl Studios, Inc.; 33, Uhl Studios, Inc.; 35 (tl), Uhl Studios, Inc.; 37, MapQuest.com, Inc.; 41, MapQuest.com, Inc.; 42 (t), MapQuest.com, Inc.; 42 (b), MapQuest.com, Inc.; 44, MapQuest.com, Inc.; 45, Leslie Kell.

Chapter 3: Page 48 (t), MapQuest.com, Inc.; 48 (b), MapQuest.com, Inc.; 49 (tr), MapQuest.com, Inc.; 50 (bl), MapQuest.com, Inc.; 53 (t), MapQuest.com, Inc.; 54, MapQuest.com, Inc.; 55 (t), MapQuest.com, Inc.; 58, MapQuest.com, Inc.; 64, MapQuest.com, Inc.; 67, MapQuest.com, Inc.

Unit 2: Page 72 (bl, t), Ortelius Design; 73, MapQuest.com, Inc.; 74, MapQuest.com, Inc.; 75, MapQuest.com, Inc.; 76, MapQuest.com, Inc.; 77, MapQuest.com, Inc.; 78–81, MapQuest.com, Inc.

Chapter 4: Page 85, MapQuest.com, Inc.; 87 (b), MapQuest.com, Inc.; 89 (b), MapQuest.com, Inc.; 95, MapQuest.com, Inc.; 97, MapQuest.com, Inc.; 101, MapQuest.com, Inc.; 104, MapQuest.com, Inc.; 105, MapQuest.com, Inc.

Chapter 5: Page 107 (b), MapQuest.com, Inc.; 108, (bl) MapQuest.com, Inc.; 109 (t), MapQuest.com, Inc.; 110, (b) MapQuest.com, Inc.; 113 (t), MapQuest.com, Inc.; 114 (bl), MapQuest.com, Inc.; 116, MapQuest.com, Inc.; 117, MapQuest.com, Inc.; 118 (bc), MapQuest.com, Inc.; 122 (b), MapQuest.com, Inc.

Chapter 6: Page 125, MapQuest.com, Inc.; 126, MapQuest.com, Inc.; 128, MapQuest.com, Inc.; 129, MapQuest.com, Inc.; 130, MapQuest.com, Inc.; 133, MapQuest.com, Inc.; 134 MapQuest.com, Inc.; 139 Uhl Studios, Inc.; 140 MapQuest.com, Inc.; 142 MapQuest.com, Inc.; 143, Leslie Kell.

Chapter 7: Page 145, MapQuest.com, Inc.; 147, MapQuest.com, Inc.; 148, MapQuest.com, Inc.; 149, MapQuest.com, Inc.; 152, MapQuest.com, Inc.; 155, Leslie Kell; 156, MapQuest.com, Inc.; 159, MapQuest.com, Inc.

Unit 3: Page 164 (bl, t), Ortelius Design; 165, MapQuest.com, Inc.; 166, MapQuest.com, Inc.; 167, MapQuest.com, Inc.; 168, MapQuest.com, Inc.; 169, MapQuest.com, Inc.; 170–175, MapQuest.com, Inc.

Chapter 8: Page 177 (bl), MapQuest.com, Inc.; 179, Stephen Brayfield; 181, Nick Rotondo; 183, MapQuest.com,Inc.; 187 (tl), MapQuest.com, Inc.; 191, MapQuest.com, Inc.; 198, MapQuest.com, Inc.; 199, MapQuest.com, Inc..

Chapter 9: Page 201, MapQuest.com, Inc.; 202, MapQuest.com, Inc.; 203, MapQuest.com, Inc.; 207, MapQuest.com, Inc.; 208, MapQuest.com, Inc.; 206, Ralph Voltz; 209, MapQuest.com, Inc.; 210, MapQuest.com, Inc.; 211 (r, l), Joe LeMonnier; 212, MapQuest.com, Inc.; 213 (tr), MapQuest.com, Inc.; 216 (tr), MapQuest.com, Inc.; 218, MapQuest.com, Inc.; 219, Leslie Kell.

Chapter 10: Page 221 (b), MapQuest.com, Inc.; 222 (bl), MapQuest.com, Inc.; 224 (bl), MapQuest.com, Inc.; 225 (br), MapQuest.com, Inc.; 226 (bl), MapQuest.com, Inc.; 228 (tl), MapQuest.com, Inc.; 229 (br), MapQuest.com, Inc.; 230 (tl), MapQuest.com, Inc.; 231 (tr), Leslie Kell; 232 (bl), MapQuest.com, Inc.; 233 (t), MapQuest.com, Inc.; 234, MapQuest.com, Inc.; 236, MapQuest.com, Inc.; 237, Leslie Kell.

Chapter 11: Page 239 (b), MapQuest.com, Inc.; 240 (br), MapQuest.com, Inc.; 241 (tr), MapQuest.com, Inc.; 245 (br), MapQuest.com, Inc.; 246 (bl),

MapQuest.com, Inc.; 250 (br), MapQuest.com, Inc.; 251 (tr), MapQuest.com, Inc.; 252, MapQuest.com, Inc.

Chapter 12: Page 255 (b), MapQuest.com, Inc.; 256 (bl), MapQuest.com, Inc.; 259 (br), MapQuest.com, Inc.; 261 (tr), MapQuest.com, Inc.; 264 (tr), MapQuest.com, Inc.; 265 (br), MapQuest.com, Inc.; 268, MapQuest.com, Inc.; 269, MapQuest.com, Inc.

Chapter 13: Page 271, MapQuest.com, Inc.; 272 (tl), MapQuest.com, Inc.; 273 (tr), MapQuest.com, Inc.; 276 (tl), MapQuest.com, Inc.; 282 (cl), MapQuest.com, Inc.; 285 (tr), MapQuest.com, Inc.; 286 MapQuest.com, Inc.; 287, Leslie Kell.

Unit 4: Page 294 (bl, t), Ortelius Design; 295, MapQuest.com, Inc.; 296, MapQuest.com, Inc.; 297, MapQuest.com, Inc.; 298, MapQuest.com, Inc.; 299, MapQuest.com, Inc.; 300–301, MapQuest.com, Inc.

Chapter 14: Page 303, MapQuest.com, Inc.; 304 (bl), MapQuest.com, Inc.; 306 (bl), MapQuest.com, Inc.; 309 (tr), MapQuest.com, Inc.; 312 (bl), MapQuest.com, Inc.; 314 (bl), MapQuest.com, Inc.; 315 (br), MapQuest.com, Inc.; 318, MapQuest.com, Inc.; 319, MapQuest.com, Inc.

Chapter 15: Page 321 (b), MapQuest.com, Inc.; 324 (bl), MapQuest.com, Inc.; 325 (br), MapQuest.com, Inc.; 326 (tl), MapQuest.com, Inc.; 328 (t), MapQuest.com, Inc.; 329, Joe LeMonnier; 330 (bl), MapQuest.com, Inc.; 332 (bl), MapQuest.com, Inc.; 333 (br), MapQuest.com, Inc.; 334 (tl), MapQuest.com, Inc.; 335 (tr), MapQuest.com, Inc.; 336, MapQuest.com, Inc.; 339, MapQuest.com, Inc.; 340, Stephen Durke/ Washington Artists; 341 (t), Ortelius Design.

Chapter 16: Page 353 (b), MapQuest.com, Inc.; 354 (tl), MapQuest.com, Inc.; 355 (br), MapQuest.com, Inc.; 358 (tl), MapQuest.com, Inc.; 359 (b), Leslie Kell; 361 (br, tr), MapQuest.com, Inc.; 363 (tr), MapQuest.com, Inc.; 364 (bl), Rosa + Wesley; 365 (br), MapQuest.com, Inc.; 366 (bl), MapQuest.com, Inc.; 367 (tr), MapQuest.com, Inc.; 369 (tl), MapQuest.com, Inc.; 370 (bl), MapQuest.com, Inc.; 372, MapQuest.com, Inc.; 373, Leslie Kell;

Unit 5: Page 344 (bl, t), Ortelius Design; 345, MapQuest.com, Inc.; 346, MapQuest.com, Inc.; 347, MapQuest.com, Inc.; 348, MapQuest.com, Inc.; 349, MapQuest.com, Inc.; 350–351, MapQuest.com, Inc.

Chapter 17: Page 375 (b), MapQuest.com, Inc.; 376 (bl), MapQuest.com, Inc.; 377 (br), MapQuest.com, Inc.; 379 (br), MapQuest.com, Inc.; 384 (tl, bl), MapQuest.com, Inc.; 387 (br), MapQuest.com, Inc.; 388 (tl), MapQuest.com, Inc.; 391 (br), MapQuest.com, Inc.; 392, (bl), MapQuest.com, Inc.

PHOTO CREDITS